TEACHING THE NEW SOCIAL STUDIES IN SECONDARY SCHOOLS

An Inductive Approach

TEACHING THE NEW SOCIAL STUDIES IN SECONDARY SCHOOLS

An Inductive Approach

Edwin Fenton   *Carnegie Institute of Technology*

HOLT, RINEHART and WINSTON, INC.
NEW YORK · CHICAGO · SAN FRANCISCO · TORONTO · LONDON

For Barbara

Preface

No single element of the new social studies is really new; each element has an ancient lineage, at least in theory. Yet the forty or so national curriculum projects launched during the last five years to reform the teaching of social studies are developing something distinctively new and different. A number of well-known elements are being restated and assembled in unique ways. In addition, actual materials and lesson plans for use in elementary and secondary school classrooms are turning theory into practice. These changes imply a pending revolution in the teaching of the social studies. What will be its nature?

It will involve three clusters of objectives: attitudes and values, the use of a mode of inquiry involving the development and validation of hypotheses, and a variety of knowledge objectives. The directors of curriculum projects do not rank these three clusters of objectives in the same order of importance; nor do they arrange in identical ways the individual objectives within each cluster. They do agree, however, that objectives must be stated in behavioral terms that can be measured by evaluating instruments available to classroom teachers. Hence, a teacher should examine carefully the literature about social studies objectives, not only to assist him in selecting materials from the flood now beginning to come from publishers but also to help him in setting reasonable objectives for his own classes. Section I of this volume focuses upon the question of social studies objectives.

A range of objectives requires a range of teaching strategies. Although the new social studies emphasizes teaching techniques near the discoverey end of the continuum, expository methods have not been completely abandoned. With the spread of team-teaching arrangements, faculties have been challenged to pay more attention to the relation between teaching objectives on the one hand and appropriate strategies and patterns of deployment on the other. Section II of this volume explores these issues. It contains in addition a number of sample materials from the new social studies designed to illustrate a variety of means for reaching specific teaching objectives.

Objectives, teaching strategies, and patterns of deployment demand a variety of teaching materials. The projects are providing them. Some tell stories or give analyses in traditional expository form. Others, designed for discovery exercises in which the teacher plays a nondirective role, consist only of selected data. Between these extremes, and in a variety of combinations, lie collections of source materials—documents, autobiographies, letters, diaries, case studies, pieces of fiction, and so forth—each used for a specific purpose. Some aim primarily at teaching cognitives skills; others raise questions of values; still others help students to learn the use of a mode of inquiry. Although most materials still remain in printed form, every project that can afford to do so has developed supplementary audio-visual aids. There is little doubt that a systems approach to the teaching of the social studies will soon be upon us. Samples of this wide range of materials can be found in both Sections II and III of this book.

The staff of each social studies project has chosen its own criteria for the selection of content. Content selection has, of course, been governed by affective and cognitive objectives. But teachers can work toward the attainment of attitudes and values and the use of a mode of inquiry by concentrating on any of a number of substantive topics. A world history teacher, for example, must decide whether to ask his students to study the civilization of ancient Egypt or to concentrate his attention upon India or China or some other subject. In general, the directors of the curriculum projects, like many curriculum developers in the past, have used a combination of three criteria for the selection of content: the needs and interests of the child, contemporary social problems about which students may need information, and important substantive knowledge drawn from the social science disciplines. On the whole, the structure of the social sciences has served as the most important guide in selection of the substantive body of knowledge to teach.

As yet no consensus about the meaning of the term "structure" has developed. Some scholars equate structure with generalizations derived from the disciplines. Others use a list of basic concepts as their definition of structure. This book identifies structure with the analytical questions that historians and social scientists ask of data. Section III contains five chapters that attempt to identify some of these analytical questions and another six chapters that demonstrate, through illustrative materials, some ways in which structure can be taught in the schools. Teachers who examine these chapters might well think about ways in which structure could be combined with the needs and interests of the child, and with contemporary social problems, to provide useful guides to content selection.

Identifying structure with analytical questions makes the structure of the disciplines the major key to hypothesis formation. Facts do not speak for themselves. They have meaning only when the minds of men order them into patterns. Social scientists have developed a large number of fruitful ways to order data, stemming from their knowledge of man and society. As historians engage in research, they often put the implications of a social science model, a generalization developed from previous research, or an earlier instance of a similar pattern of development, in the form of an analytical question which guides their search for data. These questions lead to hypotheses. They can be validated, revised, or rejected by using historical data in accordance with the rules of critical thinking. The development and validation of hypotheses are the heart of the mode of inquiry in the social studies.

What about civic education? Preparation for citizenship is implied in each of the three groups of objectives listed above: a set of attitudes and values in keeping with a democratic credo, the ability to use the mode of inquiry, and knowledge of content—such as the history of the American Constitution—that provides information about institutional settings and other data essential to a rational decision-making process. But this threefold way of looking at objectives casts civic education in a new light. It provides a framework of discussion acceptable to both the civic education camp and to those who are skeptical of the role of citizenship training in conventional social studies. It provides as well model evaluating instruments, carefully devised by our best scholars, which should enable us to determine when we have achieved some of our goals.

This volume is not just another book of supplementary readings. Although it may be used as readings in conjunction with a conventional textbook, it has been designed to replace, rather than to supplement, a text. The underlying principle can be stated simply: students who will in the future be expected to rely primarily on inductive teaching techniques should be taught inductively. Throughout their school careers, most prospective teachers have never studied history taught by an inductive approach. Hence, they have no models to imitate. Expository teaching by lecture and rote memorization from texts perpetuates itself generation after generation. Virtually the entire teaching profession now agrees that this cycle must be broken.

But before we can make a full breakthrough, patterns of teaching at all levels must change. Students who are taught in college by a textbook-and-lecture method by professional historians and social scientists have the right to question the assertion that they should teach their future high school students inductively. If critic teachers under whom student teachers learn to teach dedicate themselves to cramming into students' heads the maximum quantity of factual information, beginners may again raise legitimate questions. But in the meantime we must make a start. A logical starting place is the college methods course at either the undergraduate or the graduate level. Properly taught, this course may serve as the model which will otherwise be missing from a student's background.

To serve as a model, a methods course should provide numerous examples of actual classroom experiences. Providing such experiences has long been the function of practice teaching. Our present generation of critic teachers, however, does not yet employ inductive methods to any great extent, nor are the materials used in their classes suitable to an inductive approach. Unless the methods course can supply examples of pertinent materials and techniques, student teachers will quickly follow the time-worn paths. This volume contains numerous examples of actual social studies materials. By teaching these examples to college students as if they were a high school class, or, better yet, by having a member of the class teach his fellow-students, methods teachers can build the models they have so long desired.

This book may prove useful for in-service training programs as well as pre-service college methods courses. The principles on which it is based have been drawn from the forty or more national social studies curriculum projects which have sprung up during the last five years. Most of the articles it contains have been written during this time period. Teachers who left college a few years ago should find in this book a number of new ideas and fresh approaches to teaching. It may prove appropriate as well for summer programs such as those sponsored by NDEA, or for year-round in-service work.

Despite the fact that the new curricular projects emphasize a multi-medial approach, no reading in this volume has been devoted to the use of audio-visual aids. Such a reading was omitted deliberately, so that teachers might use pertinent AV materials in a number of lessons to demonstrate their specific use in social studies courses. Two sets of AV materials have been designed specifically with inductive principles in mind. The first consists of fourteen units for the overhead projector, published by Encyclopaedia Britannica Films under the general title "The Fenton-Wallbank World History Program." Many of these units may be used appropriately with topics covered below in Chapters 12, 14, 17, 22, 26, and 28.

Five half-hour, black and white, 16-mm films, which may be purchased or rented from Holt, Rinehart and Winston or rented from film libraries, make up the second set of AV materials. These films show classes studying the five lessons in Chapter 10. Chapter 16 contains the transcript from one of these films. Taken together, the films provide examples of one style of inductive teaching which prospective teachers can observe, criticize, and adapt.

This book, and the audio-visual materials that may be used to supplement it, have benefited materially from the criticism and advice of a number of people. Five colleagues at Carnegie Institute of Technology—Richard B. Ford, John M. Good, Mitchell P. Lichtenberg, John H. Sandberg, and Mindella Schultz—have criticized parts of the manuscript or contributed a number of valuable suggestions. Professor Lawrence Metcalf of the University of Illinois criticized an early version of the entire volume and contributed substantially to whatever merit it may now have. Two classes of students at Carnegie Institute of Technology who used the book in dittoed form have helped to eliminate a number of obscure or difficult readings and to suggest replacements. Many teachers of both high school and college students have granted permission to reprint their work; without their kindness, it could not have been written. I owe special thanks to Mrs. Dorothy J. Hanna and Mrs. Ethel Blank, who typed the entire manuscript and attended to the complicated matter of permissions with unfailing skill and good humor, and to Mrs. Natalie Fowler, who read proof and suggested a number of last-minute changes. Finally, and most important, my wife Barbara encouraged me to try a new approach to the education of social studies teachers and sustained me through the inevitable failures and disappointments that followed. Without her support the book would not have been written.

Some of the materials in Chapters 9–11, 14, 20, 22, 24, and 28 were developed at the Social Studies Curriculum Development Center established at Carnegie Institute of Technology under a grant from the United States Office of Education. Most of these chapters consist of introductions, study questions, and readings. Many of the readings are copyrighted and used both by the Center and in this volume with the permission of the authors and publishers. All of the remainder of the materials in the chapters written at the Center has been placed in the public domain. Without support from the Office of Education, these materials could not have been developed and made available to the profession. This support is gratefully acknowledged.

Pittsburgh, Pennsylvania   E. F.
February 1966

Contents

Introduction

About a decade ago a wave of reform in the teaching of mathematics, the natural sciences, and foreign languages began to reach tranquil secondary school classrooms. Reinforced by Sputnik and supported by generous grants from the National Science Foundation and private philanthropic groups, these reforms have had a profound impact upon American education. In about 1960, scholars in the fields of English and the social studies joined the reform movement. Today the social studies program in both elementary and secondary schools is in ferment.

More than forty distinct curriculum projects at all grade levels are under way in the social studies area. Kindergarten, the elementary school, the junior high school, and the senior high school have all been affected. The projects have been financed by various agencies. The Department of Health, Education and Welfare and the National Science Foundation support about half of them; private foundations sponsor most of the remainder; and a few draw funds from local school systems. They are organized in a variety of ways. The majority are located at universities, with one or two faculty members in charge; four or five are controlled by scholarly groups such as the American Anthropological Association; and a few are run by school systems, groups of universities, or independent organizations specifically designed to develop curricula. Their objectives are as varied as their structure. Some projects aim to turn out materials for one course in one discipline; others are preparing materials to fit into existing courses. The majority propose to develop entire curricula, some for a period as long as twelve years, others for three or four years. Yet beneath this diversity lies a common set of assumptions and techniques.

Taken together, the materials that these projects will publish and the assumptions and techniques upon which they are built make up the new social studies. Like the recent developments in the teaching of mathematics and science, they point in new directions without breaking entirely with the past. The directions, however, are new, the assumptions are different, the materials are fresh, and the teaching techniques include a number of new departures. Anyone who teaches in an up-to-date school system five years from now will

1

probably be using material developed or influenced by the curriculum projects. In the meantime, the teaching techniques developed in these projects can often be adapted to conventional material.

Most students learn to teach by imitating their teachers. For this reason, every subject course becomes an implicit methods course. Miss Jones, teaching history by a question-and-answer technique designed to test the ability to recall factual information, implicitly endorses a teaching method. Similarly, Professor Smith, lecturing three times a week and assigning only book reviews to supplement the text, establishes a model for his students to imitate. Neither of these models will prepare students for the new social studies. Each is essentially expository rather than inductive, and each relies upon textbooks rather than upon materials geared to a discovery method. If a methods course is also taught from a conventional text, students can reach the classroom with no inductive teaching models to imitate.

This book has been designed for college teachers or leaders of in-service groups who wish to provide a model of inductive teaching for their students. Most methods books digest what the author knows about teaching into expository chapters. This one, however, contains readings about teaching, learning theory, and the social studies curriculum, as well as samples of materials suitable for inductive teaching in high school social studies classes. Each reading contains an introduction to link it to the remainder of the volume and study questions chosen to emphasize important matters. Professors using the book will probably choose to teach it inductively, just as teachers of the new curricula will employ inductive teaching techniques. Thus the college professor will become the model for his students to imitate and criticize. Professors may ask some of their students to teach lessons from the sample materials included in the volume to their classmates, as if the remainder of the class were high school students enrolled in a social studies course. This procedure can provide useful insights into the demanding art of teaching.

Numerous surveys indicate that the status of the social studies in the secondary schools has reached a new low. Tired of memorizing long lists of facts and generalizations from textbooks, students have turned their attention to other disciplines that present more stimulating materials or a more challenging intellectual experience. Yet the future of the democratic way of life may depend in part upon the kind of instruction given in social studies classes. So may the ability of millions of students to live rich lives amid the abundant opportunities of our affluent society.

This volume represents an invitation to join a movement that is reinvigorating the teaching of the social studies in this country. Articles by many of the leaders of the new social studies have been included in this volume. Even more leaders have contributed ideas which have worked their way into articles written by others. No one represented here, either directly or vicariously, would argue boldly that he had final answers to the problems that beset the typical social studies teacher. Everyone involved in the new social studies agrees, however, that improvements can be made and that the heart of the problem lies with the classroom teacher. To this fine calling we invite you as colleagues to join in an exciting and serious endeavor, that of helping young people to discover themselves, the nature of the society in which they live, and the significance of their heritage.

I
MAINLY WHY

Why should we teach the social studies? What are appropriate objectives? Answers to these two questions vary as much as the men who ask and answer them. Although everyone seems to agree that the social studies are a "good thing," there is no consensus about specific objectives. Yet we must know why we teach if we are ever to assess the results of our teaching.

The readings in Section I deal with various aspects of the why question. They examine the objectives of past curricula and investigate contemporary claims. What cognitive skills should be taught in social studies classes? Can we—and should we—stress the development of attitudes and values? What are the best criteria for the selection of content? Why are contemporary scholars stressing the structure of the social science disciplines? How is citizenship training related to these questions? These issues and others like them concern every teacher of the social studies.

CHAPTER 1 Teaching the Social Studies: The Traditional Textbook

Millions of teachers have lived through the harrowing first day of teaching. Usually they reach home exhausted but exhilarated by their first contact as a teacher with real live students. All too often, however, the exhilaration fades with a steady diet of discouragement fed by one rude awakening after another. Beginning teachers soon discover that most students have no innate zeal for learning; the majority have to be motivated, and some never learn to study with zest. They learn that many students do not know how to study or to take notes or to write essay examinations; students must be taught basic skills over and over again, and the process is often painful for inexperienced teachers. They find out that some of their colleagues cannot give them satisfactory answers to questions about curriculum or pedagogy; in this situation, beginning teachers must fall back on their own knowledge and training. Only a truly exceptional teacher in a most unusual school becomes an immediate success. The road to excellence is long and hard.

Given this situation, beginning teachers should not expect too much. A few rewards may come quickly—a friendly smile from a shy boy, a ripple of laughter from a joke, the development of a facility for asking questions, a good set of papers from a class that has been doing poorly. These are all signs that teaching will soon go well. But if teachers are to improve steadily at their craft, they must master the principles upon which good teaching rests. This book has been designed to encourage students to discover these principles for themselves.

Usually a first experience as a practice teacher or an intern comes after several days of observation. The critic teacher will take a few classes—sometimes far too many—and then turn his charges over to the neophyte. "Why don't you try Chapter 3?" he may say. "Read it, develop a lesson plan, and bring it to me for criticism." This situation parallels the one a beginning

7

teacher faces on his first full-time teaching day, except that no friendly critic is at hand.

Suppose you are in such a situation. You are assigned a class of some thirty-five tenth graders in a course in world history. Their textbook is *Story of Nations,* by Lester B. Rogers, Fay Adams, and Walker Brown (Holt, Rinehart and Winston, 1965), a standard, successful world history text that has gone through eleven editions since it was first published in 1934. Part 2 begins with Chapter 3, a discussion of the civilization of ancient Egypt, completed in Chapters 4 and 5. Part 1, consisting of the first two chapters of the book, was concerned with the formation of the earth and the life of early man. Chapter 3 is reprinted here in its entirety. As you read it, think about the following questions:

1) Why should we teach Chapter 3 to a fifteen-year-old American high school student? If we should teach it at all, should we emphasize factual knowledge, basic concepts, critical thinking, values, or some other objective?

2) Suppose we do decide to teach Chapter 3. What methods of teaching are available to us? How do we select which ones to use?

3) What content emphases in Chapter 3 are most important to teach? How should a teacher select content emphases?

EGYPT: EARLY CIVILIZATION ON THE NILE

Lester B. Rogers · Fay Adams · Walker Brown

Egypt: Geographic Setting

The Nile, the longest river in the world, drains Lake Victoria in central Africa and follows a northerly course to the Mediterranean Sea. During a portion of the early part of its four-thousand-mile journey to the north, it is called the White Nile, because of its milky-gray color. The clear waters of the Blue Nile, a tributary, join it at Khartoum (shown on the map on page 10).

Proceeding north (downstream) between Khartoum and Aswan, the Nile flows through six cataracts, or rapids. In the cataracts the water rushes over rocky beds between high cliffs and sometimes drops as much as two feet

Reprinted from Lester B. Rogers, Fay Adams, and Walker Brown, *Story of Nations* (New York: Holt, Rinehart and Winston, Inc., 1965), Part 2, Chap. 3, pp. 15–22.

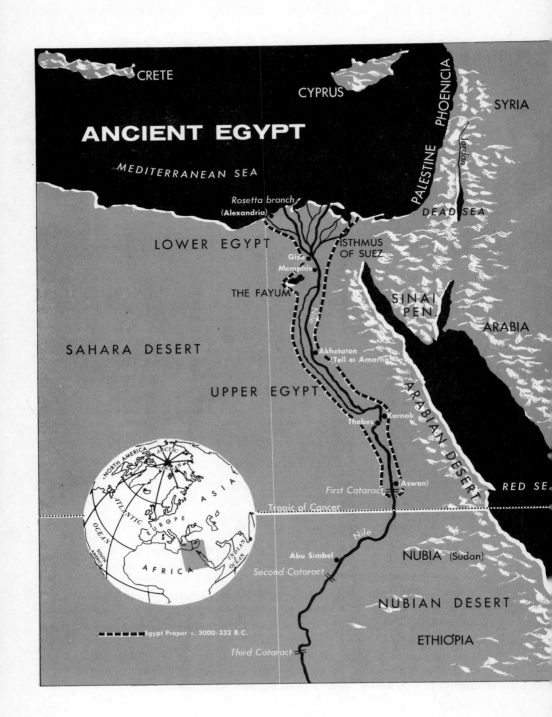

CRETE

CYPRUS

SYRIA

PHOENICIA

PALESTINE

ANCIENT EGYPT

MEDITERRANEAN SEA

Rosetta branch
(Alexandria)

DEAD SEA

LOWER EGYPT

ISTHMUS
OF SUEZ

Giza
Memphis

THE FAYUM

Nile

SINAI
PEN.

ARABIA

SAHARA DESERT

Akhetaton
(Tell el Amarna)

UPPER EGYPT

ARABIAN DESERT

Thebes • *Karnak*

RED SEA

First Cataract • *(Aswan)*

Tropic of Cancer

Nile

Abu Simbel

Second Cataract

NUBIA (Sudan)

NUBIAN DESERT

------- Egypt Proper c. 3000-332 B.C.

ETHIOPIA

Third Cataract

each mile. Beyond the northernmost, or First Cataract, the Nile has cut a narrow valley ten to thirty miles wide in the rocky, brown, desert plateau that stretches away on either side. This narrow strip of land along the river is fertile and green because it is watered by the Nile floods. Historians call this river valley Upper Egypt.

About six hundred miles farther north, beyond Memphis, the river divides into two branches (seven in ancient times), and the narrow valley widens into a steaming, marshy, triangular plain. This region, comprising about 150 miles from Memphis to the sea, is called the Delta, or Lower Egypt. Its hot, humid climate is less comfortable than that of Upper Egypt, where the air is dry.

The ancient Egyptian civilization, which we are about to study, was almost entirely confined to the Delta and the narrow valley of Upper Egypt. Although a few Egyptians settled south of the First Cataract, the rough waters made transportation farther upstream difficult. Notice that ancient Egypt was protected by natural boundaries on all sides: the Mediterranean Sea to the north, the Libyan Desert to the west, the Nubian Desert (today the Sudan) to the south, and the Arabian Desert and Red Sea to the east. The strip of land between the Red Sea and the Mediterranean, called the Isthmus (*iss-mus*) of Suez, was Egypt's only land link with Asia.

Egypt: Perspective

A hundred years ago men knew very little about the history of ancient Egypt. Occasionally, robbers dug into an ancient tomb to steal its contents, but for the most part the secrets that lay buried beneath the sands remained hidden from men. After all, what possible value could there be in bothering to study a wasteland of desert split by a muddy river?

Then, in the middle of the nineteenth century, two men armed themselves with shovels, picks, and other tools. Venturing into the Nile Valley, they began to dig in the ruins left by men who had lived thousands of years ago. The remarkable discoveries they made sent other archaeologists scrambling into the region, until today historians know more about life in Egypt five thousand years ago than they know about life in North America only five hundred years ago.

What accounts for the popularity of Egypt as a hunting ground for historians? For one thing, Egypt's climate favors the work of archaeologists. Over the centuries, the dry heat has preserved remains of the ancient Egyptian civilization and has prevented the deterioration that in most other regions has reduced valuable relics to dust. Then too, the Egyptian custom of preserving an amazing variety of objects in their tombs has made the tombs virtual museums of Egyptian history.

But until only recently the most important reason for the interest in Egypt was that scientists regarded the region as the home of the first civilized people. Now, although it appears that equally early civilizations also developed along other river valleys, the importance of Egypt in the puzzle of ancient man remains great. Underlying all of man's interest in ancient Egypt is his desire to know more about his forebears, to discover what kind of people lived in the world at the dawn of history, and to search for clues to their lives and their achievements. In Part 2 you will share some of the excitement of that search.

The Nile Has Influenced the Story of Egypt

GEOGRAPHY MADE EGYPT A CRADLE OF CIVILIZATION

EGYPT IS THE GIFT OF THE NILE

Geography and climate show their importance in Egypt more clearly than in any other ancient country. Nearly all of North Africa is desert and has a hot, dry climate. Along the banks of the Nile, however, the landscape changes dramatically into a green, fertile valley. This natural garden spot provided the setting for one of man's first great civilizations, that of the Egyptians.

Twenty-five hundred years ago, Herodotus (heh-*rod*-oh-tus), a Greek historian, was correct when he said: "All Egypt is the gift of the Nile." Since it seldom rains in the Nile Valley or in the surrounding deserts, all water, including that for drinking and bathing, comes from the river. Even the fertile soil of Egypt is a gift of the Nile, for with unfailing regularity floods have deposited a new layer of soil in the valley each year.

To most ancient Egyptians, the cause of the Nile floods was a mystery. Only a few guessed that the flooding was the result of heavy rains in the mountains of Abyssinia (ab-ih-*sin*-ee-uh), the source of the Blue Nile. Modern explorers have confirmed this belief. From June to September, melt-

The Nile Today. Transportation on Egypt's great waterway has not changed much since ancient times. The prevailing winds blow south, but the river current flows north, so boats can travel easily in either direction.

Trans World Airlines Photo

ing snow and heavy rainfall turn the Blue Nile into a thundering torrent. The sudden increase in water and soil, which the Blue Nile dumps into the White Nile at Khartoum, causes the level of the river downstream to rise gradually and spill onto the flat, sunbaked fields of Egypt. The flood reaches its crest in October. Then the river level slowly drops, leaving a new layer of rich mud ready for planting. As the fields become a broad green carpet of waving grain, the Nile continues to recede until a new cycle begins in the following year.

Metropolitan Museum of Art

Fishing and Fowling. The waters of the Nile provided staples for the Egyptian diet. This wall painting from an Egyptian tomb shows the man on the right spearing fish while his companion hunts birds with a boomerang-like stick. The figures look flat because painters apparently did not know how to achieve three-dimensional effects.

In addition to supplying water and soil, the Nile also served ancient Egyptians as a highway linking Upper and Lower Egypt. Boats traveling north can glide easily with the current, while those going south need only to hoist a sail to take advantage of steady winds from the north.

EGYPT WAS PROTECTED BY SEA AND DESERT

Doubtless one of the reasons for the development of civilization was Egypt's natural protection from enemy invasion. The surrounding seas and deserts assured the Egyptians of peace and enabled them to devise better ways of living instead of constantly defending themselves from attackers. The Isthmus of Suez was the only easy point of entry, and, as long as Egypt was strong, she guarded that. Not until she became weakened from within did she fall prey to enemy invaders.

MEN OF THE NEW STONE AGE SETTLED IN THE NILE VALLEY

Eleven thousand years ago, North Africa was covered with forests and grassy plains through which men of the Old Stone Age wandered in search of food and shelter. During the last centuries of the Old Stone Age, the climate gradually grew hotter and drier, eventually turning the hunting grounds into the Sahara Desert. As a result, beginning about 5000 B.C., these hunters were forced to retreat eastward to the still fertile Nile Valley. There they happily discovered that geography had given them ideal conditions for a permanent home: sun, fertile soil, water, and natural protection from invasion.

During the New Stone Age, these ancestors of the Egyptians grew wheat, barley, vegetables, and flax along the banks of the Nile. The river also supplied them with waterfowl, fish, and even mud from which they made bricks to build their huts. The papyrus (puh-*pi*-rus) reeds that grew thickly along the marshes furnished these early farmers with material for rope, sandals, thatched roofs, and even light fishing boats. In the graves of these early settlers, archaeologists have found copper and polished stone tools, carved figures, pottery, and ivory combs. Thus while the continent of Europe was still an undeveloped wilderness, these ancient men in Egypt were well on their way to becoming civilized.

EGYPTIAN GOVERNMENT WAS BORN OUT OF ATTEMPTS TO CONTROL THE NILE FLOODS

For nearly two thousand years the farmers along the Nile made few changes in their way of life; but as the population increased, it became necessary to raise more food. Men enlarged their fields by digging ditches to drain the marshlands and by building canals to bring the water to the nearby desert. They soon learned that by erecting dikes they could conserve some of the flood water for irrigation in the dry season. This reservoir of water enabled them to grow two or three crops a year.

Because so much digging, draining, and irrigating required a great deal of co-operative effort, farmers began to live together in villages instead of in their own fields. Leaders were needed to organize the work and to make sure that each man did his share of digging and took no more than his share of water. Gradually a few capable leaders brought several villages under their control and developed a system of government. Finally, around 4000 B.C., two powerful leaders succeeded in uniting the groups of villages into the two kingdoms of Upper and Lower Egypt.

Hieroglyphics. The massive pillars of the great Temple of Karnak are covered with hieroglyphics, the writing of ancient Egypt.

Rupert Leach from Shostal

THE DETAILS OF GOVERNMENT CREATED A NEED FOR WRITING

As the villages were organized into kingdoms, government became more complicated and written records became a necessity. For example, farmers insisted that the tax collector write down how much grain they owed and whether they paid it so that they could not be taxed twice in the same year.

To meet this need for records, the Egyptians developed a system of writing. At first they simply drew pictures of objects, such as a cricle for the sun or a four-legged animal with horns for a cow. But it was hard to make cows look different from sheep or other animals and impossible to draw a picture of a word like "beautiful" or "begun." So they slowly learned to use pictures to represent not only objects but also certain sounds or syllables. Eventually they developed these pictures into an alphabet of twenty-four letters, which they used together with the original picture writing. Thus Egyptian writing came to include three kinds of symbols, representing objects, syllables, and letters, all mixed together. This system of writing was called hieroglyphics (hy-er-oh-*glif*-iks). It was clumsy and complicated. Later, the Egyptians developed a much simpler form of hieroglyphics called *hieratic* writing to meet the everyday needs of government and business.

RECORDS WERE WRITTEN ON A KIND OF PAPER

The Egyptians developed a convenient way of keeping records by writing with a reed pen on a kind of paper made by weaving dried papyrus reeds. Instead of cutting the sheets of paper into pages and binding them like books, they fastened them together end to end to make a strip that was sometimes as long as a hundred feet. The strips were rolled into scrolls and stored in jars. Egypt's dry climate preserved them so well that many can still be read.

15

Written records are one of the foundations of modern civilization. They enable each generation to use and add to the knowledge gained by its forerunners. Without some form of writing, such as the ancient Egyptians invented, civilization might never have advanced beyond the Stone Age.

THE ROSETTA STONE PROVIDED THE KEY
TO EGYPT'S SECRETS

For centuries scholars knew almost nothing about ancient Egypt because they were unable to read hieroglyphics. It was not until the end of the eighteenth century that French soldiers digging a fort near the Rosetta branch of the mouth of the Nile turned up an extraordinary stone which became the key to Egypt's past. The "Rosetta Stone" was covered with inscriptions in three languages: Greek, hieroglyphics, and an unknown writing which later proved to be a simplified, popular kind of Egyptian writing. Scholars from many countries tried to read the Egyptian writing on the Rosetta Stone.

The Oriental Institute, The University of Chicago

The Rosetta Stone. This slab of stone, found in 1799 near the mouth of the Nile, was the key to the translation of hieroglyphics. It is covered with an identical text in hieroglyphics at the top, in a simpler Egyptian writing in the center, and in Greek below.

Twenty years later, a French scholar, Champollion (shahn-paw-*lyawn*), correctly guessed that the three inscriptions were exactly the same message written in three different languages. This discovery enabled him to translate the hieroglyphics and paved the way for scholars who unlocked the secrets contained in other Egyptian inscriptions.

THE NILE FLOODS LED TO THE DEVELOPMENT OF GEOMETRY AND THE CALENDAR

Experience with the Nile floods brought home to the Egyptians the necessity of developing an accurate system of measuring distance and time. Each year's food supply depended on how much water the flood brought to the land. One year the river might rise so high that it would wash away dikes and villages. The next year it might be so low that it would not even fill the irrigation ditches. You can understand why the people felt it was important to foresee what the Nile would do. At several points along the river the Egyptians built stone stairways called Nilometers on which they measured the level of the water each year. If the water reached a certain point by July, they knew whether to build their dikes higher or deepen their canals.

Because the annual floods often washed away boundary lines, the Egyptians needed a simple and accurate way to measure land. They devised a method of marking out angles and calculating areas that enabled them to redraw the original boundary lines. Thus geometry, the science of space measurement, was born.

Metropolitan Museum of Art

Geese. Egyptian art was usually symmetrical, as can be seen in this painting.

The Egyptians learned to measure time as well as space. They noticed that the average number of days between the peaks of the Nile flood was the same, 365, and that when the Nile reached its height, Sirius, the Dog Star, always appeared on the horizon. From this information and from observation of the moon, they constructed a calendar of 365 days divided into twelve months of thirty days each. The five days left over they set aside for feasting. This first calendar told the Egyptians when to expect the flood and when to start planting.

CHAPTER CHECK-UP

1. In which direction does the Nile River flow?
2. How were the Egyptians able to navigate their boats in both directions on the Nile River?
3. What was the weak point in Egypt's natural defenses against invasion?
4. What geographic conditions favored the growth of a civilization in the Nile Valley?
5. Why did Stone Age men settle in the Nile Valley?
6. What was the main occupation of the ancient Egyptians?
7. How did the earliest Egyptian writing differ from our method of writing today?
8. What is papyrus and how was it used by the ancient Egyptians?
9. Why was the development of writing such an important step in history?
10. How was the Rosetta Stone a key to our understanding of ancient Egypt?

CHAPTER 2

Setting Objectives in the Social Studies: The Cognitive Domain

Most lesson plans, unit outlines, and courses of study designed for the social studies begin with a list of objectives. All too often this list is too diffuse and imprecise to serve as a useful guide to learning activities. But since teachers learn from other teachers, imprecisely stated objectives continue to reappear year after year in much the same form. All of us know that we should define our objectives before we plan a curriculum, a course, a unit, or a single lesson. This chapter is designed to raise some of the questions involved in the entire problem of setting proper educational objectives.

Most teachers emphasize knowledge objectives in their classroom teaching. They tend to teach students facts, emphasizing names, dates, and events for their own sake. In practice, many of the social studies teachers devote so much time and energy to teaching facts that other important instructional goals are neglected. Yet dozens of retention studies prove that students soon forget facts they have learned by rote.

Proponents of the new social studies often set forth three groups of objectives for social studies instruction. They are:

1) Knowledge: the ability to recall or recognize ideas or phenomena that a student has experienced in the same form or in a similar form at an earlier time.

2) Abilities and skills: the ability to find appropriate information and techniques in a student's experience to help him solve new problems or cope with new experiences. In the social studies, the modes of inquiry of historians and social scientists are an important part of these abilities and skills.

3) Affective objectives: the development of attitudes, understandings, and values that will promote a democratic way of life and help each student to develop a personal philosophy. *Perpetuate our culture.*

19

Before we can assess the relative weight that should be allotted to each of these three objectives, we must understand precisely what they are. The reading in this chapter discusses the nature of cognitive objectives: knowledge, and abilities and skills. It is taken from a volume edited by Benjamin S. Bloom of the University of Chicago, whose ideas have had a profound impact on the new curricula. The appendix to the reading contains a summary of Bloom's entire cognitive classification system. Affective objectives will be discussed in Chapter 3. As you study the excerpt from Bloom, think about the following questions:

1) What does Bloom mean by the term "educational objectives"? What are the sources from which objectives can come? Should the major yardstick for one's objectives be a philosophy of education or a psychology of learning?

2) How can a teacher best justify the acquisition of knowledge as an important goal for social studies instruction? How can he best justify the acquisition of abilities and skills? society is constantly changing

3) Can teaching only for knowledge or for intellectual abilities automatically accomplish other objectives or must other desired behaviors be aimed at specifically? Yes

4) Using content from Chapter 1, devise a simple strategy designed to teach for one of the skills or abilities listed in the appendix to the reading in this chapter.

EDUCATIONAL OBJECTIVES AND CURRICULUM DEVELOPMENT

Benjamin S. Bloom · David R. Krathwohl

Problems of developing curriculum and instruction are usually considered in relation to four major types of questions.[1]

1. What educational purposes or objectives should the school or course seek to attain?

From *Taxonomy of Educational Objectives: Handbook I, The Cognitive Domain,* by B. S. Bloom and D. R. Krathwohl, 1956, pp. 25–43. Used by permission of David McKay Company, Inc.

[1] The content of this section has been largely drawn from Ralph W. Tyler, "Achievement Testing and Curriculum Construction," *Trends in Student Personnel Work,* E. G. Williamson, Ed., Minneapolis, Minn.: University of Minnesota Press, 1949, pp. 391–407.

2. What learning experiences can be provided that are likely to bring about the attainment of these purposes?

3. How can these learning experiences be effectively organized to help provide continuity and sequence for the learner and to help him in integrating what might otherwise appear as isolated learning experiences?

4. How can the effectiveness of learning experiences be evaluated by the use of tests and other systematic evidence-gathering procedures?

We are here concerned primarily with the first of these questions: the formulation and classification of educational objectives.

By educational objectives, we mean explicit formulations of the ways in which students are expected to be changed by the educative process. That is, the ways in which they will change in their thinking, their feelings, and their actions. There are many possible changes that can take place in students as a result of learning experiences, but since the time and resources of the school are limited, only a few of the possibilities can be realized. It is important that the major objectives of the school or unit of instruction be clearly identified if time and effort are not to be wasted on less important things and if the work of the school is to be guided by some plan.

The formulation of educational objectives is a matter of conscious choice on the part of the teaching staff, based on previous experience and aided by consideration of several kinds of data. The final selection and ordering of the objectives become a matter of making use of the learning theory and philosophy of education which the faculty accepts.

One type of source commonly used in thinking about objectives is the information available about the students. What is their present level of development? What are their needs? What are their interests? Another source for objectives is available from investigations of the conditions and problems of contemporary life which make demands on young people and adults and which provide opportunities for them. What are the activities that individuals are expected to perform? What are the problems they are likely to encounter? What are the opportunities they are likely to have for service and self-realization?

Another source of suggestions for objectives comes from the nature of the subject matter and the deliberations of subject-matter specialists on the contributions their subject is able to make to the education of the individual. What is the conception of the subject field? What are the types of learning which can arise from a study of that subject matter? What are the contributions that the subject can make in relation to other subjects?

It is likely that a consideration of these three sources will result in a suggested list of objectives which require more time and effort than the school has at its disposal. The problem of selecting among possible objectives as well as the determination of relative emphasis to be given to various objectives requires the use of some guiding conceptions. The philosophy of education of the school serves as one guide, since the objectives to be finally included should be related to the school's view of the "good life for the individual in the good society." What are the important values? What is the proper relation between man and society? What are the proper relations between man and man?

Finally, educational objectives must be related to a psychology of learning. The faculty must distinguish goals that are feasible from goals that are unlikely to be attained in the time available, under the conditions which are possible, and with the group of students to be involved. The use of a psychology of learning enables the faculty to determine the appropriate placement of objectives in the learning sequence, helps them discover the learning conditions under which it is possible to attain an objective, and provides a way of determining the appropriate interrelationships among the objectives.

It should be clear from the foregoing that objectives are not only the goals toward which the curriculum is shaped and toward which instruction is guided, but they are also the goals that provide the detailed specification for the construction and use of evaluative techniques. . . . A test of the achievement of students is a test of the extent to which the students have attained these educational objectives. An achievement test is an adequate and valid test if it provides evidence of the extent to which students are attaining each of the major objectives of the unit of instruction.

The cognitive objectives derived from a process like that described in the foregoing paragraphs may, for discussion purposes, be divided into two parts. One would be the simple behavior of remembering or recalling knowledge and the other, the more complex behaviors of the abilities and skills. The following section discusses these two divisions in turn, considering their nature, their appearance in the taxonomy, and their place in the curriculum.

KNOWLEDGE AS A TAXONOMY CATEGORY

Probably the most common educational objective in American education is the acquisition of knowledge or information. That is, it is desired that as the result of completing an educational unit, the student will be changed with respect to the amount and kind of knowledge he possesses. Frequently knowledge is the primary, sometimes almost the sole kind of, educational objective in a curriculum. In almost every course it is an important or basic one. By knowledge we mean that the student can give evidence that he remembers, either by recalling or by recognizing, some idea or phenomenon with which he has had experience in the educational process. For our taxonomy purposes, we are defining knowledge as little more than the remembering of the idea or phenomenon in a form very close to that in which it was originally encountered.

This type of objective emphasizes most the psychological processes of remembering. Knowledge may also involve the more complex processes of relating and judging, since it is almost impossible to present an individual with a knowledge problem which includes exactly the same stimuli, signals, or cues as were present in the original learning situation. Thus, any test situation involving knowledge requires some organization and reorganization of the problem to furnish the appropriate signals and cues linking it to the knowledge the individual possesses. It may be helpful in this case to think of knowledge as something filed or stored in the mind. The task for the individual in each knowledge test situation is to find the appropriate signals and cues in the problem which will most effectively bring out whatever knowledge is filed or stored. For instance, almost everyone has had the experience of being unable to answer a question involving recall when the question is stated in one form, and then having little difficulty in remembering the necessary information when the question is restated in another form. This is well illustrated by John Dewey's story in which he asked a class, "What would you find if you dug a hole in the earth?" Getting no response, he repeated the question; again he obtained nothing but silence. The teacher chided Dr. Dewey, "You're asking the wrong question." Turning to the class, she asked, "What is the state of the center of the earth?" The class replied in unison, "Igneous fusion."

John Dewey's story also illustrates the rote recall nature of some knowledge learning. The emphasis on knowledge as involving little more than remembering or recall distinguishes it from those conceptions of knowledge which involve "understanding," "insight," or which are phrased as "really know," or "true knowledge." In these latter conceptions it is implicitly assumed that knowledge is of little value if it cannot be utilized in new situations or in a form very different from that in which it was originally encountered. The denotations of these latter concepts would usually be close to what have been defined as "abilities and skills" in the taxonomy.

Whether or not one accepts this latter position, it is sufficient to note that knowledge by itself is one of the most common educational objectives. The most cursory reading of the standardized tests available or of teacher-made tests would indicate that tremendous emphasis is given in our schools to this kind of remembering or recall. A comprehensive taxonomy of educational objectives must, in our opinion, include all the educational objectives represented in American education without making judgments about their value, meaningfulness, or appropriateness. Knowledge, therefore, is one of our taxonomy categories.

The knowledge category in particular and, as noted earlier, the classifications of the taxonomy in general range from the simple to the more complex behaviors and from the concrete or tangible to the abstract or intangible. By simple we mean elemental, isolable bits of phenomena or information, e.g., "the capital of Illinois is Springfield," or "Arkansas contains much bauxite." Thus, our base subclassification is titled "knowledge of specifics." At the upper end of the knowledge category the subclassifications refer to more complex phenomena. Thus, remembering a theory is a more complex task than remembering a specific such as the capital of a state. Knowledge of the theory of evolution, for instance, would be very complex. Accordingly, the subclassification at the complex end of the knowledge category is titled the "knowledge of theories and structures."

The knowledge categories may also be viewed as running from concrete to abstract. Thus, in general, knowledge of specifics will refer to concrete, tangible phenomena: "Insects have six legs"; "Most glass is brittle." But the more complex categories, as, for example, the name "knowledge of theories and structures" implies, tend to deal with abstract phenomena. . . .

WHAT IS KNOWABLE

One of the major problems with regard to knowledge is determining what is knowable, for there are different ways in which something can be said to be known. Adding to this problem is the fact that different criteria of accuracy and authenticity are applied to knowledge in different areas, at least the knowledge to be learned in school. To a large extent knowledge, as taught in American schools, depends upon some external authority; some expert or group of experts is the arbiter of knowledge. Some information is the result of little more than convention and consensus. That is, a group of workers or experts in the field has come to some agreement on the ways in which particular terms will be defined, on the particular referents for selected symbols, or the most effective or practical ways in which to organize a field or attack problems in it. For instance, lexicographers appear to make many arbitrary decisions in preparing a dictionary. The symbol system for punctuation is solely a matter of convention. Memorizing the conjugation of verbs and the declension of nouns is accepted as the proper approach to learning some foreign languages. Other information is known as the result of logical tests of consistency either by definition or by some logic of relationship. Certain kinds of geometry, mathematical propositions, and mathematical models are examples. Finally, some knowledge or information is known as the result of some historical, experiential, or pragmatic test. Thus, historical information is known as the result of a number of observations which are in agreement or which satisfy particular historical tests of their authenticity. Scientific information is known as a result of some observation, experiment, or test which meets the canons of scientific methodology.

It should also be noted that the validity, accuracy, and meaningfulness of information are relative in many ways and always are related to a particular period of time. Thus, what is known in 1955 was not known in the same way in a previous era and will presumably undergo some changes in the future. Compare the way we pictured the atom twenty years ago with today's view of it.

There is also a geographical and cultural aspect to knowledge in the sense that what is known to one group is not necessarily known to another group, class, or culture. It must be clear from all this, that knowledge is always partial and relative rather than inclusive and fixed.

JUSTIFICATION FOR THE DEVELOPMENT OF KNOWLEDGE

Knowledge or information may be justified as an important objective or outcome of learning in many ways. Perhaps the most common justification is that with increase in knowledge or information there is a development of one's acquaintance with reality. Such reality may represent what is known by convention or definition, what are known as the findings or outcome of inquiry in the various fields, what are known as the more fruitful ways of attacking problems in the field, or what are known as the more useful ways of organizing a field. It is assumed that as the number of things known by an individual increases, his acquaintance with the world in which he lives increases. But, as has been pointed out before, we recognize the point of view that truth and knowledge are only relative and that there are no hard and fast truths which exist for all time and all places. Nonetheless, most educators hold it desirable that the learner increase his knowledge of what is currently known or accepted by the experts or specialists in a field, whether or not such knowledge, in a philosophical sense, corresponds to "reality."

The selection of knowledge as an educational objective usually assumes some stability in the world, in the culture, or in the subject field. If the knowledge learned at one time is not regarded as very useful or accurate at another time, there would be little point in the student learning it. It is likely that the stability of knowledge varies considerably with the field or problem under consideration. Some fields or topics are undergoing such rapid transition that what is known at one time is not accepted or is altered shortly thereafter. Under such conditions the acquisition of knowledge could not be justified for its own sake but would have to be justified in relation to the other educational objectives, a position which is discussed next.

Another justification for the teaching of knowledge is that it is quite frequently regarded as basic to all the other ends or purposes of education. Problem solving or thinking cannot be carried on in a vacuum, but must be based upon knowledge of some of the "realities." The intellectual abilities represented in the taxonomy assume knowledge as a prerequisite. Knowledge becomes either the material with which the problem solving deals or it becomes the test of the adequacy and accuracy of the problem solving. Thus in fields undergoing rapid transition, knowledge may be taught, not so much with the expectation that it will prove eternally "true," but as a basis for learning the methodology of the field and as a basis for attacking the problems therein. Even the manipulative and motor skills assume some knowledge about the materials, methods, or tools that are used. Further, in another sense, all of the affective classifications make use of or are based upon knowledge. Thus, it is generally held that interests are developed as the result of an increase in information; likewise, attitudes and appreciations are regarded as having some base in knowledge or information. Even the objectives involving personal adjustment are quite frequently based upon the notion that a person must have some knowledge about himself before he can proceed to resolve his conflicts, anxieties, or other individual difficulties. It is clear that justification of knowledge for all these uses will usually involve knowledge in relation to other objectives, rather than knowledge for its own sake.

Still another justification for the development of knowledge as an objective of education arises from the status of knowledge in our own culture. Many workers assume a positive relationship between increase in knowledge and increase in maturity. In fact, quite frequently the increasing maturity of individuals or groups is judged in terms of their increasing knowledge about themselves or about the world in which they live. Knowledge is also frequently regarded as an important criterion of brightness or intelligence. This is reflected in intelligence testing where vocabulary or knowledge questions predominate and are regarded as signs of intelligence. In many schools, knowledge is regarded as the primary index of the level of education an individual has attained. This is indicated by the content of our standardized achievement test. The layman frequently regards knowledge and education as being synonymous. The great emphasis on radio quiz programs and tests of either historical or contemporary information which appear in newspapers and magazines further reflects the status of knowledge in our culture. There is little doubt that our culture places tremendous weight on knowledge or information as an important characteristic of the individual.

Many teachers and educators prize knowledge to some extent because of the simplicity with which it can be taught or learned. Mass methods, such as lectures, audio-visual methods, printed material, and the like, can be readily used for the acquisition of information. Quite frequently we tend to think of knowledge as something which is learned as the result of simply presenting it to the learner in one form of communication or another. Clearly related to this is the ease with which it is possible to gauge the extent to which the student has acquired knowledge. Practically all teachers have considerable confidence in their ability to build tests of knowledge. Because of the simplicity of teaching and evaluating knowledge, it is frequently emphasized as an educational objective out of all proportion to its usefulness or its relevance for the development of the individual. In effect, the teacher and school tend to look where the light is brightest and where it is least difficult to develop the individual.

Requiring that a student learn certain knowledge assumes a prediction that the student is likely to be able to make some use of the knowledge in the future. Thus, knowledge about phenomena relevant to the specialization of the engineer is maximally useful if the student is to become an engineer. Requiring the student to learn about engineering phenomena means that we can predict that he will be an engineer or that the knowledge will transfer to

Easy to evaluate

Mono
Lea - Raphael

other areas where he is likely to be able to use it. Knowledge required of students prior to their making a firm vocational choice will need to have more general relevance and widespread usefulness than after a firm choice is made. Extensive knowledge requirements in rapidly changing specialized fields need to be checked against the best possible prediction of what knowledge will be of continuing use and what knowledge is necessary for a grasp of the current known field. The teacher and the curriculum specialist must take all these factors into account in determining what knowledge to select.

Undoubtedly the greatest predictability arises within the school itself where it may be known that the knowledge learned in one class will be used in one way or another in a subsequent course. Conversely, there is least predictability in the attempt to relate what is learned in the classroom to what the student may need as a citizen or specialist.

Our general understanding of learning theory would seem to indicate that knowledge which is organized and related is better learned and retained than knowledge which is specific and isolated. By this we mean that learning a large number of isolated specifics is quite difficult simply because of the multiplicity of items to be remembered. Further, they cannot be retained very well if they are kept in such isolation. Thus one hundred nonsense syllables would be more difficult to learn than an equal number of syllables in a meaningful poem. Specifics can be learned in relation to a general abstraction, and as a result can be remembered or retained best in this relationship. When learning takes place in this way, it is possible for an individual who remembers the generalization to proceed relatively easily to some of the specifics subsumed under that generalization. On the other hand, generalizations or abstractions are relatively difficult to learn unless they are related to appropriate concrete phenomena. A generalization isolated from the phenomena it covers is very difficult to learn and very hard to retain. As a matter of fact, some definitions of intelligence regard the abstractness of the ideas an individual can understand as a good index of the level of intelligence.

Curricular Decisions To Be Made about Knowledge Objectives

Four decisions to be made with respect to the nature of the knowledge objectives included in the curriculum should be noted. These relate to "How much knowledge should be required learning?"; "How precisely need the student learn the required knowledge?"; "How is knowledge best organized for learning?"; and "How meaningful need required knowledge-learning be to the student?"

Decisions with respect to "How much knowledge should be required learning?" must strike a balance between attempts to include all the knowledge the individual might conceivably acquire in a particular subject and only that knowledge which is most basic to the subject. Rarely does the educator lean toward the latter of these two alternatives. Some educators frequently assume that the knowledge which the expert or specialist needs to possess about a field or topic and the knowledge which the beginning student may reasonably be expected to learn are identical. Such an assumption tends to overestimate the student's ability to learn and retain information. These educators must decide whether the student's time and effort are best used in becoming acquainted with the major knowledge in the field or in thoroughly mastering that knowledge which is basic to further learning in the field. For instance, in the field of mathematics it would be possible for the student to become aware of the existence and nature of the major mathematical techniques or to concentrate on learning the fundamentals which would permit him to later pick up these techniques on his own.

A second decision, the degree of precision to be required of the student, is not unrelated to the first. Thus, requiring the student to "become aware of the existence and nature of the major mathematical techniques" would presumably permit the student some latitude in the precision of his recall of the details of the techniques. On the other hand, to "thoroughly master that mathematical knowledge which is basic to further learning" implies a rather high standard of precision in the learning of this material. This decision about the precision to be required of the student exists at all levels of knowledge. Thus, even in the simplest type of objective such as knowledge of terminology, it is quite conceivable for a student to learn definitions of terms at many different levels of accuracy and precision. Usually greater precision is required at later stages of training. Thus, the student is introduced to an item of knowledge at a general but accurate level, gradually making finer and finer distinctions as he uses the item until he has reached the more detailed and precise level of the expert.

A third decision relates to the best organization of knowledge to facilitate learning. As previously noted, the cases of the specialist and the student are not identical. The organization the specialist finds most useful is not necessarily the organization that provides the easiest learning path for the student. The decision to be made is whether to use an organization externally imposed by some authority or expert as compared with an organization that fits the internal state of the learner at his particular stage of development.

A fourth decision with respect to the nature of knowledge objectives in the curriculum relates to the immediate as opposed to the future need of the student for this information. A student can memorize a body of information whether or not he finds immediate use for it or whether it meets any of his present needs. This is particularly true once the student becomes habituated to this kind of learning, as many of our students have. Many schools orient their students in this direction by the use of grades, examinations, and competition. It is likely that if the teacher believes the learning of knowledge is important or can communicate the importance of it to the students, there will be little difficulty in obtaining learning of even the most artificial and esoteric *prevate* kinds of information.

THE NATURE OF ABILITIES AND SKILLS

Although information or knowledge is recognized as an important outcome of education, very few teachers would be satisfied to regard this as the primary or the sole outcome of instruction. What is needed is some evidence that the students can do something with their knowledge, that is, that they can apply the information to new situations and problems. It is also expected that students will acquire generalized techniques for dealing with new problems and new materials. Thus, it is expected that when the student encounters a new problem or situation, he will select an appropriate technique for attacking it and will bring to bear the necessary information, both facts and principles. This has been labeled "critical thinking" by some, "reflective thinking" by Dewey and others, and "problem solving" by still others. In the taxonomy we have used the term "intellectual abilities and skills." The most general operational definition of these abilities and skills is that the individual can find appropriate information and techniques in his previous experience to bring to bear on new problems and situations. This requires some analysis or understanding of the new situation; it requires a background of knowledge or methods which can be readily utilized; and it also requires some facility in discerning the appropriate relations between previous experience and the new situation. *transfer, have to see a relationship*

Recall

ARTS OR SKILLS + KNOWLEDGE = ABILITIES

Sometimes in educational achievement testing we wish to distinguish between what we might call "intellectual abilities" and "intellectual arts and skills." "Arts and skills" refer to modes of operation and generalized techniques for dealing with problems. In testing for arts and skills, the problems and materials are of such a nature that little or no specialized and technical information is required. Whatever information is required is assumed to be part of the general fund of knowledge of the group being tested. The emphasis in testing is on the examinee's competence in using a generalized method of operating or dealing with a new problem situation. The arts and skills emphasize the mental processes of organizing and reorganizing material to achieve a particular purpose.

The intellectual abilities, on the other hand, refer to situations in which the individual is expected to bring specific technical information to bear on a new problem. They represent combinations of knowledge and intellectual arts and skills. In solving problems requiring intellectual abilities, the student is expected to organize or reorganize a problem, to recognize what material is appropriate, to remember such material, and to make use of it in the problem situation. In the case both of abilities and of skills, the problems are intended to be new and unfamiliar to the student.

Although this distinction between intellectual abilities and intellectual skills may be made in achievement testing, it is rather difficult to classify educational objectives and test items as abilities or skills without a full knowledge of the prior experience of the students. It is for this reason that the distinction has been omitted in the taxonomy and is only briefly mentioned here.

JUSTIFICATION FOR THE DEVELOPMENT OF INTELLECTUAL ABILITIES AND SKILLS — *Problem solving*

Justification for the development of intellectual abilities and skills can readily be derived from a consideration of the nature of the society and culture in which we live, the knowledge that is available to us, and the kind of citizen the schools seek to develop. Further justification may be derived from what is known in educational psychology about the permanence of various kinds of learning and the extent to which various kinds of learning can be transferred to new situations.

The development of problem-solving skills (intellectual abilities and skills) is not equally necessary in all societies and cultures. It is possible to imagine a society or culture which is relatively fixed. Such a society represents a closed system in which it is possible to predict in advance both the kinds of problems individuals will encounter and the solutions which are appropriate to those problems. Where such predictions can be made in advance, it is possible to organize the educational experiences so as to give each individual the particular knowledge and the specific methods needed for solving the problems he will encounter. Probably the nearest one can come to such a closed system in our culture is in some aspects of military life. For instance, if one is training an individual to be a radio technician for military work, it is frequently possible to know in advance exactly what kind of radio circuits he will have to work with. Under these conditions it is possible to reduce the amount of training to only these particular radio circuits and to teach the individual how to solve all the foreseeable difficulties he will encounter in working with them. Such training can be quick and efficient, but it is highly restricted since it is applicable to only a very limited range of situations.

Whatever the case in the past, it is very clear that in the middle of the 20th century we find ourselves in a rapidly changing and unpredictable culture. It seems almost impossible to foresee the particular ways in which it will change in the near future or the particular problems which will be paramount in five or ten years. Under these conditions, much emphasis must be placed in the schools on the development of generalized ways of attacking problems and on knowledge which can be applied to a wide range of new situations. That is, we have the task of preparing individuals for problems that cannot be foreseen in advance, and about all that can be done under such conditions is to help the student acquire generalized intellectual abilities and skills which will serve him well in many new situations. This places faith in the intellectual virtues as providing some form of stability for the individual who must find or make some order in his world.

However, even in the relatively stable culture or society, we do have to recognize that all knowledge is partial and that each situation the individual encounters has some unique characteristics. Forced to act, the individual has the task of taking what knowledge he has (which is only partially appropriate to a situation) and determining its relevance to the new situation. Since each situation is unique, the individual must be able to recognize which essential characteristics of the new situation are related to situations he has already encountered; then he must apply the correct knowledge and method with appropriate modifications. Clearly it is impossible to give the individual all the knowledge he will ever need for every new situation he will encounter. It is possible, however, to help him acquire that knowledge which has been found most useful in the past, and to help him develop those intellectual abilities and skills which will enable him to adapt that knowledge to the new situations. *Problem solving*

The importance of the intellectual abilities and skills is further illustrated by our recognition of the individual's ability to independently attack his problems as a desirable sign of maturity. Individuals are expected, as they mature, to solve problems on their own and to make decisions wisely on the basis of their own thinking. Further, this independent problem solving is regarded as one indication of the individual's adjustment. It is recognized that unless the individual can do his own problem-solving he cannot maintain his integrity as an independent personality.

Closely allied to this concept of maturity and integrity is the concept of the individual as a member of a democracy. Citizens are expected to make important and independent decisions about governmental problems and about their political future. It is clear that many of these decisions require problem solving of a very high order. It is impossible to tell an individual in advance how to vote or even the bases on which he should vote. These are matters he must decide repeatedly throughout his life whenever a major election takes place. But more than specific elections and voting is the concept of individuals in a democracy as independent decision-makers who, in the last analysis, are responsible for the conduct of a democratic political system as well as a democratic way of life.

The above justifications for the development of intellectual abilities and skills reflect a number of value components in relation to the concept of the good life. The following two reasons have to do primarily with the efficiency of the learning process.

As we have defined intellectual abilities and skills, they are more widely applicable than knowledge. If we are concerned with the problem of transfer of training, by definition we would select intellectual abilities and skills as having greater transfer value.

A second reason for the efficiency of intellectual abilities and skills in learning is their permanence. From psychological theory (e.g., reinforcement theory) it would seem reasonable to expect greater permanence of learning for those outcomes of education which can be generalized and applied in a number of different situations throughout the individual's formal educational experience than for those outcomes which are so specific that they are likely to be encountered only once or at the most a few times throughout the educational program. It would seem desirable to determine whether research evidence is in support of our logical and pedagogical distinctions. While only a few studies in the literature deal with this problem, the findings are in general support of the foregoing.

Finally, the foregoing discussion has illustrated the importance of the abilities and skills for both the individual and his society, and it has noted the learning efficiency of the abilities and skills. But common observation would indicate that individuals in general tend to avoid real problem solving. When presented with problems, they usually apply a limited stock of techniques to them and are frequently satisfied if a partial solution is obtained. If the techniques do not work, there is a strong tendency either to reorder the problem completely (that is, to make it a new problem) or to escape from it entirely. Rarely do individuals stay with a difficult problem for any considerable length of time and try increasingly varied procedures for attacking it. Yet, we need more than ever to help students develop problem-solving methods which will yield more complete and adequate solutions in a wide range of problem situations. It is to be hoped that the taxonomy's analysis of this area will facilitate the exploration of new methods of teaching for high-level problem solving and assist in evaluating these methods.

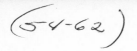

Appendix to Chapter 2
CONDENSED VERSION
OF THE TAXONOMY OF
EDUCATIONAL OBJECTIVES

Benjamin S. Bloom · David R. Krathwohl

KNOWLEDGE

1.00 KNOWLEDGE

Knowledge, as defined here, involves the recall of specifics and universals, the recall of methods and processes, or the recall of a pattern, structure, or setting. For measurement purposes, the recall situation involves little more than bringing to mind the appropriate material. Although some alteration of the material may be required, this is a relatively minor part of the task. The knowledge objectives emphasize most the psychological processes of remembering. The process of relating is also involved in that a knowledge test situation requires the organization and reorganization of a problem such that it will furnish the appropriate signals and cues for the information and knowledge the individual possesses. To use an analogy, if one thinks of the mind as a file, the problem in a knowledge test situation is that of finding in the problem or task the appropriate signals, cues, and clues which will most effectively bring out whatever knowledge is filed or stored.

1.10 KNOWLEDGE OF SPECIFICS

The recall of specific and isolable bits of information. The emphasis is on symbols with concrete referents. This material, which is at a very low level of abstraction, may be thought of as the elements from which more complex and abstract forms of knowledge are built.

1.11 KNOWLEDGE OF TERMINOLOGY

Knowledge of the referents for specific symbols (verbal and non-verbal). This may include knowledge of the most generally accepted symbol referent, knowledge of the variety of symbols which may be used for a single referent, or knowledge of the referent most appropriate to a given use of a symbol.

* To define technical terms by giving their attributes, properties, or relations.
* Familiarity with a large number of words in their common range of meanings.

From *Taxonomy of Educational Objectives: Handbook I, The Cognitive Domain*, by B. S. Bloom and D. R. Krathwohl, 1956, pp. 201–207. Used by permission of David McKay Company, Inc.
* Illustrative educational objectives selected from the literature.

1.12 KNOWLEDGE OF SPECIFIC FACTS

Knowledge of dates, events, persons, places, etc. This may include very precise and specific information such as the specific date or exact magnitude of a phenomenon. It may also include approximate or relative information such as an approximate time period or the general order of magnitude of a phenomenon.

* The recall of major facts about particular cultures.
* The possession of a minimum knowledge about the organisms studied in the laboratory.

1.20 KNOWLEDGE OF WAYS AND MEANS OF DEALING WITH SPECIFICS

Knowledge of the ways of organizing, studying, judging, and criticizing. This includes the methods of inquiry, the chronological sequences, and the standards of judgment within a field as well as the patterns of organization through which the areas of the fields themselves are determined and internally organized. This knowledge is at an intermediate level of abstraction between specific knowledge on the one hand and knowledge of universals on the other. It does not so much demand the activity of the student in using the materials as it does a more passive awareness of their nature.

1.21 KNOWLEDGE OF CONVENTIONS *writing*

Knowledge of characteristic ways of treating and presenting ideas and phenomena. For purposes of communication and consistency, workers in a field employ usages, styles, practices, and forms which best suit their purposes and/or which appear to suit best the phenomena with which they deal. It should be recognized that although these forms and conventions are likely to be set up on arbitrary, accidental, or authoritative bases, they are retained because of the general agreement or concurrence of individuals concerned with the subject, phenomena, or problem.

* Familiarity with the forms and conventions of the major types of works, e.g., verse, plays, scientific papers, etc.
* To make pupils conscious of correct form and usage in speech and writing.

1.22 KNOWLEDGE OF TRENDS AND SEQUENCES

Knowledge of the processes, directions, and movements of phenomena with respect to time.

* Understanding of the continuity and development of American culture as exemplified in American life.

* Knowledge of the basic trends underlying the development of public assistance programs.

1.23 KNOWLEDGE OF CLASSIFICATIONS AND CATEGORIES

Knowledge of the classes, sets, divisions, and arrangements which are regarded as fundamental for a given subject field, purpose, argument, or problem.

* To recognize the area encompassed by various kinds of problems or materials.
* Becoming familiar with a range of types of literature.

1.24 KNOWLEDGE OF CRITERIA

Knowledge of the criteria by which facts, principles, opinions, and conduct are tested or judged.

* Familiarity with criteria for judgment appropriate to the type of work and the purpose for which it is read.
* Knowledge of criteria for the evaluation of recreational activities.

1.25 KNOWLEDGE OF METHODOLOGY

Knowledge of the methods of inquiry, techniques, and procedures employed in a particular subject field as well as those employed in investigating particular problems and phenomena. The emphasis here is on the individual's knowledge of the method rather than his ability to use the method.

* Knowledge of scientific methods for evaluating health concepts.
* The student shall know the methods of attack relevant to the kinds of problems of concern to the social sciences

1.30 KNOWLEDGE OF THE UNIVERSALS AND ABSTRACTIONS IN A FIELD

Knowledge of the major schemes and patterns by which phenomena and ideas are organized. These are the large structures, theories, and generalizations which dominate a subject field or which are quite generally used in studying phenomena or solving problems. These are at the highest levels of abstraction and complexity.

1.31 KNOWLEDGE OF PRINCIPLES AND GENERALIZATIONS

Knowledge of particular abstractions which summarize observations of phenomena. These are the abstractions which are of value in explaining, describing, predicting, or in determining the most appropriate and relevant action or direction to be taken.

* Knowledge of the important principles by which our experience with biological phenomena is summarized.
* The recall of major generalizations about particular cultures.

1.32 KNOWLEDGE OF THEORIES AND STRUCTURES

Knowledge of the *body* of principles and generalizations together with their interrelations which present a clear, rounded, and systematic view of a complex phenomenon, problem, or field. These are the most abstract formulations, and they can be used to show the interrelation and organization of a great range of specifics.

* The recall of major theories about particular cultures.
* Knowledge of a relatively complete formulation of the theory of evolution.

INTELLECTUAL ABILITIES AND SKILLS

Abilities and skills refer to organized modes of operation and generalized techniques for dealing with materials and problems. The materials and problems may be of such a nature that little or no specialized and technical information is required. Such information as is required can be assumed to be part of the individual's general fund of knowledge.

Other problems may require specialized and technical information at a rather high level such that specific knowledge and skill in dealing with the problem and the materials are required. The abilities and skills objectives emphasize the mental processes of organizing and reorganizing materials to achieve a particular purpose. The materials may be given or remembered.

2.00 COMPREHENSION

This represents the lowest level of understanding. It refers to a type of understanding or apprehension such that the individual knows what is being communicated and can make use of the material or idea being communicated without necessarily relating it to other material or seeing its fullest implications.

2.10 TRANSLATION

Comprehension as evidenced by the care and accuracy with which the communication is paraphrased or rendered from one language or form of communication to another. Translation is judged on the basis of faithfulness and accuracy, that is, on the extent to which the material in the original communication is preserved although the form of the communication has been altered.

* The ability to understand non-literal statements (metaphor, symbolism, irony, exaggeration).

* Skill in translating mathematical verbal material into symbolic statements and vice versa.

2.20 INTERPRETATION

The explanation or summarization of a communication. Whereas translation involves an objective part-for-part rendering of a communication, interpretation involves a reordering, rearrangement, or a new view of the material.

* The ability to grasp the thought of the work as a whole at any desired level of generality.

* The ability to interpret various types of social data.

2.30 EXTRAPOLATION

The extension of trends or tendencies beyond the given data to determine implications, consequences, corollaries, effects, etc., which are in accordance with the conditions described in the original communication.

* The ability to deal with the conclusions of a work in terms of the immediate inference made from the explicit statements.

* Skill in predicting continuation of trends.

3.00 APPLICATION

The use of abstractions in particular and concrete situations. The abstractions may be in the form of general ideas, rules of procedures, or generalized methods. The abstractions may also be technical principles, ideas, and theories which must be remembered and applied.

* Application to the phenomena discussed in one paper of the scientific terms or concepts used in other papers.

* The ability to predict the probable effect of a change in a factor on a biological situation previously at equilibrium.

4.00 ANALYSIS

The breakdown of a communication into its constituent elements or parts such that the relative hierarchy of ideas is made clear and/or the relations between the ideas expressed are made explicit. Such analyses are intended to clarify the communication, to indicate how the communication is organized, and the way in which it manages to convey its effects, as well as its basis and arrangement.

4.10 ANALYSIS OF ELEMENTS

Identification of the elements included in a communication.

* The ability to recognize unstated assumptions.

* Skill in distinguishing facts from hypotheses.

4.20 ANALYSES OF RELATIONSHIPS

The connections and interactions between elements and parts of a communication.

* Ability to check the consistency of hypotheses with given information and assumptions.
* Skill in comprehending the interrelationships among the ideas in a passage.

4.30 ANALYSIS OF ORGANIZATIONAL PRINCIPLES

The organization, systematic arrangement, and structure which hold the communication together. This includes the "explicit" as well as "implicit" structure. It includes the bases, necessary arrangement, and the mechanics which make the communication a unit.

* The ability to recognize form and pattern in literary or artistic works as a means of understanding their meaning.
* Ability to recognize the general techniques used in persuasive materials, such as advertising, propaganda, etc.

5.00 SYNTHESIS

The putting together of elements and parts so as to form a whole. This involves the process of working with pieces, parts, elements, etc., and arranging and combining them in such a way as to constitute a pattern or structure not clearly there before.

5.10 PRODUCTION OF A UNIQUE COMMUNICATION

The development of a communication in which the writer or speaker attempts to convey ideas, feelings, and/or experiences to others.

* Skill in writing, using an excellent organization of ideas and statements.
* Ability to tell a personal experience effectively.

5.20 PRODUCTION OF A PLAN, OR PROPOSED SET OF OPERATIONS

The development of a plan of work or the proposal of a plan of operations. The plan should satisfy requirements of the task which may be given to the student or which he may develop for himself.

* Ability to propose ways of testing hypotheses.
* Ability to plan a unit of instruction for a particular teaching situation.

5.30 DERIVATION OF A SET OF ABSTRACT RELATIONS

The development of a set of abstract relations either to classify or explain particular data or phenomena, or the deduction of propositions and relations from a set of basic propositions or symbolic representations.

* Ability to formulate appropriate hypotheses based upon an analysis of factors involved, and to modify such hypotheses in the light of new factors and considerations.
* Ability to make mathematical discoveries and generalizations.

6.00 EVALUATION

Judgments about the value of material and methods for given purposes. Quantitative and qualitative judgments about the extent to which material and methods satisfy criteria. Use of a standard of appraisal. The criteria may be those determined by the student or those which are given to him.

6.10 JUDGMENTS IN TERMS OF INTERNAL EVIDENCE

Evaluation of the accuracy of a communication from such evidence as logical accuracy, consistency, and other internal criteria.

* Judging by internal standards, the ability to assess general probability of accuracy in reporting facts from the care given to exactness of statement, documentation, proof, etc.
* The ability to indicate logical fallacies in arguments.

6.20 JUDGMENTS IN TERMS OF EXTERNAL CRITERIA

Evaluation of material with reference to selected or remembered criteria.

* The comparison of major theories, generalizations, and facts about particular cultures.
* Judging by external standards, the ability to compare a work with the highest known standards in its field—especially with other works of recognized excellence.

CHAPTER 3 Setting Objectives in the Social Studies: The Affective Domain

Affective objectives emphasize a feeling, an emotion, or a degree of acceptance or rejection. Many of the traditional objectives of social studies teachers lie in the affective domain. For example, social studies teachers try to influence the attitudes of their students toward their work. They want students to find satisfaction in responding creditably to homework assignments and classroom discussions. They want each student to examine his values, to organize them into a value system, and to develop a personal philosophy. These desires force conscientious teachers to face three problems.

The first involves the choice of interests, attitudes, appreciations, values, and emotional sets or biases to teach. About some—that students must not disrupt class discussion—there is widespread agreement. About others—that we should inculcate a particular set of ethical principles—there is virtually no agreement at all. Yet each teacher must choose to emphasize or to ignore these affective considerations both in what he teaches and in the way he teaches.

The second problem involves teaching technique. Much that we do in the affective domain results from implicit rather than from explicit instruction. We may teach students to value the opinions of others by treating the statements made by our students in class discussion with respect. We may teach students to find satisfaction in intellectual attainment by writing encouraging comments on their papers or by asking them to report to the class on extra reading they have done. We can also strive to attain affective objectives through explicit teaching, that is, by examining the value systems of others or by teaching that a certain set of values is to be preferred.

The third problem involves evaluation. As many scholars have pointed out, cognitive objectives are relatively easy to evaluate through paper-and-pencil tests. But affective objectives are another matter. Students can often guess what response a teacher wants to an affective question and answer accord-

40

ingly. Moreover, teachers hesitate to grade students on their interests, attitudes, or character development. If we are to set affective objectives, however, we must find a way to evaluate progress toward them.

Chapter 3 consists of two parts. The first is a speech given by the author to a PTA at Taylor Allderdice High School, Pittsburgh, in April 1961. This talk raises some questions that sometimes trouble teachers about the matter of teaching values in the schools. The second section of the chapter comes from the Krathwohl, Bloom, and Masia taxonomy concerned with the affective domain. Like the earlier, companion volume on the cognitive domain, this publication has had a marked impact on curriculum specialists. In the excerpts reprinted here, the authors examine the need for an affective classification and set forth the basis for their scheme. A condensed version of their classification scheme follows in the appendix to the reading. As you read, keep the following in mind:

1) Is the tripartite division of types of values taught in the schools given in Professor Fenton's paper a justifiable one? Is it possible to avoid indoctrination in teaching for affective goals? If so, how? *OPEN MINDEDNESS*

2) Does Fenton's position involve any values? if so, what? Did Bloom's argument for teaching intellectual abilities in Chapter 2 involve any values? *Yes*

3) Should a teacher make his own values clear to himself by translating them into affective objectives? Is this technique more "honest" than trying to avoid affective goals?

4) Using content from Chapter 1, devise a simple strategy designed to teach for one of the affective goals listed in the appendix to this reading.

TEACHING ABOUT VALUES
IN THE PUBLIC SCHOOLS

Edwin Fenton

Every teacher affects the value system of his students whether he likes it or not. If he is conscientious and hard working, he often communicates this attitude to his classes; if he is slovenly and lazy, a quite different set of values transmits itself to the perceptive student. A martinet, meticulous about the width of the margins on a term paper, may convey an entirely different attitude to learning from the one which a creative teacher, interested in developing ideas more than in teaching the canons of polite writing, will demonstrate. Even the teacher who tries conscientiously to avoid teaching values to his students does so; the very act of avoiding indoctrination expresses a value judgment. We cannot avoid values. We must still decide, however, the limits to which we, as teachers, have a right to go in the matter of approaching matters of value in the classroom.

Let me begin by distinguishing three types of values with which we must deal: behavioral, procedural, and substantive values. Two of these we have a right to teach; the third, in my opinion, we do not.

A behavioral value concerns procedure in the classroom. We teachers are retained by the board of education to instruct the young, and we are paid for doing our jobs. We cannot tolerate students who disrupt classes or who make our bookkeeping unnecessarily complicated by coming to school late day after day. In order to perform adequately as teachers, we must enforce certain rules of order in the classroom. Students must keep quiet when others have the floor; they must keep textbooks in good condition; they must not molest their classmates; they must not defenestrate the teacher. Each teacher has a right to teach and enforce a value system that implies these patterns of behavior. If he does not teach such values he will be unable to teach. Not only must he tell students that these values are good ones, he must also enforce rules which these values imply, even to the extent of sending Jane or Johnny to the office where they speak harshly and carry big sticks. I am prepared to defend the proposition that every teacher ought to teach behavioral values. If he does not he cannot teach effectively.

I am also prepared to defend the proposition that we ought to teach procedural values. Critical thinking is better than uncritical thinking; this canon underlies the entire scholarly world. If a student insists that his prejudices should not be challenged and defends them with an emotional appeal, he should be *forced* to subject them to the test of evidence and to defend them in the face of the full array of scholarly argument. In science classes we have a right to insist that students accept the method of experimentation as preferable to what "common sense" might tell them. In mathematics they *must* accept the structure of the deductive method. In history and the social sciences they must be willing to look at evidence for their position and to accept the method by which social scientists and historians arrive at conclusions. Unless parents and school officials give us the right to teach the validity of certain procedural values, we cannot teach our disciplines.

But substantive values are a different matter. Let me give some examples of substantive values that might be held by men in different parts of this nation or of the world. These values are not necessarily mine; I cite them only as examples to make the issue clear to all of us.

Democracy is better than totalitarianism.

The major purpose of education is to permit each individual to develop to the limit of his abilities.

Religion is a good thing, and young people ought to attend church or synagogue.

The family is the basis of society, so divorce ought not to be permitted.
If the individual wants one course of action, and society another, then
the individual ought to do as society dictates.

Money is more important than anything else.

Young people ought to go along with the crowd rather than pursue an
independent course.

Do you parents want me as a teacher to teach any of these values? Do you want to select a set of values to be taught in the schools? Do you want me as a teacher to avoid these issues entirely in class? Each teacher must make up his mind about what he wishes to do in the matter of teaching substantive issues such as these. I shall argue that he should raise them, but he should not teach a set of them as truth.

Many teachers of the social studies argue that they should instill a set of values in their students. According to this line of argument, the social studies should indoctrinate students to the end that they will accept normative standards of behavior and normative value systems in the United States. This position is implicit in many of our texts. In some elementary school textbooks the family consists of four people, two male and two female, two parents and two offspring. Fathers carry briefcases; mothers are always well groomed and lovely; no one ever loses his temper; everyone lives in a little house in the suburbs; there are no Negroes in these all-white neighborhoods. Do we really want to teach values such as these? After all, about a quarter of our marriages end in divorces. Should children from these families be forced to look upon themselves as abnormal? Do teachers have a right to teach, even implicitly, that segregation is acceptable in American society?

Foreign observers writing about the United States often comment about the diversity of our society. We are remarkably pluralistic; our population has origins in every land; our religions are as diverse as our sporting events; our political faiths and standards of behavior are remarkably disparate; the value system of different economic and social classes vary enormously. This pluralism implies diverse sets of values. Among some American culture groups, divorce is anathema; among others—particularly some Hollywood stars—it appears that consecutive polygamy has become a way of life. Some Americans are pacifists; others could hardly be more belligerent. I could multiply these examples endlessly. Each of us knows from personal experience that we disagree with each other about something. Do you want teachers telling your children what they ought to believe about matters such as these?

I think we can agree that we ought to teach them to abide by values which have been enacted into law. Most parents do not object if we teach students not to murder or not to steal—particularly where parents' lives and funds are involved. We ought to make students realize the extent to which they will be punished if they fail to pay income taxes—a sore topic in mid-April—or if they joy ride without permission in someone's automobile. Teaching these truths implies value systems, but like the behavioral values I spoke of earlier, they form the cement that holds our society together and permits it to function. Once we go beyond laws, however, who is to decide what should be taught? Will you permit a teacher to decide to teach students in a public school that a collectivist economy is better than a free-enterprise economy? Will you permit a teacher to tell his students that the major objective in life is to make money, no matter what the costs in human terms? Do you want teachers to tell students to develop their abilities to the limit, even if they must harm others in the process? Shall we teach students to conform or to be leaders or to give to charity? I do not want teachers to make such statements to my children, even if I agree with them. On the other hand, I do want teachers to raise these issues for discussion, always keeping the discussion under the control of evidence within a framework of critical thinking. Of what value is an education if it does not approach these vital issues?

Let me illustrate what I mean about the distinction between teaching values and teaching about values. If a teacher teaches substantive values about government, he may tell his students that democracy is better than totalitarianism. If he teaches about values, he raises questions about democracy and totalitarianism. He might ask students to define the objectives a government should set for itself. Then he might ask what alternative ways men have devised for attaining these objectives and insist that students examine the logical consequences of these alternatives. The goal of this procedure is not unanimous agreement; it is to persuade each student to examine goals and means for himself in order to arrive at a political philosophy by which he can guide his later life. If a student does not alter a value, this process ought to provide him with evidence to support a position he may have held as a mere prejudice. If he does change a value judgment, he has scrapped an opinion that failed to meet the test of evidence and adopted a sounder one. In either case he is better off.

I see three major bad effects from teaching values in the schools. First, we have little evidence that we can do it. Research seems to indicate that we can get movement around a pole, that is, that we can get students to change value judgments, but they change in various directions instead of moving toward a predetermined position that the teacher has decided. Second, if we decide that certain values should be taught in the schools, we either dictate what each teacher shall teach or we permit teachers who disagree with us to tell our students that certain values they might hold are wrong. I am not willing to permit either alternative. Finally, teaching certain values as desirable inclines students to believe that people in foreign lands who hold other value systems are necessarily wrong and ought for their own good to be corrected. How frightening!

If we try to avoid teaching values, or at least teaching about values, we run the danger of leading students to believe that no values are worthwhile. They might conclude that nothing really matters, that they can do anything they wish as long as they obey the law. I am willing to argue that issues of values ought to be raised in order to help students to thrash out these vital matters with their peers.

But teaching particular substantive values I shall leave to the home. If anyone, parents and not teachers should tell their children what to believe. If anyone, I want to tell my child what I think he ought to think about the role of the individual in society. I shall object vigorously to a teacher who tells my child that I am wrong or that he is wrong about a value system. I shall be equally disturbed if a teacher does not raise questions about values so that my child or yours can examine each of his feelings, his standards, and his attitudes to develop a coherent personal and civic code of behavior in keeping with the ethical principles essential to a democratic way of life.

Appendix to Chapter 3
THE NEED FOR A
CLASSIFICATION OF
AFFECTIVE OBJECTIVES

David R. Krathwohl · Benjamin S. Bloom · Bertram B. Masia

One of the reasons the cognitive domain presented us with a more easily solvable problem than the affective domain was the tremendous wealth of evaluation material we found being used for grading and certifying student achievement. Faculty, examiners, administrators, and even students accept the need for and value of such material.

When we looked for evaluation material in the affective domain we found it usually in relation to some national educational research project or a sponsored local research project (for which a report had to be written). Only rarely did we find an affective evaluation technique used because a group of local teachers wanted to know whether students were developing in a particular way. It was evident that evaluation work for affective objectives was marginal and was done only when a very pressing question was raised by the faculty or when someone wished to do "educational" research.

It is not entirely fair to imply that evaluation of the attainment of affective objectives is completely absent from the regular activities of schools and

From *Taxonomy of Educational Objectives: Handbook II, The Affective Domain,* by D. R. Krathwohl, B. S. Bloom, and B. B. Masia, 1964, pp. 15–28. Used by permission of David McKay Company, Inc.

teachers. Undoubtedly almost every teacher is on the alert for evidence of desirable interests, attitudes, and character development. However, most of this is the noting of unusual characteristics or dramatic developments when they are almost forced on the teacher's attention. What is missing is a systematic effort to collect evidence of growth in affective objectives which is in any way parallel to the very great and systematic efforts to evaluate cognitive achievement.

Erosion of Affective Objectives

We studied the history of several major courses at the general education level of college. Typically, we found that in the original statement of objectives there was frequently as much emphasis given to affective objectives as to cognitive objectives. Sometimes in the early years of the course some small attempt was made to secure evidence on the extent to which students were developing in the affective behaviors.

However, as we followed some of these courses over a period of ten to twenty years, we found a rather rapid dropping of the affective objectives from the statements about the course and an almost complete disappearance of efforts at appraisal of student growth in this domain.

It was evident to us that there is a characteristic type of *erosion* in which the original intent of a course or educational program becames worn down to that which can be explicitly evaluated for grading purposes and that which can be taught easily through verbal methods (lectures, discussions, reading materials, etc.). There is a real shift in intent that comes with time. It may be true that it is easier to teach and evaluate cognitive objectives. But we really doubt that this is the sole determining influence and believe that a number of forces are responsible for the erosion of intentions. size

School Grading and Affective Objectives

The failure to grade students' achievement on affective objectives accounts for a large portion of the erosion. Cognitive achievement is regarded as fair game for grading purposes. Examinations may include a great range of types of cognitive objectives, and teachers and examiners have little hesitation in giving a student a grade of A or F on the basis of his performance on these cognitive achievement examinations. In contrast, teachers and examiners do not regard it as appropriate to grade students with respect to their interests, attitude, or character development. To be sure, a student who is at one extreme on these affective objectives may be disciplined by the school authorities, while a student at the other extreme may be regarded so favorably by teachers that he receives whatever rewards and honors are available for the purpose (e.g., the teacher's attention, appointment to prestige classroom positions, etc.).

A considerable part of the hesitation in the use of affective measures for grading purposes stems from the inadequacy of the appraisal techniques and the ease with which a student may exploit his ability to detect the responses which will be rewarded and the responses which will be penalized. In contrast, it is assumed that a student who responds in the desirable way on a cognitive measure does indeed possess the competence which is being sampled. For instance, if we wish to determine whether a humanities course has resulted in "an interest in seeking and enjoying a wide variety of musical experiences," we may attempt to appraise the variety of musical experiences the student has voluntarily participated in prior to, during, and subsequent to the humanities course. We hesitate to trust the professed evidence that a student has developed such an interest, because we have difficulty in determining the difference between a natural or honest response and one that is made solely to please the teacher, and we may even have some question about the accuracy of the student's recall of such experiences. On the other hand, if our objective is "the development of the ability to become sensitive to and perceptive of different aspects of a musical work," we may present him with a series of musical selections which are likely to be unfamiliar to him. Then, by careful questioning, determine which elements he has perceived and which he has not. We would not hesitate to assign him a grade on the second objective, but we would have considerable hesitation about failing the student or giving him a high grade on the basis of our evidence on the first objective. However, though this difficulty with affective measures presents a series of technical problems, they could probably be solved with very substantial effort.

A much more serious reason for the hesitation in the use of affective measures for grading purposes comes from somewhat deeper philosophical and cultural values. Achievement, competence, productivity, etc., are regarded as public matters. Honors are awarded for high achievement, honor lists may be published by the Dean, and lists of National Merit Scholarship winners may be printed in newspapers. In contrast, one's beliefs, attitudes, values, and personality characteristics are more likely to be regarded as private matters, except in the most extreme instances already noted. My attitudes toward God, home, and family are private concerns, and this privacy is generally respected. My political attitudes are private; I may reveal them if I wish, but no one can force me to do so. In fact, my voting behavior is usually protected from public view. Each man's home is his castle, and his interests, values, beliefs, and personality may not be scrutinized unless he voluntarily gives permission to have them revealed. This public-private status of cognitive vs. affective behaviors is deeply rooted in the Judeo-Christian religion and is a value highly cherished in the democratic traditions of the Western world.

Closely linked to this private aspect of affective behavior is the distinction frequently made between education and indoctrination in a democratic society. Education opens up possibilities for free choice and individual decision. Education helps the individual to explore many aspects of the world and even his own feelings and emotion, but choice and decision are matters for the individual. Indoctrination, on the other hand, is viewed as reducing the possibilities of free choice and decision. It is regarded as an attempt to persuade and coerce the individual to accept a particular viewpoint or belief, to act in a particular manner, and to profess a particular value and way of life. Gradually education has come to mean an almost solely cognitive examination of issues. Indoctrination has come to mean the teaching of affective as well as cognitive behavior. Perhaps a reopening of the entire question would help us to see more clearly the boundaries between education and indoctrination, and the simple dichotomy expressed above between cognitive and affective behavior would no longer seem as real as the rather glib separation of the two suggests.

SLOW ATTAINMENT OF AFFECTIVE OBJECTIVES

Another cause of the erosion in affective objectives has to do with the immediacy of results. A particular item of information or a very specific skill is quickly learned and shows immediate results on cognitive examinations. Even more complex abilities may be learned in a one-semester or one-year course, and the evidences of the learning may be seen in the examination given at the end of the course. In contrast, interests, attitudes, and personality characteristics are assumed to develop relatively slowly and to be visible in appraisal techniques only over long periods of time, perhaps even years. Whether these assumptions are sound can only be revealed by much more evidence than is now available.

It is even possible that just the opposite may be true; namely, that affective behaviors undergo far more sudden transformations than do cognitive behaviors. What is even more probable is that certain objectives in the cognitive and affective domain may be quickly learned or developed, whereas other objectives in both domains may be developed only over a long period of time. Implicit in the *Taxonomy* is the assumption that objectives which fall into the first categories (e.g., *Knowledge, Receiving*) are likely to be learned more rapidly and more easily than objectives which fall into the later and "higher" categories (e.g., *Synthesis, Generalized set*). In any case, a useful classification of affective and cognitive objectives and behaviors would help to expose these assumptions about change (as well as the conditions required for change) in the different types of objectives, whether they be cognitive or affective.

TEACHING FOR AFFECTIVE LEARNING IN RELATION TO COGNITIVE LEARNING

Before closing this discussion of causes of the erosion of affective objectives, we should point up the distinction between objectives as goals to be worked for directly and objectives which are assumed to be the by-products of other objectives (Sawin and Loree, 1959). For a long time it was assumed that if a student learned the information objectives of a course he would, as a direct consequence of this information learning, develop the problem-solving objectives in that course. Thus the teacher's responsibility was reduced to that of providing learning experiences to develop the information in students, and the examination was designed to appraise the students' progress toward the information objectives. As a result of the research and writings of Tyler (1934, 1951), Furst (1958), Dressel (1958), and others, this belief in the "automatic" development of the higher mental processes is no longer widely held. However, there still persists an implicit belief that if cognitive objectives are developed, there will be a corresponding development of appropriate affective behaviors. Research summarized by Jacob (1957) rises serious questions about the tenability of this assumption. The evidence suggests that affective behaviors develop when appropriate learning experiences are provided for students much the same as cognitive behaviors develop from appropriate learning experiences.

The authors of this work hold the view that under some conditions the development of cognitive behaviors may actually destroy certain desired affective behaviors and that, instead of a positive relation between growth in cognitive and affective behavior, it is conceivable that there may be an inverse relation between growth in the two domains. For example, it is quite possible that many literature courses at the high-school and college levels instill knowledge of the history of literature and knowledge of the details of particular works of literature, while at the same time producing an aversion to, or at least a lower level of interest in, literary works. Clearly there is need for conclusive experimentation and research on the relations between the two domains. Here, again, the specificity which a taxonomy can introduce into both domains is likely to reveal conditions under which one conclusion is sound as well as point to situations where the opposite conclusion is tenable.

Perhaps one of the most dramatic events highlighting the need for progress in the affective domain was the publication of Jacob's *Changing Values in College* (1957). He summarizes a great deal of educational research at the college level and finds almost no evidence that college experiences produce a significant change in students' values, beliefs, or personality. Although he has been criticized for his methods, definitions, and assumptions, his critics have not responded by pointing up changes in the affective domain which he had overlooked. Jacob's work has stimulated a considerable amount of soul searching at the college level and is undoubtedly responsible for an increase in interest and research in this area. We must pay our respects to Jacob for increasing our own determination to complete this Handbook.

CLARIFICATION OF COGNITIVE AND AFFECTIVE OBJECTIVES

More than two decades of work on cognitive objectives have produced specific and meaningful results. Few serious workers now use such terms as "critical thinking," "problem solving," or "higher mental processes" as statements of objectives. These terms may be used to describe large goals and aims of education, but in describing the objectives of a course with specific sequences of learning experiences, curriculum makers have more recently made use of terms like "application of principles," "interpretation of data," "skill in recognizing assumptions," etc. These terms are further defined behaviorally, enabling teachers to analyze an examination or evaluation technique to determine whether it does or does not appraise the kinds of educational outcomes they have specified. This greater precision in specifications has, of course, evolved from a considerable amount of interaction between teachers and evaluators. General statements of objectives have been gradually refined and restated until the operational consequences for evaluation instruments became explicit. Furthermore, the consequences of these objectives for the development of learning experiences have become more and more clear as the result of the operational definitions provided by statements of behavior and evaluation instruments. The effectiveness of learning experiences in helping students attain selected objectives has also become clearer through the use of appropriate evaluation instruments in educational research. Such research has stimulated efforts to develop learning theory and learning principles which deal more directly with these highly specific educational objectives. All this is not an attempt to describe a Utopian situation in which cognitive objectives, learning experiences, and evaluation techniques have been developed so well that little further work is now needed. Far from this, we have barely scratched the surface of the tremendous potential for clarification and development of cognition.

However, the situation with respect to affective objectives is so primitive that little in the way of meaning is at present conveyed by statements of objectives. For example, here are six objectives selected from the literature, which purport to state outcomes in the affective domain:

1. The student should develop an attitude of faith in the power of reason and in the methods of experiment and discussion.
2. The student should develop attitudes of intelligent self-criticism in matters of effective expression and correct form of writing.
3. The student should develop an appreciation for the rights and feelings of others.
4. The student should have deep wells of feeling that manifest themselves not only in a passionate hatred of injustice, a "divine discontent," and an unwillingness to be a passive bystander in the presence of violently pressing social issues, but also in active and joyous identification of his own happiness with the larger social good.
5. The student should become interested in good books.
6. The student should develop an appreciation of classical music.

It will be noted that each of these states a general term like "interest," "attitude," or "appreciation" followed by an object such as books, music, people, etc. What is meant by "interest" may range from simply knowing that the object exists to a passionate devotion to this type of object or activity. For example, some possible interpretations of objective 5 may be the following:

> The student should be able to distinguish between good books and not-so-good books.
>
> The student should want to know more about what makes a book good.
>
> The student should read an increasing number of books which experts classify as good.
>
> The student should express a desire to read more good books.
>
> The student should purchase good books for his personal library.

An evaluator attempting to develop an evaluation instrument to appraise growth toward objective 5 could infer almost anything he desired and construct the instrument accordingly. However, in that case the specification of the objectives of instruction would pass from the teachers to the examiners. This would represent a shift in control of instruction and outcomes from the teachers responsible for the learning experiences to the evaluators who devise the instruments for appraising the results of instruction. We regard this as an undesirable shift, since it places educational direction (and control) in the hands of a small number of instrument makers. Furthermore, it is likely that those teachers who, through vague statements of objectives, have yielded control over objectives to the examiners will not make major contributions to the development of learning experiences which will enable students to grow in the ways specified by the objectives.

THE CONTRIBUTION OF A TAXONOMY OF AFFECTIVE OBJECTIVES

If affective objectives and goals are to be realized, they must be defined clearly; learning experiences to help the student develop in the desired direction must be provided; and there must be some systematic method for appraising the extent to which students grow in the desired ways.

It is our hope that the *Taxonomy* will be of service in defining more clearly the objectives in this domain. If it does nothing more, it will serve to indicate that many of the present objectives in this domain are so general as to be meaningless.

It is our hope also that the *Taxonomy* will help teachers become aware of the techniques which are available for appraising growth of students toward various categories of objectives and for assessing other affective changes, whether intended or not. Perhaps this will further stimulate the development of better methods of evaluation in this domain.

Finally, it is our hope that the *Taxonomy* will provide a bridge for further communication among teachers and between teachers and evaluators, curriculum research workers, psychologists, and other behavioral scientists. As this communication process develops, it is likely that the "folklore" which we have presented in the beginning of this chapter can be replaced by a somewhat more precise understanding of how affective behaviors develop, how and when they can be modified, and what the school can and cannot do to develop them in particular forms.

THE SEARCH FOR AN AFFECTIVE CONTINUUM

Perhaps the most difficult part of the task of building the affective domain of the *Taxonomy* was the search for a continuum that would provide a means of ordering and relating the different kinds of affective behavior. It was presumed that the affective domain, like the cognitive, would be structured in a hierarchical order such that each category of behavior would assume achievement of the behaviors categorized below it. But it did not appear likely that the principles of "simple to complex" and "concrete to abstract" would provide as appropriate a basis for structuring the affective domain as they had provided for the cognitive domain. Some additional construct had to be found.

An analysis of affective objectives was undertaken to determine their unique characteristics. It was hoped that among these we would find what was needed to structure an affective continuum. . . .

As has already been indicated in previous chapters, the materials from which this continuum was to be educed were the objectives dealing with interests, attitudes, values, appreciation, and adjustment. These terms were all found to have too wide a variety of meanings to serve, themselves, as the focal points through which to construct a continuum. . . .

This analysis found, for instance, that objectives dealing with interests describe behavior ranging all the way from the student's merely *being aware* that a given phenomenon exists (so that he will at least give it his attention when it is present) through behavior where he is increasingly willing to attend and respond to a phenomenon, to behavior where he is expected to *avidly seek out the phenomenon* in question and to be totally absorbed in it. Throughout the range, it is expected that the student will *feel positively* toward the phenomenon, but at the "high interest" end he is expected to be fairly enamored of it.

The term "attitude" was also found to include objectives with a wide range of behaviors. On the one hand, it is used to describe the involvement of the student who is willing to grant that he has a *positive feeling about something* when he is asked about it. At the other extreme, it is expected that his commitment is such that *he goes out of his way* to express it and even seeks instances in which he can communicate it to others. Objectives dealing with attitudes frequently require the individual to have *a clear conception* of his attitude which he can verbalize.

When we speak of an individual as holding a value, the same range of behavior described for attitudes comes into play. Further, both the terms "attitude" and "value" may refer to behavior which has either rather specific referents as its object, e.g., one's next-door neighbors, or much more general and pervasive referents, e.g., all minority groups. In the latter instance, although the terms "attitude" and "value" are still usually employed, the behavior is often better described as a bundle of attitudes *organized* into an attitude cluster or a value complex.

The term "appreciation," like "interest," may refer to such a simple behavior as a person's being aware of a phenomenon and *being able to perceive it*. It may require that the individual be able to verbalize it (in which instance it may become almost a cognitive rather than an affective objective). It may require only that the individual *experience a pleasant feeling* when he perceives the phenomenon.

Of the terms analyzed, the widest range of meanings is probably accorded the term "adjustment." Central to any definition of adjustment is an *interrelation of one aspect* of the person *with another* in such a way that within this organization some kind of balancing may take place. The term may refer to such behaviors as appear in the social interaction between two persons, or it may *refer to one's whole outlook on life*. It may refer to the internal balancing of self-concept and self-ideal or to the balancing of overt behavior with some role concept. . . .

At one stage in our work in this domain [the affective] it was hoped that by appropriately delimited definitions of such terms as interest, attitude, value, etc., we could build the components into a string of guideposts tied to the common terms in the field. But such definitions were difficult to devise, and their meanings tended to drift into the connotations and denotations which these terms encompassed in common parlance. When we abandoned this, we tried to fit the components into the various theories of learning and theories of personality which were extant in the field. While we were able to find the components in almost all the formal theories, we did not find any one theory which structured the components into a single continuum and which sufficiently clarified the meanings of a representative range of objectives chosen from the literature.

The more we carefully studied the components, however, the clearer it became that a continuum might be derived by appropriately ordering them. Thus the continuum progressed from a level at which the individual is merely *aware of* a phenomenon, being *able to perceive it*. At a next level he is *willing to attend* to phenomena. At a next level he *responds* to the phenomena with a *positive feeling*. Eventually he may feel strongly enough *to go out of his way* to respond. At some point in the process he conceptualizes his behavior and feelings and *organizes* these conceptualizations into a structure. This structure grows in complexity as *it becomes his life outlook*.

This ordering of the components seemed to describe a process by which a given phenomenon or value passed from a level of bare awareness to a position of some power to guide or control the behavior of a person. If it passed through all the stages in which it played an increasingly important role in a person's life, it would come to dominate and control certain aspects of that life as it was absorbed more and more into the internal controlling structure. This process or continuum seemed best described by a term which was heard at various times in our discussions and which has been used similarly in the literature: "internalization." This word seemed an apt description of the process by which the phenomenon or value successively and pervasively become a part of the individual.

When we tried this concept as an organizing principle, we found we were able to construct a meaningful continuum. When we tried it with objectives, we found it helpful in delimiting and describing them and in classifying them into this structure. Our method of choice of an organizing structure was a combination of analytic and pragmatic criteria. The process termed "internalization" was chosen because it encompassed and combined the components which were present when we analyzed the behaviors implied by objectives belonging in the domain. It gave an ordering to these components which appeared to be reasonably parallel to some of our theories about how learning takes place with affective objectives. It helped to define operationally the kinds of tasks a teacher faces in this domain. It appeared to provide a means for cutting through the tangle of conflicting and inadequate learning theories without tying the structure to any one of them. It was consistent with the behavioral point of view of education which places the focus of learning within the individual, and it constructed a continuum of his behavior. It helped to simplify and clarify the meaning of both terse and lengthy complex affective objectives if we analyzed them from this point of view.

Appendix to Chapter 3
A CONDENSED VERSION
OF THE AFFECTIVE DOMAIN
OF THE TAXONOMY OF
EDUCATIONAL OBJECTIVES

David R. Krathwohl · Benjamin S. Bloom · Bertram B. Masia

1.0 RECEIVING (ATTENDING)

At this level we are concerned that the learner be sensitized to the existence of certain phenomena and stimuli; that is, that he be willing to receive or to attend to them. This is clearly the first and crucial step if the learner is to be properly oriented to learn what the teacher intends that he

From *Taxonomy of Educational Objectives: Handbook II, The Affective Domain,* by D. R. Krathwohl, B. S. Bloom, and B. B. Masia, 1964, pp. 176–185. Used by permission of David McKay Company, Inc.

will. To indicate that this is the bottom rung of the ladder, however, is not at all to imply that the teacher is starting *de novo*. Because of previous experience (formal or informal), the student brings to each situation a point of view or set which may facilitate or hinder his recognition of the phenomena to which the teacher is trying to sensitize him.

The category of *Receiving* has been divided into three subcategories to indicate three different levels of attending to phenomena. While the division points between the subcategories are arbitrary, the subcategories do represent a continuum. From an extremely passive position or role on the part of the learner, where the sole responsibility for the evocation of the behavior rests with the teacher—that is, the responsibility rests with him for "capturing" the student's attention—the continuum extends to a point at which the learner directs his attention, at least at a semiconscious level, toward the preferred stimuli.

1.1 AWARENESS

Awareness is almost a cognitive behavior. But unlike *Knowledge,* the lowest level of the cognitive domain, we are not so much concerned with a memory of, or ability to recall, an item or fact as we are that, given appropriate opportunity, the learner will merely be conscious of something—that he take into account a situation, phenomenon, object, or stage of affairs. Like *Knowledge* it does not imply an assessment of the qualities or nature of the stimulus, but unlike *Knowledge* it does not necessarily imply attention. There can be simple awareness without specific discrimination or recognition of the objective characteristics of the object, even though these characteristics must be deemed to have an effect. The individual may not be able to verbalize the aspects of the stimulus which cause the awareness.

> Develops awareness of aesthetic factors in dress, furnishings, architecture, city design, good art, and the like.
>
> Develops some consciousness of color, form, arrangement, and design in the objects and structures around him and in descriptive or symbolic representations of people, things, and situations.[1]

1.2 WILLINGNESS TO RECEIVE   *Tolerate*

In this category we have come a step up the ladder but are still dealing with what appears to be cognitive behavior. At a minimum level, we are here describing the behavior of being willing to tolerate a given stimulus, not to avoid it. Like *Awareness,* it involves a neutrality or suspended judgment toward the stimulus. At this level of the continuum the teacher is not concerned that the student seek it out, nor even, perhaps, that in an environment

---

[1] Illustrative objectives selected from the literature follow the description of each subcategory.

crowded with many other stimuli the learner will necessarily attend to the stimulus. Rather, at worst, given the opportunity to attend in a field with relatively few competing stimuli, the learner is not actively seeking to avoid it. At best, he is willing to take notice of the phenomenon and give it his attention.

> Attends (carefully) when others speak—in direct conversation, on the telephone, in audiences.
>
> Appreciation (tolerance) of cultural patterns exhibited by individuals from other groups—religious, social, political, economic, national, etc.
>
> Increase in sensitivity to human need and pressing social problems.

1.3 CONTROLLED OR SELECTED ATTENTION

At a somewhat higher level we are concerned with a new phenomenon, the differentiation of a given stimulus into figure and ground at a conscious or perhaps semiconscious level—the differentiation of aspects of a stimulus which is perceived as clearly marked off from adjacent impressions. The perception is still without tension or assessment, and the student may not know the technical terms or symbols with which to describe it correctly or precisely to others. In some instances it may refer not so much to the selectivity of attention as to the control of attention, so that when certain stimuli are present they will be attended to. There is an element of the learner's controlling the attention here, so that the favored stimulus is selected and attended to despite competing and distracting stimuli.

> Listens to music with some discrimination as to its mood and meaning and with some recognition of the contributions of various musical elements and instruments to the total effect.
>
> Alertness toward human values and judgments on life as they are recorded in literature.

2.0 RESPONDING

At this level we are concerned with responses which go beyond merely attending to the phenomenon. The student is sufficiently motivated that he is not just 1.2 *Willing to attend,* but perhaps it is correct to say that he is actively attending. As a first stage in a "learning by doing" process the student is committing himself in some small measure to the phenomena involved. This is a very low level of commitment, and we would not say at this level that this was "a value of his" or that he had "such and such an attitude." These terms belong to the next higher level that we describe. But we could say that he is doing something with or about the phenomenon besides merely perceiving it, as would be true at the next level below this of 1.3 *Controlled or selected attention.*

This is the category that many teachers will find best describes their "interest" objectives. Most commonly we use the term to indicate the desire that a child become sufficiently involved in or committed to a subject, phenomenon, or activity that he will seek it out and gain satisfaction from working with it or engaging in it.

2.1 ACQUIESCENCE IN RESPONDING — *GRUDGINGLY TRY*

We might use the word "obedience" or "compliance" to describe this behavior. As both of these terms indicate, there is a passiveness so far as the initiation of the behavior is concerned, and the stimulus calling for this behavior is not subtle. Compliance is perhaps a better term than obedience, since there is more of the element of reaction to a suggestion and less of the implication of resistance or yielding unwillingly. The student makes the response, but he has not fully accepted the necessity for doing so.

— Willingness to comply with health regulations.
— Obeys the playground regulations.

2.2 WILLINGNESS TO RESPOND

The key to this level is in the term "willingness," with its implication of capacity for voluntary activity. There is the implication that the learner is sufficiently committed to exhibiting the behavior that he does so not just because of a fear of punishment, but "on his own" or voluntarily. It may help to note that the element of resistance or of yielding unwillingly, which is possibly present at the previous level, is here replaced with consent or proceeding from one's own choice.

Acquaints himself with significant current issues in international, political, social, and economic affairs through voluntary reading and discussion.

Acceptance of responsibility for his own health and for the protection of the health of others.

2.3 SATISFACTION IN RESPONSE

The additional element in the step beyond the *Willingness to respond* level, the consent, the assent to responding, or the voluntary response, is that the behavior is accompanied by a feeling of satisfaction, an emotional response, generally of pleasure, zest, or enjoyment. The location of this category in the hierarchy has given us a great deal of difficulty. Just where in the process of internalization the attachment of an emotional response, kick, or thrill to a behavior occurs has been hard to determine. For that matter there is some uncertainty as to whether the level of internalization at which it occurs may not depend on the particular behavior. We have even questioned whether it should be a category. If our structure is to be a hierarchy, then each category should include the behavior in the next level below it. The emotional component appears gradually through the range of internalization categories. The attempt to specify a given position in the hierarchy as *the* one at which the emotional component is added is doomed to failure.

The category is arbitrarily placed at this point in the hierarchy where it seems to appear most frequently and where it is cited as or appears to be an important component of the objectives at this level on the continuum. The category's inclusion at this point serves the pragmatic purpose of reminding us of the presence of the emotional component and its value in the building of affective behaviors. But it should not be thought of as appearing and occurring at this one point in the continuum and thus destroying the hierarchy which we are attempting to build.

> Enjoyment of self-expression in music and in arts and crafts as another means of personal enrichment.
> Finds pleasure in reading for recreation.
> Takes pleasure in conversing with many different kinds of people.

3.0 VALUING   *Motivated by individuals commitment To value*

This is the only category headed by a term which is in common use in the expression of objectives by teachers. Further, it is employed in its usual sense: that a thing, phenomenon, or behavior has worth. This abstract concept of worth is in part a result of the individual's own valuing or assessment, but it is much more a social product that has been slowly internalized or accepted and has come to be used by the student as his own criterion of worth.

Behavior categorized at this level is sufficiently consistent and stable to have taken on the characteristics of a belief or an attitude. The learner displays this behavior with sufficient consistency in appropriate situations that he comes to be perceived as holding a value. At this level, we are not concerned with the relationships among values but rather with the internalization of a set of specified, ideal, values. Viewed from another standpoint, the objectives classified here are the prime stuff from which the conscience of the individual is developed into active control of behavior.

This category will be found appropriate for many objectives that use the term "attitude" (as well as, of course, "value").

An important element of behavior characterized by *Valuing* is that it is motivated, not by the desire to comply or obey, but by the individual's commitment to the underlying value guiding the behavior.

3.1. ACCEPTANCE OF A VALUE   *Emotional Acceptance*

At this level we are concerned with the ascribing of worth to a phenomenon, behavior, object, etc. The term "belief," which is defined as "the emotional acceptance of a proposition or doctrine upon what one implicitly considers adequate ground" (English and English, 1958, p. 64), describes quite well what may be thought of as the dominant characteristic here. Beliefs have varying degrees of certitude. At this lowest level of *Valuing* we are concerned with the lowest levels of certainty; that is, there is more of a readiness to re-evaluate one's position than at the higher levels. It is a position that is somewhat tentative.

One of the distinguishing characteristics of this behavior is consistency of response to the class of objects, phenomena, etc. with which the belief or attitude is identified. It is consistent enough so that the person is perceived by others as holding the belief or value. At the level we are describing here, he is both sufficiently consistent that others can identify the value, and sufficiently committed that he is willing to be so identified.

> Continuing desire to develop the ability to speak and write effectively.
>
> Grows in his sense of kinship with human beings of all nations.

3.2 PREFERENCE FOR A VALUE *willing to seek it out.*

The provision for this subdivision arose out of a feeling that there were objectives that expressed a level of internalization between the mere acceptance of a value and commitment or conviction in the usual connotation of deep involvement in an area. Behavior at this level implies not just the acceptance of a value to the point of being willing to be identified with it, but the individual is sufficiently committed to the value to pursue it, to seek it out, to want it.

> Assumes responsibility for drawing reticent members of a group into conversation.
>
> Deliberately examines a variety of viewpoints on controversial issues with a view to forming opinions about them.
>
> Actively participates in arranging for the showing of contemporary artistic efforts.

3.3 COMMITMENT — *complete certainty*

Belief at this level involves a high degree of certainty. The ideas of "conviction" and "certainty beyond a shadow of a doubt" help to convey further the level of behavior intended. In some instances this may border on faith, in the sense of it being a firm emotional acceptance of a belief upon admittedly nonrational grounds. Loyalty to a position, group, or cause would also be classified here.

The person who displays behavior at this level is clearly perceived as holding the value. He acts to further the thing valued in some way, to extend the possibility of his developing it, to deepen his involvement with it and with the things representing it. He tries to convince others and seeks converts to his cause. There is a tension here which needs to be satisfied; action is the result of an aroused need or drive. There is a real motivation to act out the behavior.

> Devotion to those ideas and ideals which are the foundations of democracy.
>
> Faith in the power of reason and in methods of experiment and discussion.

4.0 ORGANIZATION *of values into a system*

As the learner successively internalizes values, he encounters situations for which more than one value is relevant. Thus necessity arises for (*a*) the organization of the values into a system, (*b*) the determination of the interrelationships among them, and (*c*) the establishment of the dominant and pervasive ones. Such a system is built gradually, subject to change as new values are incorporated. This category is intended as the proper classification for objectives which describe the beginnings of the building of a value system. It is subdivided into two levels, since a prerequisite to interrelating is the conceptualization of the value in a form which permits organization. *Conceptualization* forms the first subdivision in the organization process, *Organization of a value system* the second.

While the order of the two subcategories seems appropriate enough with reference to one another, it is not so certain that 4.1 *Conceptualization of a value* is properly placed as the next level above 3.3 *Commitment*. Conceptualization undoubtedly begins at an earlier level for some objectives. Like 2.3 *Satisfaction in response,* it is doubtful that a single completely satisfactory location for this category can be found. Positioning it before 4.2 *Organization of a value system* appropriately indicates a prerequisite of such a system. It also calls attention to a component of affective growth that occurs at least by this point on the continuum but may begin earlier.

4.1 CONCEPTUALIZATION OF A VALUE

In the previous category, 3.0 *Valuing,* we noted that consistency and stability are integral characteristics of the particular value or belief. At this level (4.1) the quality of abstraction or conceptualization is added. This permits the individual to see how the value relates to those that he already holds or to new ones that he is coming to hold.

Conceptualization will be abstract, and in this sense it will be symbolic. But the symbols need not be verbal symbols. Whether conceptualization first appears at this point on the affective continuum is a moot point, as noted above.

> Attempts to identify the characteristics of an art object which he admires.
>
> Forms judgments as to the responsibility of society for conserving human and material resources.

4.2 ORGANIZATION OF A VALUE SYSTEM

Objectives properly classified here are those which require the learner to bring together a complex of values, possibly disparate values, and to bring these into an ordered relationship with one another. Ideally, the ordered relationship will be one which is harmonious and internally consistent. This is, of course, the goal of such objectives, which seek to have the student formulate a philosophy of life. In actuality, the integration may be something less than entirely harmonious. More likely the relationship is better described as a kind of dynamic equilibrium which is, in part, dependent upon those portions of the environment which are salient at any point in time. In many instances the organization of values may result in their synthesis into a new value or value complex of a higher order.

> Weighs alternative social policies and practices against the standards of the public welfare rather than the advantage of specialized and narrow interest groups.
>
> Develops a plan for regulating his rest in accordance with the demands of his activities.

5.0 CHARACTERIZATION BY A VALUE OR VALUE COMPLEX

At this level of internalization the values already have a place in the individual's value hierarchy, are organized into some kind of internally consistent system, have controlled the behavior of the individual for a sufficient time that he has adapted to behaving this way; and an evocation of the behavior no longer arouses emotion or affect except when the individual is threatened or challenged.

The individual acts consistently in accordance with the values he has internalized at this level, and our concern is to indicate two things: (*a*) the generalization of this control to so much of the individual's behavior that he is described and characterized as a person by these pervasive controlling tendencies, and (*b*) the integration of these beliefs, ideas, and attitudes into a total philosophy or world view. These two aspects constitute the subcategories.

5.1 GENERALIZED SET

The generalized set is that which gives an internal consistency to the system of attitudes and values at any particular moment. It is selective responding at a very high level. It is sometimes spoken of as a determining tendency, an orientation toward phenomena, or a predisposition to act in a certain way. The generalized set is a response to highly generalized phenomena. It is a persistent and consistent response to a family of related situations or objects. It may often be an unconscious set which guides action without conscious forethought. The generalized set may be thought of as closely related to the idea of an attitude cluster, where the commonality is based on behavioral characteristics rather than the subject or object of the attitude. A generalized set is a basic orientation which enables the individual to reduce and order the complex world about him and to act consistently and effectively in it.

Readiness to revise judgments and to change behavior in the light of evidence.

Judges problems and issues in terms of situations, issues, purposes, and consequences involved rather than in terms of fixed, dogmatic precepts or emotionally wishful thinking.

5.2 CHARACTERIZATION

This, the peak of the internalization process, includes those objectives which are broadest with respect both to the phenomena covered and to the range of behavior which they comprise. Thus, here are found those objectives which concern one's view of the universe, one's philosophy of life, one's *Weltanschauung*—a value system having as its object the whole of what is known or knowable.

Objectives categorized here are more than generalized sets in the sense that they involve a greater inclusiveness and, within the group of attitudes, behaviors, beliefs, or ideas, an emphasis on internal consistency. Though this internal consistency may not always be exhibited behaviorally by the students toward whom the objective is directed, since we are categorizing teachers' objectives, this consistency feature will always be a component of *Characterization* objectives.

As the title of the category implies, these objectives are so encompassing that they tend to characterize the individual almost completely.

Develops for regulation of one's personal and civic life a code of behavior based on ethical principles consistent with democratic ideals.

Develops a consistent philosophy of life.

CHAPTER 4 Citizenship As an Objective in the Social Studies

Several of the social studies curriculum projects have been designed to encourage the development of good citizens. The most notable of these projects, sponsored by the American Heritage Foundation, is located at the Lincoln Filene Center for Citizenship and Public Affairs at Tufts University. Another at the University of Chicago is investigating the political socialization of the child. Several groups have been founded to encourage the teaching of the Bill of Rights in the school. All of this activity will certainly lead to increasing discussion of the role of citizenship training in the schools.

Students are often expected to learn the virtues of our political and cultural heritage through discussion of the Constitution and the Bill of Rights. They also study diagrams of government structures as if they gave insight into what constitutes civic responsibility. But knowledge of what already exists in the form of political credos or institutions does not insure the understanding or proper use of our inheritance. Teachers often neglect to get their students to internalize the essential democratic credo as they concentrate on the study of institutions.

The characteristics and attitudes that shape a child's future political orientation and understanding of the political process are vital elements in the building of good citizenship. Learning stated goals of political responsibility and obtaining a passing acquaintance with the structure of governmental systems are not enough to insure political maturity in the student. Our society and the world at large are changing so rapidly that today's student must have more enduring resources in order for him to apply the best of his cultural heritage to new and difficult political decisions. To isolate and strengthen the attitudes that insure the survival of the social order is no small task, but it is one our schools must face.

The following selections approach the problem of citizenship training in different ways. In a provocative essay, Ruth Benedict suggests that the study

63

of comparative societies can help us discover how best to transmit our particular cultural heritage to students in a rapidly changing environment. In the second essay, Franklin Patterson, the Director of the Lincoln Filene Center, offers a definition of citizenship within the Western tradition and discusses educative procedures that he feels would strengthen a child's realistic view of his democratic culture. The following questions are pertinent to both essays:

1) Should social studies education try to help preserve American culture by passing on its values? if so, how? Should teachers endorse the values of their culture over those of other cultures? Should positive attitudes toward the democratic law-making process be taught, beyond simple compliance with laws as a procedural necessity? *Internal sanctions are necessary*

2) What does Benedict use the word "democracy" to mean? How does Patterson use the word? Do these two definitions imply similar objectives, procedures, and content for social studies instruction?

3) How best can citizenship be defined for the education of the young so that they can function in a changing world and yet adhere to the ideals of our democratic society?

4) What do we mean by political alienation? How can it be prevented? Does the aim of preventing it lead to teaching any particular method or content?

TRANSMITTING OUR DEMOCRATIC HERITAGE IN THE SCHOOLS

Ruth Benedict

Controversies about education in recent years have in one way or another turned upon the issue of the role of the schools in transmitting our cultural heritage. There have been those who have blamed the schools for every "un-American" trait they believed to be increasing in our society. Some of these critics place on the schools responsibility for the decreasing religious affiliations in our cities and rural areas; some attack them for the moral relativism they see in our decade. Such criticisms assume that an educational system

Reprinted from Ruth Benedict, "Transmitting Our Democratic Heritage in the Schools," *American Journal of Sociology*, Vol. XLVIII, No. 6, May 1943, 722–727, with the permission of The University of Chicago Press. Copyright 1943 by the University of Chicago.

can, of and by itself, have such far-reaching effects as these; and this same assumption is just as basic in a very different argument: that education should shoulder the responsibility for ushering in a new social order. In so far as these critics and exhorters have argued only that some particular set of facts should be taught in our schools—American history or the Bible or Thomas Aquinas or the achievements of the T.V.A.—there is no need for further discussion; the school curriculum can easily be improved without claiming that our educational system makes or breaks the social order. But the assumption made by these critics has consequences of its own which go far beyond the changes in curriculum they urge. It is an assumption that can be examined in the light of comparative studies of other cultures, and such an examination can throw light on the whole relation of education to social change.

It is instructive to study a long series of societies, identifying those where culture is relatively stable and those where it is highly unstable. One does not find that those which are stable educate their children in one fashion and those which are unstable in another. There are a great many different ways of rearing children: they may be treated like little adults from birth and divide their day into work and play almost exactly as their parents do; they may be little outlaws who consider the adults fair game, pillaging their fields and evading responsibilities; they may be privileged beings whose every wish is gratified, however inconvenient. But none of these or other ways of rearing children correlates with whether or not the culture is reproduced in the next generation. Stability of culture over generations is not a function of the particular kind of education that is given to children. It is a function rather of social conditions in the whole tribe or nation. Anthropologists have to study rapidly changing cultures over and over again, and usually with sinking hearts. When a Plains Indian tribe is put on a reservation, the differences between older and younger generations are very great, and transmission of culture most inadequate. The livelihood techniques the parents knew can no longer be used, for the buffalo have disappeared from the plains, and horses can no longer be raided from other tribes. The older ways of life no longer work, and with them go the religious rites that guaranteed them and the respect which the young once showed their elders. These drop out, and the tragedy is that it is hard to replace them. Then one generation is not like another: transmission of culture has been interfered with by all the external and internal conditions which are present in an unstable society. Sometimes the anthropologist can study cultural change under more favorable conditions: when incentives to activity are increased; when there is more leisure because iron tools, for instance, have been introduced; and when the arts of life therefore flourish and new developments take place.

Under such social conditions—whatever the method of education—transmission of culture is achieved only in part. But a homogeneous society faced by no new circumstances sufficiently drastic to disturb its balance transmits its culture generation after generation, no matter how it breaks the rules of education that seem to us essential. Our problems in transmission of culture arise from the rapidity of social changes in our society; and no method of education can prevent this. The choices open to our school systems are only whether they will cling to the teaching of subjects and attitudes which the child can no longer use profitably in the world in which he will live or whether they will give him equipment he can use. They cannot possibly make a stable world of an unstable one. Those critics who blame the schools for the changes they resent in our culture are making the educational system a scapegoat for vast changes in the structure of modern society which they do not take into account.

Once we are sufficiently skeptical about the notion that schools—or parents—have it in their power to indoctrinate our children so that they will maintain the status quo, we can face the crucial problem of the relation of education to the social order. All the problems in this relationship, whatever the tribe or nation studied, concern the degree to which the method of education fits the requirements of that society. It is not a matter of identifying some good educational policies and some bad ones. The "best" education can be a weakness in a society that does not give the adolescent scope to put his learning into practice; it can breed sullenness and frustration. The "worst" can be well adapted to all that will ever be required of him as an adult.

Nothing is more striking in some primitive societies than the rapid intellectual development of children which flattens out somewhere in early life so that a man of twenty, perhaps, has already all the skills and all the knowledge of a man of fifty. This fact has sometimes been read off as an inherent characteristic of simpler peoples; it is said that their mental powers are capable of only a limited development. It would be truer to say that they do not expand if the society requires nothing further of them. If men can supply their needs of livelihood and gain prestige among their fellows without adding to their skills or their knowledge, they early reach a mental plateau. This is not a characteristic of all primitive societies, for in many tribes a man must accumulate "wisdom" and special techniques throughout his life in order to take any desired position in the society. It is this continuing stimulus to mental achievement supplied by the responsibilities society puts upon its members which in any society, our own included, prevents the arrest of intellectual development.

Not only intellectual development but also training of the emotions and will-power are relative to the social order in which they occur. Life in some primitive cultures requires tough and violent people if they are to carry on; they can fill their roles with less cost to themselves and to their fellow-men if they have been reared not to expect universal kindness. Primitive people are generally more permissive to their children than we are, and their methods of child-rearing often seem to us extraordinarily attractive. They are not all of them the better for it. In some tribes where sorcery is a common practice and greatly feared, children are believed to be unaffected by black magic. They live in a charmed circle. At adolescence they become liable to all the machinations of their fellow-tribesmen, and they are unprepared. Sorcery in such tribes is a daily terror the intensity of which is possible just because the children were secure and happy in their childhood. There are other tribes where the maladjustment between education and adult requirements is quite the opposite. Life in the band is co-operatively regulated; all members share the labors and the rewards of labor. But the boy's education is, as they say, "like breaking a colt." He must be humiliated by his elders, and they send him on lying errands to make game of him. He must be chased out of bed to jump into icy water. He is taught that he has only himself to depend on. "Rely on no one. Your hands are your friends. Your feet are your friends. Your eyes are your friends. Rely on these." The education he is given does not fit the cooperative arrangements of band life; and the aggressions, the mean gossip, the bickering of tribal life, are objective measures of the lack of consonance between child-training and the kind of character structure which can operate to advantage in the culture.

In our own culture there are of course many inconsistencies between education and the world for which it offers training. I shall not discuss the curriculum, though it is obvious that in any changing society the curriculum must be reconsidered constantly. The matters which are affected when we try to make our education consonant with our total cultural life go far beyond the curriculum. They include attitudes which our children learn in the course of studying their lessons and the institutional organization of our schools. And we cannot plan without analyzing our own culture. The more clearly we see its general outlines, the more wisely we shall propose.

We are constantly in danger in our schools of underestimating the cultural changes that occur in such a society as ours. Education in our world today must prepare our children to adapt themselves to unforeseeable conditions. It must give them a basis upon which they can make their own decisions in situations not yet on the horizon. The controversies of our decade will die out or be re-embodied in quite different events. The phrasing will change. In the first decade of this century the duty of thrift was one of the absolute values on which all my teachers were agreed. Starting little bank accounts was a learning activity which would bear the fruit of the good life from childhood to old age. The object was to create in school a sentiment for valuing accumulation rather than for present expenditure. My schoolmates and I have lived through the nemesis of this teaching, through periods when one's whole duty was to spend and the hoarder was antisocial. Then, too, we were taught that the world was through with war and that in our day and age ethics and humanitarianism were so developed that the voice of the whole earth was unanimous for peace. We have lived through the first World War and the Long Truce, and today we do not know where the second World War will take us. The absolute values of peace which we were taught in school are something for which people are jailed.

A clearer analysis of our culture would have made it unnecessary for that generation of school children to unlearn painfully these lessons they had been taught. If, instead of trying to educate us to recognize an absolute good in hoarding, our teachers had chosen out of the cultural values of American civilization that pre-eminent one of initiative and independence, if they had been able to teach us that according to our abilities we could get somewhere if we showed initiative and independence and that we would be honored for them by our fellow-men, they could have subordinated saving money to the due place which it holds in an American scheme of things. They could have put their teaching on the ground that some attainable goals are worth saving for. If, instead of pacifism, they had taught us that peace was the dearest possession of any people and the one most worth giving one's greatest efforts to perfect, if they had taught us that war was the greatest calamity but one which, no matter what men's ethical sentiments were, would follow from certain acts, the generation they taught would not have had to unlearn the lesson.

"Transmitting our culture" in a changing society means self-examination and a certain detachment; for, unless our analyses are good, our teachings may go into limbo with the passing of some special set of circumstances. A stable society is not faced with such necessities. It can inculcate saving for generation after generation, or it can inculcate stripping one's self of all possessions. If these are integrated in the whole economic pattern of their culture, they can be taught to each generation in minute detail. Stable societies, too, have teachings either about the glories of war or about the virtue of peacefulness; these are consequences of the state of warfare or lack of warfare in which they live, and generation after generation maintains the status quo. The great challenge of education in our changing world today is that it requires so much more of our educators than a stable society need require.

This challenge is intensified when we try to state what we mean by transmitting our heritage of democracy. Here, too, we must stress those things without which our culture would be unrecognizable. Fortunately, in America there is a certain basic agreement. In contrast to European and South American nations, the United States from the first has had a tradition of liberty and opportunity, and despotic power has been at a minimum. It is true that there are marked divergencies in current definitions of what democratic heritage we want to transmit, divergencies which turn upon whether the speaker is demanding liberty and opportunity for a special group to which he belongs or whether he is demanding these privileges for all Americans on the same terms. What is essential to all of them, however, is that they identify our way of life with adequate scope for personal achievement. All the definitions are drawn from experience in our culture where initiative and independence are traits every man wants for himself.

The transmission of our democratic heritage means primarily, then, preparing children in our schools to act as adults with initiative and independence.

Who is to say that initiative & independence are more imp than co-operation?

Our culture does not go about this with the directness that is characteristic of many tribes which set this same goal. With us, children are dependent, and yet as adults they must be independent. They are commanded as children, and as adults they command. This is in strong contrast to those societies which make no qualitative differences between children and adults. The qualities they value in grown men they boast of also in little boys even if the child flouts his father or even strikes him. "He will be a man," his father says. Such tribes do not have the problem we have in our culture: the unlearning of dependence and docility when the child reaches man's estate. Nevertheless, this discontinuity in the life-cycle is basic in our culture, and we have used it to good advantage. We greatly prolong infancy, and we define it as a period of learning. We give ourselves, therefore, the opportunity to equip our children with all that a long-continued and uninterrupted course of teaching can give them. We do not always take full advantage of our opportunity, of course, but the opportunity is there. The child on the threshold of manhood has spent years sitting at the feet of the older generation, and his teachers have had a remarkable chance to pass on to him all they know and value.

One great danger we face under this system is not that the child will be rebellious or insufficiently docile—but that he will learn his lesson of docility too well. Our schools impose the school schedule, the subject matter, the personnel, the forms of discipline; in all these matters the child takes what is offered. As long as he accepts these arrangements as the condition of his progress toward adulthood, his docility in these matters need not interfere with a later independence. But the training is overwhelmingly in docility rather than in self-reliance and independence, and many adults have obviously been overinfluenced by this training. They find dependency hard to relinquish. Progressive education, with its greater encouragement of the kind of behavior the child will need as an adult in our culture, is clearly on the right track. There are many classroom customs which could be introduced and which could give the child greater experience in responsibility and initiative. All such methods bridge the gap between school and life and lessen the numbers who find it difficult or impossible to make the transition.

The spread of progressive education is at least in part a compensation for increased restrictions on children's opportunities for independence and responsibility in our modern cities. In the earlier days of our democracy, village and even city life provided more chances for genuine autonomy. Boys shouldered their fishing rods and organized their own games and filled their free time according to their own ideas. A bully at the fishing hole was the affair of the older boys who swam there. Their chores, too, were genuine responsibilities. A boy might have to milk the cows and tend store, but his work belonged in the scheme of things. He was doing the things his father also did. Today he listens to the radio or plays in supervised playgrounds or on the street with one eye on the policeman. His father's work is away from home and he cannot contribute to it. The changed conditions in our cities make it harder for the child to get experience in the kind of behavior upon which success in his adult life will depend; and, unless our schools offer such opportunities, the persistence of childhood dependency into adulthood—our so-called "regressions"—will inevitably become a greater social problem.

Just as our system of child-rearing runs the danger of inadequately transmitting our cultural heritage because the child may learn the lesson of dependency too well, so, too, it may fall short because he learns too well the lesson of external sanctions for moral behavior. Our moral tradition is based on internalized sanctions; we do not regulate private life by constant external supervision as is the custom in some European countries and in many native tribes of Africa. Our democracy needs as many individuals as possible with the capacity for self-discipline, individuals who will subordinate immediate and shifting wishes to a chosen goal. But self-discipline is not a lesson which is learned directly by enforced discipline. In many societies the step from one to the other is never made. It is not automatic. In our culture we make the transition the hard way, and all our psychiatric discussions of the punishing superego are documentation of this difficulty. For our transition internalizes not the actual consequences of the compromising act but the outside punisher himself, a punisher who when he is internalized can be overwhelmingly inhibiting. Many societies follow a different course. From earliest childhood they inculcate genuine self-discipline, and individuals in such societies do not have to make such extensive transitions as are common in our culture. Parents in such tribes are not so afraid as we are of placing responsibility for his acts genuinely in the child's hands. If the baby sells his tanned-skin dress to a white man for a dime, no adult punishes him; they would consider that extraneous to the issue. The dress was his, and he alone is responsible for what he has done with it. But at the next feast he has no fine dress to wear. He learns the consequences of his act; he does not learn the punishing parent. Even very extreme disciplines are left in the child's hands. From our point of view these disciplines seem arbitrary and out of all proportion to the goals sought. They may be rubbing one's self with nettles or letting wads of grass burn into one's skin or drawing blood from sensitive parts of one's body. The point is that even these are readily assumed by the child himself, not imposed by an outside authority. Democratically organized societies have often fared well by giving the child experience in genuine self-discipline. They put upon the child responsibility for going out to seek a vision and for taking the initiative in obtaining his own instruction in hunting. Data from such societies make it clear that absence of enforced discipline does not necessarily mean license or laziness. This notion, so common in conventional discussions of our educational system, can arise only in a society which has systematically minimized opportunities for preadult self-discipline.

These specific points of strain in our educational system occur just because of the contrast in our culture between the child's world and the adult world, and all our problems are acute at the period of transition itself. Gradually our schools are coming to realize that it is just at this transition period where they have failed the child. Vocational training and job-placement assistance are being provided, but the problem is only partly met, as statistics in unemployment and criminology abundantly show. Primitive democratic societies which, like us, require one set of behavior for the child and another for the adult have remarkable basic likeness in their procedure at the period of transition. They have great graduating ceremonies—the conclusion of puberty rites—and automatically give the graduates as a group their new responsibilities as adults, providing them with the necessary tools and equipment. They do not leave the transition to each adolescent's fumbling attempts, and they do not put obstacles in the way of his access to the means of production. It seems fair to say that it is at this point of transition from childhood dependency to adult independence that our culture most often fails adequately to transmit our democratic heritage and that our educators must work with our social planners if our current wastage is to be lessened.

These examples of what education can do to insure the transmission of our democratic heritage are not based on "the nature of the child" or on an absolute standard of what a mature individual should be or of what a good society is. They depend upon surveying some of the major wastages in our civilization and upon citing ways in which some other cultures have met similar situations. Such knowledge of comparative cultures can often be useful; and it highlights the truth that our democracy, with its special demand for initiative and independence, is a special way of functioning as a human being that has to be learned. All that we know about the learning process we need to apply socially to this task of transmitting our democratic heritage in a changing world.

seems to consist of initiative & independence, & probably self-discipline according to her.

POLITICAL REALITY
IN CHILDHOOD
Dimensions of Education
for Citizenship

Franklin Patterson

An individual's political behavior is integrally related to his total experience and behavior as a person. Gordon Allport once observed:

> The political nature of man is indistinguishable from his personality as a whole, and . . . [the latter] is not the sum-total of his specific reactions, but rather a congruent system of attitudes, each element of which is intelligible only in the light of the total pattern. A man's political opinions reflect the characteristic modes of his adjustment to life.[1]

Exploration of this integral relationship has been a task of political science in the past two generations. . . .

Such studies confirm not only the integral relationship of political behavior to the total personality but the vital influence of early life experience on later political orientations and actions. Subsequent investigations have tended to support Merriam's 1931 observation that

> . . . the process of politicalization begins far down the scale both in organization and in years. The point of departure for civic education is the child. . . . Social and political attitudes are determined far earlier than commonly supposed, many of them in fact in pre-school years. Observations show that political party allegiance in the United States is often fixed at the age of eight or ten years, as a result of social contact and pressure, but more fundamental attitudes determining the character of political behavior may be reached earlier in many cases.[2]

Peck and Havighurst, in their study of a group of children from ten to seventeen years of age, found that "characteristic personality and character patterns . . . [were] largely laid down by age ten and changed little thereafter."[3] Other studies tend toward similar findings.

Thus is verified what common sense told us all along. The child is the

Reprinted from Franklin Patterson, "Political Reality in Childhood, Dimensions of Education for Citizenship," *National Elementary School Principal*, May 1963. Copyright 1963, Department of Elementary School Principals, National Education Association. All rights reserved.

[1] Allport, Gordon W. "The Composition of Political Attitudes." *American Journal of Sociology* 35: 238; 1929–30.
[2] Merriam, Charles Edward. *The Making of Citizens: A Comparative Study of Methods of Civic Training.* Chicago: University of Chicago Press, 1931. pp. 331–32.
[3] Peck, Robert F.; Havighurst, Robert J.; and others. *The Psychology of Character Development.* New York: John Wiley & Sons, Inc., 1960. p. 157.

father of the adult citizen. The child is whole; his character and citizenship are dimensions of his total self. What happens to him at an early age, what he is and does in school and elsewhere, will bear heavily on the kind of person and citizen he becomes. Thus in *The Republic,* Plato addressed himself to "the problem of instilling in youth the qualities of character necessary for effective citizenship." So, too, must we.

THE IDEA OF CITIZENSHIP

Before we turn to the problem of educating for effective citizenship, it is important, however, to consider the definitions we use. The prevalence of cant and cliché in defining "citizenship" is matched only by the industry of those who have sought instead to make the term more educationally manageable by dissecting it into detailed "behavioral outcomes." Unfortunately, neither glittering generalities nor a list of molecular "behaviors" will serve as an adequate general guide in thinking about citizenship. Behavioral and operational descriptions are useful in specific curriculum planning and research. But we need, first, something that will help us get to the heart of the matter, a definition sufficiently abstract to be at once flexible and accurate.

The idea of citizenship within the Western tradition has been stated with admirable and deceptive simplicity by D. W. Brogan, the British political scientist:

> What is this idea? It seems to me to have two aspects. The first—possibly the most important, certainly the most novel—aspect is the assumption that every citizen has the right to be consulted on the conduct of the political society and the duty of having something to contribute to the general consultation. The second aspect is the converse of the first. The citizen who has a right to be consulted is bound by the results of the consultation. His duties flow from his rights.[4]

In understanding Brogan's definition, it is necessary to note that he uses the term "political society" instead of "government." In doing so, he recognizes that government, complex as it is, is only one of many organized and informal structures of power, influence, and relationship in which the citizen finds himself. The individual enters into a political society at many levels and in different roles.

The Detroit Citizenship Education Study led by Stanley E. Dimond was operated under somewhat broader definitions. During the five years, 1945–1950, the Detroit Study involved the faculties and children of eight schools; four of the schools were elementary. No other study of comparable depth in terms of teacher development and child study is available in the civic education field. The Detroit Study held that:

[4] Brogan, D. W. *Citizenship Today: England, France, The United States.* Chapel Hill, North Carolina: University of North Carolina Press, 1960. pp. 4–5.

Citizenship as it relates to school activities has a two-fold meaning. In a narrow sense citizenship includes only legal status in a country and the activities closely related to the political functions—voting, governmental organization, holding of public office, and legal rights and responsibilities. Citizenship, in addition, has also acquired a broad meaning almost synonymous with those desirable personal qualities which are displayed in human associations. . . . For this Study, then, citizenship means the relations of the individual to his government and, in addition, his relations to other members and groups in a democratic society.[5]

Implicit in both Brogan's and Dimond's definitions are factors of knowledge, value, and skill which it is the business of education to make explicit. These may be stated in various ways. They need to be articulated in terms of the varying contexts and situations in which the democratic citizen is an actor. The heart of the matter, at whatever level, is what Brogan calls "consultation." It is in this transactional process that democratic citizenship is expressed, whether one is dealing with the political economy of a primary school reading group or an election to the United States Senate.

The heart of all politics, in Lasswell's words, is "who gets what, when, how."[6] What makes the polities, governance, and societal relationships of a democracy distinctive is the process of consultation in which all citizens can expect to share. Through this process, they have the right to be heard and the responsibility to have something worth saying in decisions about who gets what, when, and how. And they have the obligation to stand by the decisions that are so reached.

Such consultation is learned behavior. It involves, as Jean D. Grambs once said, having people who *know*, who *care*, and who *can do*. It involves helping very young children acquire the idea of citizenship in their lives in the two aspects Brogan emphasizes. And it involves for the larger society, swept by complexity and change, the maintenance and invention of "devices for reconciling social order with individual freedom and initiative, . . . for making the immediate power of a country's rulers subject to the ultimate power of the ruled."[7] Such devices are hard to come by in any age; in our time of intricate bigness, this seems especially so. The rights and obligations of consultation not only must be learned; they must be won, again and again. It is the difficult privilege of today's school to help them be learned and won anew.

---

[5] Dimond, Stanley E. *Schools and the Development of Good Citizens.* Detroit, Michigan: Wayne University Press, 1953. p. 36.
[6] Lasswell, Harold D. *Politics: Who Gets What, When, How.* New York: McGraw-Hill Book Company, 1936. Republished in *The Political Writings of Harold D. Lasswell.* Glencoe, Illinois: The Free Press, 1951. pp. 295–461.
[7] Huxley, Aldous. *Brave New World Revisited.* New York: Harper & Brothers, 1958. p. 57.

The Best of Times, the Worst of Times

Writing about our times and the social studies, C. W. Hunnicutt and Jean D. Grambs have remarked that "the chief characteristics of the world in which we teach are *change* and *uncertainty*."[8] Some years ago, Ralph Tyler wrote that our personal lives are affected by a civilization which features increasing mechanization, increasing complexity, increasing commercialization, increasing impersonality, and continuous, chaotic stimulation. Innumerable observations of an analogous sort have been made about the times that we and our children live in. These are, as always, "the best of times and the worst of times," depending on which part of the scene you view and what refraction you use.

— hopeful

Jerome Bruner, for example, is sanguine about man's capacity for handling the increased stimulation which surrounds him in a rapidly changing technological civilization. Bruner argues that people are getting incredibly good at cognitively ordering and dealing with external events. John R. Seeley takes a different view, seeing today's individual confronted by gigantic monoliths (big government, big business, big labor, etc.) on the one hand, and an infinitude of unrelated fragments (his life experience) on the other. In context, both Bruner and Seeley probably are correct. Considering the present acceleration of change, it is remarkable that men are able to ride the whirlwind as well as they do; our hope must be in Bruner's direction, i.e., that man's cognitive apparatus can keep up with the changes he creates.

At the same time, all too ample evidence exists that there is a widening margin of possible breakdown in human affairs, a gap between our technological brilliance and our handling of the consequences of technology. Old answers for new problems may be as bad as no answers at all. Yet we tend to depend on obsolete solutions for many reasons. Our perceptions of phenomena are apt to be stereotyped. Since behavior is deeply influenced by what we "see" in a situation, and since much of what we "see" is the memory of an earlier perception, our reactions to new situations are often unrealistic. Our times require a conception of problem-solving as a process for developing "solutions to problems for which no man has a ready answer."[9] A productive, flexible approach to problem-solving: (a) includes substantial reliance on the communication and corrective feedback processes of consultation; (b) is difficult to develop after early adolescence; and (c) is more possible to achieve by personalities whose basic needs are adequately met than by those with deep unmet needs.

[8] Hunnicutt, C. W., and Grambs, Jean D. "The Social Studies Under Fire." *The Elementary School Journal* 56: 210; January 1956.
[9] Tyler, Ralph W. "We Are Learning More and More About Human Behavior. What Are the Implications for Education?" *NEA Journal* 44: 428; October 1955.

Reactions: 1. withdrawal
2. projection
3. Identification
4. rational activism

The Problem of Political Alienation

There is also evidence that many citizens today do not feel that they are a part of the political process. This feeling, called "political alienation," pervades a proportion of the electorate who view themselves as politically powerless and their vote as meaningless.

> Political powerlessness is the feeling of an individual that his political action has no influence in determining the course of political events. Those who feel politically powerless do not believe that their vote, or for that matter any action they might perform, can determine the broader outcome they desire.[10]

Expression of the feeling of political alienation may take any of several forms. One of these is political withdrawal, in which the person removes his interest and activity from politics. A second form of expression is projection, in which the citizen displaces the anger and resentment which arise from political alienation onto some other person or group whom he "blames." Identification with a charismatic leader is a third way a person may attempt to deal with his feelings of political alienation: the individual seeks to gain a feeling of power and meaning by incorporating within himself the attitudes held by a leader he perceives as powerful. Withdrawal as a mode of expression may be the result of a conscious, rational estimate of the political situation and one's desires, or it may be an irrational response to conditions. Projection and identification are irrational modes of expression, and they are regressive in the sense that they are more characteristic of child than adult behavior.

A different level of response to one's feelings of political alienation is rational activism: political action based on a realistic assessment of the political situation. Rational activism is behavior founded on relatively undistorted perception of political reality and on logical reasoning.

Now we come to a basic dilemma in developing programs of education for citizenship. We are committed to a liberal Western definition of citizenship, very much like Brogan's statement of it. Yet this pervasive, ideal definition itself can operate so as to *create* political alienation.

A transactional theory of the relation of citizens to one another and to the state, with the government viewed as a neutral agency which settles disputes according to principles of reason and justice, is what we accept and teach. But our simplification of this theory in classroom practice can result in a kind of "copybook civics" which leads a child to have unrealistic perceptions of the citizen's role and the nature of governance. Murray Levin states this case in its most extreme form:

> Feelings of alienation will arise in individuals who accept the classical democratic theory because it demands more of the individual citizen than he

[10] Levin, Murray B. *The Alienated Voter: Politics in Boston.* New York: Holt, Rinehart & Winston, Inc., 1960. p. 60.

can realistically fulfill and promises more than can be delivered. . . . The theory also fails to account for the necessary roles of leadership and exaggerates the active role of the masses. Those who do lead are therefore regarded as potential usurpers of what rightfully belongs to the electorate. The theory also leads its followers to believe that bargaining and compromising, . . . so essential to democratic politics, is necessarily evil. . . .[11]

For citizenship education, such a view, if correct, means that we must not instill in children a Utopian image of the citizen and his government. If we do so, we are unwittingly contributing to his later disillusionment when he encounters the political process directly. There will be limits—his own and those externally applied—on the possibilities of consultation. There will be less than human perfection in the political world he grows up into. Politics will be a healthy, earthy part of all government, private and public, and he had best know and accept it in realistic terms.

He will live in times laden with change and uncertainty and remarkable opportunity. He can realize his birthright as a citizen best to the degree that he is helped to achieve political maturity rather than a fantasy about the citizen role and government. To achieve political maturity, he must be helped toward a level of rational activism in which he can "perceive the realities of the political structure, hold political goals which are potentially operational, and attempt to develop institutions through which these goals may be realized."[12] And all of this still within the central values of democratic life, of which the Brogan definition is a clear cut example.

Such a view means that the education of citizens in a modern democracy cannot afford to be mythological in its orientation because the end product, alienation, will erode the system in ultimate practice. It means that a major amount of attention in early and later education must be paid to the building of rational political maturity strong enough to meet the challenges of reality.

ELEMENTS IN CIVIC EDUCATION

At least three emphases suggest themselves as being vital to this mission:

1. *Intellectual Honesty.*   Political maturity is apt to begin and grow in childhood if we are straightforward in our treatment of the political facts of life, not deploring all that is less than familiar, congenial, or perfect in our system. Bruner says it well:

> Most important of all, the educational process must be free of intellectual dishonesty and those forms of cheating that explain without providing understanding. I have expressed the conviction elsewhere that any subject can be taught to anybody at any age in some form that is honest. It is not honest to present a fifth-grade social-studies class with an image of town government as if it were a den of cub scouts presided over by a parent figure interpreting

[11] *Ibid.,* pp. 73–74.
[12] *Op. cit.,* p. 63.

the charter—even if the image set forth does happen to mesh with the child's immediate social experience. A lie is still a lie—even if it sounds like familiar truth.[13]

Part of our task is to recognize that there are structures of knowledge realistically pertinent to the idea of citizenship at every level of individual learning. Another part is to devise strategies of education which will help children discover these structures and internalize them for use in their own behavior. But neither of these parts of the task can be accomplished without the kind of intellectual honesty of which Bruner speaks. And intellectual honesty about the political process in any of its myriad forms captures the essential excitement of the subject. Children, for good reason, often find the social studies a crashing bore because we empty the subject of its natural vitality before making it available.

2. *Historical Models Plus Jurisprudential Consultation.*   Out of his work with children, Donald W. Oliver offers an approach to education for citizenship which deserves wide attention and trial. Essentially, Oliver has sought a formula which would enable teachers to help children toward two fundamental kinds of learning: the acquisition of basic values of our culture and the development of capability to dissect and interpret our culture with the tools of rational inquiry. Space does not permit detailed review of Oliver's approach, but in barest outline it has the features noted here.

First, he proposes the use of dramatic narrative history to establish a firm foundation of value models early in the child's life. One illustration of what Oliver means is Sandburg's treatment of the Lincoln family in 1817–1819, when Nancy Hanks Lincoln died and Abe's father remarried. Oliver feels that narrative history, handled in various media, but always with as much power and beauty as possible, can help children to find concrete images of the courage, suffering, adventure, cooperation, and aggressive impulses from which America has sprung. In case one thinks that present materials already do this, it is instructive to compare the selection from *The Prairie Years* with most current elementary textbooks.

Second, Oliver proposes emphasis on a consultation-oriented approach to what he calls political process values, meaning largely those classes of rights which are the foundation of our freedom: freedom of expression, freedom to evaluate and change governmental leaders, due process of law, etc. Oliver calls this approach *jurisprudential,* focusing "upon the earnest use of free speech and open debate," guided by established rules of evidential proof, for students to determine themselves what man's proper relationship to government is in terms of particular public issues.

Oliver's jurisprudential approach uses controversy and its resolution through proof and persuasion as a vehicle for giving children experience in personal

---

[13] Bruner, Jerome S. *On Knowing; Essays for the Left Hand.* Cambridge, Massachusetts: Harvard University Press, 1962. p. 124.

and group policy decisions. The protocols of Oliver's experimental use of this vehicle reflect a carefully conceived teaching strategy aimed at responsible consultation about meaningful issues, not at producing random-talk democracy. His approach requires the use of narrative background texts, illustrative cases, dilemma cases, argumentative dialogue, persuasive documents, case-play, and the construction of personal briefs.

3. *Study and Practice of Self-government.*   Much that is sentimental and not a little that is artificial has been written about the uses of self-government as a part of school experience. But in elementary and secondary schools alike one finds little that could honestly go by this name; there is, I suppose, an understandable wariness about the whole subject. At the secondary level, the term "self-government" is eschewed altogether by the National Association of Secondary School Principals, who prefer to speak of student councils.

Yet a good deal of experience, primarily in small experimental private schools, suggests that self-government can genuinely help children grow as citizens. Both in terms of Brogan's definition and the wider meaning attached to citizenship by the Detroit Study, planned experience for children in self-government would seem to be as essential as it is logical. But this is not to say that such experience can be casual or a fake and be of much use.

Marion E. Turner's unusual verbatim reports of the conversations of a group of children four to nine years of age who learned to call meetings when some member created a disturbance is a rare record of experimentation with self-government in childhood education. Rules, using parliamentary procedures, were made to prevent similar disturbances, and when these rules were broken, the children established their own system of penalties and restraints.

Turner dealt with what are essentially political aspects of interaction in childhood society and sought to use "power factors in children's play" as subject matter. That is, she used conflict and conflict resolution in childhood relations as a means for introducing children to the political process. And from the verbatim reports, it would appear that in her three-year experiment, children gained a notable level of self-control and ease in consultation procedures without adult steering.

Of Turner's experiment and record, Theodore M. Newcomb has said:

> Those who have wondered at how early an age children are capable of taking an interest in the collective management of their own members' behavior will probably have to revise their estimates downward. And those—if there be any—who had correctly estimated that the capacity exists as early in life as does the capacity to participate in school activities . . . [will find] that the early capacity can be cultivated with remarkably successful results.[14]

At any rate, Turner's unusual report should encourage us to think again about experiences in self-government as a useful component of citizen education.

[14] Turner, Marion E. *The Child Within the Group; An Experiment in Self-Government.* Stanford, California: Stanford University Press, 1957, pp. vii–viii.

Toward a Realistic View

The emphasis on intellectual honesty about politics and governance, the use of value models based on rich historical narrative, the deliberate involvement of students in jurisprudential study of political process values as exposed in particular issues of real significance, and the utilization of self-government as a conscious educative procedure are far from a panacea. But taken together, they can help to introduce children to a realistic view of their relationship to a democratic culture in which lasting values are to be found and yet unceasingly reinterpreted in the changing context of life.

Social scientist mode of inquiry

Synonomous

CHAPTER 5 Structure As an Objective in the Social Studies

3 basic Approaches

Each teacher may choose one or more of a number of approaches to teaching the social studies. He may begin with the child, taking him at his own stage of development and trying to move him ahead. He may begin with basic problems of the society, confronting his students with these problems in an attempt to teach them to solve social dilemmas successfully. He may choose instead to teach the traditional disciplines to his students.

We have no conclusive evidence about which of these approaches is the best. Most teachers combine them. No one could successfully ignore the stage of emotional and intellectual development of his students. Very few teachers are able to resist referring to contemporary problems, even in courses in ancient history. Because teachers are trained by subject specialists in universities, they are accustomed to a disciplines approach. Most of us combine elements of these three basic approaches in our classes. In the new social studies, spurred by the work of Jerome Bruner, the structures of the disciplines are receiving increased attention.

Professor Bruner's little book _The Process of Education_ may eventually prove to be the most influential volume ever written about curriculum development. Bruner's emphasis upon structure and his bold assertion that any topic can be taught to any child at any age have become part of the working assumptions of most curriculum developers. The literature about curriculum development is filled with references to Brunerian concepts, and speeches at meetings of professional associations abound with references to his work. Bruner has become a latter-day John Dewey.

Most of the new curriculum projects have adopted the structure of the disciplines as the major criterion for the selection of content in the social studies. The directors of several projects are devoting all of their time to the identification of structure. Other projects have already identified major structural elements and are developing materials to help students find these elements for themselves. Section III of this volume contains five chapters that suggest the structure of social studies disciplines as well as a number of sample student readings designed to help students discover structure.

Chapter 5 consists of a condensation of Bruner's book. Four topics are discussed: the importance of structure, readiness for learning, intuitive and analytical thinking, and motives for learning. In addition to insights into the development of the curriculum, Bruner's material contains many suggestions about methods of teaching. The entire essay implies that methods of teaching and the materials for teaching cannot be separated.

As you read, keep the following in mind: *BASICS*

1) What does Bruner mean by structure? What is the purpose of teaching the structure of a discipline?
2) Why does Bruner endorse a discovery approach to the teaching of structure? Do the benefits he claims for the teaching of structure derive mainly from the students' new knowledge of structure or from their use of the discovery approach?
3) What does Bruner's claim that any concept can be taught to normal children in some form at any age imply for the process of curriculum development?
4) Are Bruner's objectives in both the cognitive and affective domains? Do they have implications for the development of good citizens?

THE IMPORTANCE OF STRUCTURE

Jerome Bruner

The first object of any act of learning, over and beyond the pleasure it may give, is that it should serve us in the future. Learning should not only take us somewhere; it should allow us later to go further more easily. There are two ways in which learning serves the future. One is through its specific applicability to tasks that are highly similar to those we originally learned to perform. Psychologists refer to this phenomenon as specific transfer of training; perhaps it should be called the extension of habits or associations. Its utility appears to be limited in the main to what we usually speak of as skills. Hav-

Reprinted by permission of the publishers from Jerome Bruner, *The Process of Education*. Cambridge, Mass.: Harvard University Press, Copyright 1960 by the President and Fellows of Harvard College, pp. 17–32, 38–40, 46–48, 50–60, 66–68, 71–73, and 80, with omissions.

ing learned how to hammer nails, we are better able later to learn how to hammer tacks or chip wood. Learning in school undoubtedly creates skills of a kind that transfers to activities encountered later, either in school or after. A second way in which earlier learning renders later performance more efficient is through what is conveniently called nonspecific transfer or, more accurately, the transfer of principles and attitudes. In essence, it consists of learning initially not a skill but a general idea, which can then be used as a basis for recognizing subsequent problems as special cases of the idea originally mastered. This type of transfer is at the heart of the educational process— the continual broadening and deepening of knowledge in terms of basic and general ideas.

The continuity of learning that is produced by the second type of transfer, transfer of principles, is dependent upon mastery of the structure of the subject matter, as structure was described in the preceding chapter. That is to say, in order for a person to be able to recognize the applicability or inapplicability of an idea to a new situation and to broaden his learning thereby, he must have clearly in mind the general nature of the phenomenon with which he is dealing. The more fundamental or basic is the idea he has learned, almost by definition, the greater will be its breadth of applicability to new problems. Indeed, this is almost a tautology, for what is meant by "fundamental" in this sense is precisely that an idea has wide as well as powerful applicability. It is simple enough to proclaim, of course, that school curricula and methods of teaching should be geared to the teaching of fundamental ideas in whatever subject is being taught. But as soon as one makes such a statement a host of problems arise, many of which can be solved only with the aid of considerably more research. We turn to some of these now.

The first and most obvious problem is how to construct curricula that can be taught by ordinary teachers to ordinary students and that at the same time reflect clearly the basic or underlying principles of various fields of inquiry. The problem is twofold: first, how to have the basic subjects rewritten and their teaching materials revamped in such a way that the pervading and powerful ideas and attitudes relating to them are given a central role; second, how to match the levels of these materials to the capacities of students of different abilities at different grades in school.

The experience of the past several years has taught at least one important lesson about the design of a curriculum that is true to the underlying structure of its subject matter. It is that the best minds in any particular discipline must be put to work on the task. The decision as to what should be taught in American history to elementary school children or what should be taught in arithmetic is a decision that can best be reached with the aid of those with a high degree of vision and competence in each of these fields. To decide that the elementary ideas of algebra depend upon the fundamentals of the commutative, distributive, and associative laws, one must be a mathematician in a position to appreciate and understand the fundamentals of mathematics.

Whether school children require an understanding of Frederick Jackson Turner's ideas about the role of the frontier in American history before they can sort out the facts and trends of American history—this again is a decision that requires the help of the scholar who has a deep understanding of the American past. Only by the use of our best minds in devising curricula will we bring the fruits of scholarship and wisdom to the student just beginning his studies. . . . .

Mastery of the fundamental ideas of a field involves not only the grasping of general principles, but also the development of an attitude toward learning and inquiry, toward guessing and hunches, toward the possibility of solving problems on one's own. Just as a physicist has certain attitudes about the ultimate orderliness of nature and a conviction that order can be discovered, so a young physics student needs some working version of these attitudes if he is to organize his learning in such a way as to make what he learns usable and meaningful in his thinking. To instill such attitudes by teaching requires something more than the mere presentation of fundamental ideas. Just what it takes to bring off such teaching is something on which a great deal of research is needed, but it would seem that an important ingredient is a sense of excitement about discovery—discovery of regularities of previously unrecognized relations and similarities between ideas, with a resulting sense of self-confidence in one's abilities. Various people who have worked on curricula in science and mathematics have urged that it is possible to present the fundamental structure of a discipline in such a way as to preserve some of the exciting sequences that lead a student to discover for himself. . . .

That the method of discovery need not be limited to such highly formalized subjects as mathematics and physics is illustrated by some experimentation on social studies carried out by the Harvard Cognition Project. A sixth-grade class, having been through a conventional unit on the social and economic geography of the Southeastern states, was introduced to the North Central region by being asked to locate the major cities of the area on a map containing physical features and natural resources, but no place names. The resulting class discussion very rapidly produced a variety of plausible theories concerning the requirements of a city—a water transportation theory that placed Chicago at the junction of the three lakes, a mineral resources theory that placed it near the Mesabi range, a food-supply theory that put a great city on the rich soil of Iowa, and so on. The level of interest as well as the level of conceptual sophistication was far above that of control classes. Most striking, however, was the attitude of children to whom, for the first time, the location of a city appeared as a problem, and one to which an answer could be discovered by taking thought. Not only was there pleasure and excitement in the pursuit of a question, but in the end the discovery was worth making, at least for urban children for whom the phenomenon of the city was something that had before been taken for granted.

How do we tailor fundamental knowledge to the interests and capacities of children? This is a theme we shall return to later, and only a word need be said about it here. It requires a combination of deep understanding and patient honesty to present physical or any other phenomena in a way that is simultaneously exciting, correct, and rewardingly comprehensible. In examining certain teaching materials in physics, for example, we have found much patient honesty in presentation that has come to naught because the authors did not have a deep enough understanding of the subject they were presenting.

A good case in point is to be found in the usual attempt to explain the nature of tides. Ask the majority of high school students to explain tides and they will speak of the gravitational pull of the moon on the surface of the earth and how it pulls the water on the moon's side into a bulge. Ask them now why there is also a bulge of less magnitude on the side of the earth opposite to the moon, and they will almost always be without a satisfactory answer. Or ask them where the maximum bulge of the incoming tide is with respect to the relative position of the earth and moon, and the answer will usually be that it is at the point on the earth's surface nearest to the moon. If the student knows there is a lag in the tidal crest, he will usually not know why. The failure in both cases comes from an inadequate picture of how gravity acts upon a free-moving elastic body, and a failure to connect the idea of inertia with the idea of gravitational action. In short, the tides are explained without a share of the excitement that can come from understanding Newton's great discovery of universal gravitation and its mode of action. Correct and illuminating explanations are no more difficult and often easier to grasp than ones that are partly correct and therefore too complicated and too restricted. It is the consensus of virtually all the men and women who have been working on curriculum projects that making material interesting is in no way incompatible with presenting it soundly; indeed, a correct general explanation is often the most interesting of all. Inherent in the preceding discussions are at least four general claims that can be made for teaching the fundamental structure of a subject, claims in need of detailed study.

The first is that understanding fundamentals makes a subject more comprehensible. This is true not only in physics and mathematics, where we have principally illustrated the point, but equally in the social studies and literature. Once one has grasped the fundamental idea that a nation must trade in order to live, then such a presumably special phenomenon as the Triangular Trade of the American colonies becomes altogether simpler to understand as something more than commerce in molasses, sugar cane, rum, and slaves in an atmosphere of violation of British trade regulations. The high school student reading *Moby Dick* can only understand more deeply if he can be led to understand that Melville's novel is, among other things, a study of the theme of evil and the plight of those pursuing this "killing whale." And if the student is led further to understand that there are a relatively limited number of human plights about which novels are written, he understands literature the better for it.

The second point relates to human memory. Perhaps the most basic thing that can be said about human memory, after a century of intensive research, is that unless detail is placed into a structured pattern, it is rapidly forgotten. Detailed material is conserved in memory by the use of simplified ways of representing it. These simplified representations have what may be called a "regenerative" character. A good example of this regenerative property of long-term memory can be found in science. A scientist does not try to remember the distances traversed by falling bodies in different gravitational fields over different periods of time. What he carries in memory instead is a formula that permits him with varying degrees of accuracy to regenerate the details on which the more easily remembered formula is based. So he commits to memory the formula $s = \frac{1}{2} gt^2$ and not a handbook of distances, times, and gravitational constants. Similarly, one does not remember exactly what Marlowe, the commentator in *Lord Jim*, said about the chief protagonist's plight, but, rather, simply that he was the dispassionate onlooker, the man who tried to understand without judging what had led Lord Jim into the straits in which he found himself. We remember a formula, a vivid detail that carries the meaning of an event, an average that stands for a range of events, a caricature or picture that preserves an essence—all of them techniques of condensation and representation. What learning general or fundamental principles does is to ensure that memory loss will not mean total loss, that what remains will permit us to reconstruct the details when needed. A good theory is the vehicle not only for understanding a phenomenon now but also for remembering it tomorrow.

Third, an understanding of fundamental principles and ideas, as noted earlier, appears to be the main road to adequate "transfer of training." To understand something as a specific instance of a more general case—which is what understanding a more fundamental principle or structure means—is to have learned not only a specific thing but also a model for understanding other things like it that one may encounter. If a student could grasp in its most human sense the weariness of Europe at the close of the Hundred Years' War and how it created the conditions for a workable but not ideologically absolute Treaty of Westphalia, he might be better able to think about the ideological struggle of East and West—though the parallel is anything but exact. A carefully wrought understanding should also permit him to recognize the limits of the generalization as well. The idea of "principles" and "concepts" as a basis for transfer is hardly new. It is much in need of more research of a specific kind that would provide detailed knowledge of how best to proceed in the teaching of different subjects in different grades.

The fourth claim for emphasis on structure and principles in teaching is that by constantly reexamining material taught in elementary and secondary schools for its fundamental character, one is able to narrow the gap between "advanced" knowledge and "elementary" knowledge. Part of the difficulty now found in the progression from primary school through high school to college is that material learned earlier is either out of date or misleading by virtue of its lagging too far behind developments in a field. This gap can be reduced by the kind of emphasis set forth in the preceding discussion. . . .

A word is needed, finally, on examinations. It is obvious that an examination can be bad in the sense of emphasizing trivial aspects of a subject. Such examinations can encourage teaching in a disconnected fashion and learning by rote. What is often overlooked, however, is that examinations can also be allies in the battle to improve curricula and teaching. Whether an examination is of the "objective" type involving multiple choices or of the essay type, it can be devised so as to emphasize an understanding of the broad principles of a subject. Indeed, even when one examines on detailed knowledge, it can be done in such a way as to require an understanding by the student of the connectedness between specific facts. There is a concerted effort now under way among national testing organizations like the Educational Testing Service to construct examinations that will emphasize an understanding of fundamental principles. Such efforts can be of great help. Additional help might be given to local school systems by making available to them manuals that describe the variety of ways in which examinations can be constructed. The searching examination is not easy to make, and a thoughtful manual on the subject would be welcome.

To recapitulate, the main theme of this chapter has been that the curriculum of a subject should be determined by the most fundamental understanding that can be achieved of the underlying principles that give structure to that subject. Teaching specific topics or skills without making clear their context in the broader fundamental structure of a field of knowledge is uneconomical in several deep senses. In the first place, such teaching makes it exceedingly difficult for the student to generalize from what he has learned to what he will encounter later. In the second place, learning that has fallen short of a grasp of general principles has little reward in terms of intellectual excitement. The best way to create interest in a subject is to render it worth knowing, which means to make the knowledge gained usable in one's thinking beyond the situation in which the learning has occurred. Third, knowledge one has acquired without sufficient structure to tie it together is knowledge that is likely to be forgotten. An unconnected set of facts has a pitiably short half-life in memory. Organizing facts in terms of principles and ideas from which they may be inferred is the only known way of reducing the quick rate of loss of human memory.

Designing curricula in a way that reflects the basic structure of a field of knowledge requires the most fundamental understanding of that field. It is a task that cannot be carried out without the active participation of the ablest scholars and scientists. The experience of the past several years has shown that such scholars and scientists, working in conjunction with experienced teachers and students of child development, can prepare curricula of the sort we have been considering. Much more effort in the actual preparation of curriculum materials, in teacher training, and in supporting research will be necessary if improvements in our educational practices are to be of an order that will meet the challenges of the scientific and social revolution through which we are now living.

There are many problems of how to teach general principles in a way that will be both effective and interesting, and several of the key issues have been passed in review. What is abundantly clear is that much work remains to be done by way of examining currently effective practices, fashioning curricula that may be tried out on an experimental basis, and carrying out the kinds of research that can give support and guidance to the general effort at improving teaching.

How may the kind of curriculum we have been discussing be brought within the intellectual reach of children of different ages? To this problem we turn next.

READINESS FOR LEARNING

We begin with the hypothesis that any subject can be taught effectively in some intellectually honest form to any child at any stage of development. It is a bold hypothesis and an essential one in thinking about the nature of a curriculum. No evidence exists to contradict it; considerable evidence is being amassed that supports it. . . .

But the intellectual development of the child is no clockwork sequence of events; it also responds to influences from the environment, notably the school environment. Thus instruction in scientific ideas, even at the elementary level, need not follow slavishly the natural course of cognitive development in the child. It can also lead intellectual development by providing challenging but usable opportunities for the child to forge ahead in his development. Experience has shown that it is worth the effort to provide the growing child with problems that tempt him into next stages of development. As David Page, one of the most experienced teachers of elementary mathematics, has commented: "In teaching from kindergarten to graduate school, I have been amazed at the intellectual similarity of human beings at all ages, although children are perhaps more spontaneous, creative, and energetic than adults. As far as I am concerned young children learn almost anything faster than adults do if it can be given to them in terms they understand. Giving the material to them in terms they understand, interestingly enough, turns out to involve knowing the mathematics oneself, and the better one knows it, the better it can be taught. It is appropriate that we warn ourselves to be careful of assigning an absolute level of difficulty to any particular topic. When I tell mathematicians that fourth-grade students can go a long way into 'set theory' a few of them reply: 'Of course.' Most of them are startled. The latter ones are completely wrong in assuming that 'set theory' is intrinsically difficult. Of course it may be that nothing is intrinsically difficult. We just have to wait until the proper point of view and corresponding language for presenting it are revealed. Given particular subject matter or a particular concept, it is easy to ask trivial questions or to lead the child to ask trivial questions. It is also easy to ask impossibly difficult questions. The trick is to find the medium questions that can be answered and that take you somewhere. This is the big job of teachers and textbooks." One leads the child by the well-wrought "medium questions" to move more rapidly through the stages of intellectual development, to a deeper understanding of mathematical, physical, and historical principles. We must know far more about the ways in which this can be done. . . .

There has been little research done on the kinds of concepts that a child brings to these subjects, although there is a wealth of observation and anecdote. Can one teach the structure of literary forms by presenting the child with the first part of a story and then having him complete it in the form of a comedy, a tragedy, or a farce—without ever using such words? When, for example, does the idea of "historical trend" develop, and what are its precursors in the child? How does one make a child aware of literary style? Perhaps the child can discover the idea of style through the presentation of the same content written in drastically different styles, in the manner of Beerbohm's *Christmas Garland*. Again, there is no reason to believe that any subject cannot be taught to any child at virtually any age in some form.

Here one is immediately faced with the question of the economy of teaching. One can argue that it might be better to wait until the child is thirteen or fourteen before beginning geometry so that the projective and intuitive first steps can immediately be followed up by a full formal presentation of the subject. Is it worthwhile to train the young inductively so that they may discover the basic order of knowledge before they can appreciate its formalism? In Professor Inhelder's memorandum, it was suggested that the first two grades might be given over to training the child in the basic logical operations that underlie instruction in mathematics and science. There is evidence to indicate that such rigorous and relevant early training has the effect of making later learning easier. Indeed the experiments on "learning set" seem to indicate just that—that one not only learns specifics but in so doing learns how to learn. So important is training per se that monkeys who have been given extensive training in problem solving suffer considerably less loss and recover more quickly after induced brain damage than animals who had not been previously thus educated. But the danger of such early training may be that it has the effect of training out original but deviant ideas. There is no evidence available on the subject, and much is needed. . . .

There has been much written on the role of reward and punishment in learning, but very little indeed on the role of interest and curiosity and the lure of discovery. If it is our intention as teachers to inure the child to longer and longer episodes of learning, it may well be that intrinsic rewards in the form of quickened awareness and understanding will have to be emphasized far more in the detailed design of curricula. One of the least discussed ways of carrying a student through a hard unit of material is to challenge him with a chance to exercise his full powers, so that he may discover the pleasure of full and effective functioning. Good teachers know the power of this lure. Students should know what it feels like to be completely absorbed in a problem. They seldom experience this feeling in school. Given enough absorption in class, some students may be able to carry over the feeling to work done on their own.

There is a range of problems that have to do with how much emphasis should be placed on acquisition, transformation, and evaluation in a learning episode—getting facts, manipulating them, and checking one's ideas. Is it the case, for example, that it is best to give the young child a minimum set of facts first and then encourage him to draw the fullest set of implications possible from this knowledge? In short, should an episode for a young child contain little new information but emphasize what can be done to go beyond that bit on one's own? One teacher of social studies has had great success with fourth-graders through this approach: he begins, for example, with the fact that civilizations have most often begun in fertile river valleys—the only "fact." The students are encouraged in class discussion to figure out why this is the case and why it would be less likely for civilizations to start in mountainous country. The effect of this approach, essentially the technique of discovery, is that the child generates information on his own, which he can then check or evaluate against the sources, getting more new information in the process. This obviously is one kind of learning episode, and doubtless it has limited applicability. What other kinds are there, and are some more appropriate to certain topics and ages than others? It is not the case that "to learn is to learn is to learn," yet in the research literature there appears to be little recognition of differences in learning episodes.

With respect to the optimum length of a learning episode, there are a few commonsense things one can say about it, and these are perhaps interesting enough to suggest fruitful research possibilities. It seems fairly obvious, for example, that the longer and more packed the episode, the greater the payoff must be in terms of increased power and understanding if the person is to be encouraged to move to a next episode with zest. Where grades are used as a substitute for the reward of understanding, it may well be that learning will cease as soon as grades are no longer given—at graduation.

It also seems reasonable that the more one has a sense of the structure of a subject, the more densely packed and longer a learning episode one can get through without fatigue. Indeed, the amount of new information in any learning episode is really the amount that we cannot quite fit into place at once. And there is a severe limit, as we have already noted, on how much of such unassimilated information we can keep in mind. The estimate is that adults can handle about seven independent items of information at a time. No norms are available for children—a deplorable lack.

There are many details one can discuss concerning the shaping of learning episodes for children, but the problems that have been mentioned will suffice to give their flavor. Inasmuch as the topic is central to an understanding of how one arranges a curriculum, it seems obvious that here is an area of research that is of the first importance.

The "*spiral curriculum.*" If one respects the ways of thought of the growing child, if one is courteous enough to translate material into his logical forms and challenging enough to tempt him to advance, then it is possible to introduce him at an early age to the ideas and styles that in later life make an educated man. We might ask, as a criterion for any subject taught in primary school, whether, when fully developed, it is worth an adult's knowing, and whether having known it as a child makes a person a better adult. If the answer to both questions is negative or ambiguous, then the material is cluttering the curriculum.

If the hypothesis with which this section was introduced is true—that any subject can be taught to any child in some honest form—then it should follow that a curriculum ought to be built around the great issues, principles, and values that a society deems worthy of the continual concern of its members. Consider two examples—the teaching of literature and of science. If it is granted, for example, that it is desirable to give children an awareness of the meaning of human tragedy and a sense of compassion for it, is it not possible at the earliest appropriate age to teach the literature of tragedy in a manner that illuminates but does not threaten? There are many possible ways to begin: through a retelling of the great myths, through the use of children's classics, through presentation of and commentary on selected films that have proved themselves. Precisely what kinds of materials should be used at what age with what effect is a subject for research—research of several kinds. We may ask first about the child's conception of the tragic, and here one might proceed in much the same way that Piaget and his colleagues have proceeded in studying the child's conception of physical causality, of morality, of number, and the rest. It is only when we are equipped with such knowledge that we will be in a position to know how the child will translate whatever we present to him into his own subjective terms. Nor need we wait for all the research findings to be in before proceeding, for a skillful teacher can also experiment by attempting to teach what seems to be intuitively right for children of different ages, correcting as he goes. In time, one goes beyond to more complex versions of the same kind of literature or simply revisits some of the same books used earlier. What matters is that later teaching build upon earlier reactions to literature, that it seek to create an ever more explicit and mature understanding of the literature of tragedy. Any of the great literary forms can be handled in the same way, or any of the great themes—be it the form of comedy or the theme of identity, personal loyalty, or what not. . . .

Many curricula are originally planned with a guiding idea much like the one set forth here. But as curricula are actually executed, as they grow and change, they often lose their original form and suffer a relapse into a certain shapelessness. It is not amiss to urge that actual curricula be reexamined with an eye to the issues of continuity and development referred to in the preceding pages. One cannot predict the exact forms that revision might take; indeed, it is plain that there is now available too little research to provide adequate answers. One can only propose that appropriate research be undertaken with the greatest vigor and as soon as possible.

INTUITIVE AND
ANALYTIC THINKING

Much has been said in the preceding chapters about the importance of a student's intuitive, in contrast to his formal understanding of the subjects he encounters. The emphasis in much of school learning and student examining is upon explicit formulations, upon the ability of the student to reproduce verbal or numerical formulae. It is not clear, in the absence of research, whether this emphasis is inimical to the later development of good intuitive understanding—indeed, it is even unclear what constitutes intuitive understanding. Yet we can distinguish between inarticulate genius and articulate idiocy—the first represented by the student who, by his operations and conclusions, reveals a deep grasp of a subject but not much ability to "say how it goes," in contrast to the student who is full of seemingly appropriate words but has no matching ability to use the ideas for which the words presumably stand. A careful examination of the nature of intuitive thinking might be of great aid to those charged with curriculum construction and teaching.

Mathematicians, physicists, biologists, and others stress the value of intuitive thinking in their respective areas. In mathematics, for example, intuition is used with two rather different meanings. On the one hand, an individual is said to think intuitively when, having worked for a long time on a problem, he rather suddenly achieves the solution, one for which he has yet to provide a formal proof. On the other hand, an individual is said to be a good intuitive mathematician if, when others come to him with questions, he can make quickly very good guesses whether something is so, or which of several approaches to a problem will prove fruitful. . . .

Questions about the nature of intuitive thinking seem to center upon two large issues: what intuitive thinking is, and what affects it.

One can say many more concrete things about analytic thinking than about intuitive thinking. Analytic thinking characteristically proceeds a step at a time. Steps are explicit and usually can be adequately reported by the thinker to another individual. Such thinking proceeds with relatively full awareness of the information and operations involved. It may involve careful and deductive reasoning, often using mathematics or logic and an explicit plan of attack. Or it may involve a step-by-step process of induction and experiment, utilizing principles of research design and statistical analysis.

In contrast to analytic thinking, intuitive thinking characteristically does not advance in careful, well-defined steps. Indeed, it tends to involve maneuvers based seemingly on an implicit perception of the total problem. The thinker arrives at an answer, which may be right or wrong, with little if any awareness of the process by which he reached it. He rarely can provide an adequate account of how he obtained his answer, and he may be unaware of just what aspects of the problem situation he was responding to. Usually intuitive thinking rests on familiarity with the domain of knowledge involved and with its structure, which makes it possible for the thinker to leap about, skipping steps and employing short cuts in a manner that requires a later rechecking of conclusions by more analytic means, whether deductive or inductive.

The complementary nature of intuitive and analytic thinking should, we think, be recognized. Through intuitive thinking the individual may often arrive at solutions to problems which he would not achieve at all, or at best more slowly, through analytic thinking. Once achieved by intuitive methods, they should if possible be checked by analytic methods, while at the same time being respected as worthy hypotheses for such checking. Indeed, the intuitive thinker may even invent or discover problems that the analyst would not. But it may be the analyst who gives these problems the proper formalism. Unfortunately, the formalism of school learning has somehow devalued intuition. It is the very strong conviction of men who have been designing curricula, in mathematics and the sciences particularly, over the last several years that much more work is needed to discover how we may develop the intuitive gifts of our students from the earliest grades onwards. For, as we have seen, it may be of the first importance to establish an intuitive understanding of materials before we expose our students to more traditional and formal methods of deduction and proof.

As to the nature of intuitive thinking, what is it? It is quite clear that it is not easy either to recognize a particular problem-solving episode as intuitive or, indeed, to identify intuitive ability as such. Precise definition in terms of observable behavior is not readily within our reach at the present time. Obviously, research on the topic cannot be delayed until such a time as a pure and unambiguous definition of intuitive thinking is possible, along with precise techniques for identifying intuition when it occurs. Such refinement is the goal of research, not its starting place. It suffices as a start to ask whether we are able to identify certain problem-solving episodes as more intuitive than others. Or, alternatively, we may ask if we can learn to agree in classifying a person's style or preferred mode of working as characteristically more analytic or inductive, on the one hand, or more intuitive, and, indeed, if we can find some way to classify tasks as ones that require each of those styles of attack. It is certainly clear that it is important not to confuse intuitive and other kinds of thinking with such evaluative notions as effectiveness and ineffectiveness: the analytic, the inductive, and the intuitive can be either. Nor should we distinguish them in terms of whether they produce novel or familiar outcomes, for again this is not the important distinction.

For a working definition of intuition, we do well to begin with Webster: "immediate apprehension or cognition." "Immediate" in this context is contrasted with "mediated"—apprehension or cognition that depends on the intervention of formal methods of analysis and proof. Intuition implies the act of grasping the meaning, significance, or structure of a problem or situation without explicit reliance on the analytic apparatus of one's craft. The rightness or wrongness of an intuition is finally decided not by intuition itself but by the usual methods of proof. It is the intuitive mode, however, that yields hypotheses quickly, that hits on combinations of ideas before their worth is known. In the end, intuition by itself yields a tentative ordering of a body of knowledge that, while it may generate a feeling that the ordering of facts is self-evident, aids principally by giving us a basis for moving ahead in our testing of reality. . . .

What can be said about the conditions in which intuitive thinking is likely to be particularly effective? In which subjects will mastery be most aided by intuitive procedures followed by checking? Many kinds of problems will be best approached by some combination of intuitive and other procedures, so it is also important to know whether or not both can be developed within the same course by the same teaching methods. This suggests that we examine the mode of effective operation of intuition in different kinds of fields. One hears the most explicit talk about intuition in those fields where the formal apparatus of deduction and induction is most highly developed—in mathematics and physics. The use of the word "intuition" by mathematicians and physicists may reflect their sense of confidence in the power and rigor of their disciplines. Others, however, may use intuition as much or more. Surely the historian, to take but one example, leans heavily upon intuitive procedures in pursuing his subject, for he must select what is relevant. He does not attempt to learn or record everything about a period; he limits himself to finding or learning predictively fruitful facts which, when combined, permit him to make intelligent guesses about what else went on. A comparison of intuitive thinking in different fields of knowledge would, we feel, be highly useful.

We have already noted in passing the intuitive confidence required of the poet and the literary critic in practicing their crafts: the need to proceed in the absence of specific and agreed-upon criteria for the choice of an image of the formulation of a critique. It is difficult for a teacher, a textbook, a demonstration film, to make explicit provision for the cultivation of courage in taste. As likely as not, courageous taste rests upon confidence in one's intuitions about what is moving, what is beautiful, what is tawdry. In a culture such as ours, where there is so much pressure toward uniformity of taste in our mass media of communication, so much fear of idiosyncratic style, indeed a certain suspicion of the idea of style altogether, it becomes the more important to nurture confident intuition in the realm of literature and the arts. Yet one finds a virtual vacuum of research on this topic in educational literature.

The warm praise that scientists lavish on those of their colleagues who earn the label "intuitive" is major evidence that intuition is a valuable commodity in science and one we should endeavor to foster in our students. The case for intuition in the arts and social studies is just as strong. But the pedagogic problems in fostering such a gift are severe and should not be overlooked in our eagerness to take the problem into the laboratory. For one thing, the intuitive method, as we have noted, often produces the wrong answer. It requires a sensitive teacher to distinguish an intuitive mistake—an *— PROB* interestingly wrong leap—from a stupid or ignorant mistake, and it requires a teacher who can give approval and correction simultaneously to the intuitive student. To know a subject so thoroughly that he can go easily beyond the textbook is a great deal to ask of a high school teacher. Indeed, it must happen occasionally that a student is not only more intelligent than his teacher but *prob* better informed, and develops intuitive ways of approaching problems that he *intuitive* cannot explain and that the teacher is simply unable to follow or re-create for *Thinking* himself. It is impossible for the teacher properly to reward or correct such students, and it may very well be that it is precisely our more gifted students who suffer such unrewarded effort. So along with any program for developing methods of cultivating and measuring the occurrence of intuitive thinking, there must go some practical consideration of the classroom problems and the limitations on our capacity for encouraging such skills in our students. This, too, is research that should be given all possible support.

These practical difficulties should not discourage psychologists and teachers from making an attack on the problem. Once we have obtained answers to various questions raised in this chapter, we shall be in a much better position to recommend procedures for overcoming some of the difficulties.

MOTIVES FOR LEARNING

In assessing what might be done to improve the state of the curricular art, we are inevitably drawn into discussion of the nature of motives for learning and the objectives one might expect to attain in educating youth. Obviously, matters of such enormous scope can be considered only briefly here. Yet certain issues seem to be particularly in need of closer scrutiny in relation to the designing of curricula. . . .

Somewhere between apathy and wild excitement, there is an optimum level of aroused attention that is ideal for classroom activity. What is that level? Frenzied activity fostered by the competitive project may leave no pause for reflection, for evaluation, for generalization, while excessive orderliness, with each student waiting passively for his turn, produces boredom and ultimate apathy. There is a day-to-day problem here of great significance. Short-run arousal of interest is not the same as the long-term establishment of interest in the broader sense. Films, audio-visual aids, and other such devices may have the short-run effect of catching attention. In the long run, they may produce a passive person waiting for some sort of curtain to go up to arouse him. We do not know. Perhaps anything that holds the child's attention is justified on the ground that eventually the child will develop a taste for more self-controlled attention—a point on which there is no evidence. The issue is particularly relevant in an entertainment-oriented, mass-communication culture where passivity and "spectatorship" are dangers. Perhaps it is in the technique of arousing attention in school that first steps can be taken to establish that active autonomy of attention that is the antithesis of the spectator's passivity. . . .

Several tentative recommendations have already been made in the spirit of suggesting needed research. Principal among these were increasing the inherent interest of materials taught, giving the student a sense of discovery, translating what we have to say into the thought forms appropriate to the child, and so on. What this amounts to is developing in the child an interest in what he is learning, and with it an appropriate set of attitudes and values about intellectual activity generally. Surely we shall not by presently conceivable reforms create a nation of devoted intellectuals, nor is it apparent that this should be the major guiding aim of our schools. Rather, if teaching is done well and what we teach is worth learning, there are forces at work in our contemporary society that will provide the external prod that will get children more involved in the process of learning than they have been in the past. . . .

To sum up the matter, motives for learning must be kept from going passive in an age of spectatorship, they must be based as much as possible upon the arousal of interest in what there is to be learned, and they must be kept broad and diverse in expression. The danger signs of meritocracy and a new form of competitiveness are already in evidence. Already it is possible to see where advance planning can help. Such planning and the research to support it should be given high priority.

CHAPTER 6 Some Criteria for Selecting Content

Every teacher selects the content he wishes to emphasize in a social studies course. In the past, all too many teachers have left the major task of selection to the author of their textbook. By following the text chapter by chapter, they have given up the right to select the material their students will study, and as a result they have often offered inferior courses lacking sound philosophical justification.

If teachers knew about the way in which some texts were written, they might be less willing to adhere slavishly to the author's outline. Some publishers examine the competing texts in a field in order to determine what subjects are discussed by all their major rivals for the market. They then list these topics for their authors, suggesting that the new book should touch each of the issues presented in the old books. Teachers assigned the task of developing a course of study from the product that results then usually accept the structure of the book and organize a set of assignments and classroom procedures designed to get through it within the school year.

Entire curricula are sometimes developed by teachers with little more creative thought than they devote to course outlines. Most schools follow one of the patterns suggested by a national committee chosen to make recommendations for social studies content. The most common curriculum pattern for the secondary schools—the one recommended by the Commission on the Reorganization of Secondary Schools in 1916—places geography in seventh grade, American history in eighth, civics in ninth, world history in tenth, American history in eleventh, and problems of democracy in twelfth. Most schools pay little attention to organizing the work of these courses in cumulative and sequential fashion. Indeed, many teachers in the upper grades cannot name the author or title of the books their students have studied in junior high school. Hence, they often fail to design courses that consciously pick up subject threads or cognitive skills learned in previous years.

The essay in Chapter 6 was written by Professor Donald W. Oliver of Harvard University. Professor Oliver directs a major curriculum development project supported by a grant from the United States Office of Education. In the excerpt that follows he examines some of the criteria that were used in the past to justify the selection of content in the social studies and then suggests criteria of his own. His content selection implies a revolution in the entire structure of the social studies sequence, as well as fundamental changes within each individual course. As you read, keep the following questions in mind:

1) How have curriculum developers in the past justified the selection of content for the social studies? What are Oliver's criticisms of these justifications?

2) Why does Oliver believe that curriculum decisions should be based on a value position? Do you agree with him? Do his choice of affective goals and his methods of reaching them imply indoctrination?

3) Which would be more useful preparation for handling future social problems, understanding the structure of history and the social sciences or understanding how to solve typical social conflicts? Are typical social conflicts easier to identify objectively than the structure of a discipline?

4) For which of the goals described by Krathwohl, Bloom, and Masia can Oliver's teaching strategies be used? Can the content and methods of teaching that Oliver advocates be used to reach the objectives described by Benedict? by Patterson? by Bruner?

THE SELECTION OF CONTENT IN THE SOCIAL SCIENCES

Donald W. Oliver

THE PROBLEM

Introduction.   The problem of defining adequate criteria for the selection of social science content to be taught in the secondary school has become increasingly acute for at least two reasons. First, the methodology and accumulated substantive knowledge of the various social sciences have ex-

Reprinted from Donald W. Oliver, "The Selection of Content in the Social Studies," *Harvard Educational Review*, Vol. 28, No. 1, Winter 1957, pp. 271–276, 278–284, and 291–300, with omissions.

panded tremendously in the last decade. A relatively new branch of social science, the behavioral sciences, has developed a methodology and an approach to human problems and society that is influencing disciplines such as political science and economics which have been traditionally historical. Second, with a growing emphasis on the belief that man might collectively control his own destiny if only he could cooperate with his fellow men, pressure to teach a direct morality of cooperation and brotherly love has become much greater. As a result of these two trends, the social science content taught in the public schools has been expanded to include principles of group understanding and group dynamics derived from the behavioral sciences as well as a broad ethic of collective responsibility.

Once the social science curriculum is consciously molded by the belief that direct morality should be taught via social science content—rather than the use of such content only to clarify moral issues—the door is open to an inevitable expansion of the social studies into ethical areas which have to be thought through clearly.

The Social Sciences As Disciplines and As General Education.   Before presenting a review of some criteria for the selection of content in the social studies, a distinction should be made between the teaching of various social sciences as disciplines and the teaching of social sciences as subject-matter which, presumably, will contribute to the general intellectual competence of all the citizenry. We can illustrate this distinction with the following example. Suppose that a university scholar of the Jacksonian Period in American history is asked why he wishes to teach students the Jacksonian Period in American history. He might reply that it is because it happens to be his field of scholarly competence; and from a disciplinary point of view, need he answer more? His rationale for presenting some data and not other data bearing on the Jacksonian Period rests only on the assumption that a particular selection of data will represent a more accurate picture of the period. This historian might also include in his justifications of such content the hope that a spark of interest would be generated in his students (if it were not already there), and that after studying this content, the student might then pursue the subject of Jackson for the sake of knowing—for scholarship alone. This justification asserts that the methodology and substantive knowledge of the various social science disciplines may be taught simply as an attempt to perpetuate scholarship. The same justification might hold for teaching large numbers of students introductory courses in the disciplines. Although only a small percentage of those introduced to a particular content area in such a course might actually enter training in a scholarly field, the procedure can certainly be defended on the basis of the difficulty of recruiting academic personnel who may make significant contributions to their own disciplines and to the culture as a whole.

The selection of specific content for general education is a more difficult problem. How does one justify choosing particular content areas and giving them priority over others? Trends in the present secondary school curriculum suggest that educators are seeking to solve the problem by introducing courses in which a wider and wider range of content is taught, e.g., the yearly extension of "United States History" courses to include contemporary events; and the current popularity of the courses commonly called "World Civilization," which literally cover recorded history from the first caveman to the last atom. Even if it is possible to teach such a course, there is still the problem of selecting particular content to put into the exhaustive chronological scheme. Perhaps teachers feel that because the chronology is complete, the selected content which parallels the chronology is also complete. This notion is, of course, absurd.

Assuming that it is impossible to teach the complete methodology and/or substantive content in any or all of the social sciences, and assuming that some information and understandings are in fact more valuable than others in educating citizens to exercise their social responsibilities, the problem of selecting specific content areas—and justifying this content—inevitably arises.

Some Major Attempts to Define and Justify Social Studies Content

The problem of selecting and justifying social studies content in the secondary school is certainly not new. National committees of the American Historical Association, the National Education Association, and other scholarly organizations have periodically attacked the problem. We shall discuss four such attempts before presenting our own position with respect to this problem. The intention here is not so much to deal with the historical impact of the various reports as with an analysis of the philosophical difficulties that have become apparent in the short period of time that social scientists and educators have wrestled with them.

The four reports which we shall discuss are: The Report of the Committee of Seven of the American Historical Association published in 1899; The Report of the Committee on the Social Studies of the Commission on the Reorganization of Secondary Education of the National Education Association, published in 1916; The work carried out in the 1930's as part of the activities of the Commission on Social Studies of the American Historical Association; and the Preliminary Report of the Committee on Concepts and Values of the National Council for the Social Studies published in 1956. . . .

The report of the National Education Association published in 1916 represented a major change in thinking about the nature and purpose of social science education when contrasted with the 1899 report of the American Historical Association. The Committee of Seven apparently assumed that history was the only social science that could make a contribution to secondary education; that four years of history arranged chronologically was necessary; and that the appropriate techniques of teaching such content should consist mainly of feeding the learner codified historical literature and seeing to it that all the material was properly consumed. The National Education Association's report of 1916 showed certain striking reversals of this kind of thinking: it explicitly considered the frame of reference of the learner as important in the selection of materials; it dealt with history as only one of a number of social science disciplines capable of making a contribution to the secondary school student. It went so far as to suggest the institution of a "problems of democracy" course in the senior year of high school in which the student would ". . . study actual problems, or issues or conditions, as they occur in life, and in their several aspects, political, economic, and sociological." It is partly as a result of this committee's report that the term "social studies" gained respectability and came into common use.

Perhaps the most striking aspect of the 1916 report was its shift in the basis for justifying historical content. While in the 1896 report history was assumed to have a vague but generally beneficial effect upon the entire thinking process of the student, the 1916 report justified the teaching of history in terms of its immediate utilitarian value in understanding current and future problems. It is, perhaps, this shift in thinking about social studies objectives that raised the whole question of what is appropriate content for teaching. As long as there existed in the minds of educators a sacred body of historical knowledge, the only problem was rationalizing why it should be taught. Since 1916 this sacred body of knowledge has become less secure as other social sciences have risen to challenge the fruitfulness of the historical approach as a way of thinking about social issues; and history itself has assumed more and more the burden of becoming a social science rather than an impressionistic narration of the past. By 1916 the sanctity of historical literature had diminished to the point where educators (and some historians) refrained from prescribing a certain pat body of history as absolutely necessary for the education of the young. The "problems of democracy" course suggested by the 1916 report, which attempts to focus the findings from several social sciences upon concrete social problems, offered an alternative to the strictly chronological basis of content selection advocated by previous reports.

The most thorough and extended study of the teaching of social studies in the secondary school was undertaken in 1929 by the American Historical Association's Commission on the Social Studies. This group undertook surveys and research projects which resulted in no less than seventeen volumes published between 1932 and 1942. They made no recommendations for specific content at specific grade levels, but rather devoted considerably more energy to the careful formulation of objectives and the rationale for various types of content.

While the 1896 report assumed that history was "good for people" and proceeded to give reasons to support its belief; and while the 1916 report of the National Education Association turned an about-face by assuming that the good citizen is the objective of social studies instruction and then fumbled for appropriate content with which to build the good citizen; the Commission seemed to ask more basic questions: what is a good citizen? what is a good society?

The Commission's discussion proceeds logically from certain basic values to the learning outcomes that should be achieved to the particular content that should promote this learning.

Basic values are defined on two levels: societal and individual. With respect to individual values, the Commission states that the ". . . fundamental purpose of instruction in the social studies is 'the creation of rich, many-sided personalities, equipped with practical knowledge and inspired by ideals so that they can make their way and fulfill their mission in a changing society which is part of a world complex.' "

This individual ideal is to be accomplished within a general frame of reference which is ". . . a more or less idealized picture of individual life and society deemed desirable within the limits of necessity." The function of the frame of reference is further described as a "cultural guide to action, not fixed as the law of gravitation, but still a guide. It is both abstract and concrete. In its high unity it is a summation of relations built upon concrete situations and relations. Its base is the concrete situations and relations of life—personal, community, national, and world."

The Commission, then, set forth two principles: the basic objective of social education in individual terms (the rich and many-sided personality), and the frame of reference in which such a personality is to be developed (a conception of society both desired and possible). The frame of reference is then translated into the specific social science knowledge required to achieve the desirable and possible society. . . .

The Commission's important contribution to the problem of defining objectives and content in the social studies was a recognition of the necessary ethical basis of social studies education. It presented the thesis that the validity of knowledge is relative to the scope of reality under consideration, and that when the scope is large, values of the observer will inevitably enter into the selection of those aspects of reality which are included in the historical narrative. Likewise when one is selecting those aspects of social reality which are to be presented in a formal educational setting, the values of the selector are a crucial consideration. The Commission's report further emphasized that when one selects and organizes data to be taught in the classroom, submerged or unconscious criteria will operate anyway. . . .

Obviously, the educator cannot teach all content—as Beard himself [the Chairman of the AHA's Commission on the Social Studies] admits, not because it is not desirable, but because it is not practicable. Thus the Commission's approach to defining criteria for the selection of content, while realistic in its frank acknowledgment of the limitations of empiricism, is aborted by its failure to give adequate weight to practical limitations of the formal educational setting.

In the twenty year period between the work of the Commission on the Social Studies of the American Historical Association and the Preliminary Report on Concepts and Values of the National Council for the Social Studies, American society recovered from its worst depression in the process of waging its largest war, and entered upon a period of persisting international tensions. In such a series of national crises one would suspect that educators might revise their ideas of optimistic progressivism so eloquently proposed by Beard. The report of the National Council, however, reflects a faith in social progress that far outdoes Beard, but without Beard's qualifying phrase referring to a vision of society that is both desirable and *possible*.

The 1956 Report of the National Council for the Social Studies defines twelve themes which it phrases as goals or values, each of which is supposed to imply concepts and content. The title of the report itself is "A Guide to Content in the Social Studies." It was an effort to define very general areas of concern rather than specific guides to social studies content. In summary, the Themes are:

Theme   1. Reciprocal adjustment of man and nature.

Theme   2. The adaptation of individual and group ideas to an interdependent world.

Theme   3. Recognition of the dignity and worth of the individual.

Theme   4. The use of intelligence to improve human living . . . and . . . maintenance of the free marketplace for ideas and values.

Theme   5. The intelligent acceptance of individual responsibility for personal and general welfare.

Theme   6. Increasing the effectiveness of the family as a basic social institution.

Theme   7. The intelligent and responsible sharing of power in order to attain justice.

Theme   8. The wise allocation of scarce resources in order to bring about the widest material security.

Theme   9. Achievement of adequate horizons of loyalty . . . a sane and reasoned patriotism and a global humanitarianism.

Theme 10. Cooperation in the interest of peace and welfare . . . an increase in conference and conciliation, mediation and arbitration, seeking a consensus.

Theme 11. Achieving a balance between social stability and social change.

Theme 12. Widening and deepening the ability to live more richly.

Perhaps the most interesting feature of these Themes is not that they achieved any new or striking intellectual breakthrough, but rather that there appears to be a retrogression to the days—*ante* Beard—when committees set up to determine educational objectives ignored or skimmed over important logical and ethical considerations, such as a statement of the relationship be-tween values and empirical knowledge in the teaching process. In this respect the Themes seem to represent a fair sample of the level of thinking currently going on in the social studies, and thus deserve a more careful analysis.

One of the major difficulties with the Themes is that they indiscriminately mix moral dicta with social science directives. The moral implications of knowledge are in the mind of the knower. If the Themes are interpreted as values or moral directives, they leave little choice but to seek social science data that might bear out the "fact" that the values actually do imply "correct" conduct, e.g., if war is "bad," we demonstrate historically that war has never paid off. . . .

A confusion of several conceptual levels of analysis arises from the failure to distinguish clearly among several possible definitions of knowledge. At one level there are statements about the basic moral values of society. At a second level is knowledge as the scholar sees it, which can be analyzed into several dimensions: methods of stating and testing hypotheses, predictable social phenomena, general bodies of theory, and conceptual tools for analyzing and understanding new data. At a third level are general run-of-the-mill beliefs—sometimes referred to as "common sense"—by which most of us guide our daily lives.

Obviously it is necessary to arrive at a definitive understanding of the validation processes of the social sciences before we can develop a clear con-ception of what the term "knowledge" means in the context of the Themes. Clarifying the distinction between the social science disciplines—their methods, concepts, and findings—and ethical statements relating to their function and purpose is a necessary initial step that must be taken before one can develop meaningful criteria for the selection of content. . . .

The Themes appear to assert strongly the opinion that man has the ability to identify an ultimate truth, one that would eliminate conflict as a necessary ingredient of social living. The goals of man and nature are described by the Themes in such terms as "reciprocal adjustment," "adaptation," "liberty com-patible with the rights of others," "superstition . . . not yet . . . routed," "a sturdy self-reliance coupled with an altruistic individualism," "a sane and reasoned patriotism, and a global humanitarianism," "greatest good for the greatest number," "balance between social stability and social change." All indicate, either explicitly or implicitly, a battle between conflicting forces to which some kind of verbal solution is given: either ultimate conquest of one force by another (the evil one losing, of course), or adjustment between two extremes. The philosophical question for each of these two types of solu-tion automatically follows: (a) when one force must conquer another, how is man to know the devil from the god? and (b) when there is to be some ad-justment between extremes, how are we to define moderation from extreme? The Themes implicitly assume that man can adequately distinguish moderation from extremism, and that he can distinguish between the devil and the god, hence, the potential solvability of all problems.

That man may be too puny a creature ever to assess the nature of the divine scheme—if there is one—or that he should ever be aware of his puniness and feel a deep humility before the awesome forces that surround and control him: these ideas are also a part of our cultural heritage, and perhaps should be considered when confronting the problem of selecting appropriate content in the social studies. Although the Themes make one feel that the requirements of man's happiness are a solvable riddle and present touching evidence of a tradition of American exuberance and optimism, we cannot reasonably ignore the contrary possibility: that man is by nature fated to deal eternally with certain conflicts within himself and others. The notion of original sin, for instance, is contrary to the idea that there is an ultimate fulfillment for man on earth: man's life on earth necessarily involves trial and suffering. To reject such alternative interpretations of man and society by omission rather than making a direct case would appear to reflect an unfortunate blind spot in the thinking of modern social studies educators. . . .

A Tentative Approach to the Selection of Content in the Social Studies

Criticisms of the reports of the American Historical Association's Commission for the Social Studies and the National Council for the Social Studies' Committee on Concepts and Values may be summarized as follows: (1) there is a failure to consider adequately the question of the school's right to mold personal values of the student; (2) there is considerable confusion in the use of the term knowledge and in the relationship between knowledge and values; (3) there is a failure to take into account one of the major facts of American society—namely, the ferment and conflict over competing ideas and values most of which can be allowed because of a more basic creed of mutual tolerance; and (4) there is a failure to consider the difficulty of adequately describing American society, and the increasing problem which such a description will present to scholars because of the society's dynamic qualities.

We shall attempt to offer here an approach to the selection of content that will face some of these criticisms in an explicit manner. It should be stated that the criteria we are seeking for the selection and justification of content are not within the context of teaching the disciplines for the sake of recruiting and training scholars or knowledge for the sake of knowledge, but rather to justify knowledge and an approach to knowledge that will increase the student's ability to deal effectively with broad social issues which confront all citizens of our society. . . .

An Interpretation of the Purpose of Social Science Instruction

The goals outlined below, which determine the criteria for the selection of social studies content, are closely related to the basic values, assumptions, and hypotheses we have presented. For this reason we would like to summarize the major points already made.

We have stated that one of the pillars upon which our type of society rests is the right of individuals to make personal choices regarding appropriate conduct in seeking fulfillment. When this kind of freedom exists, we assume that there tends to be disagreement and conflict within society because different individuals (who are associated with different groups) see fulfillment and the conduct leading to this fulfillment in different terms. That is, while the existence of many groups tends to promote the right of individual choice, some groups will continuously resist mutual toleration of a variety of subcultures. Society's cyclical tendency to gravitate toward conformity of values of major groups, and then to react away from such conformity we have labeled "multi-value equilibrium." We have noted that the various groups might see the multi-value society as both good and bad—good in that it guarantees protection for each group when it happens to deviate from the standards set by a more powerful group; bad in that it will not allow any single group to bludgeon the rest of the society into conformity to a single-value system.

We then tried to relate the notion of group ambivalence toward the multi-value society to the idea of a dual socialization process. The family or clan is the conditioning agent for the individual's deepest personal values, which usually include an intolerance for members of outgroups. This intolerance is then counteracted by a second socialization process which attempts to provide wider societal cohesion through the promotion of mutual toleration of all groups within society.

From this general theoretical base we now propose to set forth a justification of content for social studies education. We want to emphasize our assumption that, before any instructional procedure can be used to carry out proposed objectives, the basic processes of socialization (the unconscious internalization of social values) have already taken place. The student already has a descriptive knowledge of his culture and has internalized the specific beliefs of his family or clan as well as some of the more general beliefs and values of the total society, e.g., liberty, equality, love of country.

When the student has reached this stage of development, we propose that the relationship between personal values, the general canons of tolerance of our society, and the determination of public policy for the regulation of human affairs be made the center of the social studies curriculum in the public school. The basic core of content would consist of the study of existing and predicted conflicts caused by differing definitions and interpretations of the meaning of liberty, security, and public welfare.

Translating this into concrete educational goals, it means consciously and explicitly teaching the student to deal with the problem of defining liberty within the context of the total society. We feel that one of the essential requirements of this task is that the individual student be liberated from his own narrow value system to the point where he can see the relationship between his personal value judgments and those of other groups within society; to the point where he can see and feel sources of conflict within himself, and between himself and others; and to the point where he can handle these conflicts by predicting courses of action which will maximize the possibility of individual or group fulfillment as individuals and groups may define this fulfillment. Such prediction involves an understanding of one's own feelings and values and the feelings and values of other individuals and groups, as well as a descriptive knowledge of the general beliefs and artifacts of the society.

The object of teaching the skills that will allow the student to make reasonable predictions about methods of social control within a free society may be broken down into a number of very specific goals. It is important that one read these specific objectives in the context of the model of society and the description of the values and assumptions set forth above.

AN OUTLINE OF SPECIFIC OBJECTIVES OF SOCIAL SCIENCE INSTRUCTION IN GENERAL EDUCATION

I. Students should be taught to recognize and define areas of human conflict.

The basic values of the student should be related to larger political and social issues to the point where the words and symbols which describe these issues become charged or affectively loaded for the student in the same way as the words which describe his own values. That is, the student should learn a vocabulary that is charged—either positively or negatively—for the whole society. There should be established a common language through which the individual can describe and feel general societal conflicts. We think the individual should understand to some extent (both intellectually and emotionally) the value positions of other groups which may oppose or support his own personal beliefs.

II. With reference to specific political and social issues, students should be taught to define alternative methods of regulating human affairs that are possible from the point of view of major value positions in society.

Once the student sees an area of social conflict and can feel the value positions of various groups having an interest in this issue, his problem is to offer alternative modes of regulation which are *possible* in the light of the value positions of the groups involved. That is, the student should be taught to state alternatives which encompass both his own value orientation and those of opposing groups.

III. With reference to specific social and political issues, students should be taught to make thoughtful predictions about the consequences of various alternative methods of regulating human affairs.

After the individual has considered possible alternative approaches to the regulation of human affairs, he should be taught to make considered predictions regarding the possible consequences of the various alternatives deemed possible, and to try to assess the degree of probability with which one might predict that these consequences will, in fact, occur. Predicting consequences of social action involves the procedures and methodology of the social sciences. This is the justification of "knowledge" or evidence: it sheds light upon the probability that a given consequence will occur as a result of a social action. Any approach to the regulation of human affairs designed to meet the demands of a specific issue can conceivably have both positive and negative consequences. These possible consequences are, in fact, hypotheses, and can be tested to some extent by such available social science procedures. . . .

The objective of social science education, according to this approach, is to introduce young people into the fire and controversy that rages within a free society over ways of regulating human affairs—ways that might presumably maximize the freedom of the individual to pursue his own fulfillment as each person defines that fulfillment. In such an introduction we would hope to provide the student with a way of approaching conflicts and controversies that is more "rational" than blind adherence to some ideology which happens to be consistent with those values learned during early socialization. "Rational" does not imply a denial of the importance of personal values (or emotionality) as forces to be considered in social decisions, but rather emphasizes the ability to see social problems explicitly as conflicting affective reactions by various groups and individuals.

This approach would mean a dramatic shift in the type of content now taught in the secondary school. Since the curriculum builder would begin by inquiring into the major areas of conflict—both those we perceive in current affairs and those which will probably occur in the future—there would be a strong emphasis upon the sociological, political, and economic disciplines as well as competent journalism; and there would be less reliance upon traditional historical literature. If the issue of a deflated farm income were used as a major conflict in public policy, and the problem was to predict the consequences of alternative modes of regulation, it is apparent that the disciplinary boundaries would necessarily break down. Similar problems have occurred in the course of history and various approaches have been taken: this would provide pertinent data. Other necessary information such as the existing attitudes and feelings of actual groups in conflict today and the voting patterns of Congressmen and agencies representing various pressure groups could be derived from current sources. In addition, some understanding of general principles of economics regarding the relationship between supply, demand, and prices as well as the way these factors are deliberately manipulated by organized groups would be important.

In considering such a problem, the basic criteria for the selection of content would be (a) whether the information would enable the student to conceptualize possible alternative modes of regulating human affairs with respect to this particular conflict; (b) whether the information would give some indication of the consequences of each alternative considered; and (c) whether it would permit us to say something about the probability that these consequences would, in fact, occur.

To use this approach would mean leaving out large areas of American history. But, as we have suggested, the traditional body of historical literature would continue to be presented to children in the early school years. This is part of what we have called the societal socialization process. By the time the student encountered our curriculum, he would have a descriptive knowledge of his own culture as well as some knowledge of other cultures. (Children living in the city of Boston would have some understanding of living conditions in rural Arkansas.) However, we would not call either the combined fact-myth-legend representation of history taught in most public schools or a purely descriptive account of immediate and distant cultural settings "social studies." Our justification for calling this approach "social studies" or "social science education" rests with our concern for predicting the consequences of alternative modes of social action. We feel that there is a crucial distinction between education as an unconscious internalization of the values and beliefs of the culture and an explicitly critical attempt to stand aside from these immediate values and beliefs and make objective predictions about how to control major conflicts in the regulation of human affairs. The substantive values with which the student would be indoctrinated in this approach would relate only to the idea of basic tolerance and to the social inventions and mechanisms that protect this tolerance.

Our approach is a combination of ethics and social science, with ethical considerations paramount because of the conscious attempt to teach students the analytical tools by which they may continuously redefine legitimate areas of personal liberty. We believe that it is the particular way we treat the relationship between ethics and empirical knowledge, between emotional and intellectual perceptions of social issues, that distinguishes this approach most clearly from the approaches to social science education discussed earlier in the paper, and from the traditional university conception of the teaching of social sciences as semi-related but independent disciplines.

A Consideration of Some Difficulties in the Social Conflict Approach to the Selection of Content

One of the greatest difficulties in any "problems approach" to the selection of content consists of the definition of "problem." If one is concerned with the teaching of conflict situations, how does he decide which of the multitude of conflicts among individuals and groups are most important to the survival of a multi-value society?

In answering this question, an initial step might be to describe various types or sources of conflict. For example, a distinction can be made between conflicts arising from disagreements over prediction and conflicts arising from disagreements over values themselves. The former can arise if there is a difference of opinion regarding the consequences predicted from one or more courses of action, e.g., a disagreement over whether the establishment of public housing for low-income families will increase or decrease their dependence upon welfare agencies. The latter can arise if all antagonists agree that certain consequences will result from public action, but disagree over whether the consequences are good or bad, e.g., all factions may agree that integration in the public schools will lead to less racial self-consciousness, but will not agree on whether this is good or bad.

This example of an analysis of social conflict simply indicates that it may be possible to describe, enumerate, and categorize major conflicts over public policy. However, our ability to distinguish among different types of conflict should not mislead us into thinking that there is no real problem in defining which specific conflict situations should be placed in the curriculum. Despite the obvious difficulties of selecting conflict situations, the problem seems manageable. It might well be possible for journalists, social scientists from a number of disciplines, and men of practical affairs to define the most crucial areas of conflict that can be anticipated, as well as those which are immediately upon us. It might also be possible for these same men to discuss which alternative courses of action seem possible as ways of dealing with the conflicts, as well as probable consequences of the various alternative approaches. The information which bears upon the pressing problems of the day—as decided upon by such a group of scholars and men of practical affairs—would then become the content selected for students in the classroom. While the conflict selected might be changing constantly as a result both of the identification of emerging problems and of the increased social science knowledge, we anticipate that the core of conflict situations would remain fairly stable.

A second difficulty that must be faced by the conflict-problems approach to the selection of content concerns the question of how much the student must "know"—how much descriptive political and social experience he must have had before he can deal intelligently with major societal conflicts. No one would question the assumption that a student should know something about his culture before he arrives at our proposed curriculum. As to a definition of just what he should know, we have two very tentative suggestions, one of which has been indicated already. (1) In order to have a sense of cultural identity, the student should be familiar with the combination of fact-myth-legend he is now exposed to in history texts and social studies literature. (2) The student should have some realistic descriptive knowledge of the existing culture, including both the general and technical social science vocabulary required to talk about it. Since the current culture can be observed directly, perhaps the most effective way of teaching these constructs would be through demonstrations in the field. Most of the important terms and constructs used by the social scientists have observable referents. For instance, it is quite obvious that one can see concrete manifestations of such terms as "mass production," "slums," "mechanization of farms," "labor unions," and "social class." The problem of selecting content becomes acute only when one wishes to give order and interpretation to these terms.

The position we are taking here is that it is not necessary or useful to put such terms and constructs into an ordered interpretative narrative until the student is sufficiently mature to study the regulation of human affairs in the context of social conflict.

An issue that is closely related to the question of how much one must "know" before he studies current controversy is the relationship of history—as a discipline—to other sources of social knowledge. We realize that many educators are of the opinion that "no conscious advance, no worthy reform, can be secured without both a knowledge of the present and an appreciation of how forces have worked in the social and political organization of former times . . .—that historical-mindedness should be in some slight measure bred within [boys and girls], and that they should be given the habit, or the beginnings of a habit, of considering what has been, when they discuss what is or what should be." The general thesis is that without the tempering influence of history to give a broader perspective to the present, there is danger of great distortion in a picture of current social reality. So far as we know, there is little systematic evidence to back up this thesis. The notion that history tends to give one a broad and total perspective of current society presents only one side of the issue. History can also give one a narrow and biased view of current affairs. It all depends upon who has written the "history." History is not totality, but rather one artist's conception of what a limited selection of past events indicate might have happened. And the historian, by refusing to abandon the narrative form of summarization and generalization, is so restricted in the number of events he can present that it is doubtful whether a valid picture can be painted within these limitations.

We would certainly not deny that the process of writing history—of carefully weighing the importance of past events and sifting and selecting such events for a narrative—may have desirable effects upon the writer. But we do not teach students to write history, we teach them historical writings. If we were to teach students to write history, it would be impossible to teach them more than a small slice of chronology. We believe that there is a contradiction between teaching a wide scope of chronology through existing historical literature and teaching a discipline of mind that may come through one's attempt to validate and synthesize records of the past. If the scholarly canons are taught, this must be done within a narrow range of chronology. Given the practical limitations of time within the formal educational setting, it may be impossible to do both. But is it defensible to teach the surface area of large volumes of the past without at some point providing the student with the intensive validation techniques of the historian? So far as our approach is concerned, we conceive of historical knowledge as one source of evidence out of many to be brought to bear upon immediate and pressing social conflicts.

A third difficulty of the conflict-problems approach discussed here is its essential negativism. There is the potential danger that such an approach might place too much emphasis upon the negative aspects of social organization and would not deal adequately with the positive traditions and institutions that also characterize our society. In considering this difficulty we would emphasize that included in the conflict-problems approach is the teaching of the institutional safeguards to personal liberty that have been developed within the tradition of Western Civilization. Perhaps the teaching of such safeguards to personal liberty would take on dramatic meaning as the student came to see the severe problems of controlling and mediating conflicts within a free society. This is not to deny that our approach does explicitly set out to describe in depth the disintegrative forces in the culture. It does this, however, in the hope of directing such forces so as to prevent major disruption to the institutions which protect a heritage of liberalism.

There is, of course, a more fundamental criticism of our approach which strikes at the heart of our assumption that tension and conflict are inevitable. What right have we to establish an educational program which assumes from the beginning that a culture governed by love for others and sacrifice of self cannot be achieved through the conscious efforts of seers and educators? Our reply to such a question is that one cannot teach men to love without telling them what is worth loving—and except for the teaching of love for liberty and tolerance this is not possible in a system of public education established by a multi-value society. We cannot deny the possibility that the Christian vision or a similar model of society may eventually materialize on earth. The question is whether it is the responsibility of social education to teach such a vision. We think not. We feel, rather, that it is the responsibility of social education to teach a tradition established by the toughminded jurists of Rome and England; a tradition that involves a set of concrete institutions which protect our free way of life—which give man the right to be a Christian, an agnostic, or an atheist. We further assert that while the Christian vision embodies some of the noblest aspirations of mankind—as do many ideologies—it makes assumptions about the nature of man and the road to his fulfillment which are too narrow to be enforced in a free society. The teaching of harmony and love as totalitarian goods contradicts other possible, and very legitimate, interpretations of man's road to fulfillment.

Conclusion

Our approach to the selection of content may be stated simply as one in which the central core of the curriculum would be the study of those human affairs fraught with conflict or tension which might threaten the integrity of a free society. We have pointed out that this does not preclude the teaching of the fact-myth-legend content usually referred to as "history" or "citizenship education" in the public schools. The type of social studies program proposed here is a tough-minded scientific approach which presents immediate and future conflict situations in the hope of inducing the student to utilize social processes and to make social predictions and decisions that will keep such conflicts within reasonable limits. This approach to social studies objectives, we feel, clearly recommends some specific content areas and indicates an explicit relationship between the basic values and assumptions with which we begin and the specific objectives and content with which we end. At this point we can see the necessity of careful research into whether learning outcomes defended here can be effected through a series of definable learning treatments. This research is now being carried forward by a number of investigators, including a group at Harvard.

Our severest critics—and this, of course, is only speculation—will consist mainly of two groups: those who wish to maintain historical literature as the bulwark of the social studies curriculum of the high school; and those who wish to teach, overtly or covertly, an ideology of love and harmony as solutions to the inevitable tensions and stresses within society. Our answer to these hypothetical critics will be a simple challenge: let them say what content should be taught; let them justify it by means of a philosophical scheme that is consistent with the values and assumptions of a liberal democratic society. Most important, let them demonstrate that the content and the procedures by which it is presented do, in fact, lead to the changes in social behavior they believe are desirable. It is our conviction that American society is too pressed by existing and impending tensions to continue to rely upon pious hopes and emotional arguments in defense of teaching any subject matter that is so closely related to the preservation of our basic freedoms.

II

MAINLY HOW

In reality we cannot separate discussion of why we teach from talk about how to teach it. The two questions are inextricably intertwined. For example, many social studies teachers use the discussion method because they set the ability to express oneself clearly as a major objective of their course. Here the why question has dictated the answer to the how question.

Nevertheless, it seems indispensable to concentrate on ways to teach various skills and procedures in the social studies. Note-taking, writing essay tests, reading charts and graphs, and similar skills are essential to the training of good students. They deserve explicit attention in a course on methods of teaching. But while they are being discussed, students should not lose sight of the larger issue of why we teach these skills. Only by asking why consistently can each of us hope to develop a coherent philosophy of teaching.

II

MAINLY
HOW

CHAPTER 7 The Discovery Method

"Tell 'em what you're going to say; say it; then tell 'em what you said." This ancient bit of advice to the novice speaker has been taken far too seriously by many social studies teachers. Their teaching has become telling. The textbooks they use are expository, filled with facts and generalizations for students to learn and give back on examinations designed primarily to test recall. More than any other factor, this technique of teaching probably accounts for the well-known unpopularity of the social studies in the schools. One survey after another reveals that students rate their social studies classes the dullest and least useful of their academic courses.

Until the curriculum reforms of the past decade, expository teaching characterized all the disciplines in the secondary school. Then the mathematicians and scientists broke through, developing new techniques of presenting materials and new devices for engaging students in the process of finding things out for themselves. These new techniques usually pass under two names: the discovery method and inductive teaching.

Instead of thinking of two diametrically opposite ways to teach—straight exposition opposed to pure discovery—we ought to realize that teaching techniques can be placed along a continuum. At the one end lies a lecture or a question-and-answer technique designed to transmit a prescribed body of information from teacher to student. At the other end lies a nondirective, student-centered approach. A teacher might begin the school year by asking students what they want to learn and how they want to learn it and then act as a consultant as each student designs and carries out projects for himself. Dozens of variations dot the continuum between these extremes.

Without exception the social studies curriculum projects pay homage to techniques near the discovery end of the continuum. Textbooks have been supplemented with or replaced by books of readings or packages of materials. Films like the four produced by the Lincoln Filene Center at Tufts University pose problem situations in practical politics and leave the resolution of the problems for discussion by students in the classroom. Lesson plans emphasize techniques that encourage students to make generalizations from factual evidence and to check the hypotheses they form with additional evidence. These techniques and materials will work a revolution in teaching in the schools.

Not that they are new. Thousands of teachers have taught inductively for years. They have been hamstrung, however, by lack of appropriate materials and by a compulsion to "cover" whatever happens to be in their textbook. They have also been hampered because they have had few models of inductive teaching to imitate. Herein lies the challenge to teacher-training institutions and to supervisors who organize in-service workshops: How can we provide models of new teaching techniques for teachers to emulate?

The two readings in this chapter indicate the long period during which scholars have been interested in an inductive approach and suggest ways to teach by discovery. The first, from the pen of John Dewey, describes reflective thinking as the goal of instruction. The second, by Jerome Bruner, discusses a discovery approach in general terms. As you read them, think about the following questions:

1) What does Dewey mean by reflective thinking? What does Bruner mean by the discovery method? How are the two related?

2) Under what conditions does reflective thinking arise? What does your conclusion imply about the kinds of problems particularly appropriate for discovery teaching? about methods of presenting material for discovery work?

3) According to Dewey, what is the difference between suggestions and hypotheses? What conditions favor fruitful hypothesis formation? How does this issue relate to Bruner's theories about structure?

REFLECTIVE THINKING

John Dewey

The two limits of every unit of thinking are a perplexed, troubled, or confused situation at the beginning and a cleared-up, unified, resolved situation at the close. The first of these situations may be called *pre*-reflective. It sets the problem to be solved; out of it grows the question that reflection has to answer. In the final situation the doubt has been dispelled; the situation is *post*-re-

Reprinted from John Dewey, *How We Think* (Boston: D. C. Heath and Company, 1933), pp. 106–116.

flective; there results a direct experience of mastery, satisfaction, enjoyment. Here, then, are the limits within which reflection falls.

FIVE PHASES, OR ASPECTS, OF REFLECTIVE THOUGHT

In between, as states of thinking, are (1) *suggestions,* in which the mind leaps forward to a possible solution; (2) an intellectualization of the difficulty or perplexity that has been *felt* (directly experienced) into a *problem* to be solved, a question for which the answer must be sought; (3) the use of one suggestion after another as a leading idea, or *hypothesis,* to initiate and guide observation and other operations in collection of factual material; (4) the mental elaboration of the idea or supposition as an idea or supposition (*reasoning* in the sense in which reasoning is a part, not the whole, of inference); and (5) testing the hypothesis by overt or imaginative action.

We shall now take up the five phases, or functions, one by one.

THE FIRST PHASE, SUGGESTION

The most "natural" thing for anyone to do is to go ahead; that is to say, to *act* overtly. The disturbed and perplexed situation arrests such direct activity temporarily. The tendency to continue *acting* nevertheless persists. It is diverted and takes the form of an idea or a suggestion. The *idea* of what to do when we find ourselves "in a hole" is a substitute for direct action. It is a vicarious, anticipatory way of acting, a kind of dramatic rehearsal. Were there only one suggestion popping up, we should undoubtedly adopt it at once. But where there are two or more, they collide with one another, maintain the state of suspense, and produce further inquiry. The first suggestion in the instance recently cited was to jump the ditch, but the perception of conditions inhibited that suggestion and led to the occurrence of other ideas.

Some inhibition of *direct* action is necessary to the condition of hesitation and delay that is essential to thinking. Thought is, as it were, conduct turned in upon itself and examining its purpose and its conditions, its resources, aids, and difficulties and obstacles.

THE SECOND PHASE, INTELLECTUALIZATION *of level of Problem*

We have already noted that it is artificial, so far as thinking is concerned, to start with a ready-made problem, a problem made out of whole cloth or arising out of a vacuum. In reality such a "problem" is simply an assigned *task.* There is not at first a situation *and* a problem, much less just a problem and no situation. There is a troubled, perplexed, trying situation, where the difficulty is, as it were, spread throughout the entire situation, infecting it as a whole. If we knew just what the difficulty was and where it lay, the job of reflection would be much easier than it is. As the saying truly goes, a question well put is half answered. In fact, we know what the problem *exactly* is simultaneously with finding a way out and getting it resolved. Problem and solution stand out *completely* at the same time. Up to that point, our grasp of the problem has been more or less vague and tentative.

A blocked suggestion leads us to reinspect the conditions that confront us. Then our uneasiness, the shock of disturbed activity, gets stated in some degree on the basis of observed conditions, of objects. The width of the ditch, the slipperiness of the banks, not the mere presence of a ditch, is the trouble. The difficulty is getting located and defined; it is becoming a true problem, something intellectual, not just an annoyance at being held up in what we are doing. The person who is suddenly blocked and troubled in what he is doing by the thought of an engagement to keep at a time that is near and a place that is distant has the suggestion of getting there at once. But in order to carry this suggestion into effect, he has to find means of transportation. In order to find them he has to note his present position and its distance from the station, the present time, and the interval at his disposal. Thus the perplexity is more precisely located: just so much ground to cover, so much time to do it in.

The word "problem" often seems too elaborate and dignified to denote what happens in minor cases of reflection. But in every case where reflective activity ensues, there is a process of *intellectualizing* what at first is merely an *emotional* quality of the whole situation. This conversion is effected by noting more definitely the conditions that constitute the trouble and cause the stoppage of action.

The Third Phase, the Guiding Idea, Hypothesis

The first suggestion occurs spontaneously; it comes to mind automatically; it *springs* up; it "pops," as we have said, "into the mind"; it flashes upon us. There is no direct control of its occurrence; the idea just comes or it does not come; that is all that can be said. There is nothing *intellectual* about its occurrence. The intellectual element consists in *what we do with it*, how we use it, *after* its sudden occurrence as an idea. A controlled use of it is made possible by the state of affairs just described. In the degree in which we define the difficulty (which is effected by stating it in terms of objects), we get a better idea of the kind of solution that is needed. The facts or data set the problem before us, and insight into the problem corrects, modifies, expands the suggestion that originally occurred. In this fashion the suggestion becomes a definite supposition or, stated more technically, a *hypothesis*.

Take the case of a physician examining a patient or a mechanic inspecting a piece of complicated machinery that does not behave properly. There is something wrong, so much is sure. But how to remedy it cannot be told until it is known *what* is wrong. An untrained person is likely to make a wild guess—the suggestion—and then proceed to act upon it in a random way, hoping that by good luck the right thing will be hit upon. So some medicine that appears to have worked before or that a neighbor has recommended is tried. Or the person fusses, monkeys, with the machine, poking here and hammering there on the chance of making the right move. The trained person proceeds in a very different fashion. He *observes* with unusual care, using the methods, the techniques, that the experience of physicians and expert mechanics in general, those familiar with the structure of the organism or the machine, have shown to be helpful in detecting trouble.

The idea of the solution is thus controlled by the diagnosis that has been made. But if the case is at all complicated, the physician or mechanic does not foreclose further thought by assuming that the suggested method of remedy is certainly right. He proceeds to act upon it tentatively rather than decisively. That is, he treats it as a guiding idea, a working hypothesis, and is led by it to make more observations, to collect more facts, so as to see if the *new* material is what the hypothesis calls for. He reasons that *if* the disease is typhoid, *then* certain phenomena will be found; and he looks particularly to see if *just* these conditions are present. Thus both the first and second operations are brought under control; the sense of the problem becomes more adequate and refined and the suggestion ceases to be a *mere* possibility, becoming a *tested* and, if possible, a *measured* probability.

THE FOURTH PHASE, REASONING (IN THE NARROWER SENSE)

Observations pertain to what exists in nature. They constitute the facts, and these facts both regulate the formation of suggestions, ideas, hypotheses, and test their probable value as indications of solutions. The ideas, on the other hand, occur, as we say, in our heads, in our minds. They not only occur there, but are capable, as well, of great development there. Given a fertile suggestion occurring in an experienced, well-informed mind, that mind is capable of elaborating it until there results an idea that is quite different from the one with which the mind started.

For example, the idea of heat in the third instance in the earlier chapter was linked up with what the person already knew about heat—in his case, its expansive force—and this in turn with the contractive tendency of cold, so that the idea of expansion could be used as an explanatory idea, though the mere idea of heat would not have been of any avail. Heat was quite directly suggested by the observed conditions; water was felt to be hot. But only a mind with some prior information about heat would have reasoned that heat meant expansion, and then used the idea of expansion as a working hypothesis. In more complex cases, there are long trains of reasoning in which one idea leads up to another idea known by previous test to be related to it. The stretch of links brought to light by reasoning depends, of course, upon the store of knowledge that the mind is already in possession of. And this depends not only upon the prior experience and special education of the individual who is carrying on the inquiry, but also upon the state of culture and science of the age and place. Reasoning helps extend knowledge, while at the same time it depends upon what is already known and upon the facilities that exist for communicating knowledge and making it a public, open resource.

A physician today can develop, by reasoning from his knowledge, the implications of the disease that symptoms suggest to him as probable in a way that would have been impossible even a generation ago; just as, on the other hand, he can carry his observation of symptoms much farther because of improvement in clinical instruments and the technique of their use.

Reasoning has the same effect upon a suggested solution that more intimate and extensive observation has upon the original trouble. Acceptance of a suggestion in its first form is prevented by looking into it more thoroughly. Conjectures that seem plausible at first sight are often found unfit or even absurd when their full consequences are traced out. Even when reasoning out the bearings of a supposition does not lead to its rejection, it develops the idea into a form in which it is more apposite to the problem. Only when, for example, the conjecture that a pole was an index pole had been thought out in its implications could its particular applicability to the case in hand be judged. Suggestions at first seemingly remote and wild are frequently so transformed by being elaborated into what follows from them as to become apt and fruitful. The development of an idea through reasoning helps supply intervening or intermediate terms which link together into a consistent whole elements that at first seemingly conflict with each other, some leading the mind to one inference and others to an opposed one.

Mathematics as Typical Reasoning.   Mathematics affords the typical example of how far can be carried the operation of relating ideas to one another, without having to depend upon the observations of the senses. In geometry we start with a few simple conceptions, line, angle, parallel, surfaces formed by lines meeting, etc., and a few principles defining equalities. Knowing something about the equality of angles made by parallel lines when they intersect a straight line, and knowing, by definition, that a perpendicular to a straight line forms two right angles, by means of a combination of these ideas we readily determine that the sum of the interior angles of a triangle is equal to two right angles. By continuing to trace the implications of theorems already demonstrated, the whole subject of plane figures is finally elaborated. The manipulation of algebraic symbols so as to establish a series of equations and other mathematical functions affords an even more striking example of what can be accomplished by developing the relation of ideas to one another.

When the hypothesis indicated by a series of scientific observations and experiments can be stated in mathematical form, that idea can be transformed to almost any extent, until it assumes a form in which a problem can be dealt with most expeditiously and effectively. Much of the accomplishment of physical science depends upon an intervening mathematical elaboration of ideas. It is not the mere presence of measurements in quantitative form that yields scientific knowledge, but that particular kind of mathematical statement which can be developed by reasoning into other and more fruitful forms—a consideration which is fatal to the claim to scientific standing of many educational measurements merely because they have a quantitative form.

THE FIFTH PHASE, (TESTING THE HYPOTHESIS BY ACTION)

The concluding phase is some kind of testing by overt action to give *experimental corroboration,* or *verification,* of the conjectural idea. Reasoning shows that *if* the *idea* be adopted, certain consequences follow. So far the conclusion is hypothetical or conditional. If when we look we find present all the conditions demanded by the theory, and if we find the characteristic traits called for by rival alternatives to be lacking, the tendency to believe, to accept, is almost irresistible. Sometimes direct observation furnishes corroboration, as in the case of the pole on the boat. In other cases, as in that of the bubbles, experiment is required; that is, *conditions are deliberately arranged in accord with the requirements of an idea or hypothesis to see whether the results theoretically indicated by the idea actually occur.* If it is found that the experimental results agree with the theoretical, or rationally deduced, results, and if there is reason to believe that *only* the conditions in question would yield such results, the confirmation is so strong as to induce a conclusion— at least until contrary facts shall indicate the advisability of its revision.

Of course, verification does not always follow. Sometimes consequences show failure to confirm instead of corroboration. The idea in question is refuted by the court of final appeal. But a great advantage of possession of the habit of reflective activity is that failure is not *mere* failure. It is instructive. The person who really thinks learns quite as much from his failures as from his successes. For a failure indicates to the person whose thinking has been involved in it, and who has not come to it by mere blind chance, what further observations should be made. It suggests to him what modifications should be introduced in the hypothesis upon which he has been operating. It either brings to light a new problem or helps to define and clarify the problem on which he has been engaged. Nothing shows the trained thinker better than the use he makes of his errors and mistakes. What merely annoys and discourages a person not accustomed to thinking, or what starts him out on a new course of aimless attack by mere cut-and-try methods, is a stimulus and a guide to the trained inquirer.

THE SEQUENCE OF THE FIVE PHASES IS NOT FIXED

The five phases, terminals, or functions of thought, that we have noted do not follow one another in a set order. On the contrary, each step in genuine thinking does something to perfect the formation of a suggestion and promote its change into a leading idea or directive hypothesis. It does something to promote the location and definition of the problem. Each improvement in the idea leads to new observations that yield new facts or data and help the mind judge more accurately the relevancy of facts already at hand. The elaboration of the hypothesis does not wait until the problem has been defined and adequate hypothesis has been arrived at; it may come in at any intermediate time. And as we have just seen, any particular overt test need not be final: it may be introductory to new observations and new suggestions, according to what happens in consequence of it.

There is, however, an important difference between test by overt action in practical deliberations and in scientific investigations. In the former the practical commitment involved in overt action is much more serious than in the latter. An astronomer or a chemist performs overt actions, but they are for the sake of knowledge; they serve to test and develop his conceptions and theories. In practical matters, the main result desired lies outside of knowledge. One of the great values of thinking, accordingly, is that it defers the commitment to action that is irretrievable, that, once made, cannot be revoked. Even in moral and other practical matters, therefore, a thoughtful person treats his overt deeds as experimental so far as possible; that is to say, while he cannot call them back and must stand their consequences, he gives alert attention to what they teach him about his conduct as well as to the nonintellectual consequences. He makes a problem out of consequences of conduct, looking into the causes from which they probably resulted, especially the causes that lie in his own habits and desires.

In conclusion, we point out that the five phases of reflection that have been described represent only in outline the indispensable traits of reflective thinking. In practice, two of them may telescope, some of them may be passed over hurriedly, and the burden of reaching a conclusion may fall mainly on a single phase, which will then require a seemingly disproportionate development. No set rules can be laid down on such matters. The way they are managed depends upon the intellectual tact and sensitiveness of the individual. When things have come out wrong, it is, however, a wise practice to review the methods by which the unwise decision was reached, and see where the misstep was made.

THE ACT OF DISCOVERY

Jerome Bruner

Maimonides, in his *Guide for the Perplexed*, speaks of four forms of perfection that men might seek. The first and lowest form is perfection in the acquisition of worldly goods. The great philosopher dismisses this on the ground that the possessions one acquires bear no meaningful relation to the

Reprinted from Jerome Bruner, *On Knowing*. Cambridge, Mass.: The Belknap Press of Harvard University Press, Copyright © 1963 by the President and Fellows of Harvard College, pp. 81–96, with footnote omissions.

possessor: "A great king may one morning find that there is no difference between him and the lowest person." A second perfection is of the body, its conformation and skills. Its failing is that it does not reflect on what is uniquely human about man: "he could (in any case) not be as strong as a mule." Moral perfection is the third, "the highest degree of excellency in man's character." Of this perfection Maimonides says: "Imagine a person being alone, and having no connection whatever with any other person; all his good moral principles are at rest, they are not required and give man no perfection whatever. These principles are only necessary and useful when man comes in contact with others." The fourth kind of perfection is "the true perfection of man; the possession of the highest intellectual faculties. . . ." In justification of his assertion, this extraordinary Spanish-Judaic philosopher urges: "Examine the first three kinds of perfection; you will find that if you possess them, they are not your property, but the property of others. . . . But the last kind of perfection is exclusively yours; no one else owns any part of it."

Without raising the question of whether moral qualities exist without reference to others, it is a conjecture much like the last of Maimonides' that leads me to examine the act of discovery in man's intellectual life. For if man's intellectual excellence is the most his own among his perfections, it is also the case that the most personal of all that he knows is that which he has discovered for himself. How important is it, then, for us to encourage the young to learn by discovery? Does it, as Maimonides would say, create a unique relation between knowledge and its possessor? And what may such a relation do for a man—or, for our purposes, a child?

The immediate occasion for my concern with discovery is the work of the various new curriculum projects that have grown up in America during the last few years. Whether one speaks to mathematicians or physicists or historians, one encounters repeatedly an expression of faith in the powerful effects that come from permitting the student to put things together for himself, to be his own discoverer.

First, I should be clear about what the act of discovery entails. It is rarely, on the frontier of knowledge or elsewhere, that new facts are "discovered" in the sense of being encountered, as Newton suggested, in the form of islands of truth in an uncharted sea of ignorance. Or if they appear to be discovered in this way, it is almost always thanks to some happy hypothesis about where to navigate. Discovery, like surprise, favors the well-prepared mind. In playing bridge, one is surprised by a hand with no honors in it and also by one that is all in one suit. Yet all particular hands in bridge are equiprobable: to be surprised one must know something about the laws of probability. So too in discovery. The history of science is studded with examples of men "finding out" something and not knowing it. I shall operate on the assumption that discovery, whether by a schoolboy going it on his own or by a scientist cultivating the growing edge of his field, is in its essence a matter of rearranging or transforming evidence in such a way that one is enabled to go beyond the

Stimulation of methods to encourage student to investigate further for himself.

evidence so reassembled to new insights. It may well be that an additional fact or shred of evidence makes this larger transformation possible. But it is often not even dependent on new information.

Very generally, and at the risk of oversimplification, it is useful to distinguish two kinds of teaching: that which takes place in the *expository mode* and that in the *hypothetical mode*. In the former, the decisions concerning the mode and pace and style of exposition are principally determined by the teacher as expositor; the student is the listener. The speaker has a quite different set of decisions to make: he has a wide choice of alternatives; he is anticipating paragraph content while the listener is still intent on the words; he is manipulating the content of the material by various transformations while the listener is quite unaware of these internal options. But in the hypothetical mode the teacher and the student are in a more cooperative position with respect to what in linguistics would be called "speaker's decisions." The student is not a bench-bound listener, but is taking a part in the formulation and at times may play the principal role in it. He will be aware of alternatives and may even have an "as if" attitude toward these, and he may evaluate information as it comes. One cannot describe the process in either mode with great precision of detail, but I think it is largely the hypothetical mode which characterizes the teaching that encourages discovery.

Consider now what benefits might be derived from the experience of learning through discoveries that one makes oneself. I shall discuss these under four headings: (1) the increase in intellectual potency, (2) the shift from extrinsic to intrinsic rewards, (3) the learning of the heuristics of discovering, and (4) the aid to conserving memory.

Intellectual Potency.   I should like to consider the differences among students in a highly constrained psychological experiment involving a two-choice machine. In order to win chips, they must depress a key either on the right or the left side of the apparatus. A pattern of payoff is designed so that, say, they will be paid off on the right side 70 percent of the time, on the left 30 percent, but this detail is not important. What is important is that the payoff sequence is arranged at random, that there is no pattern. There is a marked contrast in the behavior of subjects who think that there is some pattern to be found in the sequence—who think that regularities are discoverable—and the performance of subjects who think that things are happening quite by chance. The first group adopts what is called an "event-matching" strategy in which the number of responses given to each side is roughly commensurate to the proportion of times that it pays off: in the present case, 70 on the right to 30 on the left. The group that believes there is no pattern very soon settles for a much more primitive strategy allocating *all* responses to the side that has the greater payoff. A little arithmetic will show that the lazy all-and-none strategy pays off more if the environment is truly random: they win 70 percent of the time. The event-matching subjects win about 70 percent on the 70-percent payoff side (or 49 percent of the time there) and 30 percent of the time on the side that pays off 30 percent of the time (another 9 percent for a total take-home wage of 58 percent in return for their labors of decision).

But the world is not always or not even frequently random, and if one analyzes carefully what the event matchers are doing, one sees that they are trying out hypotheses one after the other, all of them containing a term that leads to a distribution of bets on the two sides with a frequency to match the actual occurrence of events. If it should turn out that there is a pattern to be discovered, their payoff could become 100 percent. The other group would go on at the middling rate of 70 percent.

What has this to do with the subject at hand? For the person to search out and find regularities and relationships in his environment, he must either come armed with an expectancy that there will be something to find or be aroused to such an expectancy so that he may devise ways of searching and finding. One of the chief enemies of search is the assumption that there is nothing one can find in the environment by way of regularity or relationship. In the experiment just cited, subjects often fall into one of two habitual attitudes: either that there is nothing to be found or that a pattern can be discovered by looking. There is an important sequel in behavior to the two attitudes.

We have conducted a series of experimental studies on a group of some seventy schoolchildren over a four-year period. The studies have led us to distinguish an interesting dimension of cognitive activity that can be described as ranging from *episodic empiricism* at one end to *cumulative constructionism* at the other. The two attitudes in the above experiments on choice illustrate the extremes of the dimension. One of the experiments employs the game of Twenty Questions. A child—in this case he is between ten and twelve—is told that a car has gone off the road and hit a tree. He is to ask questions that can be answered by "yes" or "no" to discover the cause of the accident. After completing the problem, the same task is given him, though this time he is told that the accident has a different cause. In all, the procedure is repeated four times. Children enjoy playing the game. They also differ quite markedly in the approach or strategy they bring to the task. In the first place, we can distinguish clearly between two types of questions asked: one is intended to locate constraints in the problem, constraints that will eventually give shape to an hypothesis; the other is the hypothesis as question. It is the difference between, "Was there anything wrong with the driver?" and "Was the driver rushing to the doctor's office for an appointment and the car got out of control?" There are children who precede hypotheses with efforts to locate constraint and there are those who are "potshotters," who string out hypotheses noncumulatively one after the other. A second element of strategy lies in the connectivity of information gathering: the extent to which questions asked utilize or ignore or violate information previously obtained. The questions asked by children tend to be organized in cycles, each cycle usually given over to the pursuit of some particular notion. Both within cycles and between cycles one can discern marked differences in the connectivity of the children's performances. Needless to say, children who employ constraint location as a technique preliminary to the formulation of hypotheses tend to be far more organized in their harvesting of information. Persistence is another feature of strategy, a characteristic compounded of what appear to be two factors: sheer doggedness and a persistence that stems from the sequential organization that a child brings to the task. Doggedness is probably just animal spirits or the need to achieve. Organized persistence is a maneuver for protecting the fragile cognitive apparatus from overload. The child who has flooded himself with disorganized information from unconnected hypotheses will become discouraged and confused sooner than the child who has shown a certain cunning in his strategy of getting information—a child who senses that the value of information is not simply in getting it but in being able to carry it. The persistence of the organized child stems from his knowledge of how to organize questions in cycles and how to summarize things to himself.

Episodic empiricism is illustrated by information gathering that is unbound by prior constraints, that is deficient in organizational persistence. The opposite extreme, what we have called cumulative constructionism, is characterized by sensitivity to constraint, by connective maneuvers, and by organized persistence. Brute persistence seems to be one of those gifts from the gods that make people more exaggeratedly what they are.

Before returning to the issue of discovery and its role in the development of thinking, there is a word more to say about the ways in which the problem solver may transform information he has dealt with actively. The point arises from the pragmatic question: what does it take to get information processed into a form best designed to fit some future use? An experiment by R. B. Zajonc in 1957 suggests an answer. He gave groups of students information of a controlled kind, some groups being told that they were to transmit the information later on, others that they were merely to keep it in mind. In general, he found more differentiation of the information intended for transmittal than of information received passively. An active attitude leads to a transformation related to a task to be performed. There is a risk, to be sure, in the possible overspecialization of information processing. It can lead to such a high degree of specific organization that information is lost for general use, although this can be guarded against.

Let me convert the foregoing into an hypothesis. Emphasis on discovery in learning has precisely the effect on the learner of leading him to be a constructionist, to organize what he is encountering in a manner not only designed to discover regularity and relatedness, but also to avoid the kind of information drift that fails to keep account of the uses to which information might have to be put. Emphasis on discovery, indeed, helps the child to learn the varieties of problem solving, of transforming information for better use, helps him to learn how to go about the very task of learning. So goes the hypothesis;

it is still in need of testing. But it is an hypothesis of such important human implications that we cannot afford not to test it—and the testing will have to be in the schools.

Intrinsic and Extrinsic Motives.   Much of the problem in leading a child to effective cognitive activity is to free him from the immediate control of environmental rewards and punishments. Learning that starts in response to the rewards of parental or teacher approval or to the avoidance of failure can too readily develop a pattern in which the child is seeking cues as to how to conform to what is expected of him. We know from studies of children who tend to be early overachievers in school that they are likely to be seekers after the "right way to do it" and that their capacity for transforming learning into viable thought structures tends to be lower than that of children achieving at levels predicted by intelligence tests. Our tests on such children show them to be lower in analytic ability than those who are not conspicuous in overachievement. As we shall see later, they develop rote abilities and depend on being able to "give back" what is expected rather than to make it into something that relates to the rest of their cognitive life. As Maimonides would say, their learning is not their own.

The hypothesis I would propose here is that to the degree that one is able to approach learning as a task of discovering something rather than "learning about" it, to that degree there will be a tendency for the child to work with the autonomy of self-reward or, more properly, be rewarded by discovery itself.

To readers familiar with the battles of the last half-century in the field of motivation, this hypothesis will be recognized as controversial. For the traditional view of motivation in learning has been, until very recently, couched in terms of a theory of drives and reinforcements: learning occurs because a response produced by a stimulus is followed by the reduction in a primary drive. The doctrine is greatly but thinly extended by the idea of secondary reinforcement: anything that has been "associated" with such a reduction in drive or need can also serve to reinforce the connection between a stimulus and the response that it evokes. Finding a steak will do for getting a food-search act connected with a certain stimulus, but so will the sight of a nice restaurant.   *pleasure leads to seeking stimulus again*

In 1959 there appeared a most searching and important criticism of this ancient hedonistic position, written by Robert White, reviewing the evidence of recently published animal studies, of work in the field of psychoanalysis, and of research on the development of cognitive processes in children. Professor White comes to the conclusion, quite rightly I think, that the drive-reduction model of learning runs counter to too many important phenomena of learning and development to be either regarded as general in its applicability or even correct in its general approach. Let me quote some of his principal conclusions and explore their applicability to the hypothesis stated above.

I now propose that we gather the various kinds of behavior just mentioned, all of which have to do with effective interaction with the environment, under the general heading of competence. According to Webster, competence means fitness of ability, and the suggested synonyms include capability, capacity, efficiency, proficiency, and skill. It is therefore a suitable word to describe such things as grasping and exploring, crawling and walking, attention and perception, language and thinking, manipulating and changing the surroundings, all of which promote an effective—a competent —interaction with the environment. It is true, of course, that maturation plays a part in all these developments, but this part is heavily overshadowed by learning in all the more complex accomplishments like speech or skilled manipulation. I shall argue that it is necessary to make competence a motivational concept; there is *competence motivation* as well as competence in its more familiar sense of achieved capacity. The behavior that leads to the building up of effective grasping, handling, and letting go of objects, to take one example, is not random behavior that is produced by an overflow of energy. It is directed, selective, and persistent, and it continues not because it serves primary drives, which indeed it cannot serve until it is almost perfected, but because it satisfies an intrinsic need to deal with the environment.[1]

I am suggesting that there are forms of activity that serve to enlist and develop the competence motive, that serve to make it the driving force behind behavior. I should like to add to White's general premise that the *exercise* of competence motives has the effect of strengthening the degree to which they gain control over behavior and thereby reduce the effects of extrinsic rewards or drive gratification.

In 1934 the brilliant Russian psychologist Vygotsky characterized the growth of thought processes as starting with a dialogue of speech and gesture between child and parent. Autonomous thinking, he said, begins at the stage when the child is first able to internalize these conversations and "run them off" himself. This is a typical sequence in the development of competence. So too in instruction. The narrative of teaching is of the order of Vygotsky's conversation. The next move in the development of competence is the internalization of the narrative and its "rules of generation" so that the child is now capable of running off the narrative on his own. The hypothetical mode in teaching, by encouraging the child to participate in "speaker's decisions," speeds this process along. Once internalization has occurred, the child is in a vastly improved position from several obvious points of view—notably that he is able to go beyond the information he has been given to generate additional ideas that either can be checked immediately from experience or can, at least, be used as a basis for formulating reasonable hypotheses. But over and beyond that, the child is now in a position to experience success and failure not as reward and punishment but as information. For when the task is his own rather than a prescribed matching of environmental demands, he becomes his

[1] R. W. White, "Motivation Reconsidered: The Concept of Competence," *Psychological Review*, no. 66 (1959), pp. 317–318.

own paymaster in a certain measure. Seeking to gain control over his environment, he can now treat success as indicating that he is on the right track, failure as indicating that he is on the wrong one.

In the end, this development has the effect of freeing learning from immediate stimulus control. When learning leads only to pellets of this or that in the short run rather than to mastery in the long run, then behavior can be readily "shaped" by extrinsic rewards. But when behavior becomes more extended and competence-oriented, it comes under the control of more complex cognitive structures and operates more from the inside out.

The position of Pavlov is interesting. His early account of the learning process was based entirely on a notion of stimulus control of behavior through the conditioning mechanism in which, through contiguity, a new conditioned stimulus was substituted for an old unconditioned stimulus. But even he recognized that his account was insufficient to deal with higher forms of learning. To supplement it, he introduced the idea of the "second signalling system," with central importance placed on symbolic systems, such as language, in mediating and giving shape to mental life. Or as Luria put it in 1959, the first signal system is "concerned with directly perceived stimuli, the second with systems of verbal elaboration." Luria, commenting on the importance of the transition from first to second signal system, says:

> It would be mistaken to suppose that verbal intercourse with adults merely changes the contents of the child's conscious activity without changing its form. . . . The word has a basic function not only because it indicates a corresponding object in the external world, but also because it abstracts, isolates the necessary signal, generalizes perceived signals and relates them to certain categories; it is this systematization of direct experience that makes the role of the word in the formation of mental processes so exceptionally important.[2]

It is interesting too that the final rejection of the universality of the doctrine of reinforcement in direct conditioning came from some of Pavlov's own students. Ivanov-Smolensky and Krasnogorsky published papers showing the manner in which symbolized linguistic messages could take over the place of the unconditioned stimulus and of the unconditioned response (gratification of hunger) in children. In all instances, they speak of these as *replacements* of lower first-system mental or neural processes by higher second-system controls. A strange irony, then, that Russian psychology, which gave us the notion of the conditioned response and the assumption that higher-order activities are built up out of colligations of such primitive units, has rejected this notion while much of the American psychology of learning until quite recently has stayed within the early Pavlovian fold—as, for example, a 1959 article by Spence in the *Harvard Educational Review*, reiterating the primacy of conditioning and the derivative nature of complex learning. It is even more

[2] A. L. Luria, "The Directive Function of Speech in Development and Dissolution," *Word*, no. 15 (1959), p. 12.

noteworthy that Russian pedagogic theory has become deeply influenced by this new trend and is now placing much stress upon the importance of building up a more active symbolical approach to problem solving among children.

In this matter of the control of learning, then, my conclusion is that the degree to which the desire for competence comes to control behavior, to that degree the role of reinforcement or "outside rewards" wanes in shaping behavior. The child comes to manipulate his environment more actively and achieves his gratification from coping with problems. As he finds symbolic modes of representing and transforming the environment, there is an accompanying decline in the importance of stimulus-response-reward sequences. To use the metaphor that David Riesman developed in a quite different context, mental life moves from a state of outer-directedness, in which the fortuity of stimuli and reinforcement are crucial, to a state of inner-directedness in which the growth and maintenance of mastery become central and dominant.

The Heuristics of Discovery.   Lincoln Steffens, reflecting in his *Autobiography* on his undergraduate education at Berkeley, comments that his schooling paid too much attention to learning what was known and too little to finding out about what was not known. But how does one train a student in the techniques of discovery? Again there are some hypotheses to offer. There are many ways of coming to the arts of inquiry. One of them is by careful study of its formalization in logic, statistics, mathematics, and the like. If one is going to pursue inquiry as a way of life, particularly in the sciences, certainly such study is essential. Yet whoever has taught kindergarten and the early primary grades or has had graduate students working with him on their theses—I choose the two extremes for they are both periods of intense inquiry—knows that an understanding of the formal aspect of inquiry is not sufficient. Rather, several activities and attitudes, some directly related to a particular subject and some fairly generalized, appear to go with inquiry and research. These have to do with the *process* of trying to find out something and, though their presence is no guarantee that the *product* will be a great discovery, their absence is likely to lead to awkwardness or aridity or confusion. How difficult it is to describe these matters—the heuristics of inquiry. There is one set of attitudes or methods that has to do with sensing the relevance of variables—avoiding immersion in edge effects and getting instead to the big sources of variance. This gift partly comes from intuitive familiarity with a range of phenomena, sheer "knowing the stuff." But it also comes out of a sense of what things among many "smell right," what things are of the right order of magnitude or scope or severity.

Weldon, the English philosopher, describes problem solving in an interesting and picturesque way. He distinguishes among difficulties, puzzles, and problems. We solve a problem or make a discovery when we impose a puzzle form on a difficulty to convert it into a problem that can be solved in such a way that it gets us where we want to be. That is to say, we recast the difficulty into a form that we know how to work with—then we work it. Much of what we speak of as discovery consists of knowing how to impose a workable kind of form on various kinds of difficulties. A small but crucial part of discovery of the highest order is to invent and develop effective models or "puzzle forms." It is in this area that the truly powerful mind shines. But it is surprising to what degree perfectly ordinary people can, given the benefit of instruction, construct quiet interesting and what, a century ago, would have been considered greatly original models.

Now to the hypothesis. It is my hunch that it is only through the exercise of problem solving and the effort of discovery that one learns the working heuristics of discovery; the more one has practice, the more likely one is to generalize what one has learned into a style of problem solving or inquiry that serves for any kind of task encountered—or almost any kind of task. I think the matter is self-evident, but what is unclear is the kinds of training and teaching that produce the best effects. How, for instance, do we teach a child to cut his losses but at the same time be persistent in trying out an idea; to risk forming an early hunch without at the same time formulating one so early and with so little evidence that he is stuck with it while he waits for appropriate evidence to materialize; to pose good testable guesses that are neither too brittle nor too sinuously incorrigible? And so on and on. Practice in inquiry, in trying to figure out things for oneself is indeed what is needed—but in what form? Of only one thing am I convinced: I have never seen anybody improve in the art and technique of inquiry by any means other than engaging in inquiry.

Conservation of Memory.   I have come to take what some psychologists might consider a rather drastic view of the memory process. It is a view that in large measure derives from the work of my colleague, George Miller. Its first premise is that the principal problem of human memory is not storage but retrieval. In spite of the biological unlikeliness of it, we seem to be able to store a huge quantity of information—perhaps not a full tape recording, though at times it seems we even do that, but a great sufficiency of impressions. We may infer this from the fact that recognition, the ability to recall with maximum promptings, is so extraordinarily good in human beings and that spontaneous recall, with no promptings, is so extraordinarily bad. The key to retrieval is organization or, in even simpler terms, knowing where to find information that has been put into memory.

Let me illustrate with a simple experiment. We present pairs of words to twelve-year-olds. The children of one group are told only to remember the pairs and that they will be asked to repeat them later. Others are told to remember the pairs by producing a word or idea that will tie them together in a way that will make sense. The word pairs include such juxtapositions as "chair-forest," "sidewalk-square," and the like. One can distinguish three styles of mediators, and children can be scaled in terms of their relative preference for each: generic mediation, in which a pair is tied together by a superordinate idea: "chair and forest are both made of wood"; thematic mediation, in which the two terms are imbedded in a theme or a little story: "the lost child sat on a chair in the middle of the forest"; and part-whole mediation, in which "chairs are made from trees in the forest" is typical. Now the chief result, as you would predict, is that children who provide their own mediators do best—indeed, one time through a set of thirty pairs, they recover up to 95 percent of the second words when presented with the first ones of the pairs, whereas the uninstructed children reach a maximum of less than 50 percent recovered. Also, children do best in recovering materials tied together by the form of a mediator they most often use.

One can cite a myraid of findings to indicate that any organization of information that reduces the aggregate complexity of material by imbedding it into a cognitive process a person has constructed for himself will make that material more accessible for retrieval. We may say that the process of memory, looked at from the retrieval side, is also a process of problem solving: how can material be "placed" in memory so that it can be obtained on demand?

We can take as a point of departure the example of the children who developed their own technique for relating each word pair. The children with the self-made mediators did better than the children who were given ready-made ones. Another group of children were given the mediators developed by this group to aid them in memorizing—a set of "ready-made" memory aids. In general, material that is organized in terms of a person's own interests and cognitive structures is material that has the best chance of being accessible in memory. It is more likely to be placed along routes that are connected to one's own ways of intellectual travel. Thus, the very attitudes and activities that characterize figuring out or discovering things for oneself also seem to have the effect of conserving memory.

CHAPTER 8 Methods, Materials, and the Size of the Class

Most of American education still goes on in schools built like egg cartons. Every room in the building is the same size and approximately the same shape. Each holds the same number of students: twenty-five in the fortunate suburbs, forty in overcrowded city schools. Each is controlled by one teacher isolated in his classroom-castle except for occasional visits from principals or supervisors. Bells set to ring at forty-minute intervals shift classes of students from one room to another shaped and furnished exactly like the first. Our schools are plagued by sameness, by routine, and by a frightening lack of imagination.

Change is at last under way. Here and there around the country significant experiments with new ways of grouping students, new technology, new buildings, and new methods of staff utilization are working a quiet revolution which no one entering the teaching profession can afford to ignore. This fresh air ventilating the traditional classroom has brought a host of problems to teachers and those who design materials for the schools. A decade or so ago an eleventh-grade social studies teacher could comfortably ask which American history text was best for his class of 35 students. Now a host of new questions presses upon him: Should I teach American history in the eleventh grade? If I do, what parts of it can I teach best to 150 students in a single room, what parts to groups of 15, and what should I leave for independent study? How can I make the best use of the overhead projector, the tape recorder, movies, filmstrips, slide-tapes, and the opaque projector? How can I best deploy the staff to get a maximum contribution from each individual? How can I use teacher aids and specialists drawn from the community? How can I reorganize my time and the time of my students to better advantage? What material is best for each purpose, and where can I get it?

Chapter 8 poses the challenge of these new educational arrangements to teachers. It contains two readings. The first is a defense of expository teaching and an attack on the discovery method, an issue that is closely related to

To explain

teaching techniques in classes of different size. The second article summarizes recommendations about teacher and pupil deployment made by an official of the National Association of Secondary School Principals. As you read them, think about the following questions:

1) According to Professor Ausubel, on what assumptions is discovery teaching based? Are his charges accurate as applied to Bruner? Would Dewey agree with Ausubel that problem solving is unteachable to many students?

2) Ausubel argues that learning can take place only when the learner is able to relate new information to something he already knows. How might this conclusion be related to the argument that it is important to teach the structure of a discipline?

3) Suppose you were going to organize a school along the lines that Trump suggests. Where might it be most appropriate to employ discovery methods? expository techniques? How could the two ways of teaching be used in a complementary fashion?

RECEPTION VERSUS DISCOVERY LEARNING IN CLASSROOM INSTRUCTION

David P. Ausubel

Formal education has two principal objectives with respect to the cognitive development of the individual: (a) the long-term acquisition and retention of stable, organized, and extensive bodies of meaningful, generalizable knowledge, and (b) growth in the ability to use this knowledge in the solution of particular problems, including those problems which, when solved, augment the learner's original store of knowledge. These objectives, therefore, although related and mutually supportive, do not overlap completely. In the first place, quite apart from its usefulness in problem-solving, the acquisition of knowledge is a legitimate objective in its own right. Second, the goal of most kinds and instances of problem-solving activity is to facilitate everyday living and decision-making—not to discover knowledge that is of sufficient general significance to merit permanent incorporation into cognitive structure. The inductive derivation of concepts and generalizations from diverse instances is an exception to this statement, but is only a conspicuous feature of concept attainment during childhood (before a really large quantity of subject matter is

Reprinted from David P. Ausubel, "Reception versus Discovery Learning in Classroom Instruction," *Educational Theory,* Vol. 11, January 1961, 21–24.

incorporated). For the most part, in the formal education of the individual, the educating agency merely transmits ready-made concepts, categorical schemata and relational propositions.

Many educators contend, however, that the use of problem-solving techniques beyond the elementary school years should neither be limited to the application of knowledge to particular problems of transitory significance, nor constitute the exclusive methodological prerogative of scientists and scholars engaged in pushing forward the frontiers of knowledge. They maintain that these techniques should be used generally, in preference to verbal reception learning, in acquiring the substantive *content* of subject-matter—in much the same manner as the method of inductive derivation of concepts and generalizations during childhood. Their reasoning is essentially based on the following premises: (a) that abstract propositions are forms of glib verbalism unless the learner constructs them directly out of his own nonverbal, empirical experience; that "generalizations are products of problem-solving . . . and are attainable in no other way"; and (b) that discovery methods enhance the learning, retention, and transferability of principles.

It has already been shown, however, that although the first premise (apart from the gratuitous assumption about the indispensability of independent problem-solving for generalization) is warranted during the elementary school years, it does not validly apply to learning that takes place during and after adolescence. Students do not independently have to solve the intellectual problems they perceive in the content of learning materials in order for the solutions to have meaning and transferability for them. The deference to authority implied in accepting already discovered relationships has been condemned out of all reason. If students were required independently to validate every proposition presented by their instructors before accepting it, they would never progress beyond the rudiments of any discipline. We can only ask that established knowledge be presented to them as rationally and non-arbitrarily as possible, and that they accept it tentatively and critically as only the best available approximation of the "truth."

The second premise regarding the superior learning, retention, and transferability of material learned by the discovery method needs to be examined more closely. Although experimental findings tend to be inconclusive because of the confounding of variables (e.g., failure to hold constant the rote-meaningful and the inductive-deductive dimensions while varying the reception-discovery factor), it is plausible to suppose that the greater effort and vividness associated with independent discovery lead to somewhat greater learning and retention. One might expect the advantages conferred by discovery techniques to be even greater with respect to transferability, since the experience gained in formulating a generalization from diverse instances, for example, obviously facilitates the solution of problems involving this generalization. None of these advantages, however, seems sufficiently impressive to compensate for the unalterable fact that empirical problem-solving methods of instruction are incomparably more time-consuming than the method of verbal presentation. Problem-solving, manipulative, nonverbal, and inductive procedures undoubtedly have their place in promoting and reinforcing particular understandings that are difficult to grasp on a purely verbal basis (especially in fields such as mathematics with its own distinctive language), and in testing for the meaningfulness of verbal reception learning. Feasibility as a *primary* technique for transmitting the substantive content of an intellectual or scientific discipline, however, is quite another matter.

The development of problem-solving ability is, of course, a legitimate and significant educational objective in its own right. Hence it is highly defensible to utilize a certain proportion of classroom time in developing appreciation of and facility in the use of scientific methods of inquiry and of other empirical, inductive and deductive problem-solving procedures. But this is a far cry from advocating (a) that the presentation of scientific and other subject-matter should be organized in whole or part along the lines of inductive discovery, and should require nonverbal understanding and application of principles before the latter are introduced verbally; and (b) that the enhancement of problem-solving ability is the major function of the school. To acquire facility in problem-solving and scientific method it is not necessary for learners to rediscover every principle in the syllabus. Since problem-solving ability is itself transferable, at least within a given subject-matter field, facility gained in independently formulating and applying one generalization is transferable to other problem areas in the same discipline. Furthermore, overemphasis on developing problem-solving ability would ultimately defeat its own ends. It would leave students with insufficient time in which to learn the content of a discipline; and hence, despite their adeptness at problem-solving, they would be unable to solve simple problems involving the application of such content.

Aptitude in problem-solving also involves a much different pattern of abilities than those required for understanding and retaining abstract ideas. The ability to solve problems calls for qualities (e.g., flexibility, resourcefulness, improvising skill, originality, problem sensitivity, venturesomeness) that are less generously distributed in the population of learners than the ability to comprehend verbally presented materials. Many of these qualities also cannot be taught effectively. Although appropriate pedagogic procedures can improve problem-solving ability, relatively few good problem-solvers can be trained in comparison with the number of persons who can acquire a meaningful grasp of various subject-matter fields. Thus, to ignore the latter individuals and concentrate solely on producing talented problem-solvers would be educationally indefensible. Because of the different patterns of abilities involved, we also cannot assume that the learner who is unable to solve a given set of problems *necessarily* does not understand but has merely memorized the principles tested by these problems. Unfortunately, however, there is no other feasible way of testing for meaningfulness.

The method of verbal presentation does not necessarily constitute a deductive approach to instruction. For one thing it is entirely possible to follow an inductive order of presentation. But even when principles are presented first, the deductive designation is often inappropriate since much of the following material is correlative rather than supportive or illustrative in nature, and provides as much of a basis for deriving more inclusive new generalizations as for deriving subsidiary principles and solving subsidiary problems.

Misuses of the method of verbal learning are so well-known that only the following more flagrant practices need be mentioned: premature use of verbal techniques with cognitively immature pupils; arbitrary, cookbook presentation of unrelated facts without any organizing or explanatory principles; failure to integrate new learning tasks with previously presented materials; and the use of evaluation procedures that merely measure ability to recognize discrete facts or to reproduce ideas in the same words or in the identical context as originally encountered. Although it is entirely proper to caution teachers against these frequent misuses of verbal learning, it is not legitimate to represent them as inherent in the method itself. An approach to instruction which on logical and psychological grounds appears appropriate and efficient should not be discarded as unworkable simply because it is subject to misuse. It would seem more reasonable to guard against the more common misapplications, and to relate the method to relevant theoretical principles and research findings that actually deal with long-term learning and retention of large bodies of meaningful, verbally presented materials. The latter research, of course, still remains to be conducted. But until it is, the efficient programming of verbal learning is impossible, and devices such as "teaching machines" can do no better than present automatically, with somewhat more immediate reinforcement, the same materials currently presented by teachers.

SUMMARY AND CONCLUSIONS

Much of the opprobrium currently attached to verbal learning stems from failure to distinguish between "reception" and "discovery" learning and to appreciate the underlying basis of meaningfulness. It is widely accepted, for example, that verbal learning is invariably rote (glib verbalism) unless preceded by recent nonverbal problem-solving experience.

Most classroom instruction is organized along the lines of reception learning. Independent discovery of what is to be learned is not required: the content of the learning task is typically presented, and only has to be internalized and made available (functionally reproducible) for future use. This learning is meaningful provided that the learner has a set to relate the learning material to cognitive structure, and that the material is in fact logically (non-arbitrarily) relatable thereto. Only approximately before the age of twelve is direct empirical and nonverbal contact with data necessary for relatability to cognitive structure (i.e., for potential meaningfulness). At no stage does the learner have to discover principles independently in order to be able to understand and use them meaningfully.

Thus, after the elementary school years, verbal reception learning constitutes the most efficient method of meaningfully assimilating the substantive content of a discipline. Problem-solving methods are too time-consuming to accomplish this objective efficiently, but are useful for communicating certain insights and for measuring the meaningfulness of reception learning. The promotion of problem-solving ability, however, is a legitimate educational objective in its own right as long as it is not overemphasized.

The method of verbal reception learning will be restored to its rightful place in classroom instruction only when it is related to relevant but still-to-be-conducted research on the nature and conditions of long-term meaningful learning of large bodies of verbally presented material.

ORGANIZING FOR CHANGE

J. Lloyd Trump

Those who work in local schools and those who support them can also adopt any one of three basic attitudes toward change. They can turn their backs on the times we live in and oppose change. They can wait while others study and demonstrate, thus delaying action in their own schools, denying potential advantages to students, and limiting possible improvements in job satisfactions of teachers. Or, they, too, can spearhead change by encouraging experimentation with new ideas and by helping the public who supports the schools understand the nature of the changes and the results accomplished.

The factors that determine the rate of change are varied and complex, differing in each community. A variety of initial steps are suggested here so each school may find its own pace.

Starting Team Teaching

Team teaching can start in a limited way by periodically combining the classes of two teachers so that one or the other of them can teach those phases of a subject he is most interested in and most competent to handle. If no better space is available, the combined classes can meet in one of the classrooms.

Reprinted from J. Lloyd Trump, "Organizing for Change," in J. Lloyd Trump and Dorsey Baynham, *Focus on Change* (Chicago: Rand McNally & Company, 1961), pp. 105–119.

This simple arrangement is possible whenever a minimum of two sections or classes are scheduled at the same time in the day.

Two next steps could logically follow the first:

> The two teachers could work together in a deliberately systematic way, planning presentations or units of study.
>
> An expanded team which cuts across subject matter lines could be organized by adding one or more teachers to the team.

In an example of the first of these suggestions, students would be given a test at the beginning of a unit or division of class work. Those who did very well on this pretest would be scheduled by the team teachers to spend a major portion of their time in the library, laboratory, or some other appropriate place, depending upon the subject area. The rest of the class could be taught by the two teachers in groups of different sizes set up for different purposes. Arrangements and group size could be extremely flexible, depending on what individual students needed most.

In an example of the second, a teacher of United States history, a teacher of United States literature, teachers who know the music and arts of the country, and specialists who can improve students' writing and speaking could team together to teach various phases of the culture of this country. The size of the teams and the number of students involved would depend on the size of the school. This approach would provide a natural synthesis of subject matter and the most competent teaching in the various subject areas.

Not all teachers should be required to become members of teaching teams. As more teachers and more students are involved in team teaching activities, however, greater flexibility in scheduling and more effective use of the special talents of different teachers will result.

Some suggestions for making teaching teams more effective were given in earlier sections of this book. The teachers should have a common free period for planning and evaluating. Clerks and instructional assistants should be provided, and technological aids to instruction should be available. When a team needs consultant help, steps should be taken to obtain it. The principal and other supervisors should work closely with the teaching team.

CHANGING STAFF PATTERNS

The use of community consultants—specialists or experts in specific areas where they are more competent than any member of the staff—to give presentations to students is a relatively easy first step in changing staff patterns. Service clubs, religious groups, women's clubs, parent-teacher associations, other organized groups, local newspapers, and radio and television stations can be enlisted to assist the school in developing resource files of community consultants. Teachers can then plan to call on these persons for assistance when needed. Because community consultants, individually, are used infrequently, it is not ordinarily necessary to pay for their services. Recordings should be made and pictures taken of presentations by these specialists so that future generations of students may benefit from them without the necessity of calling the consultants back to the school.

Providing clerical help for teachers is another easy way to start changing staff patterns. Teachers could be asked to list the clerical work they do, estimate the amount of time spent doing it, and indicate what they would do instead if they had clerical assistance. A recommendation, based on this information, could then be made to the board of education that clerks be employed to do some of the listed work. A small start could be made by employing one clerk to assist the total teaching staff. Rules will be needed for the cooperative use of the clerk's services.

A first step in the employment of instruction assistants might be to hire aides to help English teachers grade themes. Job specifications should be worked out by the faculty. Ordinarily, the assistant should mark only mechanical errors on themes, leaving evaluation of content to the teachers, and then report these errors to the teachers so that remedial measures can be taken by them. An article or an advertisement in local newspapers ordinarily will produce a number of applicants for the position of instruction assistant. The assistant will be selected with the same care as in the case of any other member of the staff.

Another possibility in the employment of assistants is hiring someone to supervise playgrounds and study halls and to perform other tasks in which neither clerical nor subject matter competence is necessary. Instruction assistants and persons employed as general aides are usually hired only on a part-time basis.

The use of educational specialists from outside the school district is important in improving job satisfactions and making efficient use of professional competences. Many teachers now in service have not been adequately trained to use modern technology in instruction or to perform some other tasks. As a result, they feel insecure and threatened. Specialists in technology, the group process, counseling, and in other aspects of instruction need to be brought into the school to work with teachers. These specialists can come from the central office of large school systems, from nearby higher education institutions, or from state departments of education. Benefits from the use of such consultants will be immediate and significant if both teachers and consultants examine carefully their respective roles.

Yet another simple and often readily available way to provide teacher assistants is to use teacher education students from nearby higher education centers. Many competent college students already have part-time jobs. They would profit more in many instances if those jobs involved working in schools. College schedules usually are sufficiently flexible to make possible this work in elementary and secondary schools. One or more persons from the college need to be asked to work with school teachers and administrators in planning and evaluating the program, which could start very simply and expand as the need and opportunities developed further.

Teaching assistants, ultimately, must be woven into the patterns of the teaching teams. Thus, the leader will be able to coordinate and supervise the entire program, so that teachers can reap maximum benefits from the assistance. The constant re-examination of what constitutes professional tasks for teachers and what may be done by clerks, instruction assistants, general aides, and community consultants constitutes an important new approach to the development of a profession of teaching.

Lightening Class Loads

Teachers need time for professional tasks now omitted entirely or treated lightly in school programs. Today's teachers are scheduled for too many class hours per week, and the classes are *uniformly* too large. This report earlier recommended that teachers spend an average of 15 hours per week with groups of students and most of that time with no more than 15 students per class. Such a schedule provides the time for neglected professional tasks, many of which are essential for quality teaching today.

The recommended teaching load will be logistically and financially feasible only if the changes suggested in this report are made in a coordinated program. First steps will constitute a paradox: they will require *more* teacher time and energy than does the teaching load in the usual school arrangement. Teaching teams must meet to plan and prepare for instruction and, eventually, to evaluate results. Large-group teaching and the accompanying instructional aids must be carefully planned and developed. Instruction assistants and clerks must be supervised. Small-group discussion techniques must be studied.

A partial answer to the paradox that more time and energy will be needed in initial phases of the changeover is to employ teachers to attend a summer workshop for three weeks or more, to make plans and develop materials. Instruction assistants, clerks, and consultants should be employed for at least part of the workshop time.

Another possible answer, by itself not so desirable as the first, is to employ the teachers one Saturday or more per month to plan and prepare. During regular school days, teachers' schedules should be shortened by one period or more as another time-making device during early stages of the new program.

Reorganizing Instruction

The easiest first step in reorganizing instruction is to provide for large-group classes of from 100 to 150 students three or four, and then more, times a semester. On an average, teachers in conventional classes spend about one-fourth of their time talking to students. Increasing the number of students will mean very little change in this face-to-face instruction, and if teachers have time to plan better what they might say and what audio-visual aids they might use, the presentations are likely to be improved. Viewing films and taking examinations offer other easily managed opportunities for organization of large-group classes.

If two or more classes in the same subject, or at the same grade level, are scheduled for the same period, it is relatively simple to combine them on occasion for large-group instruction. A teacher who is especially competent or who has made a study of some phase of a subject makes a presentation to the combined groups. Teachers thus can gain confidence and see some potential advantages in the reorganization of instruction. Of course, the potential gains will be limited until the number of large-group sessions is fairly substantial and assistants are provided to help with large-group class routines.

Reorganizing instruction can begin with provision for large groups only, but significant improvement in the quality of education will be delayed until small-group discussion and independent study are included in a systematically planned pattern.

Effective small-group instruction and independent study are difficult to initiate. Teachers can gain some experience with small groups in conventional classes by assigning half the class to work in the library and retaining the remaining 15 or so students for classroom discussion. This division allows teachers to know students in a small-group setting. It also provides them with opportunities to learn to listen, to observe, to correct a point or raise an issue, to know when to enter the discussion, and, in general, to help students think better and discuss better. None of these is likely to happen if the other half of the class, for whom the teacher feels an equal sense of responsibility, remains in the classroom.

What students do in independent study must be quite different from what they do in today's homework. A beginning can be made by setting aside one or two periods a month where the emphasis is completely on creativity. Students will not be told what to do but rather will be given questions and suggestions and, most important of all, an opportunity to undertake a task related to the subject on their own initiative. There will be very great differences in students' creativity in the beginning, with some students accomplishing virtually nothing. Teachers will have to content themselves with total class gains and to work persistently to stimulate those students who lag behind.

In the initial stages of reorganizing class size according to the purposes of instruction, it may seem advisable to provide more small groups than the percentage recommended earlier in this report. Ultimately, the average division of time, which will include many variations for individual students and groups and at different age levels, will be about 40 per cent for large-group instruction, 20 per cent for small-group discussion, and 40 per cent for independent study.

A total program of reorganized instruction is easiest to start with the more able students in the senior year. These are the students who will work best in small groups, assume responsibility in independent study, and require less careful preparation by teachers of large groups. This does not imply that the reorganization of instruction proposed in this report is not appropriate for all students. It means simply that a school may wish first to try out the ideas experimentally with older, more able, and more mature students.

Using New Technological Aids

Most schools already possess more technological aids to instruction than they are using. Reasons for failure to use them were given earlier in this report. Prior to purchasing additional aids, steps must be taken to facilitate their use. Teachers need time to plan and prepare, facilities must be simplified, and students' schedules must be modified.

One of the most helpful instructional aids is the tape recorder, which can be used advantageously to give repetitive instructions and explanations, and a soundproof recording studio should be provided so teachers can learn to prepare tapes. They also need access to catalogues of commercially prepared tapes. To gain experience, tapes may first be tried out in conventional-size classes and then used in combined groups of several classes simultaneously, in a team situation. Such an arrangement saves both time and money.

The overhead projector is a simple, relatively inexpensive, and effective teaching tool. Teachers may first use the projector as they would a blackboard. Then they may use it to display students' work for analysis and correction. Finally, they may use it to project transparencies with colored overlays, which can be purchased but which they can also learn to prepare themselves. Lists of commercially available transparencies and directions for arranging facilities for making transparencies are available. As with the tape recorder, teachers may first use the overhead projector in a conventional classroom, but real economies of time and money result when the projector is used for large-group instruction.

Film strips and 2-by-2-inch slides represent another inexpensive and simple approach to the use of technological aids. A list of commercially available slides and film strips should be accessible, but both can be prepared locally if facilities are available. As in the case of other technological aids, these can be used in individual, conventional classes, but their maximum contribution to the saving of time and money results from use in large-group instruction.

Automated instruction devices (teaching machines) may be tried out experimentally as they become available. In the beginning, teachers doubtless will want to supervise student work with these self-teaching mechanical and electronic aids, but the major contribution of such devices will come when students are allowed to use them in relatively independent ways.

The use of television, films, video tapes, and other technological aids to instruction should be approached in the same manner as indicated in the foregoing paragraphs. In each case they can be used in conventional classrooms, but the greatest benefits result from their use in large-group instruction and in independent study. In the former they save money by allowing more pupils to participate; in the latter they save time by allowing teachers to make more efficient use of their professional competencies, and provide students with opportunities to develop responsibility for learning.

A first step in curriculum reorganization involves an analysis of what is now being taught and studied by students in conventional classrooms, study halls, libraries and laboratories, and in the usual assignment of homework. Teachers in a subject area should then ask themselves which of these purposes could be better served by large-group instruction, by small-group discussion, and by increased independent study by students.

In effect, these are the questions that teachers will answer for each unit in their present courses:

> What content and purposes could students of different levels of ability learn and accomplish for themselves with little or no help from me?
> What content and purposes require motivation, explanation, demonstration, or other presentation by me or by some other competent person?
> What content and purposes *actually* require personal interaction among students and between me and the students?

The answer to the first of these three questions provides leads to the development of *independent study*. The second question and its answers suggest possible programs of *large-group instruction*. The answer to the third question calls for *small-group discussion* in classes with 15 or fewer students in a setting where personal interaction is closer than in conventional classes. Incidentally, the amount of personal interaction now present may be quite small in conventional classes.

The teachers could further provide their own guidelines to more flexible curriculum organization by answering the following questions:

> Which of the following instructional methods is best used (for specific content and purposes): the voice of the teacher, physically present; films; television; slides; books; other instructional aids?
> Which of the following school areas is best used (for specific content and purposes): a classroom, and of what size; laboratory; library; other areas?

Such an analysis is not intended first as investigation of what is now being taught or of the present purposes of the school. Instead, it is intended simply as an aid in making decisions about the most effective methods and best school settings for accomplishing present purposes.

One way to conduct this reappraisal is to establish a file for each unit in a course. Different colored pages can be used to record answers to the foregoing questions and the pages arranged in each unit file according to the purpose and the content of each specific lesson.

In using this approach to reorganizing curriculum, two possible pitfalls should be avoided. The first is the temptation to redefine goals. Some re-examination of objectives is bound to occur in answering the foregoing questions, but redefinition of goals does not constitute the opening attack on curricular reorganization, and many meetings spent in redefining goals merely postpones reorganization by that much time.

Changing the methods of evaluation, too, may be avoided at first. Teachers may continue to use the testing procedures they have evolved for a considerable time, plus available standardized tests that have been conventionally used. In later stages of the reorganization, of course, they and others will realize that conventional evaluation methods do not measure such highly important goals as development of independent responsibility for learning, growth in creativity and inquiry, ability to think and discuss effectively in small groups, and development of satisfaction in learning. In the process of working toward these goals, teachers are likely to discover improved methods of evaluation, but in the meantime they should rely on their own professional judgment and not delay necessary improvements until more satisfactory evaluation devices are available.

Curricular reorganization requires continual study. Ultimately, teachers will need to consider redefinition of goals, changes in content, and problems of evaluation, of sequence, of differentiation for students with varying ability and interests, and many others. The first steps, however, can and should be simple.

TEACHING TEAMS

	REGULAR SCHEDULE		COMBINED
period	*English* teacher **X**	*History* teacher **Y**	teachers **X** or **Y**
1	section **A**	section **B**	sections **AB**
2	section **B**	section **A**	sections **AB**

	REGULAR SCHEDULE			COMBINED
period	*English* teacher **X**	*History* teacher **Y**	*Science* teacher **Z**	teachers **X, Y** or **Z**
1	section **A**	section **B**	section **C**	sections **ABC**
2	section **B**	section **C**	section **A**	sections **ABC**
3	section **C**	section **A**	section **B**	sections **ABC**

Modifying Schedules

The purpose of schedule modification is to make it more flexible so that students and teachers can break out of the conventional, standard-size period, five days a week, each period slated for a self-contained classroom. First steps in schedule modification may take several directions.

One of the simplest methods of schedule modification is the "back-to-back" arrangement whereby two regular groups of students, totaling perhaps 50 to 60, are kept together for two or three class periods, as shown in the accompanying chart. Thus, Miss X or Mr. Y may present material to both sections combined to save time and effort. If the enrollment permits the combination of 75 to 90 students, the potential flexibility is even greater, as shown in the second chart. Teachers can easily try out various procedures, such as working with larger-than-usual or smaller-than-usual student groups, experimenting with various types of presentations, or taking two- or three-hour field trips, without being interrupted by the schedule for other classes.

Changing the length of periods constitutes another type of schedule modification. A school day may be divided into 15- or 20-minute modules, and different classes may meet for varied number of modules—one, two, three, five, or any number desired—depending upon the purpose of the class. Under the module system, the schedule may also provide that a class meet on certain specified days of the week, instead of every day. A school can change to the modular use of time by rescheduling only a few classes in the first stages of schedule modification.

Another possible step in schedule modification is to leave open one or two periods near the middle of the school day, with no regularly scheduled classes. During this time, students can be scheduled for a variety of activities—large-group instruction, small-group discussion, laboratory work and work in other areas, or independent study—without conflicting with regular classes which are scheduled during other periods of the school day.

A more radical type of modification, followed in some schools for many years, is provided by scheduling classes for four days a week. One full day a week then can be kept free of regular classes. A regularly scheduled day, preferably Wednesday, the mid-point of the week, can be used for classes of varied sizes, for independent study, and for other learning activities so that they will not conflict with conventional classes.

These suggested methods of schedule modification should be used only as first steps and not as ultimate goals. The school of the future will provide much more flexibility in the use of time than the foregoing modification suggests.

MEETING INDIVIDUAL DIFFERENCES

The first step in serving individual differences among teachers and students is to plan specific, individual programs only with and for those teachers and students who are particularly interested. This means starting in a small way but being ready to expand individual programming as more staff members and more students indicate interest.

The wishes and talents of individual teachers should be considered. Not all teachers should be expected to work as members of teaching teams, to instruct large-group classes or to guide small discussion groups. But those teachers who are interested in any of the approaches suggested here and are able to experiment should be given an opportunity to do so. Administrators should not place priority on any one approach as being preferable to others because the approaches are interrelated and equally important.

If one or more teachers want to try a new approach, the administration should be ready to make schedule changes, redeploy students so that the new approaches are logistically and financially feasible, try to obtain necessary educational facilities, seek consultant help if needed, and take other necessary steps. These steps should be taken, however, in a manner that will not antagonize those teachers who wish to continue conventional methods. Thus, all individual differences among the staff are recognized and individual teachers are protected from the inequalities which result from uniform practices rigidly followed.

Much the same procedure can begin a program for dealing with individual differences among students. For example, students who wish to spend more than the usual amount of time in a laboratory and whose teachers and counselors believe this would be advantageous should find it possible to do so. Administrators make whatever schedule changes are necessary, see that facilities are available and supervision is provided, and take other steps toward the success of these individual experiences.

Pressure need not be placed on all teachers and all students to participate in the new program. But the school can learn a great deal from those teachers and students who wish to try new approaches and individual differences can be recognized in ways that are impossible when school programs are based upon arbitrary and clerical, rather than professional and personal, decisions.

CHAPTER 9 Teaching the Mode of Inquiry: History

In many secondary schools, history is a chronicle of past events that students are expected to memorize. In some schools, history becomes those events that are described in the textbook chosen for the course. Class recitations check upon the thoroughness with which students have mastered the details in the book, and objective examinations of the true-and-false or fill-in variety provide a further evaluation. These procedures do not describe history as historians themselves know the subject.

History is really a way of reading and writing about events in the past. Since only a tiny proportion of all the events that have happened were recorded and saved for posterity, history cannot be an accurate record of everything in the past. Moreover, no historian in a single lifetime could read all the extant material on a topic as complicated, for example, as the Protestant Reformation. Hence, history is not even an accurate record of all the information about the past. In addition, the historian doing research selects from the mass of material that he reads those pieces of information which seem to him significant. What seems significant is conditioned by a man's conception of the nature of causation and by his personal characteristics and experiences. The very act of selecting evidence implies interpretation.

This argument leads to the conclusion that we must teach methods of interpretation if we claim to teach history. Students must learn the rules by which historians collect evidence and use it to interpret the past if they are to read or write history intelligently. They must be able to judge whether an author's conclusions are supported by the evidence he presents. They must also learn to draw their own conclusions and to present the evidence on which these conclusions are based. Unless students are taught to interpret, they are not taught history at all. Teaching the mode of inquiry of history and the social sciences lies at the heart of the new social studies.

How can we teach students to think like historians? Clearly we must devote a substantial proportion of our class time to this pursuit. We cannot leave the

150

teaching of historical method to incidental learning while we concentrate in class upon amassing factual information. One way to dramatize the importance of learning method and to raise the questions about method that a student should seek to answer through his course is to begin a year's work with a group of readings designed to encourage students to think about the ways in which historians work. The readings in Chapter 9 have been chosen for this specific purpose. They have been used as the first six days' work in a world history course. Model lesson plans for the readings will be found in Chapter 10 of this volume. Five half-hour films showing an actual class using this material are now available (Holt, Rinehart and Winston, Inc.). The transcript of a class discussion of the first of these films will be found in Chapter 16 of this book. As you read, keep the following questions in mind:

1) What is the definition of history implicit in these readings? Is this kind of history useful for citizenship training?
2) What would Professor Bruner think of the way in which this unit of work has been organized? How can one lesson build upon another?
3) How could the information and attitudes taught in this unit be recalled and strengthened during the remainder of a school year?
4) What is the difference between the mode of inquiry of the historian and the abilities and skills described by Bloom in Chapter 2?

UNIT I: INTRODUCTION TO THE STUDY OF HISTORY

Edwin Fenton

STATING THE ISSUE

Today we begin a formal study of history. Our first task is to find out what history is. Is it merely, as the dictionary says, "a narrative of events" or "a systematic, written account of events, particularly of those affecting a nation, institution, science or art, usually connected with a philosophical explanation of their causes"? Is it instead only "one man's interpretation of the past," or as Voltaire said, "a pack of tricks we play on the dead"? Or is it primarily a way of thinking, a set of rules and procedures for making interpretations?

The first six assignments in this course have been designed to encourage each student to work out his own definition of history. Notice that we do not suggest that everyone should arrive at exactly the same understanding of the term. Historians disagree with each other about the nature of their discipline. Literally hundreds of volumes have been written in an attempt to find a definition of history that everyone in the profession would accept. So far no author has reached this goal. When even experts disagree, students should not be expected to reach a consensus.

Nor should students be expected to understand the nature of history in one week's work. These six assignments merely introduce the topic and present opportunities to develop a first approximation of the nature of historical investigation. Throughout the course, students who use this book will have frequent opportunities to increase their knowledge about historical procedures and to apply historical techniques to a great variety of situations. Only by successfully applying the tools of analysis can anyone be certain that he has mastered them.

We will concentrate our study of the nature of history on a few key issues. What will a historian accept as fact? What determines how he categorizes facts into groups of related events? How does he develop and validate hypotheses? How can he deal with the problem of overcoming a mind set growing out of his entire life experience? These are the questions we will try to answer in Unit I.

Reading I: How the Historian Classifies Information

A historian who collects information from newspapers or other sources must arrange his data for his readers. His job is to decide the question he wishes to investigate and the arrangement of the evidence he uses to prove the point he wishes to make. If he did not arrange evidence, he could only list facts helter-skelter in no pattern whatsoever. No one would waste his time reading such an account.

We shall begin our study of history by investigating the problem of the arrangement of data. In order to concentrate on this problem without becoming involved in a true historical subject, we have chosen data that would not usually be considered historical at all. In class, however, we will be able to examine the implications of our conclusions for the study of history.

Below you will find a list of eighteen words. You are to arrange these words in groups of things that seem to belong to each other for some reason. For example, if we had given you the words "tiger," "pine tree," and "iron ore," you could classify them as animal, vegetable, and mineral. You can probably think of a number of additional ways to classify these three terms. Make as many classifications of the eighteen terms below as you can think of in a half hour. Come to class prepared to discuss what you have done.

shark	tuna	pike
turkey	condor	eagle
rabbit	ostrich	sheep
cat	lion	pheasant
grouse	black bass	collie dog
rainbow trout	elephant	barracuda

Reading II: How The Historian Proves a Hypothesis

Historians never collect data helter-skelter. If they did, they would take notes about everything they read. No historian operates in this fashion. He selects the data he wants to record in his notes and then selects again from his notes those pieces of evidence (facts) that he will use to prove his point. Every step in the process of writing a book or an article involves selection.

How does a historian start to select? He usually starts with a question: What caused World War I? Why did the United States become more democratic in the 1830s? What was the most important contribution of the Romans to the Western heritage? Then he begins to do research, reading, and collecting notes about his topic. Before long he starts to develop a hypothesis, a tentative answer to the question. As he gathers more data, he revises his hypothesis; he may abandon it entirely if he finds enough evidence against it. In this case, he will be forced to develop another hypothesis to guide his research. Eventually he will conclude that the hypothesis he has developed really explains the facts of the case. He is then ready to write his conclusions.

This procedure sounds far more simple than it really is. Where does he get the idea for his hypothesis in the first place? How does he decide when a hypothesis has been proved? How should he arrange his evidence to support his explanation in such a way that readers will agree with him? These are all questions we will try to answer during this course.

Today we will investigate the way in which two historians developed hypotheses and tried to prove or disprove them. The article you will read concerns the controversy about the Kensington Rune Stone, a slab marked with runic inscriptions that was discovered in Minnesota in 1898. We will introduce further evidence about this stone in class. As you read, keep the following questions in mind:

1) How does the author begin this article? Do most historians start research in a similar way?
2) What was the original hypothesis about the authenticity of the stone? What evidence made scholars think it was a forgery?
3) What was the next hypothesis about the stone? What evidence prompted a new investigation? Why have many historians decided that the stone is an authentic relic?
4) Are you convinced that the stone is genuine?

I. THE RIDDLE OF THE KENSINGTON STONE*

Thomas R. Henry

Did a group of Scandinavians reach this country—and perish under Indian tomahawks—130 years before Columbus came? Once denounced as a fraud, the message they left for posterity is now called "the most important archaeological object yet found in North America."

A challenging enigma confronts American historians. Did a Norwegian knight named Paul Knutson lead an ill-fated band of forty armored soldier-missionaries to the headwaters of the Red River in West Central Minnesota 130 years before the first voyage of Columbus? Evidence of such an expedition, accumulating through half a century, is now so substantial that some of this country's foremost archaeologists consider the case nearly proved. A few hard facts jut like mountain crags out of the clouds of New World antiquity.

The first of these facts: Late in the autumn of 1354 King Magnus Erikson, first ruler of the combined realms of Norway and Sweden, commissioned Knutson, a "law speaker"—or judge—and one of the most prominent men of his court, to recruit an expedition to rescue the souls of a vanished Norwegian colony on the west coast of Greenland. Presumably the party sailed early the next spring. It was never heard of again.

The second fact: Fifty years ago a stone slab was found clutched in the roots of a tree by a Swedish homesteader near Kensington, Minnesota. It bore what purported to be a message to posterity, carved in runic letters. It recorded an Indian massacre of a group of explorers. Assuming the relic is genuine, these explorers must have been members of Knutson's expedition. The inscription's date was 1362.

The third fact: A few weeks ago the slab was placed in the great hall of the Smithsonian Institution, in Washington. Dr. Matthew W. Stirling, chief of the Government's Bureau of American Ethnology, called it "probably the most important archaeological object yet found in North America."

When it was first discovered, the stone was denounced generally as a naïve fraud. In the half century that has elapsed since its discovery, the major objections have been met with corroborating evidence. For more than ten years, discarded and discredited by scholars, the relic had been a flagstone in a farmer's muddy barnyard. The very features which once caused experts to denounce it are now cited as bearing witness to its genuineness.

The whole case rests, of course, on the authenticity of this blue-gray slab which the highly conservative Smithsonian has just placed among its greatest treasures. It was back in the summer of 1898 that Olof Ohman, young

---

* Reprinted from Thomas R. Henry, "The Riddle of the Kensington Stone," *Saturday Evening Post*, Vol. 221, August 21, 1948.

Swedish immigrant and homesteader near the village of Kensington, in Douglas County, Minnesota, grubbed up the stump of an aspen tree at the edge of a marsh. Clutched in its roots was a flat, gravestone-shaped piece of graywacke, one of the hard glacial sandstone rocks of the region. It was about the size of a headstone in a Swedish country cemetery. Carved on one face and one edge of this slab were strange letters.

All this had no meaning and little interest to Farmer Ohman. He was a stolid, unimaginative man. The character of Ohman is significant in the effort to validate the relic. The circumstances of the stone's discovery are recorded in a sworn affidavit which Ohman made before a local justice of the peace. If Ohman had been a glib talker or student of history—especially if he ever had tried to make any money out of his find—there might be grounds for suspicion. But he was the kind of man who had no inclination—and even less capacity—to perpetrate a fraud.

He told some neighbors about the queer stone. At their suggestion he delivered it to the local bank on his next trip to the county seat for supplies. The banker had a keen interest in local antiquities, and he, in turn, sent the relic to the University of Minnesota, at Minneapolis. There Prof. O. J. Breda, one of the foremost Scandinavian scholars in America, found little difficulty in deciphering most of the inscription. The letters were Norse runes, the curious first alphabet of the Germanic peoples derived in some roundabout way from the letters of the Greeks and Romans. Some of these symbols meant nothing to Breda. In his translation, he left blank spaces where they occurred. It now is known that they represented numbers.

This is the translation as now accepted: [We are] 8 Goths [Swedes] and 22 Norwegians on (an) exploration journey from Vinland through (or across) the West. We had camp by (a lake with) two skerries [rocky islands] one day's journey north from this stone. We were [out] and fished one day. After we came home [we] found 10 [of our] men red with blood and dead. AV[e] M[aria], Save [us] from evil. [We] have 10 of (our party) by the sea to look after our ships (or ship) 14 days' journey from this island. Year 1362.

Professor Breda was not at all impressed. It was such an obvious hoax, he said, that it was not worthy of further attention from anybody. The language itself was a dead giveaway. It was a mixture of Norwegian, Swedish and what looked like old English. In the days of runic writings Swedes and Norwegians had been bitter enemies and it was incredible that they could have been partners on an expedition. The three letters AVM were Latin, not runic. The Roman alphabet had not been introduced into Scandinavia until early in the Middle Ages.

The learned runologist missed the date—1362. The figures representing it were not in the early runic alphabet. Breda quite naturally assumed that any Norsemen who could have reached central Minnesota must have come from the Greenland colonies of Eric the Red sometime in the twelfth century. There was no room here for any argument. The Kensington Stone could not have been carved by any such Greenlander. It was all a crude and silly fraud perpetrated by somebody with a superficial knowledge of runes together with a gross ignorance of Scandinavian history. The hoaxer, whoever he was, hardly could have expected to be taken seriously. He had said that the stone was carved on an island in a lake. There was no lake within twenty miles of Ohman's homestead.

Nevertheless, the relic was sent to Northwestern University, at Evanston, Illinois, for a further check by runic experts. They agreed with Breda, and the slab was sent back to the country bank, which returned it to Farmer Ohman.

What is "probably the most important archaeological object yet found in North America" very likely still would be in that barnyard had it not been for the interest of an outstanding Norse-American historian, Hjalmar R. Holand of Ephraim, Wisconsin. For thirty years he has given most of his spare time to its study in every aspect—geological, archaeological, geographic, linguistic and historical. He has taken it to twenty-three European universities for consultation with experts. One after another, the most serious objections to its authenticity have proved the strongest points in its favor. First was the discovery of the meanings of the runic number symbols and the determination of the date. These particular runes were of late origin and local usage in Norway. In the fourteenth century the Latin alphabet had been introduced, and its letters were intermingled quite often with the ancient Germanic symbols. That disposed of the apparent incongruity of the Roman letters AVM for AV(e) M(aria). This was a well-understood symbol, easy to write. It would have required a lot of space to have produced it in runes.

The biggest break, however, came about twenty years ago with the publication in a Danish archaeological journal of a copy, found by chance in the royal library at Copenhagen, of King Magnus' order to Knutson. It was translated as follows:

"Magnus, by the grace of God king of Norway, Sweden and Skaane, sends to all men who see or hear this letter good health and happiness.

"We desire to make known that you, [Paul Knutson], are to take the men who are to go in the Knorr [the royal trading vessel] whether they be named or not named, from my bodyguard and also from among the retainers of other men whom you may wish to take on the voyage, and that Paul Knutson, who shall be the commandant upon the Knorr, shall have full authority to select the men who are best suited either as officers or men. We ask you to accept this, our command, with a right good will for the cause, inasmuch as we do it for the honor of God and for the sake of our soul, and for the sake of our predecessors, who in Greenland established Christianity and have maintained it to this time, and we will not let it perish in our days. Know this for truth, that whoever defies this, our command, shall meet with our serious displeasure and thereupon receive full punishment.

"Executed at Bergen, Monday after Simon and Judah's day in the six and XXX year of our reign (1354). By Orm Ostenson, our regent, sealed."

Thus it was established that a few years before the date found on the Kensington Stone a certain Paul Knutson, one of the most prominent citizens of Magnus' kingdom, had been ordered to recruit and lead an expedition across the Atlantic. Certainly no hoaxer of the nineteenth century could have known this. The date on the stone, eight years after the issuance of the order, would have been a remarkable coincidence with history. Eight years was a reasonable time to have allowed Knutson to have come from Bergen to the headwaters of the Red River.

There can hardly be any question but that the crusade left Norway. Mr. Holand ventures a tentative reconstruction of what happened. Presumably, Knutson, guided by vague descriptions in the Icelandic sagas, proceeded to some point on the New England coast, established a base camp, and made a systematic search for the lost colony. Failing to find any trace of the Greenlanders, he must have turned northward with a considerable number of his party—perhaps leaving a small rear guard in what is now Massachusetts or Rhode Island—and finally sailed into the iceberg-filled Hudson Bay. Still there was no trace of the men he sought. And very likely his instructions from King Magnus had been quite peremptory: If you don't find them you needn't come back.

He came to the mouth of the great Nelson River, followed it southward to Lake Winnipeg, and thence by a series of lakes and portages to the Red River country, whose waters flow into the Mississippi and the Gulf of Mexico. Even today there is an almost continuous waterway from the ice-filled sea to the Minnesota lakeland where the Kensington Stone was found. This, the explorer probably thought, would have been a natural route from Greenland for the lost colonists. Also, Mr. Holand conjectures, he thought he was following the easiest route back to his base in Vinland. He did not picture North America as a continent but as a group of large islands.

This, of course, is all highly speculative. But one fact remains: If the Kensington Stone is genuine, Paul Knutson and his crusading knights were in Central Minnesota in 1362. Evidence increases for the authenticity of the relic. If Farmer Ohman told the truth about the circumstances of the stone's discovery—and this stolid, hard working, unlettered immigrant must have been leading an extraordinary sort of double life if he concocted the story—the tablet had been in the spot where he found it for at least as long as the aspen tree had been growing. Archaeologists have a reasonably accurate means of dating trees and timbers from the rings in the wood; examination of similar trees in the neighborhood has led to the conservative assumption that the tree in whose roots the rune stone was found was at least forty years old in 1898. This means that, if the relic had been "planted," the attempted deception must have taken place in the 1850's. There were then few white men in that part of Minnesota. It was inhabited by savage and hostile Sioux.

The conglomeration of languages alone was enough to convince Professor Breda that the stone was a fake. But he was thinking in terms of the language of the sagas in which had been related the exploits of Eric the Red and Leif the Lucky. This stone had been inscribed more than three centuries later. Norway then was in contact with all Europe. Some English words had been introduced into the vulgar speech. Both Swedes and Norwegians participated in the expedition. Magnus was king of both countries. It was natural enough that the "crusaders" should have spoken a slight mixture of tongues. Furthermore, these men were not scribes or scholars. Very likely their priests had been left in Vinland. But they were reasonably intelligent, literate young men. Mr. Holand's researches in the popular literature of fourteenth-century Scandinavia convince him that the words of this despairing note on stone are just about the words to be expected of such a man, especially when he was under emotional stress. Whoever carved these runes may hardly have expected to live to finish the job.

Why did he use runes at all? By that time the Latin alphabet was well known in Norway and was used in most documents. For the simple reason, Mr. Sarff explains, that runic characters had been especially adapted for carving on gravestones. They were used for that purpose in both Iceland and Norway long after they had been abandoned in ordinary writing. It was easier to carve in hard stone the straight-lined runic symbols than the roman letters with curved lines. Whoever inscribed these letters was in a hurry to finish his job. He was working on the edge of eternity.

The message stated that some of the party had been left behind to look after the boats by the sea, "14 days' journey from this island." It has been found that the expression "day's journey" was a conventional term of the time, meaning approximately seventy-five miles, or the distance which a vessel could sail in a day with a fair wind. This would be just about the correct distance to the mouth of the Nelson River. The journey probably had taken Knutson's men at least a year.

The inscription indicates that the party was encamped on an island in a lake, seventy-five miles away from another lake containing two rocky islands, on the shore of which their comrades had been massacred. It is to be assumed that they had come there for temporary security from the Indians. Ohman found the stone at the edge of a marsh. This now is dry land. Geological surveys show that the slightly elevated, rocky land from which the farmer grubbed the aspen stump was almost certainly an island in 1362. The countryside has been getting progressively drier for the past century.

Just about seventy-five miles away is the only lake with two "skerries," or rocky islands. It is Cormorant Lake, in Becker county. On its shore are large glacial boulders with triangular holes drilled in three of them. This was a common device for mooring boats along the fiords of fourteenth-century Norway. Beside one of these rocks a fourteenth century Norwegian fire steel was recently picked up. Several other such mooring rocks have been found in this section of Minnesota. The implication is that the explorers continued their journey eastward for a time, probably seeking a waterway back to Vinland. Along the course of the Nelson during the past half century various Norwegian implements have been picked up—three battle-axes, a fire steel and a spearhead. This may indicate the route followed by Knutson's men southward from Hudson Bay.

There is only a vague suggestion that some of the men left at Vinland, or with the ships at the mouth of the Nelson, returned to Norway: It is said that, in the midst of the great plague, King Magnus received news that his Greenland colony was lost without trace. Who could have been the bearer of these bad tidings? There still remains a faint possibility that among age-yellowed manuscripts in some European archives there may be found a full account of the expedition by somebody who accompanied Knutson.

Reading III: How the Historian Decides What Is Fact

In Reading II we discovered that historians use facts to validate hypotheses. We also learned that scholars often disagree about what is fact and what is not. Some historians accept a statement as fact while others reject it because of differences in their frames of reference. We studied examples of this generalization in class yesterday.

Sometimes historians have only one source for a statement of fact. In most cases, however, they have two or more sources. Often the sources will disagree. Because each author has his own frame of reference from which he views an event, he will select some of the things he sees to describe and reject others. Another eye witness might have different events to record or might interpret the same event differently. Yet the historian must rely heavily on eye-witness accounts to obtain the evidence he needs to validate a hypothesis.

Today's reading gives you an opportunity to decide which facts can be accepted from two authors who disagree on many details. Suppose that civilization on earth has been destroyed by hydrogen war. You have just landed from Mars (we won't speculate about what you look like or how you got here). You know how to read both English and Russian because your midget computer makes instant translations into Martian. In a time capsule buried on the site of ancient New York (or Nyawk, as Theodore Bikel, playing the archaeologist of the future, called it) you discover a yellowed magazine containing an account of a revolution in a place called Hungary. In another time capsule on the site of ancient Moscow you discover a fading script of a radio broadcast describing this same event. The two accounts are all the information you have. As an historian, Martian variety, it is your task to decide what the facts are. How would you go about doing so?

As you read these two articles (one actually is taken from *Time* and the other is a verbatim account of a broadcast from Radio Moscow) think about the following questions:

1) Which of these accounts, if either, do you accept? Do you think each might be right in parts and wrong in other parts?
2) Do the two accounts agree about anything? If the two accounts do agree about something, are you willing to accept it as a fact? Why or why not?
3) What are some of the issues on which the accounts differ? How would you decide which, if either, is correct?

I. HUNGARY
The Five Days of Freedom*

Time

For five frantic days Hungary was free.

From beleaguered Budapest on Tuesday the news flashed that the Soviet tanks were pulling out. Shouted the jubilant announcer: "For long years past this radio had been an instrument of lies. It lied day and night. It lied on all wave lengths . . . From this moment those who mouthed the lies are no longer . . . We who are now facing the microphone are new men." It was the voice of the people of Hungary in that hour: a great burden had been cast off.

The first to see the unfamiliar face of freedom were the young rebels. Their weapons at the ready, their faces filthy with the grime of battle, their clothes often blood-caked, they stood along the arteries of battle leading out of the battered city, happily jeering the departing Soviet tanks as they rumbled sullenly by.

TANK SMASHING

Only a few hours before, desperate battles had been fought at the Maria Theresia barracks, at the Communist Party headquarters, and at the steel mills at Csepel island. With their heavy 76-mm. guns, the Soviet tanks had attempted to blast the rebels out of their hiding places, but the "incredible youngsters" had evolved their own technique for dealing with the mighty 26-ton tanks. First they would fire on the tanks from upper-story windows, then as the big T-34s rumbled up, their great guns elevated, a small boy would leap out of a doorway, fling a pail of gasoline over the tank's engine compartment and leap back to shelter. As the tank took fire and its crew scrambled out of the turret, the young Tommy-gunner firing from the windows above would mow them down. An alternate system was to slosh a

---

* Reprinted from "Hungary—The Five Days of Freedom," *Time*, November 12, 1956. Courtesy *Time*; copyright *Time*, Inc., 1956.

bucket of gasoline across a street and throw a match in it just as a Soviet tank plunged past.

FREEDOM FIGHTERS

Now, as they began to realize what had happened and what they had done, the faces of the rebels were lit with a kind of ecstasy. There were vigorous blond students and tough-looking workers among them, but many seemed pitifully young. A correspondent noted a boy who could not have been more than ten years old holding himself at the ready with a rifle as tall as himself. Beside him was a 15-year-old girl with a submachine gun and a forage cap on her head. Grey with the fatigue of four days' ceaseless fighting, almost falling from exhaustion, they solemnly welcomed the foreigners: "We greet you in the name of the Hungarian Freedom Fighters!" Some carried machine-gun ammunition belts slung around their shoulders, and out of almost every pocket and above every inch of belt protruded hand grenades.

Premier Nagy had disowned the city's 10,000-man Communist security-police force, and the Russians had pulled out leaving the hated AVH men to their fate. Most of them had found temporary ratholes. In a huge concrete bunker below Communist Party headquarters, some 200 were said to be hiding out with political prisoners as hostages. Scores hung from trees and lampposts.

The revolution uncovered terrible evidence of AVH cruelty. On a wooded hill in Buda, in a bright new housing development reserved exclusively for ex-Premier Rakosi and his comrades, rebels found a villa with a built-in torture chamber and prison cells, one padded and soundproofed, another equipped with a powerful lamp beamed on a chair. The rebels remembered having seen closed automobiles driving up to this house at night. At Györ, in the provinces, Western newsmen were shown an AVH headquarters with tiny 2 ft.-wide standup torture cells, and a secret crematory for victims who did not survive AVH treatment. In the same modern building were technical facilities for monitoring all telephone conversations in western Hungary, including a score of tape recorders working simultaneously.

There was also fun to be had pulling down Soviet war memorials. High on Gellert Hill, antlike figures swarmed around Sculptor Szigmund Strobl's 150-ft. statue of Freedom, a graceful woman guarded by the bronze statue of a Russian soldier. Slowly the crowd, pulling on lines attached to the soldier, rocked the statue back and forth, until he tipped forward on his face. There had been no looting in the city thus far, but to walk abroad at night was to hazard being shot at (see PRESS) or stopped by some tough young rebel and made to show identity papers.

DEMOCRACY'S RETURN

Small newspapers representing political parties long believed defunct suddenly appeared. The old National Peasant Party, the Smallholders Party, and the Social Democratic Party each found its voice. Out of the disorganized Communist Party a new Hungarian Socialist Workers Party with national Communism as its aim was formed by Party Leader Janos Kadar.

What had come over Hungary, without anyone quite realizing it, was democracy.

To continue holding down the premiership, new Premier Nagy was forced to yield to the pressures of the new parties, to promise free elections, to acclaim neutrality, and, above all, to insist that the Russian troops be withdrawn, not only from Budapest, but from Hungary.

From the moment that U.S. correspondents had begun coming into free Budapest the rebels had never ceased to ask, "When are the Americans coming?" During the middle of the fighting a Hungarian had lifted up his son so that the child might touch a U.S. flag on a correspondent's car. Again and again, innocent of world affairs, they had asked if arms would come soon from America. Said one: "If the Russians come back, we can't hold out forever."

The Russians were coming back, and many Americans were leaving Budapest. Sadly the Hungarians watched them go. They had no stake in the revolution; they were at peace with the mighty Soviet Union and hoped to remain so—Hungary's bloodshed was only a drop of what the world would suffer in a total war.

II. A SOVIET TOURIST IN BUDAPEST*

E. M. Bazarina

MOSCOW

We arrived in Hungary on 19 October with other Soviet tourists. We spent four days touring this beautiful country and were everywhere given a most cordial and hearty welcome. On Tuesday, 23 October, on our way to a theatre we saw crowds of people in the streets of Budapest. They were lined up in ranks and carried placards, many of which bore the inscription "Long live Hungary!" . . . The students together with members of the intelligentsia and workers were demanding the redress of errors and omissions committed by the Hungarian Government. They were legitimate demands. . . .

On that first evening I saw from the hotel in which we were staying a man

---

* Reprinted from Richard Lettis and William E. Morris, "The Hungarian Revolt," in *The Hungarian Revolt*, ed. Melvin J. Lasky (New York: Frederick A. Praeger, Inc., 1957), pp. 126–127.

with a rifle appear in the deserted street. He took up a position in one of the drives and, taking careful aim, began shooting out the street lamps. The lamps went out one by one and darkness enveloped the street. What prompted the marksman to do this? Just hooliganism? Hardly. I think he was one of the bright sparks of the reactionary underground who wanted to create confusion and chaos in the city. Quite soon afterwards there were flashes of gunfire and sounds of battle and we saw wrecked and burning buildings in the streets of Budapest, overturned tram-cars and other vehicles. Firing would die down and then flare up again. Hostile elements were aiming at paralysing the city's life but the workers of Budapest were repelling the rebels. Detachments of armed workers tried to restore order in the streets and prevent looting. In many places, including the area around our hotel, workers' patrols were posted. . . .

One member of our hotel staff, a middle-aged man with grey hair, told us: "Our workers cannot have had a hand in this looting and rioting. It is fascism raising its head." And that is what it was. The counter-revolutionary underground was in action in Budapest. Fascist reactionary elements had arrived there from abroad. The hostile venture was gathering momentum and the Hungarian Government asked the USSR Government for aid. In response to this request Soviet military units stationed in Hungary under the Warsaw Treaty entered Budapest to help to restore order. The overwhelming majority of Hungarians welcomed this move in the hope that life in the city would quickly return to normal. I myself saw in one street how the people were welcoming the Soviet tanks.

One Hungarian, a member of the hotel staff, described the following incident to us. Firemen-volunteers, absolutely unarmed, were putting out a fire in one of the public buildings. Suddenly, from a small house opposite, shots were fired by fascist louts who opened fire on the unarmed firemen. Several of them fell. Our tank was stationed in the street. The tankmen immediately aimed their gun at the house where the bandits were entrenched. This was sufficient to make them run into a side street. Several firemen ran up to the tank and shook hands with the tankmen. This episode gives a good testimony of the attitude of the Hungarians towards the Soviet troops. However, reaction did not cease its activities. When we walked along some of the streets we saw that the walls of houses were thickly covered with counter-revolutionary posters. . . .

When Soviet troops began withdrawing from Budapest an unbridled White Terror started in the Hungarian capital. We Soviet tourists recall this time with horror. It is difficult to describe the chaos which reigned in the city where public buildings were destroyed, shops looted, and where crowds of armed bandits, obviously fascists, walked along the streets committing bestial murders in broad daylight. I shall never forget what I saw with my own eyes. I think it was on 30 or 31 October. A man in a sports suit walked along the Lenin Boulevard. He might have been one of those who tried to restore order in the city. Several armed ruffians wearing counter-revolutionary tricolours ran up to him. A horrible inhuman cry was heard. A whole crowd of bandits appeared from somewhere. I was unable to see what they were doing with their victim, but in a few minutes he was hanging on a nearby tree with an eye gouged out and his face slashed with knives.

Some time ago I read how the fascists in Germany burnt progressive literature on bonfires. We saw similar things . . . A group of some hooligans looted and set fire to the House of Books. Thousands and thousands of books were smouldering in the muddy street. We were there, witnesses of this barbarity. The works of Chekhov, Shakespeare, Tolstoi, Pushkin, and other famous authors were lying in the mud, black smoke rising. We saw an old man who lifted a few books, then carefully wiped the mud with his sleeve, pressed them to his breast and walked slowly away. Many people did the same.

In the Hotel "Peace" the atmosphere in those days was extremely tense. The counter-revolutionaries tore the red star from the front of the hotel and trod it underfoot on the pavement. We were told that the Hotel "Peace" from now on would be called Hotel "Britannia." The person who told us about it looked around and added quietly: "It doesn't matter. It will only be temporary."

More than once we were witnesses of acts which manifested the friendly attitude of the Hungarians towards the Soviet people. This friendly attitude was felt by us Soviet people, when we were leaving Budapest . . . In small groups of two or three people we made our way along the devastated streets towards the Danube in order to board a Red Cross steamer. We were accompanied by a worker . . . a young girl. She led us from one cross-road to another, fearlessly seeking the safest way. At the pier we heartily embraced her. She said: "Someone in the West wants us to pull their chestnuts out of the fire. Don't believe them, dear friends. We Hungarians are for socialism and we are with you." When we were in Czechoslovakia on our way home, we learned that the counter-revolution in Hungary was routed and that life was becoming normal in the country. Now we are at home in Moscow. We shall not forget that Hungarian girl who said that the Hungarians were for socialism and that they were with us. . . .

Reading IV: How the Historian Asks Questions

Readings I–III were concerned with the way historians develop and validate hypotheses with factual evidence. But how does a historian develop a hypothesis in the first place? And how does he go about the complicated and time-consuming process of searching for facts to support his hypotheses? How does he know, for example, that he has not overlooked some really vital possibility in a complex historical situation? If he has overlooked something vital, the explanation he has tried to develop will certainly fall short of the truth.

Historians deal with very complicated developments involving millions of people and great spans of time. Hence, they must be particularly careful to develop procedures that will help them cover the large number of possibilities inherent in any historical situation. Most historians work through a set of questions that often helps to reveal the information which has a bearing on an issue. Knowing which questions to ask becomes a vital matter. No simple checklist can cover the enormous range of historical possibilities. Every historian must always be ready to ask new questions, questions that he has never asked before, if he expects his frame of reference to expand. Still, having a few questions in mind that have proved fruitful in the past when beginning an historical investigation often prevents a scholar from overlooking a vital point.

In Reading IV, Carl G. Gustavson, a contemporary historian, explains his procedure for discovering the causes of the Protestant Reformation. He is concerned with both the development of hypotheses and ways of uncovering facts that bear on these hypotheses. Research on the causes of the Reformation, one of the most complicated of historical problems, requires particular attention to the rules of clear thinking. As you read, think about the following questions:

1) What questions did Gustavson ask? why these rather than some others? Do these questions give you a clue about what types of analytical questions are most fruitful in an historical inquiry?

2) Do you think that all historians would compile a list of questions very much like Gustavson's? why or why not?

3) Will Gustavson's questions help him to develop an hypothesis about the causes of the Reformation? If he asked different questions, might he end up with a different hypothesis?

I. THE CAUSES OF THE REFORMATION*

Carl G. Gustavson

Quite obviously the immediate cause for the Reformation is to be found in the activity of Luther between 1517 and 1521, although the selection of a specific event may bring differences of opinion . . . Identifying the initial spark, however, by no means explains the enormous extent of the conflagration which followed.

Luther's ninety-five theses immediately became the best seller of that day. Great crowds gathered to applaud him as he went to the Diet of Worms. If we can decide why he suddenly experienced this popularity, we may also gain some idea of the reason for his success. First of all, anyone who champions a cause and defies authority will attract a crowd of supporters, if only for the

---

* Reprinted from Carl G. Gustavson, *A Preface to History*, pp. 56–64, with omissions. Copyright © 1955 by McGraw-Hill. Used by permission of McGraw-Hill Book Company, Inc.

sake of the show. . . . He was hitting out at unpopular figures, always a good way to attract a following. The friar of Wittenberg was a German, a son of the people, courageously talking up to pope and emperor, speaking for the common people and expressing what many of them felt.

Could any deeper reasons be at work that produced the quick acclaim for Luther's stand? Could it be that such a sudden blaze was generated because the inflammable materials had already been gathered by others? Had there been any earlier instances of men who had preached the same viewpoint as this reformer? . . . If so, this must indicate a general trend of the time in the direction of the reform which the Protestants were to take.

The career of John Hus of Prague is apt to come to mind. His life story bears several marked resemblances to that of Luther, and his proposals were very similar to those of his successors; there was a major difference however— he was burned for his temerity. A whole century before the Lutheran Reformation some of its principles were already widely approved, as witness the obstinate refusal of the Bohemians to give up the reforms of Hus. . . . Other reformers had also preceded Luther: Peter Waldo, Wyclif, Savonarola, to mention the most prominent. Nor should the criticism of the Church by such writers as Erasmus and Valla be forgotten. Evidences of Protestant ideas appear everywhere in Western Europe during the preceding century. The monasteries were fair game for many of the leading writers of the time, the papal control of the Church roused voices in protest, and the financial dues were found irksome. Consequently, the historian may fairly assume that whatever the reasons for the Reformation were, they were operative to a considerable degree long before Luther. The Reformation could, conceivably, have begun in 1415, and it might have been postponed beyond 1520.

One point to note is that the criticism of the Church usually did not carry with it a threat to leave the institution. It was criticized, its officials castigated, its practices and policies assailed in the same spirit in which Americans treat their governmental institutions. The object was reform, not separation, the attacks representing no more a desire to destroy the Church than we expect to abolish Congress. Some people might dislike papal authority in much the same way as some Americans suspect the power of a strong President. When Luther appeared at Worms, he had no expectation of founding a separate church, and in fact he may have gone to the diet with a lurking hope of converting Charles V to his own viewpoint. Had this happened, a sweeping reform within the Church could have resulted and the universal Church remained united at least for a longer time. Even after the break had occurred, the Lutheran and Anglican churches insisted that it was the Roman Catholics who had abandoned the original idea of the Church, while they themselves were simply purifying it. . . .

Luther dared to go to Worms. Powerful reasons must have driven him to risk the fate of Hus by making this journey. The assurance that his own prince, the Elector of Saxony, was on his side and the boisterous plaudits of the multitudes undoubtedly emboldened him, but beyond all this was an inner necessity, a personal conviction of a spiritual mission, that forced him to speak his mind. Luther's actions were indubitably born of motives other than personal ambition or opportunism: biographies of the reformer fully document the gradual development of his convictions from the time he became a friar until he stood in full defiance against the existent ecclesiastical authorities. This must be accounted as an instance where spiritual force acted as a primary impulse in history.

Only a rugged, roughhewn, obstinate man could have shouldered his way to success in the circumstances—the looming figure of Luther makes the personal factor important in the causation of the Reformation. Unless the odds are too great, the victory is likely to go to the side inspired by genuine zeal for a cause. Historical movements, however much they are impelled by economic and social factors, after all are carried through by men. Their states of mind are important. Even Luther, however, could have accomplished little more than propagate his ideas if he had not found many others in the same mood. Had Luther alone, or a small circle of disciples only, held Protestant ideas, no social force of sufficient magnitude to create historical events would have existed. When tens of thousands, however, were possessed of the same general outlook, the scene was set for action, and it took only Luther's words and actions to precipitate the formation of a spiritual force of enormous extent and potency. We are dealing with a large-scale example of a social force of a spiritual nature such as was described in the preceding chapter. In time, also, the Reformation stimulated an equally powerful reaction to it in Catholicism, a renewed spiritual vigor on the Catholic side sufficient to halt the European expansion of Protestantism.

The circumstances were ready for the man, and his religious zeal furnished a focal point for the hitherto diffused causes for the Reformation. One may legitimately question if any one single force, albeit as powerful as this one, could in itself have altered the course of history. From our perspective, at least, a number of social forces seem to converge upon the developing events and carry them forward.

We have seen gunpowder and the better ocean-going vessels make possible the expansion of the European into other parts of the world. The printing press, another technological advance, served as a tool of incalculable importance in the Reformation. Someone might argue very plausibly that no Reformation could have occurred had it not been for the invention of the printing press. Without this method of spreading ideas, the Lutheran doctrines could not have been disseminated so rapidly, and, if support had not quickly manifested itself, the emperor and Church might have succeeded in suppressing the movement. The press also aided the reformers by undermining the claim of the Church to pose as the custodian of final truth, since it was now becoming possible for more persons to acquire a copy of the Bible.

Social forces emerging from economic motives, powerful as they were, must have exercised an important influence on these events. . . . Especially would the growing middle class deplore the drag on productivity caused by the clerical possession of land, the numerous church festivals, and the presumed idleness of the monks. With their ideals of thrift and industry, the middle class found many church habits irritating. Luther appealed to these feelings, with violent and exaggerated words, in his *Address to the Christian Nobility of the German Nation:* "What has brought us Germans to such a pass that we have to suffer this robbery and this destruction of our property by the pope? . . . Do we still wonder why princes, cities, foundations, convents, and people grow poor? We should rather wonder that we have anything left to eat." . . .

The thought must occur to one that the incipient restlessness should have been crushed by the imperial regime. Why did Luther "get away with it" when others before him had failed? The truth is that Charles V was in a dilemma. New on the throne, he was uncertain of his support and would hesitate before alienating his German subjects. Luther's own prince, the Elector of Saxony, was friendly to the reformers and possessed the force and prestige to raise a rebellion. The loud acclaim of the friar must have alarmed Charles and dissuaded him from a highly unpopular move. He undoubtedly underestimated the potentialities of the movement, the more so since he had grave political problems to grapple with elsewhere. The Ottoman Turks were approaching the far-flung borders of his realm, and Charles needed German unity in order to meet this threat. All in all, "the king *was* weak," not so much because of his own personality as in his inheritance of an enfeebled government from his predecessors.

The Crown was one of the institutions which should have suppressed the rebellion. The other was the Church itself. After many centuries as the universal Church of Western Europe, it had undergone both a loss of positive vitality and a diminishing strength in comparison with new emerging forces . . . The Renaissance was having a debilitating spiritual effect upon the papacy; popes who were using spiritual resources for temporal ends were blunting their own swords. Having centralized the Church, they failed to live up to their responsibilities. By making the papacy synonymous with the Church, they drew upon the Church itself a shower of invective. The fact that many believed the Church to be corrupt shook the all-important allegiance of the great masses of the people. . . .

During the fourteenth and fifteenth centuries, national kings continued to add to their power . . . The Catholic Church was faced with its perennial problem, how to keep its international character although threatened by national feelings and provincial attachments. . . .

In the northern countries, a sense of nationalism was a strong factor in the break with Rome. In Germany, where other national aspirations went unsatisfied, this was particularly true. The Reformation passed into effect in Sweden coincident with the overthrow of Danish rule. The English struggle against Spain would tend to associate the state church with national existence in that country. The native language was substituted for Latin in the churches of these regions. In nearly all instances, the advent of the Reformation brought added power and wealth to the kings or territorial princes. The institutional factor is a powerful one in the causation of the Reformation; one institution, the Church, was losing ground to another institution, the national monarchy, and the spiritual crisis precipitated by Luther offered the territorial princes of Germany and the kings of northern Europe a splendid opportunity to establish state control over the Church.

The foregoing outline, which by no means exhausts the possibilities of causation in the Reformation, does provide a check list of factors likely to be important in such a phenomenon. When a student is faced with a problem of this nature, a few general questions are of great assistance in analyzing the situation. When these are "tried on for size," some will immediately suggest causes, while others may have little relevance. The following nine should prove helpful: (1) What was the immediate cause for the event? (2) Had there been a background of agitation for the principles victorious during this episode? (3) Were personalities involved on either side whose strengths or weaknesses may have helped to determine the outcome of the struggle? (4) Were any new and potent ideas stimulating the loyalty of a considerable number of people? (5) How did the economic groups line up on the issue? (6) Were religious forces active? (7) Did any new technological developments influence the situation? (8) Can the events be partially explained by weakened or strengthened institutions? (9) Was the physical environment itself a factor in the situation? (It will be noticed that questions four through eight relate to various social forces already enumerated.) A systematic analysis of a problem of causation with the aid of these questions will ensure that all the major historical factors have been taken into consideration. . . .

One warning needs to be added. The foregoing represents an attempt to provide a systematic approach to causation for the beginner. Reasoning, however, cannot be effective without the facts. A student is using facts from a textbook, class notes, and whatever other reading is provided. The historian, while using a basically similar approach, cannot be satisfied until he finds genuine evidence upon which to base his conclusions. There is only one way to achieve this: go to the evidence itself, which is made up of the records of that age. A reading of a few of Luther's pamphlets is apt to be revealing. The historian will want to read the opinions of many people who were contemporaries of Luther and Calvin. He will examine the declarations from the Roman Catholic side of the controversy. Other factors must be investigated. If he carefully examines the record in a spirit of humility, prepared to recognize tenacious reality rather than what he wishes to find, he is then prepared to formulate a worthwhile interpretation of the events.

Reading V: How the Historian Deals with Mind Set

In Reading IV we studied the way in which a historian developed a hypothesis by asking analytical questions. Gustavson was trying to discover the causes of the Protestant Reformation. He assumed that a number of factors were at work; no major historical development is ever caused by only one event but by a combination of many. His questions were designed to reveal whether or not some of the more important causes of change in other situations were involved in this one. He conceded that all the questions he listed might not be appropriate to every topic and that an alert historian would always have to watch for unique causes if he hoped to make an accurate interpretation.

Asking analytical questions seems to be a simple matter. It is not. Everyone is conditioned by his culture, by the knowledge, beliefs, customs, and skills he acquires as a member of society. Two men from different cultures may perceive the same events quite differently. What may strike a man from one culture as particularly important may seem commonplace and not worth noting to someone from another society. A culture can give a person a mind set, attitudes toward life that condition the interpretation he will develop.

The excerpt below illustrates this point. It was written about A.D. 1000 by a monk in the monastery of St. Benedict at Fleury in France. This story was part of a two-volume work on the miracles of St. Benedict, for whom the monastery was named. As you read think about the following questions:

1) What really happened to Herbert? Was he struck by St. Benedict or did he have a heart attack? Why do you think so?
2) Why did Herbert and the monk think that St. Benedict had intervened?
3) What factors account for the interpretation of history that we find in this excerpt?

I. A MIRACLE OF THE EARLIEST DAYS OF FEUDALISM*

The castle of Sully, which is three miles from Fleury, was in the possession of a certain Herbert. Our venerable abbot Richard had given this Herbert as a benefice some lands that were church property. But Herbert, being by no means content with these, by an act of scandalous boldness seized the remaining lands reserved there for the benefit of the monks. So the abbot and the

* Translated from the original Latin in *Les Miracles de Saint Benoit*, ed. E. de Certain (Paris, 1858), pp. 107–109; Paul L. Ward, trans.

members of the monastery go all together to him, asking him to take to heart the good faith he pledged to them by oath, and to cease occupying their possessions. Since he pays little attention to their pleas, they proceed to lay the mournful burden of their complaint before King Lother and Duke Hugh, but make no progress in those quarters either. Then on their own they begin again with the man of bad faith, praying that he take pity on them and halt his oppression of them. Since he nonetheless averts his ears, they come back to his castle. All in all, for practically the whole period of Lent in that year, they poured forth their prayers of tribulation to God, amid solemn litanies, beating at the same time two pieces of brass, in order by the sound to invite the help of all who hear.

Meanwhile that man Herbert, continuing in his evil defiance and daily adding worse deeds to his bad behavior, on a certain night set out with some of his men into the district of the Gatinais. And since, according to the word of Truth, "He who walks in darkness offends, for the light is not in him," if at the least he lacks the light of virtues and is hemmed in with the shadows of vices, an inpious man tries to hide himself and his actions under the added obscurity of mundane night; but though he escapes as far as he may the gaze of human eyes, he is quite unable to flee the eyes of God, which look down on the ways of men and observe all their steps. Indeed, as the blessed Job says, with the Lord there are no shadows or shades of death, in which those who do iniquity may hide. So likewise from this impious Herbert his own light was taken, and he himself was suddenly snatched away, an ending that was long overdue. For as he, seated on the back of his horse, was choosing his way carefully with his men, all surrounded by an evening mist, suddenly he saw beside him a person in monk's clothing bearing the marks of holy wounds, whose whole covering gleamed with an ethereal brightness—as he himself told his men afterwards. And then he let out a horrible cry, for he was hit between the shoulders by a staff which the figure seemed to have in hand; and then the vision disappeared before his eyes. The riders around him, struck by the horror of his cry, try solicitously to find out what has happened to him. "Saint Benedict," he tells them, "just now standing by me, struck me a powerful blow, from which I feel now severe pain. But you faithful fellow-soldiers, follow the path back and take me to my home, and from there hurry to the tomb of the glorious saint to demand urgent forgiveness for me." They followed his orders and took him back to where they had started. Almost on the threshold of his home, in the arms of his servants, he gave up his soul; his devoted vassals, going to the monks of St. Benedict, reported what had happened and asked that the dead body be received for burial. The monks, although fearful of the indignation of the abbot, who at the moment was by chance absent, agreed and buried the body. Although they in part were quietly pleased, yet with pious compassion they did pity the man who had died, for in the first flower of his youth he was now deprived of the gift of this life and also unable to make up for the wickedness of his ways.

Language and Mind Set

Even the language a man uses may affect his interpretation of events. Each of us learns to describe his world in words. Some languages are much richer than others. Languages adapted to a particular environment often have a wide choice of words that another tongue lacks entirely. For example, Eskimos have a number of words for snow, each one with a special meaning. We have only one. This difference in language can cause different interpretations of history and different descriptions of the same events.

The following passage may make this matter clear. As you read it, think about the following questions:

1) How would a Navaho describe a Renaissance painting or a colorful costume?
2) How would we describe the same painting or the same costume in our own language?
3) How can language influence our interpretation of history?

II. LANGUAGE, THOUGHT, AND CULTURE*

Paul Henle

It would seem then to be consistent with what we know of mental set on other grounds to assume that the world appears different to a person using one vocabulary than it would to a person using another. The use of language would call attention to different aspects of the environment in the one case than it would in the other. Numerous illustrations of this sort may be given. The Navaho, for example, possess color terms corresponding roughly to our 'white,' 'red,' and 'yellow' but none which are equivalent to our 'black,' 'grey,' 'brown,' 'blue,' and 'green.' They have two terms corresponding to 'black,' one denoting the black of darkness, the other the black of such objects as coal. Our 'grey' and 'brown,' however, correspond to a single term in their language and likewise our 'blue' and 'green.' As far as vocabulary is concerned, they divide the spectrum into segments different from ours. It would seem probable that on many occasions of casual perception they would not bother to notice whether an object were brown or grey, and that they would merely avoid discussions as to whether a shade of color in a trying light was blue or green, but they would not even make the distinction.

This example must not be taken as showing that the Navahos are incapable of making color distinctions which are familiar to us. They do not suffer from

* From Paul Henle, *Language, Thought, and Culture* (Ann Arbor, Mich.: University of Michigan Press, 1958), pp. 7–8. Reprinted with the permission of The University of Michigan Press.

a peculiar form of color-blindness any more than we do since we lack words for the two sorts of black which they distinguish. The point is rather that their vocabulary tends to let them leave other distinctions unnoticed which we habitually make.

Culture and Mind Set

Today few Americans believe that miracles happen every day. This is not a mind set that plays an important part in our interpretation of events. But political attitudes may. Most Americans and most Russians are convinced that their own way of life is superior to any other. In school they learn an interpretation of history that probably conditions the way in which they perceive events. The different attitudes some of them have are clear in the following short passages.

III.
The Communist Manifesto

The history of all hitherto existing society is the history of class struggles. Freeman and slave, patrician and plebian, lord and serf, guild master and journeyman, in a word, oppressor and oppressed, stood in constant opposition to one another, carried on an uninterrupted, now hidden, now open fight, that each time ended either in the revolutionary reconstitution of society at large, or in the common ruin of the contending classes.

The Declaration of Independence

When in the Course of human events, it becomes necessary for one people to dissolve the political bands, which have connected them with another, and to assume among the powers of the earth, the separate and equal station to which the Laws of Nature and of Nature's God entitle them, a decent respect to the opinions of mankind requires that they should declare the causes which impel them to the separation. We hold these truths to be self-evident, that all men are created equal, that they are endowed by their Creator with certain unalienable Rights, that among these are Life, Liberty and the pursuit of Happiness.—That to secure these rights, Governments are instituted among Men, deriving their just powers from the consent of the governed,—That whenever any Form of Government becomes destructive of these ends, it is the Right of the People to alter or to abolish it, and to institute new Government, laying its foundation on such principles and organizing its powers in such form, as to them shall seem most likely to effect their safety and Happiness.

Do you think that a man who had been taught that the *Communist Manifesto* correctly interpreted the nature of the world would be likely to perceive events in the same way as a man who believed in the Declaration of Independence? Might mind sets like these have influenced the two men who reported events in the Hungarian Revolution about which you read in Reading III?

Reading VI: What Is History?

For the past five days we have been studying the way in which historians investigate the past. As you read and as you discussed the readings in class, you should have been developing your own interpretation of the nature of historical investigations. If you have been thoughtful, you should have already developed your own definition of history and your own conception of historical method.

For tomorrow you are to write a paper of no more than three hundred words, in which you analyze the way you would approach an historical problem. Suppose you wanted to determine the causes of the Peloponnesian wars, which were fought between Athens and Sparta near the end of the fifth century B.C. Assume that you know nothing about Athens or Sparta except that they were city states in Greece. How would you go about investigating this problem?

CHAPTER 10 Lesson Plans

All teachers are supposed to make lesson plans. Some claim that a group of questions stored in loose order in their heads is good enough. Most concede that the most important of these questions, along with a few objectives, should be committed to paper. A few consistently make elaborate plans, sometimes pages long, to guide them. Although standard forms of lesson plans have circulated for years, there is no consensus about the form that an ideal lesson plan should take.

Inductive-teaching techniques require carefully developed teaching strategies. A lecture or any other form of expository teaching solely for knowledge objectives places fewer requirements on the teacher. If the teacher wishes to communicate only a body of facts and generalizations, and if he assumes that children will learn what they hear, the teaching problem is easy. But if a teacher juggles three types of objectives at once—knowledge, abilities and skills, and objectives in the affective domain—he must know precisely what he intends to communicate if he hopes to succeed. Precise objectives become even more important than usual when a teacher employs a discussion method. He must be particularly careful if he plans to use nondirective techniques, which afford the maximum opportunity for student discovery.

The problem of setting objectives for a lesson plan parallels the difficulties that face teachers as they map objectives for an entire course of study. Course objectives must be attainable. As a general rule, it seems even more important to set specific, attainable goals for each lesson, goals that can be evaluated both while the class discussion is going on and through an examination at a later date. If goals are too general or for some other reason cannot be evaluated, teaching may well be in vain. At least, no teacher will be able to prove otherwise.

The two volumes in the *Taxonomy of Educational Objectives* contain condensed versions of the classification systems for educational objectives that

175

have been worked out by the authors. These lists of objectives are excellent guides for teachers who wish to set attainable objectives for daily lessons. Teachers should plan lessons with these lists of objectives before them until they become so skilled in their use that they need no longer refer to them. The test items in the taxonomies provide examples of types of questions teachers can ask on examinations to determine whether or not their objectives have been reached. The numbers preceding objectives in the following lesson plans provide keys to the appropriate objectives in the taxonomies (see the appendixes to the readings in Chapters 2 and 3).

In addition to statements of objectives, lesson plans usually contain two additional elements. The first is a statement of the materials to be used to accomplish the objectives. The second is an account of the teaching strategy to be employed. There is no "right" way to put teaching strategy down on paper. Moreover, inductive teaching requires a somewhat loose set of directions, because what a teacher does will be influenced in large part by student responses to questions. In addition, different sorts of materials require different teaching strategies. Lesson plans for the sort of material described by Byron Massialas and Jack Zevin in the reading in Chapter 16 are probably the most difficult of all to structure tightly.

Chapter 10 consists of a statement of unit objectives and lesson plans for five of the six readings found in Chapter 9. They were written by John M. Good, a co-director of the Carnegie Tech Social Studies Curriculum Development Center. Your teacher may wish to show you classroom films (available from Holt, Rinehart and Winston, Inc.) showing these materials being taught from the lesson plans. He may also wish to criticize the form of the plans, particularly the fact that no objectives in the affective domain are specified for each day. As you read these plans and review the material on which they are based, think about the following questions:

1) Are the stated objectives attainable within a single class period? Is any attempt made to determine whether or not students have attained the objectives?

2) Are these lesson plans designed for discovery teaching as Bruner uses the term? Are they primarily expository devices? What is the role of the teacher in these plans? Does he field questions which students bring up, tell students what the mode of inquiry is, or lead students to search for the major generalizations he wants them to learn from each lesson?

MAJOR UNIT OBJECTIVES

John M. Good

KNOWLEDGE

1) Knowledge of terminology. (1.11) To know the meaning of technical terms such as frame of reference, hypothesis, fact, analytical question, mind set, and history.
2) Knowledge of methodology. (1.25) To know the major elements in the methodology of professional historians.

ABILITIES AND SKILLS

1) Analysis of elements. (4.10) To be able to recognize unstated assumptions and to distinguish facts from hypotheses.
2) Analysis of relationships. (4.00) To be able to determine whether evidence supports an hypothesis.
3) Production of a unique communication. (5.10) To be able to report verbally and in writing the results of the process of synthesizing information learned over a period of time.
4) Derivation of a set of abstract relationships. (5.30) To be able to develop hypotheses.
5) Evaluating in terms of internal evidence. (6.10) To be able to assess the degree to which statements in an article are factually accurate using internal evidence.

THE AFFECTIVE DOMAIN

1) Willingness to receive. (1.2) Willingness to listen carefully when others speak.
2) Willingness to respond. (2.12) Willingness to answer questions and to volunteer information.
3) Preference for a value. (3.2) Willingness to examine several viewpoints on a controversial issue in order to form an opinion.

Lesson Plan: Reading I

How the Historian Classifies Information

Subject Objectives:	To know that the classification of information is a function of a person's frame of reference. To know that a person's frame of reference is a product of his entire life experience.

Skill Objectives:	Analysis of elements (4.10). To know that a classification scheme grows out of unstated assumptions about the world.
	Derivation of a set of abstract relationships (5.30). To develop hypotheses about the frame of reference leading to three classification schemes in the lesson.
Materials:	Reading I.
	Transparencies 1a, 1b, 1c, and 2.

What are we going to be doing in the first six days of the course, according to the introductory paragraphs?

Get the students to state the problem involved in the first unit of work. The students should realize that they are trying to find out how the historian proceeds so that for the rest of the course they will have a method for disciplined inquiry into the past.

GROUP WORK: Divide the class into as many groups as are manageable and ask each group to decide three ways of categorizing the eighteen creatures in the reading. After a few minutes, have each group report on the categories they chose.

This exercise will make clear the students' own frame of reference that will be contrasted with the teacher's frame of reference as revealed in the transparencies that follow. The students will probably make biological classifications for the eighteen terms.

What do all of your categories have in common?

The students should realize that their classifications stem from the biological sciences. This frame of reference can later be contrasted with the linguistic frame of reference of the teacher.

PROJECT TRANSPARENCIES 1a, 1b, 1c: These are my classifications. What do my categories have in common?
How are they different from yours?

This exercise is designed to get the students to contrast their classification scheme with the teacher's. On the transparencies, the terms are classified by number of letters in a word, number of syllables in a word, and whether a term has two words ("collie dog") or one ("shark").

INTRODUCE TERM: "Frame of reference."

Once the teacher is satisfied that the students see the basis of both schemes of classification, he should introduce the term "frame of reference," which students should be asked to define. They should indicate that the two classification schemes discussed stemmed from different frames of reference.

What does frame of reference have to do with history?

Students should see that different frames of reference will determine the historian's classification of facts, which, in turn, will influence the way in which he interprets history.

PROJECT TRANSPARENCY 2: Have students classify the names of the political leaders.
Where did you get your frame of reference to classify these men?

This exercise will show students that their education partially determines their frame of reference. They should recognize that their scheme of classification came from what they learned in the ninth grade course in comparative political systems.

Where else does one get his frame of reference?

The aim of this question is to get the students to see that <u>everything in one's background</u> influences one's frame of reference—conversation, family, school, experience, church, and so on. After the students have suggested several sources, the teacher may wish to ask, "Is there anything in your past experience that has not helped shape your frame of reference?"

Why do you think we have been learning about frame of reference in a history course?

Students need to recognize that historical interpretation depends upon the historian's frame of reference. His classification of facts and his <u>selection of facts</u> depend upon the way in which he views the world.

Lesson Plan: Reading II

HOW THE HISTORIAN DEVELOPS AND SUPPORTS A HYPOTHESIS

Subject Objectives:

To know that historians develop hypotheses as starting points for investigations. To know that historians support and revise hypotheses with factual evidence derived from documents and artifacts.

Skill Objectives:

Analysis of elements (4.10). To know the difference between a fact and a hypothesis.
Analysis of relationships (4.20). To determine when evidence supports a hypothesis.
Derivation of a set of abstract relationships

	(5.30). To develop hypotheses about the Kensington Stone.
Materials:	Reading II.
	Recording by Theodore Bikel, "Digging the Weans," from *An Actor's Holiday.*
	Student Handout: "The Stone Is a Fraud," excerpted from *American Heritage,* X, 3 (April 1959), 101–104.

What did we decide in yesterday's class?

Have students summarize the findings of the previous lesson and develop the relationship between frame of reference and the historian's mode of inquiry.

What was the major issue that this article dealt with?

This question should fix in the student's mind the basic methodological problem dealt with in the reading. The students might respond that the author was trying to prove that the Kensington Stone was authentic. The teacher should then ask for a definition of the problem in more general terms: historians try to validate hypotheses.

Have a student read the first paragraph.

Historians begin investigations with questions. This procedural matter should be discussed.

How did the historian begin? What was the next step?

Historians develop tentative answers to their questions. The students will perhaps answer that the next step was to find information to answer the question, but the teacher should indicate, by having the students carefully analyze the steps in the article, that a tentative answer to the question was assumed and then information to corroborate that answer was sought.

assumption

INTRODUCE TERM: "Hypothesis"

When the students have realized that the historians began with a tentative answer, the teacher should introduce the term "hypothesis" and ask the students to define it.

What hypothesis did the author discuss first in the article?

The hypothesis that the stone was a fraud.

What evidence did he give for this hypothesis?

Get the students to give the specific pieces of evidence used to support this hypothesis and list them on the board.

What hypothesis did he discuss next?	That the stone was a genuine relic.
How did he support his second hypothesis?	He showed that some of the original evidence used to "prove" that the stone was a forgery was inaccurate. He also cited new evidence not previously discussed. Get the students to give all of this evidence and list it on the board.
How do historians validate hypotheses?	The two previous exercises illustrate that historians search for facts with which to support hypotheses. Ask questions in several ways to be sure that students know this conclusion.
Do you think he proved the hypothesis?	Most of the students should feel that the stone's authenticity was validated. This will set up the recording that should throw some doubts in their minds.
PLAY RECORDING: "Digging the Weans." What do you think the message of this bit of fun is for us?	The tape pokes fun at historians and archaeologists who build up elaborate hypotheses on the basis of a few fragments of evidence. The question is designed to see if the students comprehend this point.
Now how many think the stone is authentic?	Many students should now have some doubts about the stone's authenticity.
PASS OUT HANDOUT: "The Stone Is a Fraud."	This handout argues that the stone is a fake.
How does this author prove the other hypothesis?	The students should realize from the handout that its author uses facts to support his hypothesis, but that he also examines the frame of reference of the historian who believes the stone is real.
Can we ever be certain that a hypothesis is proved beyond a shadow of a doubt? Can we be more certain as we collect more evidence?	The question is designed to alert students to the idea that no historical hypothesis can ever be completely validated. We can be more certain of its accuracy, however, as we collect more evidence.

Lesson Plan: Reading III

HOW THE HISTORIAN DECIDES WHAT IS FACT

Subject Objectives:	To know how historians determine what is factually accurate by seeking corroborative statements from people with different frames of reference and by analyzing the validity of statements through both external and internal evidence.
Skill Objectives:	Analysis of elements: (4.10). To recognize unstated assumptions and to distinguish between statements of fact, generalizations based on facts, and hypotheses.
	Analysis of relationships: (4.20). To determine whether factual evidence supports a particular hypothesis.
	Evaluating in terms of internal evidence (6.10). To know by the use of internal evidence whether the facts reported in a document should be accepted as accurate.
Materials:	Reading III.
	Transparency 3.

What have we learned about how historians work from our previous two lessons?

Students should summarize what they have learned so far.

From what you say, it would seem important for historians to get facts from sources in order to support their hypotheses. As historians from Mars, where did you get your facts?

This question challenges students to draw a connection between the first two lessons and this one. Students should realize that they are dependent upon documents or artifacts that are preserved from the past for the facts they obtain.

GROUP WORK: Divide the class into groups and ask each group to select three facts or generalizations from the two documents. Have a student from each group report to the entire class.

Have a student record the statements on the blackboard.

Why did you decide that these were accurate statements?

The goal of this question is to get the students to establish general criteria for a true statement. They probably will decide that statements are more probable when accounts from two different frames of reference agree on something.

PROJECT TRANSPARENCY 3: Are these statements accurate?
Where did I get them?
Why did I select facts about the United States and the Soviet Union?

This transparency includes facts that can be inferred from internal evidence in the documents..They are facts about the United States and the U.S.S.R. The exercise is set up to show students how they can learn information about authors from internal evidence in a document.

How can we decide what statements are accurate when we read records from the past?

Students should agree that statements are probably accurate when two people with different frames of reference agree about something. They should also agree that we can infer information about the authors of articles and the kinds of societies in which they live from documents. For example, the existence of these papers implies that the United States and the Soviet Union had several characteristics in common: their people were literate, they had highly developed technologies, and they had developed different ideologies.

Suppose I had only one account, how would I determine what is fact, then?

This question is included to extend the students' thinking beyond the criteria already established. They should suggest other ways of determining the accuracy of statements, namely the analysis of the language of the document to determine objectivity. (Here a look at the reference to Soviet tanks in the last sentence of the second paragraph can serve as an example of how writers can reveal their frame of reference by the way they write.) The teacher and students may wish to suggest other criteria, such as the proximity of the author to the event—was he an eye witness or wasn't he?

What criteria have we established for deciding whether or not a statement is accurate?

Students should be encouraged to summarize the criteria decided upon in the day's lesson. The teacher should see that each student gets the criteria written down in his notes.

Lesson Plan: Reading IV

How the Historian Asks Analytical Questions

Subject Objectives:	To know the kinds of ~~analytical questions~~ that historians ask. To know that the questions that a particular historian asks are a function of his frame of reference.
Skill Objectives:	Derivation of a set of abstract relationships (5.30). To be able to develop a hypothesis through the use of analytical questions.
Materials:	Reading IV.

What have we learned, so far, about how the historian works?

Again the class should begin with an attempt to summarize what has been learned and relate it to the major issue of the unit.

What did you learn about how the historian works from this reading?

The purpose of this question is to see if the students understood the major methodological point of the reading—namely, that the historian asks analytical questions in the course of his investigations.

Do you think the questions Gustavson asks are important?

The aim is to get the students to commit themselves to the position that Gustavson asks important questions in order to set up the writing exercise.

WRITING EXERCISE: Since you seem to agree that the questions Gustavson asks are important, let's see if you can remember them. Write them all down on a sheet of paper. What questions do you have?

Let the students write down the questions to see how many they can remember from Gustavson's list. Have the students report what they wrote down and have the other students write down the ones they missed. Have them write all nine of Gustavson's questions into their notes.

What answers does Gustavson give to these questions?

Go through the questions one by one and find out what answers Gustavson found to his questions. This will provide the basis for answering the next question in the lesson plan.

Why do you think Gustavson asked these particular questions?

The students should look at the answers to develop a general reason for asking such questions. They should see that the questions are designed to provide direction to the investigation and to keep the historian from overlooking data.

Can you think of any other questions you might ask? Would you ask all these questions for every investigation? Can you apply the questions to another event?	These two questions aim to get the students to develop their own questions for studying an event in the past. As students apply their additional questions and Gustavson's questions to another event, such as the American Revolution or the Civil War, they should recognize the help that questions give to historical investigations. Even if the question does not prove to be fruitful, students should realize that it is important to ask it anyway to make sure nothing is overlooked.
Where did Gustavson get these questions? Would a professor at the University of Moscow ask the same questions?	Students should see that the questions the historian asks are a product of his frame of reference.
Then how do you know you are asking the "right" questions?	Students should see that no one can identify a short list of "right" questions, but that scholars can identify a number of analytical questions that have been useful to investigators in the past. They should also recognize the usefulness of a small list of questions to be used as a starting point for investigations.

Lesson Plan: Reading V

HOW THE HISTORIAN DEALS WITH MIND SET

Subject Objectives:	To know that a historian's frame of reference is a product of his culture. To know that a frame of reference can be so rigid that it can prevent accurate reporting or interpretation of events.
Skill Objectives:	Analysis of elements: (4.10). To be able to recognize unstated assumptions. Analysis of relationships: (4.20). To be able to determine whether or not evidence supports a hypothesis. Evaluating in terms of internal evidence: (6.10). To be able to assess the degree to which the statements in an article are factually accurate.

Materials:	Reading V. Transparency 4.

What is history?	This question is again for purposes of getting the student to summarize what he has learned and also to get him thinking about the assignment that is due tomorrow. The teacher might ask the students to write a paragraph in answer to the question.
EXPLAIN ASSIGNMENT	The student's assignment is Reading VI in their book. Answer any questions they might have.
PROJECT TRANSPARENCY: Tell students to write down the first thing that comes to their mind. After a short time ask the students to tell the class what they saw.	The transparency is an ink blot that can be interpreted several ways. The point to be made with this exercise is that what people see is a function of their own frame of reference, as the following question indicates.
Why do you suppose you each saw different things?	The students, by this time, should be well aware that frame of reference conditions most of the activities of historical investigation, and their responses should indicate this conclusion.
What special problems for historians do you think this ink blot reveals?	The students should see two points: first that historians themselves see the world differently from each other and this colors their interpretations; and second, that eyewitness reporters will see different happenings in an event and will report only what they are ready to see.
Let's turn our attention to the reading. What was the story that was told in the first section of the reading? Who was its author?	The aim here should be to get the students to recount the story exactly as the monk told it, so that the elements of the monk's frame of reference are clear to the class.
Do you believe the monk's story? Why did the monk believe Herbert was stricken by St. Benedict?	This series of questions is designed to illuminate the problems of using evidence that comes from another culture where the writer's frame of reference influenced his interpretation or description of events. The fourth

Why don't you believe the monk?
Can you prove the monk was wrong?
How should you treat this piece of evidence?

EXERCISE: Have the class describe a student's clothing in Navaho.
What problem does this exercise reveal for the historian?
Now let's look at the last section of the reading.
How would persons who believed in each of the two ideas of man and revolution interpret the Hungarian revolution?
How can the historian deal with evidence that contains unstated value assumptions?

question in the series should indicate to the students that they also have a mind set about how things happen, and the teacher should encourage the students to compare their frame of reference with the monk's. The students should also be aware that a man's entire culture influences his frame of reference.

Problems of interpretation also arise out of translating from one language to another. Evidence written in one language might be distorted when it is translated into another one.

This exercise is designed to show the students that a person's values color his interpretation of history. Hence investigators should be aware of what their values are so that they will be able to recognize their role in forming interpretations. Underlying assumptions such as these always color the interpretation of the past.

CHAPTER 11 Teaching the Mode of Inquiry: The Social Sciences

Knowledge in the social sciences consists of a number of generalizations about the behavior of individuals and of men in groups and of a method to discover and validate such generalizations. For future learning, the method is more important than the generalizations themselves. Retention studies agree that most isolated facts and generalizations learned in school are soon forgotten. Information connected to the structure of a discipline and to the mode of inquiry itself, however, remains longer in a student's mind.

Most teachers teach the mode of inquiry implicitly. In courses such as problems of democracy, they require students to come to conclusions in terms of evidence, and by so doing expose students to the techniques by which social scientists develop and validate generalizations. But implicit attention to the mode of inquiry is usually not enough to assure mastery of complicated techniques. Students also should study method for its own sake in order to fix correct procedures firmly in their minds. Most of the social studies curriculum projects provide explicit training in the use of scientific method.

This requirement places three obligations upon teachers. First, it requires them to teach the steps in the mode of inquiry. During these classes teachers should pay only incidental attention to the subject material of a lesson in order to concentrate upon method. A well-trained student ought to be able to state specifically the steps required in the process of developing and validating a hypothesis. Hence, he should have opportunities to study each step in detail at several points in a course. For example, several days each year can profitably be spent concentrating on ways to develop fruitful hypotheses, with only incidental attention given to the process by which the hypotheses are validated.

Second, teachers must develop the cognitive skills essential to thinking in the social sciences. Again implicit and incidental work with the cognitive processess is not enough. Each skill must be taught explicitly over and over

188

again if students are to master it. Familiarity with the cognitive processes is indispensable to accurate work in the social sciences.

Finally, teachers must give incidental attention to the mode of inquiry when they are teaching primarily for knowledge objectives. Each lesson should emphasize not only what a student is expected to learn but how he is to learn it. Students master the cognitive skills only through repeated practice. Unless teachers are aware of the importance of the mode of inquiry and of the necessity to reinforce the process of learning it through constant use, it will not be mastered.

Chapter 11 consists of two parts. The first discusses the three methods of inquiry commonly used by social scientists. Two of these, the survey and the case study, can be used effectively in secondary school classes. The third, the experiment, presents more problems for the school, but not insurmountable ones.

The second reading consists of materials developed at Carnegie Tech's Curriculum Development Center to introduce students to some of the problems as well as the usefulness of surveys. Practical difficulties stand in the way of drawing up scientific samples and conducting interviews in the schools. Yet the results of interviews can be used to teach students to develop hypotheses, and they can be introduced to sampling techniques by discussing the sort of sample necessary to check the validity of a hypothesis. As you read, keep the following questions in mind:

1) What are the three methods of inquiry commonly used by social scientists? How can each best be taught in the schools? How can teaching the mode of inquiry of the social scientist be combined with teaching knowledge about a subject and with teaching skill objectives?

2) What is the essential purpose of the exercise in the second part of the reading? How could students profitably discuss the difference between the sample Professor Rosenberg used to develop his hypotheses and the sample that would be necessary to validate them?

3) What difference, if any, is there between the kind of evidence used by the social scientist and that which is available to the historian? Which kind of evidence permits surer conclusions? Can the methods of inquiry of the social scientist be adapted to the study of past societies?

4) In what different ways might knowledge of the mode of inquiry of the historian and the social scientist contribute to democratic behavior?

METHODS OF INQUIRY

Bernard Berelson · Gary A. Steiner

In the broadest terms, there are three designs used in the behavioral sciences: the experiment, the sample survey, and the case study.

THE EXPERIMENT

By *experiment* is meant any investigation that includes two elements: manipulation or control of some variable by the investigator and systematic observation or measurement[1] of the result. In short, it means active intervention on the phenomena of interest to see what, if any, effects are produced by the intervention.

The experiment has had a central place in the history of science. The importance of experimentation depends not so much on its precision, its objectivity, or its instruments as on the inherent efficiency of intervention in disentangling cause-and-effect relationships. Whenever its use is feasible, intentional intervention is the method that most readily exposes cause and effect; and if the behavioral sciences were able to experiment more widely on their materials they would be better equipped today with important findings. For example, we would know much more about the effects on personality of different ways of rearing children if experimentation were not precluded on moral and humanitarian grounds. And the field is currently making some progress on such basic problems as mental disease and emotional disturbance by means of physiological intervention in the nervous system accompanied by controlled observation of the behavioral results. The implantation of tiny electrodes in the brain has been used to induce fear, rage, joy, even "pleasure"; and ultimately such mapping of the brain centers that mediate emotions may have far-reaching clinical implications. Similarly, in human beings, chemical intervention has produced behavior that closely resembles certain manifestations of schizophrenia; and, in animals, certain parts of the brain have been systematically removed to see what effect that has on learned problem-solving.

From *Human Behavior: An Inventory of Scientific Findings* by Bernard Berelson and Gary A. Steiner, © 1964, by Harcourt, Brace & World, Inc., and reprinted with their permission. Pp. 18–22 and 25–27.

[1] By *measurement* the behavioral scientist typically means something broader than what the term means to the layman. The behavioral scientist considers that an attitude has been measured if it can simply be distinguished as "for" or "against," "more" or "less." Finer quantitative distinctions, of course, are also measurements, but so are dichotomies or classificatory categories in general.

THE CLASSICAL EXPERIMENT

The prototype of scientific experimentation, and in many ways its most foolproof form, is the classical experiment. The general question it answers is whether, and to what extent, one variable (called the experimental or independent variable) affects another variable (the dependent variable).

The logic is simple. Two groups are matched at the outset; one is given the experimental intervention (a piece of propaganda, a new drug that affects behavior, a French lesson taught in a new way, a special procedure that can introduce changes in working procedures in a factory); the result of the intervention is subsequently measured (i.e., its effect on attitudes, on personality, on the amount of French learned, on morale and productivity). The essentials of the classical experiment can be schematized as follows:

EXPERIMENTAL GROUP, BUT NOT CONTROL GROUP,
EXPOSED TO INTERVENTION (THE EXPERIMENTAL
OR INDEPENDENT VARIABLE)

	Before	*After*
Experimental group or subject	B_e	A_e
Control group or subject	B_c	A_c

The figures represent measurements of the dependent variable, and the effect of the experimental variable is $(A_e - A_c) - (B_e - B_c)$.

Here is an illustration of a classical experiment concerned with the effects of a new tranquilizer pill on psychotic behavior:

(1) Define the population of subjects and draw a sample—e.g., a random sample of all the patients with a given diagnosis at a certain institution.

(2) Divide the sample at random into two groups. By definition the two groups will now be similar, within limits of sampling error, on *any* measurement. Thus there is no reason to expect one group to behave any differently in the future than the other. Flip a coin to decide which will be "experimental" and which "control."

(3) Define the dependent variable ("psychotic behavior"): How will it be measured or rated? Take a "before" measurement on each group.

(4) Define the experimental variable precisely—What doses of the tranquilizer over what period of time?—and administer it to the experimental group only. The control group will probably get a placebo—a pill that looks the same but has no active ingredients— to control for the effects of autosuggestion, and even for the effect of participating in the experiment at all (since that will involve some special attention, at the least). In some cases of this kind, for extra precaution, the experiment is "double blind": not only does

the subject not know which pills he gets but, in order to control the expression of his own (conscious or unconscious) wishes in the matter, the experimenter does not know at the time either.

(5) Take "after" measurements of the dependent variable on each group.

(6) The difference between the two groups after the experiment, beyond any difference that may have existed before, is the effect of the experimental variable. In this case, it is the effect of the tranquilizer upon psychotic behavior.

The glory of the classical experiment is that its logic has no loophole. When all the conditions of the classical experiment have been met, and all four cells have been filled in, the final difference between control and experimental group *must* be due to the effect of the experimental or independent variable: both groups reflect the effects of any other variables not directly manipulated by the experimenter (such as time itself, atmospheric conditions, or the effects of having been selected to participate in the study). Thus the control group protects the experimenter against many of the common fallacies that plague less rigorous studies. Before-and-after observation of an experimental group alone is particularly vulnerable to the fallacy of *post hoc, ergo propter hoc*. Without a control group there is a temptation to attribute any subsequent change in the observed subjects to the experimental variable, whereas the change may have occurred without the experimenter's intervention.

Although there is a logical model for the classical experiment, in actual experiments the design is frequently modified for various reasons: costs, practical difficulties, and so on. In some cases, statistical approximations will do. For example, if the experimental and control groups are truly divided at random, the before-measurement may be omitted in the knowledge that the two groups will vary only within known limits of sampling error. The experiment simply consists of the administration of the experimental condition to one group and the subsequent after-measurements of both. If this after-measurement records a difference between the two groups that cannot be attributed to chance variation, it is taken to be the result of the experimental variable.[2]

Similarly, many experiments add onto the basic four-fold model. Some

---

[2] It is sometimes hard to believe, but it is still true, that when a group has been divided at random into two groups, the groups will differ by no more than chance on *any* characteristic whatsoever. The proportion of blue-eyed people in the two groups, of redheads, of people over and under 5'7", of Catholics, of those who skipped breakfast this morning, of those opposed to capital punishment or in favor of a stronger United Nations—all will be roughly equivalent. There are statistical procedures that determine the probability of a given difference having arisen simply by such random division. Therefore, when a difference is greater than that which could reasonably be expected on the basis of random division, and the groups have in fact been randomly divided, the conclusion is that the difference is not due to their division but to something that happened to them afterward.

measure the effect of the experimental variable over time: propaganda may be effective right after its administration, but how long does it last? Others assess the effects of several experimental variables within a single investigation. The simplest form of this involves two or more experimental groups, each of which is measured against a single control group. For example, the patients can be divided into three or more groups: one is the control, one gets tranquilizer A, one gets tranquilizer B, etc.

Moreover, modern statistical designs make it possible to evaluate the relative effects of a number of independent variables acting simultaneously and in combination. An investigation of classroom learning might vary the method of instruction, the sex of the teacher, the room lighting, and student motivation, all at one stage of observations; and then conclude which of these factors is the most important influence on learning, and how they act in combination.

So much for the general logic of experimental design: the principal point, worth repeating, is that the fundamental advantage of experimentation is not its precision or its instrumentation but its inherent logical rigor. . . .

THE SAMPLE SURVEY

The sample survey, as a type of research design, does not refer simply to a public opinion poll, though a properly designed poll is certainly one example of a sample survey, and probably the most familiar one. In our sense, a sample survey is properly named in that it contains the indicated two elements:

(1) *A sample:* The investigator first decides what group or "population" he is interested in (American adults, voters, women of childbearing age, college students, etc.) and then selects a sample in the statistical sense. It may be "random," "representative," "quota," "weighted," or any of a number of technical types. The main point is that the sample is so chosen as to enable the experimenter to draw conclusions regarding the entire "population" and not simply those members of the population who happen to turn up in the sample.

(2) *A survey:* The investigator then collects some measures on the appropriate characteristics of the population being studied (number of television sets or children in the household; how the members feel about Russia or religion; what they know about India or space; and so on).

Obviously there are certain questions that can be answered only by a sample survey. The question, "To what extent do American psychologists today believe that extrasensory perception exists?" can be answered by specifying a population and then asking a selected sample. No experiment will answer the question once and for all and neither will a case study. In general, whenever the investigator is interested in assessing or estimating the present state of affairs with regard to some variable that changes over time for a large group of subjects, a sample survey is the only practical way to get the answer. If the variable did not change over time, we could probably learn the answer once and for all by experiment; or if there were interest in only one or a few instances, case studies could provide the answer. These are certainly not the only conditions under which the sample survey is useful, but these are the conditions under which it is the imperative form of design.

In addition to simple measures of magnitude (How many people will vote?), sample surveys provide clues to relations between variables (and thus ultimately to cause and effect) by correlation of the various measures obtained. For example, a survey of number of children per family can provide a series of tables showing how fertility varies by families of differing class, race, rural-urban residence, religion, etc. This example, incidentally, illustrates another advantage of the sample survey in the study of relationships: many times the variables of interest are difficult or impossible to manipulate by experiment (years of schooling, race), so the only approach is to compare people who already differ on the characteristic in question and see how their behavior differs.

Such correlations are difficult to disentangle causally, because the direction of the influence is uncertain (and it is often reciprocal, which makes the matter more difficult still). To take a simple example, a correlation between reading an advertisement for a given make of car and buying the car could go either way—reading influenced purchase, purchase influenced reading. Even when the direction is clear, when one characteristic (e.g., race) antedates and is not affected by another (e.g., fertility), the nature of the causal relationship is quite complex, with several other factors usually involved (e.g., income, social position, religion, place of residence, age at marriage).

To handle change over time in certain investigations, a variant of the sample survey has been developed that is called the panel. This requires repeated measures of the appropriate characteristics on the same people, so that the investigation can study how changes were brought about over time. This method is particularly useful in campaigns that bring a variety of stimuli to the subjects' attention, and it is no accident that the method is used mainly in studies of marketing and voting. A major limitation of the panel technique is that, as the same people are queried repeatedly, they may change their behavior simply as a result of panel membership. As a control, panel responses are often checked against samples of "fresh" respondents.

The Case Study

The case study is complementary to the sample survey. The sample survey measures many people on few characteristics, usually at one point in time. The case study intensively examines many characteristics of one "unit" (person, work group, company, community, culture), usually over a long period of time. The goal of such investigations is to learn "all" about the area of interest for the one case involved. Typical case studies in the behavioral sciences might include: the life history of a psychotic; an intensive analysis of a patient's psychological disturbance;[3] an anthropological monograph describing in detail the technology and customs of a primitive culture; a detailed description and analysis of the socioeconomic classes existing in a small Southern town.

As the examples suggest, the detail and the depth of information over time that the case study provides makes this design particularly relevant for questions involving etiology and development: How does a particular neurotic manifestation emerge and change over time? What are the critical incidents that lead up to an industrial strike? How does the industrialization of a traditional society affect the family?

The chief limitation of this method is that the results are based on a sample of one, so that the degree of their generality is not known. Would another individual, another company, another community, another culture respond in the same way? In addition, the case study is often subject to the *post hoc, ergo propter hoc* fallacy, since neither a "control group" nor intervention by the investigator is provided as a safeguard.

Hence, case studies rarely *prove* anything, although they are frequently rich in clues and insights for further investigation. In many areas the case study is the idea-getting investigation par excellence. But since in this book we limit ourselves to what is more or less proved about human behavior, we shall bring in the results of case studies only when they have been verified in some way.

POLITICAL INACTIVITY
BY AMERICAN CITIZENS

Curriculum Development Center, Carnegie Institute of Technology

We are often told that the "good citizen" should participate actively in politics. Yet nearly half the eligible voters fail to cast ballots in a typical election, and millions of other citizens do not become involved in politics except to vote. Why do so many Americans avoid the duties of good citizenship? What is responsible—apathy, fear, ignorance?

[3] In fact, case studies are one of the principal sources of data on many questions in clinical psychology, since the practicing clinician is interested in specific individuals and collects intensive data on his patients. The most important questions in this area revolve around such time-bound issues as how and when the various syndromes arise, develop, and change. Thus, clinical histories have practical significance for the therapist and stimulate many hypotheses in personality theory.

Professor Morris Rosenberg, a member of the staff of the National Institute of Mental Health, tried to find out. He conducted what he termed an "exploratory study," interviewing seventy citizens of Ithaca, New York. Since these respondents were not chosen in order to obtain a cross sample of the community, Professor Rosenberg warned his readers that his results should not be taken as scientific fact. He was attempting only to develop some hypotheses that might explain political apathy, and he did not think a scientific sample was necessary for this purpose.

In the study that Professor Rosenberg published in *Public Opinion Quarterly,* he listed the answers he had received to his questions under the hypotheses he had developed. They then served as evidence for his hypotheses. This was not the way in which he received them. The people he questioned gave answers at random, and Professor Rosenberg later arranged them in the pattern into which they seemed to fall.

We have mixed them up again for you in order to put you into the shoes of a research scholar. Suppose you had asked a number of people why they did not participate more actively in politics and they had given you the replies you will find below. How would you arrange them into groups that made some sense?

Suppose, for example, that you were able to find four replies that indicated the respondents did not participate in politics because they thought this an unladylike activity. (You won't find this reply here, of course.) Four such answers ought to suggest a hypothesis worth investigating further: that some women avoid politics because they think it unladylike. Your assignment is to develop hypotheses to explain political inactivity from the data we give you.

Your teacher will give you a dittoed copy of the following quotations. To make your task easier, we suggest that you cut the dittoed sheet of answers until there is only one answer on each piece of paper. Then arrange the pieces of paper in piles, each pile containing replies that indicate the same reason for political apathy. When you have finished use a paper clip to hold similar replies together. Then on a sheet of notebook paper write the hypotheses you have developed. Make each hypothesis no more than one sentence long. Be prepared to defend your hypotheses before the class tomorrow.

SOME DETERMINANTS OF
POLITICAL APATHY

Morris Rosenberg

Some of my friends are (active in politics). Some are avid Democrats, but most of my friends are not active. We don't discuss politics much. I think it's sort of like religion. It's personal, and I don't like to get into arguments. . . . When politics comes up in conversation, I always say—"Let's talk about something else," . . . especially when ———— is around. She's such a Democrat and gets so riled up.

I personally want to be informed because my husband holds different political beliefs. We don't discuss politics very often because when we do we are likely to disagree violently. Right now I want to avoid friction—*we were just married last June*—so we try not to get into political discussions.

I remember one time going to a city council meeting when I was back in Minnesota. I was disagreeing with one of the commissioners on an important town issue. Why, the next day I received calls and a visitor asking me what exactly it was all about and what I was up to. After that I just didn't go to meetings of that sort.

Well, it's a personal subject . . . You see, in my field, there is no harm in avoiding unnecessary conflicts, and politics are subject to strong sentiments . . . I have to maintain relations among employees and management, and I try to avoid trouble points. I've always felt it wise policy to be quiet about how I vote.

No, because I never like to express my political views in public. . . . Since I have to deal with so many men, both in the plant and in the buying of (raw materials), there is no sense in making people angry at you over a local election.

Absolutely; for that reason I register *No Mark*. Actually I'm a Republican. But in the case of ————, it's different. He's a friend of mine . . . and *everybody* knew I'd support him anyway. Besides, he lives in ———— where I have my business, and (his opponent) is over in ———— (a different town). *I don't sell much over there anyway.*

I don't think I'm capable enough to take an active part (in politics). I just feel I lack the ability . . . I don't know what would be required of me. My husband and I talk it over, of course, but I don't talk about it in public because I don't know enough. I wish I knew more. Sometimes I'd like to say something.

Voting doesn't make that much difference. What can an individual do about it? He can't really do much.
My vote will always count, yet one vote one way or the other doesn't make much difference.

Quotations reprinted from Morris Rosenberg, "Some Determinants of Political Apathy," *Public Opinion Quarterly*, 18, 4, Winter 1954–1955, 352–365, with omissions.

. . . All right, but it is always the big guy he (the politician) is interested in helping . . . The only thing I have against them is that they are too damn narrow-minded (and that politics) keep the little man down.

What does the working man care about politics, anyway? What can he do, even if he did care? That's probably it . . . What can he do? Nothing should bother him anyway. The country will still go on just the same for the average working man.

Well, it seems almost useless to do a lot of work for the national group when there are so many other people for it and when you really won't have much to say about what happens anyway. A lot of those people are a lot better than I am, and a lot of them have more pull.

. . . The little man votes and that's all . . . The party usually takes over pretty much. They don't think too much about the little man.

One respondent was asked whether world peace was important to him. He replied:

It's an important problem, yes, but there isn't much we can do about it in a meeting downtown. We're concerned about it, naturally, everyone is; but just about all we can do is sit by and watch what happens. Washington does all the deciding, and we've put men there for the purpose . . . I know what it entails to pick up garbage, but I haven't the foggiest notion of what it takes to put over a treaty between two countries. I don't know whether the men in Washington are doing the best possible job or not.

The machine is too strong to do what you want.
The machines run things all around . . . Working to stop the machine could go on and on and still get no place. They'll always be there.

We say we live in a democracy because we elect our representatives. But if the people we elect are in turn chosen by people who are outside our control, then our democracy is only relative and not as pure as we think it is. . . . I think that the higher levels of party organization are closed to ordinary citizens.
Today most of the platforms of both major parties are about the same. The people it really matters to are those who are looking for special favors. Just take the issue of tidelands' oil and take a list of the visitors of the General the day before he signed the bill!
A couple of men get together in some room . . . and when they come out, the party nomination has been made. You never know.

Once a man is elected and he turns out no good, it is too late to do anything about it. They might not do what they say. Either they can't do it, or they say, "I'm in now, so I don't have to do it."

Nobody realizes how hard the Democratic Party around here does work. We'd like to get a higher caliber man to run but it's just impossible. Everybody knows the Republican will win and nobody wants to waste his time. Everyone votes Republican here whether they are good, bad or inefficient (sic) . . . In many town, local and county elections, one party dominates the area. There is not enough spirit of competition to arouse interest.

Well, I'm not interested enough. I don't take the time to read such matters. I like to read more exciting things, such as kidnap cases, and I also like the sports section a lot.

Yes, I think it's better to do something which has direct results. I don't know how party politics go or anything, and maybe I'm wrong, but it seems that you end up doing little things like telephoning or licking stamps. You don't have any control over things because everything is decided by party leaders, and you don't have much to say about what goes on. You don't get any direct results. In Girl Scouts, you see these results; you have a chance to shape the characters of the girls. I think that's more important.

Well, I would say politics are dull in comparison to other news.
Well, like this here—I see much more excitement in this story about the plane crashes than in this story about Eisenhower and the story on farm supports.

R. I didn't have the time. If I had had the time, I would have been more interested. I work each day at the Community Center and it takes up most of my free time. I also devote many evenings to work there. I feel my work there is much more important than politics.
I. Can you say why?
R. I feel I'm really able to help people directly through my work at the Center, but I don't think I have much power to help others through politics.

I don't think politics or election results will or do affect my own life very much. Regardless of who is in power, I'll keep my job and my home.

I don't follow the news too much. I feel the world will go on without me, no matter. [At a later point, asked if she felt that politics had any importance in her life, she replied] No, we go on and politics has nothing to do with us. . . . I think most people go along from day to day and take what comes. I don't think they are much interested.

No, I wasn't asked to do anything. Many of my friends were asked to help —ring doorbells, stamp envelopes, and things like that. But I wasn't asked to do anything. Had I been asked, I would have been glad to help.

You can probably class me as apathetic, except when it's brought right to my attention, but I think most people are the same way. They are not aware of, or they ignore, corruption in government until a McCarthy-type seizes it and makes a big thing out of it.

Well, a few of our friends belong to some political groups. But I wouldn't call them our most intimate friends. Not many of our close friends belong.
As a matter of fact, besides the professors' wives, I don't think too many women know much about politics. Even though a lot of them are active on the election board—canvassing and things like that—they still don't seem to know too much about politics—especially national politics.
I guess everyone else is even more passive than I am. They're all busy with household things.

CHAPTER 12 **Teaching Students To Define Terms Historically**

How can we teach students to use language precisely? All of us want them to learn to speak well and to communicate accurately to others. Many beginning teachers are shocked by the loose use of language that characterizes many class discussions. We must teach students to communicate clearly if we expect to make them into good citizens and logical thinkers.

One issue frequently misunderstood and even more frequently ignored entirely is the difficult matter of historical definition. Most high school students use words such as "democracy," "imperialism," "socialism," or "fascism" as if each of these overworked terms had simple and precise meanings. None of them has. Athenian democracy was quite different from nineteenth-century American democracy and different again from democracy as the word is used in twentieth-century Soviet Union. Unless a student understands that the word "democracy" can be used to describe quite different political and social systems, he will never be able to read history—or his newspaper, for that matter—intelligently. How do we teach him this skill?

Chapter 12 consists of two parts. The first is an excerpt from a paper by Sherrill Aberg, a teacher at Bethel Park (Pennsylvania) High School, which raises the problem of how to teach an historical definition of socialism in high school and college classes. What Mr. Aberg says about socialism can be applied with equal force to similar catch-all terms. The second part consists of a problem in which students are asked to work out for themselves an historical definition of the term "imperialism."

1) According to Mr. Aberg, what is the problem of historical definition? How does he suggest that a teacher ought to go about teaching this matter to students? Can his techniques be applied to other similar terms?

2) How is the problem entitled "The Meaning of Imperialism" set up? What is the function of the Introduction? the study questions? the readings themselves?

3) If you were planning a history course, would you include several problems

about historical definitions of terms? why or why not? What other devices could you utilize to emphasize the importance of the precise use of language?

TEACHING ABOUT SOCIALISM IN AN INTRODUCTORY HISTORY COURSE

Sherrill Aberg

The problem of historical definition is universal. All of us face the task of getting students to understand the manner in which a historian develops a definition of a term. Our students are accustomed to thumbing through Webster's when they encounter a word with which they are unfamiliar. This process teaches them implicitly that each word has one or two "right" meanings that have applied to it throughout history. Vocabulary lists kept throughout grade and high school teach the same lesson: each word can be defined succinctly, and this definition can be used in every situation. Before a student can understand the history of socialism he must unlearn the idea that this term has one and only one precise meaning.

Teaching about socialism has another level of complexity, however. Not only do students assume that they will be able to learn one pat definition, but they also think they know what that definition is. Their information comes from radio, from television, from newspapers, from their schoolmates, and most of all, from Father's *ex cathedra* pronouncements at the dinner table. To most beginning students socialism is the opposite of democracy or of Americanism. The more sophisticated divide it into subtypes: the creeping variety, sponsored by Democrats (large D), insidiously toppling one bastion of democracy after another through such dangerous devices as social security laws, federal aid to education, and subsidies to the post office; the British variety, according to a well-known group, is primarily a disguised attack upon the sacred relationship between doctor and patient; the Scandinavian variety is obviously an attempt to replace the family with free love; parlor socialism, in contrast, is harmless talk indulged in by wealthy impractical idealists; and fellow-traveling socialism is a first step down the long, dark path to communism and the grave. For some students socialism is all of these at once; at least these eclectics recognize the complexity of their subject.

Reprinted from an address given by Sherrill Aberg at Carnegie Institute of Technology, June 1961.

I want my students to leave their history course with a sophisticated knowledge of various historic types of socialism and with a clear conception of what this much-abused term has meant to different men at different times or at the same time in different cultural environments. Composing and learning an historical definition is not only good history; it is also good citizenship training. Once a citizen learns the manner in which terms are misused by writers and speakers, he is much less likely to be taken in by emotional arguments and appeals. Moreover, terms requiring historical definitions come up over and over in history courses: "feudalism," "nationalism," "democracy," and "communism" are only a few of many possible examples. Somewhere in a course every teacher ought to focus explicitly on the matter of historical definition in order to be certain that students learn exactly this aspect of the historian's art. In our course, we use "socialism" as our prime example. The most important reason for doing this is that "socialism" appears over and over again throughout the second semester; thus it provides a theme that continues to the present.

We can count almost as many types of socialism as there are socialist writers. No introductory course ought to touch on each of these esoteric varieties; instead, each teacher ought to select three or four types to study in depth. Then, to make distinctions clear, he ought to investigate the same problems for each type of socialism. Although there are a number of questions he might ask, the following list of five will help a student to understand the major similarities and contrasts among the cases he selects to study:

1. How is the socialist society to come to power, by violence, by persuading individuals to vote for a voluntary settlement, or by capturing control of the machinery of government in an election?
2. What will the new socialist economy look like? Who will own or control the means of production? How will goods be distributed?
3. How will the political machinery operate in the socialist society?
4. What, if anything, does the particular brand of socialism intend to do about normative institutions and patterns of behavior in society?
5. What is the ultimate goal of the socialist system?

Once he asks these and similar questions of such diverse groups as Utopian Socialists, Marxists, and Fabians, a student will see clearly that the three systems have little in common. For example, one espoused a nonviolent appeal to men of all classes; another was violent and based its arguments upon the premise of the class struggle; the third hoped to win power through the ballot box. The student must now explain why these differences arose, and to do this successfully, he must examine the entire cultural context that gave rise to each philosophy. To understand Marx he must learn about Hegel, about the vogue for revolutionary solutions to basic problems at mid-century, about Engels' experiences with Manchester's cotton workers, in short, about the whole galaxy of conditions that influenced the authors of the *Communist Manifesto*. He must also understand the enormous impact of the doctrine of evolution and of universal manhood suffrage if he is to understand why the Webbs helped to develop Fabianism.

One aspect of a complete historical definition remains. If a student understands the differences among socialist philosophies within one culture and can trace these differences to their cultural antecedents over a span of years, he need only study different types of socialism in different nations at the same time period to complete his picture. Parliamentary socialism in Germany and Great Britain in the late nineteenth century will serve as good examples. One variable a student should spot quickly as a partial explanation of the somewhat different types of socialist thought in these two nations is the role of the government and the attitude of Bismarck toward the socialists in Germany. Another difference can be traced to the relative power and influence of trade unions in the two societies. Students can readily comprehend the differences existing at this period in the political life of these countries.

One way to reinforce the use of historical definitions while teaching a class is to refuse to permit a student to use the word "socialism" by itself. Insist that he add an adjective—"Utopian," "Scientific," "Fabian," or "Revisionist"—an adjective carrying with it an entire cultural context. This degree of precision in the use of language will bear rich dividends in sharpening the edge of the critical tools with which a student works at his history assignments. We ought, however, to warn him that if he tries this technique on Dad at dinner he may run into trouble. Father knows best, at least in his own citadel.

Let me list for review the three aspects of an historical definition that each student should learn. First he ought to know exactly what a writer means by the word "socialism"; second he should know the cultural antecedents of the term in each instance; and third, he should know the similarities and differences between socialist systems passing under the same label at the same time period but in different countries.

THE MEANING
OF IMPERIALISM

Edwin Fenton

As we have previously noted, many historical terms are used very loosely. Such words as *democracy* and *socialism*, for instance, have been handled so carelessly that they are often more confusing than explanatory. Imperialism, which is the subject of today's reading, is another such term. Some people refer to the territorial expansion of the 16th and 17th centuries (discussed in

Reprinted from Edwin Fenton, *32 Problems in World History,* Copyright © 1964 by Scott, Foresman and Company, pp. 169–177.

Problem 15) as imperialism when they should be using a more appropriate label—colonialism. Generally speaking, 19th-century expansionism was more organized and more aggressive than that of the earlier period, and grew out of more complex motives.

In the 20th century, the use of the term *imperialism* has become even more confused. Some use it to characterize the foreign policy of the Soviet Union, others to describe the foreign policy of the United States. The English and the French, who have been practically stripped of their empires, are accused of being imperialists by the Chinese communists, who seem intent on adding to their own vast territory.

As we have seen in Problems 3 and 20, historians like to define terms according to the time and place in which they were used. The word *imperialism* belongs to the last half of the 19th century. Although it first came into use in France to describe certain aspects of society under Napoleon III, it was being applied by the end of the century to the process of European expansion abroad. Until about 1870 European nations had not tried to win political control of underdeveloped areas. Then in a rush Germany, England, France, Italy, Russia, and Belgium (as well as Japan and the United States) began to compete for this kind of colony. The term *imperialism* can be properly used to describe this development.

What were the motives of the imperialists? Marxists, such as Lenin, have argued that imperialism is merely the last stage of capitalism. According to their argument, capitalist nations extended their power overseas in order to postpone their inevitable downfall. They hoped to revive their internal economies—suffering from dwindling resources and profits—by exploiting lands and peoples abroad. On the other hand, some persons have argued that "advanced" nations felt they had a moral duty to spread their institutions and cultures to so-called "backward" peoples. Still others have held that one of the strongest factors was the desire of Western countries to control naval bases and coaling stations in case of war.

The four documents below will help you to work out an historical definition of the word *imperialism* as it was used in Great Britain and the United States about 1900. The first reading is from a book written by F. D. Lugard of the British East Africa Company, an enterprise which was instrumental in developing Kenya. Next you will read Rudyard Kipling's famous poem "The White Man's Burden," written in February 1899, shortly after the Spanish-American War. Senator Albert J. Beveridge's speech to the Senate, given on January 9, 1900, in support of a resolution to retain control of the Philippine Islands, illustrates the viewpoint of a particularly important American imperialist. Finally, the short passage from a book by Admiral Alfred T. Mahan indicates the attitude of a prominent naval officer who was a close friend of Theodore Roosevelt.

Consider the following questions as you read:

1. What were the stated or implied motives of the authors represented in these readings? Do you see selfish and selfless motives combined? Do the four writers share the same point of view?
2. How do you think educated Africans and Asians would react to the attitudes expressed in these four documents? What bearing does this issue have on international politics in the mid-20th century?
3. If you used the word *imperialist* to describe a man living about 1900, what would you want the word to mean? Would you use the same word to describe present-day Russian expansion into Europe? Why or why not?

I. THE RISE OF OUR EAST AFRICAN EMPIRE*
F. D. Lugard

The value of the Industrial mission . . . depends, of course, largely on the nature of the tribes among whom it is located. Its value can hardly be overestimated among such people as the Waganda, both on account of their natural aptitude and their eager desire to learn. But even the less advanced and more primitive tribes may be equally benefited, if not only mechanical and artisan work, such as the carpenter's and blacksmith's craft, but also the simpler expedients of agriculture are taught. The sinking of wells, the system of irrigation, the introduction and planting of useful trees, the use of manure, and of domestic animals for agricultural purposes, the improvement of his implements by the introduction of the primitive Indian plough, etc.—all of these, while improving the status of the native, will render his land more productive, and hence, by increasing his surplus products, will enable him to purchase from the trader the cloth which shall add to his decency, and the implements and household utensils which shall produce greater results from his labour and greater comforts in his social life. . . .

In my view . . . instruction (religious or secular) is largely wasted upon adults, who are wedded to custom and prejudice. It is the rising generation who should be educated to a higher plane, by the establishment of schools for children. They, in turn, will send their children for instruction; and so a progressive advancement is instituted, which may produce really great results. I see, in a recent letter, that Dr. Laws supports this view, and appositely quotes the parallel of the Israelites after their exodus from Egypt, who were detained for forty years in the desert, until the generation who had been slaves in Egypt had passed away. The extensive schools at his mission at Bandawi were evidence of the practical application of his views. These schools were literally

* Edinburgh: William Blackwood & Sons, 1893.

thronged with thousands of children, and chiefs of neighboring tribes were eagerly offering to erect schools in their own villages at their own cost. . . .

An administrative mission can, of course, only be founded in a country not under the aegis of any European Power. Under such circumstances, a mission may be justified in undertaking to some extent administrative functions, pending the absorption of the country under European protection, especially where no central native authority exists, and there is no cohesion to repel the attacks of slavetraders, or the tyranny of the dominant tribe. This, of course, is more especially the case when the community has grown up in a previously unpopulated country. . . . But when a secular administration is established, it appears to me that the missions should resign entirely into the hands of the authorized executive Government all functions pertaining to administration. . . .

One word as regards missionaries themselves. The essential point in dealing with Africans is to establish a respect for the European. Upon this—the prestige of the white man—depends his influence, often his very existence, in Africa. If he shows by his surroundings, and by his assumption of superiority, that he is far above the native, he will be respected, and his influence will be proportionate to the superiority he assumes and bears out by his higher accomplishments and mode of life. In my opinion—at any rate with reference to Africa—it is the greatest possible mistake to suppose that a European can acquire a greater influence by adopting the mode of life of the natives. In effect, it is to lower himself to their plane, instead of elevating them to his. The sacrifice involved is wholly unappreciated, and the motive would be held by the savage to be poverty and lack of social status in his own country. The whole influence of the European in Africa is gained by his assertion of a superiority which commands the respect and excites the emulation of the savage. To forego this vantage-ground is to lose influence for good. I may add, that the loss of prestige consequent on what I should term the humiliation of the European affects not merely the missionary himself, but is subversive of all efforts for secular administration, and may even invite insult, which may lead to disaster and bloodshed. To maintain it a missionary must, above all things, be a gentleman; for no one is more quick to recognize a real gentleman than the African savage. He must at all times assert himself, and repel an insolent familiarity, which is a thing entirely apart from friendship born of respect and affection. His dwelling-house should be as superior to those of the natives as he is himself superior to them. And this, while adding to his prestige and influence, will simultaneously promote his own health and energy, and so save money spent on invalidings to England, and replacements due to sickness or death. . . .

It is sufficient to reiterate here, that as long as our policy is one of free trade, we are compelled to seek new markets; for old ones are being closed to us by hostile tariffs, and our great dependencies, which formerly were the consumers of our goods, are now becoming our commercial rivals. It is inherent in a great colonial and commercial empire like ours that we go forward or go backward. To allow other nations to develop new fields, and to refuse to do so ourselves, is to go backward; and this is the more deplorable, seeing that we have proved ourselves notably capable of dealing with native races, and of developing new countries at less expense than other nations. We owe to the instincts of colonial expansion of our ancestors, those vast and noble dependencies which are our pride and the outlets of our trade to-day; and we are accountable to posterity that opportunities which now present themselves of extending the sphere of our industrial enterprise are not neglected, for the opportunities now offered will never recur again. . . .

If some initial expense is incurred, is it not justified by the ultimate gain? I have already pointed out what other nations are doing in the way of railway extension. The Government is not asked to provide the capital of the railway, but only a guarantee on the subscribed capital. . . . Independently of money spent on railways, the conquest of Algeria alone cost France £150,000,000, and it is estimated that her West Coast colonies cost her half a million yearly. Italy spends on her Abyssinian protectorate a sum variously estimated at £400,000 or £600,000 per annum. Belgium, besides her heavy expenses for the Congo railway, the capital of which she has advanced without interest, guarantees £80,000 per annum to the Congo State, and is altering her constitution in order to allow her to take over that State as a colonial possession. Germany has spent over a million sterling in East Africa, besides her expenditure on the west and south-west colonies. The parallel is here complete, for the German Company failed, and Government stepped in to carry out the pledges and obligations incurred. Even Portugal is content to support a yearly deficit on each of her African possessions, gives heavy subsidies to the mail-steamers, and £10,000 per annum to the Cable. All these nations are content to incur this yearly cost in the present, confident that in the future these possessions will repay the outlay. . . .

II. THE WHITE MAN'S BURDEN*
Rudyard Kipling

> Take up the White Man's burden—
> Send forth the best ye breed—
> Go bind your sons to exile
> To serve your captives' need;
> To wait in heavy harness,
> On fluttered folk and wild—
> Your new-caught, sullen peoples,
> Half-devil and half-child.

* Reprinted from *Rudyard Kipling's Verse, Definitive Edition,* by permission of Mrs. George Bambridge, Doubleday & Company, Inc., the Macmillan Company of Canada, Ltd., and Methuen & Company, Ltd.

Take up the White Man's burden—
In patience to abide,
To veil the threat of terror
And check the show of pride;
By open speech and simple,
An hundred times made plain,
To seek another's profit,
And work another's gain.

Take up the White Man's burden—
The savage wars of peace—
Fill full the mouth of Famine
And bid the sickness cease;
And when your goal is nearest
The end for others sought
Watch Sloth and heathen Folly
Bring all your hopes to nought.

Take up the White Man's burden—
No tawdry rule of kings,
But toil of serf and sweeper—
The tale of common things.
The ports ye shall not enter,
The roads ye shall not tread,
Go make them with your living,
And mark them with your dead.

Take up the White Man's burden—
And reap his old reward:
The blame of those ye better,
The hate of those ye guard—
The cry of hosts ye humour
(Ah, slowly!) toward the light:—
"Why brought ye us from bondage,
Our loved Egyptian night?"

Take up the White Man's burden—
Ye dare not stoop to less—
Nor call too loud on Freedom
To cloak your weariness;
By all ye cry or whisper,
By all ye leave or do,
The silent, sullen peoples
Shall weigh your Gods and you.

Take up the White Man's burden—
Have done with childish days—
The lightly proffered laurel,
The easy, ungrudged praise.
Comes now, to search your manhood
Through all the thankless years,
Cold, edged with dear-bought wisdom,
The judgment of your peers!

III. ADDRESS TO THE SENATE*

Albert J. Beveridge

The Philippines are ours forever, "territory belonging to the United States," as the Constitution calls them. And just beyond the Philippines are China's illimitable markets. We will not retreat from either. We will not repudiate our duty in the archipelago. We will not abandon our opportunity in the Orient. We will not renounce our part in the mission of our race, trustee, under God, of the civilization of the world. And we will move forward to our work, not howling out regrets like slaves whipped to their burdens, but with gratitude for a task worthy of our strength, and thanksgiving to Almighty God that He has marked us as His chosen people, henceforth to lead in the regeneration of the world. . . .

. . . The power that rules the Pacific . . . is the power that rules the world. And, with the Philippines, that power is and will forever be the American Republic. . . .

. . . It would be better to abandon this combined garden and Gibraltar of the Pacific, and count our blood and treasure already spent a profitable loss, than to apply any academic arrangement of self-government to these children. They are not capable of self-government. How could they be? They are not of a self-governing race. They are Orientals, Malays, instructed by Spaniards in the latter's worst estate.

They know nothing of practical government except as they have witnessed the weak, corrupt, cruel, and capricious rule of Spain. What magic will any-one employ to dissolve in their minds and characters those impressions of governors and governed which three centuries of misrule has created? What alchemy will change the oriental quality of their blood and set the self-governing currents of the American pouring through their Malay veins? How shall they, in the twinkling of an eye, be exalted to the heights of self-governing peoples which required a thousand years for us to reach, Anglo-Saxon though we are? . . .

* Reprinted from the *Congressional Record,* 56th Cong., 1st Sess., pp. 704, 708, 711.

Mr. President, this question is deeper than any question of party politics; deeper than any question of the isolated policy of our country even; deeper even than any question of constitutional power. It is elemental. It is racial. God has not been preparing the English-speaking and Teutonic peoples for a thousand years for nothing but vain and idle self-contemplation and self-admiration. No! He has made us the master organizers of the world to establish system where chaos reigns. He has given us the spirit of progress to overwhelm the forces of reaction throughout the earth. He has made us adept in government that we may administer government among savage and senile peoples. Were it not for such a force as this the world would relapse into barbarism and night. And of all our race He has marked the American people as His chosen nation to finally lead in the regeneration of the world. This is the divine mission of America, and it holds for us all the profit, all the glory, all the happiness possible to man. We are trustees of the world's progress, guardians of its righteous peace. The judgment of the Master is upon us: "Ye have been faithful over a few things; I will make you ruler over many things."

IV. THE INTEREST OF AMERICA IN SEA POWER*

Alfred T. Mahan

The interesting and significant feature of this changing attitude [*an increasing interest in overseas markets*] is the turning of the eyes outward, instead of inward only, to seek the welfare of the country. To affirm the importance of distant markets, and the relation to them of our own immense powers of production, implies logically the recognition of the link that joins the products and the markets,—that is, the carrying trade; the three together constituting that chain of maritime power to which Great Britain owes her wealth and greatness. Further, is it too much to say that, as two of these links, the shipping and the markets, are exterior to our own borders, the acknowledgment of them carries with it a view of the relations of the United States to the world radically distinct from the simple idea of self-sufficingness? We shall not follow far this line of thought before there will dawn the realization of America's unique position, facing the older worlds of the East and West, her shores washed by the oceans which touch the one or the other, but which are common to her alone. . . .

There is no sound reason for believing that the world has passed into a period of assured peace outside the limits of Europe. Unsettled political conditions, such as exist in Haiti, Central America, and many of the Pacific islands,

* Boston: Little, Brown & Company, 1897.

especially the Hawaiian group, when combined with great military or commercial importance as is the case with most of these positions, involve, now as always, dangerous germs of quarrel, against which it is prudent at least to be prepared. Undoubtedly, the general temper of nations is more averse from war than it was of old. If no less selfish and grasping than our predecessors, we feel more dislike to the discomforts and sufferings attendant upon a breach of peace; but to retain that highly valued repose and the undisturbed enjoyment of the returns of commerce, it is necessary to argue upon somewhat equal terms of strength with an adversary. It is the preparedness of the enemy, and not the acquiescence in the existing state of things, that now holds back the armies of Europe. . . .

When the Isthmus [*of Panama*] is pierced, this isolation will pass away, and with it the indifference of foreign nations. From whersoever they come and whithersoever they afterward go, all ships that use the canal will pass through the Caribbean. Whatever the effect produced upon the prosperity of the adjacent continent and islands by the thousand wants attendant upon maritime activity, around such a focus of trade will centre large commercial and political interests. To protect and develop its own, each nation will seek points of support and means of influence in a quarter where the United States always has been jealously sensitive to the intrusion of European powers. The precise value of the Monroe Doctrine is understood very loosely by most Americans, but the effect of the familiar phrase has been to develop a national sensitiveness, which is a more frequent cause of war than material interests; and over disputes caused by such feelings there will preside none of the calming influence due to the moral authority of international law, with its recognized principles, for the points in dispute will be of policy, of interest, not of conceded right. Already France and Great Britain are giving to ports held by them a degree of artificial strength uncalled for by their present importance. They look to the near future. Among the islands and on the mainland there are many positions of great importance, held now by weak or unstable states. Is the United States willing to see them sold to a powerful rival? But what right will she invoke against the transfer? She can allege but one,—that of her reasonable policy supported by her might.

CHAPTER 13 Teaching Students To Take Good Reading Notes

Many teachers fail to teach note-taking as a skill indispensable to the interpretation of history. Many of us rely on the outlining techniques taught in English classes for instruction in this vital aspect of our discipline. But good history notes often cannot be taken in outline form. Outlines imply that the student should adhere slavishly to the organizational pattern developed by the author of the book. But we often read for some other purpose than to learn what the author wrote in the order that he wrote it. Students should learn to read actively, not passively, and to put their own probing questions to material. Outlining a book gets in the way of this vigorous thinking process.

One reason for our failure to teach note-taking well is the time involved in checking and correcting notes. No job that a teacher does is duller than poring over a set of routine reading notes. For many students, this burdensome task is entirely unnecessary. Students can be taught note-taking without having notes corrected by the teacher. Many teachers have found the following techniques helpful:

1. Give students written instructions about note-taking. Make the instructions clear and explicit, like those that follow in the first reading in this chapter.
2. Hand out sample notes to students in class. Take your own notes on a ditto master and distribute them to students. Go over the notes in class to point out their strong and their weak points.
3. Check notes occasionally for performance. Instead of making numerous corrections on each paper, choose the best set of notes from the class, ditto it, and correct the dittoed copy. Sometimes it seems best to let students make their own corrections as a class exercise. At other times, the teacher's corrections may prove particularly helpful to students who have not grasped essential elements.

4. Work individually with students who do not develop good note-taking habits. Either a conference or a careful editing of a student's notes may be enough to get the main ingredients of good note-taking techniques across.

Chapter 13 consists of two excerpts. The first is a set of directions for note-taking taken from the syllabus for an advanced placement (college level) American history course used in the Pittsburgh Public Schools. The second is part of a pamphlet written by Professor Paul L. Ward, formerly head of the history department at Carnegie Tech and now Executive Secretary of the American Historical Association, where he is a vigorous proponent of the new social studies. As you read, think about the following questions:

1) Professor Ward's article described procedures for teaching note-taking to college students. Are these procedures practical for high school?
2) How are the note-taking directions related to the conception of history revealed in Chapter 9?
3) What is Professor Ward's conception of the nature of historical investigation?
4) How would knowledge of the structure of history and the social sciences help a student to take good notes in the way that Professor Ward advocates?

NOTE-TAKING DIRECTIONS

Pittsburgh Public Schools

Richard Hofstadter, William Miller, and Daniel Aaron, The United States: The History of a Republic *(Englewood Cliffs, N.J.: Prentice-Hall, 1957), pp. v.–vi, 46–52. Hereafter cited as text.*

Your text was written for college students enrolled in a survey course much like this one. The language and style, however, are not complex. Keep a vocabulary list of all words with which you are not familiar.

Your first three assignments are deliberately quite short. We shall use them to teach you note-taking techniques, as well as information about the colonies. Follow the directions below carefully for each of the three first assignments.

Pages v–vi are particularly important. Notice the view of our history that the authors set forth here. Always read the preface to a book. You will pick up hints about the slant of an author and sometimes an idea about the way in which his book is organized.

Take notes on the reading as follows:

1. Read the paragraph at the bottom of page 46. What, evidently, is this chapter about? Then rapidly flip over the entire chapter. Notice the headings in large type at the beginning of each section. How is the chapter organized? Now at the top of your note paper take down information about the source you are using: text, pp. 46–52. *Do this for every assignment during the year.* Next write a one-sentence summary of the contents of the chapter, describing what the authors were doing in these twenty-two pages. All of this vital preliminary work should take you no more than a few minutes.

2. Next skim the section entitled "The Colonial Population" rapidly. Read the first sentence in each paragraph. Write a one-sentence summary of what the authors were trying to do. Then return to page 47 and read, taking notes on the more vital information. Be certain to take down specific information such as names, dates, and events. As you read, keep in mind questions worth discussing and thinking about: What were the major differences between the effects of German and Ulster (North Ireland) immigration to the United States?

3. Repeat the process of skimming, summarizing, and reading to get notes for the following section on "The Southern Colonies."

4. Go over the notes you have taken. Underline the most important factual information. Some people use red ink or red pencil to make these items stand out for study at examination time. Rearrange your factual information in your own mind around the questions you have developed for yourself.

TEACHING NOTE-TAKING TO HISTORY STUDENTS AS ENCOURAGEMENT TO ACTIVE STUDY

Paul L. Ward

For beginners in history, careful instruction in note-taking need not be dull. At its best it opens to them the means of well-disciplined thinking along lines of awakening interests. Then as they proceed to sift through evidence assigned them as homework they can feel the excitement of discovering with more and more skill the real issues of the past, and the possible implications

Reprinted from Paul L. Ward, *Teaching Note-Taking to History Students: An Encouragement to Active Study*, Carnegie Papers on History Teaching, Carnegie Institute of Technology, No. 3.

of these for today's difficulties. The study of history becomes an intellectual adventure in which care brings satisfying rewards.

In the required freshman history course at Carnegie Institute of Technology we have experimented for some years on ways of bringing students to this frame of mind. Our first weeks' assignments have by now a double emphasis, on careful note-taking and on stimulating issues, that seems unusually effective. . . .

Three general points have to be emphasized to students in the first weeks of our course, to make plain the reasons for our assigned exercises. One is, of course, the practical value of note-taking. The second is the danger, in our intellectual climate, that diligence in note-taking will lead to essentially passive memorization of historical information. The third is the presence in good note-taking of two components, active investigating and scrupulous summarizing, both of which require deliberate attention.

The first of these points, the practical value of note-taking, can be put in a few simple assertions. Note-taking is a central tool in history study. In the taking of notes the historian, at any level of craftsmanship, puts to decisive use whatever skills of investigation he possesses. For the beginner to study history without paper and pen would be like his doing his mathematics exclusively in his head. The history student can work much better when he does his thinking both on paper and in the mind, rather than in the mind unaided. This is the reason for students at all undergraduate levels to take notes —"for thinking purposes," they can tell themselves—even when studying textbooks which they have bought and so will continue to have right at their elbow.

Notes are a part of thinking. Earnest students should be warned against copying off whole phrases or sentences out of desire to be accurate. We lay down the rule that anything taken from a reading must be translated into the note-taker's own words. The one exception, aside from single technical words, is the rare phrase that deserves verbatim quotation within quotation marks. Translating into one's own language promotes thought and becomes the indispensable process of digesting what is being read. As the student completes and looks back over each page of notes, the ideas should seem to him already half mastered and made his own, by their passage through his active mind. If not, he has plainly postponed the essential act of studying.

There are two subsidiary arguments that we mention in personal conferences. Any student who acquires the habit of regularly putting each item into his own words is at the very least less likely to find his mind going to sleep in the midst of studying. He should see that any string of words copied from a book into his notes is plain evidence that he has not been wide awake. Secondly, the translating habit will be the best protection against lapses into unintentional plagiarism in subsequent course papers. Beginners need to be reminded that teachers, even more than the public at large, will take any plagiarism as a direct insult to the intelligence of readers.

These comments on the value of active thought contribute to the second main point we wish our beginners to understand from the start. This is that the greatest handicap to their progress as students of history is likely to be a reliance on rote accumulation of facts. They deserve every encouragement they can be given to bend their efforts in the opposite direction, for until recently emphases within the historical profession have unfortunately encouraged acceptance of rote accumulation.

We explain that fifty years or so ago historians tended to consider the gathering of facts separate from, and essentially a preliminary to, any constructive thinking about the facts. This may have been in part a reflection of the prestige in which historians then held medieval records. Especially in France, a corps of professional archivists had developed particular skills for testing, dating, and explaining records. The writing of history often seemed to be on a quite separate scholarly level. Since then our understanding of the nature of historical work has changed, and one of the changes has been to reject the view that you must first assemble the facts before you have a right to think about what they may add up to. Marc Bloch, the great French medievalist, put it admirably in 1941 in his parting testament as historian:

> Many people and, it appears, even some authors of manuals entertain an extraordinarily simplified notion of our working procedure. First, as they are only too eager to tell you, there are the documents. The historian collects them, reads them, attempts to weigh their authenticity and truthfulness. Then, and only then, he makes use of them. There is only one trouble with this idea: no historian has ever worked in such a way, even when, by some caprice, he fancied that he was doing so.

Turning to examples of texts or documents, Bloch showed that even those

> . . . which seem the clearest and the most accommodating will speak only when they are properly questioned. . . . In other words, every historical research supposes that the inquiry has a direction at the very first step.[1]

This was a strong plea for cross-examining the evidence, starting with the first step of any inquiry. We teachers make essentially this same recommendation to our students, that they put themselves in the frame of mind of vigorous cross-examining whenever they begin on a new reading. We warn them that active reading will probably not come easily at first because it is very different from the way that most of them studied in high school. There they were required to read for each day only a small number of pages from a single textbook, and to repeat back in full detail whatever part of this reading the teacher selected for recitation or examination. Above all, while in high school they understood that the important examinations such as the College Boards would be chiefly objective-style tests, for which they should commit to memory the maximum number of separate historical facts. The limited resources of the secondary schools, the enormous demands placed on teachers by large classes and extracurricular duties, and the pressure of numbers on the national examining agencies, have combined to make memorization of

[1] M. Bloch, *The Historian's Craft,* trans. P. Putnam (New York, 1958), 64–65.

textbook facts the one method of history study that has been drilled into students.

To counter these habits, we arrange our first few weeks' instruction in note-taking to drive home the value of actively cross-examining readings of all types. Different forms of questioning are tried out. The students are asked to frame their own questions and so find out for themselves what makes a question appropriate for history study. At the same time in class discussion we find occasions to make our third general point, that effective historical inquiry is a matter of combining this active questioning with scrupulous summarizing. To press one or two selective lines of questioning, and still achieve a faithful digest, remains a characteristic problem of historical work at the highest levels of scholarly attainment. It helps the ordinary beginner to tell him so as he looks back uncertainly over his notes on the first assignments of the year.

To make the issue clear early in the course we assign students an example of a great historian's combination of selective arguing with workmanlike summarizing. Our current example is the first half of Chapter 20 in Edward Gibbon's *Decline and Fall of the Roman Empire,* which examines Emperor Constantine's conversion to Christianity. Although the language is difficult for the ordinary freshman in our classes, the remoteness of Gibbon's style of thought from our day helps students see more objectively the selective line of argument he is pressing, and the coolness and irony with which he exposes the human qualities of the first great patron of Christianity. The best of our students can see how well this bias illustrates eighteenth-century rationalism. What is impressive in these pages by Gibbon, however, is how carefully he covers the evidence and does justice to the inferences of earlier scholars, at the same time that he builds up his personal interpretation and paints in his own reactions with bold colors. Any teachers who feel uncertain of the appropriateness of valuing Gibbon's work in this way may look at the excellent statement in Mr. Per Fuglum's *Edward Gibbon* (Oslo, 1953), chapter III.

Students can thus be encouraged to see their own responsibility to be workmanlike in their note-taking, whether or not they are conscious of having selective interests. Just as Gibbon carefully provided all the proper footnotes, even though he was writing a best seller, so they should now mark down in their note-taking the identity of each reading they use, author and title and date and pages. We find it advisable throughout the year to provide reminders that these practical touches of scholarly care are not to be slighted. Now and then we find ourselves offering our personal testimony that care in handling data does ensure that historians cherishing quite different beliefs or viewpoints can communicate easily, learn from one another, and appreciate deeply each other's scholarly findings.

These, then, are the three general points we make in the first weeks of the course: the importance of note-taking, the danger of using it for rote learning, and the need both to pursue personally chosen questions and to maintain impartial summarizing. At the same time we are introducing the students to the practical details of taking notes. . . .

Active interests and a questioning attitude are at the heart of good study-ing and good note-taking. Our course deliberately employs readings of various types and qualities, to force students to be on their toes. Often when they come into class feeling that by their standards the assignment for the day is second-rate, they can quickly see what is wrong with it: the researcher or writer simply did not trouble to ask himself any vigorous questions. When no significant or exacting questions are posed, intellectual flabbiness is likely to follow, implications are missed, and presentation is weak. We therefore pro-pose to each student in his first weeks that since he is inevitably working up his understanding of history afresh, he must take responsibility for develop-ing his own questions or choosing among those that he can pick up. In either case it is up to him to make them as clear and meaningful as he can.

Pamphlets on "How to Study," available in many American schools, advise the student to pick up his book and skim the assigned pages for two or three minutes before starting to read. This is excellent advice. Before he begins to study in detail, the student should give himself a chance to see what the pages as a whole have to offer, what he should look for, and so what question (or questions) he should keep in the back of his mind as he reads. For this pur-pose he best spends those two or three minutes on glancing through the in-troductory paragraph or the final summary paragraph, whichever seems to him more informative, and then on letting his eye run down the marginal headings or over the topic sentences in scattered sample paragraphs. This preliminary skimming and judging of the reading should become a habit. Since students' previous study habits make the practice hard to acquire, our teachers must again and again specify it in assigned exercises, and furnish other reminders of its value.

But what question or questions should the student set out to answer? Plainly, his choice depends upon the nature of the materials before him, as well as upon what he brings to them. It is important for him to be flexible and perceptive in his question-asking. So we give practice on successive days with different sorts of questions, to equip him with an awareness of the range of possibilities:

"What is the main point (or points) made in the reading?"

"What is there for me to notice and bear in mind about the author (or sources used)?"

"What useful historical questions can I make up and apply here out of present-day issues that this reading reminds me of?"

"How did things happen to turn out the way they did?"

"What human angles which meant much to people of the time am I likely to be missing?"

Preliminary skimming leads naturally to the first question. What is the chief point of the reading? What is it trying to do, or does it do? This is a question for which good notes are precisely the best answer. The point the reading actually makes may not be quite the same as the author intended or announced. Our students are thoroughly familiar with today's tendency in news magazines and over the air to be heavily factual, and they recognize readily enough that being factual does not in the least stand in the way of bias and distortion. We want them to have many chances to practice note-taking on readings in which the selecting and ordering of the facts, and the coloring of incidental words, effectively present a strong interpretation or opinion. On several controversial assignments we instruct them to capture in their notes the special structure of argument in the reading, or its quiet emphases, or its key color-words, so as to expose the character of the lurking interpretation. This is note-taking to answer the pivotal question, "What is the author really doing here?"

There is, to be sure, a much more restricted sort of study question that we find ourselves providing throughout the year on the assignment sheets we pass out, one or two such study questions for nearly every reading. These are not questions directly on the main point or points of each reading, since after the first few weeks we expect the students to do the questioning of that type on their own. Moreover, they do not ask for specific answers in the notes the students take down. They are instead leading questions, chosen to call attention directly or indirectly to issues that the students need to be aware of. . . .

Even with these suggestions on the assignment sheets, students are slow to acquire the habit of thinking of one or two questions before starting to read. In class discussions we insert blunt reminders, for example by asking, "How many of you realized before you got all the way into the second reading for today how much it contradicted the first reading?" But no student is really over this hurdle until on at least one assignment in history he has found a whole succession of interesting and appropriate questions crowding in on him as he settles down to read. Success in bringing him to this point seems to require not only prodding him into sound habits of mustering study questions. It also requires confronting him again and again with historical questions that seem alive and wide open to debate.

Our second assignment every September attacks the credibility of Tacitus as witness, along six indicated lines of criticism. This group of questions arouses students' interest at once. They can appreciate that it is at the frontiers of scholarly knowledge. It puts a question mark against the major conclusion they reached in the previous class hour, the conclusion that the Germans back in Tacitus' day were primarily militarily minded. The imagination of the better students is stirred by the possibility that it was Tacitus' impulse to moralize which provided for later Germans a picture of themselves containing the elements of Nazi doctrine. And quite a lot of evidence pro and con can be assembled in students' notes, illustrating how much we can usefully and satisfyingly ask about the authors or sources of our information.

For the third assignment each student reads some eleven of the opening chapters of "The Acts of the Apostles" in the *New Testament*, using whatever edition he himself prefers, and frames two study questions of his own choice, answering each with not more than eight items of evidence from the chapters. A number of students dutifully come into class with study questions bearing on the main points of the reading, or on the essential credibility of the author, in line with the examples in the preceding class sessions. But others use their freedom of choice to submit questions more personally interesting to them, which involve matters of religious dispute. These student questions are worth looking at in class—with all due respect for religious feelings—as characteristic examples of special-interest questions, with real possibilities and difficulties for history study.

We put it to our students that they have a chance here to prepare themselves for the inevitable times ahead in life when personal or political or sectarian interests will suddenly crowd into the center of their vision. It may be quite pointless for them now to spend time learning to keep their intellectual balance on strictly milk-and-water subjects, if sound judgments are going to mean most to them in the future in situations more like strong drink, situations of aroused patriotism, for example, or personal animosity. By considering a few of the questions turned in for this assignment on "The Acts," our classes can arrive at a few rules for keeping within strictly manageable bounds questions on problems of human affairs.

Plainly a question like "Was Jesus Christ divine?" is not a proper question for purposes of this history assignment. From such examples the students can see that, to be a proper *historical* question, a question must be so put that it invites a workaday answer composed primarily of pieces of the evidence referred to. In our written instructions for "The Acts" on the assignment sheet we prepare the students for this, actually, by suggesting that the study questions they submit should not point to conclusions which "depend primarily on religious convictions for their acceptability." A down-to-earth answer, put together out of pieces of evidence collected as notes, has a chance to prove acceptable to others who do not share the questioner's religious convictions. If the student's choice of the question about Christ's divinity represents real interest, he should consider translating this interest instead into a narrower and much more manageable question. An example might be, "What are the characteristic ways in which the author of 'Acts' speaks of the relation between Jesus and God?" This is a narrow enough question, at least, to get an unambiguous and convincing answer. It would seem to be a proper historical question for this assigned reading.

Our written instructions also suggest that the study questions on "The Acts" should point to "conclusions about the early church which seem significant to history." A question is more useful for historical study, that is, if it relates to the main point of the reading—or to what is for us as readers the main point of the reading. It is also a sounder question, since the answer to it then will not consist simply of a few isolated pieces of evidence, easily open to misunderstanding. The revised question just now suggested is not ideal for beginners, for this very reason, and the one word "characteristic" has had to be inserted into it to underline its wider implications. Students should learn that a good historical question not only is sharp enough to secure an answer in the form of definite details, but also broad enough in its implications to provide the answer with meaning and confirmation.

A question is better for historical use, then, if it partly resembles the general study question that seeks out the main point of the reading. It is also better for historical purposes if it has some of the quality of the second group of study questions, which looks critically at the author or source. This is perhaps the chief change evident in the revised question above about the relation between Jesus and God. By focusing on what the author of "The Acts" says, it calls for a practical answer in terms of evidence and still has broader implications tying it, through the word "characteristic," to much else in the chapters.

Yet it has one practical defect that remains to be pointed out to the students. Since it speaks about "Jesus and God," and their relationship, the beginner may find it hard to handle in workaday fashion—whether he is a believing Christian, a skeptic, or a non-Christian. Many words that come into our thinking about history are powerfully evocative words, and at the risk of being called a Mr. Milquetoast the history student must avoid them, translating them into more colorless language just to make sure that he will do the job accurately. For the same reason he may need to bring in other evidence to provide more of a balance of contrasting interpretations.

Questions raising religious issues with respect to "The Acts" are not, we feel, to be pressed home. We move right on in the next assignment to consider Gibbon's discussion of Constantine's conversion, with its quite different flavor. Here we can attempt more specific criticisms and appreciations, because this is an instance of academic historical work, though on a matter of religion. The questions on "The Acts" remain for our students primarily vivid illustrations of difficulties that they will face on different issues, such as democracy and Communism, throughout their study of history.

The requirements of sound historical questions, then, seem to include inviting a direct answer in notes drawn from the evidence referred to, connecting by broader implications to main issues being investigated, providing for critical awareness of the author or source, and avoiding disturbingly evocative language or onesided emphasis. If the students learn a respect for these requirements, it seems unnecessary to repeat to them any of the arguments or counter-arguments of historians over the propriety of letting present-day questions influence the study of the past. . . .

Every live question that beginners bring up, whether as a study question or simply spontaneously in class discussion, is actually likely to be a "present-minded" question, and still one that the student is more or less successfully reframing as a historical question. Everything that he learns about history's methods during the year should make clearer to him that meeting the requirements for historical question-asking is a small price to pay for obtaining answers from history. These answers are, of course, historical answers, properly focused so strictly on the past moment that it is only through their overtones that they speak to the present-day situation. But it is a rare student who after careful exposure to historical method does not find such answers to his own live questions a satisfying reward for the effort required.

Every class discussion or lecture, if well handled, is an effective illustration of how to shape worth-while historical questions, and how to follow them through. Now and then a particular reading in our course—chapter IV in Pirenne's *Medieval Cities*,[2] for example—lends itself to consideration in class as a clear example of the same thing. But there is one place in our teaching where the student advancing beyond the first weeks of instruction is called upon to handle question-asking deliberately, and it is a surprisingly searching test of what skill he has gained in the privacy of his own studying. This test comes when he is asked to write an outside paper that involves a degree of independent research. Even though the subject is handed to him, he has to know how to rethink it in terms of his own interests and understandings. He has to know how to keep its cutting edge sharp and clarify its various implications, turning these into subsidiary questions when appropriate. Too often he makes even a good subject dull, that is, both uncertain in its focus on relevant detail and weak or empty of wider implications. Quite as often he fails to make the central question his own, and so mislays it along the way and winds up with no argument at all.

The most effective device we have yet found to improve the writing of course papers gets at exactly these problems, even though we first tried it solely to insure that all students were doing their work independently. A week or five days before the outside paper is due, we set aside a class hour for the students to write out their first drafts, in class and without notes or books. We tell them to write as satisfactory a draft as they can within the fifty minutes, picturing themselves as by chance talking on a train or bus with an interested stranger and trying to tell him about the paper. The point in all this, we say, is to make sure that the argument of the paper does not remain a collection of scraps of evidence and opinion but comes to life as their own argument. We collect these first drafts, scan them, and return them within twenty-four hours for the revising and filling out with evidence that will make them into proper papers for submission. Notes and drafts are handed in with the final paper. Nothing that we have previously tried has underlined so effectively the responsibility which the student must accept, when he comes to write a paper, for developing a central argument and presenting it in good order.

But we feel we have accomplished what is central if we bring him to the habit of actively framing questions as he studies. Questions of his own will inevitably guide his selection of details to put down as notes, and then his

[2] Henri Pirenne, *Medieval Cities* (Princeton, 1925).

notes can seem to him significantly independent of the teacher's preferences and the textbook's whim. They cannot then seem a dead collection for him to memorize. He is likely to keep on improving the sharpness and relevance of the questions that already enliven his note-taking.

The other element in the effective studying of history is obviously the straightforward summarizing of information, while playing down all expectations or special interests. Note-taking then focuses on picking out the minimum essentials to represent fairly all parts of the information. Summarizing may merge with question-asking so closely that, given broad enough study questions, good notes on either principle can turn out much the same. But the frame of mind of responsible summarizing is often needed and has its value as a regular ingredient of active study. When assignments in the textbook start recurring, and the novelty of the first week or two has worn off, we still urge students to take notes on all that they read as an effective use of their study time. Notes on a textbook should of course be conspicuously brief, but they can be a great help to accurate and fruitful thinking.

Note-taking when undertaken as summarizing should by all means be made as efficient as possible. It must make allowances for active and responsible selection. We recommend terse statement, with whatever abbreviations the student himself finds natural, so long as they are not the sort to trip him up later. Efficient summarizing requires setting the notes down on the page in whatever arrangement saves time initially and allows for quickest scanning later in review. But to give students more precise instructions than these runs the risk of turning note-taking back into a passive chore performed with a sense of virtue by the diligent.

We have to admit that note-taking requires more time than taking no notes at all. During the first few weeks we urge students to recognize that throughout the year their effort must be to take notes down as fast as possible. After the initial skimming of the assignment, they should try for the least possible interruption of reading. Pen or pencil should be still moving when the eyes go back to read. We ask beginners not to leave their note-taking for a second reading, and not to make a second clean copy after taking down notes the first time. The writing, as matter of mechanics, should take as little time as possible. We may collect students' notes every so often, in order to make helpful suggestions, but we do not venture to give grades on them. If encouragement is continuous from the teacher, the students' unrelenting practice soon brings a steady increase in speed. Many students will eventually admit that their reading has hardly been slowed at all.

The first notes turned in for inspection always consist too largely of general headings instead of specific evidence. "Economic difficulties" is nearly worthless for the decline of Rome. "Shortage of currency" is better because it keeps the focus sharper for the picture forming in the student's mind. Therefore the student is well advised to regard the introductory remarks in the typical first paragraph of a chapter as no more than showing him what the outline structure of his specific notes, their grouping on his page, will probably have to be. The topic sentence of a paragraph is similarly in most cases best dismissed as simply a pointer to the paragraph's central one or two details. It is these details that deserve to be jotted down, briefly, in the student's own words. We advise students to acquire, as quickly as they can, the hard-boiled attitude of a police detective, waiting with boredom for generalities and courtesies to pass by but recording the solid bit of evidence the moment it turns up. The analogy with a police detective is actually a useful one for their growing understanding of historical method. They must be sharpening their eyes for clues that may point to something else other than the surface argument. And clues are recorded much more often, and then are available in the notes to be thought over later, if each note-taker is determined not to waste his time on loose talk.

With comments like these, the students' daily note-taking can get off to a fairly smooth start, particularly because some of our assignments are in standard textbooks. Most American textbooks have the information responsibly laid out to facilitate digesting into summary form, paragraph by paragraph, at a satisfyingly even rate. Since our first assignments are source readings, followed by scholarly arguments, our students do not find it hard to understand that their style of note-taking has to be flexible. On one reading it is more of a paragraph-by-paragraph digesting, and on the next more of a selective listing of what they find in answer to their study questions.

The emphasis we place on question-asking leads the students to show, week by week, more active attention to possibly significant detail and more disposition to ask "Why?" even in the midst of summarizing. As questions come up in class on precise details, we teachers find it natural to refer the students right back to the notes that they have brought to class. Thus the strengths and weaknesses of their notes are exposed to them directly. If teachers are careful to set expectations neither too high nor too low, the students will slowly gain from this testing the confidence that they need. They see that they are actually beginning to pick up in advance the bits of evidence that are most useful for answers to unexpected and new questions. They can learn from this also the sense in which it is quite enough to have only a few of the pieces of evidence required by the fresh question. After all, no two persons' notes should be identical, let alone complete, in coverage of possibly useful evidence.

But before this time, in the first month of the course, many of the more earnest students speak up in real distress. They are taking fuller and fuller notes in spite of themselves, and this takes much too much time. We insist that good notes are brief notes, and warn against their inspecting the forest by trying to pat each tree trunk. At this point, however, they are in a good position to understand that historical knowledge is in a special sense different from knowledge in, say, mathematics. Any student in history must be content to pick, for firm remembering, only one point out of each group of from five to ten new points that he registers and even thinks over on first reading. He should try to think of the one point as representative of those five to ten, pulling them together in his own mind to form a proper group. We find it a handy figure of speech, in explaining this, to say that a history student does not normally understand a point reliably unless he is aware of as much more about it, really, as there is to an iceberg under the water's surface. He can make the point bear weight safely—unless it is tied in on all sides to other things he knows—only if he knows or half-knows this much more detail about it. He should normally *not* put the supporting detail down as notes. . . .

This rule of selection may create difficulty now and then for the teachers, who must give credit for careful use of evidence but can hardly condone conclusions that turn out wrong because much has been passed over. But in our experience this difficulty is rare and confined to the first weeks. When the student has selected one fact out of seven, he is still responsible for having picked the most representative or influential one, according to his judgment. As soon as the procedure begins to work for him as it should, enough of the meaning of the facts omitted clings to each fact he selects to protect him from major errors. As students gain mastery of other aspects of historical method, their conclusions starting from different choices of details tend to converge much more than diverge. The freedom of selection offers a real freedom of interpretation and coloring, as we feel it should. We find no problem of erratic conclusions.

One of the practical reasons for making notes brief by means of this rule of selection is to help students retain control of sharply seen detail when they come to review for examinations. In good note-taking each detail that they have written down is their handle for a package of understanding that is considerably larger. These selected details must take their place in groupings on some broader scale. If the notes from the start have been put on each page with clear groupings and subordinations, the spacings and indentations make it easy for the eye at review time to divide up the information quickly into the most meaningful larger packages. To these larger packages, in turn, we suggest that brief labels or handles be attached, by the underlining of one or two key words with red pencil or the entering of these words in the margin.

These key labels should if possible *not* be generalized headings or logical summaries. Instead they should remain details as specific and vivid as the student feels he can use without confusion to represent the whole package of information. He might end up with "Sans Souci," the name of Frederick the Great's palace and park at Potsdam, as a reminder of Frederick's contempt for German culture, his relationship to Voltaire, his version of Versailles-type monarchy, his sophistication and harsh upbringing, and, more widely, for all of these together as one significant cross-section of the enlightened despotism of 1763–89. When reviewing ends with sharp items highlighted in the foreground, then the pressure during an examination brings these first to mind. If they are in any sense effective handles to more information, further needed details follow readily, in this case details about Frederick and his fellow despots. This actually has many advantages over the student's remembering the generalized phrase "enlightened despots" and then fumbling in the back of his mind for some names and precise details to fill it out.

To make these key details stand out even more clearly at review time, many students find it good practice to begin with a wide margin at the left of their notepaper, marking off by a vertical line as much as a third of the sheet. They can then enter their running notes in the right-hand two-thirds with less hesitation for indentations and spacings, since the margin allows room for more labels whenever needed for clarity. The wide margin also invites jotting down terse comments and references to other data, which may be essential for effective study. For any following review the student can easily cover up the right-hand two-thirds and let his eye dwell successively on the labels in the margin, to check his grasp of what he has on the page of notes. Even this is preliminary, however, to a last stage of effective review, which is to put notes to one side, think up a possible question, and jot down on scratch paper the key labels for the different bodies of evidence that come to mind for the answer—then try another question, and then another. Summarizing through responsible selection has plainly been done well when this final act of studying demonstrates flexible command of an adequate store of detail.

During the first weeks of the year several students protest that they do not really know what to select. Wouldn't it help to tell the whole class directly? We answer that "What to select?" is what the whole course is about. In direct proportion as any student masters both methods and subject matter of history, he will know more surely what to select for any notes as he reads. Somewhat later, after we have made it clearer that the rule of selection involves choosing a detail that will represent well the rest that must be omitted or subordinated, we can suggest the simple touchstone: "Which is the detail that will work most effectively for you?" The beginner, that is, can start with an unpretentious judgment, one which allows for his own interests and sensitivities: "This item may do, for it seems the best to remind me of the others and help me understand."

Once they have grasped this central criterion of usefulness, the students should learn some principles of selection that they can associate with being systematic. If they have already tried through notes to pin down an interpretation conveyed between the lines in a "factual" account, or if they have simply been asked often enough whether the textbook author was advancing any central judgment in the last section, they can grasp that systematic notes have to pick up both structural details and clues. The structural details are, of course, the milestone events with their place and date, the episodes that indicate the range of variation in each situation, and the characteristics that best reveal relations of cause or of parallelism between the groupings of facts. The clues, on the other hand, are the odd items that look like especially good indicators of the human situation, or even of some possible chain of causes waiting to be uncovered. These structural details and clues are best taken down with some regard for the iceberg ratio, which guards against the possibility that the account used may be too thin to be trustworthy, and so encourages the student to look at other information to fill out his understanding.

There are many other features of good notes, of course, which our teachers find occasion during the year to call to the attention of their classes. One statement of the criteria for good notes, which was drawn up to provide new members of our staff with a well-rounded picture of the essentials, follows:

1) Notes should be meaningful and specific.
   a) They should be directed purposefully toward answering some significant question or questions provided by the instructor or developed through skimming the assigned pages.
   b) They should be solidly concrete, noting who, what, where, when, and why in detail, rather than made up of loose generalizations.
   c) They should be clear as to reliability, indicating the value of the testimony supplied by the witness.
   d) And whenever this will make them more meaningful, they should point up recurrent phenomena in history, such as the role of event-making individuals, or illustrate the theories of social sciences, like supply-demand analysis in the case of American agriculture.
2) Notes should be pointed toward constructing explanations for historical events.
   a) They should include bits of information or comments in brackets by the student to highlight their relevance to the problem under examination.
   b) They should represent in true proportion the full variety of the evidence.
   c) And they should be tested, even if only in mental reflection, by arrangement on synoptic lists or charts which summarize the evidence by key details and disclose possible cause-effect relationships.
3) Notes should give the maximum help to imaginative understanding.
   a) By including samples of the tone and manner of the author in the case of primary sources, preferably through short quotations.
   b) And by indicating, wherever possible, the way people at the time looked at things.

This statement combines elements of emphasis on question-asking with elements of systematic digesting. One matter which is related to both topics requires special emphasis for students several times during the year. Especially in working up course papers, they need to look for substantial bits of evidence on both sides of each controversial issue mentioned. This is usually easy enough on the issue between Luther and Erasmus, for example. But they must make a real effort to escape being content with the "right answer" to any controversy that was settled long ago, like that over the Copernican theory. We ask them to try in their notes to do justice to the arguments and uncertainties of the past. Taking care to highlight all the relevant controversies, both in note-taking and in course papers, is to help oneself acquire more perceptiveness towards questions and more impartial understanding of the whole. The questions that men in the past might have asked are then more apt to spring to mind to supplement the questions arising from today's preoccupations.

Students' minds fortunately make no sharp separation between systematic digesting and the posing and answering of historical questions. The persistent following out of a single searching study question, the raising of one sharp question after another, and the maintaining of an over-all questioning attitude while summarizing, merge into one another and are equally appropriate on different occasions. The habit of relying on sharp detail to do the work of summaries, and the rule of selection that requires choosing among details, give the student scope in his summaries for selecting items which will also best answer his study questions. Above all, the student has some chance to work up to the conclusions he seeks by the unpretentious and satisfying method of putting together the facts of his own choice. He is not mechanically bound to the interpretation embodied in the textbook's selection and ordering of its evidence. Even at its most methodical, his note-taking calls on him to decide what he will pick, on the basis of all the knowledge and skill that he can develop. His practice of careful workmanship stimulates his interests and disciplines them at the same time.

CHAPTER 14 Getting Evidence from Charts, Tables, and Graphs

The social sciences rely increasingly upon statistics. As a result, more and more evidence is being presented in the form of charts, tables, and graphs. Our newspapers and periodicals reflect this trend. No citizen can understand articles about the economy without knowing how to read statistical information accurately. Specific practice with reading charts, tables, and graphs has become essential both for intelligent work in the social studies and for full participation as citizens in American society.

Like the mode of inquiry of the social sciences and history, the reading of statistical information receives only incidental attention in most social studies classes. Teachers use graphs and tables that appear in social studies textbooks incidentally to the main assignment in the text. Hence, attention concentrates on material in the text reading rather than on techniques of graphical presentation unless the teacher makes a special effort to teach them. This focus is appropriate most of the time, but only after a teacher knows that his students can extract information accurately from charts, tables, and graphs.

The best way to assure mastery of these skills is to concentrate specifically upon the task of teaching them in several classes throughout the year. Each teacher should deliberately select the types of graphs, tables, and charts appropriate to the course he is teaching and develop several lessons around the problems of reading them accurately. Once these are discussed thoroughly, incidental attention to the interpretation of tabular information should be enough to reinforce and maintain skills.

This chapter consists of two lessons designed originally for a ninth-grade course. After a brief introduction that places the reading in the wider context of the subject of the course, each lesson consists entirely of graphs, charts, and tables. Beneath each are a number of study questions. As you read, keep the following issues in mind:

1) Why organize lessons around charts, tables, and graphs?
2) What are the major purposes of the study questions which appear under each tabular presentation? Are there additional reading skills which are not covered by the study questions?
3) Can similar exercises be devised for types of graphs, tables, and charts which are omitted entirely from these two lessons?

THE SOCIAL BACKGROUNDS OF AMERICAN POLITICAL DECISION-MAKERS

Edwin Fenton

It is impossible to generalize about the social backgrounds of all American political leaders. Much depends upon the part of the country they are from and the importance of their office. For example, a county commissioner in a predominantly rural county in the Midwest would more often than not be a farmer. On the other hand, the mayor of a large city would probably represent a business or professional group. Since it is impossible to generalize about all political leaders, we will concentrate our investigation in this lesson on the social backgrounds of national political leaders and pay less attention to leaders at other levels of government.

By social background we mean race, religion, education, the occupation of the decision-maker, and the occupation of his father. We will try to determine whether national political leaders have social characteristics similar to those of typical Americans or whether men with certain backgrounds form a disproportionate part of our political leadership.

This is a very important question. Many Americans believe that each citizen is born with an equal chance to hold public office. In theory this is true; in practice some people seem to be born with advantages over others. In order to understand how our leaders are recruited, we need to examine their backgrounds.

For evidence about the social backgrounds of decision-makers we will use five tables taken from the standard authority on this subject, Donald Matthews, *The Social Backgrounds of Political Decision-Makers*. Under each table we have asked specific questions, all of which can be answered by examining the information in the table itself. Since one of our objectives in this assignment is to help you to learn to use information in tabular form, our procedure has been designed in part to help you extract the maximum information possible.

You should first turn to the tables and answer the questions under each table for yourself. Then come back to the study questions below and answer them. They are designed to help pull together the more specific information that you can derive from individual tables.

1) According to the criteria given in the five tables, what is the social background of a "typical" American decision-maker on the national level?
2) How do you account for the predominance of men of this particular social background in American politics?
3) Do the tables lead you to believe that the general picture is changing?
4) Does the information in the table imply that the United States has a "ruling class"? If you are not certain what the term "ruling class" means, write down what you think it means and then check it against the definition you find in the dictionary.

TABLE 1 NEGROES IN CONGRESS: 1869–1950

Congress	Number in House	Number in Senate
41st	2	1
42nd	5	0
43rd	7	0
44th	7	1
45th	3	1
46th	0	1
47th	1	0
48th	2	0
49th	2	0
50th	0	0
51st	3	0
52nd	1	0
53rd	1	0
54th	1	0
55th	1	0
56th	1	0
57th to 71st	0	0
72nd	1	0
73rd	1	0
74th	1	0
75th	1	0
76th	1	0
77th	1	0
78th	1	0
79th	2	0
80th	2	0
81st	2	0

SOURCE: Donald Matthews, *The Social Backgrounds of Political Decision-Makers*, p. 23. Copyright 1954 by Random House, Inc. Reprinted by permission.

1) In 1869 Negroes made up 14 percent of the population; today they are 10 percent. The membership of the 41st Congress was 333; today's Congress numbers 535. According to Table 1, has the Negro race been proportionately represented in Congress?

TABLE 2 RELIGIOUS AFFILIATION OF UNITED STATES SENATORS AND REPRE-
SENTATIVES 77TH, 78TH, 81ST CONGRESSES (IN PERCENTAGES)

Religion	77th Congress Senate	77th Congress House	78th Congress Senate	78th Congress House	81st Congress Senate	81st Congress House	Total Claimed Membership (1950)
Protestant	81	70	85	74	87	83	59
Congregational	7	3	6	4	6	4	6
Presbyterian	11	13	17	12	12	12	4
Episcopal	10	11	17	10	10	12	3
Unitarian	1	1	2	1	1	1	*
(group sum)	29	28	42	27	29	29	13
Methodist	22	17	18	17	17	22	13
Lutheran	2	4	2	3	4	4	7
Baptist	10	11	12	12	13	12	20
(group sum)	34	32	32	32	34	38	40
Disciples of Christ	2	3	3	3	2	0	2
Mormon	2	0	2	1	3	0	1
Society of Friends	1	0	2	0	2	1	*
Church of Christ, Scientist	1	0	1	1	1	0	**
Christian Church	0	0	0	2	4	4	*
Unspecified and other	12	6	3	8	11	12	3
Roman Catholic	11	20	10	18	12	16	34
Jewish	0	2	0	2	1	1	6
Other	0	0	0	0	0	0	1
None	4	1	3	0	0	0	0
Unknown	3	6	2	6	0	0	0
	99	99	100	100	100	100	100
	(n=96)	(n=435)	(n=96)	(n=435)	(n=109)	(n=289)	

* Less than 5%.
** Membership figures may not be published.

SOURCE: Donald Matthews, *The Social Backgrounds of Political Decision-Makers,*
p. 24. Copyright 1954 by Random House, Inc. Reprinted by permission.

1) According to Table 2, what percentage of the total religious population of the U.S. in 1950 was claimed by the Congregational, Presbyterian, Episcopalian, and Unitarian churches?

2) What percentage of Senators of the 81st Congress were members of
these four groups?

3) What was probably the more important factor in the election of these
men: their religion or the fact that most of them were probably richer,
better educated, and had more prestige in their communities than
"average" people?

TABLE 3 EDUCATIONAL LEVEL OF AMERICAN POLITICAL DECISION-MAKERS (IN PERCENTAGES)

Highest Level Attained	Presidents, Vice-presidents, Cabinet Members (1877–1934)	Supreme Court Justices (1897–1937)	United States Senators (1949–51)	United States Representatives (1941–43)	High-level Civil Servants (1940)	State Governors (1930–40)	Missouri State Legislators (1901–31)	Population Over 25 Years of Age (1940)
None	0	0	0	0	0	0	0	5
Grade school	11	0	3	0	0	3	30	54
High school	10	0	10	12	7	20	13	31
College	79	100	87	88	93	77	57	10
	100	100	100	100	100	100	100	100
	(n=176)	(n=20)	(n=108)	(n=431)	(n=242)	(n=135)	(n=2,876)	

SOURCE: Donald Matthews, *The Social Backgrounds of Political Decision-Makers*, p. 27. Copyright 1954 by Random House, Inc. Reprinted by permission.

1) According to Table 3, what percentage of the population in 1940 had a college education?
2) How many of the 431 United States Representatives counted in this survey had received a college education?
3) In which governmental positions were better-educated people found? Why do you think this was the case?

TABLE 4 OCCUPATIONAL CLASS OF FATHERS OF AMERICAN POLITICAL DECISION-MAKERS (IN PERCENTAGES)

Occupational Class of Father	President, Vice-president, Cabinet 1789–1934	High Level Civil Servant 1940	U.S. Senators 81st Congress 1949–51	U.S. Representatives** 77th Congress 1941–43	Labor Force 1890
Professional	38	28	22	31	5
Proprietors & officials	20	30	33	31	6
Farmers	38	29	40	29	26
Low salaried workers	*	3	1	0	5
Wage earners	4	10	3	9	36
Servants	0	0	0	0	7
Farm laborers	0	0	0	0	15
Unknown, unclassi-fied	0	0	1	0	0
	100	100	100	100	100
	(n=311)	(n=180)	(n=109)	(n=186)	

* Less than 1.
** Subject to substantial error because of incomplete data.

SOURCE: Donald Matthews, *The Social Backgrounds of Political Decision-Makers,* p. 29. Copyright 1954 by Random House, Inc. Reprinted by permission.

Table 4 provides information about the fathers of the political decision-makers in groups 1, 2, 3, and 4. The year 1890, mentioned in column 5, represents the approximate time that the fathers of important decision-makers of 1950 were in the labor force. On the basis of your understanding of this table, answer the following questions:

1) What was the largest single occupational class in the labor force of 1890?
2) Which were the two smallest occupational classes in the labor force of 1890?
3) Of these three, which class produced the largest number of political decision-makers? Which class produced the smallest number?
4. What percentage of the labor force was made up of low-salaried workers, wage earners, servants, and farm laborers?
5) What percentage of sons from these four classes became (1) U.S. Senators, (2) U.S. Representatives, and (3) high-level civil servants?

TABLE 5 OCCUPATIONAL CLASS OF AMERICAN POLITICAL DECISION-MAKERS (IN PERCENTAGES)

Occupational Class	President, Vice-president, Cabinet* 1877–1934	United States Senators 1949–51	United States Representatives 1949–51	State Governors 1930–40	State Legislators** 1925–35	Labor Force 1940
Professionals	74	69	69	60	36	7
Lawyers	70 }	57 }	56 }	52 }	28 }	
Others	4 }	12 }	13 }	8 }	8 }	
Proprietors & officials	21	24	22	25	25	8
Farmers	2	7	4	11	22	11
Low-salaried workers	1	0	1	1	4	17
Wage earners	2	0	2	1	3	40
Servants	0	0	0	0	0	11
Farm laborers	0	0	0	0	0	7
Unknown, unclassified	0	0	2	3	10	0
	100	100	100	101	100	101
	(n=176)	(n=109)	(n=435)	(n=170)	(n=12,689)	

* Occupations in this column are those for which presidents, vice-presidents, and cabinet officers were trained.
** Figures for the lower houses of 13 selected states and the upper houses of 12. The states are Arkansas, California (lower house only), Illinois, Indiana, Iowa, Louisiana, Maine, Minnesota, Mississippi, New Jersey, New York, Pennsylvania, Washington.

SOURCE: Donald Matthews, *The Social Backgrounds of Political Decision-Makers*, p. 30. Copyright 1954 by Random House, Inc. Reprinted by permission.

1) According to Table 5, which single occupational class produced the most political decision-makers?
2) What was the largest occupational class in the labor force in 1940?
3) Contrast the size of this class with the size of the professional class. Which occupational class produced more political decision-makers?
4) Why do you think some occupational groups produced more political decision-makers than did others?

WHAT TYPES OF POLITICAL ACTIVITY MOST ENGAGE AMERICAN CITIZENS?

Edwin Fenton

In the preceding reading we studied the reasons that many Americans are not active politically. Yet, to divide Americans into only two groups—politically active and politically inactive—would be misleading, for there are many degrees of political activity. An American who votes regularly is participating in politics, although his participation is much less than that of the professional politician. In this reading we will study various types of political activity and the degree to whch American citizens participate in each of these types.

In a previous reading we read an excerpt from Robert Dahl's book *Who Governs,* an investigation of political behavior in New Haven, Connecticut. In another part of this study, Professor Dahl tried to determine what part his respondents actually took in political activity. As you will see, some of his information was taken from historical records, but most of it came from interviews conducted with a scientifically chosen sample of 525 respondents. From their answers to his questions, Professor Dahl constructed tables and figures illustrating various aspects of political activity. If we can assume that people in New Haven are pretty much like people elsewhere in the United States and that their political behavior is similar to that of other Americans, we can learn something from these charts about the political activity of typical American urban dwellers. At least Professor Dahl's work has given us some hypotheses to investigate.

Political scientists must learn to read figures and tables accurately. Tables, charts, and graphs can provide particularly useful and accurate ways to present information. With them we can condense a large amount of information into a small amount of space. We can sometimes make information, such as the percentage of people voting for President as contrasted to those voting for mayor, much more vivid with a graph than it would be in words. All students of political science must learn to use these valuable tools well. You have already had some experience with them in this course.

The assignment for today has two purposes: (1) to study the degree to which American citizens are active participants in politics and (2) to learn to make conclusions from evidence presented in the form of tables and figures. To make this latter task easier, we have prepared questions to accompany each table. Study them carefully as you look over the data presented in the tables. Then, when you have finished answering these specific questions, turn back to the following more general questions and try to answer them for yourself in preparation for class discussion:

1) To what degree is the average citizen concerned with politics and with political activities? Support your generalizations with evidence from Table 1 and from Figures 2 and 3.

2) What relationships can you find between the degree of personal involvement a particular political activity requires and the percentage of citizens who become involved?

3) To what extent do most citizens use the sources of information about politics available to them?

4) How can you explain the degree of political inactivity revealed by these tables and figures?

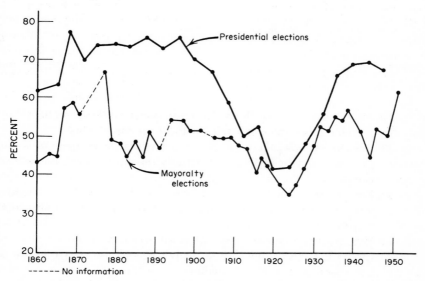

Fig. 1. Percentage of citizens 21 years old and over voting in Presidential and mayoralty elections, 1860–1950. (From Robert A. Dahl, *Who Governs?* New Haven, Conn.: Yale University Press, 1961, p. 277)

1) According to Figure 1, in what year did the largest percentage of eligible voters cast their ballots in a Presidential election? Describe the procedure by which you found your answer.

2) During what years did the smallest percentage of eligible voters vote in a Presidential election?
3) Did more people vote for President or for mayor?
4) Why is percentage of political activity figured in terms of the population 21 years and over rather than in terms of general-population statistics?
5) During the early decades of the twentieth century there was a great rise in the number of immigrants entering the United States. Can you tell whether or not this rise is reflected in Figure 1?

TABLE 1 CAMPAIGN PARTICIPATION, BY KINDS OF ACTIVITIES

	Yes	
	%	N
Does anyone from either party call you up during campaigns or come around and talk to you?	60	320
Do you talk to people during campaigns and try to show them why they should vote for one of the parties or candidates?	33	172
Do you give money or buy tickets or anything to help the campaign for one of the parties or candidates?	26	139
Do you go to political meetings, rallies, dinners, or things like that?	23	119
Have you ever taken part in a party's nominations?	9	44
Do you do other work for a party or candidate?	8	42
Have you ever held an office or had a job in a political party?	5	25
Do you belong to any political club or organization?	4	22
Have you ever held a public office?	1	6
N = 525 registered voters.		

SOURCE: Robert A. Dahl, *Who Governs?* (New Haven, Conn.: Yale University Press, 1961), p. 278.

1) As political activity calls for greater personal involvement, according to Table 1, is it more or less likely to attract participants?
2) Are more people likely (a) to attempt to convince others to vote a particular way or (b) to work actively for a particular candidate or party?
3) Can you tell from Table 1 what factors (such as lack of time, money, interest) seem to be of major importance in keeping people from participating in political activity?
1) What is the subject of Figure 2? What does this mean?
2) Of the 525 voters studied, how many vote and also engage in five or more additional political activities?
3) In how many political activities do the largest number of voters participate?
4) According to Figure 2, what percent of the group studied were nonvoters?
5) How does this compare with the number of nonvoters indicated in Figure 1?
6) How do you account for the seeming difference in these figures?

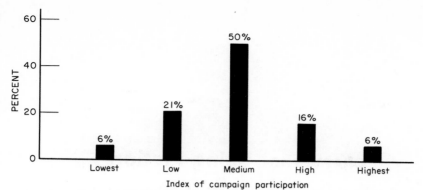

Fig. 2. Campaign participation, by number of activities. Explanation: lowest—nonvoting; low—voting and no other activities; medium—voting and one or two other activities; high —voting and three or four other activities; highest—voting and five or more activities. N = 525; 10 persons in the sample could not be classified. (From Robert A. Dahl, *Who Governs?* New Haven, Conn.: Yale University Press, 1961, p. 278)

TABLE 2 ACTION IN LOCAL AFFAIRS, BY KINDS OF ACTIVITIES

	Yes	
	%	N
When you and your friends get together, do you ever talk about New Haven politics and local affairs?	47	252
Have you ever contacted any local public officials or politicians to let them know what you would like them to do on something you were interested in?	27	141
In the past year or so have you had any contact with political or governmental officials in New Haven?	16	85
During the past year or so have you yourself done anything actively in connection with some local issue or local problem— political or nonpolitical?	13	66
N = 525.		

SOURCE: Robert A. Dahl, *Who Governs?* (New Haven, Conn.: Yale University Press, 1961), p. 279.

1) According to Table 2, what percent of the registered voters studied in New Haven indicated an interest in politics to the extent of talking about political affairs to their friends?

2) What percent indicated an active connection with some local issue?

CHAPTER 15 Using Fiction as Evidence

Should a teacher use fiction as evidence in a history course? If he should, for what purposes? How can students be encouraged to read fiction in order to increase their understanding of an historical period without assuming that knowledge gleaned from a novel can be used as evidence in the same way as events which actually took place? All these questions trouble social studies teachers.

In most history courses fiction is used in only one way. Students read historical novels in order to gain "fresh insights" into a period. But their insights are often inaccurate because they fail to differentiate between the make-believe characters in the novel and the real-life figures who might be studied in a biography. Using fiction with immature students can be dangerous unless they are trained specifically to use it. In fact, the entire practice of assigning historical novels—unless the assignments are being made solely for purposes of motivating students—seems questionable.

Fiction does have great value as evidence. In the first place, the popularity of a particular novel can give a history student insights into the sorts of reading people did in an era, insights that can provoke new hypotheses of great value. For example, the popularity of Horatio Alger in the last of the nineteenth century or of Mickey Spillane in the midtwentieth may indicate basic attitudes prevalent in the two societies. At least, this idea is worth investigating.

In the second place, fiction can be used to give real-life detail to factual accounts of an era. Students can really begin to understand the craze for investments that led to the South Sea Bubble in the early eighteenth century when they read *Robinson Crusoe*. This same novel demonstrates the vital importance of religion in the life of Englishmen of the period and reveals the emerging spirit of the entrepreneur. The very popularity of the novel indicates that middle-class English readers responded to these sentiments. But fiction cannot be used as a substitute for facts. Novels should not be assigned in place of biographies or interpretative articles. Fiction is a valuable supplement; it is not an alternative way of gathering evidence.

Chapter 15 consists of a problem based on fiction taken from *32 Problems in World History* and a discussion of how this material might be taught. As you read, keep the following questions in mind:

1) What subject objectives and skill objectives seem appropriate for this assignment? How could you reach those objectives through a class discussion?

2) How can teachers show students appropriate ways to use fiction as evidence in a history course?

3) What sources are available in a typical school library from which a teacher could gather background information as a basis for this discussion?

13TH-CENTURY FRANCE AS SEEN THROUGH A MEDIEVAL ROMANCE

Edwin Fenton

Aucassin and Nicolette is a classic example of the stories told and sung by 13th-century French minstrels. In manor houses and at fairs in medieval towns, groups of people gathered around traveling singers to hear the old familiar tales. These sessions were the medieval movie, radio, and television rolled into one. They were a window to the outside world, to romance, and to the secret thoughts of men and women.

But they were fiction. The events described probably never took place; even if their origins were factual, retelling by generations of minstrels probably distorted fact until it became fiction. Nevertheless, historians have used minstrels' tales to learn more about the Middle Ages. One aspect of life they illuminate is the development of romantic love and its importance in marriage. For hundreds of years, marriage had been largely a business matter. Then, about the 12th century, there developed the chivalric ideal of courtly love—the devotion of a knight to the lady of the castle. The lyrics of the troubadours show that at first this sentiment had little to do with man and wife. Over the years, however, the attitude began to change. If a knight should love the lady he served, why not also love his wife? The delightful romance that follows presents, among other things, a 13th-century picture of love and marriage. It develops

Reprinted from Edwin Fenton, *32 Problems in World History,* Copyright © 1964 by Scott, Foresman and Company, p. 46.

the theme of the conflict between the young, who want to marry for love, and the old, who emphasize family, wealth, and status.

Aucassin and Nicolette was written down in the early 1200's. Like most minstrel romances, it was not an original composition, but a reworked version of earlier material. Some scholars believe it may have been based on a Moorish tale. Its form of alternating prose and verse is oriental, and its hero's name may derive from the Arabic Alcazin or al-Kasim. The work survived in a single manuscript, which was rediscovered in 1752.

As you read the selections below, think about the following questions:

1. The word-portraits of Aucassin and Nicolette were probably stereotypes, not real-life descriptions. Is distortion such as this common in literature? What does it reveal about the way men often think? About what the nobility thought of themselves?
2. What can you infer about the class structure of the Middle Ages from this story?
3. What does this account reveal about the attitude of the nobility toward religion? See particularly Aucassin's remarks to the Viscount beginning "In Paradise what have I to do?"
4. What does the attitude of the vassals to Aucassin's leadership in battle indicate about the nature of personal relationships in feudalism?
5. For what type of evidence is fiction particularly useful to historians? For what should it not be used?

AUCASSIN AND NICOLETTE*

Who will deign to hear the song
Solace of a captive's wrong,
Telling how two children met,
Aucassin and Nicolette;
How by grievous pains distraught,
Noble deeds the varlet wrought
For his love, and her bright face!
Sweet my rhyme, and full of grace,
Fair my tale, and debonair.
He who lists—though full of care,
Sore astonied, much amazed,
All cast down, by men mispraised,
Sick in body, sick in soul,

---

* From *Aucassin and Nicolette and Other Medieval Romances*, translated by Eugene Mason. Dutton Paperback Series, pp. 1–3, 5–10, 13–14, and 35–38, 1951. Reprinted by permission of E. P. Dutton and Company, Inc., and J. H. Dent & Sons, Ltd.

Hearing shall be glad and whole,
So sweet the tale.

Now they say and tell and relate:

How the Count Bougars of Valence made war on Count Garin of Beaucaire, war so great, so wonderful, and so mortal, that never dawned the day but that he was at the gates and walls and barriers of the town, with a hundred knights and ten thousand men-at-arms, on foot and on horse. So he burned the Count's land, and spoiled his heritage, and dealt death to his men. The Count Garin of Beaucaire was full of years, and frail; he had long outworn his day. He had no heir, neither son nor daughter, save one only varlet, and he was such as I will tell you. Aucassin was the name of the lad. Fair he was, and pleasant to look upon, tall and shapely of body in every whit of him. His hair was golden, and curled in little rings about his head; he had grey and dancing eyes, a clear, oval face, a nose high and comely, and he was so gracious in all good graces that nought in him was found to blame, but good alone. But Love, that high prince, so utterly had cast him down, that he cared not to become knight, neither to bear arms, not to tilt at tourneys, not yet to do aught that it became his name to do.

His father and his mother spake him thus—"Son, don now thy mail, mount thy horse, keep thy land, and render aid to thy men. Should they see thee amongst them the better will the men-at-arms defend their bodies and their substance, thy fief and mine."

"Father," said Aucassin, "why speakest thou in such fashion to me? May God give me nothing of my desire if I become knight, or mount to horse, or thrust into the press to strike other or be smitten down, save only that thou give me Nicolette, my sweet friend, whom I love so well."

"Son," answered the father, "this may not be. Put Nicolette from mind. For Nicolette is but a captive maid, come hither from a far country, and the Viscount of this town bought her with money from the Saracens, and set her in this place. He hath nourished and baptized her, and held her at the font. On a near day he will give her to some young bachelor, who will gain her bread in all honour. With this what hast thou to do? Ask for a wife, and I will find thee the daughter of a king, or a count. Were he the richest man in France his daughter shalt thou have, if so thou wilt."

"Faith, my father," said Aucassin, "what honour of all this world would not Nicolette, my very sweet friend, most richly become! Were she Empress of Byzantium or of Allemaigne, or Queen of France or England, low enough would be her degree, so noble is she, so courteous and debonair, and gracious in all good graces."

Now is sung:

Aucassin was of Beaucaire,
Of the mighty castle there,

But his heart was ever set
On his fair friend, Nicolette.
Small he heeds his father's blame,
Or the harsh words of his dame.
"Fool, to weep the livelong day,
Nicolette trips light and gay.
Scouring she from far Carthage,
Bought of Paynims for a wage.
Since a wife beseems thee good
Take a wife of wholesome blood."
"Mother, naught for this I care,
Nicolette is debonair;
Slim the body, fair the face,
Make my heart a lighted place;
Love has set her as my peer,
Too sweet, my dear."

[*In the passage that follows, Count Garin, Aucassin's father, threatens the Viscount, Nicolette's guardian, and demands that she be sent away. The Viscount, in order to protect his ward, locks her in a tower of his palace. Aucassin then seeks out the Viscount, and asks for Nicolette.*]

"Fair sire," answered the Viscount, "put this from mind. Nicolette is a captive maid whom I brought here from a far country. For her price I trafficked with the Saracens, and I have bred and baptized her, and held her at the font. I have nourished her duly, and on a day will give her to some young bachelor who will gain her bread in honourable fashion. With this you have nought to do; but only to wed the daughter of some count or king. Beyond this, what profit would you have, had you become her lover, and taken her to your bed? Little enough would be your gain therefrom, for your soul would lie tormented in Hell all the days of all time, so that to Paradise never should you win."

"In Paradise what have I to do? I care not to enter, but only to have Nicolette, my very sweet friend, whom I love so dearly well. For into Paradise go none but such people as I will tell you of. There go those aged priests, and those old cripples, and the maimed, who all day long and all night cough before the altars, and in the crypts beneath the churches; those who go in worn old mantles and old tattered habits; who are naked, and barefoot, and full of sores; who are dying of hunger and of thirst, of cold and of wretchedness. Such as these enter in Paradise, and with them have I nought to do. But in Hell will I go. For to Hell go the fair clerks and the fair knights who are slain in the tourney and the great wars, and the stout archer and the loyal man. With them will I go. And there go the fair and courteous ladies, who have friends, two or three, together with their wedded lords. And there pass the gold and the silver, the ermine and all rich furs, harpers and minstrels, and the happy of the world. With these will I go, so only that I have Nicolette, my very sweet friend, by my side."

"Truly," cried the Viscount, "you talk idly, for never shall you see her more; yea, and if perchance you spoke together, and your father heard thereof, he would burn both me and her in one fire, and yourself might well have every fear."

"This lies heavy upon me," answered Aucassin.

Thus he parted from the Viscount making great sorrow.

Now is sung:

> Aucassin departed thus
> Sad at heart and dolorous;
> Gone is she his fairest friend,
> None may comfort give or mend,
> None by counsel make good end.
> To the palace turned he home,
> Climbed the stair, and sought his room.
> In the chamber all alone
> Bitterly he made his moan,
> Presently began to weep
> For the love he might not keep.
> "Nicolette, so gent, so sweet,
> Fair the faring of thy feet,
> Fair thy laughter, sweet thy speech,
> Fair our playing each with each,
> Fair thy clasping, fair thy kiss,
> Yet it endeth all in this.
> Since from me my love is ta'en
> I misdoubt that I am slain;
> Sister, sweet friend."

Now they say and tell and relate:

Whilst Aucassin was in the chamber lamenting Nicolette, his friend, the Count Bougars of Valence, wishful to end the war, pressed on his quarrel, and setting his pikemen and horsemen in array, drew near the castle to take it by storm. Then the cry arose, and the tumult; and the knights and the men-at-arms took their weapons, and hastened to the gates and the walls to defend the castle, and the burgesses climbed to the battlements, flinging quarrels and sharpened darts upon the foe. Whilst the siege was so loud and perilous the Count Garin of Beaucaire sought the chamber where Aucassin lay mourning, assotted upon Nicolette, his very sweet friend, whom he loved so well.

"Ha, son," cried he, "craven art thou and shamed that seest thy best and fairest castle so hardly beset. Know well that if thou lose it thou are a naked man. Son, arm thyself lightly, mount to horse, keep thy land, aid thy men, hurtle into the press. Thou needest not to strike another, neither to be smitten down, but if they see thee amongst them, the better will they defend their goods and their bodies, thy land and mine. And thou art so stout and strong that very easily thou canst do this thing, as is but right."

"Father," answered Aucassin, "what sayest thou now? May God give me nought that I require of Him if I become knight, or mount to horse, or thrust into the press to strike knight or be smitten down, save only thou givest me Nicolette, my sweet friend, whom I love so well."

"Son," replied the father, "this can never be. Rather will I suffer to lose my heritage, and go bare of all, than that thou shouldest have her, either as woman or as dame."

So he turned without farewell. But when Aucassin saw him part he stayed him, saying—

"Father, come now, I will make a true bargain with thee."

"What bargain, fair son?"

"I will arm me, and thrust into the press on such bargain as this, that if God bring me again safe and sound, thou wilt let me look on Nicolette, my sweet friend, so long that I may have with her two words or three, and kiss her one only time."

"I pledge my word to this," said the father.

Of this covenant had Aucassin much joy.

Now is sung:

> Aucassin the more was fain
> Of the kiss he sought to gain,
> Rather than his coffers hold
> A hundred thousand marks of gold.
> At the call his squire drew near,
> Armed him fast in battle gear;
> Shirt and hauberk donned the lad,
> Laced the helmet on his head,
> Girt his golden-hilted sword,
> Came the war-horse at his word,
> Gripped the buckler and the lance,
> At the stirrups cast a glance;
> Then most brave from plume to heel
> Pricked the charger with the steel,
> Called to mind his absent dear,
> Passed the gateway without fear
> Straight to the fight.

Now they say and tell and relate:

Aucassin was armed and horsed as you have heard. God! how bravely showed the shield about his neck, the helmet on his head, and the fringes of the baldric upon his left thigh. The lad was tall and strong, slender and comely to look upon, and the steed he bestrode was great and speedy, and fiercely had he charged clear of the gate. Now think not that he sought spoil of oxen and cattle, nor to smite others and himself escape. Nay, but of all this he took no heed. Another was with him, and he thought so dearly upon Nicolette, his fair friend, that the reins fell from his hand, and he struck never a blow. Then the charger, yet smarting from the spur, bore him into the battle, amidst the thickest of the foe, so that hands were laid upon him from every side, and he was made prisoner. Thus they spoiled him of shield and lance, and forthwith led him from the field a captive, questioning amongst themselves by what death he should be slain. When Aucassin marked their words,

"Ha, God," cried he, "sweet Creature, these are my mortal foes who lead me captive, and who soon will strike off my head; and when my head is smitten, never again may I have fair speech with Nicolette, my sweet friend, whom I hold so dear. Yet have I a good sword, and my horse is fresh. Now if I defend me not for her sake, may God keep her never, should she love me still."

The varlet was hardy and stout, and the charger he bestrode was right fierce. He plucked forth his sword, and smote suddenly on the right hand and on the left, cutting sheer through nasal and headpiece, gauntlet and arm, making such ruin around him as the wild boar deals when brought to bay by hounds in the woods; until he had struck down ten knights, and hurt seven more, and won clear of the melee, and rode back at utmost speed, sword in his hand.

The Count Bougars of Valence heard tell that his men were about to hang Aucassin, his foe, in shameful wise, so he hastened to the sight, and Aucassin passed him not by. His sword was yet in hand, and he struck the Count so fiercely upon the helm, that the headpiece was cleft and shattered upon the head. So bewildered was he by the stroke that he tumbled to the ground, and Aucassin stretched forth his hand, and took him, and led him captive by the nasal of the helmet, and delivered him to his father.

[*In the passages that follow, Count Garin refuses to keep his promise to Au-cassin, who releases his captive, Count Bougars. Aucassin's father casts him into prison, where he is visited by Nicolette.*]

. . . Her hair was golden, with little love-locks; her eyes blue and laughing; her face most dainty to see, with lips more vermeil than ever was rose or cherry in the time of summer heat; her teeth white and small; . . . so frail was she about the waist that your two hands could have spanned her, and the daisies that she brake with her feet in passing, showed altogether black against her instep and her flesh, so white was the fair young maiden.

[*Aucassin and Nicolette flee the country, but they become separated. Au-cassin returns to his home to find his father, the Count, dead, and assumes his rightful place as Count. Nicolette is captured and taken to the court of Car-*]

thage where she discovers that she is the daughter of the king. Making her way back to Beaucaire, she arrives disguised as a minstrel, to sing to Aucassin.]

> "Now I sing, for your delight,
> Aucassin, that loyal knight,
> And his fond friend, Nicolette.
> Such the love betwixt them set
> When his kinsfolk sought her head
> Fast he followed where she fled.
> From their refuge in the keep
> Paynims bore them o'er the deep.
> Nought of him I know to end.
> But for Nicolette, his friend,
> Dear she is, desirable,
> For her father loves her well;
> Famous Carthage owns him king,
> Where she has sweet cherishing.
> Now, as lord he seeks for her,
> Sultan, Caliph, proud Emir.
> But the maid of these will none,
> For she loves a dansellon,
> Aucassin, who plighted troth.
> Sworn has she some pretty oath
> Ne'er shall she be wife or bride,
> Never lie at baron's side
> Be he denied."

Now they say and tell and relate:

When Aucassin heard Nicolette sing in this fashion he was glad at heart, so he drew her aside, and asked—

"Fair sweet friend," said Aucassin, "know you naught of this Nicolette, whose ballad you have sung?"

"Sire, truly, yes; well I know her for the most loyal of creatures, and as the most winning and modest of maidens born. She is daughter to the King of Carthage, who took her when Aucassin also was taken, and brought her to the city of Carthage, till he knew for certain that she was his child, whereat he rejoiced greatly. Any day he would give her for husband one of the highest kings in all Spain; but rather would she be hanged or burned than take him, however rich he be."

"Ah, fair sweet friend," cried the Count Aucassin, "if you would return to that country and persuade her to have speech with me here, I would give you of my riches more than you would dare to ask of me or to take. Know that for love of her I choose not to have a wife, however proud her race, but I stand

and wait; for never will there be wife of mine if it be not her, and if I knew where to find her I should not need to grope blindly for her thus."

"Sire," answered she, "if you will do these things I will go and seek her for your sake, and for hers too; because to me she is very dear."

He pledged his word, and caused her to be given twenty pounds. So she bade him farewell, and he was weeping for the sweetness of Nicolette. And when she saw his tears—

"Sire," said she, "take it not so much to heart; in so short a space will I bring her to this town, and you shall see her with your eyes."

When Aucassin knew this he rejoiced greatly. So she parted from him, and fared in the town to the house of the Viscountess, for the Viscount her god-father, was dead. There she lodged, and opened her mind fully to the lady on all the business; and the Viscountess recalled the past, and knew well that it was Nicolette whom she had cherished. So she caused the bath to be heated, and made her take her ease for fully eight days. Then Nicolette sought a herb that was called celandine, and washed herself therewith, and became so fair as she had never been before. She arrayed her in a rich silken gown from the lady's goodly store; and seated herself in the chamber on a rich stuff of broidered sendal; then she whispered the dame, and begged her to fetch Aucassin, her friend. This she did. When she reached the palace, lo, Aucassin in tears, making great sorrow for the long tarrying of Nicolette, his friend; and the lady called to him, and said—

"Aucassin, behave not so wildly; but come with me, and I will show you that thing you love best in all the world; for Nicolette, your sweet friend, is here from a far country to seek her love."

So Aucassin was glad at heart.

Now is sung:

> When he learned that in Beaucaire
> Lodged his lady, sweet and fair,
> Aucassin arose, and came
> To her hostel, with the dame;
> Entered in, and passed straightway
> To the chamber where she lay.
> When she saw him, Nicolette
> Had such joy as never yet;
> Sprang she lightly to her feet
> Swiftly came with welcome meet.
> When he saw her, Aucassin
> Oped both arms, and drew her in,
> Clasped her close in fond embrace,
> Kissed her eyes and kissed her face.
> In such greeting sped the night,
> Till, at dawning of the light,

Aucassin, with pomp most rare,
Crowned her Countess of Beaucaire.
Such delight these lovers met,
Aucassin and Nicolette.
Length of days and joy did win,
Nicolette and Aucassin,
Endeth song and tale I tell
With marriage bell.

TEACHING *AUCASSIN* AND *NICOLETTE*

Edwin Fenton

Aucassin and Nicolette is a superb example of the work of thirteenth-century French minstrels. Its background, and that of similar tales, is discussed in Eugene Mason (trans.), *Aucassin and Nicolette and Other Mediaeval Romances and Legends,*[1] and in Joseph R. Strayer and Dana C. Munro, *The Middle Ages, 395–1500.*[2] I intend to spend a few minutes in class supplying background information from these sources.

Next I shall ask, "Of what value as evidence for the history of the Middle Ages is *Aucassin and Nicolette?*" Then, before the discussion has evaporated into vague generalities, I shall quickly draw attention to the fourth paragraph in the story. In this passage, the Viscount, Nicolette's guardian, explains to the love-struck Aucassin why marriage to Nicolette, a captive maiden, is out of the question. The son of a count should wed "the daughter of some count or king," the Viscount argues. Here students acquire an insight into the class structure of the Middle Ages. They will need to be reminded that minstrels sang at fairs and in manor houses before the assembled nobility. Is it likely that they would introduce the idea of marriage within one's social group if marriage outside it were common? Clearly not. This passage probably reflects patterns of marriage and conceptions of status deeply rooted in the society.

The second paragraph following the next poem (beginning "In Paradise") is a priceless statement of the lighthearted attitude of a virile knight devoted to his lady fair. Aucassin is quite willing to choose hell in preference to heaven in order to have Nicolette by his side, in the conviction that chivalrous knights and vivacious ladies with their lovers, and all "the happy of the world," will be

[1] New York: Dutton, 1951.
[2] New York: Appleton-Century-Crofts, 1942, Chap. XI.

there. This lively passage helps to destroy the image of the Middle Ages as an era dominated sternly by the church.

The poem in the middle of the selection (beginning "Aucassin the more was fain") and the prose passages preceding it are useful for two points. First, they illustrate the role of the knight as a warrior in feudal society. Notice particularly the poet's emphasis on Aucassin's proud, erect carriage and the general impression of strength and vitality conveyed by his description. This ought, at least, to make an impression on the girls in the class. Students should perceive that this passage does not describe a typical knight, but sets forth instead a stereotype of the ideal knight. Second, this selection illustrates the personal relationship that tied the members of the feudal order together. Vassals would fight vigorously only when their lord was in the midst of the fray to lead and inspire them. Here is an insight into the close web of personal relationships that held members of the feudal order together.

Immediately after discussing the poem, I shall summarize the next portion of the plot. Aucassin, borne by his charger into the midst of the battle where the clash of steel on steel assailed his eardrums, fell to his customary occupation, daydreaming about Nicolette. Naturally he was captured and "spoiled of shield and lance." Then his captors made a fatal error; they began to discuss the merits of various ways of dispatching him to the hereafter. Aucassin aroused himself; "When my head is smitten, never again may I have fair speech with Nicolette." Plucking forth his sword, which his captors had carelessly overlooked, he hacked his way through the enemy hosts, killing ten, injuring seven more, and capturing Count Bougars of Valence—all single-handedly, and all with the image of Nicolette as his cross in the sky.

I shall then ask students, "What on the Broadway stage does this remind you of?" Obviously it is pure musical comedy; "Poor Jud" was almost dead and had sprung to life again. They can revel in these musical comedy elements, particularly if their teacher reads, and hams a little, a part of the following passage:

> The varlet was hardy and stout, and the charger he bestrode was right fierce. He plucked forth his sword, and smote suddenly on the right hand and on the left, cutting sheer through nasal and headpiece, gauntlet and arm, making such ruin about him as the wild boar deals when brought to bay by hounds in the wood; until he had struck down ten knights, and hurt seven more, and won clear of the melee, and rode back at utmost speed, sword in his hand.
> The Count Bougars of Valence heard tell that his men were about to hang Aucassin, his foe, in shameful wise, so he hastened to the sight, and Aucassin passed him not by. His sword was yet in hand, and he struck the Count so fiercely upon the helm that the headpiece was cleft and shattered upon the head. So bewildered was he by the stroke that he tumbled to the ground, and Aucassin stretched forth his hand, and took him, and led him captured by the nasal of the helmet, and delivered him to his father.

Students are thoroughly acquainted with dashing heroes and beautiful damsels beset with mustachioed villains, or at least with dull, well-meaning bores, from listening to musicals. They recognize each stereotype easily— each Henry Higgins, each Liza, each Freddy—and they know how far from real life these characters are. They can also recognize stereotypes of the knight and the peasant in *Aucassin and Nicolette:*

> Aucassin was the name of the lad. Fair he was, and pleasant to look upon, tall and shapely of body in every whit of him. His hair was golden, and curled in little rings about his head; he had grey and dancing eyes, a clear, oval face, a nose high and comely, and he was so gracious in all good graces that nought in him was found to blame, but good alone.
> Tall he was and marvellously ugly and hideous. His head was big and blacker than smoked meat; the palm of your hand could easily have gone between his two eyes; he had very large cheeks and a monstrous flat nose with great nostrils; lips redder than uncooked flesh, teeth yellow and foul; he was shod with shoes and gaiters of bull's hide, bound about the legs with ropes to well above the knees; upon his back was a rough cloak; and he stood leaning on a huge club.

Read aloud consecutively, these two passages reveal the tremendous gulf yawning between the top and bottom strata of society in the eyes of the nobility. Strayer and Munro used this description of the peasant in an interesting fashion in *The Middle Ages* (p. 395).

In a passage that is not quoted, a pilgrim, sick unto death, caught sight of Nicolette's ankle and was promptly cured. This incident illustrates the chivalric conception of the role of women in society carried to the extreme. The description of Nicolette, whose ankle was just as miraculously powerful as the saint's relics that the pilgrim was presumably seeking to cure him, is worth reading to the class for the stereotype of the ideal woman of the period:

> Her hair was golden, with little love-locks; her eyes blue and laughing; her face most dainty to see, with lips more vermeil than ever was rose or cherry in the time of summer heat; her teeth white and small; her breasts so firm that they showed beneath her vesture like two rounded nuts; so frail was she about the girdle that your two hands could have spanned her, and the daisies that she brake with her feet in passing, showed altogether black against her instep and her flesh, so white was the fair young maiden.

All this is difficult to pack into a class period unless the discussion is thoroughly organized by the instructor. I shall need five minutes at the end of the class to summarize the significance of the assignment. Here we have been using fiction as evidence. We have assumed that nobles who listened to this tale, and minstrels who sang it, were familiar with similar attitudes in the society about them. Otherwise the text would have been changed. If this assumption is warranted, *Aucassin and Nicolette* gives us a firsthand glimpse into French chivalry about A.D. 1200, probably not as it existed, but as members of the nobility envisioned it in the abstract. It is from evidence in tales such as these that a part of our history has been written. High school students should be intrigued to discover that they have been consulting genuine source material. I shall read a paragraph from Joseph Strayer's *Western Europe in the Middle Ages* to indicate the type of conclusion that one author drew from similar material:

> The effect of these new ideas on the position of women demands special consideration. Marriage remained a business affair, completely outside the scope of courtly love. The new concept of romantic love, expressed in the lyrics of the troubadours and the acts of the chivalrous knights, applied almost entirely to extra-marital relations . . . and yet, while the idea of romantic love came in, so to speak, at the back door, it did spread gradually beyond its early limits. If some women were to be worshipped as almost divine and served faithfully for years, why not all? If love determined the choice of a mistress, why not that of a wife? The growth of these ideas can be easily traced in European literature, as it develops the theme of the eternal opposition between the young who want to marry for love, and the old who put first family, status, and wealth.[3]

This exercise will illustrate once more the function of the historian: to explain events in the past, using as evidence whatever material is available and pertinent. It will also reveal the remarkable amount of data that can be culled from a single, short piece of source material.

[3] New York: Appleton-Century-Crofts, 1955, p. 137.

CHAPTER 16   Learning To Ask Questions for Inductive Teaching

No art is more difficult to master than that of asking the appropriate question. The majority of questions asked in social studies classes are sterile. "Who discovered America?" cannot get a student anywhere. Fact questions such as this one demand only the recall of information memorized from a textbook reading. They cannot build a method of inquiry that will equip a student to investigate another problem in history, nor can they reveal an important generalization.

The art of asking questions cannot be learned through a series of rules. Knowing the rules does help; it is a necessary but not a sufficient condition. Only self-confidence and knowledge of subject and method can equip a teacher to ask appropriate questions consistently.

A teacher needs self-confidence enough to leave his lesson plan in order to follow a line of inquiry that a student has initiated. An answer to one question should provoke another question and another answer in turn. Unless a teacher feels sure that he has control of the work for the day, he may confine himself so closely to a prearranged lesson plan that he will fail to recognize the opportunity for a provocative question inherent in a student's answer.

A teacher must know his subject in order to develop a line of questioning that leads to a useful generalization. Good classes are often organized around only one big issue: What did economic and political changes contribute to the development of the Renaissance, or, What did the Muckrakers contribute to the Progressive movement? A teacher who does not know the history of the Renaissance or of Progressivism will not be able to lead students through a series of questions to the major variables involved in answering these questions.

A teacher must know the method of the historian for similar reasons. Will you venture a hypothesis to explain this development? What evidence should you look for to validate or to modify this hypothesis? Where might you find evidence like this? All these questions help to teach a method of inquiry and to focus the attention of students in the class on worthwhile questions.

Chapter 16 consists of two transcriptions of unrehearsed classroom discussions. The first describes a discovery approach, in which the teacher gives as little direction as possible to the students. In the second the teacher directs the line of investigation carefully toward a predetermined set of content goals. The second transcription used the material from the first day of the unit on teaching the historian's mode of inquiry, which is Chapter 9 of this volume. As you read these transcriptions, think about the following questions:

1) What sort of questioning technique is used in each of the two articles? How do the techniques differ? What does your conclusion imply about the goals of the two teachers?

2) Which of these questioning techniques seems more appropriate to challenge the creativity of students? Which would probably result in greater mastery of content? Which has the better balance between knowledge and skill objectives?

3) How can you justify the amount of time that teaching techniques such as these consume? How might Bloom; Krathwohl, Bloom, and Masia; or Bruner justify this expenditure of time?

4) The article by David Ausubel in Chapter 8 argues that only talented and creative students can derive full benefit from a discovery method. Does his criticism apply more to one of these transcriptions than to the other?

TEACHING SOCIAL STUDIES
THROUGH DISCOVERY

Byron G. Massialas · Jack Zevin

The study reported here is grounded in some of the hypotheses advanced by Jerome Bruner in his recent work. According to him, the highest state of human autonomy and perfection is achieved when the child begins to discover for himself regularities or irregularities in his physical and socio-political environments. While no earth-shaking scientific discoveries should be expected, the person who is engaged in this process is given the opportunity to make leaps into the unknown and uncontrolled world, and he learns the value of

Reprinted from Byron G. Massialas and Jack Zevin, "Teaching Social Studies through Discovery," *Social Education*, XXVIII, November 1964, 384–387 and 400. Copyright © 1964 by the National Education Association.

formulating plausible hypotheses about human interactions. It is maintained that when facts and details are put into a structured pattern, they are retained longer and can be retrieved easier when needed.[1]

The study was conducted in a Chicago public high school over a period of one academic year, and it attempted to explore further the dimensions and the implications of teaching a course in world history through discovery or, what Bruner calls, the process of "figuring out." While the general nature of the study was exploratory, some questions provided the focus of the investigation. Some of these questions were: (1) To what extent are high school sophomores with slightly above average ability capable of participating in discovery and in inquiry? (2) How can historical materials be presented in such a way that while some cues will be offered, the story will not be given away, and the student will be prompted to study independently and to acquire the heuristics of learning? (3) To what extent do the style and method of discovery operate as a potent motivational device in learning? Before dealing with these questions and presenting relevant classroom discussion, let us briefly identify some instructional procedures and classroom mechanics which will help the reader reconstruct the teaching experience.

The class was composed of 35 students, most of them about 15 years old, enrolled in a required modern world history course. The course began with the Reformation, and it generally followed the sequence of historical topics; selected social events were chosen to be investigated in some depth. All the aesthetic products of culture including art, music, literature, and architecture were drawn upon for classroom material; however, the study emphasized the use of historical documents in developing the student's ability to discover and explain his political and social environment. Secondary sources— e.g., textbooks, excerpts from monographs, magazine articles—were used only insofar as they related to the problem under attack, and they were introduced after the initial encounter with the "discovery episode." On the average, a new discovery episode was introduced every two weeks, and in the main, it consisted of a historical document, the origin, referent, and author of which were carefully deleted. The students were challenged to gather all the missing information. Although a discovery episode presupposed some general knowledge, it was not necessary for the student to have had special training or familiarity with the problem under consideration. In a situation such as this, the instructor performs a non-directive role in that he explicitly refuses to answer any of the students' questions. His task in the classroom is twofold: (1) to instigate and challenge the students, and (2) to moderate the discussion.

[1] Jerome S. Bruner. "The Act of Discovery." *Harvard Educational Review* 31:21–32; Winter 1961. For more details on the philosophical and psychological assumptions underlying the method, see B. G. Massialas, "Teaching History as Inquiry," in Shirley H. Engle, editor, *New Perspectives in World History*. Thirty-Fourth Yearbook. Washington, D.C.: The National Council for the Social Studies, 1964.

In order to illustrate the flow of classroom discussion during a discovery session, parts of the student dialogue are here reproduced. In this particular case, the students were given ten brief poems[2] and were asked to read them carefully. The participants were encouraged to discover a plausible choice for the cultural origin of the following poems.

1.

My thoughts turn to the Ancient Capital
    Long life and peace during your reign
O, Emperor.

2.

The beginning of all art
    A song when planting a rice field
in the country's inmost part.

3.

Is there, I wonder
    A man without a pen in hand—
The moon tonight!

4.

On the temple bell
    Resting, sleeping,
a firefly.

5.

A Great Lord—And Who
    makes *Him* get off his horse?
—cherry blossoms do!

6.

Snow yet remaining
    The mountain slopes are hazy—
It is evening.

7.

A crossroad sermon! True,
    It's rigamarole—but then
It's tranquil too!

8.

So brilliant a moonshine
    When I am born again—
A hilltop pine!

9.

To the Great Lord's hall
    Five or six horsemen hurry hard—
A storm wind of fall.

---

[2] From *An Introduction to Haiku* by Harold G. Henderson. Copyright © 1958 by Harold G. Henderson. Reprinted by permission of Doubleday & Company, Inc.
The selection of material was based primarily on two criteria: (a) availability of data pertaining to a central or common theme, e.g., the feudal system in Japan; and (b) careful avoidance of clues which would "give away" the puzzle.

10.

As he snoozes, the mountain stream he uses
   To wash his rice,
No simple peasant, this!

The discussion that ensued was tape-recorded and transcribed. Selected parts of the transcription are given below.

First Day

Teacher: Please read this. (*five minutes of silence*) Well now, everyone finished? What do you think of this reading? What are these?

Tim: This must be a collection of poems.

Teacher: Why?

Tim: Because each of these little pieces is in verse. Some rhyme.

George: But they're so vague. What are we supposed to do with them?

Teacher: Whatever you like. Are they really vague?

Gwen: I don't think so. Some of the poems are very interesting, maybe difficult to interpret, but interesting.

Sylvia: Yes, I think we can find clues if we try.

George: Clues for what? All this is still vague.

Bill S.: Yes, what are we supposed to find out? What do these mean? Where are they from? Who wrote them? When were they written?

Teacher: All of you should be able to supply your own answers to these questions. Who would like to make the first attempt? (*a moment of silence*)

Carolyn: Well, they're all poems, so they must have been written by a poet.

Bill S.: That's some help! How do you know they're not written by one and the same poet? They all look the same to me, same three lines, same style, all short and vague.

Carolyn: But they're on different subjects and they give different feelings. Each one gives me a different feeling.

Bill S.: Does that mean they can't be by one poet expressing himself on different subjects?

Sylvia: I have a different idea. Maybe these poems are all by different poets, but may seem to be the same because of the style. What I mean is that maybe these are the usual kind of poem for this country.

Gwen: Or, it could just be the style of a particular poet.

John: I think this is getting us nowhere. Let's forget about the poet and try to find out where it's from.

Bob: But these poems are too vague.

Diane: We're back to that again.

Teacher: Well, does everyone agree with this, or can someone offer advice or evidence to help us out? Where are these from?

Sharon: They are from Europe because an Emperor is mentioned, and lords are also mentioned a couple of times. This means there must have been an autocracy in this country. Many countries of Europe had monarchs and lords.

Bernard: At one time almost every European country had this kind of government. Maybe these poems are from Russia. Russia had an Emperor and nobles running it for a long, long time.

Diane: I think that this is from France or Germany, or Austria during the Middle Ages, because the lords seem to be very powerful; they are able to command cavalry men and to own large halls. Maybe the emperor referred to is Charlemagne.

Gwen: I think you're getting on the wrong track. This is no European set of poems, certainly not American!

Teacher: Why?

Gwen: Well, you're missing a lot of important parts of the poems that seem not to be European at all. What about the mention of a temple? Since when are Medieval churches called temples? And what about the reference to rice in one of the poems? Rice wasn't one of the European's main dishes, at least as far as I know.

Eddie: Rice is from the Orient, from China. The Chinese eat lots of rice. The poems must be translated from Chinese.

Steve: They could also be from Japan or India. I've read somewhere that these two countries produce and eat rice as their main dish.

Mary: I read recently that Southeast Asia produces a lot of rice. Vietnam exports rice, and eats some of it.

Helen: I have a suggestion, but not of another country. I think we should try to get the meaning and message of each poem and then find out where they're from. Let's start with poem 1 and work our way down.

It is apparent that the first day is spent on orientation and organization of the materials at hand. During the introductory phases of the discovery episode, the students are encouraged to come to grips with the responsibility of exercising independent judgment in pursuing a course of action. The teacher and the material, which includes only limited clues, create a sense of puzzlement. The students begin to suggest modes of attack and try to capitalize on the available springboards. For example, John proposes that the focal point of investigation should change from a quest to identify the poet to an inquiry into the national origin of the poems. This suggestion is taken up by several members of the class—e.g., Gwen, who in her first reaction to the poem, offers a hypothesis which harmonizes several problematic bits of data and refutes previous conjectures. At this point other students attempt to validate and to narrow down the proposition that the poems are of non-Western source. Helen, following up this line of investigation, concludes the deliberations of the first day by suggesting that each poem be thoroughly scrutinized and analyzed before returning to the main source of perplexity.

SECOND DAY

Here the students are considering Helen's suggestion, and they are studying each poem in depth. Only discussion relating to three of these poems (8, 9, and 10) is reproduced here.

Helen: This poem (Number 8) is written by a Buddhist or a Hindu because it contains a belief in rebirth. As far as I know, only these two religions teach this belief.

George: I think it's called reincarnation. That means that you are born over and over again into new bodies or forms, although your soul remains the same.

Helen: Well, I think this poet is a Buddhist or Hindu because he believes this idea. He wants to be born again as a pine tree on a hilltop so he can enjoy beautiful moonlit nights. Does anyone disagree?

Mary: I don't. Now we have a better idea of where these poems are from. They have to be from the Orient, and they have to be from a country with Buddhists or Hindus living in it. They can't be from anywhere else.

Gwen: Yes, and according to the ninth poem, these would have to be from a country in which great lords are important people. The ninth poem repeats the fourth poem, and the great lord is said to own a hall. This must be like a castle.

Steve: The lord seems to have soldiers or cavalry working for him. Then the poem changes subject and tells of a storm wind of the fall.

Gwen: Maybe the poet is trying to tell us in a roundabout way that a war or fight is brewing. That's why the cavalry is reporting to the great lord. I don't think his poem is peaceful like the others at all. It's a poem that tells us of troubles in the country. People were fighting each other and each great lord probably had soldiers working for him.

Sharon: That's called a feudalistic system. These poems have to be from a feudalistic country. We have to find out which Oriental countries were feudalistic—or still are.

George: That might be a help. Find out which Oriental countries had feuding societies and feudal lords.

Sharon: I agree about the wars, but I don't think your suggestion will help because all those feudal societies used to have little wars.

Steve: Like England during the War of the Roses and France during the tenth and eleventh centuries?

Tim: I think you are right. You have also missed something important. If there are great lords in this country, there are most likely other lords, lesser ones in the set-up as well. This sounds very close to feudalism. Usually, however, feudalism is a system of many powerful nobles and a weak king.

Sharon: Well, that fits pretty well. We definitely know that the lords of this country are powerful, armed, and have castles of some kind, while the emperor is spoken of as being in his ancient capital. It seems to me that he's out of the picture.

Bill: But we really can't tell for sure.

Sharon: Well, at least we know that the nobility is powerful, and if that's true, then the emperor must have that much less power or say-so on everything.

Teacher: Good point. Now what about a volunteer for the last poem?

Bernard: The last one is about a lazy peasant. I guess it's a kind of joke because the peasant is taking a nap while the water washes his rice, which I guess is in some sort of sack hanging in the water. Say! That's pretty clever.

Diane: Some people, including the poet, must have thought peasants were simple-minded, and the poet is showing us that this isn't so, because here's a peasant who can get his work done and sleep at the same time.

Bernard: By the way, I think this poem and the second one about rice prove that rice is very important in the life of the people of this country, and it also shows that these two poems are by different people.

Mary: Why do you say that? We decided before that we couldn't be sure of that.

Bernard: Well, in the second poem those who plant the rice are praised and in the last poem peasants are made fun of.

Karen: That could still be that same poet in a different place or mood.

In the above discussion the students are subjecting the poems to a detailed examination. All shades of meaning and locational clues are explored. In part, they seem to be working in sequential steps or plateaus; once they have determined that the poems are of Buddhist or of Hindu origin then they strike out to reach a new plateau which would incorporate more data and eliminate fruitless speculations. In their attempt to explain the existence of "great lords" they begin to draw certain logical inferences, e.g., if powerful lords are in control the monarch must be correspondingly weak. It should also be noted that in the process of "figuring out" the puzzle, the participants draw from personal accumulated knowledge which, on several occasions, provides the missing parts and clarifies certain ambiguities and vagueness in the material. For example, they are trying to interpret the poems in terms of a theory of feudalism. The discussion pertaining to the last poem is a clear illustration of an attempt to reconcile contradictory information and place it in the framework of a more inclusive and warranted hypothesis.

THIRD DAY

Teacher: Now that you've analyzed all of the poems, where do you think they're from?

George: We've ruled out the West, and this has to be from countries under the influence of Buddhism or Hinduism, the only religions preaching reincarnation.

Eddie: That limits our choices to India, China, or Japan.

Eileen: Or Southeast Asia. The question is which one?

Steve: It seems as though each of these places fills the bill. All are countries that are literate, religious, feudalistic at one time or another, and dependent on rice for a main part of their diet.

Eddie: Well, wait a minute. Now that I think of it, China may not be a good choice. It doesn't fit in with what we've been saying about these poems. China had a very powerful emperor who ruled through a civil service. As far as I know there was no nobility in China except for the emperor's household.

Bill V.: But wasn't there an earlier period in Chinese history in which feudalism was the form of government?

Mary: Well, at least we can eliminate most of Chinese history.

Tim: I think it's India. Great Lord could be a translation for Maharaja, but I'm not sure if India has had emperors. Did it?

Teacher: You can find out, can't you?

Bill S.: Oh, please tell us where it's from. I can't wait any longer.

Teacher: But why should I when you can find out for yourself? Doesn't someone have any helpful suggestions?

Diane: I think it's from India, too. The mention of rice, temples, peasants, and the religious tone to several of the poems make me think of India.

Gwen: But what you've said could apply to almost all of Asia, India, and the East.

Tim: I think we can rule out China altogether because I remember reading that Buddhism and the idea of rebirth were introduced into China after China already had a system of absolute emperors who ruled through a civil service, and I think there were no powerful nobles.

Bob: If all of that is correct, then China is ruled out; but that still leaves us with Japan, India, and Southeast Asia.

Mary: These poems must be from a mountainous country because of the mention of mountains in several of them.

Gwen: Northern India is very mountainous, so are parts of Southeast Asia, and all of Japan is that way.

Randy: Maybe it's Japan. Up until very recently Japan was a feudal country with lords, barons, and soldiers called Samurai, including a very shy, weak emperor. It is also a Buddhist country filled with ancient temples and preachers of religion. Japan sounds like a very good choice.

Bill S.: It could still be Northern India or Southeast Asia some time long ago.

Bernard: I believe there were emperors in India rather recently, called Moguls, or something like that.

Karen: What about the style of these poems? They seem pretty unusual. Maybe we can check into this by looking at sample poems from all over Asia until we hit on the same type. Maybe that will help us find a definite answer.

(Bell rings)

During the third day of class deliberations, the students begin to limit the range of alternative choices or hypotheses; based on the previous analysis, they assert that the country in question will have to be Oriental, and that it will have to be under the cultural influence of Buddhism and/or Hinduism. Once this has been determined, a search for specific countries within the given cultural region takes place. Here they attempt to match alternative countries with the criteria that they have established. They further delimit the field of choice by rejecting those Oriental nations which deviate from the image they have constructed based on their interpretation of the poems. Throughout this process, they draw inferences which aid them in the defensible elimination of unwarranted hypotheses, e.g., the rejection of China as a possible choice by Tim and Bob, which takes the form of what Hunt and Metcalf call an "if-then generalization."[3] The primary goal of the group is the discovery of an answer that harmonizes all the evidence and integrates the ten poems. However, they soon realize that whatever data are at their command, they are not sufficient to support conclusively any of the proposed solutions. The realization of this difficulty motivates them to seek additional sources, especially those which include more detailed and authoritative information.

Fourth Day

Bill W., Steve, Tim, and Karen: We have final proof. We found it.

Karen: We checked these poems against Indian, Chinese, Japanese, and

[3] Maurice P. Hunt and Lawrence E. Metcalf. *Teaching High School Social Studies.* New York: Harper & Row, Publishers, 1955.

any other Oriental types of poems we could find, and we found out that this type of poem is Japanese only, and is called a *haiku*.

During the last phase of the discussion, the students offer concluding suggestions which are based on newly obtained evidence. For the most part, the additional proof was the result of the collation of the poems under investigation with all other relevant material which was accessible in the library. This line of inquiry was in part instigated by Karen's suggestion at the conclusion of the third day, which directed attention to the form and style in addition to the content of the poems.

SUMMARY

The following four points provide the major results of this research:

1. Without exception the students were able to participate directly in the process of discovery and inquiry. This process entailed a number of related tasks—identifying and defining the problems at hand, devising alternative plans of attack, formulating working hypotheses from the given data and their previous learning experiences, testing the hypotheses by drawing logical inferences and by gathering relevant information, and arriving at a theory or "grand generalization" which draws together all bits of data and supporting hypotheses. It is interesting to note that the process of discovery moves from a stage of hunch and intuition to a stage of in-depth analysis and, finally, to the point where knowledge-claims are based on concrete, documentary evidence. While this is the general direction followed in the discovery episode, speculative or "intuitive" thinking may be found, to a great or lesser degree, in all of the phases; when there is a gap in knowledge the student reaches out in uncharted and largely unknown realms of interpretation and thinking. From this observation the complementary nature of intuitive and analytic thinking may be seen.

2. Historical materials are used as raw data or as archeological remains from which students may reconstruct a society at a given place and period. The historical document furnishes the springboards for inquiry into human thought and action and the evolution of social institutions. In the process of reconstructing the event, historical hypotheses are often checked against contemporary phenomena; the students employ both historical and social science concepts, research techniques, and methods of analysis.

3. The way material is presented coupled with the non-directive behavior of the teacher, leads to the creation of a new psychological climate. The students now become increasingly independent and they begin to question the authority of secondary material. They generally adopt an attitude of intelligent doubt, and they tend to propose new ideas and explanations that must be carefully defended. The class is given the opportunity to exchange ideas and analyze different views and interpretations.

4. The method of discovery has a highly motivating effect on students. Almost without exception, the students, directly or indirectly, demonstrate a great deal of personal involvement with the material under discussion. During the duration of the study there was wide classroom participation and intensive utilization of library resources. The motivating effect of the discovery episode is due, in large part, to the game-like situation which reinforces the element of perplexity and incentive to explore. The teacher indirectly encourages student exploration by stubbornly refusing to provide ready-made answers.

The reader should keep in mind the exploratory nature of this study and the fact that the writers are offering observations based on rather limited samples. This research should, hopefully, provide a point of departure for further experimentation in this area. It would be advisable to undertake further study in which a variety of materials is given to students who represent all levels of education and who have a wide range of intelligence.

TRANSCRIPT OF A CLASSROOM DISCUSSION IN WORLD HISTORY

Edwin Fenton · Students of Peabody High School, Pittsburgh

Teacher: I guess we're really ready to start. Let me begin by asking Wayne back there what we're going to be doing during the first six days of this course.

Student: Studying the way historians gather facts, how they accept facts and general history.

Teacher: Is that all we're going to be doing is studying how historians gather facts and learn how to accept them?

Student: Coming to a conclusion of what a good definition for history is.

Teacher: Eva, do you agree with this or do you have anything to add to it?

Student: Well, they want us to work out our own definition of history and not all of our definitions will be the same.

Teacher: You want to work out what your own definition of what history is and you mean that some of you may come up with a definition that is different from what mine would be. Paul, do you want to add something to this?

Student: Well, I think we're also learning how to interpret facts.

Teacher: So, really, what we're getting at then is what history is which involves facts and the interpretation of facts. Is that right? And we'll be working at this for five or six days. Bill, do you think at the end of five or six days you'll really know what history is and be able to say this precisely?

Student: Well, nobody can tell what history really is—I mean you can learn a fact or maybe a hundred facts of history each day for your whole life for even a thousand years and you'd never know all facts about history.

Teacher: What you're really saying then—implying, is that history *is* a collection of facts, and one of the things you want to decide is whether or not it's true that history is a collection of facts. Well, let's worry for a few minutes about the assignment I gave you last night. I have listed here on a transparency those eighteen terms I asked you to put into categories.

SHARK	LION
TURKEY	BLACK BASS
RABBIT	ELEPHANT
CAT	PIKE
GROUSE	EAGLE
RAINBOW TROUT	SHEEP
TUNA	PHEASANT
CONDOR	COLLIE DOG
OSTRICH	BARRACUDA

What I'd like to do now is divide the class into three parts and ask the people in each of the three sections of the class quickly to choose someone to report for us and then to try to agree on three statements—on three ways of categorizing this information. I want you to agree on three categories and then get ready to report. Let me ask the people in the front row and you four in the second to gather in a minute in this corner, and the people in the third row, you two on the end to gather near that blackboard and the rest of you to gather over there. You're to do two things: first, choose a chairman very quickly, don't take time with it, and then spend just two or three minutes (no more) agreeing on three categories. All right, let's go. Just leave your things—don't move the chairs—leave your paper at your desk. (*The students break into three groups to discuss a few minutes. Then the teacher says:*)

Teacher: I think we're ready now, will you go back to your seats, please. We have a blackboard back here and I'll have Sandy write on it—Sandy, will you get a piece of chalk? What I want you to do is report the categories to us and we'll have Sandy write them on the board. Start at the top, Sandy, so you have room. Mark, were you a reporter?

Student: Yes.

Teacher: Stand up will you so that we can hear you and you'll all have to turn around this way a bit.

Student: My first category was carnivorous, herbivorous, and omnivorous.

Teacher: Okay, tell me what they mean. What does "carnivorous" mean?

Student: Those are meat eaters.

Teacher: Meat eaters and what else?

Student: Plant eaters and both.

Teacher: Carnivorous, herbivorous——

Student: ——and omnivorous.

Teacher: And what's "omnivorous"?

Student: That's both.

Teacher: Do you mean like we are?

Student: Yes.

Teacher: All right, write "omnivorous."

Student: Our second——

Teacher: Now wait until she gets it written out. I would like all of you to get these categories down in your notes as well. Get your note paper and as Sandy writes them, you write them too.

Student: Our second classification was species—mammals, fowl, and scales (fish).

Teacher: Mammals, fowl, and fish. Are all of you getting it down? What's your third one, Mark?

Student: Our third was domesticated and wild.

Teacher: Give me some examples of domesticated.

Student: Like the collie, the cat, sheep, rabbits——

Teacher: All right, and wild?

Student: And wild would be like the shark, lion, elephant.

Teacher: Fine. Thank you. Let me have the report from the second group that was on the side. Wait a minute, I couldn't hear you. What did you say, Robbie?

Student: We've almost the same thing as them.

Teacher: Well, tell us what you got.

Student: We have whether they're carnivorous or vegetarian.

Teacher: I think what you ought to do is just put two marks there. Go to the right-hand side and put—no, up next to one—two ones to indicate that two people classified them that way. That's fine.

Student: We have their environment—that would determine whether they were amphibians, reptiles——

Teacher: Like what?

Student: Like a snake is a reptile——

Teacher: Well, give me your categories, Robbie.

Student: Environment.

Teacher: Environment is not a category. They all have environments. Are there different environments?

Student: Ocean, land, or jungle.

Teacher: Well, land is one and what instead of water?

Student: Sea.

Teacher: I'm trying to see—a black bass.

Student: Yes, a black bass.

Teacher: Now, wait a minute, a black bass doesn't live in the ocean, does he?

Student: Water.

Teacher: Water. Fine. Land would be one and water would be a second and what else?

Student: Air.

Teacher: Air. All right, so this is coming from their environment. What's another way to categorize?

Student: We also have wild and domestic.

Teacher: Oh, do the same thing there—indicate the two of them, will you. Thank you, Robbie. Who's reporting for the third group? Would you stand so we can see you?

Student: We have prehensile and nonprehensile.

Teacher: Wow, what does that mean?

Student: Well, the opposing thumb which means you can grasp things.

Teacher: I see, which a black bass does not have.

Student: No. Vertebrate or——

Teacher: Now wait a minute. Which one is prehensile?

Student: There's a monkey on there, isn't there?

Teacher: No.

Student: Oh, well.

Teacher: I'm not sure you have a prehensile. Put it down anyway. Sharon, what other one?

Student: Vertebrate and invertebrate.

Teacher: Vertebrate and nonvertebrate.

Student: And breathing by lung and breathing through a gill.

Teacher: Lung as against gill. Are all of you getting all of these down in your notes? That's "gi," "gu" is the bird. Question?

Student: Which ones are the invertebrates?

Teacher: Which ones are the invertebrates? Carl, is there one that's an invertebrate there?

Student: Invertebrate—shark.

Teacher: The shark has a vertebra, hasn't it? Look, I'd like all of you to check on the prehensile and the vertebrate, nonvertebrate for the next time. I don't want to discuss it right now. Whether there are—what you may have are all vertebrate here or you may have all—none of them prehensile. But that doesn't matter. It is possible to put them in categories of vertebrate or invertebrate. All of them might be in one of the categories, which is all right. Let me check your notes to see if you got all of this as I work my way back here. (*Teacher passes up the aisles checking notes as he walks.*) Did all of you take the notes exactly as she did on the board? You didn't have to, you know, if you could think of a better way to do it. There are many good ways to take notes and you might have done them—I think that's a better way to take them than she had.

Teacher: Let me now ask you what all your categories had in common. Sheldon, what do you think? What do all of your categories have in common?

Student: They have vertebrae. If they're mammals, or how they get air—that seems to be the most common one in all three.

Teacher: Well, maybe I didn't ask the question in a way that really makes this clear. Let's let a few other people try to answer and see if we can reach a consensus. Aileen, your hand was up. What do you think?

Student: They all have something to do with life, they're all essential to life.

Teacher: All the categories are essential to life.

Student: Anything that's living can be put into these categories.

Teacher: Oh, I see. These, in one way or another, have something to do with the fact that they're all living creatures. Is that it?

Student: Yes.

Teacher: Harold, would you like to add something more about this?

Student: Well, we all picked the ones which we knew were the most frequent, which we hear about and talk about most. Well, we picked the ones which were most usual.

Teacher: Now what do you mean "are most usual," Harold? I think this is a very interesting idea.

Student: Which are common with more of the animals.

Teacher: Well, let me ask it another way around, Harold. Let's suppose you had a brother in third grade, if we asked him to do this exercise, would he have come up with categories like this?

Student: It all depends. I think if he knew more about science he would pick up the ones that are most general, which we have picked.

Teacher: You said if he knew more about science—what do you mean by this?

Student: Well, when you're in third grade they don't emphasize science as much as we know it and they probably wouldn't—they probably would think of the same ones but they would put them in a different way of saying it.

Teacher: Now what are you really saying about the source of your classification scheme? Let me ask Gregory this. Gregory, what is he saying about the source of your classification scheme? Where does it come from?

Student: It comes from what you really know about the animals.

Teacher: Yes, but where did you learn about them?

Student: In school.

Teacher: And where in school, English class?

Student: Well, it depends which grades you're in. For instance, in third grade you might pick it up from conversation, you might be doing something which pertains to animals.

Teacher: Well, Gregory, if you had to pick one subject you studied in school from which this classification scheme had to come, which one would you choose?

Student: Biology.

Teacher: Biology. May I ask how many of you are studying biology? Just one. How many of you studied some biology in elementary school, somewhere along the line? All of you. Do you really agree— Cynthia, let me ask you, do you really agree with Harold that your classification schemes come out of science?

Student: Aw, yes.

Teacher: Would you like to see my classification scheme? I don't know what I'd do if you said no because I'm going to show it to you anyway. (*Teacher shows the transparency that follows.*)

3	4	5	6	7	8
CAT	LION	SHARK	TURKEY	OSTRICH	ELEPHANT
	TUNA	EAGLE	RABBIT		PHEASANT
	PIKE	SHEEP	GROUSE		
			CONDOR		

Now let me ask you by what strange twist of mind I've done this. What do the numerals three, four, five, six, seven, and eight mean? How many of you think you know? Paul, you think you know. What does it mean?

Student: Number of letters in the word.

Teacher: Number of letters in the word. You mean there are three letters in "cat" and four in "lion" and so on. All right, let me try another one of mine. Have a look at it and see if you can decide the basis on which I categorized it. Sheldon.

1	2
TURKEY	RAINBOW TROUT
SHARK	COLLIE DOG
LION	BLACK BASS
SHEEP	

Student: The words with one word in it and the animals with two words in it.

Teacher: Turkey has one word and——.

Student: Rainbow trout has two.

Teacher: And rainbow trout has two. All right, let me try another one. How many of you get it? Faith, let's try you on this one.

1	2	3
CAT	LION	ELEPHANT
SHARK	OSTRICH	COLLIE DOG
GROUSE	CONDOR	RAINBOW TROUT
	TUNA	
	RABBIT	
	TURKEY	
	BLACK BASS	

Student: Syllables, like cat has one, monkey and lion have two, and elephant has three.

Teacher: Cat has one, lion has two, and elephant has three. It's the number of syllables in a word. Well, you got those very quickly. What do my categories have in common? How many of you think—see we decided that your categories had in common that they came from science. Cheryl, what do my categories have in common?

Student: They have to do with words, syllables, and letters.

Teacher: I had trouble hearing you, Cheryl.

Student: They were to do with words and syllables and letters like you'd learn in reading and spelling.

Teacher: So evidently my terms don't come from science—or rather my categories don't come from science. Is that right, Cheryl?

Student: Right.

Teacher: Yes. Robbie, would you like to add something to what Cheryl said?

Student: No.

Teacher: Go ahead, I bet you do.

Student: Well, different people know more about different things and what you know reflects how you characterize it.

Teacher: Well, do you think an English teacher would likely characterize them in this way?

Student: Yes.

Teacher: All right, I think you're quite right. A science teacher might categorize them the way you do and an English teacher might categorize them the way I did. Now let me ask you if you can figure out from what I said just now what we mean by the term "a frame of reference." Robert.

Student: A frame of reference is when you're doing a certain assignment what different books, or what different thoughts you have when you're doing it. Most of us fit in science categories, we were thinking mostly from a science aspect of doing it.

Teacher: From a science frame of reference.

Student: Yes. But if you know mostly about English then you'd do it to the construction of each word like how many letters are in it or something.

Teacher: So that's a frame of reference coming out of English, is that right?

Student: Yes.

Teacher: Now, this is a history class, it's not biology and it's not English; let me ask you what the problem of a frame of reference has to do with a historian. Why should we be fooling around with science terms and talking about frames of reference from science and English in a history class? Mont, would you like to try this one?

Student: Well, historians might look at historical events, but there are different frames of references, they might classify them differently.

Teacher: Well, so what. Don't the facts speak for themselves, Mont?

Student: If you read two different history books you'll find two different things written about different events. If you read a southern history book you might find a different look at the battles of the Civil War than you would from a northern history book.

Teacher: And what would determine the interpretation you are arguing?

Student: The frame of reference that the author used.

Teacher: Are you really arguing that there's no truth in history, that all of this just depends upon somebody's frame of reference?

Student: It's all fact, but it just depends upon what frame of reference you look at it through.

Teacher: David, would you like to comment on this? This is a very interesting idea if it's true, Mont, because what it really means is that we had better learn about frames of reference and interpretation if what you say is accurate. David.

Student: Well, the historian's job is to interpret the facts, to find out which is fact and which is not fact—this is his most important job, I think.

Teacher: You mean the facts don't speak for themselves and the interpretation is not implicit in the fact?

Student: Well, it's hard to interpret the facts—the historian's job is to interpret the facts because not anybody can do that because each person has a different frame of reference.

Teacher: Frank, would you like to add another comment before we go on?

Student: The historian's job is to find the facts, but it is also to put what facts he thinks are most important. And he might look at it in a different way and put a different fact up—more important than another person might.

Teacher: All right, let me give you some historical information this time and ask you to write down in your notes some ways to classify this sort of information. Here I've given you a group of names of Americans. I'd like you now to spend a couple of minutes (no more than two minutes) putting these names into some kinds of categories in the same way you started some categories for the animals and fish and birds, a minute ago. Just spend a couple of minutes doing it. Take them on the same note page.

CHIEF JUSTICE EARL WARREN
GOVERNOR WILLIAM SCRANTON
SENATOR JOSEPH CLARK
MAYOR JOSEPH BARR
SECRETARY OF STATE DEAN RUSK
COUNCILMAN JAMES JORDAN
ASSEMBLYMAN HARRY MARKOVITZ
REPRESENTATIVE WILLIAM MOOREHEAD
PRESIDENT LYNDON JOHNSON

(*Several minutes elapse.*) Let's see what you've done with these. Who would like to volunteer one category into which these have fallen? Howard, would you like to give us one?

Student: One category——

Teacher: Wait a minute. Wayne, would you go and erase the board and copy these down for us?

Student: One category I put mine in is the federal government—people in the federal government and the three divisions of government.

Teacher: Well, tell me what the other divisions are.

Student: Well, the, my second category was on the state level.

Teacher: Federal, state, what else?

Student: Local, I have for my third category.

Teacher: Local. Federal, state, local would be one. Would all of you agree that all of these people fit into one of those three categories? One of them's in the national—we really shouldn't say federal, we should say national, state, and local. Now what else?

Student: Elected and appointed.

Teacher: Elected and appointed. Some of these people were elected. Give me one who was elected.

Student: President Lyndon Johnson.

Teacher: Now one who was appointed.

Student: Assemblyman Harry Markowitz.

Teacher: No, he'd be elected, wouldn't he?

Student: Secretary of State, Dean Rusk.

Teacher: That's right, the Secretary of State would be appointed. What's another category? Get these down in your notes as we get them here. Yes.

Student: The legislative, judicial, and the executive branch of the government.

Teacher: Give me one example of the legislative.

Student: I can't see too well but if there's a congressman or a council——

Teacher: There is a congressman, William Moorehead, there.

Student: Well, then, he'd be in the legislative. President Johnson would be in the executive. Chief Justice Earl Warren would be in the judicial.

Teacher: All right, we could get a large number of other categories, but let's hold it here at the moment. Thank you. Why did you categorize them like this? Why did you do it this way? Mark, why do you think that you would categorize them in this way?

Student: In our ninth-grade social studies course they sort of changed our frame of reference to look at things from this sort of viewpoint.

Teacher: So you've lifted this really from your ninth-grade course. Is that it? And this is the frame of reference that's been given to you? What's he implying, Harold, about where a person gets a frame of reference? Where does it come from?

Student: It comes from the things that he learns and he dwells upon most. The thing he has the most knowledge about.

Teacher: And he learns where, Harold?

Student: Well, in this case it's in school, but really——

Teacher: All right, this is one place—he learns it in school. Dan, can you think of some other places from which a historian gets a frame of reference?

Student: In the newspapers, or literature, TV, and radio.

Teacher: TV, radio, newspapers, and literature. Where else might a historian get some things? Gregory, what are some other places?

Student: By word of mouth from listening to other people.

Teacher: Just in conversation? Where else, Sheldon?

Student: Other historians.

Teacher: Other historians. Linda?

Student: In his home, the way he's brought up affects his reference.

Teacher: In his home. Robert?

Student: Or you can say his environment.

Teacher: His whole environment. Let me ask you what places—name one place—one sort of experience a person can have which wouldn't have a chance of affecting his frame of reference. (*Pause.*) Do you mean none of you can think of a way? Have you, Cheryl?

Student: An experience——

Teacher: Yes, one experience he has that has no chance of affecting his frame of reference.

Student: Being born.

Teacher: Maybe you're right. I would like to ask a psychiatrist about this, but since I don't know let's suppose that he's one year old—from then on does everything really affect it? What do you think?

Student: I think that everything affects him because anything that passes through his life (maybe he doesn't know right offhand) but taken subconsciously, I think that everything affects him.

Teacher: So if you're right your argument is (and I can see one person who disagrees) that every experience of a person's life affects his frame of reference and therefore it affects the way a historian cate-

gorizes material. And this, in the long run, must affect the interpretation of history. Is that right? We'll spend a considerable
amount of time this year building up a frame of reference for all
of you because if this assumption that Sandy came to back there—
if the conclusion rather she came to is right, it's obvious that all
of your education and all of your dinner table conversations with
friends in one way or another affects your frame of reference. And
if this is so, then what we had better do is start to make our own
frame of reference clear in our own mind.

CHAPTER 17 Essay Testing *— make as objective as possible.*

The entire subject of essay testing is filled with controversy. Much of this controversy results from the failure t~~o state test objectives~~ clearly. Most professional testers assume that the major objective of an essay test is to rank the performance of students reliably on a scale from best to least. Many teachers, on the other hand, assume that one of the major functions of essay testing is to teach students to write well. Still other teachers will argue that only through writing essay tests and short papers can students really learn to be historians.

If history is really a way of reading and writing, then writing history— either in the form of essay tests or as short papers—is indispensable to the mastery of the discipline. Writing history should reinforce good habits of reading; the reverse of this process is equally true. When students read a text or an article they should search out the interpretation of the author and assess the evidence he gives to support that interpretation. When a student writes an essay he should write an interpretation and give factual evidence to support it. Reading and writing support each other.

Should an essay test be used for both of these purposes—ranking students and teaching them to interpret—at once? When teachers grade essay examinations together, they soon learn how easy it is for ~~two equally competent~~ *reliability* people to rank the same essay quite differently. A number of experiments even indicate that the same person ranking the same set of papers at two different times often fails to rank them in the same order. Essay tests are not a reliable way to rank students. We should face this conclusion squarely.

But should they be abandoned for this reason? They serve other functions well. They give a student practice in writing, although such practice may not lead to improvement unless the teacher points out the student's mistakes. They also help to ~~teach the method of the~~ historian, although people who make this claim would probably not be able to support it through any testing instruments we now have.

275

All of these issues are discussed in the two readings in this chapter. The first consists of a few pages from a well-known text in measurement and evaluation. Here the authors point to the difficulties inherent in the problem of ranking essay tests accurately and suggest some ways to overcome this shortcoming. The second article, written by a former Pittsburgh high school teacher, strongly supports essay testing, although it does not make a case for the essay as an accurate ranking device.

As you read, keep the following issues in mind:

1) What should be the objectives of an essay test? *reliable*
2) Do the authors of these two articles agree about the qualities that a good essay question should have? why or why not?
3) How can a teacher assign and evaluate essay questions, given the fact that they take so long to correct?
4) For which of the skills listed by Bloom in Chapter 2 are essay examinations appropriate? Do Bruner's ideas about structure provide hints about the focus of content in essay questions?

ADVANTAGES AND DISADVANTAGES OF ESSAY TESTS

Robert L. Thorndike · Elizabeth Hagen

Consider the following answers written by two eighth-grade students to the question "Compare the powers and organization of the central government under the Articles of Confederation with the powers and organization of our own central government today."

STUDENT A

Our government today has a president, a house of representatives, and a senate. Each state has two senators but the number of representatives is different for each state. This is because of compramise at the Constitutional Convention. The Articles of Confederation had only a Congress and each state had delegates in it and had one vote. This Congress couldn't do much of anything because all the states had to say it was alright. Back then Congress couldn't make people obey the law and there wasn't no supreme court to make people obey the law. The Articles of Confederation let Congress

Reprinted from Robert L. Thorndike and Elizabeth Hagen, *Measurement and Evaluation in Psychology and Education* (New York: John Wiley & Sons, Inc., 1961), pp. 43–47 and 53–56.

declare war, make treaties, and borrow money and Congress can do these things today. But Congress then really didn't have any power, it had to ask the states for everything. Today Congress can tell the states what to do and tax people to raise money they don't have to ask the states to give them money. Once each state could print its own money if it wanted to but today only the U. S. Mint can make money.

Student B

There is a very unique difference between the Central Government under the Articles of Confederation and the National Government of today. The Confederation could not tax directly where as the National Government can. The government of today has three different bodies—Legislative, Judicial, and Executive branches. The Confederation had only one branch which had limited powers. The confederate government could not tax the states directly or an individual either. The government of today, however, has the power to tax anyone directly and if they don't respond, the government has the right to put this person in jail until they are willing to pay the taxes. The confederation government was not run nearly as efficiently as the government of today. While they could pass laws (providing most of the states voted with them) the confederate government could not enforce these laws, (something which the present day can and does do) they could only hope and urge the states to enforce the laws.

These two answers together with three other answers written by students in the same class were given to two groups of graduate students in courses in measurement or evaluation. Both groups of students were provided with a model answer to the question and given the following instructions:

Instructions: The essay question was a part of a social studies test consisting of fifty objective items and one essay question. The students were given 25 minutes to write their answers to the essay question. You have been given the answers written by five of the students. The class that these five students were in was a heterogeneous one. Twenty-five points is the maximum score for the question. Please grade each paper using the model answer provided. The grade is to reflect completeness and accuracy of the answer—not quality of English expression, spelling, or grammar.

Suppose that *you* grade these two answers in accordance with the instructions given above before you read any further. Record the scores that you would give the answers.

Now look at Table 3.1, which shows the scores actually given to all five answers, including these two. Every one of the answers receives scores spreading over about 20 points of the possible range of 25. Any one of the papers might have gotten a score as high as 18; any one might have gotten a score as low as 5. The responses of students A and B were judged to be outstandingly good by some raters, poor by others. The inconsistency of the judgments is demonstrated most forcefully. A single rating of any one of these papers tells us very little about how that same paper will be rated by someone else. Why is this? What makes the appraisal of an essay response so undependable?

Let us admit to start with that the dice were somewhat loaded against the

TABLE 3.1. GRADES GIVEN TO FIVE ANSWERS TO ESSAY QUESTION

Score	Student A	Student B	Student C	Student D	Student E
25	6	5	—	6	—
24	2	2	—	4	—
23	4	3	—	4	—
22	3	9	2	5	—
21	8	2	—	4	—
20	32	21	6	24	—
19	6	1	—	3	—
18	14	11	3	12	1
17	6	8	3	2	1
16	4	2	2	4	—
15	23	23	18	34	4
14	4	1	3	5	—
13	2	2	3	2	1
12	4	13	9	7	6
11	1	3	6	1	2
10	6	11	33	4	25
9	1	4	9	1	5
8	—	6	9	3	6
7	2	3	3	—	—
6	—	—	3	3	16
5	3	—	11	2	50
4	—	—	1	1	7
3	—	1	3	—	15
2	—	—	1	—	1
1	—	—	—	—	—
0	—	—	2	—	1

graders in this little experiment. Most of them were not social studies teachers, though the majority had had some teaching experience. (Previous experience has indicated that social studies teachers will show about as much variation.) Furthermore, they had not taught the class, and did not know anything about the general level of performance in this and similar groups.

One major reason for the wide range of scores found in Table 3.1 is that different raters maintained very different standards for rating *all* the papers. Different raters used quite different parts of the scale of scores. Though it was most common for a rater to spread his scores between about 5 and 20, a few awarded no grade higher than 10 to *any* of the answers while others assigned no grades below 15. These last two groups were operating in entirely different score ranges and showed no overlap. The best for one group was lower than the poorest for the other. Judges differed not only in the average level at which they rated the papers, but also in how much they spread out their scores. Some were very "conservative," bunching all their ratings close together, while others tended to spread them widely over the whole range. Such differences in grading standards are very real in actual school situations—as every student knows —and provide one main source for inconsistency in grading essay responses.

However, the judges were also not very consistent in the rank order in which they arranged the 5 papers. In Table 3.2 we have shown how often

TABLE 3.2. RANK ORDER ASSIGNED TO EACH OF FIVE ESSAY QUESTIONS

Rank	Student A	Student B	Student C	Student D	Student E
1	44	29	2	33	1
1.5	13	12	1	11	—
2	28	23	8	31	1
2.5	12	10	5	17	—
3	24	32	19	23	—
3.5	1	6	9	5	3
4	3	16	55	9	11
4.5	3	1	18	1	20
5	1	1	13	—	94

each paper was ranked first, how often second, and so on. (Tie ranks have been indicated as 1.5, 2.5, etc.) In this table we see that every one of the 5 answers was ranked first by somebody, and every answer was either last or tied for last. There is some consensus that student E wrote the poorest answer and student C the next poorest, but practically no agreement as to the relative standing of the other three. Students A, B or D could easily have been judged best of the group or only average. Thus, there is not only a marked difference in *absolute* standard from judge to judge, but also inconsistency in the *relative* judgment of one paper in comparison with the others. Inconsistency in relative judgment is characteristic not only of different raters but also of the same rater at different times. Thus, when the evaluation class was asked to grade the papers a second time 3 weeks later (without advance notice that this was to be done), a third of the ratings differed from the original rating by 5 points or more (out of the possible range of 25 points). Only a third of the papers kept the same rank in the group of 5 on the second grading.

The results that we have presented illustrate the situation that commonly prevails in evaluating essay responses. The responses vary in many ways and by infinitely small degrees. Raters approach them with differing standards of severity and looking for different things. As a result the evaluation of these responses is generally highly subjective and quite unreliable. We shall consider later in the chapter what can be done to deal with these very real problems. . . .

IMPROVING THE CONTENT OF AN ESSAY TEST

The following paragraphs present and discuss several suggestions for improving the questions that go into an essay test. These are not scientifically established principles, but they reflect the judgment of experienced test makers.

1. *Before Starting to Write the Essay Question, Have in Mind Explicitly What Mental Processes of the Student You Want to Bring Out by the Question.* If you want to use the essay question to determine the extent to which a student can *use* his information then the question must be phrased in such a

way that the student must do such things as solve a problem that has not been directly taught, or point out relationships that have not been explicitly pointed out before.

2. *In General, Start Essay Questions with Such Phrases as "Compare,"* *"Contrast," "Give the reasons for," "Present the arguments for and against,"* *"Give original examples of," and "Explain how or why."* These words will help to present tasks requiring the student to select, organize, and apply his knowledge. Don't start essay questions with such words as "what," "who," "when," and "list." These words are likely to present tasks requiring only the reproduction of information.

3. *Write the Essay Question in Such a Way That the Task Is Clearly and* *Unambiguously Defined for Each Examinee.* A question such as "Discuss the factors and influences that led to the writing and adoption of our Constitution," is global, vague, and ambiguous. First, what does the teacher mean by the word "discuss"? Second, does the teacher want the student to start with the Magna Charta in 1215 or with the settlement of the colonies or with the end of the Revolutionary War? Third, does the teacher want the student to stop with the beginning of the Constitutional Convention in 1787 or with the ratification of the Constitution? Fourth, what does the teacher mean by "factors and influences"? The score that the student receives for his answer is likely to depend to a large extent on how lucky he is at guessing what the teacher wanted.

A better way to phrase this question so that each examinee will interpret the question in the same way would be:

> Explain how each of the following influenced the provisions written into our Constitution by the delegates to the Constitutional Convention.
> A. The Magna Charta, the Petition of Right, and the English Bill of Rights.
> B. The fear of tyranny or rule by one man or one group.
> C. The problems that arose in trying to operate under the provisions of the Articles of Confederation.
> D. The fear of the small states that they would be controlled by the large states.
> E. Business rivalries between states.

The question as it has been rephrased guarantees a more common basis for response. In one sense it breaks the one question up into five. The analysis also makes clear that on the original question (and also the revised one) students will require a relatively long time to write an adequate answer.

4. *The Words "What do you think," "In your opinion," or "Write all you* *know about . . ." Almost Never Belong in an Essay Question to Measure Academic Achievement.* The use of these phrases is common on teacher-made essay tests. But when a teacher asks: "Why do you think that the Articles of Confederation provided a poor basis for the formation of our central government?" he is not really interested in the student's opinion. He actually wants

to determine whether the student knows the fundamental weaknesses of the Articles of Confederation, as stated by the teacher or text. Therefore the question would be better if written: "Why did the Articles of Confederation prove to be unworkable as a framework for our national government?"

The only time when the use of "you," "in your opinion," or "do you think" is justified in an essay question (or any other type of test question) is when the purpose of the question is to obtain an expression of attitudes (which really cannot be graded) or to determine how good a logical defense a student can make of the position that he has taken. In the latter instance, the teacher should *not* be particularly interested in which position the student takes and should evaluate the answer given only on the basis of how well the student defends or supports his position.

5. *Be Sure That the Students Do Not Have Too Many or Too Lengthy Questions to Answer in the Time Available.* An essay test should not be a test of speed of writing. Good essay questions demand that the student consider the question, think about his answer, then write it. These processes take time and the younger the student or the more complex the question, the longer is the required time. In order to answer adequately the revised question on p. 280, the typical eighth grader would probably need from 45 to 60 minutes. In most essay tests given in the classroom, three to five such questions are given to be answered in a single classroom period. This practice may encourage both sloppy thinking and sloppy writing on the part of the student.

6. *Do Not Use Both Essay and Objective Questions in the Same Test when the Time for Testing is Limited.* Quite frequently teachers use both objective and essay questions on the same test. It is not unusual to see a teacher-made test consisting of thirty to fifty multiple-choice questions and one to three essay questions, all of which are to be answered in a 50-minute period. This practice is undesirable first because there is not enough time for the student to answer adequately all of the questions and second because there are very difficult problems in combining the scores on the two different kinds of items. (See Chapter 17.)

7. *Have Each Examinee Answer the Same Questions. Don't Offer a Choice of Questions to be Answered.* When an essay examination is being used to appraise achievement of the objectives of a common program of study, each examinee should be required to answer the same questions. Giving a choice of questions reduces the common base upon which different individuals may be compared. It adds one further source of variability to the subjectivity and inaccuracy that already exist. A choice of questions may have a public-relations value with the examinees, but it has no justification from the point of view of effective measurement.

Scoring Essay Examinations

A number of steps may be taken to mitigate the subjectivity and reduce some of the biases in evaluating the answers to an essay examination. These are mostly attempts to break up the process of evaluation into a series of more specific, fractionated judgments made upon a common base and applied to an anonymous product. Specific suggestions are outlined below.

1. *Decide in Advance What Factors Are to Be Measured. If More than One Distinct Quality Is to Be Appraised, Make Separate Evaluations of Each.* If facts are considered important, score for facts. If organization is important, give a rating upon organization. If mechanics of English, sentence structure, spelling, punctuation, etc., are considered a significant outcome, give a rating upon mechanics. However, do not contaminate the rating for knowledge or understanding with appraisal of mechanics. It is hard to isolate quality of organization from extent of factual information, but if the essay question is to serve its distinctive purpose an attempt should be made to do so.

2. *Prepare a Model Answer in Advance, Showing What Points Should Be Covered and How Many Credits Are to Be Allowed for Each.* This will provide a common frame of reference for evaluating each paper. After the preliminary model has been prepared, it should be checked against a sample of student responses to the question. The model and the scoring scheme should be modified in the light of these answers. They can now be used as the yardstick for assigning credits to each paper in turn.

3. *Read All Answers to One Question before Going on to the Next.* A more uniform standard can be maintained for a single question and for a short period of time. There is more chance to compare one person's answer with another's and thus to build up a "feel" for the answers. There is less contamination of judgment by what that same examinee had written on the previous question.

4. *Grade the Papers as Nearly Anonymously as Possible.* The less you know about *who* wrote an answer, the more objectively you can grade *what* was written.

5. *Greater Reliability Can Be Obtained by Averaging Independent Ratings.* If the importance of the test merits the expenditure of the extra effort, a more dependable appraisal can be obtained by having one or more additional raters each give an independent rating of the responses.

TEACHING STUDENTS TO WRITE ESSAY EXAMINATIONS

Frances A. Hess

History students must learn to write essay examinations. If we expect our students to learn to perform the task of an historian, that is, to amass and interpret evidence on a particular historical event or period and then come to conclusions logically based on that evidence, then the only effective way to test the student's proficiency is through an essay exam or a research paper. Only by reading our students' essays can we as teachers see just how well each one is able to perform as an historian. Far too frequently, college professors and high school teachers blithely assume that students who discuss well in class will be able to express their ideas effectively on paper without additional assistance from the instructor. All too often, however, these same students have no idea how to go about writing a good essay, for they may not have had previous instruction in this area. Good essay writing is not an inherited trait; it is an acquired characteristic.

At the beginning of the year, before the first essay exam, it is important to take considerable time to explain to students just what constitutes a well-written essay. One excellent way to do this is to present them with a sheet of pointers on "How to Write a Good Essay Examination." This gives them a convenient reference throughout the year. At the same time this instruction sheet has an additional value: In the process of writing and explaining it, we as teachers are making absolutely sure that we can be articulate about what we are asking our students to do. Grading essay exams becomes far easier when we know what the standards of a good essay are. Many of our students have been getting A's for years for mere verbiage and volume and honestly do not know how to give a concise, specific, and well-organized answer to a challenging question such as, "To what extent can we call the royal absolutism of Louis XIV his personal success, and to what extent was it a product of events and developments of the preceding seventy years?" Students will flounder in answering this question unless they have been carefully instructed in appropriate means of attack. First of all, they must realize that when they answer this question they are expected to present a tightly organized, sustained, and well-substantiated argument on the nature of Louis XIV's absolutism. If a student fails to take a position on this issue, then he is not answering the question. It is at this particular point of writing an argument, that is, taking a position on

Reprinted from an address given by Frances A. Hess at the Eighth Annual Advanced Placement History Conference, Carnegie Institute of Technology, June 1961. Mrs. Hess taught an Advanced Placement European History course at Taylor Allderdice High School, Pittsburgh.

the issue raised, that students have great difficulty at the start of the year. If they cannot even identify the central issue in the question, they tackle the question in hit-or-miss fashion. They need careful and frequent explanation of this procedure of defining the issue and formulating the argument, and many opportunities to practice it, followed by detailed teacher criticism.

After the student has analyzed the question and formulated his argument, he should make an outline so that he will cover all evidence relevant to his argument and can organize the development of his essay. It seems to be a student's natural instinct to look at the question and just plunge in, afraid to "waste" a minute in thought or organization. Here is where we must constantly remind students of the necessity of outlining and assure them that outlining and stopping to think are distinctly not to be confused with wasting time.

An argument on the issue raised and a well-planned outline will not guarantee an essay of A quality. Students must also be taught the basic form of an essay. We should insist that they always write an introductory paragraph, in which they state and define their argument in the topic sentence and then indicate the major points they will develop to prove this argument. If we insist that students do this, they will be far less likely to avoid the issue and merely write a description of Louis XIV's absolutism or rephrase the question instead of taking a definite stand on it. In the body of the essay the students must be expected to substantiate their position with accurate and specific evidence. Each paragraph should be clearly and obviously related to the principal argument by a topic sentence connecting the particular subissue to the main line of thought. Students who write a good introductory paragraph often get lost as they develop their essay and fail to write a sustained argument. Under the pressure of time, many students just fade away at the end of an essay, or else they introduce new material in the conclusion. They should be cautioned, instead, to budget their time and never forget an effective and valid conclusion pulling the entire essay together.

Once the basic techniques have been explained, the students need many opportunities to write essay exams and a great deal of critical guidance from the instructor. A twenty-minute quiz or a full period exam every two or three weeks may appear to be a tremendous amount of blue-book reading for the instructor (and it's not easy!), but it seems to be the most effective way to train students in essay writing. The rapid progress of the students is encouragement enough for the teacher. In addition to essay exams on each unit of work, students also need practice in pulling several units together.

Although we give our students many opportunities to write essay exams, we shall not see much progress unless we take the time and effort to grade each examination very carefully. Much more significant to our students than the grade we give them are the detailed, written comments pointing out the specific strengths and weaknesses of each paper. These commentaries are definitely time consuming, but they are the only way students can gain insight into their individual problems of essay writing. One or two general comments are not enough; specific criticisms interspersed along the essay are of much more value to the student.

Both individual conferences with students requesting them and ten or fifteen minutes of class time spent in general comment on the essays when we return them have proved to be invaluable ways to help students improve in essay writing. Another method of tackling the essay-writing problem is to give students dittoed copies of a good and a poor paper with the teacher's critique. By analyzing and discussing these samples as well as their own individual papers, students get a much clearer idea of what they should be doing. Later in the year, we can give them a copy of an A paper, without any teacher comment, leaving the analysis up to the students. Occasionally having students grade each others' quiz papers also helps them gain insight into their own difficulties. Naturally, this procedure should not be attempted early in the year. To give students additional practice in analyzing essay questions and in formulating an argument, it is a good idea to start class occasionally by presenting students with an essay question based on the day's assignment, allowing them ten minutes or so to write their introductory paragraph, and then using these paragraphs as basis for class discussion.

During the year, as we stress essay writing and correct individual exam papers, there are a number of points that should be emphasized. Students must realize that the style of writing and the proper use of the English language are very important aspects of good essay writing. If we do not keep emphasizing spelling, grammar, and accuracy in the use of words, students will concentrate solely on the ideas themselves and thus fall far short of excellence. Students must not be allowed to get away with glittering generalities and vague phrases or statements, such as ". . . the people rose up against the French government," nor should they be permitted to dismiss Napoleon by labeling him a "dictator" and completely ignoring his achievements. Students need to be reminded constantly to let their knowledge show through! Their evidence must be as precise as possible. They should discuss particular Renaissance artists and their characteristics rather than uttering a few platitudes about Renaissance art in general. Many students tend to take a black-or-white position when confronted with a question such as this one:

> The rise of the strong national monarchy is the single most significant development in European history in the period 1400–1600. The economic, religious, social, and cultural changes that took place in this two-hundred year period all resulted from this one development.
>
> Evaluate this statement carefully, discussing the extent of its applicability to historical developments in this period.

They argue either that the political development caused all other changes or that it had nothing to do with them. Students should be made to realize that they must always view the question or statement critically; they can accept part of it and modify other parts. We must impress our students with the importance of defining terms in an essay. They cannot do a good job in discussing whether genuine freedoms in the West have been won by evolutionary change or violent revolution without first defining "evolution" and "revolution" and making clear what they mean by "genuine freedoms." We must also take our students to task for not answering the question asked or for narrowing its scope too much. The following question presents a broad issue:

> The basic characteristics of the Renaissance can be adequately summed up by these phrases: classicism, secularism, and individualism.
>
> Test this generalization by applying it to three of the following areas: religion, politics, economics, the intellectual field, and the arts and seeing whether it is an adequate and an accurate description.

In answering this, students discuss what the basic characteristics of the Renaissance are, and not just whether the terms "classicism," "secularism," and "individualism" are applicable.

Time spent instructing students in essay writing does not guarantee success. Too much time and effort are wasted during an examination period if students have not reviewed the material purposefully and intelligently. Since most students do not know how to review effectively, we must help them to develop satisfactory methods of reviewing for an exam. After floundering through one or two essays, students will soon realize the value of organizing ahead of time the mass of material they have studied and of searching for the major threads in the particular time block to be covered.

We may spend many hours teaching our students to write essay exams, but all this effort will come to naught unless we give them questions that are challenging and pose problems that force them to use their analytical and critical powers, to pull together the material they have studied, and to make judgments. If on a Renaissance test we ask only about the political developments of the period, the students may have no opportunity to demonstrate their knowledge, or lack of knowledge, of the period as a whole. I am the first to admit that writing good essay questions is extremely difficult: it is an art that comes only with much practice. However, a well-worded, challenging question is extremely important. A quotation about peace settlements in general, which students are asked to apply to the Congress of Vienna or to Versailles, is a far more effective type of question than just asking students to "Evaluate the peace settlement of 1815 or 1919." The traditional and exceedingly boring "List" or "Describe" question does not test the student's proficiency as an historian. A question like the following requires careful analysis by the student:

> French, Russian, and Austro-Hungarian history, 1860–1914, represent a failure on the part of the government to come to grips with any of the basic problems it faced. In Germany and England, in this period, we see quite the opposite situation. The governments did successfully resolve most of the basic issues they faced.
>
> Evaluate this statement in the light of three countries you select as case studies.

This question tests both the mastery of the students of the 1860–1914 period and their ability to analyze the issue, evaluate the evidence, and organize their argument.

Furthermore, students are not likely to do very well on essay tests unless they are given an opportunity in the daily class discussion to use the analytical and interpretative powers we demand of them on an exam. In class discussion, students should be concerned with analyzing the basic issues raised by the assignment, formulating an argument, and substantiating it with precise evidence. During class we have an excellent opportunity to poke holes in the sweeping generalization and to make students be specific and accurate in their use of evidence and logical in their argument. Daily lectures give students little opportunity to grapple with difficult issues such as, "Why did the French Revolution come in 1789 and not in 1715?" and give the teacher no chance to evaluate the student's progress.

I am sure we agree that teaching students to write essay exams is no easy task, and certainly requires infinite energy, patience, and skill on the teacher's part. Essay exam writing must occupy a key place in any history course. We must take all the time necessary to make clear to our students what the elements of good essay writing are, and then must give them every possible opportunity to become skilled in this particular art. Rare is the student who will succeed without constant guidance and criticism. If we do take the time to work with our students on essay writing, if we try to write challenging exam questions, and if we give students many opportunities to tackle complex issues in class discussion as well as on examinations, then our students should become more proficient as historians.

CHAPTER 18 **Objective Testing**

Like most arts, testing must be learned slowly and at considerable cost. Professional testing companies such as the Educational Testing Service spend thousands of dollars to develop a single multiple-choice test. First, test experts draw up specifications. ETS then hires item writers to contribute original questions. Test experts review these questions and select those that seem suitable for the purposes of the examination. Sometimes questions that have been used on previous examinations are introduced. Next, several versions of the test are tried out on groups of students. An item analysis is then made and the best questions are chosen for the final examination to be published. No classroom teacher can hope to duplicate this process.

Good testing takes time. Beginning teachers often take hours to develop a few items for a multiple-choice examination. Yet the process of evaluation is indispensable to good teaching. Unless we can find out what our students have learned, we will never be able to assess the success of our teaching or to plan succeeding lessons intelligently. A few simple rules may prove to be helpful:

1. State to yourself, and then write down, the exact purpose of the test. Ask yourself questions. Are you trying to find out whether or not your students have learned the factual information in a particular unit of study? Are you trying to rank students according to their abilities? Do you want to diagnose the strengths and weaknesses of individual students?
2. Plan the test questions carefully. Write out a test plan in detail.
3. If you are testing skills, write a number of questions designed to test the mastery of each skill. These questions will then yield subscores for each skill or for parts of one skill.
4. Provide a separate answer sheet such as the one at the end of the illustrative items. Punch or drill out the correct answers on a key to make scoring as efficient as possible. Then collect all copies of the test questions so that the same exam can be used again.

5. Analyze your test after you have given it.
6. Start a file of good test questions. Put each question on a separate card and on the back of the card note the appropriate data about where and when the question was used and about its relative difficulty.

Chapter 18 has two parts. The first is a set of specifications for a mid-semester test in American history at the eleventh-grade level. The three teachers who were contributing questions drew up these "specs," wrote items to meet them, and then edited the final version. The second part of the reading consists of illustrative social studies items developed by the Educational Testing Service.

As you read, think about the following issues:

1) Why should a teacher develop test specifications such as these?
2) What are the types of objective questions contained in the list of illustrative social studies items?
3) How do items designed to test for knowledge differ from those designed to get at skills or at objectives?

AMERICAN HISTORY TEST SPECIFICATIONS: MIDSEMESTER EXAMINATION

Anna Quattrocchi · Edwin Fenton

A. *General Specifications*
   1. Although variation in item difficulty is desired, the average difficulty of items should be such that 60 percent of an *average ability* group of eleventh graders will make correct responses.

Number of Questions

B. *Types of Abilities to be Measured*

28	1. Recall of information, ideas, and definitions
14	2. Comparison of two or more events or ideas
14	3. Application of generalizations and definitions
14	4. Judgment of relative significance
70	

C. *Types of Items in Terms of the Form They Take*

28	1. Discrete multiple-choice items, with or without much stimulus material as quotations
14	2. Sets of multiple-choice items based on passages or round-tables (4–7 items in each set)

14   3. Grouped identification sets (5–8 items in each set)
14   4. Sets of multiple-choice items based on charts, graphs,
⌣ 70   maps, or cartoons (4–7 items in each set)

Content topics within major chronological periods.

25 questions   1. Exploration and Settlement
              A. European backgrounds
              B. Exploration and settlement by French, Spanish, and
                 Portuguese
              C. The settlement of the English colonies
23 questions   2. Rivalries and revolt
              A. Old rivalries (first part of Chap. 3)
              B. The colonies and the mother country
              C. The causes of the American Revolution
              D. The Revolutionary War
22 questions   3. Establishing a new government
              A. The Articles of Confederation
              B. The Development of the Constitution
              C. The Federalist period

Each of the three teachers in the course should choose one of the three major content topics listed above. She should then write questions covering this content and testing for the types of abilities under B, listed above. Each question should be written on a separate piece of paper in order to make editing easy. A chart, map, graph, passage, roundtable or grouped identification, although it might contain as many as eight questions, would, of course, go on one piece of paper. In order to obtain a correct balance of the types of items under C, listed above, each of the three teachers ought to write the indicated number of the types of items listed below. The page references refer to the multilithed sheet entitled "Illustrative Social Studies Items," which has been distributed.

    A. One map, chart, or graph with 4 to 7 items (see pp. 4–6)
    B. One set of items based on passages or roundtable with 4 to
       7 items (see pp. 8–9)
    C. One grouped identification with 5 to 8 items (see p. 4, top)
    D. Twelve discrete multiple-choice items (see pp. 1–3). Some
       of these items ought to call for knowledge of material in the
       two bodies of content information assigned to other teachers.
       Students will then be asked questions forcing them to use
       information from more than one content area.

WARNING: Please use the style used on the sheet entitled "Illustrative
                 Social Studies Items." Observe capitalization, punctuation,
                 and other peculiarities. This practice will make editing
                 much easier.

ILLUSTRATIVE SOCIAL STUDIES ITEMS

Educational Testing Service

1. To which of the following features of American life did *both* the administrations of Woodrow Wilson and Franklin D. Roosevelt contribute?
   I. The banking system
   II. Old-age insurance
   III. Government regulation of business
   (A) I only
   (B) II only
   (C) I and III only
   (D) II and III only

2. The policy of the Open Door in China was designed to
   (A) divide Chinese territory among the great powers
   (B) compel the Chinese to open their ports to foreign trade
   (C) preserve equal trading rights for all foreigners in that country
   (D) restore full sovereign rights to China

3. All of the following are means of combating inflation EXCEPT
   (A) establishing price controls and rationing
   (B) reducing the volume of currency and credit
   (C) reducing taxes
   (D) increasing productivity

4. Elections of members to the British House of Commons and to the United States House of Representatives are most similar with respect to the
   (A) length of the election campaign
   (B) cost of the election campaign
   (C) number of other officials elected on the same ballot
   (D) proportion of the total number of seats to be filled

5. Franklin D. Roosevelt was LEAST successful in securing congressional support for
   (A) unemployment relief
   (B) a social security program
   (C) a reform of the court system
   (D) monetary reform

6. "Just as the superior race should rule over inferior races, so within the superior race power should be given to superior individuals."
   This statement represents the ideas of
   (A) the enlightened despots of the eighteenth century
   (B) Marxian Socialists

Reprinted with the permission of Educational Testing Service, Princeton, N.J.

(C) leaders of the medieval Church

(D) twentieth-century Fascists

7. "The United States has a trade surplus of 3 billion dollars a year, but that is not enough to cover military expenditures and other payments abroad amounting to 7.5 billion dollars a year."

The imbalance of 4.5 billion dollars could be reduced if there were an increase in

(A) exports of consumer goods

(B) expenditures of American tourists abroad

(C) imports of raw materials

(D) income for foreign investors in American industry

8. Beginning with the earliest, what is the correct chronological order of the following?

   I. The Yalta Conference
   II. The Potsdam Conference
   III. The Berlin Blockade
   IV. The admission of the Federal Republic of Germany to NATO

(A) I, II, III, IV

(B) I, III, IV, II

(C) II, I, III, IV

(D) II, I, IV, III

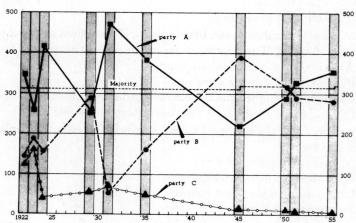

9. The graph above represents the political composition from 1922 to 1955 of which of the following?

(A) The German Bundestag

(B) The French National Assembly
(C) The Italian Chamber of Deputies
(D) The British House of Commons

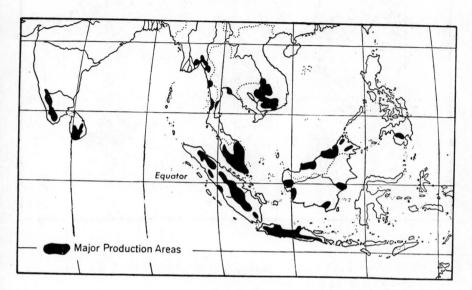

Equator

— Major Production Areas —

10. The map above would be used to show some of the major areas for world production of
(A) natural rubber
(B) coffee
(C) cotton
(D) iron ore

Questions 11–13 refer to the following treaties.
(A) Hay-Bunau-Varilla Treaty
(B) Adams-Onis Treaty
(C) Clayton-Bulwer Treaty
(D) Treaty of Guadalupe Hidalgo

11. An agreement transferring East Florida to the United States

12. An agreement which established the boundary of Texas at the Rio Grande

13. An agreement not to seek exclusive control over any Central-American canal

Questions 14–16 refer to the following map.

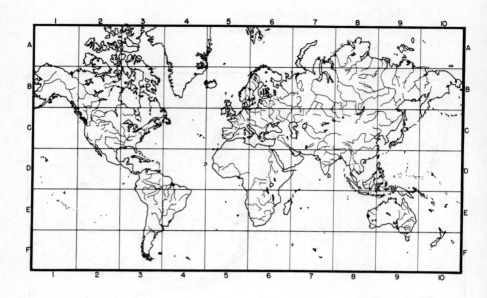

14. On the Mercator projection above, land in which of the following squares is most exaggerated in size?
    (A) 2-C
    (B) 4-E
    (C) 5-D
    (D) 8-A

15. The Ural Mountains are in
    (A) 5-C
    (B) 6-D
    (C) 7-B
    (D) 8-C

16. Territory of nations where Muslims constitute a majority of the population is located in all of the following squares EXCEPT
    (A) 6-C
    (B) 6-E
    (C) 7-D
    (D) 8-D

Questions 17–18 refer to the following graph.

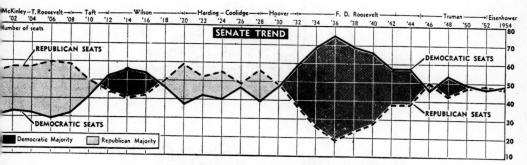

17. The peaks that appear on the chart for such years as 1920, 1928, and 1936 are explained by the fact that
    (A) control of the Senate frequently shifts from one party to the other
    (B) senators are frequently re-elected
    (C) senators have six-year terms
    (D) a victorious presidential candidate often carries some senatorial candidates into office with him

18. Which of the following took place in each of the years shown on the graph?
    (A) The election of the President and the entire Congress
    (B) The election of the President, the House of Representatives, and one-third of the Senate
    (C) The election of the House of Representatives and one-third of the Senate
    (D) The election of all of the House of Representatives and two-thirds of the Senate

Questions 19–20 refer to the following cartoon.

By *Willard Combes, in* The Cleveland Press

19. The cartoonist would probably favor
    (A) greater representation for rural areas
    (B) gerrymandering of urban areas
    (C) equitable representation on the basis of income
    (D) equitable representation on the basis of population

20. The cartoon would not have been as appropriate in the nineteenth century because
    (A) the Populist party protected the farmer against city bosses
    (B) farmers were less interested in politics
    (C) a larger portion of the population was then rural
    (D) the federal government exercised more supervision over the states

Questions 21–23 refer to the following statement.

   "This compromise helped to keep the peace for four decades by admitting two states and by the mere drawing of a line. Only when this compromise was set aside, first by an act of Congress and then by a decision of the Supreme Court, did the conflict which has been called inevitable occur."

21. The President at the time of the compromise was
    (A) James Monroe
    (B) Andrew Jackson
    (C) John Quincy Adams
    (D) James K. Polk

22. The act of Congress referred to was the
    (A) Bland-Allison Act
    (B) Fugitive Slave Act
    (C) Force Act
    (D) Kansas-Nebraska Act

23. The Supreme Court decision mentioned was
    (A) Chisholm *v.* Georgia
    (B) Mississippi *v.* Johnson
    (C) Dred Scott *v.* Sanford
    (D) Marbury *v.* Madison

Questions 24–26 refer to the following points of view on the meaning of freedom.

Speaker I: This nation was founded on the principles of freedom, and this means freedom to buy and sell without artificial restriction. When you tell a man what he may or may not do with his property, you have sown the seed of totalitarianism.

Speaker II: Freedom does not mean the freedom to starve. When the unrestricted use of property causes economic panic and unemployment, there arises a need for regulation and artificial stimulation which will restore the nation's economic health and set our system right again.

Speaker III: Freedom is a term that the weak use to excuse their follies. The rights of individuals to the use of property must be submerged in the struggle to fulfill the destiny of the state, the nation, and the race.

Speaker IV: Freedom in any society is directly related to the ownership of property, particularly the means of production. The state is the pawn of the propertied. Therefore, the workers can never be free until they eliminate the present owners of the means of production and seize control of the state and the economy.

24. Which speaker would most strongly oppose a planned economy?
    (A) I
    (B) II
    (C) III
    (D) IV

25. The ideas of Franklin D. Roosevelt's New Deal are best conveyed by Speaker
    (A) I
    (B) II
    (C) III
    (D) IV

26. The philosophy underlying the Bolshevik Revolution of 1917 is best expressed by Speaker
   (A) I
   (B) II
   (C) III
   (D) IV

III

MAINLY WHAT

Separating why from how and what is artificial at best. Some of the readings at the beginning of this volume were filled with information both about how social studies should be taught and about what content to stress. In like manner the readings in Section III contain insights into questions of why and how we should teach social studies. Focusing on the what question permits each discipline to speak for itself and gives teachers and students an opportunity to think through the demands that each proponent sets forth.

This section contains five sets of chapters, with two or three chapters in each set. The first in each case consists of a discussion of the major substantive issues from a discipline —the structure—that a well-known scholar thinks must be taught in the social studies. The remaining chapters in each set consist of sample materials through which a few of these issues may be taught. The last reading in the section sets the new social studies in the wider curriculum reform movement.

CHAPTER 19 Political Science

Political science is a huge field with an ancient lineage. Most political science departments in universities offer courses in political philosophy, comparative government, constitutional law, international politics, American national government, state and local government, and public administration. Thousands of books are published in these fields every year. How much of the information contained in these books should be taught to students in the public schools? Should it be taught in separate courses in political science or as part of courses in civics or history? These two questions plague curriculum developers.

There are other vital questions. Should the schools concentrate their attention on the substantive knowledge of political science or upon the methods by which political scientists work? Should they set citizenship education as one of their major goals? How can political science best be learned in the schools? What part of it can be absorbed through participating in mock elections or student government? How early should a child's exposure to political science begin?

In the article that follows, the author suggests an analytical scheme for political science. He identifies four major categories of analysis that can be used to study any political system at any point in time or space. Each major category has a number of subdivisions. Although other political scientists might devise other major categories, the article still provides an extremely useful discussion of major aspects of political science. The entire volume of which this reading is a part deserves careful study by every student of the social studies.

As you read, keep the following questions in mind:

1) What are the major elements of the scheme of analysis provided by Macridis?

2) How can a scheme of analysis such as this one be useful in a practical way as a guide to the selection of content, to teaching strategy, and to the process of note taking?

3) How would Dewey use this scheme of analysis? What aspect of Bruner's thought does it represent?

COMPARATIVE POLITICS: A SCHEME OF ANALYSIS

Roy C. Macridis

A General Scheme for Comparative Analysis

PROBLEMS OF ANALYTIC SCHEMES

Every student of politics has an implicit or explicit scheme of analysis. Such a scheme is often nothing more than a series of concepts with which the student attempts to order the political reality he is observing. In many instances, the student does not feel obligated to tell in advance what his questions are, in what categories they are put, or how they are related to each other. . . .

An analytical scheme should be formulated in such a way as to be applicable to as many political systems as possible. This calls for the development of general and abstract analytical categories in the light of which particular phenomena and institutions in as many countries as possible can be studied and whole systems compared. To give an illustration: Most comparisons have dealt with concrete institutional structures—parliaments, political parties, bureaucracies, and the like. Assumed in such comparison is the notion that the functions of seemingly similar institutions in different countries are comparable, that the institutions themselves correspond to analogous processes. This, for instance, is the case when the Supreme Soviet is compared to the American Congress or when "elections" in the Soviet Union are compared with elections in the United States or England. The same is naturally true when comparisons are made between the one-party system and multiparty or two-party systems. A better way to proceed is to study these

Condensed from Roy C. Macridis, *The Study of Comparative Government*, pp. 34–62. Copyright © 1955 by Random House, Inc. Reprinted by permission.

institutions and processes in the light of abstract analytical categories descriptive of functions.

The formulation of questions calls, therefore, for an a priori conceptual design. It should be pointed out, however, that given the present state of political science, there is no such conceptual design and every student is free to develop his own concepts. His only obligation is to formulate them as clearly as possible and to show their relevance and superiority to other concepts on the basis of (1) their generality and (2) their analytical utility in identifying concrete institutional realities in terms of the functions they perform or of the particular processes to which they correspond.

The Political System: Four Categories of Analysis

For the purpose of illustration a scheme will be developed here composed of four basic analytical categories in the light of which political systems can be studied and compared. They are the following: (1) the deliberative process and decision-making as a function of politics; (2) the power configuration and its social and political aspects; (3) ideology and its role in political motivation and institutional organization; and (4) the organization of political authority. This conceptual frame can give us relevant categories for the study of both political morphology and political dynamics. We shall try here to analyze each one of the categories suggested, to illustrate their utility for the study of structures, and to indicate their importance in the study of the operation of a system. . . .

The Political System:
Decision-Making

Politics involves the performance of certain social functions. The making of decisions for the attainment of certain purposes—adjustment of conflict, change, adjudication—is probably the most prevalent social function of politics. Political decisions are, however, those which emanate either from authorized persons or from organs which are known and recognized by the community. The use of sanctions to enforce the made decision does not constitute a unique characteristic of the political process. Otherwise, the decisions of a corporation to increase prices and its ability to use sanctions for the maintenance of such process could be called political. The characteristic phenomenon of politics is the legitimization of force, the development of a state of mind among the members of the community according to which decisions made by certain organs or persons are, generally speaking, obeyed. . . .

Decision-making is an analytical concept which involves a set of questions or categories in the light of which concrete institutional realities can be identified, described, and compared.

Who Makes the Decisions?

In every system we shall find persons or organs through which decisions are made. The chieftain of a primitive tribe, the medieval courts, the administrative official in a modern democratic state, the legislatures—all make decisions. We very often associate the decision-makers with the political elite of a given system and this is generally correct provided we understand clearly that there is a difference between political elites and other kinds of elites. If we define an elite as the "wielders of power and influence," then we shall have to indicate in every comparative study we make whether the political elite is the *real* elite or not. We may well find, in other words, that the officials or the organs that are ostensibly responsible for the decision-making process are mere puppets manipulated by other groups. In such a case, the understanding of the location of political power involves the careful study of the relationship between the political elites and the actual wielders of power. The question of who makes the decisions cannot be resolved therefore by an examination of a system's constitution or formal legal structure. Very often we have to unearth the persons or groups of persons that control or influence directly the formally recognized officials who seem to make decisions.

How Are Decision-Makers Selected?

Each system has its own particular way of selecting political leaders. There are, however, some general categories under which all forms of selection can be classified. In some societies, the mode of selection is *ascriptive,* i.e., it depends upon the status and birth of certain individuals. In other societies, selection depends upon *achievement,* the demonstration of individual effort and capacity. Charismatic leaders and many of the elected officials in a democratic society are of this second type. In other political systems, including very often democratic systems, selection depends upon a combination of ascription and achievement. This was the case, for instance, with nineteenth-century England, and the House of Lords continues to demonstrate the existence of some vestiges of an ascriptive mode of selection. . . .

Composition of Political Elites

Political leaders in any particular society exhibit ideological traits and skills that should be carefully studied for the purpose of comparative analysis. More particularly, it is relevant to ask whether they belong to any identifiable social or economic or religious group, whether they are identified with a particular region, whether they use symbols and media of communication alien to the rest of the population, and what techniques they employ to wield power and maintain their position of leadership. Here again the study of the various symbols and techniques used by political elites is extremely important for the purpose of comparing them with reference to the performance of their respective systems. A comparative study of the composition of a political elite and the symbols and techniques it uses will often throw much more light upon the differences or similarities between two systems with reference to decision-making than a comparative study of their formal political organs.

In many systems the formally and legally established political leadership does not actually make the political decisions. In such cases, the location of the real power to make and enforce decisions should be sought out and studied. We ought to study the qualifications of the actual wielders of power, the channels through which they operate, the reasons why they refuse to assume a recognized and formal position of political leadership, their relationship to the political elites, and their modes and techniques of control.

Wherever, therefore, there is a difference between the real and apparent wielders of power, the student must face and attempt to answer a number of questions. The first is simply: Why the differentiation? The second question is the significance of this differentiation with reference to the dynamics of the system—namely change, adjustment, and the achievement of goals. The third one relates to the over-all performance and stability of the system, for if actual power is divorced from legal recognition, it might be at least hypothetically inferred that the system is either highly traditional and stable or that it is highly unstable, involving a continuous conflict between the formal political elites and the real decision-makers. . . .

KINDS OF DECISIONS

There are, to begin with, certain *fundamental decisions* that affect the position of the decision-makers themselves as well as the whole pattern of decision-making in a given system. Sometimes such decisions are made on the basis of prescribed processes, i.e., a constitutional amendment, such as the Reform Act of 1832, while in other systems such over-all decisions are made through nonprescribed techniques such as a revolution. An extremely important aspect of comparative analysis is to determine in advance the existence or nonexistence of prescribed forms for fundamental decision-making in any political system. For there is prima-facie evidence that constitutional and democratic systems in which fundamental decisions are made by formal processes involving the participation of the bulk of the community are, generally speaking, less susceptible to violence and revolution than systems where fundamental decisions are not made by recognized processes or are left in the hands of small political elites.

A second type of decision are those we usually refer to as *legislative enactments*. They affect the status and the rights of many persons in the community and they establish new techniques and procedures for the making of decisions in the community.

A third type of decision are those affecting a small number of persons or individual cases. Such decisions are actually of an *administrative* or *judicial* type, and in most instances they correspond to techniques through which decisions of the second type are made applicable to specific cases.

Decisions of the second and third types are related to certain concrete political institutions in any given political system. Legislative decisions are made by representative assemblies, political parties, the electorate, or by other established organs, such as a council of elders, a priesthood, or the body of tribal warriors. The task of the student of comparative government is to identify the particular political organs and procedures through which such decisions are made before attempting to compare them. To assume, as is often done, that all legislatures or all representative assemblies make such basic decisions and that they are, as a result, comparable is to be deceived by appearances. We may find that some comparative studies of concrete political institutions that have been assumed to make basic decisions, such as the British Parliament and the U. S. Congress, are essentially misleading; the legislative function of the British Parliament is, in fact, of secondary importance.

It must also be made clear that when we attempt to identify the institutions and processes through which decisions are made we ought to include all the organs that we can identify irrespective of where we find them. A comparative study of the Soviet Union and the United States should attempt to relate the Party structure and procedures for decision-making in the former with the Congress and the President in the latter. In other words, the institutions through which basic decisions are made differ in various systems, and comparisons must be based on actual functions rather than on appearances. By the same token, the study of the army or the church or of economic associations from the standpoint of decision-making may yield important findings for the understanding of the phenomenon of decision-making in a given system.

It is also necessary to attempt to discuss the manner in which various types of decisions are made in a system and to analyze in some detail the deliberative process. All types of decisions involve some kind of deliberation ranging from direct consultation between the decision-maker and his consultants in a simple despotic system to the elaborate co-operative studies made by a network of functionally divided agencies in a complex bureaucratic system. In fact, the differences between authoritarian and democratic systems with reference to the decision-making process is often a matter of degree.

STEPS IN THE DELIBERATIVE PROCESS

The deliberative process involves two steps: (1) the formulation of a problem; (2) the clarification of the problem with reference to other issues facing the society.

Formulation of a Problem. A problem requiring a decision emerges in various areas of social and political life. A depression, the impossibility of maintaining high production quotas because of poor skills in the labor force, the demands of certain groups for the satisfaction of newly felt wants are some of the many factors that can be responsible for the creation of a problem. In different systems problems are defined in different manners. In a democratic society the press, various associations, religious and economic groups constantly confront the properly constituted agencies of the government with new problems. In authoritarian systems, the party often performs the same function. Its members are sensitive to people's reactions and they are very quick to transmit reports of discontent or positive suggestions to the higher echelons of the party. So much attention has been paid to the control aspects of the party in an authoritarian system that very little study has been made of this particular function. In other systems, particularly in traditionalist societies, there are no channels for the formulation of problems. In fact, in such societies the very emergence of a problem requiring deliberation and decision has an explosive force that undermines the cohesiveness of the social and political institutions. The introduction of Western technology in various colonial areas is an illustration of this phenomenon which is only too clearly perceived in our days, particularly after the withdrawal of the stabilizing control exerted until recently by the colonial powers.

The process of discussion and examination of a problem, after it has been raised but prior to the formulation of a decision, which is really at the heart of the deliberative process, takes a number of forms depending upon the type of political system in which the problem emerges. Sometimes deliberation is limited to the political elite; at other times deliberation brings the existing political elite into conflict with newly created social and economic elites, as was the case prior to the French Revolution. At times the emergence of a problem splits the political elite into two camps, each vying for political leadership and control. The emergence of a problem in that case may lead to violence or to a broadening of the participation of the members of the community in the deliberative process since the elite groups vying for control have often to appeal to the community for support. But in either case, the emergence of a problem has revolutionary implications involving either a challenge to the existing political leadership of the system or the pitting of one type of elite against another.

The persistence of a problem situation which presses for articulation and formulation may leave the existing political leadership apathetic until the gulf between it and the bulk of the community becomes so deep that nothing but violence can result. This was the case with the French nobility prior to the French Revolution and more particularly with the Russian ruling classes throughout the nineteenth century. Their typical reaction to the existing problems was one of increasing differentiation from the masses of the people —in manners, language, and political orientation.

Clarification of the Problem.   The clarification of a problem takes various forms. In a democratic system, problems are debated through every available channel of communication. The press, the radio, the schools and universities, and various pressure groups try to relate the problem to other issues facing the society. The political parties attempt a more precise formulation which gives an opportunity to the bulk of the community to choose between alternative solutions. In authoritarian, one-party systems the party attempts to do the same thing, though the community is hardly offered a choice between conflicting viewpoints. In this case, however, the party performs a function remarkably similar to that performed by the varied free agencies in democratic systems. It assists the population in a deliberative process in which the problem is thrashed out. The basic difference is that the party never gives to the population an opportunity to accept or reject the solution arrived at. In other systems, the process of clarification is restricted to a small group of consultants or to the bureaucracy or takes the form of magic and divination.

Legislatures have traditionally played a very important role in the deliberative process. For once the contours of the problem are defined by the parties or through other formal and informal means, a sharper formulation and ultimately the making of a decision is needed. The legislative bodies reflecting the opinion of the community attempt to clarify the problem, to relate it to other existing problems, and to suggest a solution. But at the same time—and this is primarily a recent phenomenon—an increasingly complex network of institutions parallels the task of the legislative bodies: advisory committees, the bureaucracy acting through hundreds of functional committees, and specialized bodies—scientists, economists, and various experts —participate in the discussion of the particular problem. The role of the expert and his intrusion into the deliberative process is one of the most significant developments of our day. In all technologically advanced societies there is a constant interplay between legislator and bureaucrat, between politician and expert, between interest groups and various functional committees. In many instances, this interplay is not haphazard but well institutionalized. In other cases, particularly those involving deliberation in new problem areas, the interplay is unorganized. Comparative study addressed to this question will again show that there is a marked similarity between political systems that have been traditionally considered to be dissimilar—such as, for instance, the deliberative process in Nazi Germany and in England, or in the United States and the Soviet Union.

Before we come to the discussion of the content of a decision it would be worthwhile to note that in a number of political systems the raising of a problem is no longer a matter of political agitation or party initiative. A number of administrative agencies define problem areas on the basis of study and documentation. There are, in other words, rational techniques for the identification of a problem in a modern advanced society—administrative agencies, groups of experts, *ad hoc* appointed committees, and special executive agencies. A comparative study of these institutional arrangements will throw light on some of the new institutions developing in a number of contemporary states and will show their significance and relationships to the other institutions of the state. . . .

The Political System: Power

A second general category under which data should be collected and carefully interpreted for the purpose of comparative study is that of power. The pursuit of power by individuals or groups is, like decision-making, one of the most universal characteristics of social and political activity. The paterfamilias, the priest, the chamber of commerce, the landowner, and the entrepreneur not only seek and exercise power over certain other human beings but attempt to entrench themselves into positions from which social and political power can be effectively wielded.

Political power must be defined not in terms of influence or domination or control but in terms of authority. It is that segment of social power which is exercised by *recognized* and *accepted* organs to achieve certain commonly shared objectives and purposes of the society. Power, as we have seen, has been transformed into authority through the use of the appropriate political ideology and institutions. It is, generally speaking, the power exercised by the state and its organs, though it is likely to find some of its characteristics in systems where there is no political organization like the state. . . .

Group Theory and the Theory of Class

Two broad theories have been developed for the purpose of relating social groupings endowed with social power to the political process and decision-making: the *group theory* of politics and the *class theory*, both of which may be used for the purpose of comparative analysis.

Group Theory. The group theory postulates that decision-making is the resultant of the activity of organized groups. They all impinge on the decision-making process and more generally on all aspects of the deliberative process and the sum total of group activities becomes translated into a decision. According to this theory, the reality of politics is hidden below the surface of the properly constituted and recognized organs through which decisions are articulated. It is hidden in the continuous struggle for power and influence upon which groups are constantly engaged.

Comparative analysis can be fruitfully pursued in the light of this theory by isolating in various systems some groups and comparing their relationships to the respective political organs of the system. No a priori statement as to which groups we should select and observe can be made, though the study of the American system throws some light on the importance of some groups. The groups to be studied are generally economic interest groups, professional associations, religious groups, special purpose groups (i.e., veterans). The impact of these groups upon political activities and processes should be studied in various countries in terms of a number of key factors: their national or regional character; their general or specialized character; their structure and membership; their leadership and resources; the techniques they use to mobilize opinion; their relationship to political parties or to other quasi-public institutions; the degree of internal autonomy and the nature of their internal organization. With reference to their techniques of action, particular attention should be given to the secret or open way in which they act; to their attitude to violent action; to their efforts to use persuasion rather than pressure; to their dependence on foreign powers.

It is equally important to attempt to study the ideology of the particular groups within a society. . . .

Class Theory.   The theory of *class struggle* which is an integral part of Marxist doctrine has been in part discredited because of its rigidity and its identification with dialectical materialism. For all practical purposes it may be argued that the Marxist theory has not been borne out by historical developments because the political organs of a number of Western systems have altered significantly the class configuration and class conflict. But despite this, the class concept might be useful for comparative study at least with reference to some political systems. For instance, it would be most unfortunate to attempt to understand and describe the revolutionary process in Russia in the early part of the twentieth century or the French Revolution of 1789 without making use of the class concept. It would be equally unfortunate to try to understand some Western and non-Western systems such as, for instance, the Latin American political systems or those of Japan or India without the use of the concept of class.

The class concept proposed here is in fact a variant of the group theory. It simply postulates that at certain times and under certain conditions a number of groups tend to coalesce in order to protect certain common interests and values or to challenge a given set of values. It is a concept that applies with particular force to systems in which we do not find some of the prerequisite conditions we associate with a democratic system—freedom of debate, political parties, implementation of social goals through orderly decision-making, freedom for various groups to present their points of view and attempt through persuasion to influence decision-making. In default of such institutional arrangements groups gravitate toward a center that is generally determined by economic interests and this center represents what we may loosely call a class. . . .

Another subjective element associated with class configuration to which more attention has been paid recently is that of *leadership*. The human element here—the subjective factor—that provides the leadership can come from any particular group of the society. Family ties, group affiliations, pecuniary motives are swept aside and persons who normally would be expected, because of their family ties and economic interests, to provide the leadership for the class that defends the status quo are often found on the opposing side, whereas unemployed and disinherited may fill the ranks of the elite that supports the status quo. . . .

THE INSTRUMENTS OF POWER

In a number of systems, particularly non-Western political systems, the instruments of power and control are usually to be found outside of the frame of the existing political institutions. Very often such political institutions as may be identified are mere organs in the hands of a class which maintains itself in power. They are not instruments for the mitigation of conflict between various economic and interest groups but rather instruments for the elimination of conflict through force. The more force is used, however, for the maintenance of the interests of certain groups, the more we find a tendency on the part of the disfranchised groups to coalesce. The more such groups coalesce, the greater the intensity of force employed by the holders of power. The phenomenon of polarization of the society into groups, those who defend the status quo and those who challenge it—that is, the phenomenon of class conflict—becomes clearly apparent in any such society. . . .

The Political System: Ideology

The third broad category of the analytical scheme proposed here is that of political ideology. By political ideology is understood the patterns of thought and belief related to the state and the government that constitute at one and the same time a source of obedience and consent and a mechanism of control. As De Toqueville writes, "without such common belief no society can prosper; say, rather, no society can exist; for without ideas held in common there is no common action, and without common action there may still be men, but there is no social body. In order that society should exist . . . it is necessary that the minds of all the citizens should be rallied and held together by certain predominant ideas." To put it briefly, the role of political ideology is to legitimize the organized force of the state. . . .

Ideology naturally refers to the whole complex of motivation and pattern of behavior that characterizes a society. As Professor Lowenstein puts it, "An ideology is a consistent and integrated pattern of thoughts and beliefs, or thoughts converted into beliefs, explaining man's attitude toward life and his existence in society, and advocating a conduct and action pattern responsible to, and commensurate with, such thoughts and beliefs." Political ideology, however, refers to the same patterns of belief and behavior that are related to the decision-making agencies of the system and to the manner in which the power configuration of the society is shaped and the relations between power groups established.

There are four significant aspects of ideology to which comparative study can be addressed: (1) the source of the dominant political ideology; (2) the diffusion of ideologies, an aspect which pertains to a range of problems such as the acceptance of an ideology, the mode of diffusion, the modifications brought about in a system by the impact of alien ideologies; (3) the function of ideology as an instrument of social control; and (4) the relationship between ideology and the organization of political authority in any given system.

The Sources of a Dominant Political Ideology

Myths and values that shape social and political conduct obviously emerge either within the system or are borrowed from outside in one way or another. The process of borrowing may be due to imitation or imposition or assimilation; it may involve a selective acceptance or rejection and it may result in a synthesis in which indigenous and foreign values are fused into a single pattern. . . .

It is the task of the student, therefore, to identify the existing ideological pattern in a given society, and to attempt to trace it to the particular dominant groups from which it originates and to assess its general content and effectiveness. With respect to this latter point, it is necessary to examine the techniques through which the existing ideology is maintained. The school system, the use of media of communication, the particular methods of propagation—coercion, intimidation, inculcation—are extremely important. Finally, an examination of the existence of competing political ideologies within a given system is of great relevance for the purpose of assessing the strength or weakness of the political leadership. For one of the clearest indices of instability in a given system is the existence of political ideologies that are either hostile to each other or are incompatible.

The relationship between ideology and the dominant groups of a society suggests a number of questions. What is the relationship between the type of group and the content of an ideology? How do changing economic conditions affect the predominant groups and their ideology? Conversely, what is the impact of ideology upon group stratification in a given society and its relationship to social and economic changes? When can we accurately talk about a "rigid" ideology, one that resists change? What are the characteristics of an "elastic" ideology, one that can accommodate itself to new patterns of thought and change?

Diffusion of Ideologies

It is probably a truism to say that political ideologies have a tendency to spread from the area in which they were developed to adjacent areas, to lose some of their original characteristics in the process, and to blend with the ideological traits of other areas. History reveals clearly the impact of some of the political ideologies of the Greeks upon Rome, of Rome upon the Western world, of the United States upon the Latin American countries and upon the Asiatic world, of the Soviet Union upon some Eastern European and Asiatic countries. Such an expansion is naturally organically related to social, economic, and power factors. But in all cases, it takes place through a process of selection and rejection whereby only certain elements of a given ideology are being accepted and other elements rejected. . . .

It may be hypothesized, for instance, that a well-integrated political system will be more resistant to outside ideologies than an unstable society, or that a prosperous society in which there is equitable distribution of wealth among its members will be less receptive to outside ideological influence than a society in which there is poverty or a sharp division in the distribution of wealth. It may be finally argued that the nature of the political system itself is an important conditioning factor accounting for reception or rejection. If there is a sharp division between power and responsibility or between the ruling class and the masses of the society, new ideologies will be more readily accepted either by the ruling class or by the masses.

The Intellectuals

In almost all cases, comparative analysis here ought to be focused upon the most sensitive social and political groups through which ideologies are maintained and propagated or, as the case may be, challenged—the intellectuals. The study of the intelligentsia in any society may well prove to be the best indicator of the stability of a given political ideology, or, conversely, of the receptivity of the system to new political ideologies. The intellectuals manipulate the ideological symbols of a given society. The teacher, the writer, and the priest are some of the channels through which power becomes translated into legitimacy and the governors thereby linked with the governed. A number of criteria about the role of the intellectual in a given society may lead us to some significant conclusions about the internal cohesion of the system and its reactions to different ideologies. The social status of the intellectuals, the degree and extent to which they are valued by the society, their political and economic status, their relationship to the governing class, and the responsibility they have for the performance and the maintenance of the system are certainly definite and observable criteria on the basis of which we may foresee with a fairly high degree of accuracy the susceptibility of the system to foreign ideologies and to internal change.

A far more difficult problem, but one imperative for policy-orientation, is the study of a situation in which a country is exposed to two conflicting ideological systems. This is the situation today in a number of former colonies that have acquired independent status and are exposed to Western and Soviet ideological influences. Could we surmise on the basis of concrete social, economic, political, and historical determinants the impact of the two ideologies? Naturally, this is not so much a problem of studying the rejection or acceptance of one or the other ideology *in toto* but rather of speculating as to which political ideology will exert a preponderant influence on the given country. Where shall we look for an answer? To the class structure? To the various social and political elites? To the intellectuals? To the tenacity of the existing symbols and myths? To the particular social division of the society with reference to the existing distribution of wealth? To the historical past of the country which in itself reveals certain patterns of behavior? There is hardly any doubt that all these factors enter into our scheme of analysis and that they should be carefully considered in any empirical investigation by the student of comparative politics before he attempts to develop any more elaborate theories. They should be advanced in the form of problems on the basis of which studies of specific areas can be made before we attempt to generalize and compare. The questions suggested here simply indicate possible interrelationships. Some of them may be modified in the process of empirical investigation and data-gathering and new and more relevant ones may be formulated. . . .

CRITERIA FOR THE CLASSIFICATION OF POLITICAL SYSTEMS AND INSTITUTIONS

Political scientists have attempted to classify political systems according to certain basic criteria that have stood the test of time and can be quite useful for comparative study. Such criteria are related to: (1) the organization of political authority; (2) the relation between the established political authority and the members of the community; and (3) the position of the individual.

The Organization of Political Authority.   The complex of institutions that constitute the organization of political authority is referred to as the state. Though the term has fallen into some disrepute, it still has great utility. For the state is indeed an inclusive concept that covers all aspects of policy-making and enforcement. The main weakness of the concept, for the purpose of comparative study, however, is precisely its inclusiveness. To compare the British "state" to the French "state" would indeed be synonymous to comparing the political systems of the two countries.

We may avoid the difficulty by referring to the "governments," a term which expresses the concrete institutional organization through which the most important political functions, namely decision-making and enforcement, are performed.

The Organization of Political Authority and Decision-Making. Certain general types of governmental organization may be defined with reference to decision-making. For instance, Max Weber's three types of authority depend on whether decisions are made on rational grounds, traditional grounds, or charismatic grounds. These three types correspond to different patterns through which decisions are made. In the first case, decisions are made through a highly differentiated apparatus of government involving established and accepted procedures of conduct and an organization of structures based upon community recognition; in the second, decisions will be made only in terms of conformity to certain traditional or customary rules of conduct. In traditional types, we shall find little differentiation of the governmental structure, little application of knowledge to the making of decisions. Finally, in the charismatic type of authority, decisions flow from the leader without any appeal to knowledge or to tradition and without any development of institutionalized channels through which the decision must be expressed in order to receive acceptance.

Enforcement of Decisions. Political systems employ various means through which decisions become enforceable. Enforcement is closely correlated with the degree of acceptance of an institution or particular decisions by the community. As long as the particular institutions or process through which a decision is made are respected, there is every expectation that the decision will be generally obeyed. This is the case, for instance, to refer again to Max Weber's categories, with a constitutional system, or a traditional system, or even a charismatic system as long as the charisma lasts. Obedience is due in the one case to the fact that procedures are valued or because tradition or the charisma has established patterns of loyalty or obedience. But again, it is likely that at a certain point a decision may be challenged or not be obeyed. When we have a series of cases where decisions are disobeyed, we have a direct challenge to the decision-making institutions as well. The performance of a political system viewed from the standpoint of decision-making can be assessed, therefore, with reference to a number of objective criteria such as compliance, extent and types of noncompliance, the loss of prestige and the weakening of legitimacy claims on the part of the decision-making organs. . . .

Relationship between Established Political Authority and the Individual. Another important criterion for the comparative study of institutions and processes is that of the relationship between the individual and the state. A number of categories can be used for studying this relationship and it is quite likely that only when we have assessed their particular significance and their interrelationships will we be able to come up with some fruitful generalizations about some of the political phenomena already mentioned: stability and instability, change, and achievement of social goals.

Recruitment. The relationship between the individual and the organized political authority may be studied with reference to the mode of recruitment of political leadership. To what extent is leadership openly recruited? To what extent is recruitment based upon certain conditions? To what extent is recruitment limited to considerations that are unrelated to individual effort or ability? The study of the political leadership in England as compared to that of the French aristocracy throughout the eighteenth century will suggest some important differences. The impact of the extension of the franchise upon political leadership in various countries again offers us a good experimental situation for comparative study.

Education. The relationship between the members of the community and the established political authority can take a number of forms. The least investigated of all is what may be called the *apathy* of the bulk of the community toward political authority and the particular groups that wield power over it. This is characteristically the phenomenon that we observe in the great majority of the Latin American states, and, to some extent, the same phenomenon was observed among American Negroes for some time after the Civil War. In the great majority of cases, apathy can be traced to historical factors such as the exclusion of a conquered people from participation in the political process, to ethnic and racial factors, to sharp cultural differences between the leadership and the rank and file, and to educational and linguistic differences.

The reverse of apathy is, of course, the direct participation of an entire community in all decisons. This is often the case with small, primitive, homogeneous, tribal communities, or occasionally with advanced communities of a small size in which the level of education is high and the degree of class differentiation relatively small, as in Athens for a few decades before the Peloponnesian War.

Between these two extremes, we have situations in which relationships between the established political authority and the members of the community range from apathy through various degrees of participation. Such variations are largely due to the level of education of the members of the community. It may indeed be advanced as a general proposition that the higher the level of education of the bulk of the community, that is, the more diffused the mastery of skills and communication symbols, the higher the degree and intensity of participation. The political forms and the character of participation may vary here, but this same phenomenon can be observed in democratic as well as authoritarian societies. It most definitely cannot be observed, however, in aristocratic, military, or traditional societies.

Political Participation. The participation of the individual in decision-making is a separate criterion for comparative analysis, and it should be studied with reference to both the formal structures of a system as well as to some of the informal arrangements. The student of politics should examine:

1. The constitutions and existing institutions. Such matters as the electoral system, the right to vote, limitations upon the freedom to vote should be studied comparatively in two or more systems.

2. Provisions concerning the eligibility of candidates.
3. The process of nominations. If he finds that eligibility and nominations depend upon certain conditions that involve discrimination against some, the student can conclude that there are rigidities in the system which make it likely that participation will be open to some but not to others. For instance, the nomination of a candidate in elections in the Soviet Union is controlled by the Communist Party. This is prima-facie evidence that participation is restricted.
4. Whether or not more than one party exists. The existence of more than one party generally indicates wider participation of members of the community than when there is only one party.
5. Whether the systems being compared allow associational freedom. The freedom to belong to associations of various types is often directly related to the freedom to have more than one political party. The existence of many associations is again prima-facie evidence that participation is free to many members of the community. But as with the political party, the student should inquire into the ways in which associations are formed and act. If he discovers that their formation and action is dependent upon government authorization and that such authorization involves discrimination against certain political, religious, or cultural groups, he can conclude that participation is not open and free. The Soviet Union, for instance, has what appears to be a very vigorous associational life. On closer observation, however, we find that these associations are entirely controlled by the political authority.
6. The available information and knowledge on the basis of which citizens are asked to make decisions and participate in the decision-making process. To the extent to which information about social and economic problems or about foreign policy is withheld, participation is hampered. Again it will be the task of the student of comparative politics to identify the most significant institutions that provide information to the members of the community and to compare them as to impartiality, effectiveness, accessibility to the public, and the like. It is equally important to undertake the task of discovering the persons or groups in charge of the various instruments that disseminate information. Finally, the role of the government in disseminating information should be studied and evaluated since there has been a uniform tendency, at least among most Western European governments, to establish specialized agencies to collect and analyze data and present it to the public.
7. The institutions through which the responsibility of the persons in the government can be assessed and enforced in some way. We associate responsibility with those processes that render the decision-makers accountable to the community and provide the community with

political and legal sanctions. Political sanctions involve periodic elections, legislative review with the possibility of censure or removal, and financial control by a representative assembly. Election is an important sanction, or rather instrument, for insuring effective responsibility only when it is possible for groups and political parties to criticize openly the persons wielding political authority.

The Position of the Individual.   The position of the individual in the system is another important criterion for classification and comparison. Traditionally, political speculation has dealt with many intangible values centering on the individual and his position in a given system, such as "justice" or the "good life." These terms, slippery as they may be, in the sense that they involve ethical categories, continue to preoccupy the student of politics and a fortiori the student of comparative politics. In fact, as has already been pointed out, one of the most important contributions comparative government can make is to indicate through the comparative study of institutions the proper type of corrective action for the realization of certain value goals. . . .

The test of any system is the opportunities it provides to the individual to live peacefully with his fellowmen, that is, internal security and the development of institutions for the adjustment of individual and group conflict. A political system should provide men with opportunities for employment and economic security as well as for political participation. This means that the system should provide for education and freedom in the widest possible sense of the word—freedom of thought and expression, religious freedom, and freedom of association and political action. Above all, men must be treated by the government on a footing of equality. This means that they should not be differentiated on any basis other than ability and achievement; it also means that no handicaps should be placed for any reason whatsoever upon the potentiality of a man's development.

To translate these principles into measurable or at least researchable propositions for the purpose of comparative analysis is a difficult but by no means impossible task. A survey of the legal systems of a number of countries may reveal, for instance, the existence of legal disabilities or the degree to which the courts are accessible to all, irrespective of education or ability to pay. It will, in fact, indicate whether the system is in general motivated by a concern for the individual or whether it tends to subordinate the individual to the interests of the state or to certain political and social groups. The study of party structures will indicate the extent to which individuals can voice their opinions, participate actively in the nomination of candidates, or themselves run for office. The study of communication systems will indicate the degree of control by public or private persons and whether and how the systems are used to propagate the dominant political ideology. A comparative study of the distribution of national incomes in a number of systems may suggest that in some the individual share varies so greatly as to give to a few a disproportionate advantage over others. The comparative study of educational systems will show that in some societies the development of skills and the acquisition of knowledge is limited to a minority; or it may indicate that, though the acquisition of skills and knowledge is being made accessible to all, education is not used for the free development of individual initiative and thought but rather as an instrument through which conformity to the dominant ideology is being inculcated.

CHAPTER 20 Political Science: Examples

The three examples of readings in political science are taken from the first three days of a course in comparative political systems designed for able ninth-grade students. This course begins four years of a sequential and cumulative curriculum in the social studies written at the Curriculum Development Center, sponsored by Project Social Studies, at Carnegie Institute of Technology. It has been taught experimentally for two years in six schools in Pittsburgh, Pennsylvania.

The entire course has been organized around four major issues in contemporary political science. They are:

1. Who are the political leaders? What are their attributes? How are they recruited? How do they gain and maintain support?
2. How are decisions made on the local, intermediate, and national levels in the executive, legislative, and judicial branches (if levels and branches exist in the particular political system)?
3. What is the role of the individual citizen in the political system? How can he gain access to his leaders? What are his responsibilities and his rights?
4. What is the ideological foundation of the political system?

Students seek to answer these four groups of questions for three societies: the primitive society of the Plains Indians, a modern totalitarianism, the Soviet Union, and a modern democracy, the United States. The study of other types of governments and of other issues in political science are left to later courses in the sequence.

Readings I–III introduce all four groups of questions to the students. Each reading contains an introduction, questions for study, and a reading deliberately kept short because it is the first work done in a new school year and the first exposure to inductive material for many students.

A classroom film based on the second reading is available for rent or sale (Holt, Rinehart and Winston, Inc.). Your teacher may wish to show it to you. As you read, keep the following questions in mind:

1) What are the purposes of these three readings? How would you teach them to accomplish these purposes? How would you evaluate your success?
2) Why begin a course in this manner? What alternative ways of beginning a course in comparative political systems can you think of?
3) How would you organize a course that begins like this one and is concerned with the issues discussed in the Introduction?

UNIT I: INTRODUCTION

Edwin Fenton · Howard Mehlinger
STATING THE ISSUE

Every society has some form of government. Governments develop naturally whenever people live in groups. They have a number of functions. They settle conflicts that arise among people in the same group. They provide services to the community, such as protection from fires, which individuals cannot provide for themselves. They also protect a group or a nation from its external enemies. All of us can think of a number of additional things that government does.

What should be the proper function of government and what should be left to the individual? This question has always concerned mankind. As society becomes more complex, the activities of government seem to grow. Traffic laws, once few in number and simple to understand, are now numerous and complicated. But the essential question remains: which areas of life should government control? Many of our treasured freedoms depend upon the way we answer this question.

Many forms of government have appeared in the past. Some have been dictatorships in which one man has ruled. Others have been organized as oligarchies in which a group of men held power. Still others have been ruled democratically. The institutions of government have been equally varied. Parliament, Congress, the King's Council, and the Supreme Soviet are all names of governmental institutions. Government is of endless variety.

Despite their differences, governments at all times and in all places have faced similar political problems. Rather than organize this course around the various forms that governments have taken, we have chosen to structure it around four of these universal problems: the recruitment, training, and functions of political leaders; the procedure for making and carrying out political decisions; the role of the individual citizen; and the ideological foundation of the government.

We will concentrate our attention upon three types of governments: a modern democracy, a modern totalitarianism, and a primitive government typical of nonliterate societies. As we study these three types of political systems, we will raise questions and develop methods of analysis that can be applied to other types of governments. In this way every student will develop tools of analysis that should help to make him a good independent thinker.

The first three lessons in this course examine political leadership, decision-making and the role of the individual in a World War II prisoner of war camp. How did the 160 American prisoners decide who their leader would be? How did they make decisions? What was the role of the individual citizen? Why did they choose a particular way to organize their society rather than some other? These are the questions with which we begin this course.

Reading I: Leadership in Stoerpenberg Camp

Leadership plays a vital role in every political system. Whether the leader is a dictator who has seized and maintained power by force or a democratically elected official subject to the will of the electorate, the basic problem remains the same: all governments require political leaders. Each society must develop ways to recruit and train these leaders. Everywhere leaders must win and maintain support for they cannot lead if no one will follow. Leaders must communicate with citizens and be responsive to their wishes; no leader however strong can afford to antagonize continuously those whom he leads.

What are the attributes (personal characteristics) of political leaders? How are leaders different from those they lead? Are the characteristics of leaders in all societies the same, or do leaders differ from one society to another? Social scientists who study political systems frequently ask questions such as these.

Learning to ask questions will be one of the most important objectives of this course. Learning becomes sterile when it consists only of committing to memory a large amount of factual information. Many studies indicate that students rapidly forget most of the facts they have learned unless the facts are organized in such a way that one reminds a person of another. Good questions often provide the framework on which we can build our factual knowledge. More important, good questions often provide a technique for studying new bodies of information. If a student knows what questions are vital to the study of one society's political system, he will ask them of another. Asking these questions will often help to make facts meaningful.

For tomorrow you are to read Part 1 of a short essay that describes the political system in an American prisoner of war camp in Stoerpenberg, Germany. As you read, think about the answers to the following questions:

1) How were the leaders in the POW camp recruited? That is, how did the men persuade some of their fellows to "go into politics"? Was this process of recruiting leaders different from the one that now exists for American government?
2) What were the leaders like? What were their backgrounds and their most important character traits?
3) What formal government process was set up? How were "laws" made and carried out? What role did the leaders play in the process of lawmaking?
4) How did leaders and followers communicate with each other?

STOERPENBERG CAMP (PART I)*

Gerald Haines

There were a hundred and sixty of them. They had been counted by the Germans and the count had been checked. They moved about the building peering out the windows at the drab winter landscape, or sat around the tables, now and then dropping down on a bunk, hands under head, to lie staring at the ceiling. One hundred and sixty American prisoners of war, who had been captured in the Battle of the Bulge two months ago, were now organized as a prisoner of war labor unit at Stoerpenberg, somewhere in western Germany.

During the first two days they had nothing to do but lie on their beds and wait to be fed. As men drifted from one bunk to another, they began to talk about their situation. They discovered that they were all privates who had been in combat units of one kind or another. They represented a fair cross-section of the United States, with men from every region of the nation included. Some of the men who had been able to talk to the guards had discovered that the camp was at the edge of a large town. The prisoners were to be used as laborers in nearby fields or for general utility work about the town.

The prisoners were housed in a gymnasium that had been part of a group of factory buildings. It evidently had been used as a workers' recreation center. At one end of the building a few tumbling mats and gymnastic bars were all that remained of the building's former equipment. An aisle formed by two rows of tables ran down the center of the building. Behind the tables, on each side, were rows of double-decked bunks, while at the far end of the gym-

* Reprinted with the permission of the Human Relations Department, The University of Kansas.

nasium three rooms were partitioned off from the central part. The center room was fitted with washing troughs; to the north was a storage room, and to the south a lavatory. At this end of the building on the outside lay a long narrow plot of ground used as an exercise yard for the prisoners. Within the building and the exercise yard the American prisoners formed a little society of their own.

By the second day the men had picked out bunks and taken regular places at the tables. There were ten tables, so sixteen men were grouped at each. Men who had known each other before they were captured tended to cluster together. None of the men could have known anyone else in the group for more than two months, but under the circumstances, any familiar face was a welcome sight. A few men who had not yet made friends tended to drift to the table closest to their bunk.

On the third day the German officer in charge told the prisoners to choose a group leader. This leader would pass on to the group the regulations and orders of the German officers and would be responsible for carrying out rules for health and sanitation made by the prisoners.

After the interpreter told the prisoners this, they began to discuss the matter among themselves. They were seated around the tables where there was enough space for two or three of them to get together. They decided to hold an election. Very shortly men began to move from table to table campaigning for their favorite. Finally a few men were selected as candidates. Votes were taken by a show of hands. If a proposed candidate seemed to have a fairly large number of people behind him he was considered in the running, and if not, his name was dropped. The choice soon narrowed down to a few men. Each man was presented to the group by his backers who made campaign speeches in his favor. After the speeches were finished, a final vote was taken by a show of hands. The choice was George Kent, a man of good physical appearance, who had demonstrated a commanding personality and superior social presence during the election of the leader. A college graduate, Kent had at one time been an acting sergeant, and had distinguished himself in battle.

Kent immediately brought up the vital matter of how food was to be distributed. In a prisoner of war camp with limited rations, food was of vital importance to everyone and was without doubt the subject most constantly on every prisoner's mind. Kent suggested that the entire ration of food should be divided into ten parts, one for each table, and then distributed at the tables to the men. In order to supervise this final distribution of food, he suggested that each table elect a table leader to take charge. The men quickly responded to this suggestion. Gathered around the tables, they talked informally, and finally each table chose its representative. The men who were finally chosen as leaders had a few characteristics in common. Several were college graduates and the remainder all had finished high school. A number of them had acted as noncommissioned officers at one time or another. Every one of them was a good talker who could communicate well with his fellows.

Shortly after the table leaders were chosen, several of them suggested to Kent that they set up a council to govern the unit. Kent agreed. In the following weeks the council met regularly. It consisted of Kent and the ten table leaders. At each meeting Kent passed on orders and information from the German administration of the camp so that the table leaders could inform the men in their group. The members of the council also discussed living arrangements, such as the choice of bunks, and made assignments to clean-up details.

If a man felt that he had a legitimate "gripe" he complained to his table leader. If the table leader was unable to settle the matter on the spot, he would bring it before the council at the next meeting. Most matters brought up in this way were settled at the council, but when a new problem seemed to be particularly important, it was referred to the tables for discussion and a referendum. Through this procedure the men were able to make rules by which they could govern themselves.

Reading II: Decision-Making in Stoerpenberg Camp

Government exists to make decisions about matters of vital concern to the people of a society. The government of your family decides how to spend your father's pay check. The leaders of the family—your parents—probably make this decision without asking your advice, but they may consult you about other matters, particularly those in which you are most actively involved, such as the amount of time to be spent on homework.

Societies more complicated than the family organize elaborate institutions to make decisions. Our President, Congress, and court system compose an enormously complicated decision-making process involving elections, political parties, and many other similar institutions. Learning about how decisions are made in the national political arena will occupy several weeks of our time later in the course.

Today we shall deal with a much simpler matter—the way in which political decisions were made in Stoerpenberg Camp. To make these decisions, the prisoners set up simple political institutions, as our reading yesterday revealed. They had a leader, ten table leaders organized as a council, and 160 voters. They did not try to set up an executive (president), legislature (congress), and judiciary (courts) because their society was so simple that one set of institutions and people could perform all three of these tasks. The leader and table leaders passed laws, subject to referendum by the voters (the legislative function), carried out laws (the executive function), and interpreted laws by applying them to specific cases (the judicial function).

Studying the manner in which decisions were reached in the camp may reveal to us some interesting questions worth exploring when we investigate more complex political systems. The purpose of today's assignment is to raise some of these questions. Think about them as you read.

1) Who took initiative to bring up suggestions for laws in the camp? Can people who have parallel positions in American society take similar action?
2) Who decided whether or not a question brought up for discussion was worth taking to a referendum? Could these people control what was discussed? Does every suggestion from a voter reach the floor of Congress?
3) How were laws made? How were they carried out?
4) What happened when a man broke the unwritten code? What role did Kent play in this incident? What did it reveal about who really had power in the society? Does our President have a similar position?

STOERPENBERG CAMP (PART II)*

Gerald Haines

In a few weeks the camp was functioning very effectively. The men were organized into compact units. The routine of their lives had been worked out with each man having certain duties to perform in a regular rotation for the benefit of all. Behind this formal organization was the code of the group. The code was not formal—no one had written it down or made speeches about it —yet everyone knew what it was and lived by it, or knew what to expect if he did not.

The first and most important rule of this informal code was that no prisoner would steal from another, particularly that he would not steal food or tobacco. Stealing from the Germans was quite all right as long as a prisoner did not get caught. If he were caught, the prisoner's duty was clear—to identify himself as the sole participant and to bear the brunt of German displeasure. There were a few other important parts of the code. Everyone was expected to keep as clean as possible, although keeping clean required a great deal of effort. As to the work being done for the Germans, it was quite all right to do as little as possible as long as a prisoner did not get caught.

Within two weeks after the 160 prisoners had been thrown together in the gymnasium at Stoerpenberg, they had developed a small but complete society. They had organized a government; they had made some laws; they had worked out an economic organization to distribute food; they had built up a social structure; and they had accepted an informal code which everyone obeyed.

In the third week of March, 1945, as the result of an incident among the members of Table Five, the leaders of the work unit suddenly found them-

*Reprinted with the permission of the Human Relations Department, The University of Kansas.

selves with a difficult problem. One of the men at the table was accused of stealing food and the uproar over it threatened to break up the society. One of the members of Table Five was a man named Court. From the very first, Ainslee, the table leader of Number Five, had been aware that Court did not fit into any of the informal groups at the table, nor did he seem to have friends at any of the other tables. His manner was listless and apathetic. He seemed withdrawn from the life about him and his reactions seemed rather slow and confused when any situation arose that required him to participate in some activity. His personal habits were very lax to the point that he was filthy, even though a room for washing was available. Ainslee thought that Court was mentally ill or had suffered some intense experience during his capture.

Whatever the reasons, Court was one of the few men who did not actively participate in the life of the group. His sole interest was food. Soon he began to save the bread from his daily rations. Each day he added another small portion to his store. He concealed the chunks of bread about his clothing and bunk. Court was very suspicious of his fellow-prisoners and spent much of his free time carefully checking his hoard. By the middle of March much of the bread he had managed to save was stale and unpalatable. He was not seen to eat any of it, but he seemed to get satisfaction from handling it and knowing that it was there when he wanted to look at it.

Bartrum, a tall, heavy man from Table Five, had been observing Court's behavior carefully. In casual conversations with others, he pointed out the futility of Court's actions. Many others agreed with him and, because food was so scarce, some felt that it was wrong for one man to waste what could be used so well by others.

Each evening the men of the work unit stood in the aisle to be counted by one of the German noncommissioned officers. Late in March Bartrum was late to formation. Immediately after the men were dismissed, he returned quietly to his bunk. A short time later the men around Table Five were startled by hoarse cries. Court was moving around and around his bunk, searching here and there, uttering moans and weeping. Ainslee and several others moved quickly over to Court to discover that much of his hoard of bread had been stolen. In a few minutes a large crowd had collected about Court's bunk. The news of his loss passed quickly among them. The low hum of many voices began to comment on the fact that Bartrum had been late to head count. The men began to suspect that he was the thief.

Ainslee had decided to go to Kent to organize a search among the members of the group when a few of the men walked over to Bartrum's bunk and began looking around. Bartrum protested when suddenly one of the men found a chunk of bread tucked away at one end of the bunk. He shouted aloud and turned upon Bartrum. A thick knot of men rapidly swirled about him, cursing, shouting, and striking at him. Bartrum attempted to fight clear, stammering incoherently, as more and more men joined the melee. The room was filled with uproar which spread rapidly until every man in the room was involved.

Kent, the group leader, quickly caught the significance of the cries of the outraged men around Bartrum and realized that if he did not act quickly Bartrum might be killed. Throwing himself into the crowd, he fought his way to Bartrum. Seizing him by the collar, Kent managed to get on top of a table where he could be seen above the mob, still holding Bartrum firmly. At first he could not make himself heard, but as more and more of the men saw who it was that held Bartrum, they became more quiet. Taking a deep breath Kent tried again, "Okay," he said, "I hate the — as much as you do, but this isn't the way to do it." Howls of protest greeted his statement but Kent kept on talking, arguing that Bartrum must be handled by regular procedure and not by a mob. Meanwhile several of the table leaders had fought their way to Kent and now began to ring about him. Slowly the protests began to lessen. Kent bore down on the fact that the group would have its chance to take action after the council had tried Bartrum. As the crowd became quieter, Kent felt that the immediate danger was over. Calling to the table leaders to come with him, he jumped down from the table and, holding tightly to Bartrum, pushed his way through the men. They let him pass. The leaders walked with Kent and Bartrum to the end of the room. Here on the old tumbling mats they sat down to consider what they should do.

Bartrum's trial was conducted with some formality. Kent presided and asked most of the questions. Bartrum began by denying the theft but soon admitted his guilt, justifying himself by saying that the bread was being wasted and should do someone some good. He surprised the council by saying that he was ready to accept any punishment that seemed fitting.

The council, after some deliberation, passed sentence on Bartrum. First, they placed him in isolation for a month; no one was to speak to him or have anything to do with him at all. Second, during this same month he was assigned to do two hours of additional work in the barracks each night after the work unit had returned from the fields. Finally, he was to replace from his own bread ration an amount equal to the bread he had stolen.

After passing the sentence, the table leaders returned to their tables and consulted their men. In general, most of the men seemed satisfied and only a few felt that the sentence was too light. After each table had voted to accept the decision, the leaders returned to Kent and informed him of the results. Kent then sent Bartrum back to his bunk with a stern reminder that if he did not carry out his sentence properly the next action would be very severe.

During the following two weeks, Bartrum was cut off from his fellow-prisoners. No one spoke to him. Each evening he put in his two hours of extra labor. Each day he turned over part of his bread ration to Court who either ate it or stored it away with the rest of his hoard. Ainslee supervised the return of the stolen rations and kept an accurate day-by-day record. He appointed a different man each day to make sure that Bartrum worked steadily during his extra hours in the evening. By refusing to have anything to do with Bartrum, every member of the group helped to enforce the rest of the sentence.

Two weeks after the sentence began, the gymnasium was hit by a bomb during an Allied air attack. The Germans then bundled the American prisoners into small groups to distribute them among a number of other work camps. The society which they had formed came to an end. Most of the prisoners never saw each other again.

Reading III: The Role of the Citizen in Stoerpenberg Camp

During the last two days we investigated two parts of the political system set up by American prisoners in Stoerpenberg Camp. First we studied the leaders of the political system to find out about their backgrounds and their character traits. Then we investigated the process of making political decisions in the camp. We discussed three major issues: who took the initiative to bring up suggestions for laws, who decided whether or not a suggestion was worth discussing, and how the laws were made and carried out. Today's lesson concludes our study of the society in Stoerpenberg.

What a person learns from a reading depends in part upon the questions he has in his mind as he reads. You have already read the Stoerpenberg article to learn about leadership and decision-making in the camp. Today we are asking you to read the entire article, Parts I and II, again, this time with a new set of objectives in your mind. We would like you to investigate the role of individuals in this society. Information about this topic can be found throughout Readings I and II. Do not, of course, read the two introductions again.

In American society political activity occupies a comparatively small amount of the time of a typical citizen. Occupied with a job, a family, a group of friends and innumerable opportunities to go to movies, watch television, attend baseball games, or listen to a symphony orchestra, the attention of American citizens is often focused on these activities instead of on politics. Any American who considers entering politics must recognize that his time is a scarce resource that he must spend very carefully, dividing it among numerous activities. But time was not so scarce a resource in Stoerpenberg Camp. The prisoners there had little to do except work for part of the day in the fields and run their own society during their off-duty hours. This helped to make the nature of their political system quite different from ours. It particularly affected the role of the individual in politics.

Moreover, politics in Stoerpenberg Camp was concerned with matters essential to the life of every prisoner. Whether or not food was distributed fairly was influenced by the political system. Whether his quarters were kept clean and whether the rules established by the group were obeyed were all intimately connected to politics. This close relationship between the political system and the most important parts of a prisoner's daily life is quite different from the relationship between politics and everyday living in our own society. Hence, politics became more important to the prisoners than it sometimes is to us. Certainly, no one in the Camp would be offended if a man became deeply involved in political activity.

A number of other factors made political life in the Camp quite different from what it is in present-day American society. For example, all the prisoners had complete information about every political issue. They knew that their fellow-citizens in the camp would be anxious to discuss political affairs and would work closely with them toward the solution of fundamental problems. Since the society was so small, every citizen had an opportunity to have his thoughts heard and his suggestions for laws considered by the council. Finally, the influence of an individual in the camp was limited only by his personality and by the way in which his ideas were received by his fellow citizens.

As you reread Part I and Part II of the Stoerpenberg Camp essay, think about the following specific questions:

1) How important was political activity to the lives of the Stoerpenberg prisoners?

2) Court was not involved to any great degree in the political activity of the camp. Did other prisoners notice this and seem to resent it? Would your conclusion be as true of an American citizen who was not involved deeply in political activities?

3) How did the prisoners get information about political matters? Is it as easy to get complete information in a modern urban industrial society?

CHAPTER 21 Economics

The economists were the first professional association to initiate a move-ment for the reform of the social studies curriculum. A distinguished National Task Force on Economic Education, under the chairmanship of Professor George L. Bach of the Carnegie Institute of Technology, studied the state of economics teaching in the schools and issued a report in 1961. One volume of the report, *Economic Education in the Schools* (New York, 1961), contained the findings and recommendations of the Task Force. The other, *Study Materials for Economic Education in the Schools*, evaluated published mate-rials for the teaching of economics.

The National Task Force was able to build upon work in economics educa-tion carried on by the Joint Council on Economic Education. For years this organization has been sponsoring workshops under the direction of state and local leaders all over the nation. Millions of dollars were expended in this effort, yet the report of the National Task Force indicated that much re-mained to be done. After making suggestions for the sort of economics under-standings that citizens should have, the Task Force recommended the develop-ment of a series of telecasts for national television. Professor John R. Coleman of Carnegie Institute of Technology was chosen as national teacher for these telecasts. With the assistance of Professor John Haefner of the State Univer-sity of Iowa, who took charge of 30 telecasts directed to teachers, Professor Coleman made 150 half-hour kinescopes, which have since been shown widely around the nation.

The economists then turned their attention to developing materials. They have organized a number of centers in colleges and school systems around the country where writers develop materials and try them out in elementary and secondary school classes. As a guide to these groups, the Joint Council in 1964 engaged a number of scholars and teachers to prepare two pamphlets: *Devel-opmental Economic Education Program: Economic Ideas and Concepts* and

Developmental Economic Education Program: Suggestions for Grade Place-
ment and Development of Economic Ideas and Concepts (each available from
the Joint Council for $1). New materials will be published as they are de-
veloped at the three major centers.

Thus the economists are fully engaged with the problems of economics education. The fact that they are not yet satisfied with their results indicates the
dimensions of the problems that face social studies teachers. The problems
will be compounded in the near future when other disciplines launch projects
that may result in new courses in sociology, political science, anthropology, or
any of several other disciplines. Can each discipline have its own course,
preferably in the senior year? Clearly not. Will each discipline turn out materials to be placed within a conventional curriculum? Not likely. How can
teachers learn all the new disciplines? Not without special work, which social
studies teachers must face in the near future.

In the meantime, we have much to learn from the experience of the economists. Chapter 21 consists of articles by two of their outstanding leaders. The
first selection, by George L. Bach, consists of a refinement of the recommendations of the Task Force report. The second selection, by Dean John R. Coleman, contains his reflections and recommendations for economics education.
Both selections were written after several years of continuous efforts in the
field and contain the considered judgments of their authors. As you read, keep
the following in mind:

1) What is economics? What should be the objectives of an economics
   course? Can the study of economics examine the structure of the discipline
   and at the same time prepare students for active citizenship in a democracy?

2) What analytical scheme underlies the discussion of economics in Professor Bach's article? How can his discussion throw light on what we ought
   to study about traditional economic systems or about a command system
   such as that of the Soviet Union?

3) What are some of the implications of the efforts of the National Task
   Force on Economic Education for reform of the curriculum? Do the conclusions drawn by Professor Coleman apply to reform in other disciplines
   as well as economics?

WHAT ECONOMICS SHOULD WE TEACH?

George L. Bach

Economics is not a set of pat answers or of simple rules or principles. Economics is a body of concepts and working relationships which, when intelligently used, can help in reaching reasoned judgments about economic issues. Economics is a way of thinking, and a tool kit to be employed in thinking through problems as they arise, whether simple or complex.

Thus, properly taught, economics does not lend itself to indoctrination. On the contrary, it is the antithesis of indoctrination, since its main usefulness is to help people reach their own judgments on economic issues.

Such reasoned consideration of economic issues is vital to a well-functioning democratic process.

These three points summarize perhaps the most important things to be said about what economics we should teach. They reflect the views of leading economists over many years, and of thoughtful laymen as well. Two widely read quotations emphasize what might be called the first lesson of economics:

> The theory of economics does not furnish a body of settled conclusions immediately applicable to policy. It is a method rather than a doctrine, an apparatus of the mind, a technique of thinking which helps its possessor to draw correct conclusions.
>
> J. M. KEYNES, from the Introduction to the Cambridge Economic Handbook Series.

> Those seeking to forward special interests and those who believe that the teaching of economics should be indoctrination will find scant comfort in this report. For it stresses, above all, the development of objective, reasoned consideration of economic issues as a basis for thoroughly understanding and wise choice. Its spirit is the spirit of working democracy.
>
> DONALD K. DAVID and T. W. SCHULTZ, from Preface to the Report of the National Task Force on Economic Education.

It is no accident that the quotations above are from men of divergent backgrounds and political persuasion—two very different economists and a leading businessman-educator. For the point of view they express is one with which all who understand the essence of economics would, I think, agree. The way to resolve the question, "What economics should we teach?" is not to merchandise this brand of economics or that; it is to help people learn to reason independently on the economic issues they inevitably face.

But to teach this first lesson well is not enough. More is needed. Ob-

Reprinted from George L. Bach, "What Economics Should We Teach?" *Challenge, The Magazine of Economic Affairs*, Institute of Economic Affairs, New York University, March 1964.

viously, individuals differ widely in ability and interest. With any amount of time and energy some will learn vastly more economics than others. *To face the problem in its hardest and most practical form, I presume that our goal is to teach a majority of our youngsters that minimum amount of economics they might reasonably learn in, say, not more than a semester or so of high school or college study of economics.* This is a base minimum. But even this would be a much larger investment of time in economic education than now prevails for the majority of our population.

To achieve this minimal goal, beyond primary stress on lesson No. 1, I suggest that we need to provide four simple things:

1. A rough overview of the way our economic system works.
2. An awareness of some of the big economic problems of the day.
3. A rough understanding of a *few* major institutions of our economic society and fundamental economic concepts and relationships needed to understand the issues that the average person faces in his personal life and as a voter.
4. Some experience in applying these concepts and relationships to a few typical economic problems.

Overview of the System.   Every participant in the American economic and political system needs to have at least a rough overview of the way our preponderantly private enterprise, but mixed, economic system operates. By this I do not mean anything like the elaborate general equilibrium, mathematized model found in economic theory textbooks. Instead, I mean a very simple, rough picture.

One might begin with a look, first, at *the large private sector of the economy.* Consumers basically determine what is produced by the way they spend their dollars in the marketplace. Businessmen, trying to make a profit, produce the things they think consumers will buy at profitable prices, and in doing so draw labor and capital into those activities where consumer demands are strongest. In this process, workers and other owners of productive resources (land and capital) find that by and large they can earn the biggest incomes in those industries where consumer demands are strongest—that is, where they contribute most toward producing the goods and services that consumers want to buy.

In this interrelated process, market prices act as a regulator that keeps the system *producing,* for the most part, what consumers want and *paying* out incomes for the production of those goods and services. When demand goes up relative to supply, profits and prices generally rise; this both calls forth more production and temporarily pulls purchases back down toward supply when prices rise. Conversely, if demand falls, profitability declines and prices tend to fall; then businessmen and workers in these industries tend to find more attractive alternatives elsewhere. By and large, the businessmen who foresee and meet the demands of consumers most efficiently (at lowest cost) make the largest profits; those who guess wrong suffer losses.

Thus the system relies on the initiative of consumers, businessmen, workers and capitalists to look out for their own individual interests; and in the process, competition in the marketplace basically allocates resources to produce the largest quantity of wanted goods and services. Competition plays a central role, because it is competition that assures consumers of the goods and services they want at the lowest prices consistent with covering costs and reasonable profits.

The economy grows (the total amount of goods and services produced increases) when our total productive capacity grows and there is adequate money demand to buy all the goods and services that the economy can produce. The total output of the economy (gross national product) depends basically on the supply of resources (labor, capital, land, etc.), on our technology (the efficiency with which we organize our resources), and on the initiative and entrepreneurial ability of our businessmen. When we save part of our incomes and invest in more productive resources (buildings, machinery, schools, highways, and the like), this increases our productive capacity and we grow faster. But even when productive capacity grows, there must be adequate total money demand in the marketplace to buy this amount of goods and services; otherwise there will be unemployed men and machines—recession or depression. Conversely, if total money demand exceeds the production capacity of the system at substantially full employment, prices generally will rise, a phenomenon we call inflation.

Government (including federal, state and local levels) plays three major roles in our economic system.

First, government intervenes to establish rules to make the system work effectively—especially to prevent fraud, to protect contracts and to maintain reasonable competition.

Second, government participates directly in the allocation of resources through levying taxes and spending tax receipts to provide "collective" goods and services (national defense, public education, highways, general government, and the like). The public votes for these through the democratic process; generally they cannot be provided at all or as well through the private marketplace. Government taxes draw spendable income away from private consumers and businesses, and the ensuing government spending diverts resources away from producing for private uses (autos, clothing, and the like) to public goods (highways, defense, and the like). Thus the people must choose how they wish to use their resources—through millions of individual consumer and business expenditures in the marketplace or through collective decisions implemented through governments.

Third, in recent decades the federal government has intervened to help keep aggregate demand roughly in balance with the total productive capacity of the system, to avoid depressions and inflation. The total output of the economy is bought by three large groups of spenders: consumers, business firms and governments. Often private spenders spend more or less than just the right amount to buy all the goods available at high-level employment.

Then government may increase or decrease its spending to achieve a better balance between total supply and total demand.

When government spends more than it currently collects in taxes, this ordinarily expands total (public plus private) expenditures. Conversely, when the government collects more in taxes than it currently spends, this commonly has a depressive effect on total spending. Thus government "surpluses" may be used to help check inflation when aggregate demand is too large, and government "deficits" may be used to help prevent depressions when aggregate spending is too small. The government also attempts to help stabilize aggregate demand through its control of the supply of money. The Federal Reserve (the nation's "central bank") may increase total spending through making it easier for banks to lend when depression threatens, and may restrict total spending when inflation threatens.

This is, of course, a drastically simplified overview of the way our economic system operates. But if the layman has at least such a minimal overview, he has some framework within which to understand the big economic issues which face him—taxes, antitrust laws, the cost of local education, and the like.

Acquaintance with Big Problems. Unless people are aware of issues, they cannot be expected to form reasoned judgments about them. The evidence is amazing, but clear, that a large portion of the American public has little or no knowledge of even the big, front-page economic issues of our day.

For example, in 1961 nearly half of a large national sample of the voting-age public did not even know that the federal government was running a deficit—and this in spite of the fact that federal finances had been a major issue in the Presidential campaign of 1960 and continued to be front-page news during 1961. In 1948, when the Taft-Hartley controversy was at its peak, a comparable national survey showed that one-third of the voting-age public had never even heard of Taft-Hartley, and another third had no opinion on it or its contents. Local studies have repeatedly shown that many voters are unable to identify economic issues specifically placed on the ballot—for example, bond issues to finance new local schools.

Clearly, economic education must teach students and adults to be aware of some of the big issues that exist. The cliché that the American people learn all the economics they need to know from the newspapers and TV simply does not stand up under examination.

Concepts and Institutions. The professional economist has a large tool kit of concepts, relationships, facts, and the like, which help him in his analysis of the complex economic problems we face. Which are the most fundamental of these that we ought to try to teach to everyone?

First, a negative. To spend much time teaching detailed facts is waste. We know that the human memory is very short for unused facts. A few big facts are important—some orders of magnitude on the main sectors of the economy. But most facts are better learned when they are needed. They are relatively easy to come by once one knows what facts to look for and ask about.

Second, it *is* important for everyone to be acquainted with a few of the main institutions in our economy, such as the corporation, labor unions and banks.

Third, and most important, a few simple but fundamental economic concepts can help greatly in understanding economic issues. These need not be technical, or mathematical, or even very difficult. The fundamental concepts are those of the *market,* in which buyers (*demand*) and sellers (*supply*) meet and in this meeting determine *prices; competition,* which tends to drive prices down toward cost of production, plus a reasonable profit; *interdependence* among various prices and markets so that what happens in one part of the economy has side effects on others; economic *production,* as any activity that helps to convert resources into goods and services for which consumers will pay in the market; *productivity,* the amount of production obtained from varying amounts of labor, capital and other resources; and *income* as payment for productive services rendered.

Looking at the area of growth and business cycles, central concepts are *aggregate demand*—the total demand of private consumers, private businesses and governments for goods and services; *saving* and *investment,* or *capital formation; gross national product* as the measure of the total output of the economy; *price level,* an average of many prices; *potential high-employment output* of the economy, and the notion of comparing aggregate demand with this potential maximum output to predict unemployment or inflation; *money* and its role in changing aggregate spending; the *federal budget* and the way in which it may add to or deduct from total aggregate demand; *economic growth* and its sources.

It is easy to add more concepts. But a rough grasp of only these, with the overview of the system previously outlined, can help the layman to reach reasoned judgments on many economic issues. For example, if the economist sees a surplus of a commodity in a market, say wheat, he instinctively thinks probably the price is too high—using the concepts of the market and of supply, demand and price in that market. If he sees widespread unemployment, he instinctively thinks aggregate demand is probably inadequate—using the concept of aggregate demand and comparing it with the high employment potential output of the economy. If, in a period of prosperity, someone suggests increasing government spending (for a moon shot or more education), instinctively he thinks this is an alternative to using the resources in the private marketplace in response to consumer demands. If a "fair trade" law permits producers to prescribe a price below which their products cannot be sold, he instinctively thinks this is a restriction on price competition which will probably mean higher prices for consumers—again using the concepts of competition, supply, demand and prices in the marketplace.

These simple examples indicate how fundamental concepts can help us understand what is going on in the economy.

Experience in Applying Concepts.   Guided experience in applying such concepts as the above is the fourth stage in teaching minimal economic understanding.

In economics, as in most other fields, making rational choices among alternative policies on big or little issues generally involves at least four steps:

First, define the problem. What are the facts? What issues are raised? Where are we in relation to where we want to go?

Second, identify our goals or objectives, and give them some rough order of priority.

Third, look for the principal, feasible ways of attaining these objectives.

Fourth, analyze the consequences of each likely line of action, and, on the basis of this analysis, choose the one that promises to be best.

These are nothing more than the stages in a sound businessman's thinking as he makes an important decision. They are the same steps that a good physician or a good engineer follows in solving his problems. The same kind of orderly thinking also underlies rational economic choice for individuals and families. We have come full circle—back to the first lesson of economic education. How can we help people make reasoned judgments on economic issues through applying economic concepts in the framework of the overall operation of our economy?

Other Economic Systems.   Thus far I have written entirely about the American economic system. But I believe that every informed American should have at least a general impression of how other major economic systems operate, especially communism. All economic systems face the same basic problem of using their resources most effectively in satisfying their economic needs. Most economies are mixed, neither purely private enterprise nor Communist, neither purely controlled by individual spending nor centrally directed. Moreover, most economies are continually changing in the way they make their economic decisions and carry them out. Thus a brief analysis of how a Communist system, for example that of the U.S.S.R., does operate—pointing out major differences and similarities with our system, and some of the major changes in both over recent decades—is an important part of what we should teach about economics.

Is this enough?   Is this amount of economic understanding enough? Clearly the answer is "no." John Doe needs to know much more if he is to deal effectively with the complexities of the economic problems he faces. But the amount of economics outlined above is feasible even for a typical high school youngster with no more than a semester or so to devote to this subject. It is obviously feasible for college students; indeed, much more can be done there. But limited as it is, this amount of economics could eliminate much of the nonsense on economic issues we hear in today's public discussions. It would not, indeed, be much. But it would be vastly more than there is today.

For those who set their sights higher, the Report of the National Task

Force on Economic Education provides recommendations much like those outlined above, but more ambitious in coverage and depth.

Economics *is* a difficult subject. Economic problems *are* complex and confusing to the layman. Thus I cannot emphasize too much that what I have outlined above is intended only as a hopefully practical, bare minimum. To teach less is shocking and inexcusable. To teach much more to students going on to take multiple courses in economics in colleges and graduate schools is a sound investment, indeed.

SECOND THOUGHTS ON ECONOMICS IN THE SCHOOLS

John R. Coleman

Such a short time ago we were being assailed on all sides for "failing our economic ABC's" and for being a "nation of economic illiterates" (albeit the wealthiest illiterates the world has yet seen). Now, if I read the signs correctly, economics is "in." From many parts of the country, we get evidence of a deeper concern and a firmer commitment to action on the subject of economic education for secondary school students. Indeed, there is even a certain faddishness to the movement, which presents us with new opportunities and new problems too.

Interest in this subject is of course not entirely new. Too many men and too many organizations, such as the Joint Council on Economic Education, have worked too long for us simply to ignore the past. The National Council for the Social Studies did not wait until the 1960's to discover the importance of economics. But no one will deny that the interest has increased sharply since the appointment of the National Task Force on Economic Education in 1960. The Task Force Report came at the right time to have maximum impact: the ferment in secondary school education made this an auspicious time for a plea that we include more analytical, more objective, more demanding, and more stimulating economic units in the education of tomorrow's decision-makers.

Now that we are past the first burst of this new enthusiasm, it is time to take stock and to sum up some of the early lessons from our shared concern

Reprinted from John R. Coleman, "Second Thoughts on Economics in the Schools," *Social Education,* February 1965, pp. 74–78. Copyright © 1965 by the National Education Association.

for the education of our students. Here I propose to offer a personal summing-up and then to offer a still more personal suggestion about the most fruitful way in which we might proceed with one part of the job, the economics course at the twelfth grade level.

What then have we learned about economic education since 1960?

LESSONS FROM THE FIELD 1961–64

1. *While teacher receptivity to economic education is high, teacher confidence in handling economic ideas is low.* No one who has stepped off the college campus and entered the world of the secondary school can help but be impressed with the open-mindedness of so many teachers and administrators towards curriculum revision. (Indeed a college administrator can only look with envy at what he sees in high schools.) There is, in my judgment, far more hunger for economic materials than there is aversion toward them.

But the blunt truth seems to be that this hunger is not matched with feelings of confidence about the use of the materials. We must not delude ourselves here: an understanding of basic economic concepts is *hard* to come by. That surface understanding of these concepts is so widespread is due to the fact that all of us in a free society are economists by definition. That a deeper, more sophisticated understanding is so rare is due partly to the inherent difficulty of precise thought in any complex field; but it is probably due in larger part to a mass of uninspired and irrelevant teaching by the teachers' own instructors, the college economists. In classroom after classroom across this country, tomorrow's teachers (and today's teachers who are seeking advanced credits) are sitting through courses that scarcely lift their sights or their desire to go on learning. They are watching, in all too many cases, a parade of economic ideas better attuned to making the instructor look good in the eyes of his fellow economists than to meeting the needs of students who have no intention of becoming economics majors. Until the economics professors become more concerned about themselves as teachers—and hence more selective in what they do, more imaginative in how they teach, and more aware of what modern learning theory can tell them about their work—the prospects for the economic competence of high school teachers are not too bright.

But, even with the best college teaching of economics, the job will be less than half done. The secondary school teachers must *want* more and more exposure to that teaching if they are to develop that confidence which underlies any rich classroom performance. Our lot as professionals in the last half of the twentieth century is to be caught up in a time when continuing learning has become urgent business. At the moment when we stop exposing ourselves to newer and deeper ideas in our field, we lose our labels as professionals. Once we could have carried the label for a longer time on the strength of what we learned in the past; now the line between the professional and the hack is drawn in a matter of a year or two. And, given the rate at which knowledge increases, the line once drawn in any man's life is unlikely to be erased.

The moral is clear and relentless. Whatever else we do to seek forward strides in economic education, we cannot move ahead one inch unless the teachers grow in competence and confidence. We waste time and human resources if we try to by-pass the teachers and reach out directly to the high school students. No aids—no textbooks, no learning machines, and certainly no television films—can compensate for an insecure teacher; but those aids—those textbooks, those learning machines, and maybe even those television films—can complement the secure teachers.

The urgency then of more and better workshops and in-service programs in economics for teachers of the social studies is great. We have both to make up for the inadequacies in the teaching and the learning of economics in the past and to recognize the exploding interest in new economic concepts and applications. If we would settle for routine teaching by lectures and cut-and-dried texts, it wouldn't matter much whether social studies teachers were well-grounded in economics; presumably a teacher can parrot words as easily as a student. But, if we believe in inductive teaching—in leading each student to the threshold of his own mind—then our teachers must have that extra degree of confidence that permits them to lead a discussion where the precise directions can never be set in advance. The inductive method demands more than the skill of keeping the discussion going; it demands keeping it relevant to a few key targets, forcing students to sort out the facts from the value judgments in what they say, and employing the newly acquired analytical tools wherever they are appropriate. This is difficult teaching, inspiring when done by the experts who know their subject and their students, but sham when done by others.

2. *Economic education calls for a deeper partnership between secondary school teachers and college economists.* An alert outside observer who looked in on our world of education would surely be surprised by the extent to which we have compartmentalized our activities. Leaving aside the much maligned colleges of education, the contacts between the box labeled "secondary school" and the box labeled "college" have too often been confined to diplomatic letters between senior counsellors and admissions officers. This gap is more than wasteful; it is now dangerous, because unless the college faculties learn more about the ferment in today's high schools and more about the rising potential of the high school senior, there is every likelihood that college will be a big bore for its new recruits.

But there are some signs that the gap may be closed. You know of advanced placement and curriculum development projects where college and high school faculty members worked together to build more demanding and stimulating courses, and where both parts of the team benefited from their shared insights and experiences. The most obvious gain on the high school teacher's side has been that he returned to his class more confident of his own grasp of evolving ideas in a particular field of inquiry. The most obvious gain on the college professor's side is that he can never again be so complacent about his own teaching once he has seen the best of the high school teachers.

And so it is with economics. Perhaps there are exceptions; perhaps there are secondary school teachers who have worked without the help of professional economists in designing the kinds of rigorous and relevant courses we need. (But I doubt if there is a single professional economist who can design a teachable economic course or unit for the high schools without the aid of the high school teacher who is to use it.) All of the promising projects I know about, however, are joint endeavors. The high school teacher brings to the best of these projects (1) a feeling for what the student is like in maturity, skills and interests, (2) a grasp of the total educational program into which the economic units are to be fitted, and (3) a sense of what he or she can reasonably and comfortably accomplish in the classroom. The college economist brings (1) a richer grasp of the fundamentals of the field, (2) a battery of examples from which the teacher may choose those most likely to hit the target, and (3) a set of expectations as to what the economically illiterate high school graduate should know.

Whether this partnership works depends on whether the partners grow in their respect for one another's special skills. Condescending attitudes, rigid convictions of one right way to do things, turning away at the first sign of barriers in the road, unwillingness to challenge one another on the appropriateness of each of the proposed materials—all these things can upset the partnership. But all of these traps are avoidable as men on each side of the artificial line see their mutual stake in getting the job done well.

A last word on this point: just as it is a folly of conceit for the college economist to assume that he is the never-to-be-attained-but-always-to-be-sought-after answer to the high school teacher's prayer, so too it is naïve for the high school teacher to expect that college economists will be coming around in large numbers volunteering their help. The economist has other interests—and his profession has unfortunately not yet made it clear that it will confer accolades for work in secondary school curriculum development. Those who want the help of the economists will have to seek them out. But this is not an impossible task. Attitudes are changing here. One example: had anyone told me five years ago that Carnegie Institute of Technology, a school without a department of education but with many prospective teachers among its students, would become engrossed in secondary school problems, I would have dismissed the idea as fantasy. Yet today this involvement in curriculum building is, without any doubt, one of the three or four most exciting thrusts on our entire campus. Economists, historians, English teachers, fine artists, scientists—we are all in it with expanding zeal.

3. *The clearest lesson from the current push for economic education is*

that we may be trying to do too much in breadth and too little in depth. If there is any one adverse impact from the landmark report of the National Task Force, it is that it may have seemed to ask too much in describing the minimum literacy that a high school graduate needs. The report was not meant as a checklist, yet it is in danger of becoming one. Witness, for example, the new books and the new courses that proclaim they carefully followed the Task Force Report; they seem to have done a better job of making sure that all of the Task Force's subject areas were touched upon than of heeding the pleas for fundamental understandings and for stimulation in the materials. Then, too, teachers may misread the Report's intent and ask, "How can I possibly do all this?" The answer to these teachers must be, "You can't—and you shouldn't try." What we must do is to settle, not apologetically but gladly, for a few things done well. We must, in short, not confuse coverage with understanding.

Perhaps we could get rid of some of our guilt feelings at leaving a few of our favorite subjects out of the high school curriculum if we remembered the "5-year-out" test. This is the test under which we ask ourselves before each class, "What difference will today's material make five years after the student leaves school?" Once asked, the question becomes a fine winnower; a lot of otherwise important ideas get left in a heap marked "Please discard" outside the classroom door. And then there is a chance to do what the Task Force was suggesting all along: that we concentrate on developing a way of thinking about economic issues.

The critical assumption here is that facts, and even institutions, get out of date rather quickly, but a way of thinking lasts. If sloppy thinking—careless use of data, weak logical constructions, unstated and unexamined assumptions—can survive the economics classes, then it has a good chance of lasting for long years to come. But if the teacher pounds away at precise thought and takes pride in the class period where some of the subject coverage was sacrificed to make a few telling points about sound analysis, there is good hope for the future. Who knows? We may even turn out a generation of voters who, if they do not know all of the institutions around them, at least know a good debate when they hear one. That generation will then be more intolerant than we proved to be in 1964 when confronted with a dreary debate about economic freedom, a debate in which terms were seldom defined, data were seldom offered or called for, and real alternatives were seldom examined. Our goal in economic literacy is not an abstract intellectual exercise; it is the application of straight thinking to complex but real problems.

In the first months of designing an economics project in social studies, the idea of dong one or two things well is probably not hard to sell; the testing period comes a little later when each member of the team says, "But we can't leave *this* entire subject out." (Textbooks have a similar life history. The first edition may be selective in coverage, but before the second edition appears the publisher has thrust irate letters from the field under the author's nose. The theme of the letters is simple: "Why didn't you include. . . . ?") There is no easy answer to this drift. It will only be halted when we discover how little that we thought we had "covered" has any lasting impact on our students.

But the teacher who can discipline himself or herself this way must inevitably ask, "Fine, but *which* few things shall I cover?" I do not think there can be any simple answer here. I propose to offer one candidate for the central theme of the senior course in this paper, but it is only one man's choice. The more important point to make is that the choice should be made on a number of grounds and not on any single one. For each classroom, the right subjects to focus on are probably: (1) those where the teacher is most comfortable; (2) those where the subject matter is most relevant to the students' interests and capacities; (3) those where the chance to use simple analytical tools is clearest; and (4) those where the available teaching materials are both sound and lively. If we use those criteria, we need offer no apologies to anyone for our selectivity or our selections.

4. *Economic materials for the secondary schools are improving in quality and quantity, but still suffer from dullness.* Acceptance of the importance of economics in the education of secondary school students has naturally enough led to a demand for better teaching materials. And there has been a response: we have more textbooks, more supplementary pamphlets, and more economic units in the Problems of Democracy books. The writers or consultants are often good economists. But something is still missing. That something is sparkle.

Where in all of the array of materials, and where in the classroom, is the excitement that is economics? Where is the sense of an unfolding science where new techniques are at man's fingertips? Where is the sense of unresolved issues, of free men grappling with choices that involve trade offs— a little more success in achieving full employment coming at the expense of a little less success in maintaining stable prices, for example?

Most materials that I have seen are antiseptically sterile. Why? If it is because we are frightened of controversy and unsettled issues, then we have given the extremists in our midst a bigger victory than they deserve. Unable to get us to teach their propaganda, they may however have been able to keep us from teaching what is lively and relevant.

Most of the materials seem, too, to be ill-suited to inductive teaching. They follow the old pattern: they tell us what they are going to tell us, tell us it, and then in a neat, closed-door type of summary tell us what they have told us. They bow to liveliness by the welcome addition of good pictures and graphs; but they miss liveliness when it appears in the guise of contrasting ideas and unresolved issues. From such materials, the student is more likely to carry away apparent answers than he is to carry away questions. And this seems deplorable to me when any answer must be somewhat tentative and an inquiring mind seems most worth preserving.

Perhaps one of our weaknesses as teachers, as textbook publishers, or as educational administrators is that we have set our sights so firmly on the high school and college years as a part of *becoming* that we lose sight of them as a part of *being*. The student's years throb with an impulse of their own. Yet we often fail to recognize or build upon his special interests in the classroom. We fail to make the class hours an end in themselves—a joyful end—as well as a means toward the further end of growth.

High school students are surely ready to make their first attempts at coming to grips with issues that will stimulate them again and again in later years. They are participants in a society that:

1. tries to combine the pursuit of incentive and risk with the pursuit of minimum security for all;
2. tries to keep alive the game of competition with its unique rule that every competitor should try hard but no one should win the whole prize;
3. tries to keep free choices dominant by expanding, not restricting, government's role in our lives;
4. tries to unlock secrets in science—physics yesterday, mathematics today, biology tomorrow—and to promote technological breakthroughs that make many of our ways of running our economic affairs out of date and that challenge man's very ability to live with the change he pursues so relentlessly.

These issues must come into the classroom, and they will come in if we are more imaginative in the materials we prepare together. We should be working now in building case materials from the real world that confront students with the dramatic, unfolding issues around them. We should be building class units that demand that students use primary data, tables for example that have no accompanying text saying, "As the Table shows . . ." and thereby stopping discussion right on the spot. We should be developing films that do more than describe; they should raise more "how" and "why" questions than they answer. (Some of our current materials proceed on the assumption that they should "lay it out cold"; but it is unclear whether the antecedent of "it" is the subject matter or the student body.) We should be using classroom debates, disciplined not by the stultifying rules of the debate societies but by the ceaseless asking of the question, "What is the evidence?" We should be using economic examples to construct exercises in logic that challenge the ability to think more clearly than the student—and maybe the teacher—has ever had to think before.

In short, we should prove once and for all that dullness and economics are not synonymous.

One Approach to Economics: Comparative Systems

Those then are some lessons from our recent experiences in improving economic education. If they are valid, they apply as well to ninth grade as to twelfth; they apply as well to the civics course as to those points in American and World History where economic issues arise. For the rest, let me direct some comments specifically to one part of the high school program only: the twelfth grade course that carries the formal label of economics. I do this not because it is the most important part of economic education (for it is ordinarily an elective only) but because I have a pet idea to advance.

Against the background of a strong plea for a few things done well in any one course, my candidate for the central theme in the twelfth grade course is comparative economic systems. It is in no sense *the* way to do the job; it is *a* way. The course should choose a few key questions about how men conduct their economic affairs in different places and times. How have they decided what to produce? How have they distributed their product? How have they sought security and stabilization? What attention have they paid to growth?

Two natural candidates for such a study are the U.S.A. and the U.S.S.R. in the 1960's. Perhaps they should dominate the course, but one or more quite different societies should be included for contrast and comparison: perhaps the Eskimos in the 19th or 20th century, the Masai in East Africa at the same time, the French under the manorial system, or the Chinese today.

What special advantages lie in the comparative systems approach?

1. *It gives us the chance to stress the commonality of economic problems: the unending problem of allocating limited resources among unlimited ends.* To see the wealthy American, the aspiring Russian, and the impoverished Eskimo all struggling with the choice question is to drive home a lesson that does not seem to get across easily through other routes and yet that must get across if there is to be intelligent decision-making on economic issues.

2. *It gives us the opportunity to illustrate the variety of ways men have organized themselves to make these choices and it lets us relate those ways to the environments in which they arose.* The key word here is *variety*. Men have never used one or two ways to make economic decisions, and any talk of a single "wave of the future" or of a "black and white choice" is absurd. Economic systems are best seen not as a simple choice between, say, a laissez faire market society and a fully planned society, but rather as a spectrum with those choices as polar types.

The rise to new influence of Professor Liberman in the U.S.S.R. is not a frustration to the teacher who taught with the aid of the spectrum. If Liberman's ideas for the use of more and more market devices take hold, he will simply move the U.S.S.R. a little further away from the completely planned end of his spectrum. And he will paint the U.S.A. too as an economy in flux. The spectrum will help his students avoid the dangerous ethnocentricity that sees only two ways of doing things: the right way and the way followed by all societies outside the U.S.A. These students may never play the shoddy game of calling it a fair comparison when he sets *ideals* of the U.S.A. alongside the *practices* of all other nations.

The comparative approach also confronts us with the chance, indeed the necessity, to relate institutions to our environments. It demands that we cross disciplinary lines. For example, one cannot talk of the rise of communist authoritarianism without seeing it against the backstop of czarist rule. It is incongruous to talk of the American economy's domestic challenges without talking too of the political and social milieu in which egalitarianism and individualism struggle side by side for attention.

There is a hazard here. A course that seeks to be all things to all social scientists is doomed to be nothing to any of them. But the choice is not between the pure, unadulterated economics course on the one hand, and hash, on the other. We can keep economics as the core of the course and still introduce key ideas from other disciplines. Students can think across these lines; so too can their teachers.

3. *The comparative system approach can be useful in teaching and using a few key analytical tools.* Part of the appeal of economics, at least to the professionals, lies in the rich body of analytical tools that can be applied to a range of problems. Yet what seem like the simplest and most useful of those tools, demand and supply analysis in markets, turns out to be difficult to communicate to many students. I suspect that their problem is one of motivation more than of intrinsic difficulties in the analysis. All too often, these students fail to see the relevance of the tools. The beauty—and even the limitations—of the price system does not get across to them because they do not see the fundamental allocation problem clearly enough. One of the strong by-products of the comparative approach is that, when students see how limited resources are allocated under alternative systems, they return to look at their own system with heightened curiosity. Now the pricing system becomes interesting because there is something else with which to compare it.

4. *The comparative systems approach encourages the student to recognize and to study his own values.* As he looks at alternative economic systems, the alert student must ask, "But which way is best?" The question is a good beginning; it can lead to a realization that what is good for one man or one society or one time may not be for another. To participate in the class search for yardsticks to apply to the societies which he is studying is to confront values—others' and his own—more sharply. But let it be clear that the ultimate objective here is to get the student to think through his own values, not to accept some one else's, not even the teacher's.

Discussion of values does not lessen the need for objectivity in the classroom. The worlds of "what is" and "what ought to be" are both relevant in economic education. Our experience is that students at the college level do not make this distinction between them very well; but this only means that we have to work that much harder at promoting clear thinking in both worlds.

Emotionalism runs high, of course, when one talks about comparative systems. Yet I cling to the view that competent, fair, and interested teachers can lift their students' abilities to make discriminating judgments that will strengthen, not threaten, the free society. And that, after all, is one of our purposes in economic education.

CHAPTER 22 Economics: Examples

The examples of readings in economics are taken from a unit in the course in comparative economic systems designed for able ninth-grade students by the Curriculum Development Center at Carnegie Institute of Technology. This course follows one in comparative political systems, from which Chapter 21 was taken. Both courses have been taught experimentally for two years.

The economics course was planned by Professor John R. Coleman, the author of one of the readings in Chapter 22. Like many economics courses, this one is concerned with the problem of scarcity and of the various ways in which men have allocated scarce resources among competing wants. Students are led to examine four major issues:

1) How does a society decide what goods to produce? (the "what" question)
2) How does a society decide how to produce these goods? (the "how" question)
3) How does a society decide how to distribute its goods? (the "for whom" question)
4) What is the role of a society's value system in determining the answers to the previous three questions?

The course contains materials from which students can discover how three types of economics systems answer these questions: a traditional economy (Alaskan Eskimos), a predominantly market economy (the United States), and a predominantly command economy (the Soviet Union). Other types of economic systems are left to later courses in the four-year sequence being written at the Center.

The first unit of the course examines the role of values in judging the worth of an economic system. The second unit explores the economy of the Kwakiutl Indians and examines the role played by traditions in answering the basic economic questions. Unit III, which follows, begins an exploration of the way in which a free market society solves its economic problems. Two of the readings are taken from an excellent collection of case studies in American business history written as a project organized by the Newton (Mass.) Public Schools and the Harvard Business School. Later in the year, students examine a number of public policy questions that require them to use information and techniques learned in the early units. As you read, think about the following questions:

1) What are the purposes of the readings in this unit? How would you teach to accomplish these purposes? How would you evaluate your success?
2) How does this unit seem to be connected to the ones that preceded it? How could the information and analytical techniques used in this unit be employed for studying issues of public policy?
3) Why do you think the course begins with a study of the structure of economics rather than with issues of public policy on which citizens may have to vote?

UNIT III: ECONOMIC DECISIONS IN THE MARKET ECONOMY

Curriculum Development Center, Carnegie Institute of Technology

STATING THE ISSUE

In the market economy, just as in the traditional one, man is faced with scarcity and is forced to make choices. In the market economy, just as in the traditional, man's choice will be influenced by the values he holds. But while traditional societies will tend to answer economic questions in terms of what was done in the past, the market economy reaches decisions in large part through consumer preferences that make themselves felt through a price system. A market is an informal coming together of buyers and sellers, each seeking to satisfy his own desires and each seeking his best self-interest. Prices, as we shall see, act as signals in these markets, giving cues to producers as to what they ought to produce. Thus, the price is to the market economy what the custom of the past is to the traditional economy or the governmental order is to the command economy. The next four lessons deal with the making of economic decisions in a market economy.

Reading VIII: Bridging the Gap between a Traditional Economy and a Market Economy— The Concept of a Spectrum

During the last three days we have been studying an economic system in which most decisions were made in keeping with traditions inherited from the past. Tomorrow we shall begin an extensive study of an economic system in which most decisions are made by a dynamic and invisible mechanism referred to as the market. In studying the market system, we shall use the American economy as an example, although it is true that, just as all traditional societies are not identical in structure to the Eskimo society we examined, neither are all market societies the same.

By now you should all be critical enough of published material to recognize that in describing the Eskimo economy we carefully chose to tell you about those customs which illustrated the points about Eskimo society we wanted to highlight for the purpose of making a particular point. Space limited our telling you all about the Alaskan Eskimos and our specific goal, explaining how traditional economies operate, would only have been blurred by too much detail. But, as a reader, beware—you can easily be led astray by even the most reputable of sources through being given only that evidence which indicates a limited point of view. If space permitted we might have presented some alternative evidence indicating that, while the Eskimos functioned primarily in accordance with tradition, there are areas where change was accepted and customs molded to fit new needs. For example, in some areas white settlers introduced wood for home building rather than blocks of ice. Many Eskimos abandoned tradition and began building shelters of wood. Again, missionaries in introducing the practices of Christianity led the Eskimos away from tradition in the direction of change. So, the Eskimo society is certainly not an example of pure tradition and complete opposition to change. Tradition plays a bigger part there than in our economy, but these are relative matters, not absolute ones.

Today we are going to examine the pure market economy. (Later we will want to modify this picture by seeing some ways in which our economy uses markets in most decisions, but also has elements of tradition and command in it.) In 1776, Adam Smith, an English economist, published *The Wealth of Nations*, an analysis of why western European economies of that time functioned as they did. This book is still considered a classic of interpretation of how a market economy operates under conditions of pure competition. Today's reading is divided into two parts. The first part consists of excerpts from Adam Smith. The second will introduce the concept of a spectrum of economic systems. As you read the few short passages in Part I, consider the following question:

1) According to Smith, how does the market society provide answers for the economic questions, what, how, and for whom?
2) At what points does Smith's theory seem an accurate description of the American economy?

I. THE WEALTH OF NATIONS*
Adam Smith

It is not from the benevolence of the butcher, the brewer, or the baker, that we expect our dinner, but from their regard to their own interest. We address ourselves, not to their humanity but to their self-love, and never talk to them of our own necessities but of their advantages. . . .

But it is only for the sake of profit that any man employs a capital in the support of industry; and he will always, therefore, endeavour to employ it in the support of that industry of which the produce is likely to be of the greatest value, or to exchange for the greatest quantity either of money or of other goods. . . .

[Every individual] generally, indeed, neither intends to promote the public interest, nor knows how much he is promoting it. By preferring the support of domestic to that of foreign industry, he intends only his own security; and by directing that industry in such a manner as its produce may be of the greatest value, he intends only his own gain, and he is in this, as in many other cases, led by an invisible hand to promote an end which was no part of his intention. Nor is it always the worse for the society that it was no part of it. By pursuing his own interest he frequently promotes that of the society more effectually than when he really intends to promote it. I have never known much good done by those who affected to trade for the public good. . . .

When the price of any commodity is neither more nor less than what is sufficient to pay the rent of the land, the wages of the labour, and the profits of the stock employed in raising, preparing, and bringing it to market, according to their natural rates, the commodity is then sold for what may be called its natural price. . . .

The actual price at which any commodity is commonly sold is called its market price. . . .

The market price of every particular commodity is regulated by the proportion between the quantity which is actually brought to market, and the demand of those who are willing to pay the natural price. . . . Such people may be

* Reprinted from Adam Smith, *The Wealth of Nations* (New York: Random House, Inc., 1937), pp. 14, 55–57, 423.

called the effectual demanders. . . . A very poor man may be said . . . to have a demand for a coach and six; he might like to have it; but his demand is not an effectual demand. . . .

When the quantity of any commodity which is brought to market falls short of the effectual demand, all those who are willing to pay . . . cannot be supplied with the quantity which they want. . . . Some of them will be willing to give more. A competition will immediately begin among them, and the market price will rise more or less above the natural price, according as either the greatness of the deficiency, or the wealth . . . of the competitors, happen to animate more or less the eagerness of the competition.

When the quantity brought to market exceeds the effectual demand, it cannot be all sold to those who are willing to pay the whole value of the rent, wages and profit, which must be paid in order to bring it thither. Some part must be sold to those who are willing to pay less, and the low price which they give for it must reduce the price of the whole. The market price will sink . . . according as the greatness of the excess increases more or less the competition of the sellers, or according as it happens to be more or less important to them to get immediately rid of the commodity. . . .

When the quantity brought to market is just sufficient to supply the effectual demand and no more, the market price naturally comes to be either exactly, or as nearly as can be judged of, the same with the natural price. The whole quantity upon hand can be disposed of for this price, and cannot be disposed of for more. The competition of the different dealers obliges them all to accept of this price, but does not oblige them to accept of less.

The quantity of every commodity brought to market naturally suits itself to the effectual demand. It is the interest of all those who employ their land, labour, or stock, in bringing any commodity to market, that the quantity never should exceed the effectual demand; and it is the interest of all other people that it never should fall short of that demand.

II. THE SPECTRUM

Curriculum Development Center, Carnegie Institute of Technology

> 1. How precise a measuring device is the spectrum?
> 2. Can you devise a system for "measuring" economic systems that would be more precise?

At the beginning of this course you learned that the economic decisions of all societies could be described as falling within one of three patterns: traditional, market, or command. In looking at the Eskimos, we discovered that while this particular traditional economy made most economic decisions in accordance with custom, some decisions were made outside the pattern of the traditional economy.

As you read the brief excerpts from Adam Smith, you surely felt some discrepancy between Smith's picture of the pure market economy and economic decisions as they are made in the United States today. Yet, basically, the American economy is as much a market system as any other in the world today.

All of this suggests then that the differences among societies are matters of degrees: in one society relatively more decisions are made on the basis of custom than on the basis of the market, and in another society relatively more decisions are made on the basis of the market than on the basis of custom. No society is a pure model of any one of the three types of economy. It might be better to go beyond the simpler picture of three neat classifications and to think instead of a whole array of economic systems. Along this array there will be extremes, but most economies will probably fall somewhere along the spectrum between the extremes, meaning that we will find some elements of both ends of the spectrum in them.

For example, a spectrum might be constructed on which societies could be arranged in accordance with what proportion of their economic decisions were made by custom, what proportion by the market.

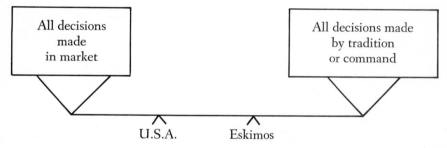

Obviously, the United States would be positioned somewhere to the left of this spectrum, the Eskimos somewhere to the right. (Will they be at fixed points along that line, or will they be moving along it as the years pass? If they are moving, in which direction are they changing?)

Another way to position or compare societies economically might be by the degree to which wealth is distributed to meet needs of individuals as opposed to distribution primarily for the society as a collective body.

Where would you position the United States on this spectrum? Where should the Eskimos be placed?

The advantage of the spectrum device is that it enables us to avoid over-simplifications in comparing economies. It should help us not to think of "blacks" and "whites" in economic systems, but rather to think of various shades of "grey" in between the extremes. These differences in shades may still be important—but they are matters of degree. Keep in mind then that the differences about which we will be talking in the weeks ahead are differences of degree only. And recall that a society's standing in relation to any other society will always depend upon what criteria you choose as bases for comparison along the spectrum. For example, if you were to compare the Eskimo society with the American society on the basis of how much freedom the individual has, you might find the differences not too great. If, on the other hand, you were to compare them on the basis of flexibility, or willingness to change, you might find them far apart along the spectrum.

Prepare for use in class tomorrow a list of criteria by which we might reasonably compare the traditional Eskimo society with the American market economy.

Glossary

1. *Market economy*—an economy in which prices are established by the forces of supply and demand.
2. *Self-interest*—motivated to act in accordance with what is to your own advantage.
3. *Spectrum*—the range of differences extending from one extreme to another.
4. *Criteria* (pl.)—specific qualities or standards by which something can be judged.

Reading IX: How One American Firm Answered the Basic Questions

During the next two days, you will read an account of the way in which an American business firm came face to face with the basic economic questions—what should be produced, how should it be produced, and for whom. These two readings will give you an opportunity to look at economics from the point of view of one business firm.

The Dennison Manufacturing Company has its general offices in Framingham, Massachusetts. Founded in 1844, it has developed in line with a growing economy. Today it has seven major divisions making and selling a large number of products. Each new direction that the company has taken has forced its management to make basic economic decisions.

As you read, keep the following questions in mind:

1) What influenced the managers of the company in deciding what products to manufacture?

2) What factors influenced their decisions concerning how each product would be produced?

Also as you read, list those developments in the Dennison story that you think typify growth within a market economy.

THE DENNISON MANUFACTURING COMPANY (PART I)*

By 1844, Andrew Dennison, a shoemaker of Brunswick, Maine, was experiencing the difficulty of competing successfully in a rapidly changing American economy. Like centuries of cobblers before him, he made shoes in his own shop. He would measure the foot size of a customer, then cut and stitch the leather by hand to fit each person's foot. This was slow and expensive.

Near Boston, shoemakers had long since begun to specialize. If several men worked together, each making a particular part of the shoe, shoes could be produced more quickly and cheaply. By adopting *standard* shoe sizes in a range of widths and lengths people could make shoes in one place to be shipped to others. A customer could buy *ready-made* shoes less expensively than he could have a cobbler make him a pair.

Andrew Dennison could not compete with these mass-produced shoes, and looked about for a better way of earning a living. Andrew's two sons had moved to Boston to engage in the jewelry business. One of them, Aaron, was a successful watchmaker who later helped establish the Waltham Watch Company. For his business he bought from France small jewelry boxes similar to those used by jewelers today to display their merchandise. The trip across the ocean on a sailing ship, however, made their delivery uncertain and their price high. Aaron took some sample boxes home to his father and two sisters with the idea that copies, made in the United States, would sell more cheaply and be more dependably delivered than the French boxes.

Andrew was persuaded to set up manufacturing of jewelry boxes. Using what money he had, he bought cardboard, fabric, wood, glue, and tools and, with the help of his family, started making jewelry boxes in his own home. To establish a price for his boxes, he added up his total cost for materials, wages, and transportation, including shipping the raw materials to Brunswick and the

* Adapted with the permission of the copyright owner, from *Casebook in Business History and Economic Concepts, For Use in Secondary Schools,* edited by Ralph W. Hidy and Paul E. Cawein. Copyright © 1963 by the City of Newton, Massachusetts. (A commercial version of these case studies will be published late in 1966.)

finished boxes to Boston. Then he added twenty per cent to this cost which he would keep for himself as *profit*. His son, Aaron, the jeweler, who had originally recognized the existing *market* for cheaper boxes, sold the boxes to jewelers in Boston and New York.

Before long, Andrew Dennison was able to increase his profit to forty per cent. He did this in two ways. First, he raised his prices, although he still made sure that his prices were less than those of the French box makers. Secondly, he decreased the costs of *manufacturing* the boxes. By searching out new sources and buying larger shipments, he learned to obtain his raw materials more cheaply. The fact that each store originally demanded boxes of different sizes and shapes made producing them slow work at first. He had learned a lesson from the changes in shoemaking, however. By persuading the stores to settle for a limited variety of boxes in standardized sizes, he cut his producing costs.

Soon Andrew's second son, Eliphalet, became involved in the business. His father's comment that he "suffers his outgoes to exceed his income" indicates that Eliphalet may have been somewhat careless with his money, more willing perhaps to *risk* it than his somewhat conservative father. Indeed, this son had not been very successful in the jewelry business in Boston. In 1849, he began to purchase supplies for the box business as an agent of his father. More important, he began to use his talents as a salesman to *market* or find buyers for his father's boxes.

Eliphalet recognized markets for other products similar to boxes, and knew that the more products they could sell the more money they could make. He was anxious to expand the business by *diversifying*, or manufacturing other products he was sure would sell. Soon the Dennisons hired neighbors to help, and were selling cards, fine cotton, tissue paper, and tags. They purchased their supplies in even larger quantities. Many of the new growing businesses in the United States found it cheaper to buy boxes and tags from Dennison, who specialized in their production, than to make their own as they traditionally had.

The location of the Dennison business in Brunswick, Maine, was unnecessarily far from major markets. Delays in transportation by wagon over the poor New England roads occasionally caused loss of orders. Eliphalet suggested moving the business to Boston, where the new railroads would provide fast regular delivery to New York and other eastern markets. His father, however, did not wish to leave his home town.

In 1855, Andrew Dennison agreed to sell the business to Eliphalet so that he could move it to Boston. Eliphalet had little cash, so he bought the business on *credit*, that is, he agreed to pay his father part of his earnings every year until $9,000 was paid. Eliphalet now rented a building in Roxbury, later to become part of Boston, and hired people in the area to work for him.

In 1858 Eliphalet added merchandise tags to his list of products. These were large tags for addresses or prices, with strings to tie them to packages or other articles for shipping. After eyes for the string were cut by machines, the tags were sent out to families who tied the strings to the tags. Since the tag had been designed by the Dennisons, Eliphalet applied for and received a *patent* from the United States Patent Office in Washington. This was a legal document, good for seventeen years, prohibiting others from duplicating the tag without Dennison's permission. To expand his market, Eliphalet bought the business of a New York tag importer. Now he could sell tags to those companies which had previously bought from the New York Company as well as to his original customers. Tags quickly became one of the most important products of the company, more important by far than the original jewelry boxes.

The Dennison Manufacturing Company grew rapidly, and as the company expanded its profits increased. Measured by almost any standards, its first few decades in business were immensely successful. During both 1863, and 1864, profits came to almost 125 per cent of the *capital invested* in the company.

These large profits in the early stages of the business were used for *dividends* and for expansion. Each of the persons who had supplied some of the money invested either in the original company or in later expansions received a yearly dividend, or share of the profits proportionate to the amount of his original investment. Some of the profit, however, was used for expansion. Equipment for manufacturing larger boxes, gummed labels, and sealing wax was added. Branch offices to expand sales were established in Philadelphia, Chicago, Cincinnati, and St. Louis.

Originally, the Dennison Manufacturing Company was an *individual proprietorship,* that is, it was the property of one individual, Andrew Dennison. He had supplied all of the capital or money to start the business, and he was personally *liable* for its affairs. If the company contracted a large debt, for instance, Andrew was responsible for paying it to the full extent of his savings, his home, and any other valuable property he personally owned. On the other hand, he could run the business exactly as he saw fit and keep all of the profits which he did not use to expand.

In 1863, after Eliphalet had been the individual proprietor for a while, he decided to take in three partners. He wanted to expand the business. He needed a larger *inventory,* or supply of merchandise on hand, so that he could fill orders as fast as they arrived. He also wanted to move to larger quarters and increase production and sales. All of these things required money. So many new young businesses were trying to borrow money that bankers were cautious, and borrowing was difficult. Therefore, Eliphalet took on the three partners who supplied the needed capital and became part owners of the firm. Among them they contributed $8,000 to Eliphalet's business, which had an estimated value of about $15,000. The partnership agreement stated that each partner would receive *dividends* and have a voice in the company's management proportionate to his investment. Since Eliphalet had still contributed over half of the capital for the expanded business, he continued to have most influence over it.

The growth of the company was not without problems. One of the more delicate policy decisions concerned the methods of selling merchandise. Most of Dennison's sales came to be made through wholesale *distributors.* Instead of selling small numbers of tags to each of their *consumers,* that is the companies and businesses who used their products, the company simplified the process by selling a large shipment to wholesale distributors, then letting them worry about selling to consumers in their areas.

In 1870, however, Dennison's became unhappy about this method of selling. In order for a distributor to make a profit, the company had to sell him products for 40 per cent less than the price he charged the consumers. This limited the manufacturer's profit. Furthermore, the fact that distributors did not always carry all of Dennison's products cut down on its potential market.

To remedy this situation, the company started sending out salesmen to compete with its distributors in selling to consumers. Aroused at loss of sales, distributors threatened to stop carrying Dennison products. The company feared it would lose sales. Modern advertising was unknown, the companies and stores which used its products had frequently never heard of Dennison. They were accustomed to buying from the local distributor, whom they knew personally, regardless of what kind of labels he sold. The company feared that they would be unwilling to give their business to a strange salesman who said he represented the Dennison Manufacturing Company. Dennison management decided it was running too great a risk, withdrew its salesmen, and continued to market its products through local distributors.

The Dennison Company, like many others, started in the home. The family members worked under the direction of the father. Later a few neighbors were hired. Hours were informal. If an employee's husband were ill, it did not matter if she stayed home a few days or kept irregular hours. Perhaps she would work late another time. If the neighborhood gadabout came in at noon now and then, it was not a matter of major concern.

When Eliphalet moved to a factory in Roxbury and started hiring strangers to work for him, the labor situation changed. Then it was necessary to set down specific rules and hours. Still, however, Eliphalet probably knew most of his employees by name, and if they were doing something wrong he could call them into his office to scold them personally.

As the business continued to grow, however, the roster of employees grew so long that one manager could not possibly know them all. No longer did laborers work with a sense of loyalty to "the boss." Managers tended to forget how workers felt about things. Discipline became a matter of rules rather than of personal relationships.

As a part of the rapid expansion of American business during the nineteenth century, the Dennison Manufacturing Company grew from a small home industry to a moderately large manufacturer. The growth of other businesses, most of which needed tags and labels, created an expanding market. An ample supply of natural resources and adequate amounts of labor and capital, combined with new, efficient transportation, stimulated rapid growth in many parts of the American economy. Dennison owner-managers rode the wave of that growth, and sales and profits continued at a very high rate.

GLOSSARY

1. *Market*—the buying or selling of a particular good or service
2. *Diversifying*—giving variety to
3. *Credit*—securing money, goods, or services in the present against the promise to pay for them in the future
4. *Dividends*—the earnings or profits that a corporation pays to its stockholders
5. *Individual proprietorship*—a business owned and managed by one individual, who assumes the risk and receives the profits
6. *Liability*—an obligation to pay what is owed to creditors
7. *Partnership*—a business owned and managed by two or more individuals, who combine their money, capital and abilities, assume the risk, and receive the profits
8. *Distributor*—an agent or agency for marketing goods
9. *Consumers*—those who use economic goods

Reading X: How One American Firm Answered the Basic Questions

Yesterday you studied the early history of the Dennison Manufacturing Company. Today we will take up the story beginning just after the Civil War. In the years at the end of the nineteenth century, the Dennison Manufacturing Company went through a number of vital changes as it faced new problems in the growing American economy. Most of these changes in one way or another involved the basic economic questions.

The study questions that you were assigned for yesterday also apply to today's assignment. Reread them before you begin work on this lesson. In addition, keep the following questions in mind:

1) How did the owners of the Dennison Manufacturing Company benefit from increased earnings? How did Dennison workers benefit? Did consumers benefit? Did the government benefit?
2) What is the relation between how a company's sales dollars are divided and the answer to the basic economic question, for whom are goods produced?

THE DENNISON MANUFACTURING COMPANY (PART II)*

In 1878 the company changed from a partnership to a far more complicated legal organization known as a *corporation*. The history of corporations is older than the history of the United States. The Virginia Company, the Plymouth Company, and the Massachusetts Bay Company were all organized as corporations. Since 1800, almost every American enterprise requiring large amounts of capital has been organized as a corporation.

Essentially a corporation enables a large number of people to act as though they are one legal entity, or one individual person. This has three main advantages. In the first place, the corporation itself, and not its individual owners, is *liable* or responsible for any debts or law suits against it. This means that the individual who owns part of a corporation can only lose as much money as he has *invested* in it. Unlike the individual proprietor or the partner, he cannot be forced to use his home, his savings, and his other personal belongings to pay debts incurred by the company. If too many debts accumulate against a corporation, it can legally go *bankrupt* without touching the personal fortunes of its owners. Of course, after the income tax was effected in 1913, corporations also had to pay income taxes, although they were given a special rate.

Secondly, although a corporation may have a time limit set in its *charter,* it is not dependent on the life of any of its owners. In a partnership, the death of a partner means that the business must be completely reorganized. A corporation, on the other hand, can continue to exist, within the time limits of its charter, as long as its policies are successful and its owners, the stockholders, are satisfied. Should the stockholders become dissatisfied, they may change the board of directors or even vote to dissolve the corporation. If this happens, all of its property will be sold and its debts paid; then any money left will be paid to the owners in proportion to how much they originally invested.

The third advantage of a corporation, that it can raise great sums of money, is a direct result of the way in which it is formed. The entire value of a company, its *stock,* is divided up into a great number of shares, which represent the ownership by the stockholders. For instance, the Dennison Manufacturing Company at the time of its incorporation in 1878 was capitalized at $150,000. Eliphalet Dennison and his son owned two-thirds of the company, and Metcalf, one of the original partners, held the remaining third. The stock of

* Adapted with the permission of the copyright owner, from *Casebook in Business History and Economic Concepts, For Use in Secondary Schools,* edited by Ralph W. Hidy and Paul E. Cawein. Copyright © 1963 by the City of Newton, Massachusetts. (A commercial version of these case studies will be published late in 1966.)

$150,000 was divided into 1,500 shares each originally valued at $100. The Dennisons received 1,000 shares, and Metcalf 500. Printed *stock certificates* were legal proof of a *stockholder's* part ownership. If the company had wished to raise another $10,000 for expansion, the board of directors could, after going through certain legal channels, issue 100 new shares of stock in the company to anyone who wished to buy them.

Dividends and control of the company are generally divided proportionately among all of the stockholders in a corporation. During each year, the managers reinvest some profit, if any, and distribute the rest among their stockholders as dividends. Each share of stock gives an owner the right to a dividend if one is paid. Usually each share also entitles its holder to one vote in electing a *board of directors* responsible for guiding the company. In this case, the Dennisons had two-thirds of the votes in electing the board of directors. These directors need not themselves hold stock, but they must come before the stockholders each year to report on the business. If the stockholders are dissatisfied, they may elect a new board or make changes in the existing one.

Should a stockholder wish to sell one or more of his shares of stock, he must find a buyer. If the corporation is a private one, he must find the buyer himself. Most large corporations, however, are public; this means that their stock is listed on a public exchange like the New York Stock Exchange. This is a place where any person can buy or sell shares of stock through *brokers* or middlemen who buy and sell stock for others in return for a fee.

The *price* of a certain stock on the exchange corresponds not to the original value of the company but to the demand for its stock. For example, a company might have begun with capital stock worth $50,000 issued in five hundred $100 shares. If investors expected that company to be very successful, they might compete with one another to buy its stock until the shares were selling at as much as two or three hundred dollars a share. On the other hand, if the shareholders expected the company to fail, they might all try to sell their stock and be unable to find buyers for it until they sold it for as little as forty or fifty dollars. If a company either grows fast or pays consistently good dividends, buyers are likely to bid its stock up.

Since a share of stock is the property of its owner, he is the one who makes the profit or absorbs the loss when he sells his share for more or less than he paid for it. Some investors sell their shares of stock in corporations frequently, hoping to make profit by always selling for more than they paid. Others hold their stock for many years, hoping to receive regular returns in the form of dividends.

The legal basis for a corporation is a charter granted by the state in which the company has its home, Massachusetts in the case of Dennison. This charter states the terms under which the corporation must operate, indicating, for example, how much stock may be sold and what the powers and responsibilities of the board of directors shall be. In 1934, the Securities Exchange Commission (SEC) was created by the Federal government to regulate the activities of corporations which sell stock on the public exchange. They are required to register with the SEC, to issue an annual report of their activities to stockholders, and to obey certain fair practice rules set up by the exchange.

During the early part of this century, as a result of deaths and sales by stockholders, much of Dennison's stock was sold to people outside the company. If this practice continued, control of the company would eventually fall to stockholders not directly interested in the company. These people might wish to take all the profits in dividends instead of reinvesting them to insure the future success and growth of the company.

In 1911, in order to take votes away from outsiders, the Dennison Corporation reclassified all of its stock as *preferred stock*. This stock was called preferred because it always pays a set dividend and because, if a company fails, holders of preferred stock are paid off first; Dennison, for example, agreed to pay a dividend of $8 a share on its preferred stock. Holders of this stock, however, were not allowed to vote for the board of directors. If Dennison failed for two years in a row to pay the promised $8 dividend, then preferred stockholders would be allowed to vote again. Although the owners of preferred stock have the advantage of being always paid a set dividend, during a period when profits are high, the dividends on preferred stock remain the same. The dividends on *common stock*, however, vary with profits. Sometimes they are very high, sometimes very low, or nonexistent.

During the period between the Civil War and World War I, for the first time the Dennison Manufacturing Company met serious *competition*. Just after the Civil War, crepe paper produced domestically, that is, in the United States, forced Dennison to cut its prices in half for paper it imported from England. The patent on Eliphalet's merchandising tag ran out in 1880, and competitors started copying it freely. Dennison was forced to cut its prices by 12 per cent. Competition also forced the company to cut gummed label prices from 75 to 50 cents per carton. During this period, salesmen were frequently given the right to adjust prices themselves to obtain orders. Prices were being formed, not by the cost of producing the merchandise, but by competitive pressure in the market. In its effort to control the market for its products, Dennison bought out some of its competitors, advertised its wares, invented new products to meet new demands, and developed new methods of marketing.

One method of eliminating a competing company is to buy it. Dennison would offer the owners cash payment for their business. If Dennison's offer was high enough, they might agree to sell. Then Dennison could sell its products to the customers who had previously bought from that company. Buying out competitors is very expensive, however, and when it was discovered that some men were starting competing businesses with the sole purpose of selling out to Dennison for more than they were worth, Dennison discontinued this method of limiting competition.

Advertising was also used to meet growing competition. When a consumer thought of tags, Dennison wanted him to think of Dennison tags. To this end the company bought advertisements in city and town directories. To appeal to home consumers it advertised in popular magazines like the *Ladies Home Journal* and *The Youth's Companion*. In 1893 it established a booth at the Chicago World's Fair to display Dennison products.

As the way of life in the country changed, the Dennison Company tried to invent new products that would appeal to consumers. New styles of jewelry boxes and cases were introduced. Merchandise was made available in a greater variety of colors. Glues and pastes were added to Dennison's list of products. Paper napkins proved very profitable. A pamphlet, "The Art of Sealing a Letter," was circulated to stimulate sale of sealing wax. Demonstrators were sent to retail stores to give instructions on how to make such things as paper flowers and window decorations out of crepe paper. Occasionally, a new product, like wooden boxes for the British parcel post, had to be dropped because it did not sell.

Meanwhile, Dennison attempted to cut its costs by increasing efficiency in marketing. By 1890, increased advertising had so associated the name of Dennison with paper products that now it was able to do what it had tried unsuccessfully to do in 1870. Although Dennison continued to market through distributors, it sent its own *salesmen* out to deal directly with the businesses, manufacturers and retailers who used their products. Regular sales districts were established so that salesmen came to know both the area and their customers personally. . . .

Eliphalet's grandson, Henry S. Dennison, became president of the company in 1917. Since he had previously been works manager, he brought an interest in production to the board of directors. Under his leadership a continuous effort was made to increase production efficiency and speed. Production costs were carefully watched. The price set on merchandise began to be based not only on the pressure of competition but also on the cost of producing each item. This meant generally lower prices but a more dependable profit.

Heavy sales at the turn of the century put a strain on the whole management to continue at high volume of production. In 1900 sales totalled over two million dollars, and in 1910 they passed the five million mark. To continue his high pressure production, in 1912 Dennison concentrated almost all of its production facilities at one site in Framingham, Massachusetts. For the first time in many years new equipment was developed or purchased to speed production of shipping tags and boxes. Although the substitution of machinery for hand processes was expensive at first, the increased profits from heavy sales provided the necessary investment capital.

In 1901 an outside expert suggested that production could be made more efficient by the establishment of new departments to control *inventories* of raw materials and of finished goods. The raw materials department tried to keep supplies steady. Excess stock of any one material tied up the company's money where it was not needed. On the other hand, to run out of a material could stop production altogether. The finished products department made sure that the merchandise inventory in the warehouse was sufficient to supply branch stores and salesmen. By determining what items were in demand, it guided the factory with regard to what products were currently needed.

Another way in which the Dennison Manufacturing Company met competition and cut production costs was by reorganizing the company so that all of the different departments worked smoothly together. In 1906 six merchandising committees were established, one for each of Dennison's six *lines:* tags, jeweler's items, adhesives, crepe, Christmas items, and *consumers' goods* (items like napkins sold directly for home use). Each committee consisted of men from three categories: salesmen concerned with demands and competition; producers concerned with methods and costs of production; and directors concerned with long term expansion and profit. By 1911 the committee chairmen, located in Framingham, were devoting full time to coordinating all facets of the business.

The merchandising committee on tags handled the problem of keen competition in the selling of certain types of tags. . . .

In the 1920's, a period of general prosperity in the country, Dennison did continue to expand. It increased production facilities by opening a box factory near Marlboro, Massachusetts. It established Dennison companies in Canada and England to sell products throughout the British Empire. The company also began to export merchandise, setting up sales offices in South America and Europe. In 1929 it formed a special research department to develop new products and methods. . . .

Glossary

1. *Corporation*—a business organization owned by the stockholders and legally (if not actually) controlled by the common stockholders through the right to vote for the board of directors
2. *Bankrupt*—use by debtor as a legal method for relieving himself of financial obligations he is unable to meet
3. *Stock*—certificates of ownership interest in a corporation, sold in units referred to as shares
4. *Stockholders*—those who own stock certificates
5. *Board of directors*—a group chosen by the stockholders of a corporation to manage the enterprise
6. *Public exchange*— the place where stocks and bonds are bought and sold according to recognized rules
7. *Broker*—an agent who buys or sells stocks, bonds, commodities, or services, usually on a commission basis
8. *Charter*—document issued by legislative authority granting privileges and duties of incorporation

Reading XI: How an American Firm Might Answer the Basic Questions

For the past two days you have studied the ways in which one American firm operating within a market economy answered the basic economic questions. Today we are going to examine the way in which a typical American child might first come face to face with these questions.

Suppose you had a brother in the fourth grade who wanted to make some money this summer. Your mother might suggest that he set up a small business for himself, a lemonade stand, for example. Ignorant in the field of economics, your brother might turn to you for advice.

Write an outline containing an analysis of the types of economic decisions you brother will have to make. In summarizing problems to be met, keep in mind the fact that your brother will be operating in a market economy. Recall, in general, the problems faced by the Dennison Manufacturing Company. In a way, the problems faced by big business are magnified versions of the same problems faced by small business.

Keep your outline under one page in length. Outline your thoughts in short clear phrases. *Do not use complete sentences in outlining.* Bring your outline to class tomorrow so that we can discuss it. After our class discussion, you may amend your outline. Your amended outline will then form the basis of a paper you will write tomorrow night.

Reading XII

There is no reading for tonight. In lieu of a reading you will write a paper based on the outline developed yesterday. Your paper should not be more than two pages in length. As you write, keep in mind the rules for essay writing discussed last semester.

Remember, your brother has come to you as an economic consultant. A good consultant knows that if a client is to be satisfied with his service, certain standards must be met.

1. You must first recognize the core of your client's problem and define his problem in terms that he can understand.
2. You must, without being offensive, identify your client's primary goals and objectives.
3. You must see and interpret for your client the alternatives confronting him in reaching his objectives.
4. You must clearly point out to your client the possible consequences of pursuing each alternative.
5. You must provide your client with the information necessary for him to make an intelligent and informed choice. Keep in mind it is your responsibility to communicate in terms that can be understood by your client, whoever he may be.

CHAPTER 23 The Behavioral Sciences

The very term "behavioral sciences" is new to most high school teachers and, for that matter, to many members of university faculties. Not that the fields of study in the behavioral sciences are new. For almost a century the leading universities have offered scattered courses in sociology, anthropology, and psychology, the three disciplines that form the heart of the behavioral sciences. But few universities even now offer courses labeled "behavioral sciences," and even fewer have departments that are so named.

There is no doubt, however, that the behavioral sciences are increasing in importance. A number of journals bear testimony to this new branch of learning. By publishing in anthropological or psychological journals sociologists indicate that the lines separating the three disciplines are becoming blurred. The publication in 1964 of Berelson and Steiner's *Human Behavior: An Inventory of Scientific Findings* (New York: Harcourt, Brace & World) further testifies to the development of a science of human behavior cutting across academic departments. A few courses in the behavioral sciences are even offered in the secondary schools, most notably at the Mark Twain Summer Institutes held each year in Clayton, Missouri. Schools elsewhere will, at the very least, soon be including methods and insights from the behavioral sciences in their social studies offerings.

But there are more pressing reasons for understanding the behavioral sciences. Even if separate courses are not taught in one or more of these disciplines, the content of the behavioral sciences occupies an important place in every high school social studies curriculum. Not only courses in civics and problems of democracy but also history courses consistently employ insights and techniques from the three behavioral sciences. Students cannot understand history well unless they employ these disciplines.

Chapter 23 consists of an analysis of the content of the behavioral sciences. It begins by differentiating them from the wider field of the social sciences and then examines the major concepts from this area in some detail. Hence, the chapter forms a companion piece to Chapters 19 and 21, which explore the structure of political science and economics. As you read it, keep the following questions in mind:

1) What are the major concepts of the behavioral sciences? How can these concepts be turned into an analytical scheme like the one in Chapter 19?
2) How can these concepts, or the analytical scheme that can be made from them, be used as a guide to content selection? Can they be used in a course in political science? the history of the non-Western world? civics?
3) Suppose you decided to teach students the structure of the behavioral sciences. How would you go about it? What guidance could you get from authors studied previously in this volume?

ANTHROPOLOGY, SOCIOLOGY, AND SOCIAL PSYCHOLOGY

Meyer F. Nimkoff

The writer has assumed an ambitious task: to set forth in a single chapter a number of the leading concepts or "big ideas" of cultural anthropology, sociology, and social psychology which high school students of the social studies ought to know. From a pedagogical standpoint it would be better to devote a separate chapter to each discipline, and better still to deal in a single chapter with just one or two significant ideas, but space considerations prevent this. The teacher, with a semester or term at his disposal, would do well to consider the advisability of presenting in each class session only one or two "big ideas" treated as fully as time permits. This is the way to build up in students "a sagacity for the significant."

At the outset, a word of caution may be desirable about the discussion that follows. The writer is a sociologist. In dealing with anthropology and social psychology he may be subject to some bias, although he trusts not. In any case, let the reader beware.

The warrant for listing the disciplines in the order given in the title of this chapter is historical. Anthropology is the oldest, and social psychology the youngest, of the three. However, no rigorous attempt will be made here to treat the three disciplines separately, since our interest is primarily in

Reprinted from Meyer F. Nimkoff, "Anthropology, Sociology, and Social Psychology," in Erling M. Hunt *et al., High School Social Studies Perspectives,* pp. 29–50. Copyright © 1962 by Houghton Mifflin Company. Reprinted by permission of the publisher, Houghton Mifflin Company.

some of the many concepts which are shared by anthropology, sociology, and social psychology.

The warrant for treating anthropology, sociology, and social psychology apart from economics and political science is that the first three are general sciences of man, whereas economics and political science are special sciences. The political scientist deals only with the political process and with political institutions, whereas the cultural anthropologist and the sociologist are concerned with a wide range of social institutions—familial, religious, legal, educational, and economic, as well as governmental. The reason for this broad interest is that the anthropologist and the sociologist are seeking general principles applicable to social organization. History is also a general subject, but it is set apart by its special descriptive emphasis on unique events and movements from the other social sciences, which are characterized by a quest for generalization. The boundaries between the disciplines, however, are hard to draw. Originally anthropology concerned itself mainly with the study of primitive or non-literate societies; but recently it has been focusing on small groups and villages in modern societies. Social psychology developed as an offshoot of both psychology and sociology and, as the name implies, its primary concern is the way the group affects the behavior of the individual.

Culture

THE CULTURE CONCEPT

The central concept of all three disciplines is *culture,* a phenomenon so vast that the student could examine it for a lifetime and still not encompass everything there is to know about it. One way to understand culture is to learn how it began and developed. Culture, as we experience it in the middle of the twentieth century, is the result of nearly a million years of living and learning on the part of mankind, and of transmitting what has been learned. Herbert Spencer called culture the *superorganic,* a useful term because it is readily differentiated from *inorganic* and *organic.* The planet on which we live, however it may have originated, had at first no living thing upon it. In the beginning all was inorganic matter. Then, in the course of a long period of time, life appeared. To the inorganic, the organic was added.

In the earliest animal life there was little or no learning from other animals. Instead, behavior was regulated by simple response to stimuli, as in the response of the moth to a bright light. More complicated behavior was regulated by a built-in mechanism, or instinct, exemplified by the wasp, which builds a nest, lays its eggs, provides food for the young, and seals up the nest whether or not it has ever seen another wasp do these things.

Eventually some animals developed the capacity to learn not only in a random manner from experience but systematically from others of their own kind, through imitation and communication. A familiar example is the way a mother cat teaches her young to catch and kill mice. The capacity to learn is a function of the nervous system; hence the capacity is highly developed among the vertebrates, which have a highly developed nervous system with a central cord. The monkeys and apes have the best learning capacity except for man, but they are limited by their inability to develop true speech or language. There is probably a biological basis for this difference, although its exact nature is obscure. In any case, language provides a medium for transmitting culture, and, especially in its written form, a method of preserving culture from generation to generation.

To the inorganic and the organic realms, then, there was added the superorganic, behavior learned by man as a member of society and persisting through tradition.

Of central importance in the culture concept is the idea that such behavior is learned from the group and that it is not inherent or biological. There are essentially two modes of adaptation to environment, the biological and the cultural. The polar bear has made an adaptation to the Arctic region in part by developing a coat of fur, a biological adaptation, whereas the Eskimo, who lives in the same frigid region, has learned to protect himself by building an igloo—and, we might add, by appropriating the skin and fur of the polar bear. The Eskimo has made a cultural adjustment to his environment.

The cultural adjustment is in many ways superior to the biological. For example, the polar bear has biologically adjusted to the cold North but will fare poorly in the temperate or tropical zones. Man is the only large animal found in all zones and parts of the earth, and this is because he has learned to adjust to the requirements of the various regions by developing an appropriate culture.

IS CULTURE BIOLOGICALLY DETERMINED?

Since man is the only animal with a substantial culture, it may be assumed that a certain degree of evolution of the brain case is a necessary precondition to the development of the superorganic. However, there has, in the last 10,000 years or so, been no significant change in the biological nature of man, yet during this time the changes in man's culture have been tremendous. The growth of the superorganic has plainly not had to depend on any continuing biological evolution of man's brain. If man were to develop biologically into a superman, his culture would no doubt be benefited. But no such evolution is in prospect and man's present biological capacities appear to be sufficient for the continued growth of culture.

The question as to whether culture is biologically determined has another aspect—namely, does the biology of man dictate its content? The answer is that heredity sets limits to culture and determines its broad outlines but does not fix details. Hereditary capacities are responsible for the fact that man lives mainly on the surface of the earth and not in the seas or in the air. But man's heredity does not preclude his living for limited periods in submarines or airplanes. Man's biology determines that every culture will have family life, but his biology does not tell us whether that family life will be monogamous, polygynous, or polyandrous. The biological nature of *Homo sapiens* may exert a strong preference for one cultural trait rather than another. Thus man, a biped, prefers stairs to ramps, which would better suit a quadruped. But the biological predispositions of man are not imperative. One would never guess from the bioglogical nature of man that monogamy would be the cultural requirement of an ever increasing number of societies.

Still another aspect of the question of the relation of biology to culture is whether the different races of man differ in their capacity for culture. This is an important question, all the more because of the widespread existence of race prejudice and the practice of bolstering the case for discrimination on the grounds of racial inferiority. On this point the evidence of anthropology is clear. Mankind is one. All men belong to one species of animal. There are variations in intelligence among individuals; but races are very large aggregates of individuals and families, and it is not clear that there are differences in intelligence among races.

RACE PREJUDICE

The response of an individual or a group to members of another race may be neutral, favorable, or unfavorable. In the United States the attitude of whites toward Negroes is often unfavorable. The feeling is called race prejudice, and the accompanying treatment, discrimination. (Prejudice may, however, exist without discrimination, and discrimination without prejudice. Prejudice is a general attitude and may be directed toward many objects, such as religion, politics, or economic practices, as well as race.) Race prejudice is exceptionally difficult to eradicate because of the high visibility of the objects of prejudice. A person can more readily change his religion, politics, language, dress, and manners than the color of his skin! Prejudice is literally the habit of prejudging the behavior of others. Individual variations in prejudice are associated with differences in frustration in early childhood; those with more prejudice are generally those who experienced more frustration. Frustration leads to aggression, one form of which is prejudice against others. Where the prejudice is collective or nearly unanimous in a large segment of society, the causes are to be found in ethnocentrism and fear of the consequences if the status quo were to be reversed, that is, if those long discriminated against were to become politically dominant.

THE VARIABILITY OF CULTURE

The ordinary observer of human customs is probably impressed by their variety above all else. He notes not that all people eat food but that Russians like steak, fish, and yoghurt for breakfast, that Filipinos eat the meat of dogs, that East Indians do not customarily use knives and forks but the thumb and the first two fingers of the right hand, and so on. It is the differences that we stress and not the underlying uniformities of function, because it is the differences that intrigue or vex us, as the case may be, as travelers or observers. All people speak a language, but the differences make it difficult if not impossible to communicate. The differences in culture are at the basis of conflicts and misunderstandings.

Difficulty with the unfamiliar is reinforced by a fairly universal tendency to assume that one's own culture is superior to all others. This is a kind of group egotism, to which the name *ethnocentrism* has been applied, and it is as difficult to eradicate as individual egotism, presumably because egotism, whether individual or collective, has the functional value of bolstering self-regard and is useful in the struggle for survival. In inter-societal relations, however, there is also value in holding correct and even sympathetic ideas of the culture of other people. One culture may be superior to another, at least in certain particulars, but, if so, this is established by the facts of the case and not by mere assertion or assumption.

A common reaction to customs that differ from one's own is to regard them as queer or peculiar. That is, the initial response is often to pass judgment on them. A more objective viewpoint is likely to be achieved if judgment is suspended and an effort first made to understand the practice. When understood, it often appears to be quite reasonable.

CONFORMITY

Although customs vary from society to society, in any given society there is pressure to conform to the prevailing practices. This is recognized by the maxim, "When in Rome, do as the Romans do." The degree of compulsion varies with the significance attached to the behavior in question. On some things, such as which shoe one puts on first in the morning, the group may be indifferent. On other things, such as what one may eat for breakfast, the group may approve a wide range of choice. But on still other matters, such as ideas of physical modesty, the group may be quite rigid and compulsive; these ideas, the *mores*, concern what is regarded as in the moral interests of the society, and the mores are sacred. In the United States in the second half of the twentieth century the mores include monogamy, democracy, and free enterprise.

So powerful are the mores that William Graham Sumner (1840–1910), who introduced the term into social science, in his book *Folkways* entitled one chapter "The Mores Can Make Anything Right and Prevent the Condemnation of Anything." A century or more ago the mores of the United States made slavery right. Some cultures approve the eating of human flesh, at least that of the enemy. Even incest has been approved in some instances, as in the brother-sister marriages among royalty in ancient Egypt. Ethicists who use what they consider to be absolute rather than relative standards of ethics would qualify Sumner's statement that the mores can make anything right. The mores, they claim, can only make anything *seem* right.

CULTURAL CHANGE AND CULTURAL LAG

One of man's characteristics is that he can make an object of himself. He can be self-conscious and self-critical. In the same way he can be critical of his culture and seek its change or improvement. In any case, one salient feature of culture is change, which in simple, rudimentary societies is minimal but in modern, industrialized societies is very rapid indeed. Most innovations, which are the building blocks of culture, represent combinations of old elements. It follows that the broader the cultural base, the more numerous will be new inventions and discoveries. The growth of culture is governed by an exponential or accelerating rate of change. If the beginnings of human culture are arbitrarily set at 100,000 years ago, then 90,000 years were required to advance from the Old Stone to the New Stone Age. Bronze came in 2000 years ago, iron 1000 years ago, steam and steel 200 years ago, atomic energy within the last decade or so. This prompted one anthropologist to comment:

> We may liken the progress of mankind to that of a man one hundred years old who dawdles through kindergarten for eighty-five years of his life, takes ten years to go through the primary grades, then rushes with lightning rapidity through grammar school, high school, and college.[1]

A culture that is undergoing rapid change may not change evenly in all parts. Some parts may experience considerable change, other parts little or no change. The elements that show little or no change are said to manifest cultural *lag*. If the parts of a culture are initially in balance or harmony, then a change in one part while a correlated part does not change throws those two parts out of adjustment and there is a strain between them. If the members of the society are aware of this strain and are disturbed by it, we say it constitutes a social problem. Many, although by no means all, social problems involve cultural lag. In modern times in Western society, the most extensive changes have been occurring in technology, and adaptive behavior has lagged. For example, as a result of industrialization and urbanization there has been a continued increase in the percentage of wives employed outside the home for pay. About one wife in three now holds a job in the United States, but the household adjustments of these women lag. The wives have added a large new responsibility by working away from home, while their husbands as a rule have not assumed a commensurate share of responsibility for the home. Adjustments are possible, with baby sitters, day nurseries, nursery schools, dishwashers, deep freezers, processed foods, and

[1] Robert Lowie, *Culture and Ethnology* (New York: Douglas C. McMurtie, 1917), p. 78.

assistance by husbands with domestic chores. But in general the adjustment tends to be slow and insufficient, creating domestic tensions.

GROUP INTERACTION

A prerequisite to culture is group interaction. This is evident from the fact that culture is the social heritage and a heritage is not social unless it is shared. Culture is learned by the individual from the group and is kept intact in part by being transmitted from generation to generation. Some of those who wish to draw formal lines of distinction between sociology and anthropology say that sociology is the discipline which concerns itself with the nature, conditions, and consequences of group interaction, whereas anthropology is the science of culture, one of the products of group interaction. Another product of group interaction, personality, is the concern of social psychology. In actuality, these formal distinctions are not always observed and practitioners who are regarded as sociologists, anthropologists, or social psychologists, as the case may be, often deal with problems which overlap the boundaries.

PRIMARY AND SECONDARY RELATIONS

Until relatively recent times the great majority of people throughout the world lived in small groups or communities. This is still true of hunting societies, and even of predominantly agricultural societies, such as that of India, where perhaps 80 per cent of the population live in villages. The Eskimo hunters live in bands often numbering no more than fifteen to twenty-five persons. In such small groups all the adult members are well acquainted with one another. Charles Horton Cooley (1864–1929), a sociologist, was greatly impressed by the intimate social relations of these small, homogeneous groups, especially by the consequences of such intimacy. He called such groups *primary groups,* and identified the family, the play group, and the neighborhood as the three universal primary groups. He called them primary for two reasons, because they are first in time in the experience of the individual and because they are first in importance in influencing personality.

By contrast, modern industrial societies are characterized by large, urban communities with a heterogeneous population and a high rate of physical mobility. There were, of course, some cities in the earlier, agricultural societies, but they accounted for only a small part of the total population. Transportation was poorly developed, which discouraged mobility and tended to give a quality of primary relations in the local communities. Now, in the United States and other highly industrialized countries, more than half of the population live in cities or in nearby communities dominated by urban influences. The quality of the social interaction in these mass societies, Cooley noted, is different from that in folk societies. In cities interaction is impersonal. In a small place one gets to know the whole person, everything about him. In the city one gets to know only certain facets of a person's life, the aspects or ideas with which one comes in contact. Cooley called such groups *secondary groups,* and meant that they are of secondary importance in shaping the human personality.

One of the more important consequences of living in a closely knit group is the sense of belonging that usually results. One feels at home in such a group, if one does not misbehave. And misbehavior is less likely than in a larger society. The small group exercises strong control over its members. The opinion of others is greatly esteemed and a good reputation is highly valued. Gossip is feared and serves as an important censuring agent, more powerful than police action in a modern city. The whole life of the individual is wrapped up in the community and there is no recourse to any outside group. In these circumstances there is little crime. One gains little by theft, since possessions are few and everybody knows who owns what.

The mass society, on the other hand, offers ample privacy for the individual, since he is surrounded by strangers who do not care about him. The privacy may indeed be excessive, much more than the individual wants, and he can be utterly lonely. People, people everywhere but not a one to know. Many, however, enjoy the freedom which the city affords. Some use it to transgress against custom or the law.

As we have noted, a secondary or mass society is composed of heterogeneous elements and is characterized by a high rate of physical mobility. Consequently it is not likely to be so well integrated as a simple folk society. In rudimentary, primitive societies unaffected by outside influences, there is, for example, usually only one church, whereas in the United States there are at present a number of major churches, and one of them, the Protestant Church, has more than 200 denominations.

A major problem of modern mass society is how to achieve the unity which is necessary for effective functioning. The cohesion required may not be so complete as, say, in a primitive village, but there is a limit beyond which separatist elements cannot be permitted, if the society is to function efficiently as a unit. There must be consensus on essential values and a feeling of satisfaction with belonging to the group, called *morale.* The individualism of modern urban society is kept within bounds by the development of codes and laws to supplement the unwritten folkways and mores, by the availability of newspapers and radio and television programs to supplement gossip and word-of-mouth dissemination of local news, and by the establishment of new organizations, such as baseball teams, to which the loyalty of the whole group can be devoted. Primary-group relationships sometimes continue, if in attenuated form, among neighbors. Urban residents have friends within the city, even if they do not live nearby. A certain modicum of intimacy in human relations appears to be a requirement for social life, if it is to be satisfying. Indications of this are to be seen in formal organizations, such as factories, where the work routine is impersonal and where the workers informally form cliques in quest of fellowship. In the Army, a highly formal organization, the authorities have taken cognizance of the need for some offsetting human element by encouraging the "buddy system," in which soldiers are paired off with the tacit understanding that each will look after the other, especially when the going is rough.

IN-GROUP-OUT-GROUP RELATIONS

In the preceding paragraphs attention has been directed to certain problems having to do with the unity and efficiency of the group. We consider next the relationship between groups. An important observation here is that groups generally differentiate importantly between their own members and outsiders. We see this in the distinction we make between those who are members of our own family and those who are not, kin and non-kin. Among primitive peoples, especially, who often live in relative physical isolation from other societies, the stranger has to establish his identity if he visits a new community, and this may not be easy to do. That is why banishment from the group was in earlier times such a severe punishment.

Toward members of one's own group one tends to be friendly; toward outsiders, strange or even hostile. These differential attitudes are often accompanied by two divergent sets of values, one set for home consumption, the other for export. To steal from one's own is almost universally condemned, but to steal from the enemy may be heartily approved.

No principle of inter-group relations is more important than the generalization that inter-group conflict increases intra-group solidarity and morale. The enemy at the gate brings cooperation within the camp. We see this in nations in the readiness during wartime to accept discipline, hardship, and rationing which in other circumstances would not be tolerated. We also see it specifically in the cooperation of Jews in support of the young state of Israel in the face of continued boycott and hostility by the Arabs. Financial support for Israel rises as the outside pressure mounts and declines as the pressure subsides. Politicians know this principle well and often use it to their advantage by summoning up a scapegoat in order to divert attention from pressing internal problems.

ROLE AND STATUS

Societies are made up of individuals and groups that differ in traits, such as sex and occupation, which can be classified, and traits, like income and age, which can be scaled. Individuals with different attributes perform different tasks. These functions, prescribed by the culture, are called by the sociologist *roles*. Division of labor is an effective device for getting work done.

Ascribed roles are those which are assigned to the individual by society.

The business of society cannot of course be left entirely to chance and the uncertainty of variations in individual competence. Age and sex are universally the most important bases of ascription of roles and therefore of social participation. Everywhere appropriate behavior is indicated and differentiated for infants, boys, girls, adult men, adult women, old men, and old women. In many cultures adolescence is clearly demarcated as an age-class, but not in the United States. Here the indeterminate nature of adolescence is said to lead to confusion and stress in the minds of adolescents, who are not clear as to their role in society. They are no longer accorded the privileges of younger children, yet they are not granted the rights of adults. In Polynesia, adolescents are relieved of most domestic and community responsibility and are free to prepare for marriage.[2] They are reported to be free of the stress which is so common among American adolescents. Societies which, like the Samoan, are organized on a kinship basis are said to be relatively free of organized age groups. A society such as that found in the United States, however, is said to foster the development of all kinds of peer groups, such as clubs, gangs, cliques, Scouts, fraternities, and youth movements, because the youth are prevented from attaining full social status through identification with the heterogeneous-age members of the family.[3]

Society not only assigns roles to individuals on the basis of such traits as sex and age but it evaluates the roles as superior, inferior, or equal. This ranking of roles is called *status*. Thus in many societies the status of women is said to be inferior to that of men. This usually means, among other things, that the political influence of women in community affairs is less than that of men. In the home, in domestic affairs, the influence of women may be greater. Status varies with role.

In addition to ascription of role and status on the basis of age and sex, at birth every individual is automatically assigned to the social class of his family, if the society is characterized by social classes. By social classes we mean two or more broad groups of individuals, based on occupation and property and characterized by differences in life-chances, cultural traits, prestige, and power. In ancient Rome, for instance, there were the slaves, the large plebeian or common class, and the five superior classes.

Social classes are important because they affect one's opportunities, behavior, associations, prestige, and power. For instance, studies in the United States show that, despite free medicine for the poor and the advantages of public health services, infant mortality is greatest among those families with the lowest incomes. The poorest people are those most frequently sick. The chances that a high school graduate will go to college are almost two and one-half times greater if his father is a professional man than if he is a

[2] Margaret Mead, *Coming of Age in Samoa* (New York: W. W. Morrow & Company, 1928).
[3] S. N. Eisenstadt, *From Generation to Generation: Age Groups and Social Structure* (Glencoe, Ill.: The Free Press, 1956).

factory worker. In the main, the low-income classes tend to vote the Democratic ticket in national elections; the high-income classes, the Republican ticket. The high-income Protestants tend to belong to the Episcopal, Congregational, and Presbyterian churches; the lower-income Protestants, to the Baptist, Lutheran, and Methodist churches. In Elmtown, investigation of students attending the same high school showed that 61 per cent of the boys and girls had dates with members of the same social class, 35 per cent with members of an adjacent class, on a five-class basis.[4] As to the distribution of power, a study of a Southern city of 500,000 reports that the principal policy-makers in this city number forty, and of this number more than half are identified with big business.[5]

The United States is said to be an "open-class" society, in which it is not uncommon for individuals to move up or down the social ladder. In every society there is some social mobility. Where there is little social mobility in a society, the classes are said to be "closed"; and if social role and status are quite rigidly fixed by heredity, the society is said to have a caste system. England, with its traditions of aristocracy, is often given as an example of a society with closed classes; and India as a caste society, with its priestly Brahman, military Kshatriya, mercantile Vaisya, and artisan or laboring Sudra, as well as the group which is entirely apart, the Outcastes.

The question as to how much social mobility there is in a society is an important one. It has long been assumed that the rates of mobility in the United States are higher than in England, but recent studies fail to establish this.[6] However, in the United States in recent decades there has been a decrease in the percentage of unskilled workers and an increase in white-collar workers, largely because of advancing technology. Also, since 1929 there has been less inequality in income. Traditionally classes have developed distinguishing characteristics, such as special titles, dress, speech, and manners. The influences moderating the effects of class in the United States in relatively recent times are the high rate of physical mobility, mass production, and free universal education. Modern communication inventions also tend to break down the barriers between groups.

The concept of social class, developed by social philosophers and social scientists since Aristotle, was given great vitality by Karl Marx, who emphasized the idea of a class struggle between the haves (those who own the means of production) and the have-nots. Marx taught that all history is a struggle for power, economic and political. He saw the emergence of the middle class but thought that it would disappear. The rich would get

[4] August B. Hollingshead, *Elmtown's Youth: The Impact of Social Classes on Adolescents* (New York: John Wiley & Sons, Inc., 1949).
[5] Floyd Hunter, *Community Power Structure* (Chapel Hill, N.C.: University of North Carolina Press, 1953).
[6] Seymour Martin Lipset, *Political Man: The Social Bases of Politics* (Garden City, N.Y.: Doubleday & Company, Inc., 1960).

richer and the poor poorer until the power of the ruling class (i.e., the bourgeoisie) was threatened by the oppressed class (i.e., the proletariat), as in the French, Russian, and Chinese revolutions. Marx erred in his conclusions about the middle class, which in the West is becoming the dominant class. He erred also in his teaching that the law of all social life is class struggle. As a rule the classes in a society live together in a state of accommodation, not conflict. Socially inferior classes accept their subordinate position without serious protest. Class conflict is the exception, not the rule. If this were not so, it would be difficult to achieve a stable society.[7]

This does not mean that there are not grave conflicts of interest in modern societies. Indeed, a student who would acquire a realistic understanding of modern society would do well to note the varied interests that exist and the competition among them for economic and political power. Even in the Soviet Union, which boasts of being a classless society, certain groups are favored and rewarded differentially. University professors in Russia, especially those in engineering and the natural sciences, receive salaries significantly higher than their counterparts in the United States, plus perquisites like a country home, a car, and a chauffeur. On the other hand, doctors in the Soviet Union are relatively underprivileged compared with doctors in the United States. The reason Soviet professors receive such high salaries is that the Russian leaders attach the highest priority to scientific innovation. As to the doctors in Russia, it is said that perhaps 75 per cent of them are women. When any good, like money or political power, is in short supply, competition results, and some get more of what there is to get, although a society can adapt rules of the game to minimize these differences. Competition and conflict, if not excessive, define issues and fix roles and position.

PERSONALITY

The social psychologist is interested in how human beings learn and how their personalities are shaped. The three principal determinants of personality are the constitutional, the social, and the cultural factors. By constitutional factors we mean the biological causes, centering in the genes as they mature in a variable environment. One such constitutional factor, for example, is intelligence, which is both a part of personality and an influence upon other facets of personality, such as habits and attitudes. The social factor has to do with one's relations to other people, and it has to do specifically with the *nature* of these other people—whether they are more or less intelligent, kind, articulate, and so on. The kind of associates one has, especially during the early, formative years of one's life, has an important bearing on the kind

[7] Nothing is more important for the serious student of society that to know how to distinguish between speculative theory and scientific theory. Scientific theory consists of generalizations supported by facts. Marx, like many another "theorist" or social philosopher, is famous, but his theory of class struggle is false.

of personality one develops. Kimball Young, sociologist at Northwestern University, has called these influences "personal-social," to differentiate them from the third set of influences, the cultural. The latter are the codified behavior patterns, the customs and ideas of how to do things which exist in the society and constitute the social tradition to which the growing individual is exposed.

The culture offers the individual a choice among a limited number of roles. Thus he chooses an occupation, influenced both by constitutional factors, including intelligence, and by the opinions of his associates: his parents, his friends, and his teachers. Once he enters into an occupation, whether he has actively chosen it or whether it has been to some extent chosen for him, he will follow it with an individual degree of success or efficiency. There may be tension between the demands of the role and one's interest or skill in it. Edward, Prince of Wales, became King of England but abdicated the throne in order to be free to marry the woman he loved, Wallis Simpson. He had been prevented from marrying her because she was a commoner and a divorcee. Although the role conflict, between occupation and marriage, is apparent, there are some who wonder whether he was temperamentally suited to be King. There are many individuals playing roles in society for which they are not suited, either because of some constitutional factor or because of attitudes derived from inter-personal experience. Especially important in the latter category are self-images.

THE IDEA OF SELF

There is of course nothing more important for the individual than his self-concept; and it is useful to inquire how the idea of the self develops. It develops in relation to other persons, and especially the opinions of others about oneself. The very young child learns to care about others because his needs are satisfied by others. These others surround the child, listen to him, observe him, and judge him. Their instruments are praise and blame. Also, the child learns the opinions of others by role-taking. In the process, the self becomes an object to itself—which we identify as self-consciousness. George Herbert Mead (1863–1931) observed that the role-playing of children passes through three progressive stages: the first, consisting of meaningless imitative acts, about the second year of life, as when a child imitates his father in "reading" a magazine, albeit the magazine is held upside down; the second stage, the play stage, around the third year, exemplified by playing store and taking successively the roles of buyer and seller; the third stage, when the child becomes a member of a team, as in baseball, and learns to relate his role to the roles of all the other players simultaneously, in the interests of efficiency. He learns to be a good member of the team, which means ideally that he anticipates in his imagination the roles of all the other players and is prepared to make necessary adjustments to any contingency that may occur. He learns also to abide by the rules of the game. Learning the rules is a step toward what Mead calls playing the role of "the generalized other." The team with its rules is a miniature society. The whole community is a "generalized other" with which individuals become identified, in varying degrees. If the identification is successful, the values of the community become the values of the individual. He internalizes them or incorporates them into his neural structure.

Along with Mead, Charles Horton Cooley observed that the adjustments one makes to the expectations of others are a highly important key to one's personality. Cooley used the phrase "the looking-glass self" to emphasize the point that one's conception of self is a reflection of the opinions of others about oneself. More precisely, it is an evaluation of those opinions. In reality one lives in one's imagination. Impressions are all we go by. We have impressions of the impressions we make on others, and impressions of the judgments others pass on our actions. Usually our impressions have some substantial basis in fact, such as the overt behavior of others toward us and the agreement between our impressions and those of friends and acquaintances, but sometimes the impressions we hold of the opinions of others are erroneous. What matters, of course, is the conviction of the individual as to how things are, his "definition of the situation." Whatever seems real to a person, whether it is in fact real or not, is real in its consequences.

Because the opinions of others mean so much to us, we go through life, says Cooley, adjusting to the expectations of others. That is why we behave differently in different situations. We are ashamed to seem cowardly in the presence of a brave man, stupid in the company of a bright man, and vulgar before a holy man. We are like chameleons, taking on the protective coloring of our environment, provided the persons with whom we associate are those whose judgment we value or whose favor we court.

THE SIGNIFICANT OTHERS

To each of us, some judges are more significant than others. We value especially the opinions of those with whom we have a relationship of intimacy and affection, and those who hold power over us. This means in most cases that in our early childhood it is our parents who are our most significant others; and, usually, mothers even more than fathers.

An individual at any given time is a member of a number of groups. For personality, what matters most is not one's membership groups but one's *reference groups,* the groups from which one takes one's values. Edwin Sutherland (1883–1950), the criminologist, advanced the theory that an important cause of crime lies in what he called differential association. According to this theory, individuals become criminals by associating with criminals and appropriating their values. There is some evidence to support this theory, such as the fact that in some gangs with a criminal culture the youth learns how to commit crimes in much the same way as children in school learn how to read. But the theory is deficient, because it does not tell us why some children who associate with criminals do not commit crimes. The answer is that criminals are not for them a reference group. It is preferential, not differential, association that matters most, the individuals with whom one would like to associate because one admires their values, whether in fact one associates with them or not.

Some children have been observed who lack reference groups completely. These are children who in early life were rejected by their parents, and who in turn rejected their parents. They are children who trust nobody. Such children have been aptly described by a psychiatrist who risked even repeated physical attacks upon his person before he could, by unfailing kindness and devotion to their interests, convince them of his true concern.[8]

It is an interesting question: Whose opinion do you value most? There are some, like the children just described, who value no one's opinion. There are others so narrowly conditioned that they value only the opinions of a single person, or perhaps of a few persons. Such a conditioning may be the result of exceptional identification of a child with, say, his father, who has an unusually strong and independent personality. In later life such a child may be quite original and daring, indifferent to the opinions of the crowd. Most persons are broadly conditioned and highly responsive to public opinion.

REFERENCE GROUPS AND RELATIVE DEPRIVATION

Reference groups not only set the standard for our values; they also set the standard for some of our satisfactions or dissatisfactions. For example, the Negroes in the United States feel deprived because they do not have equality of opportunity for education. The reference group is the white population. It does not much matter to the Negroes that their chances of going to college in the United States are greater than those of most of the white population of England. The English are not a reference group for American Negroes on this point. However, this illustration is somewhat deficient, because there is some absolute deprivation among Negroes, even those with education. A better example is the feeling of college professors that their salaries are too low. There is seldom any actual want or deprivation. The comparison is with the salaries in business, or even the salaries of, say, railroad engineers. Professors in state university X compare their salaries with those in state university Y and if they are different one of the two groups will feel deprived.

As the standard of living rises in the United States, absolute deprivation, especially in food, clothing, and shelter, is fast disappearing. Ours has been called an "affluent society,"[9] the first large society ever to have conquered the problem of poverty of the masses.

[8] Fritz Redl and David Wineman, *Children Who Hate* (Glencoe, Ill.: The Free Press, 1951).
[9] John Kenneth Galbraith, *The Affluent Society* (Boston: Houghton Mifflin Company, 1958).

Relative economic deprivation is also on the decline as the leveling tendencies in the American economy continue. But problems of relative psychological deprivation (envy) are on the increase, as improved transportation and communication facilities bring people into closer contact with one another and increase their awareness of variations in privileges and rewards.

LEARNING THEORY

The foregoing discussion has been concerned with the role of others in the learning process. In this connection it is desirable to consider also the learning process itself.

Although much attention has been given by social psychologists to the learning process, it is still not fully understood. One of the more useful explanations of how we learn is that advanced in the so-called *learning theory*. This theory holds that the essential factors involved in learning are four: a drive, a cue, a response, and a reward. The motivation for behavior is a drive of some kind, either organic like hunger or psychological like ambition. In an experiment in which chimpanzees learned to work a food-dispensing machine, the situation was as follows: The chimpanzees were hungry. They were in an experimental laboratory equipped with food-dispensing machines and chips of various shapes and colors, only some of which would work. The machines and the chips constituted the cues or stimuli. The response was to insert a chip into the machine. If the right kind of chip was used, the chimpanzee was rewarded with food. At first the chimpanzee might hit on the right chip by chance, but repeated treats would bring more successes. "The law of effect," or the reinforcement principle, came into play: Repeated rewards for certain responses to stimuli establish those responses. The reverse law is the law of extinction: If responses which formerly brought desired rewards fail over a period of time to elicit the rewards, the responses are abandoned.

Without hunger, either organic or social-psychological, there is little or no learning. This is the explanation for the "principle of satiation." A glutted rat will not run a maze. Does this principle provide a clue to the serious problems besetting Sweden, described as an egalitarian paradise where a fully developed welfare state looks after the people from cradle to grave? Yet Sweden is reported to have one of the highest suicide rates of any modern nation. Does a high degree of security in the welfare state deprive the individual of initiative and the need to struggle?

The opposite of satiation is deprivation, the more or less chronic denial of the satisfaction of one's drives. When this occurs, according to the principle of deprivation, the individual thinks of little else. There is a story of soldiers on a special assignment stationed for a long period of time away from normal community life. Some of these soldiers walked fifteen miles to a railroad juncture to see a passing train on the chance that there would be a woman aboard. There was no conversation, just the sight of a woman looking out the train window. This behavior occurred despite the fact that there are outlets for the sexual drive other than heterosexual ones, outlets which may be used when the heterosexual outlets are blocked. (When satisfaction of both sex and hunger are effectively denied for long periods, sex drops out of consciousness altogether and thoughts and dreams of food become uppermost, according to evidence supplied by refugees from Nazi concentration camps.)

There are a number of theories of learning besides "learning theory," although the latter is probably the most general and most thoroughly substantiated. It represents the psychological wing of social psychology, and is an offshoot of the earlier theory of conditioning. The theory of symbolic interaction, which represents the sociological wing of social psychology, focuses mainly on how one acquires (learns) the idea of self as an abstract entity, stressing the importance of the acquisition of language and its influence on the individual, as in the development of conscience.

PSYCHOANALYTIC THEORY

Another significant theory with which all students of personality should be familiar is psychoanalytic theory, also concerned with how we learn; in this case, how we learn to feel about ourselves and others. Psychoanalytic theory deals primarily with emotional development, with efforts to organize the affective aspects of self and to handle instinctual urges. Psychoanalytic theory, once popular in university circles, is now almost unmentionable in certain quarters because the attempts to test psychoanalytic concepts by experimental and other empirical methods have not been rewarding. Without verified data, there is of course no science. But the phenomena with which psychoanalytic theory deals may be too complex and subtle for testing by present scientific approaches. The meaning of dreams may be obscure but the reality of dreams is clear. Even psychologists dream.

One of the more significant areas of psychoanalytic theory is the realm of the unconscious, into which it is said instinctual sexual impulses are often repressed by the constraints of culture. What is repressed often finds expression in devious ways, as in dreams and slips of the tongue. The idea advanced by Freud that there is a hidden part of personality, like the submerged part of an iceberg, of which the individual is generally unaware but which exerts profound influence on behavior, was—when it was first propounded—a revolutionary idea.

CULTURE AND PERSONALITY

Freud emphasized primarily the *id,* that is, the instinctual or biological determinants of behavior. Although his idea of repression acknowledged the influence of culture, Freud did not sufficiently understand or recognize the role of culture. He did not, for instance, allow sufficiently for the fact of cultural variability in his theory of the Oedipus complex. This theory may be appropriate to modern Western society, but it is by no means applicable to all societies. Neo-Freudians pay more attention to differences in cultural patterns.

A more pronounced emphasis on the cultural determinants of personality is provided by the so-called "culture-and-personality" viewpoint, represented mainly by cultural anthropologists, sometimes in collaboration with psychiatrists.

One problem in this area is to account for differences in group personality, as between societies. These can be shown to be entirely of cultural origin. Race is not a factor, since members of different races living in the same society and having the same opportunities behave alike, whereas members of the same race living in different cultures behave differently.

The differences in personality between societies or nations are differences in degree of common personality traits rather than the possession of mutually exclusive traits. It is not correct to say that Frenchmen are excitable and Englishmen phlegmatic, but it is correct to say that Frenchmen are more excitable than Englishmen. This is an average picture, with much overlap, and some Britons are, of course, more excitable than some Frenchmen. In the same way we can say the Japanese stress formal courtesy more than do most other nations, the Pueblo Indians were more peaceful than the Plains Indians, and so on. These differences in traits of personality, although only differences in degree, are often of considerable practical importance, both for intra-group and for inter-group relations.

The preceding paragraph has dealt with the problem of differences in personality in different cultures. Within any given society, differences in personality are to be accounted for in terms of variations in constitutional factors, inter-personal relations, and sub-cultural patterns, and the inter-relationship of all three. Constitutional factors may have a direct effect on personality, as in the case of degree of intelligence and activity of the endocrine glands. The constitutional factors may also have an indirect effect on personality, as when some biological trait such as red hair is selected by the group for special attention, or a trait like tall stature is selected for special approval in men and disapproval in women. As to inter-personal relations, there are variations, too, many of a fortuitous nature, since no one selects his parents or has much to say about how many brothers and sisters he has. Some parents are more nervous than others, and nervous parents tend to produce nervous children if there is much association between them when the children are small. Nervousness is of course only one influential trait, and there are a great many others. Finally, there are differences in culture even within a single society, especially a complex society like the United States. The type of codified behavior patterns one is exposed to depends on the ethnic group and the religion to which one belongs, the region, and the occupation of one's parents, among other things.

The foregoing issues are important, but even more important is the question whether some cultures create more strain than others. Is there more social-psychological maladjustment in some societies than in others? We have already referred to the fact that the suicide rate in Sweden is relatively high. The natives of Formosa have a very low incidence of mental disorders. How account for such variations? The problem is complex, but one wing of the "culture-and-personality" school looks to the patterns of infant care prevailing in a culture for clues as to the nature of the basic personality pattern. Are infants loved or neglected? And if they are cared for, is the care permissive or rigid? According to whether it is the one or the other, the child is thought to develop a strong or a weak ego. In the Marquesas Islands, and, again, among the Alorese, mothers are reported as rejecting their infants, who grow up nervous and insecure. Among primitive peoples generally the situation is far different. Usually the children are warmly loved and even indulged. The infants are fed whenever they are hungry and pacified when they cry, and they sleep when they will, not by schedule.

The environmental stress leading to personality disorders is sought, then, in the experiences of infancy and early childhood, especially in seclusive tendencies and feelings of inferiority resulting from lack of affection. Childhood is a relatively sheltered time, and often early strains do not lead to breakdown until tested by the stress of adulthood or near-adulthood, with its conflict of personal desires and social standards, its confused moral codes, and its competitive struggles.

The foregoing constitutes a review of some of the most important findings and issues of the three social sciences, anthropology, sociology, and social psychology, as the writer conceives them. In conclusion, one further thought. At the high school level one hears the phrase "social studies," whereas at the college level there is more reference to the social sciences and "social studies" is less often heard. Are anthropology, sociology, and social psychology studies or sciences? The anthropologists, sociologists, and social psychologists who are engaged in research want to make their disciplines as respectable as the physical sciences by using the same means, namely scientific method, exact and quantitative. In the view of many of these researchers, philosophy, ethics, values, and means and ends of social action have no legitimate place in the social sciences, since they cannot be supported by incontrovertible evidence.

There are also those who think the completely scientific position is unrealistic and even dangerous. Precision in knowledge, they say, is undoubtedly a laudable objective; but if precision is the sole criterion, then we shall often be limited to dealing only with irrelevant and trifling matters, because scientific knowledge is lacking or incomplete on many basic problems. Meantime, many urgent social problems press for solution. Intelligent students of society cannot afford to abdicate their responsibility as citizens and leave decisions entirely to those who have power but who may be less well-informed. We must often make decisions on the basis of incomplete, imperfect knowledge, striving all the while to improve our knowledge of society. We must recognize, too, that scientific knowledge about man is more difficult to come by than knowledge about the atom. Einstein was once asked why progress in physics was greater than in sociology. "That is easy," said Einstein. "Society is more complex."

There is a greater investment of money and effort in research in natural science than in social science. If as much money and support were given to the socal sciences the results would be impressive. In terms of priority, our society has yet to be persuaded that Alexander Pope is right, that "the proper study of mankind is man."

CHAPTER 24 **The Behavioral**
Sciences: Examples

Chapter 11 described the three methods commonly used by behavioral scientists: the experiment, the survey, and the case study. All three of these methods can be used and are being used in the secondary schools. This volume contains examples of each method in use. Chapter 26, for example, illustrates an experiment in geography. Chapter 12 contains an example of the use of a survey. By far the most common method of the behavioral scientist used in the schools, however, is the case study.

Practical considerations make both the experiment and the survey difficult to use in the schools. Sophisticated experiments require a knowledge of mathematics beyond the grasp of many high school students. Few schools have laboratories in which students can run animals under controlled conditions as they can do in many college psychology departments. Students can be given the observations of a behavioral scientist written in simple English and asked to work with the data provided, however. This practice is sure to spread as the new curricula are published.

Conducting surveys is also awkward. Many schools frown on the practice of requiring students to interview citizens in their homes or on the street as part of a survey. In a number of schools students have drawn up survey instruments and administered them to groups within the school itself. This practice has great promise. If it proves to be impractical, students can be provided with data from an actual survey to work with.

By far the largest amount of available data for use in high school classes comes from case studies. Literally thousands of articles have been written by behavioral scientists to describe cases they have investigated. These articles can be used in almost any social studies course. They are a particularly valuable source of subject data and of practical lessons in scientific methodology.

The reading in this chapter consists of such a study. In its present form it is taken from a tenth-grade unit on apartheid in the Republic of South Africa developed at the Curriculum Development Center at Carnegie Institute of Technology. Your instructor may also ask you to review the survey in Chapter 12 or to look ahead to the experiment in Chapter 26. As you read, think about the following questions:

1) Why divide the article into two parts? How could the two parts be incorporated into a unit on South Africa?
2) Why focus the attention of the students on method in one of the parts of this reading and on subject in the other part?
3) What are the dangers of using case studies? the advantages?

Reading XII: Finding Out about Bantu Life in a South African City

Curriculum Development Center, Carnegie Institute of Technology

Thousands of Bantu tribesmen have been forced to make the transition from pastoral or agricultural life to urban conditions. This transition has affected every aspect of their lives. In cities they live in strange houses crowded together under conditions unknown in their native kralls. Instead of tending cattle the men work in the cities and the women, no longer farming or caring for the home, sell illegal beer, work as servants, take in washing, or sometimes become prostitutes. Families are disrupted because the women are outside the home. A large number of children are sent by their parents to be reared in the country; the remainder often run out of control through the crowded courtyards. In these conditions, systems of values, the customary sanctions that kept order, and even the religious beliefs of the Africans tend to change. Imagine how difficult it would be to grow up in such a society, in which nothing is safe or sacred and where ancient traditions no longer explain the meaning of life.

In order to find out about the effects of moving from a traditional to a modern society, anthropologists have studied and lived among the Bantu in their city homes. They have written accounts of their study, which include not only their conclusions but also the methods they used to gather evidence and to make inferences from it. These records give us valuable insights into the mode of inquiry of anthropology. Readings XII and XIII come from one of these reports written by Dr. Ellen Hellmann. As you read XII, concentrate on the method of inquiry that is being used. Think about the following questions.

1) What techniques of gathering information did Dr. Hellmann employ? Do you think the information she received was reliable? Could she trust her informants? Why did she describe her research techniques to her readers?
2) How did Dr. Hellmann report her information? Look at paragraphs 7 through 10. Then read the last paragraph in Reading XIII. How do the

two passages differ from each other? How did Dr. Hellmann build her interpretation?

3) Why was the material culture of the West adopted so readily by the residents of the slum yard? For what social purposes are some material objects used? Did some natives buy pianos for the same reasons that some Americans buy expensive new automobiles?

INVESTIGATING CONDITIONS AMONG THE BANTU IN JOHANNESBURG*

Ellen Hellmann

[The] growing inclination of the African to settle his wife and children in the urban center where he earns his livelihood indicates a tendency on his part to divorce himself from his rural bonds and to regard the town as his permanent home and not as the place of his solely temporary employment. The children of these families will, in all likelihood, eventually form a permanent and stable urban population, entirely dissociated from a rural background. Many of them—the potential citizens of a town—have been reared in a slum yard. Such yards represent for many Africans their first, and perhaps only, experience of a home.

Their impressions of Johannesburg, should they return to the Reserves, will be colored by this environment. Should they remain permanently in Johannesburg, even though they change their residence, the influence of their earlier environment must inevitably remain with them. In addition to forming the social setting for the Africans there resident, these yards, the centers of the illicit beer-brewing trade, are also a favored meeting resort for a great number of other Africans during their leisure hours. . . .

Rooiyard is typical of many such yards which exist all over those suburbs of Johannesburg where Africans are still permitted to reside. During the course of writing this article, Rooiyard was condemned by the local authorities as insanitary, a demolition order was granted, and the Africans were served with notices of eviction. Rooiyard is therefore no longer in existence. But, except for a difference in locality and slight variations in layout and construction, a description of Rooiyard, its manners and customs, is equally applicable to any other similar yard in Johannesburg, and for this reason I propose to continue using the present tense in my description of it.

Rooiyard, in New Doornfontein, Johannesburg, was chosen as a subject for investigation because it appeared to be typical of yards in general in Johannes-

* Reprinted and abridged from Ellen Hellmann, "Native Life in a Johannesburg Slum Yard," *Africa,* Vol. VIII, No. 1, 1935, 34–62. London: International African Institute.

burg and especially of yards in New Doornfontein, which is a suburb especially favored by the Africans owing to its central situation. Rooiyard has no special distinguishing marks and it bears a reputation neither more nor less unenviable than other yards which I visited during the course of several tours. . . .

The material for this report was gathered during a period of one year's investigation. I commenced working in Rooiyard in March 1933 and continued till April 1, 1934. During December, January, and February I discontinued daily visits to Rooiyard, but for the rest of the time I spent practically every morning, with the exception of Sunday mornings, in Rooiyard. At the commencement of my investigation I spent both mornings and afternoons there, but soon confined my work, in the main, to the mornings. I found the mornings best because then the women were generally in or about their rooms. In addition, there are far fewer beer customers in the mornings and, as was proved to me time and again, my presence in a room, while beer was being sold, was not welcome. My visits to Rooiyard over the week end were infrequent, and I only paid one night visit there. Initially I was intimidated by the earnest warnings of the police and the health inspectors against visiting Rooiyard during these hours of most active beer-selling. Although it would be an exaggeration to speak of danger—actual or potential—to the investigator in Rooiyard at night or over week ends, the drunken disorder of the yard and the definite hostility to my presence at these times did discourage me. At night, especially, in the gloomy alleyways in which the swaying and stumbling forms of drunken Africans were dimly discernible, I felt compelled to agree that Rooiyard was no place for the field worker.

The material I have been able to collect is by no means as complete as I would have wished it to be, as the difficulties which I encountered in endeavoring to build up a relationship of confidence with my informants were considerable. First and foremost comes the fact that the population of Rooiyard is actually a criminal class. This is an unavoidable result of the beer-brewing activities which, though illegal, are a necessary condition of their economic survival. This continuous conflict with the authorities has made the Africans in the yard, especially the women who are responsible for the making and selling of beer, extremely suspicious of all Europeans. I expended considerable pains and no little eloquence in my attempts to explain the nature of my work. Some women were, after a while, inclined to regard my presence as inoffensive or even to regard me as a friend, but, apart from the open hostility which I was in some cases unable to overcome, the general attitude was one of amused indifference. The men, perhaps owing to their more intimate contact with Europeans during the course of their work, were less hostile, but I did not have occasion to interview them to any considerable extent as they were usually absent from the yard. The shifting nature of the Rooiyard populace was also a hindrance. Several times I succeeded in gaining the confidence of an informant only to find that she was about to leave the yard owing to arrears of rent, a desire to return home, or for the purpose of taking up employment. Often, too, after having trained an informant to keep a daily budget of expenditure— a valuable index of confidence—I found that the more hostile elements in the yard had been at pains to warn my informant of the dire results which must inevitably follow such a reckless committal to paper of her vital statistics. The blame for the increased frequency and thoroughness of police beer-raids in Rooiyard during the last few months was also attributed to me. The language medium presented no difficulty as most of the Africans spoke English or Afrikaans with some measure of fluency.

Rooiyard consists of 107 rooms and covers an area of five stands with a total extent of 1,183 square yards. As a result of the large number of rooms which are built on this confined space, a state of extreme congestion prevails. The yard is roughly triangular in shape. Fifty-seven rooms are built on the boundary and face the yard and 15 rooms, 7 on one side and 8 on the other side of the triangle, face the street. In the center of the yard there is a double line of 35 rooms, built back-to-back and facing the rooms which skirt the yard, thus dividing the yard into two sections with rooms on either side and alleyways, about 15 feet to 20 feet in width, in the center. The 15 outer rooms and 14 of the inner rooms are built of brick and have cement floors, the remainder of the rooms being rickety constructions of old corrugated iron and thin wooden planks. The brick rooms vary in size from 10 feet by 11 feet to 11 feet by 12 feet. The partitioning walls, abut 10 feet in height, do not reach the roof, which at its apex is about 15 feet high. The other rooms vary in size from 8 feet by 11 feet to 11 feet square, with a height of from 8 to 10 feet. The flooring boards are, in the majority of these 78 rooms, rotten. Some rooms have no flooring at all and the bare earth forms the floor. The doors of the rooms are badly fitted and have no proper locks, being fastened from the outside by a padlock and from the inside by a bent nail or rough contraption of wire. Each room is fitted with two windows, but as one window often gives access to an adjoining room, it is usually covered with a plate of tin. Cross ventilation is not possible in the 64 rooms which are built back-to-back. In summer the rooms are unbearably hot and in winter the cold winds which enter through the gaps and holes in the walls necessitate the constant burning of large coal-braziers, introducing an element of danger and rendering the atmosphere in the rooms extremely unhealthy. Very few of the roofs are rainproof, window-panes are often missing, and the level of the floor is in a number of rooms below the level of the yard. In wet weather the rain water flows into the rooms, carrying with it the debris from the yard, and the discomfort of the occupants under these miserable conditions requires very little emphasis. The yard has a narrow entrance. Flanking the entrance inside the yard stand two cement garbage bins which serve the whole yard. The occupants are served by 6 latrines, three for men and three for women, but they are usually in such a bad state of repair and so neglected that the children shun them, as is amply testified by the condition of the alleyways inside the yard and of the pavements surrounding it. There is a "washing room" adjoining the lavatories, consisting of 4 corrugated iron walls with a cement floor and containing two water-taps, one or the other of which is never in working order. This single tap serves all the residents of the yard, and owing to the inevitable congestion a long queue of women waiting to fill their paraffin-tins with water for domestic purposes is a common sight.

The alleyways in the yard and the pavement on to which face the outer rooms are cluttered with an important part of the essential possessions of the Rooiyard Africans. Here stand the motley tins, ranging from one-gallon oil tins to large petrol drums, which are used for the preparation and storage of beer. The cooking-braziers are placed outside the rooms as the smallness of the rooms, which have to serve the needs of the whole family, does not permit of cooking operations being performed inside. Large packing-cases used for fire-wood occupy much of the available space outside each room. The repeated requests of the Health Inspector that the yard be cemented have remained unheeded, and after rains it is like a quagmire. In dry weather it is usually littered with an assortment of refuse and debris. Six Sotho women have each constructed a *lapa* (courtyard) of clay and cow-dung in front of their rooms, and these little courtyards form oases of cleanliness and order in the midst of the general litter of the yard. The Africans know that they should throw all refuse into the cement bins at the entrance of the yard. But when they see the refuse bins constantly overflowing and only desultory efforts made to keep the yard clean, it is small wonder that they themselves display no vital interest. They are fully aware of the insecurity of their tenure in Rooiyard and have not come to regard the place as their "home." It is merely, owing to the force of circumstances, their temporary refuge. Candles provide the sole means of illumination. At night it is difficult to conceive that Rooiyard, dark and eerie, and lit only by the fitful gleam of candles and the glowing coals in the bra-ziers, is situated in the midst of a progressive city.

The interiors of the greater number of the rooms present a striking contrast to the unsavory disorderliness of the yard. Although the ceilings are often covered with cobwebs, the floors are well scrubbed and the belongings of the family tidily arranged. That this cleanliness is achieved only by the tireless expenditure of energy and labor is conclusively proved by the constant pre-occupation of the Rooiyard woman with her washing, scrubbing, polishing, and dusting. It is no mean feat on the part of the African woman to keep the small and congested abode of her family in such good order, for the Rooiyard environment does not offer any stimulus towards greater effort.

The fittings of the rooms reveal the eagerness with which the material cul-ture of Western civilization is being adopted. Every stage of transition is exemplified in the rooms of Rooiyard, from the paucity of furniture of the new arrival from the kraal to the comparative opulence of the fittings of the African who has had several years of urban residence. There are only three rooms which do not boast a bed—invariably the first purchase—and the three families in these rooms are all recent immigrants from rural areas. All the remaining rooms in Rooiyard are furnished with at least one bed, which is always raised on bricks so that the space under the bed may be utilized for the storage of the boxes and trunks containing the possessions of the family. Curtains, usually of cheap chintz, are always hung in front of the bed so that the parents, who occupy the bed, may be ensured some measure of privacy from the prying eyes of their children, who sleep on the floor. Rough, backless benches for the accommodation of beer customers are necessary accessories to every household. The possession of furniture is one of the few criteria of social status in Rooiyard, and the gradual entry of a family into the realms of prosperity synchronizes with its gradual acquisition of new articles of furniture. When a family moves to another room in town or goes home to the country, the furniture, a visible proof of progress, is taken with it.

One of the best furnished rooms contains a bed costing £1, a sideboard costing £13 10s. 0d., a table and four chairs costing £9, and a gramophone costing £8 15s. 0d. The walls are tastefully papered with wallpaper instead of being plastered with old newspaper posters as is commonly the case. Linoleum, a much coveted article in Rooiyard, covers the floor. The voluminous curtains in front of the bed and the windows are of silk. Numerous framed pictures, chiefly of film stars, adorn the walls. A rough wooden table accommodates the paraffin cooker and domestic utensils. This table and the inevitable benches are the only articles of native manufacture in the room.

Not many rooms are as completely furnished as this one, some Africans using packing-cases as substitutes for the articles cited above. In other rooms a couch serves the purpose of chairs. One woman is the proud possessor of a second-hand organ which is, however, more valuable as an economic than a cultural asset, as its melodious strains serve to attract beer-customers to this room. Two families have purchased pianos, but as the owners are dependent on casual friends to play them, they are manifestly concessions to a desire for enhancing personal prestige and do not fulfil any practical function.

All these purchases are made possible by the hire-purchase system. The average wage of the Rooiyard man is 18s. 1d. per week. The wife supplements this income mainly through the sale of beer, but nevertheless cash purchases remain an impossibility for practically all Africans. Hence most purchases are made "by time," as is the current expression in Rooiyard. Payments are usually effected at the rate of £1 per month, and it is unusual for Africans to commit themselves to payments for more than one article at a time.

There is very little evidence of the survival of Bantu material culture in Rooiyard. With the exception of a few recently arrived Shangaan women who still wear their tribal costume, consisting of voluminous double-pleated skirts of print lavishly adorned with beads, clothing and personal adornments are predominantly Western. The young girls prefer lipstick and powder to the facial tattooed lines of the older women. Even the time-honored *imbeleko* is giving way to the blanket. Saucepans, pots and pans, and, above all, the ubiquitous tins have ousted domestic utensils of native manufacture. The facilities for the purchase of ready-prepared mealie meal and ready-stamped mealies have rendered the wooden pestle and mortar and winnowing basket nearly obsolete. Some few women still possess these articles and occasionally use them for the more economical preparation of food for a "party." That this absorption of European material culture is not a transient and fluctuating, but a cumulative and permanent process, is not to be doubted. African handicrafts are dying out in the country. In urban areas the art is considered superfluous. The children do not become acquainted with the utensils of native manufacture, nor would they know how to handle them. The persistent endeavors of the African to absorb European material culture are limited only by his poverty. He aspires to possess the amenities which the invading culture has to offer him and a great part of his labor is conditioned by this desire. It is only his utter poverty that restricts and hinders him and gives rise to the malapropisms of culture contact as exemplified by the picture of half-naked children huddling together for warmth under a piano. At present the African is eagerly grasping whatever lies within his economic reach, but the next step will be the sifting of essential from nonessential.

Reading XIII: Life in a Johannesburg Slum Yard

Curriculum Development Center, Carnegie Institute of Technology

Reading XII concerned methods of investigating life among the Bantu living in a Johannesburg slum yard. Reading XIII concerns life in the yard and has somewhat less emphasis upon the method of investigation and upon the way in which data are reported. Instead it details the daily round of life in the yard and contains the conclusions, that the author drew as the end product of her investigation.

Readings IX and X both described life among the Bantu in their native villages. There tradition set the pattern of living. Separated into small villages and dependent upon herds and agriculture for their living, the Bantu lived out their lives much as their ancestors had except that intertribal wars no longer played a vital role in the society. But most of the remainder of the life of the natives had been unaffected by contact with the West. Only in mining towns and manufacturing cities had the Bantu been forced to adapt to the ways of an alien culture. As the pastoral economy that sustained their lives fades away before population growth and the encroachments of the whites on the best lands, more and more of the natives will be forced into towns and cities.

What will happen to them there? Are they equipped with the skills and the desire to adjust to a modern society? The social structure of a Johannesburg slum yard gives us evidence about these questions. They are questions vital to the future of the Republic of South Africa. If natives can adjust to modern life in one generation, then the problem of integrating them with a white society will be far less difficult than if several generations are required. If the customs of native and white are similar enough that the two groups can live comfortably side by side, then apartheid may not seem so essential to the Afrikaners. The problems of adjustment may give us some insights into the reasons why the Boers want to keep the Africans in their own preserves. As you read, think about the following questions.

1) What happened to tribal loyalites and distinct tribal ways in the yard? why?
2) Why did women have to work? Why is the illegal beer business so popular? why beer rather than some other beverage or food?
3) What happened to the family solidarity of yard dwellers?
4) Why does fine or imprisonment bear little stigma for these Africans?
5) How have some yard residents tried to adapt tribal customs to slum life?
6) Why is neither Christianity nor the old tribal religion satisfactory to residents of the yard? How is the attitude to religion related to the attitude to magic?
7) How might a Boer use the evidence from this article to defend apartheid?

THE BANTU AND THE CITY SLUM*

Ellen Hellmann

The permanent population of Rooiyard at the beginning of September 1933 consisted of 235 adults and 141 children. These 376 inhabitants were accommodated in 105 rooms, and of the two remaining rooms one was used as a tailoring shop and the other as a church. The average number of occupants per residential room was 3.58. But this low average cannot be accepted at face value, as there is a large shifting population in Rooiyard which cannot be assessed and which consists of relatives and friends who have come to seek refuge while unemployed or to spend a holiday in the city of which they have heard so much. Apart from 11 Indians and 5 Cape Coloreds, the remainder of the population is of Bantu stock, practically every South African Bantu tribe being represented. Of the residents 5 per cent consist of natives of Rhodesia and there are, in addition, one Negro from America and one native of Nyasaland. Of the families 40 per cent are Sotho, 27 per cent are Nguni (including Zulu, Xhosa, Swazi, Fingo, and Ndebele) and 2 per cent are Shangaan. The remaining families are mixed, husband and wife belonging to different tribes. Despite the numerical preponderance of the Sothos, no one single tribe pre-

---

* Reprinted and abridged from Ellen Hellmann, "Native Life in a Johannesburg Slum Yard," *Africa*, Vol. VIII, No. 1, 1935, 34–62. London, International African Institute.

dominates. The Africans of Rooiyard, unlike tribal Africans, are characterized by a pronounced individualism. There are no bonds which integrate the different families in Rooiyard, nor is there any greater cohesion between families of the same tribe. Each family fends for itself and shows but a casual and passing interest in its neighbors.

Temporary friendships, born of common residence and proximity, do exist, but are more frequent between women of the same tribe. This is due more to the facility of intercourse consequent upon speaking the same language, than to a sense of tribal solidarity. But the contacts thus formed are so fleeting that a family will depart from Rooiyard without informing its erstwhile friends either of the day of its departure or of its new address. Possibly the competition which exists between the women as rival beer-sellers is a deterrent to the creation of a greater intimacy and the formation of more permanent bonds. As would be expected, Zulu and Sotho are the two main language media, although it would be a safe generalization to add that length of urban residence and consequent multiplicity of contacts is correlated with a mastery of more Bantu languages.

Although the majority of the inhabitants of Rooiyard have not severed their connection with the country—there is constant going to and fro to relatives in the country for puberty rites, funerals, and conclusions of mourning ceremonies—and hence cannot be considered as a permanently settled urban class, a census of the period of residence in Rooiyard of one hundred families indicates a relatively high degree of permanency of residence. The average period of residence, 17.94 months, points to a greater permanency than obtains among the poorer section of the white population. This high average is in reality maintained by 40 of these families which constitute the more permanently settled section with an average length of residence of 37.27 months. The other 60 families form a relatively shifting population with an average length of residence of 5.05 months. . . .

The Africans resident in Rooiyard are not blind to the unsatisfactory features of their environment. They complain bitterly of the high rents, which they rightly maintain are out of all proportion to value received. They revolt against the filth and congestion of their surroundings. They inveigh against the appalling state of the sanitary arrangements. But despite its obvious disadvantages, there is an incessant demand for accommodation in Rooiyard. As the number of yards in the central suburbs of Johannesburg decreases as a result of the closure policy of the Municipality, so the demand for rooms in the still existing yards increases. "Skokiaan Yard," the popular designation for yards of which Rooiyard is an example, indicates their nature. They are the centers, *par excellence,* for the brewing and selling of beer. Total prohibition has been enjoined upon the Africans of Johannesburg, but the illegality of beer-brewing only hampers but does not discourage the women brewers from continuing their occupation. It has been estimated that a minimum income of £6 per month is essential to the well-being of a family of 4 in Johannesburg.

In Rooiyard the standard of living varies enormously, some childless couples spending £8 per month while a family of 7 managed to subsist, during a month of great hardship and unemployment, on £2 2s. 11d. (excluding rent). The evidence from Rooiyard proves conclusively that the earnings of the male head of the family, averaging 18s. 1d. per week, cannot cover the unavoidable living expenses of a family. Hence it is imperative that the wife supplement her husband's income. Domestic service is becoming increasingly more difficult to obtain and often places the wife under the obligation of residing at her place of employment, consequently separating her almost completely from her family. Among one hundred women in Rooiyard, only 10 per cent earned £1 or more at a legitimate occupation. The remaining women were entirely dependent upon thir beer business to augment the family income. The central position of Rooiyard and its accessibility are great attractions to beer customers, and this fact is one of the two most important reasons for the reluctance of the Africans of the yard to move to the locations. "What about my business?" is the common counterquery to questions concerning their unwillingness to leave Rooiyard. Its proximity to the area where the majority of Africans are employed confers one other direct benefit. The Africans are saved considerable expenditure on conveyance. Orlando, the new location to which the Africans are as far as possible being transferred, is 10 miles from the center of Johannesburg. The train fare of 8s. 6d. per month is, according to European standards, not excessive. But it is a great drain on the meager African income. While the distance from the town militates against a beer business, it also increases the obstacles which a woman has to surmount in the pursuance of a legitimate occupation. Some women augment the family income by part-time domestic service. In the intervals they return to Rooiyard and attend to the needs of their children. Such employment would become impracticable were they to reside in a location. Other women take in washing for Europeans. The time and expense involved in fetching washing from Johannesburg, transporting it to the location and returning it again, make this form of occupation unprofitable. These reasons, founded upon economic necessity, actuate the distaste of the African for the locations and their determination to live in a central area.

A more detailed analysis of one hundred families reveals that the breaking up of the family is one of the first results of slum residence. The total number of children born to the hundred wives of these families, many of whom are still of child-bearing age, is 360, of whom 239 still survive. Although accurate figures could not be obtained on this point, the general impression gained was that the majority of deaths occurred in the first year of the child's life. Of these 239 children, 127 are living with their parents in Rooiyard, 104 with relatives in the country, and 8 are either married or are residing at the place of their employment. In the case of 35 families all their children are resident in Rooiyard. There are 34 families in which the children are separated, one or more living in the country with relatives and the remainder living with their parents in Rooiyard. In 23 families all the children are in charge of relatives in the country. The remaining 8 women are childless. This means that in more than half of the families investigated—to be precise 57 per cent—the parents are living in Johannesburgh, while some or all of the children are separated for long periods from their parents and from each other.

The two main reasons for this severance of the family are economic necessity and the need for the moral training of the young. The Bantu woman is under tribal conditions an economic asset, and on her work in the fields the family is dependent for its subsistence. Despite the changed nature of her work, the African woman is of no less economic importance in an urban area. But she is no longer able to combine her work with the care of her children. At her home the nature of her work in the fields enabled her to take her children with her, to educate her daughters and to give them the training which would fit them to become, in their turn, the workers of the tribe. In Johannesburg the two means by which a woman can augment the revenue of the family—beer-brewing or a legitimate occupation such as domestic service—are both incompatible with the adequate care of children. Beer-brewing subjects the mother of the family to the constant danger of arrest and imprisonment, with the consequent necessity of leaving the children to the casual and intermittent care of a neighbor. Other employment removes the mother of the family from her home and leaves the children unattended. The uncertainty of regular employment and, in many cases, the desire to shift the burden of the maintenance of the children on to relatives at home are also factors instrumental in effecting a division of the family.

The unhealthiness of Rooiyard surroundings, the lack of playing-fields, and cramped quarters prompt many parents to leave their children at home in healthier surroundings. In addition to these purely utilitarian motives, concern for the moral welfare of their children is also instrumental in determining parents to send their children home to the country. The parents are aware of the inadequacies of such educational facilities as are available to them, as well as of the many harmful influences which will be brought to bear on their children from their earliest years in the Rooiyard surroundings. Daughters especially are not infrequently sent to relatives in the country, there to be secluded after their menses have commenced, and are then not permitted to return, for "here," say some mothers, "the girls only learn washing and ironing and running round with boys. At the kraal the girls learn all jobs and then get married."

Under tribal conditions, though the children do not receive a formal training according to European conceptions, they are gradually instructed, chiefly by their parents, in the performance of such tasks as will be required of them as adult men and women. Slowly and imperceptibly they absorb the precepts of the tribe and reverence for tribal traditions and tribal taboos is inculcated. The sanctions of the tribe become a living force to them. In all this gradual training the parents do not work single-handed. They are largely assisted by their kinspeople and, above all, by tribal institutions which provide for the "gradual initiation of the individual into the various strata of the society." The whole social organization helps to mold the potential tribesman into the requisite social norm. And finally come the initiation rites, impressive in their insistence on and dramatization of tribal discipline and tribal solidarity, and symbolical of the transition from childhood to adulthood with its new duties and new obligations.

[In Rooiyard parents can spare little time from their economic pursuits to train their children for adult life; the school replaces the informal training that is a part of the tribal environment, but school attendance is lax and is not enforced.]

The parents quite frankly admit that they have no control over recalcitrant children. Their impotence to control their children and their lack of parental authority is a source of dismay to a large number of urban Africans. The individualism which is characteristic of the families of Rooiyard has already been commented upon. Each family is an isolated unit. There is no framework of a social organization in which each family and each individual may find a rightful place. There is no common body of public opinion against which the individual hesitates to offend. African public opinion has not yet emerged owing to many factors, among the chief of which are mutual distrust between members of different tribes, lack of organized institutions which may cross-sect society and integrate its members, and instability of residence. Hence one extremely valuable method of controlling the members of African society does not, as yet, function. The criminal sanction has been so widely applied to what are, to the Africans, trivial misdemeanors, that conviction and imprisonment carry no social stigma. Offenses in respect of illegal possession of Native liquor, pass laws, and Native taxation, which are treated as criminal offenses, are mainly economic in their implication to the African. The penalty is either the payment of a fine or imprisonment, and the latter, entailing a loss of employment, is an equally severe drain on financial resources. But such offenses, considered to be inspired by the white man and to be an unavoidable concomitant of his régime, do not outrage African public sentiment. In Rooiyard, where there were 65 convictions for illegal possession of Native liquor in a period of twelve months, an offense of this nature is considered merely as an unfortunate but inevitable vicissitude in the career of the beer-brewer. Economic pressure is the one force which permeates and activates the life of the African of Rooiyard. The need for employment and the fear of losing it play an important part in maintaining an equilibrium in African urban society. But the existence of a constant demand for labor, created by European dependence on African labor, has, by widening the scope of activity for the younger Africans, brought about their economic emancipation. Girls and boys of fifteen and onwards feel that they can fend for themselves and are not dependent on their parents for the necessities and, more important still, for the luxuries of life. This demand for African labor also affects the parental control of the rural Africans, for, as was frequently explained, even there a child, either male or female, will often say to its parent, "I can go to town and get better food there than you give me." . . .

A responsible and educated African living in a location where 18,000 Africans reside, said, with the exaggeration of bitterness, "You will not find five peaceful homes here." He spoke of the increase of illegitimate children and maintained that in one year twenty girls of 13 to 14 years of age had borne illegitimate children. He commented on this as contributing to domestic quarrels, as the maintenance of an additional child creates a definite additional economic burden. But he dwelt on the alarming prevalence of adultery as constituting the main reason for family dissension. Although it would not be justifiable to attempt statistics of the number of harmonious households in Rooiyard—and there are certainly marriages in which there is evidence of great understanding, harmony, and affection between husband and wife— the abundant evidence of the great prevalence of adultery and prostitution in Rooiyard, and the continuous references to quarrels and fights between husband and wife, point to the disruption of family life. Only a few women admitted that they had one or more *nyatsi* (backdoor husband), but all informants readily and emphatically testified that their neighbors had "sweethearts." Several women were known to have accumulated comparative wealth from the proceeds of prostitution. The common practice of prostitution in Rooiyard is a natural outcome of the poverty of the Africans and of the nature of the main activity of the women. The women are all beer-brewers, and consequently attract to their rooms many men, the majority of whom are either single or far removed from their wives whom they have left in the country. Many women, hard pressed to balance expenditure and revenue and importuned by men in varying stages of intoxication, must be expected to succumb to prostitution as an additional means of supplementing their incomes. Many husbands are kept in ignorance of their wives' infidelity. Some husbands, intent on leading their own lives undisturbed, do not demur. Frequently, however, the husband, on discovering his wife's infidelity, attempts to revenge himself by attacking her lover. The fights, which are such a common feature of Rooiyard life, are practically without exception caused by competition for the favors of a woman or by the desire for revenge on the part of the deceived husband. The statement of a well-tested and reliable informant, a Manyika resident in Rooiyard, an intelligent observer, holding himself aloof from but keenly apprehensive of the prevailing conditions which he describes, states the situation tersely. He says, "All the men in the yard have sweethearts. I can see plenty of people, strange men come to the yard. The women sleep with them. This happens in the daytime when the husbands are away. All the women, only the old not, have men who sleep with them. I could sleep with any of them if I wanted. All the women make a business of it. Nobody tells the husbands. Many women are married by *lobola* only, no court." In an environment where adultery, illegitimacy, and prostitution, even if not completely condoned, are accepted as social norms, and where *lobola* is regarded as payment, the foundations of marriage must inevitably totter. It is a logical conclusion to an unfortunate concatenation of circumstances, in which economic pressure is of great importance, to find extreme disruption in family life.

Economic necessity was the driving force which impelled the Africans of Rooiyard to migrate to Johannesburg. Their lives as seen in Rooiyard bear witness to a continuous struggle to overcome their all too evident poverty. It is a queer paradox that appears in Rooiyard—a combination of Bantu insouciance and of the European enthusiasm for economic gain. The owner of a sewing machine will not lend her machine to a friend but demands the tariff fee of 1s. per day. There is much evidence of a commercialization of Bantu culture. The festivals of tribal life have been converted into the "parties" of urban existence which have become an integral portion of the life of the urban African, largely owing to the fact that, in addition to beer-drinking, they form the whole of the urban African's recreational facilities.

[In such parties, at which the guests contribute money to defray the cost, the emphasis is placed on economic gain, with a loss of the traditional significance of the occasion. Another innovation is taking up a collection from every room in the yard to cover the funeral expenses of a resident who has died.]

Despite the rapid absorption of European material culture, and despite the changes which are being wrought in Bantu institutions as a result of the transition from a subsistence economy to a money economy, little progress has been achieved in loosening the stranglehold which magic has over the Africans. Practically all the Africans have either been converted to Christianity or have been baptized in their childhood. Only six of one hundred women do not belong, nominally at least, to one of the numerous Christian sects which are represented in South Africa. . . . The majority of women find that the time taken up by the domestic tasks and by their beer-selling activities does not leave them sufficient leisure time to attend church services. To judge by the Africans of Rooiyard, Christianity has failed. The minister at the home of these Africans has preached the brotherhood of all men. These Africans come to town and there, where the contrast cannot but fail to make itself felt, they find the white man dominant and the Africans occupying a definitely inferior position. . . . It appears that the inability of the church to alleviate the disabilities from which the Africans suffer has contributed largely to the indifference and apathy which they now manifest towards the white man's religion. Time and again men and women said, "At the kraal I went to church. In Johannesburg I don't go." But skepticism towards Christianity has not, in the case of the Africans of Rooiyard, brought about a reversion to their tribal belief. A few families give proof of the constancy of their faith in the belief of their fathers by invoking the *amadlozi* (dead ancestors) in joy and in distress by propitiating them according to traditional rules, and by offering to them a little of their food before they eat and a gourd of their beer before they drink. A few of the more educated Africans, disillusioned in the white man's religion, advocate a return to their own religion. But the great majority of Rooiyard Africans have tacitly renounced Christianity and have been too long dissociated from tribal religion to find solace in it now. The urban African, cast adrift between two religions, cannot look to religion to help him in the perplexities and difficulties which unavoidably present themselves in the new and unaccustomed conditions of life in an urban center. Magic fulfils this need. In Rooiyard there is a constant demand for the services of the *inyanga* and of his medicines. He fulfils the functions of both lawyer and doctor, for in addition to remedial medicines he gives much practical advice to his patients. In the event of illness most Africans, but not all, prefer the services of the *inyanga* to those of a European medical practitioner. . . . Very numerous are the demands for protective medicines which will guard the family from succumbing to the poisons of sorcerers. The belief in *abathakathi* (sorcerers) receives added stimulus in an environment where neighbors are strangers, mutually distrustful of each other and also competitors in the beer trade. Each tribe believes that another tribe is in possession of more potent medicines than their own, which will make their beer customers desert them and which will harm their children. . . .

The aim of this survey in which only a few of the most salient characteristics of the Rooiyard populace have been discussed, has been to show that while there is ample evidence of a rapid absorption of Western material culture, the assimilation of Western spiritual culture is proceeding at a far more leisurely pace. This lag in European cultural assimilation is deplored, not so much because of the inherent superiority of European culture, but because urban contacts between the two cultures usually result in a shattering of Bantu culture and consequently deprive the urban African of the supports and restraints which a stable social organization provides. The African is straining onward in an attempt to satisfy his ever-increasing needs in the way of food, clothing, and furniture. But the low wage level and the resultant inability of the male head of the family to provide for the needs of the family have caused a disruption of the immediate family. In the drive to town families are separated from their kinsfolk and form isolated units in a town. The restraints of tribal discipline do not affect the urban African, and no substitute discipline has, as yet, emerged from out of the chaotic welter of transition. The old sanctions have lost their force and the sanctions which order European life are not yet applicable to African life. Lest this picture should appear exaggerated, it may be well to point out that this survey deals with a people who are living under the most unfavorable conditions. These Africans form what is, technically, a criminal populace whose whole endeavor is to outwit the police, by whom they are continually harassed in the course of their illicit beer-brewing activities. Their contacts with Europeans have been mainly confined to such contacts as occur in the course of employment. They have lost touch with their home missionary, and in urban life they find that the church can do little to relieve their economic distress or to alleviate their social and legal disabilities. From the pedlars and hawkers, both European and Asiatic, who find in these yards a profitable custom, they learn the art of bargaining and the art of swearing. Oftentimes it has been noticed that women, who could not frame a coherent sentence in English, have, during the course of a quarrel, interspersed the argument in their home tongue with a wide selection of abusive and obscene English swear words. This is perhaps symptomatic of the process of contact. The Africans of Rooiyard are really an outcast populace, difficult of approach by the European because of their suspicious antagonism. But the gratitude with which young girls and boys speak of the time spent with their Pathfinder and Wayfarer units reveals that their great need is for European contacts, which are not directed solely towards exploiting them economically or converting them to Christianity. Whether such contacts become available or not, the approximation of the lives of some of the families in Rooiyard, admittedly as yet a small number, to the European model points to the conclusion that out of the chaos and confusion which exists in this transition period, there will emerge a people who will adopt such elements of European culture as may enable them to attain to an ordered and economically secure social life.

CHAPTER 25 Geography

Many students who have taken what passes for geography in the grades have learned to hate it. They spend endless hours learning the major products of the American states or memorizing the names and locations of seas, cities, countries, and mountains. This is not geography as the professional geographer knows it, nor is it geography as the specialist teacher of the subject handles this fascinating science. This travesty of geography is not even useful. Students quickly forget facts they have memorized when they have no structure around which to cluster the facts and no mode of inquiry that can be useful as an aid in analyzing a new situation.

Much geography teaching is not one but two revolutions behind. The older of these two revolutions emphasizes the study of geographic areas or regions. This point of view developed in the nineteenth and early twentieth centuries and is still the emphasis of most contemporary geographers. A second revolution has been in the making since the end of World War II. In the last two decades geographers have been increasingly interested in the application of statistics and other mathematical tools to the study of geography. This newest of the geographic revolutions has made no perceptible dent upon the teaching of geography in the schools, or for that matter, in many of the colleges and universities.

Geography is taught in two major ways in the schools. Many school systems, particularly in the elementary grades, offer entire courses in geography. In addition, world geography or courses with similar emphases, are taught in many senior high schools. The elementary school courses reach most students; those in the high school are more commonly electives and touch only a minority.

The second major way in which geographic information is taught is as part of other social studies courses, particularly history. In many history courses, however, geography is simply locational. Students study the routes of explorers, the location of cities or of battles, and the boundaries of countries. With more sophisticated teachers, students may examine the influence of the Nile River on the civilization of Egypt or the impact of the Erie Canal on the development of American society, but only a few lucky ones are challenged to go beyond these data to the underlying geographic concepts. Before this pattern can be broken, teachers must learn the structure of the discipline of geography, which can prompt them to undertake assignments in which geographic generalizations will be implicit.

In the reading that follows Professor Clyde F. Kohn of the Department of Geography, the University of Iowa, suggests new approaches to the teaching of geography in the schools. The following questions are pertinent:

1) What is Kohn's opinion of the hypotheses advanced by Bruner?
2) According to Kohn, what reforms must be made before the structure of geography can be taught adequately?
3) What does Kohn mean by the words "location" and "distribution"?
4) What should be the basic aim of geographic instruction in the schools? Is this aim similar to what is advocated by the other authors in this unit?

BASIC CONCEPTS OF GEOGRAPHY AND THEIR DEVELOPMENT IN THE CLASSROOM

Clyde F. Kohn

My desire, and willingness, to speak at this joint assembly of the National Council for the Social Studies and the Association of American Geographers grew out of a classroom experience of my own this past summer. Early in a five-week course at a major university, I gave a series of lectures on the structure of geographic knowledge to some fifty elementary and secondary school teachers. Toward the end of the five-week period, page proof for a sixth-grade social studies textbook began to arrive. To see if the class could apply their newly developed understanding of the structure of geographic knowledge to some of the material in the text, I read certain passages dealing with the early settlement of Southeast Asia, as follows:

Reprinted from a speech given by Clyde F. Kohn to the 1963 convention of the National Council for the Social Studies and the Association of American Geographers.

In the densely forested highlands of the Philippines and the Malay Peninsula live groups of Negritos. Like the Papuans, they are Australoids, but they are very small. The tallest measure less than five feet. Negritos seem once to have occupied much of Southeast Asia. They were, as they are now, hunters and gatherers of wild food in the great tropical forests. Also, then as now, their numbers were small and the population density low.

The Mongoloids who came later were larger, stronger, and had a more advanced culture than the original inhabitants. They settled on the better land while the little people retreated into the hills.

These early Mongoloids came into Southeast Asia about 10,000 years ago from what is now southern China. They followed the uplands, which they farmed, cultivating root crops such as the cassava and the yam. The method of farming they used is now called "shifting cultivation," and it, too, survives in Southeast Asia's museum of cultures. Sometimes it is called by the more descriptive name of "slash and burn" farming.

Migrations into Southeast Asia went on for centuries. Those who came later brought better tools and better methods of farming, and a new crop, rice. As these later migrants spread over the mainland of Southeast Asia, they settled in the river valleys and on the small coastal lowlands. Their first choice was always the land that was best for rice. The areas they chose are still the most densely populated parts of mainland Southeast Asia.

After reading these passages to the class, I raised this question: How would you handle this material in the classroom? Should it be treated as a specific set of facts to be learned—that is memorized—by the pupils? If so, would they not be rapidly forgotten after the pupils had passed the inevitable test on their ability to recall the detailed information? Or is there another way of dealing with these specific facts so that the pupils might develop a "regenerative" power? In other words, are there basic concepts, or fundamental generalizations involved in this mass of detail that will help pupils reconstruct the facts when needed?

In carrying out the discussion, I expected that the students would realize that the passages I had read could be viewed as specific instances of some basic concepts in geography. To my concern and dismay, I found that the vast majority of the class did not readily view the set of facts in this way. They were prone, instead, to view these early migrations into Southeast Asia as bits of specific, detailed information rather than as instances of more general ideas.

As we think about concepts in geography this morning, I should like to have you keep this experience in mind, for I shall want to refer to it later on for illustrative purposes.

But, before we go further, I would like first to review two developments in teaching that I believe have a significant bearing on our topic.

The first of these has to do with the contributions that Professor Bruner is making to educational theory and the application of these contributions to learning in geography. The second is related to the role of geography in the educational program.

Professor Bruner, as you are undoubtedly well aware, advocates that the key to knowledge and understanding lies in the structure of a given field of learning. He suggests that we help our pupils develop the fundamental principles or generalizations of a subject, together with the special strategies of inquiry that are employed by specialists in that subject. This theory calls for helping the learner think in terms of the basic concepts, or primary ideas, of a discipline, and to learn to think as a practitioner of that discipline thinks. Acceptance of this theory has some interesting ramifications. Does geography have a basic structure? If so, what is it? What kinds of learning experiences should be planned, for different levels of maturity, to help children think as geographers? What tools are available to accomplish this task, and what skills are needed to utilize these tools effectively? We shall want to think about all of these questions as we deal with the teaching of geography, but let us first turn to the second development in education that has an important bearing on the teaching of geography. Namely, what is the place of geography in our educational program?

For many years in this country, geography has been taught as a part of the social studies program. The quantity and quality has varied from locality to locality and from state to state, depending on a number of factors—the philosophy and preparation of educators, including supervisors, curriculum specialists, leaders in the social studies area of learning, principals and other school administrators; on the academic preparation and interests of classroom teachers; and on the materials, including textbooks, selected for use in the learning process. Some educators have favored more and better instruction in geography; many have belittled its role in the school program. A few teachers have been adequately prepared in the field; most have not. A few textbooks deal with facts in a geographic manner; most integrated social studies books do not. As a result, the quantity and quality of instruction in geography varies markedly from place to place throughout the nation. Concern has been expressed from time to time, not only by geographers but by statesmen and others interested in the general well-being of our country, about the lack of geography instruction in our schools and the kind of geography that is taught. Currently there is much concern about the almost complete lack of geography instruction in our secondary schools, despite the fact that an understanding and concern for peoples and places throughout the world is basic to our modern way of life. Few high schools require a course, for example, in the study of our world today, its patterns and cultures.

There are some in the field of the social studies who put forth the idea that the elementary school program might be developed in terms of geographic concepts and ideas, but that the secondary school social studies program should deal with "sterner" stuff. Behind such a commitment lies the belief that the study of geography is "kid stuff," a belief that I must deny in no uncertain terms.

But the explanation for the lack of sound geographic instruction is even more basic than I have indicated. It lies in the fact that many believe that geography can be taught as an adjunct to history, economics, political science, sociology, or anthropology. Yet, if the basic tenets of the Bruner theory of learning are to be accepted, then such a practice cannot be condoned. Geography cannot be assimilated or integrated with history or with any one of the social sciences and still retain its identity. If the key to knowledge and understanding lies in the structure of a given field of learning, then learning in geography will take place only when children learn to think in terms of the basic concepts of geography and to think as practitioners of that discipline think. These objectives cannot be achieved so long as isolated facts having geographic significance are taught only as they are related to historic events. Geography can make a solid contribution as a social study only if its structure is made clear to the student and when it is permitted to play its role as a unified field of knowledge.

Having said this, let me hasten to add that the study of facts from a geographic point of view can be coordinated with the other social sciences in a well-planned social studies program. A multidisciplinary, well-coordinated social studies program can be developed wherein each of the disciplines are clearly identifiable and taught. This possibility has been demonstrated by at least one group of social scientists working together on the development of materials for use in the elementary schools. These materials call for looking at the various parts of the world first from one disciplined point of view, and then from another, permitting time enough so that the learner can develop the special strategies of inquiry that are employed by each of the individual fields of learning—history, geography, economics, political science, anthropology, and sociology.

THE STRUCTURE OF GEOGRAPHY

Does geography have a structure of its own, and if so, what is it? Although several traditions can be identified in the development of geography as a discipline, basically geographers, no matter what their traditional orientation, are concerned with the location and distribution of things as they occur on the face of the earth. As the philosopher Kant recognized two hundred years ago, all facts empirically derived can be studied in three fundamental ways—according to their temporal relations; according to their spatial relations; and according to similarity of form and behavior. That according to form and behavior may be either government, economics, sociology, or anthropology, depending on the forms or behaviors under consideration.

When we say that geography is the study of the location and distribution of phenomena, both natural and man made, we need to refine both terms, "location" and "distribution." The location of something may be dealt with in one of three ways. We can think of it in terms of "nominal" location, which is simply the naming of some part of the earth. For example, we give a specific part of the earth the name "California" and locate this area by means of that name. Unfortunately, too much of what is taught in the classroom as geography is merely the memorization of nominal locations. I do not imply by this statement that nominal locations should not be taught, but I do wish to emphasize that the time given to nominal locations both in class work and in testing is quite often at the expense of relations that are far more significant.

A second way of looking at location is in mathematical terms—that is, in terms of latitude and longitude. It is only by the use of these precise measurements that we can, after all, locate places on the face of the earth specifically and accurately.

The third kind of "location" is derived from the mathematical location of places and things and is commonly referred to as "relative location" or situation. Since this is one of the basic concepts of geography, I shall discuss it later on rather than at this point.

When geographers speak of "distributions," they are thinking of "sets of locations," as, for example, the distribution of cities over a million or the distribution of particular types of farms or the distribution of specific temperatures at a given time, and so on. All such spatial distributions have three characteristics of significance to geographers: pattern, density, and areal extent. By pattern we mean the arrangement of specific locations within the distribution. For example, we may find the set of locations arranged in a linear pattern, a rectangular pattern, a clustered pattern, and so on. Density generally refers to the number of locations within a distribution per unit of area, as, for example, the density of population per square mile. Areal extent, on the other hand, refers to the area that is covered by the distribution being studied—the area occupied by manufacturing, for example, or the areal extent of coal deposits, and the like. Thus when a geographer studies distributions he studies the pattern, density, and areal extent of sets of locations.

Out of the fact, or truism, that natural and man-made phenomena are unequally distributed over the face of the earth comes a series of basic concepts to which I should now like to direct your attention.

1. The first of these is the concept that phenomena on the face of the earth are spatially associated. Let us refer to this primary idea as *the concept of areal association*. We find as we examine a set of locations that the pattern, density, and areal extent of these locations can be explained in terms of a second set of locations. Hence the geographer tries to determine the spatial correlation of things within an area. This can be done mathematically by using appropriate statistical techniques, or it can be done through the visual correlations of maps.

Let us at this point return to the illustration of Southeast Asia. You will recall that the distribution of Negritos is spatially related to the distribution of hilly and mountainous uplands. These little people do not occupy the river valleys and deltas where the great majority of Southeast Asiatics live. As later migrations of Mongoloids came into the area, the more primitive Negritos retreated to the less desirable lands and found security in the hilly, tropical-forested uplands. Here is a specific illustration of the principle that when areas are invaded by people of higher cultures, occupants of lower cultures retreat to less hospitable areas, be they dry, high, or cold. That is, the more advanced people occupy the more desirable areas.

2. A second fundamental concept of the geographer is that locations on the face of the earth are interconnected. This notion is commonly referred to as the *notion of spatial interaction*. When water for an irrigation project is dammed high in the mountains and led by a feeding system of interconnected locations, the set of locations involved in this particular interaction system provide for the flow of water from a point of origin (the dam) to a point of destination (the field of crops). Also involved are the facilities (irrigation ditches, etc.) that contain and direct this flow. In like manner, the geographer might study the flow of people, products, ideas, telephone messages, and so on.

Both the concept of areal association and the concept of spatial interaction are related to the concept of "relative location," to which I referred earlier as the third way of viewing location. The study of relative location involves a number of component elements: (1) the distance and direction one location is from another; (2) the character of the area that separates the two locations; (3) the facilities available for getting from one location to the other; and (4) the speed with which one may travel the distance between the two places. Thus the concept of relative location involves both natural and cultural characteristics. The cultural elements are, in turn, an outgrowth of the technology of a society. Let us simply recall that with the development of intercontinental air travel, the location of most places throughout the world relative to each other has changed drastically. And with this change has come the need for re-thinking economic, political, military, and social activities.

3. A third basic concept in geography grows out of the fact that change is an established condition of modern life. The areal associations and spatial interactions of phenomena with which geographers are concerned are not static relationships. They are constantly in a stage of flux, giving rise to *the concept of fluidity* in the discipline of geography. This concept gives rise to a host of hypotheses concerning trends in areal associations and spatial inter-actions. We saw this in our example of the settlement of Southeast Asia. When rice was introduced into the area, people were able to move down from the higher and drier hilly uplands to make a living in the marshy floodplains and deltas of the major river valleys. But this change was not possible until man had discovered how to make use of rice to satisfy his body needs for food.

In like manner, many changes are taking place in modern times, resulting in new patterns of population, manufacturing, farming, and the like. The Industrial Revolution, which had its beginning 200 years ago in England, is now spreading rapidly throughout the underdeveloped parts of the world. A new technology is being introduced into areas that heretofore have been in-habited by preindustrial, or traditional, societies. Likewise, tremendous changes are taking place even in the highly developed parts of the earth. The advances in the sciences and engineering within our own country during the past half a dozen years are having significant results in terms of changes in demographic, economic, social, and political patterns.

4. A fourth basic concept is related to and an outgrowth of the previous three. Geographers have discovered that not only do spatial associations and interactions of locations vary in time but also that they may vary over space. For example, in one part of the world, such as in the middle latitudes, the vast majority of people live on low-lying plains. This is not true, however, in many tropical lands. Here we find the more densely settled areas in the *tierra templada* zone of mountainous lands, leaving much of the low-lying lands uninhabited or only sparsely settled.

As a result of these variations in the areal associations of phenomena, we have different kinds of areas, which the geographer commonly refers to as *regions*. Thus, the fourth basic concept in geography is the *concept of regionality*. Geographers attempt to study the character of regions on the face of the earth by noting how the distribution of natural and cultural phenomena are interrelated.

5. Finally, the fifth basic concept that I wish to call to your attention this morning is the concept that in carrying on the basic human activities of living, man is and has always been, and probably always will be, closely related to the earth on which he lives. This concept is commonly referred to as the *concept of man-land relations*. Again, it does not differ significantly from the earlier concept of areal association, but it does suggest a different set of problems with which students might deal in the classroom. For example, it gives rise to the concept of natural resources and raises the issue of conservation, or the wise use of our natural resources. As a result, the geographer becomes concerned with the soil, plant, and animal life and with the mineral and water resources available to a given society; and he becomes interested in the way that a specific group of people relate themselves to conditions of their natural environment—that is, to land forms and climate.

Thus growing out of the facts of location and distribution on which the study of geography focuses, we find that there are at least five basic concepts, or primary ideas, that can be investigated—the concepts of areal association, spatial interaction, fluidity, regionalism, and man-land relations.

Organization of a Geography Curriculum

With these basic concepts in mind, let us turn to the second problem of interest: How might instruction in geography in the elementary and secondary schools be organized and implemented to achieve an understanding of these basic concepts? In answering this question, three topics need to be considered: thinking processes in geography, providing for individual differences, and the organization of a program of study in geography.

Nothing in recent years has stimulated elementary and secondary school teachers more than the challenge to develop the thinking processes of those they teach. Although the ways of bringing about an improvement in thinking have been widely debated, everyone seems to agree that its development is a basic goal of education, and that instruction in the several disciplines included in the school program should be directed to this end. Hence it is important to note how instruction in geography contributes to the development of the learner's ability to think.

One or more of a number of thinking processes are involved in the teaching of geography:

1. *Perception.* This process involves the ability to discriminate and differentiate the properties of objects or basic human activities and to interpret their meaning. Learners perceive when they have sensory experiences either real or vicarious.

2. *Association.* This is the process of linking or relating symbols—words, signs, and the like—with things that are experienced. For example, a learner may associate words such as "river" and "lake" with what he perceives in the real world or map symbols with actual surface features, or routes of transportation with the movement of goods or people from one place to another.

3. *Concept attainment.* This includes the process of discriminating specific properties of objects and events and abstracting or generalizing common elements so that they can be classified or grouped together. As children mature, they enrich or deepen concepts developed earlier in their school experience.

Perceptual, associative, and conceptual thinking processes are constantly called upon in the teaching of geography because much of the content of our discipline is both descriptive and analytical, and the learner must build the large vocabulary, concepts, and generalizations needed to understand the location and distribution of both natural and cultural phenomena. Also, he must develop concepts of location, of size and shape, of pattern, of density, and of areal extent, and so on. In order to handle all these concepts teachers need to help elementary and secondary school students develop a highly specialized vocabulary based on meaningful concepts. Despite this, little has actually been researched in how young people perceive, associate, and attain concepts in the study of geography. We do know, however, that if learning is to take place, specific attention needs to be given to the detailed and precise perception of the spatial characteristics of the objects and of the human activities that are commonly included in units of study in geography. We also know that if students do not clearly differentiate the orientation, magnitude, and areal extent of natural and cultural objects, they will not develop a clear and accurate understanding of their areal associations or spatial interactions. Thus, these three processes are essential to learning in geography and need to be stressed by the teacher in setting purposes, directing the learner's observations, guiding discussions, and evaluating outcomes.

The remaining three thinking processes are dependent on the three that I have already discussed. They are relational thinking, critical thinking, and creative thinking.

1. *Relational thinking.* This includes the process of relating facts, understandings, and concepts to form generalizations of one kind or another. In geography, we recognize this process of establishing generalizations regarding the areal association and spatial interactions of places, people, and events.
2. *Critical thinking.* Although often associated with relational thinking, I would like to differentiate this process by suggesting that it include the use of standards, values, and purposes to evaluate the effectiveness of some action. In other words, critical thinking involves the consideration of different points of view regarding some event or activity having geographic significance.
3. *Creative thinking.* This process involves expressing thoughts and feelings in original ways. For a learner, creative thinking may be a new interpretation, a grasp of new relationships of phenomena, an original synthesis or expression of ideas, a new proposal or hypothesis, a new way of doing something.

In the development of these six thinking processes, we need an approach that will let all of them remain naturally blended, yet one that will permit teachers to emphasize specific processes when necessary. Also, we need a flexible approach that will enable a teacher to work not only with his entire class but with groups within his class and with individual pupils.

Thus a classroom practice that might be proposed—and it is by no means a new one—is that instruction in geography be organized in terms of problems having geographic significance, that is, location and distribution. Such an approach brings together the six thinking processes that have been listed and enables the learner to use them in dealing with content that has geographic significance. Another feature of using the problems approach is that it enables a teacher to obtain a blend of individual and group work. Through such an approach, the gifted, the average, and the less able child can each be challenged. The amount of time needed to complete activities can be varied; individualized readings can be provided; individual preparation of reports, maps, and outlines can be encouraged; small groups of children with common instructional needs can be organized; home study related to individual needs can be assigned; special activities for both the academically talented and the less able children can be provided; the kind and amount of practice and direct supervision of children's work can be varied; and levels of expectancy appropriate to each child's capabilities can be more easily set.

Finally, to develop the six thinking processes and to provide for individual differences teachers need to consider patterns of organizing geographic knowledge. This calls for consideration of the scope of problems to be developed in the elementary and secondary schools and the sequence or grade placement of the problems to be solved. In terms of scope, instruction in geography should include problems in physical, economic, social, and political geography, and the study areas selected should eventually include all parts of the earth as well as the world as a whole. In terms of sequence there is no one pattern that can be said at this time to be more efficient than another. I have long advocated, as some of you know, that the sequence of problems and study areas be organized from grade to grade in terms of "scale." In the early or primary grades, problems dealing with the locality in which the child lives or with localities elsewhere in the world, that is, large-scale studies, can be handled, I believe, most effectively. Children can more readily grasp the area associations of phenomena and the spatial interrelations of two or more locations if they can observe them readily in familiar surroundings or in photographs—both useful only in large-scale studies. In the middle and upper grades problems dealing with the location and distribution of things and events at the national level can be introduced, thus focusing attention on problems involving an "intermediate scale." At the high school level problems dealing with the location and distribution of things and events on the world level, that is, problems at a "world scale," are more interesting and challenging to young people. However, at each level of instruction the teacher may want to introduce geography-oriented problems of each of these scales. Underlying these statements is the belief that the program of instruction in geography, that is, its scope and sequence, should be preplanned and not left to chance, that the educational needs of children can be determined in advance and not set day by day. On the other hand, problems selected for study at each grade level should be flexible enough to allow for modification in light of individual differences among children, their backgrounds, and changing community conditions.

Summary

In summary the following propositions may be advanced:

1. The key to instruction in geography, as Bruner indicates, lies in the structure of geography itself.
2. The basic concepts in geography can be taught only when the discipline is recognized as a unified field of study.
3. The basic concepts in geography can be introduced at an early age—even in the primary grades—and the complexities of these concepts can be unraveled through the school years.
4. Real geography learning is concept-centered rather than fact or symbol-centered, and instruction in the classroom can be directed to the development of the learner's ability to think—relationally, critically, and creatively.
5. The most effective way of teaching children to think as geographers think is by means of posing problems concerning the location and distribution of things, using the basic concept of geography as the source of hypotheses and the form of generalizations.

6. The scope and sequence of instruction in geography should take into account factors of child growth and development, the teaching and learning processes, and the social and psychological factors that contribute to variations in the total educational process.

7. That, although geography must be considered as a unified field of learning in and of itself, a coordinated program of social studies can be developed for all grade levels, wherein each of the disciplines, including geography, is clearly identifiable and taught.

CHAPTER 26 Geography: Examples

In the immediate future, imaginative materials designed to teach the new geography will have to come from teachers rather than from textbooks. Most texts remain behind the advances made in teaching the subject. Even those whose scholarship is up-to-date are expository rather than inductive. In this situation, teachers are thrust upon their own resources.

Fortunately many teachers, once they are engaged in developing new materials, find the challenge exciting and produce excellent results. The reading for today consists of descriptions of two assignments in geography developed by secondary school teachers associated with the High School Geography Project. This project grew out of the concern for geographic education on the part of the Association of American Geographers and the National Council for Geographic Education. A joint committee of these two organizations, meeting first in 1958, established the High School Geography Project to improve the content of geography courses and to develop new instructional materials. A group of geographers has been working together since 1961. The two assignments described in this chapter are some of the results of these labors.

The first paper, by Dr. Bertha Boya Thompson, describes an exercise in problem solving used while a class was studying food production in the United States. The second paper, written by John Neal, explores the way in which the mode of inquiry of the geographer can be used to solve problems within a student's own environment. A number of similar geographic exercises are described in the volume from which these two selections were taken. As you read, think about the following questions:

1) What skill objectives are implied by each of the two assignments in Chapter 26? what knowledge objectives?
2) What are the steps in the mode of inquiry used by the students in Dr.

Thompson's class? Can this method of investigation be transferred to other problems in geography?

3) What provided the stimulus for the study described by John Neal? What does a teacher need to know in order to develop projects like this one?

4) What form might a course based on principles and problems such as the ones in Chapter 26 take? What might the "text" look like?

5) Which of the two inductive teaching techniques used in Chapter 16 has been employed by Dr. Thompson?

AN EXPERIMENT IN PROBLEM-SOLVING

Bertha Boya Thompson

In the experimental high school geography course developed at Talawanda High School during the academic year, 1962–63, the problem-solving method of instruction was introduced in a unit of study on food production in the United States. As one of their assignments, students were asked to construct a dot map showing the distribution of wheat production in the fifteen leading wheat-producing states for 1959. While collecting data from the agricultural census for that year, the statistics for wheat production in Ohio for 1954 and 1959 were noted by the students. A question arose as to why wheat production in Ohio had decreased from 45 million to 29 million bushels during this five-year period.

One student asked if he might make two dot maps of wheat production for Ohio, one for 1954 and the other for 1959, to see whether or not the decline was general throughout the state (Figures 1A and 1B). Upon completion of the two maps, the student concluded that a decrease did occur in all counties, but that in some counties the decline appeared to be significantly greater than in others. The student's failure to hold an identical or uniform dot size caused some slight inconsistencies in his observations.

The following "explainers," or hypotheses, were suggested by the class to account for the general decrease in production for the years 1954–59, and for the place-to-place differences observed on the completed maps:

Reprinted from Bertha Boya Thompson, "An Experiment in Problem-Solving," in *Selected Classroom Experiences: High School Geography Project,* ed. Clyde F. Kohn, Geographic Education Series No. 4, 1964, National Council for Geographic Education, Illinois State Normal University, Normal, Ill., pp. 1–14.

OHIO
WHEAT PRODUCED DURING
1954

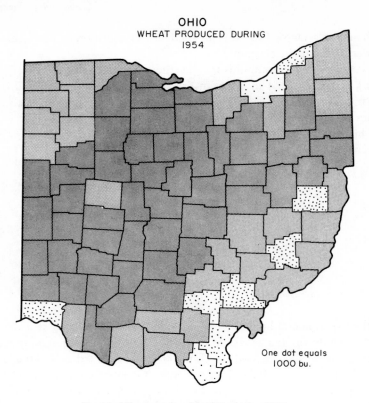

One dot equals
1000 bu.

Fig. 1A. Wheat produced in Ohio during 1954.

1. The decrease in wheat production in Ohio from 1954 to 1959 was associated with a decline in the demand for United States wheat on the world market.
2. The decrease in wheat production in Ohio from 1954 to 1959 was associated with a change in the diet of the American people.
3. The decrease in wheat production in Ohio from 1954 to 1959 occurred because 1959 was a non-wheat year in the crop rotation pattern.
4. The decrease in wheat production in Ohio from 1954 to 1959 was associated with a decline in county wheat acreage allotments.
5. The decrease in wheat production in Ohio from 1954 to 1959 occurred because other crops were able to compete successfully for acreage previously used for wheat.
6. The decrease in wheat production in Ohio from 1954 to 1959 occurred because farm land had been taken out of crop production and used for other activities such as manufacturing, urban development, recreation, and mining.

418

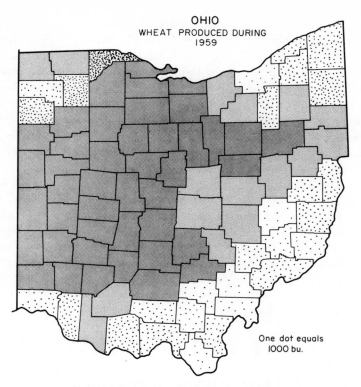

OHIO
WHEAT PRODUCED DURING
1959

One dot equals
1000 bu.

Fig. 1B. Wheat produced in Ohio during 1959.

Testing the Hypotheses: Rejection and Acceptance

After examining available data, a student reported that the United States had exported 567 million bushels of wheat in 1958, 623 million in 1959, and 712 million in 1960. He regretted his inability to secure data for 1954, but on the basis of the data obtained concluded that the increased sales from 1958–1960 did not indicate a decline in world demand for United States wheat. Hence, the first hypothesis was rejected. In other words, the decline in wheat production in Ohio between 1954 and 1959 was not due to any decline in the demand for United States wheat on the world market.

The instructor then placed the following production and sales data for Ohio on the chalkboard:

The Production and Sales of Wheat in Ohio (1954 and 1959)
Production   1954—45,202,350 bushels   1959—29,499,714 bushels
Sales   1954—38,365,231 bushels   1959—26,115,667 bushels

It was quickly noted that a larger percentage of the wheat produced in 1959 had been sold than in 1954. The class recognized that this indicated no decrease in the percentage of sales and thus rejected the second hypothesis. It was concluded that the decline in wheat production in Ohio from 1954 to 1959 did not reflect a change in the diet of the American people.

The student who proposed the third hypothesis secured wheat production data for the ten-year period, 1950 to 1959. He analyzed and graphed these data in order to determine whether or not the decrease was recurrent in any kind of recognizable pattern. He recommended that the third hypothesis be rejected, and that the class accept the conclusion that the decline in wheat production in Ohio from 1954 to 1959 was not associated with a non-wheat year in the crop rotation pattern.

To test the fourth hypothesis, which most students thought was the major reason for decreased production, data were obtained from the Agricultural Stabilization and Conservation Committee in Columbus, Ohio. Based on their analysis of these statistics, the class decided to accept the hypothesis as one of the important causes of decreased production. They were surprised to find, however, that the decrease in county acreage allotments was not so significant as they had anticipated. The following table gives some examples in which large production decreases were accompanied by relatively small declines in acreage allotments:

	Wheat Production (in bushels)		Wheat Acreage Allotments (in bushels)		
	1954	1959	1954	1959	Difference
State Total	45,000,000	29,000,000	1,753,914	1,557,896	196,018
Paulding Co.	654,765	110,609	26,701	26,553	148
Adams Co.	308,018	71,532	13,423	12,296	1,127
Ashtabula Co.	335,821	87,280	13,109	12,769	340

It was decided that the other hypotheses had to be investigated in detail, particularly when it was noted that the farmers of Ohio actually planted less than the county acreage allotments permitted, as follows:

COMPARISON OF ALLOTTED AND PLANTED ACREAGE IN OHIO (1954 AND 1959)

Year	Allotted Acreage	Planted Acreage	Difference
1954	1,753,914	1,740,000	13,914
1959	1,557,896	1,264,000	293,896

One student argued that these data could be explained by increased technological knowledge, that is, farmers could get more from less acres, so less was planted to wheat. Since many thought this was the explanation, the instructor gave wheat crop yields as 27 bushels per acre in 1954 and 24.5 for 1959. The students were surprised. The instructor then asked them to multiply the 1,264,000 acres planted in 1959 by the difference in yields between 1954 and 1959. The students readily saw that more would have been produced in 1959 if farmers had been able to reach the 1954 yield. It was at this point that the students decided that unfavorable weather conditions might have accounted for the decreased yields. Hence, a seventh hypothesis was introduced: "The decrease in wheat production in Ohio from 1954 to 1959 was associated with an unfavorable growing season during the year in which the 1959 census was taken." An interview was arranged with the vocational agriculture teacher and his class to secure information relative to critical periods in the growth of winter wheat and, in addition, possible crop competitors for wheat acreage. The students then checked the acreage for other crops for 1954 and 1959. Only corn and soybeans showed an increase, with corn increases too small to be significant. It was decided that further testing of the fifth hypothesis relative to crop competition would be necessary, and that a soybean map should be made to see if areas of decreased wheat production were also areas of increased soybean production.

In order to supply relevant data for testing the sixth hypothesis, it was noted that the number of farms in Ohio declined by 37,000 from 1954 to 1959. To the unbelieving students, the instructor explained that 7,000 of these were attributed to a redefinition of the term, "farm." Some of the decline, however, was attributed to the merging of farms, for the average farm size of Ohio increased from 112.9 acres to 131.9 acres in the five-year period from 1954 to 1959. Other contributing factors suggested were increased urban sprawl, the development of new parks, and strip mining. The field consultant on the High School Project, Professor Henry J. Warman, suggested that the decline in proportion of all land in farms or the change in the number of acres of farmland cultivated might be used as indicators of competition from other activities.

Committees were selected to map the dependent variable, that is, the phenomenon whose spatial variation was to be explained. In this instance, the dependent variable was the variation in changed wheat production from 1954 to 1959 in Ohio by counties, and the tentative independent variables (the possible explainers) were: (1) county wheat acreage allotment changes, (2) monthly differences in temperature and precipitation, (3) changes in soybean acreage, and (4) changes in farm acreages. Changes in wheat acreage were mapped to depict the dependent variable and to facilitate visual correlation.

A simplified quantitative system was devised for constructing the necessary maps (Figure 2). The differences between the 1954 and 1959 data were determined for each county, for both the dependent and independent variables (with the exception of the temperature and precipitation changes). The average county change was calculated for each variable. The symbols +, −, and 0 were placed upon each map according to fixed criteria. For example, in the case of farm acreage changes, a "+" was placed in a county if the county decrease was equal to the state average or greater; an "O" was placed in a county if the decrease was less than the average for the state. A "−" was placed in a county if an increase occurred.

Fig. 2. Farm acreage change, Ohio, 1954–1959.

The "weather data committee" placed its information upon each of their maps using areas determined by the state climatologist. Two different colors, blue for 1954–55 and red for 1958–59, were used in recording the temperature and precipitation data on each of the climatic maps constructed. The 1954 data were placed above the 1959 data as shown in Figure 3. Five-inch and six-inch isohyets for a 48-hour period were placed on the January map.

After all the maps had been constructed, they were placed upon the bulletin board. Students were urged to check the extent of spatial covariance visually. Later a class period was set aside to test hypotheses 5, 6, and 7 using this method of visual correlation. During this period students concluded that the map depicting changes in wheat production indicated that all counties had experienced a decrease in wheat production with the greatest declines in the southwestern, the central, and northwestern parts of the state (Figure 4). Similar results were noted using the map showing changes in wheat acreages.

One student noticed that the greatest decrease in wheat acreage allotment occurred in areas where the greatest changes in wheat production occurred

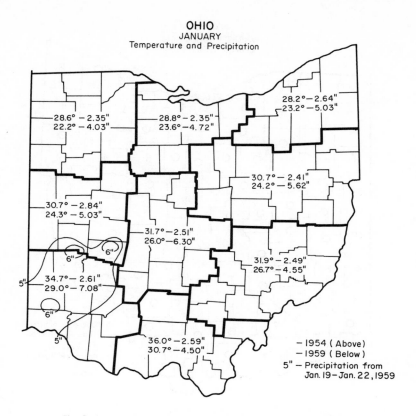

OHIO
JANUARY
Temperature and Precipitation

28.2° − 2.64"
23.2° − 5.03"

28.6° − 2.35"
22.2° − 4.03"

28.8° − 2.35"
23.6° − 4.72"

30.7° − 2.41"
24.2° − 5.62"

30.7° − 2.84"
24.3° − 5.03"

31.7° − 2.51"
26.0° − 6.30"

31.9° − 2.49"
26.7° − 4.55"

6"

6"

5"

34.7° − 2.61"
29.0° − 7.08"

6"

5"

36.0° − 2.59"
30.7° − 4.50"

− 1954 (Above)
− 1959 (Below)
5" − Precipitation from
Jan. 19 − Jan. 22, 1959

Fig. 3. January temperature and precipitation, Ohio, 1954–1959.

(Figure 5). In light of this observation, the students' previous judgment relative to the wheat acreage allotment hypothesis (hypothesis 4) was reaffirmed. However, one exception was noted in the southwestern part of the state where a greater than average decrease in production occurred but where government allotment decreases were less than the average for the state. Students also observed that a less than average decrease in wheat acreage allotment change and a less than average decrease in wheat acreage change occurred in the southeast. Here, however, there was an above average decrease in total farm acreage. These observations plus their knowledge of urban sprawl, park development, strip-mining, and reforestation in Ohio led to the acceptance of the sixth hypothesis. It was concluded that the decrease in wheat production in Ohio from 1954 to 1959 was positively associated with competition for land by other activities.

In looking at both the wheat acreage and soybean acreage maps (Figures 6A and 6B), the students concluded that where greater than average wheat acreage decreases occurred in western Ohio, soybeans showed an increase. Thus, on the basis of these observations they accepted the fifth hypothesis

OHIO
WHEAT PRODUCTION
Change 1954—1959

+ = Decrease greater
    than 178,000 bu.
O = Decrease less
    than 178,000 bu.
— = Increase

Fig. 4. Wheat production, Ohio, 1954–1959.

and concluded that the decrease in wheat production in Ohio from 1954 to 1959 was associated in part with the successful competition of other crops for acreage once planted in wheat. This judgment was reaffirmed when weather conditions were later investigated. The students proposed that the winter wheat crop might have been destroyed by inclement weather conditions, and that a spring planting of soybeans might have replaced the wheat crop.

Some wetness in the northwest was noted in November, 1958, for those counties where an above average decrease occurred; severe temperatures with much less precipitation and no snow cover in December of that year might have caused freezing; and flood-like conditions occurred in January of 1959 in two of the areas of greater than average decline. The isohyets of 5 and 6 inches for a 48 hour period include most of these areas (Figure 3). Frozen flood waters in lowland areas possibly caused suffocation of the wheat plants. The above average precipitation of May and June, 1959, did not co-vary with an above average decrease. The "adverse weather condition hypothesis" was therefore accepted, and the class concluded that the decline in wheat

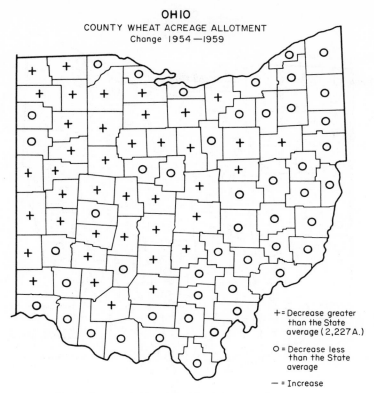

OHIO
COUNTY WHEAT ACREAGE ALLOTMENT
Change 1954—1959

+ = Decrease greater
than the State
average (2,227 A.)

O = Decrease less
than the State
average

— = Increase

Fig. 5. County wheat acreage allotment, Ohio, 1954–1959.

production in Ohio from 1954 to 1959 was associated with an unfavorable growing season for the year on which the 1959 figures are based.

Summary

Of the seven hypotheses proposed by the students, three were quickly rejected; but, on the basis of available data, four were accepted as possible "explainers" for changes in wheat production in Ohio between 1954 and 1959. Whereas, in the beginning, several students believed that their particular hypothesis was the *only* explanation, they all agreed that the solution was much more complex than they had anticipated originally. They were satisfied, however, that through the use of statistics and the process of visual correlation they had determined the major factors contributing to the decline in wheat production in Ohio for the years indicated.

+ = Decrease greater
than 5,341 acres

O = Decrease less
than 5,341 acres

— = Increase

Fig. 6A. Wheat acreage, Ohio, 1954–1959.

TEACHING THE PRINCIPLES
OF INDUSTRIAL LOCATION

John P. Neal

During the academic year, 1962–63, two experimental courses in geography were taught at Newton High School, Newtonville, Massachusetts, as part of the High School Geography Project. Both classes were offered at the twelfth grade level. The 58 students in the two classes were enrolled either in the commercial or lower college preparatory curricula, and had been selected and grouped homogeneously by the IBM data process. The median I.Q. for these students was 101. Of the total only three had taken a prior

Reprinted from John P. Neal, "Teaching the Principles of Industrial Location," in *Selected Classroom Experiences: High School Geography Project,* ed. Clyde F. Kohn, Geographic Education Series No. 4, 1964, National Council for Geographic Education, Illinois State Normal University, Normal, Ill., pp. 15–19.

OHIO
SOYBEAN ACREAGE
Change 1954–1959

+ = Increase greater
than 3.716 acres
O = Increase less
than 3.716 acres
— = Decrease

Fig. 6B. Soybean acreage, Ohio, 1954–1959.

high school course in geography. At midyear a letter-grade breakdown of all marks received by these students within the social studies department showed that 6 per cent had received A's; 29 per cent, B's; 35 per cent, C's; 21 per cent, D's; and 5 per cent, F's.

The learning experiences discussed in this paper arose out of a local incident. In the fall of 1962, the Raytheon Manufacturing Company, an electronics firm employing approximately 36,000 workers, experienced the loss of several governmental contracts, thereby causing a general reduction of employees. As a result, the life-motif of many of the students of Newton High School was disrupted by a sharp decline in parental income. For youngsters reared in an overall atmosphere of affluence, such an event was catastrophic. Class questions were raised as to reasons for this situation. From a pedagogical standpoint, the "felt-need" for some rational explanation was readily apparent, and the class was motivated to find answers, if possible, for the questions raised.

Few of the learners realized, however, that here was a problem with distinct geographic overtones. The students, like many other groups, were confronted with a problem, the geography, economics, and politics of which dwindled in significance before the problem itself. Since the business of the class was to learn geographic principles and concepts, the geographic dimensions of the problem received center-stage. The instructor made it a point, however, to refer to other aspects of the issue whenever it seemed appropriate.

After the problem had been defined with clarity, the students indicated their desire to know why particular industries locate in or migrate from specific locations; why California firms could affect Massachusetts payrolls; and why some locations seem to attract particular kinds of industries having like problems. After introductory remarks by the teacher and class discussions based on readings in several economic geography textbooks, the students listed the generally accepted criteria for industrial location—presence of natural resources, markets, and power. In addition, they noted that some industries appear to be "footloose." Other criteria, including political stability, a developed circulatory system, availability of skilled labor and investment capital, and general cultural advantages of one site over another were ruled secondary to the problem, and thus omitted from the investigations.

The Study of Resource-Oriented Industries

To study the relations of natural resources to plant location, the paper and pulp industry, the frozen concentrated juice industry, and the fishing industry were selected. The "case study" approach was used in all instances. In studying the fishing industry, field work in the Boston-Gloucester area by a class committee proved to have a high educational value to both students and teacher. Following an initial investigation, the shellfish aspect of the fishing industry began to intrigue the field workers to a marked degree. As a result, fishermen were interviewed; the executive officers of Howard Johnson's, a major buyer of fish, were consulted; and an executive of a leading fish-packing house, Gorton's, was contacted. The class also reviewed a copy of a study sent to the then Governor of the Commonwealth, Governor Volpe, including recommendations for improving Massachusetts fisheries. As the class expanded its study to include the fresh waters of the Charles River, the teacher was contacted by a member of the Massachusetts State Legislature who wished to duplicate the classroom method of using 95 vertical aerial photographs to reconstruct the Charles River Basin for an indoor "field trip." The state legislator was also concerned with offshore fishing and river pollution.

It was during this activity that the class became aware of the many facets entering the matrix of the problem. Pollution of clam flats and lobster beds, applications of the Pure Food and Drug Act, impact of Canadian imports, unionism, urban sewage disposal practices, and conservation organizations were found to be elements in the distribution of commercial fisheries. The opportunity for exciting digression was always present. For example, in the Gloucester case, the question was raised as to why Italian descendants tended to go on one-day fishing runs whereas Portuguese descendants tended to go on four-day, or more, voyages? Or, whatever became of the "Old Yankee" fisherman so dominant during the nineteenth century? The field workers required an entire class hour to report findings and to give a limited demonstration of equipment related to this resource-oriented industry. The findings which follow indicate the many geographic avenues the class pursued during the investigative process.

1. *Changes in dietary habits is a part of the changing American culture.* This fact was established by asking students and their parents, "Did you, when you were young, take cod-liver oil in your orange juice every morning?" The affirmative response of the parents, speaking from their childhood experiences, and the negative response of the students gave evidence of a change in dietary habits. The results were inverse when fried clams, now in short supply, were placed in the paradigm.

2. *The feeding areas of fish are changing.* According to several of those consulted during the study, the temperature of the North Atlantic appears to be getting warmer. The fish, therefore, are migrating farther north to maintain the same temperature and feeding habits. This means that a New England fishing vessel must range farther from home port in order not to return a "broker," that is, a vessel whose catch does not meet expenses.

3. *The technology of fishing is changing.* New ways of catching fish with larger nets mean that there may be fewer fish in the future to catch. One "old salt" reported that thirty years ago it was difficult to see the shallow bottom of the Grand Banks because the fish were so plentiful. Now fishermen not only see the bottom, they can also see the few fish that remain there to feed. Modern dragging nets scoop up seaweed and other plant life along with the fish!

4. *Foreign fishing fleets are changing in composition.* Because the oceans belong to all nations to share alike, several nations have fished the North Atlantic for centuries. Recently the appearance of Soviet fishing vessels in increasing numbers has been reflected in smaller American catches and in an increase in the number of "brokers." Since monetary profit is not a direct factor in the Soviet governmental motive, their vessels fish in concentrated numbers and follow a checkerboard pattern. This pattern is efficient in cleaning out an area, but it cannot be utilized by profit-seeking fishermen.

The use of the word "changing" in these findings was seized upon by the teacher in order to introduce the dynamic character of industrial geography. Although not related to the principles of resource-oriented industries, the class was quick to note that the cotton textile industry is a classic example of a migrating industry. They had heard about the impact of this migration on the local economy of such industrial towns as Lowell, Lawrence, and others in the Merrimac Valley. It so happened that a series of television debates between two candidates for the United States Senate spotlighted this very topic at the time it was being discussed by the class.

To map the migration of the cotton textile industry, data on spindles-in-operation were obtained from several volumes of the *Statistical Abstract of the United States*. It may be noted that slower learners were helped to visualize this migration by constructing a chronological series of dot maps or bar graphs. When secured by staples these maps could be flipped rapidly with the fingers and gave a motion picture effect of the movement of spindles-in-operation from the New England states to the Southern Piedmont. The more advanced students studied other aspects of the migration of the cotton textile industry.

THE STUDY OF MARKET- AND POWER-ORIENTED INDUSTRIES

In addition to studying industries which were resource-oriented, such as the paper and pulp industry, the frozen concentrated juice industry and the fishing industry, the class studied an industry which was market-oriented and one that was power-oriented. For a market-oriented industry, the class selected for study the location of a Coca Cola Bottling plant. Such plants are generally small in size, and have limited market areas. Thus they tend to be located quite near their customers.

The power principle was examined by studying the aluminum industry. In this instance, readings and brief lectures were relied upon, although aspects of the historic location of early New England textile mills at small waterfalls were introduced to tie this principle to the dynamic role of man's changing technology. The old Lowell mill, built at a falls on the Charles River in Waltham, Massachusetts, is only a few miles from the high school. Using this mill as an example, the power principle and the dynamic nature of our culture were related.

The concept of "footloose" industries developed rapidly out of the foregoing studies. The Commonwealth of Massachusetts was defined by the students as a political unit within an industrial region of such plants. The case of the now defunct Waltham Watch Company was used to focus student attention on problems related to footloose industries. Another, and extremely interesting reason for selecting the Waltham Watch Company, was the fact that the present Raytheon Manufacturing Company, the industry which motivated the study of industrial location in the first place, now occupies the site formerly occupied by the Waltham Watch Company. The class was quick to recognize this fact as an example of industrial sequent occupance.

At this point, a chalkboard chart was constructed by the teacher to show the "geographer's way" of developing locative principles. The chart was predicated on cost-distance-per-ton-mile of inputs of raw materials and outputs of finished products. The chart aided in summarizing locative principles in terms of the "value-added" concept. It appeared to be helpful for reflecting on understandings developed during the actual case studies.

Although the chart completed the formal classwork on the problem of industrial location and change, later units of study, both topical and regional, afforded opportunities to evaluate the student's ability to apply the principles learned to new situations. It was gratifying to note that many students did refer to them during the remainder of the course, and in several instances used them in their oral and written work.

As a concluding note, however, it should be stated that not all the class mastered all the concepts and principles. Courses have a way of ending before they are really through. Nonetheless, the learning experiences did provide new insights into industrial location and changes in the location and distribution of industrial plants.

CHAPTER 27 History

History remains the center of the social studies programs in most American schools. The typical curriculum still includes two years of American history in the eighth and eleventh grades and a year of world history, usually in the tenth. Although some school systems are experimenting with different grade placements, few are trying to reduce the total amount of time devoted to history in order to include more of the remaining social sciences.

Yet history courses seem to satisfy no one. One major complaint concerns the inability of a teacher and his students to "cover" the material. By this teachers usually mean that they feel obliged to get through the entire text-book during the school year. But each year the texts get longer and the demands on social studies teachers to teach current events and to undertake a bewildering array of extra projects grow more pressing.

The problem of coverage cannot be solved without precise criteria by which to determine the content of a course. Advising teachers to "posthole," that is, to study a few periods in depth and to span the time between them with strands of connective narrative, does not solve the problem. Teachers still must decide where to sink their postholes and what goals to set when they embark on a study in depth.

A second complaint focuses around teaching techniques that demand only the accumulation of factual information. In many history classes, students read their texts, learn the facts and generalizations they find there, and reproduce this information on examinations. This kind of teaching, and the books on which it is based, is dull and leads to unmotivated students and poor achievement.

Reform is at last under way. Since 1960 at least thirty books of readings containing source materials have been published for the use of history students in secondary schools. The authors of the volumes have established carefully selected criteria for the inclusion of content. Most are suitable for

432

inductive teaching rather than for the expository teaching, either by question-and-answer recitation or by disguised lectures, that characterizes history classes in most schools. Several major curriculum reform projects, including ones centered at Amherst College, Educational Services, Inc., and Carnegie Institute of Technology, are now preparing materials for whole courses of study in history that utilize inductive approaches.

History may be more poorly taught than other parts of the social sciences because it is far more complicated. While a political scientist or an economist may concentrate his efforts upon one social science discipline, a historian must explore all of them in order to know enough to examine entire societies in the past. He wants to know about economic organizations, political institutions, social structure, art, religion—in short, every aspect of the lives of the people he writes about. To do so, he should understand the point of view of each of the social sciences, for from them he draws the analytical questions useful to give order and meaning to the disparate facts his research uncovers.

Because history draws upon the other social studies disciplines, we have placed the chapters concerned with it at the end of this section. Chapter 27 consists of two parts. The first examines the structure of history; the second comments implicitly upon structure by analyzing the new emphasis upon teaching history by a discovery method. As you read, keep the following questions in mind:

1) How is the structure of history related to the structure of the other social sciences? What does this relation imply about the placement of history in the curriculum as it is related to the placement of other social studies?
2) Do his data and the influence of the times in which he writes limit the historian's use of analytical questions drawn from the social sciences?
3) Do the different modes of inquiry of the historian and the social scientist described by Richard Brown imply a difference in the nature of these disciplines?
4) How can the approach to teaching discussed in the first article in this chapter be used appropriately with the conception of history described in the second article?

PROBLEMS OF HISTORICAL ANALYSIS

Social Science Research Council

SEQUENCE, CAUSE, PREDICTION

The central problem of history is the analysis of change, and historians, whether they wish it or not, furnish the materials to guide or at least to justify policies, opinions, and predictions.

There are two kinds of contribution that historians can make to an understanding of human behavior. One is descriptive. In the descriptive function, events that actually took place and the order in which they occurred are identified. This function is "scientific" in the sense that it establishes credible evidence ("facts") by the critical use of documents. But if the investigator stops at this point and declines to analyze the *how* and the *why* of the temporal sequences that he describes, he is mistaking the initial task for the actual problem. The truly scientific function begins where the descriptive function stops. The scientific function involves not only identifying and describing temporal sequences; it also involves explaining them.

When we speak of explaining or understanding a given sequence of events, we mean that we undertake to give reasons for those particular events or, in other words, to explain why they occurred in that particular order. To do so is to make a statement about causation. No understanding of causation can come from a mere descriptive statement of sequence. When causal relationships enter into the interpretation we have gone far beyond description; we have begun to explain.

The social sciences do not solve the problem of analyzing time sequences but they do contribute to the historian's understanding of why men, groups, and societies behave in the way they do. They provide ways of looking at the evidence that research experience has shown to be helpful. The first step in the analysis of historical time sequences is not close scrutiny of "the documents," but rather an informed understanding of the factors that condition life in the world around us. If the historian cannot understand the behavior of individuals and groups in his own time and in his own culture, he is unlikely to be able to understand life in an earlier period and in a different cultural context. There are, to be sure, serious dangers involved in reading history backwards and in interpreting the past in the light of the present. But the historian's attempt to dissociate himself from contemporary conflicts and ideologies scarcely implies that he should strip himself of his priceless human experience. Nor does it imply that he should deny himself the use of the tech-

Reprinted from "Problems of Historical Analysis," *The Social Sciences in Historical Study: A Report of the Committee on Historiography,* Bulletin 64 (1954), Social Science Research Council, pp. 86–105, with omissions.

niques that social scientists have devised for analyzing contemporary situations and events. The only argument for dissociating oneself from the present is the persistent need for objectivity. . . .

There is, however, one important sense in which the demands made upon the historian are greater than those made upon the specialized social scientist. Like other social scientists, the historian can break down by analytic methods the complex of factors involved in human interaction; but because he is a historian, he must also undertake to appraise larger interrelationships and attempt a general synthesis. The analysis of interrelations goes on in all social science, but the attempt to make a general synthesis of all major factors at work in a given conjuncture of events is peculiar to historical studies. It is true that monographic studies in history may isolate special segments for intensive analysis; but the conscientious historian, even when engaged upon monographic research, never permits himself to forget the final goal, namely, comprehensive synthesis. Further, the historian not only strives for an understanding of the total situation *as it is* at any given point of time, but also undertakes to explain how that situation *came to be*. From the historical point of view an event is not something isolated. It is not, as the botanist's specimen is sometimes erroneously held to be, something distinct which can be transfixed with a pin and fastened to a board with a label attached. Both are always parts of a process, the precipitates of the interplay of dynamic factors operating through preceding events and probably continuing to operate through succeeding events. The significance of each lies in its relations to a past and to a future.

Reasons such as these make it vital for the social science historian to keep himself informed about the concepts and hypotheses developed by the nonhistorical social sciences. The historian's task is of considerably greater complexity than the task facing any of the nonhistorical social sciences. The complex of factors operative in a given situation is what intrigues the historian. Historical complexities, while baffling, are not unresolvable. But if we are to understand them, the use of a wide variety of carefully chosen analytical tools is required. Given adequate tools and skill in their use, the problem is not insuperable. Factors can be identified and analyzed, even though the data do not provide adequate comprehension of all particulars. The tendencies to which the factors give rise can be evaluated, for they are not without knowable effects and direction. Interpretative synthesis is possible, and the problem is one of "discovering in the data the modes and tendencies of action and intreaction." . . .

CONCEPTS AND HYPOTHESES AS ANALYTICAL TOOLS

In trying—as all historians do—to interpret their data and to select certain facts as significant for their analysis, historians engage in a form of mental activity very similar to that of the policy maker and the forecaster. The only type of historical research that neither implicitly nor explicitly makes use of theory is the purely narrative chronicle which simply records events without indicating interrelationships. Any other type of historical research must necessarily *select* those events that are recorded and those that are emphasized as significant. But if the historian selects, he does so according to some criterion. This criterion of selection is not inherent in the data; it is supplied by the historian.

Were the products of the historian's work regarded merely as entertainment, without either practical or pedagogical value, there would be no reason to choose principles of selection and interpretation. The historian could then be as arbitrary as he chose, and no one could dispute him. Similarly, no problem would exist if he were interested solely in supporting the ideology of a particular group, for then others would already have supplied him with principles. But if the historian is prepared to take responsibility for his results, if he is willing to vouch for them as valid interpretations of the past and reliable guides for the formation of future policies, then he has a duty to justify his choice of principles of selection and interpretation, to justify them not only to his own conscience but also to his professional colleagues and to all who permit his work to influence their opinions. History as social science rests on the postulate that history can be more than entertainment and more than ideology. History as social science insists that principles of selection and interpretation must be rationally chosen and rationally established; and it suggests that this can be done only by making the theories upon which it is based explicit and open to objective appraisal. . . .

In social science inquiry it is helpful to think of theories not as means of summing up a mass of data already obtained, but as means of guiding the search for data and of assisting the process of analysis and interpretation. Theories in this sense are explanatory devices. They are constructed experimentally and they are evaluated in terms of how well they enable us to discover, analyze, and explain the evidence.

Any historian, therefore, who attempts to use social science theories in his work must clearly understand that he is taking part in an experiment. These theories are not statements of eternal and immutable truth; they are, rather, statements that *may possibly provide valid explanations.* The task of the social science historian and of all other social scientists is to discover, by a process of testing and experiment, which theories are valid in whole or in part, how they relate to other theoretical formulations, and how other theories having greater validity may be constructed. The test of validity in this context is a practical one: How well does this theory *explain* the evidence? Does it help us to *understand?* . . .

As far as the social science historian is concerned, it will probably be most helpful if he thinks of hypotheses as questions that he asks of his data. Historians are understandably reluctant to accept as their primary task the testing of general theories which other social scientists have developed, and perhaps it is well that this should be so. For the historian the value of social science concepts and theories lies in the fact that they extend the range of questions that he can put to his data, and at the same time provide some indication of the kinds of data required if his questions are to be answered.

The more the historian is concerned with interpretations, with interrelations of all kinds, including causal interrelations, the greater is his need for an understanding of the social sciences. But social science approaches to history can never be applied mechanically. To talk glibly of developing concepts and testing hypotheses is simple; but rules of procedure of this kind will no more produce competent historians than an elementary handbook on chess can produce a Capablanca. The richer the intellectual and cultural equipment of the historian, the richer and more illuminating the results of his research will be. The use of social science approaches in historical research is merely a means, and only one, through which the historian can attempt to apply his intellectual faculties to better advantage.

Historians in the United States have become increasingly familiar with the use of conceptualized approaches. As a consequence, they have been driven to re-examine the nature and function of historical knowledge. Despite apprehensions, observes a member of the former Committee on Historiography, "the use of social science generalizations by the historian is increasing." More frequently, he notes, historians are setting themselves the task of discovering single cases that illustrate a social science generalization, and single cases that contradict it; and he comments on the appearance of numerous comparative studies designed to test the application of a social science generalization to similar sequences or trends. *The steady growth of historical analyses by means of concepts and hypotheses illustrates the extent to which history has already developed as a social science.* Further development depends upon a twofold expansion: an increasing use of concepts from allied fields, and greater exploitation of those ways of conceptualizing already employed and refined by historians. . . .

STRUCTURE AND PROCESS

Historians who have made social science part of their thinking are not satisfied to regard history only in terms of events. There are two other ways of viewing and interpreting the subject matter of history. One is in terms of the *structure* of the situation in which events take place. A business firm, a political party, a revolution, a university, a casual meeting of two acquaintances— all these may be described correctly as systems of human interaction, characterized by a greater or lesser degree of organization. The degree and mode of organization in a situation is its *structure*. The concept of structure enables us to build a theoretical bridge between the unique individual, with all his particularities and idiosyncrasies, and the environment in which the individual acts. Individual behavior and the structure of the social environment are viewed not as independent, but as interdependent. Human beings exist as parts of social organizations, and their behavior is patterned by the roles they play in those organizations and by controls enforced through a multitude of power-wielding groups, who in turn are responsive to well-established cultural traditions. An adequate explanation of a particular segment of human behavior (such as the career of a statesman) must therefore take account of the structure of the situation in which this behavior takes place. It is this structure that channels behavior into particular lines, limiting freedom of action in some directions, opening up wider possibilities in others.

Equally useful, and in the same sense scientific, is the approach to historical events in terms of *process*. Changes in a structure are frequently not random or haphazard, but follow definite patterns through time. For example, economists and other social scientists speak of "the process of industrialization." They mean that the changes that occur in a society when it moves from a predominantly agricultural to a predominantly industrial state follow a recognizable course which can be identified and analyzed *as a separable phenomenon*. Structure and process are closely related concepts, since the changes that are identified as constituting a process are always changes in a structure. They reflect the interaction of the parts of that structure. The process of industrialization, for example, consists in a complex series of changes in the size and composition of the labor force, the techniques and organization of production, the relationships of capital and labor, and many other factors. By calling it a process we refer to the fact that these changes follow a pattern which can be described and analyzed.

The related concepts of structure and process provide a highly useful guiding thread in the analysis of causation. They are fundamental to any systematic study of change. They enable the historian to penetrate beneath the superficial manifestations of change and to seek an explanation in terms of underlying trends and conditioning factors. For example, to analyze the history of the American family, one needs to study its internal structure (the interrelated roles of father, son, daughter, mother, uncle, and other kin), its relationship to the culture and society of which it is a part (the effects of industrialism, urban living, wider educational opportunities, the "emancipation" of women, and similar elements), and the processes through which changes in internal structure are affected by, and in turn affect, its external relationships. Or again, one would analyze the outbreak of World War I not so much in terms of assassinations and ultimatums as in terms of the social (especially the political and economic) structures of the national states involved, the structure of international relations (perhaps with particular emphasis on international trade and investment and the struggle for markets and raw materials), and the process by which conflicts arising from internal strains in the structures of national states were reflected in and aggravated by conflicts in the international sphere.

An approach that uses the concepts of structure and process, in short, leads us to ask questions that cannot be answered merely by identifying the succession of events. Events are of the moment, episodic; process and structure have duration in time, recognizable patterns, and a high degree of continuity. An approach that focuses on underlying trends and movements makes it possible to see particular events and the actions of particular men in a larger, more revealing perspective. . . .

Approach to the History of Culture

Analysis of the interplay of cultural factors in the context of history is no easy task. Human beings in every time and place are largely unconscious of the conditioning effect of their cultural traditions; and the documents and other artifacts they leave do not give the historian self-evident explanations of the influence of the culture on individual actions. But it is not impossible for the historian (and the cultural anthropologist) to achieve some understanding of what seems to people in a particular time and place to be normal and natural, i.e., what they take for granted. He can often observe better than the historical actors in the situation the peculiarities of their culture as contrasted with others. He can develop the implicit from the explicit. He can separate for analysis parts of the cultural tradition, for example, practical skills and factual knowledge (technological); the institutional tradition (organizational); and intellectual and emotional orientation (ideational). These may all be viewed as structures with recognizable patterns; and their processes of change may be identified and analyzed. They are interconnected, and the interplay in the relations between them constitutes a basic problem for historical research.

One convenient way of analyzing the interplay of the parts of a culture is in terms of the groups of persons who transmit or diffuse the bodies of knowledge and tradition. Particular groups (priestly, military, commercial) that play an active part in transmitting important skills, learning, or traditions are said to serve as *carriers* of the culture. When Dixon Ryan Fox wrote of "Culture in Knapsacks," he was dealing with the carriers of culture from the eastern seaboard of the United States to the frontier. Since the carriers of culture are men, they may be studied as groups and individuals. Culture is pluralistic; there is no universal man who carries the whole culture. A psychological concept, the human tendency toward highly selective perception, may be serviceable here. Individuals or groups carry and diffuse those elements of the cultural tradition that are rooted in their own experience and meaningful in terms of their particular intellectual and emotional orientation. Thus each group and each individual carries only part of the culture. In particular, it is that part of the whole culture that provides the occupational learning, sets the norms, and sanctions the interests of the group or groups with which the individual is chiefly identified. A good example of the analysis of the carrying of a part of Western culture is Hayes' study of nationalism, specifically the gradual transmission of its intellectual and emotional orientation downward, in vertical diffusion from higher social groups to lower ones.

But men make traditions as well as carry them. Traditions are at once forms of social learning and group interpretations of past experience. New factual knowledge, acquired by diffusion or by discovery and invention, permits a new interpretation of the cultural tradition, for example, the development of a new form of social organization; and eventually this modification, too, becomes an accepted part of the interpretation of past experience. Thus culture grows and changes usually by small increments, as inherited traditions and ways of acting are continually modified by the necessity of meeting new problems. Typically this cumulative reinterpretation and reshaping of the cultural tradition takes place covertly and without any conscious awareness of the direction of change; but there are occasions when people pause and take stock, as it were, perhaps at a time of crisis when the adequacy of the accepted cultural tradition in providing an effective solution to an urgent problem is put to the test.

There are, therefore, discontinuities as well as continuities in cultural change. There are times of cultural disorganization and even cultural crisis, when elements of the inherited tradition, such as basic patterns of behavior, work routines, and emotional and intellectual attitudes, are seriously disrupted and the culture seems to lose much of its internal cohesion. Ordinarily such discontinuities are followed by the emergence of new cultural patterns and new interpretations of the cultural tradition. In the depression of the 1930's the widespread disruption of traditional ways of acting and thinking in the United States—the feeling of being lost in a world from which the old familiar landmarks had disappeared—was a symptom of partial cultural disorganization. And in some but not all respects one might cite the New Deal to illustrate cultural emergence. In dealing with periods of rapid cultural change of this type, it is important to inquire to what extent the existing cultural tradition provided an adequate and effective solution to immediate problems; the emergence of cultural change, of a redefinition of the cultural tradition and of its potentialities, indicates a discrepancy between the problem and its traditional solution. It is in this context that consideration of the "vitality" and "creativity" of cultures becomes relevant. . . .

A Convergent Approach

Historians of different temperaments and training will prefer different ways of combining and varying social science concepts in the analysis of particular problems; and an experimental attitude—a willingness to put different approaches to the test—is of course to be encouraged. One way of tackling the problem may be suggested here, purely as an illustration. A strictly scientific treatment would start with the identification of a problem. Most historians, however, like to focus on concrete events and to proceed by narrative exposition; they are likely therefore to begin with the dramatic context—the situation, the persons, the location in space and time. As a method of presentation in contradistinction to a method of analysis, this has much to recommend it.

Nevertheless, since the concepts and hypotheses to be used depend upon careful formulation of the problem, the historian will contrive to define his problem and indicate how he intends to handle it in the initial setting of the historical stage.

Since the historian is dealing with the behavior of human beings in a social context, he will then proceed (we refer now to his order of analysis rather than to his method of presentation) to analyze the structure of the various situations in which his *dramatis personae* find themselves. What social roles do they play? What systems of sanctions do they encounter in playing these roles, what groups or individuals exert these sanctions, and how effectively are they enforced? Do we find conflict and inconsistency between patterns of sanctions or between those patterns and the predispositions of the actors? Are there processes of change at work? If so, is the behavior of the persons being studied consistent with these long-term tendencies? These and many other more specific questions will at once suggest themselves. In fact, any historian who has grasped the concept of social structure will find examples awaiting analysis at every turn: groups, individuals in groups, groups as functioning parts of society, demographic aspects of groups, their position with respect to possession of goods or wealth, their attendant position of power in economic relations, their political influence, their position in respect to command of the means of violence, and their position in respect to ideas and the manipulation of symbols. For analysis of group action, particularly in the political sphere, the historian may find Lasswell's categories suggestive, especially manipulation of symbols, control of goods, and control of the means of violence.

The historian who is concerned with social change in the broadest sense, and in particular with the role of ideas, may find helpful certain approaches that can be derived from anthropology and the sociology of knowledge. Analyses focused on the roles that particular men and groups play in generating and diffusing new knowledge and other cultural elements serve to correct the inadequacy of an abstract linear treatment of an idea as it changes through time. Ideas have functions for the groups that hold them; an adequate explanation of the history of an idea must include some analysis of the functions that this idea performed for different groups. A linear treatment of an idea, on the other hand, tends to emphasize its development in terms of its own inner logic, and thus to slight its meaning in particular contexts.

Analysis of the changing function of ideas in time and space places intellectual development in its social setting and can attempt to show the role of ideas in cultural change. For example, historians have frequently observed how a new idea opens up possibilities of change in a culture that were not perceived and perhaps not present before. A case in point is the early development of modern science, which was inspired by the idea that natural phenomena were not unpredictable, reflecting the haphazard operations of some supernatural agency, but followed "laws" that could be discovered by the exercise of reason. Such a cultural accretion opens up new potentialities for growth; it extends the limits of the possible. This concept of the *potentiality* of a culture at different points of time clearly needs more refinement and critical examination than it has yet received, but it may nevertheless be useful. When observing a culture that seems stagnant, for example, or one which is changing very slowly, a historian might well investigate the factors—physical, social, and cultural—that set limits to the possible range of alternative directions of growth. Balancing this concept of potentiality, then, we have the concept of *options* or alternatives; and both these concepts rest upon the concept of a culture as a *state of knowledge. The state of knowledge at a given time, when analyzed, may reveal the limits of the possible; that is, that some of the supposed options were not real options, or that the supposed options fell short of the potentialities that in fact existed.*

It is important that the historian, in using the concepts of culture and social structure, should not implicitly assume a greater degree of homogeneity than is actually present. To reify a culture or a social structure, as some writers have abstracted the state, to regard it as something that can exist independently and apart from the behavior of its individual members, would be to fall into the fallacy of misplaced concreteness. Even a tightly integrated society, indeed a totalitarian one, exhibits a measure of plurality. All groups participate in the transmission and interpretation of culture, but their participation is partial, and occurs at different levels and with different degrees of intensity. Each group in pursuing its interests sees a future, judges potentialities, estimates the limits of the possible, and asks, "What can be done?" Even when a group regards its interests as identical with those of the larger society of which it forms a part, its judgment of potentialities and options is likely to be highly autistic. What it sees will depend on where it stands. A social evil, for example, may go unrecognized or be accepted as inevitable for generations, until some influential group, in the light of new knowledge or a reinterpretation of its interests, decides that it is to be defined as an evil and that something can be done about it. *Potentialities arise from the introduction of new knowledge, particularly factual knowledge, and therewith new experiences and new moral ideas; but the movement to realize a potential may have to wait for a long period until changes in group relations permit positive action.*

Judgments by groups as to what can be done provide historians with documents from which they can infer the various alternatives that different segments of a society take to be real choices. These options may not have been real alternatives, and it is proper to raise the question which were realistic appraisals of the possible and which were not. Even though subjectively held and possibly unrealistic, these group appraisals of potentiality are objective data in the historical context and provide the historian with some of his most useful evidence, particularly in regard to the process by which competing groups in society achieve and retain positions of dominance. Competing groups appeal to those parts of the cultural tradition that best rationalize their interests and best sanction their judgment of potentiality. This competition injects into the historical record an appearance of multiple choice; and the process by which competition and conflict is worked out so that finally one and only one choice is made presents the historian with classic problems of multiple causation.

Thus, in the approach suggested by concepts used in other social sciences, the historian is concerned with finding a valid explanation of particular sequences of events; he develops this explanation by relating the concrete sequence to underlying tendencies and processes of change in the structure of the society and culture. He starts with the unique historical situation and, while setting his stage, states his problem. He then analyzes the structure of the situation at several different but related levels—the immediate context, the groups involved, the structure of the society, and the cultural tradition—with particular emphasis on the processes and potentialities of change at each of these levels and how they influenced individual behavior. His conclusion, if his analysis is successful, is a generalized statement of the nature and meaning of the sequence of events in this particular culture, and an *explanation* of the sequence in terms of the causal influences affecting it. On the monographic level, a general synthesis of this variety is not necessarily called for. Research would be in order on any particular segment of the causal nexus and on any particular level of analysis.

HISTORY AS DISCOVERY: AN INTERIM REPORT ON THE AMHERST PROJECT

Richard H. Brown

I do not need to tell you people who are so closely connected with education that there is raging on every side nothing less than a revolution in American education. I do not need to tell you, either, I suspect, that that revolution is coming most slowly in the teaching of the social studies, most slowly of all perhaps in history. But it is coming there as well, even in history, and I am here this morning to tell you a bit about our project, which is designed, quite frankly, to give it a push.

The revolution is, in fact, long overdue, nowhere more so than in the teaching of history. As a nation we have little sense of our history. We have less sense of what history is. What passes for it far too often is a frightful blend of antiquarianism and patriotism. The critical qualities, the reasoned temper and

Reprinted from an address given by Richard H. Brown at the 25th Annual Convention of the National School Boards Association, April 1965.

judgment and perspective that a study of history ought to provide are precisely those intellectual qualities which, as a society, we lack the most. And I am sorry to have to tell you that I think the over-all situation is growing worse, even while there are signs of possible improvement. New curricula in the social sciences and humanities seem to be ushering aside history, organizing courses that teach sociological and anthropological concepts set down in historical periods, making a bow to history as fact even while they usher it out the door as intellectual discipline. "The time may come, not more than ten years from now," as an official of the American Historical Association has put it quite candidly, "when historians may wake up to discover that what happened to the classics has happened to history." He could not have been more right.

It was concern about these matters that gave birth to our work, four years ago. That work was begun at a meeting of history teachers from the schools and from the four colleges in the Amherst area. The group had scarcely assembled before the question was thrown out to the college teachers in the group as to what it was they assumed about their students' preparation when they came into their first college history course. The answer was, quite simply, that they assumed nothing, that they had found they could assume nothing except a considerable aversion for history and a kind of bland patriotism, which was frequently more an impediment than a help. The next question was what should they be able to assume, and to this the answer that came back out of the group as a whole was that they should be able to assume not so much a knowledge of facts—these were after all readily available—as a sense of what facts were, of what history was. Above all they should be able to assume a capacity to doubt, to ask questions, to criticize. To do this, the high school teachers in the group replied, they had to be able to give the student not just the factual narrative of "answers" that one found in a textbook but hisorical evidence about which the student could ask questions and from which he could seek to draw his own conclusions. Starting with a few hundred dollars from the four colleges, and the goal of a single unit, we set out to make such materials available. We have been at it ever since, at a steadily accelerating rate.

This summer we shall be preparing materials not only for the fast high school student but for the slow one, for the culturally deprived, the junior high school, and for adult education. The project has grown into a full-fledged research and development project. We are now not only producing materials but seeking to use them to assess what happens, and what can happen, in the study of history at all those levels at which it is taught by the person who is not himself a professional historian. The work is under the advisory supervision of a national committee of educators and scholars, known as the Committee on the Study of History. It is supported by the U.S. Office of Education and sponsored by Amherst College. We maintain two offices, one at Amherst, which is the center for summer writing camps at which groups of teachers prepare the experimental units; another at the Newberry Library in Chicago, which is the center of operations in the winter when materials are tried out in a group of approximately fifty participating schools scattered from coast to coast.

What we are doing, in brief, is trying to find out as much as we can about the implications of a *method* of studying history. That method is the so-called "discovery" method, which encourages inductive learning. Because of its similarity to the approach taken in the new math and the new physics we have been called the "new history." It is a pretentious term, but the reference is perhaps illuminating. In all, the emphasis is on giving the student not the conclusions of the scholars but the raw materials with which the scholar works, asking him to formulate the question and work his way through to his own conclusions, developing, in so doing, a sense of the structure of the discipline. In history, as in the other fields, the goal is to get him to develop his critical and conceptual faculties, to give him some sense of the nature of fact, of the limits of generalizations, and of the relationship between hypothesis, evidence, and proof—in short to encourage him to relate knowledge to inquiry and to help him develop the intellectual tools of inquiry.

We are not, I am delighted to say, the only group taking this approach. Various publishing projects are now under way providing suitable materials; social science curriculum revision projects are doing the same. Nor is it a new approach. In one way or another good teachers have used it for years. But it is an approach the implications of which for the study of history have never been adequately explored. It is the exploration of those implications—for the student learning, for the teacher teaching, and for the training of the teacher who will teach—that is the primary concern of our work.

One of the notions at which we are taking dead aim is the notion popular among teachers at all levels, and among publishers and historians as well, that the use of original evidence, to the extent that it is difficult, is proper fare only for the better student—that sources are, to use one of the most wretched words in the whole vocabulary of education, properly to be seen only as "enrichment." If it were true that the use of sources is in its nature more difficult, and it seemed to be the case nonetheless that this was the only sensible way of studying history, we ought to accept the responsibility to teach it this way, its difficulty notwithstanding.

But in fact one of the things in which we are most interested is the possibility that the use of sources may be the *best* way to present history to the slow learner, to the culturally deprived, to the young student—to all those whose experience and maturity is markedly different from the teacher and the textbook writer and the publisher. To give him the raw materials of knowledge—the evidence—rather than what someone on a different wave length has said about it, is to invite him to grapple with truth on his own, to start from where he is, to fit it into his own experience, to make it something useful and therefore worthwhile to him. To be sure, the fledgling inquirer of twelve may see in evidence something different from the inquirer of sixteen, and he in turn something different from the young man of twenty. But so also will one historian see in evidence something different from another; and something different from what he himself has seen at another time. The historian would be the last to say that knowledge of the past is absolute. Why is it not therefore true that it is the process of grappling with truth that is most important for the student to learn, more important by far than a set of textbook truths-that-are-not-quite-truths, thrown together for the occasion.

It is logical that this should be the approach to teaching history. If the goal of formal education is to equip one to educate himself through life—and who would dispute that that is its goal?—it makes infinitely more sense to train the student to be a sophisticated and careful inquirer than it does to fill him full of facts. It is more important that he come to appreciate what a fact is, how it comes to be, and how one uses it than it is that he memorize it. We are coming slowly and painfully to recognize this in American education, as we draw away from the rote learning of the past. The historian, traditionally conservative, is recognizing it perhaps most slowly, and most painfully, of all. But the fact of the matter is, and no historian would deny it, that the nature of history is inquiry. If there is merit in the argument that the good scholar makes the best teacher—and I genuinely believe there is—it lies precisely in the fact that he is thereby best able to realize this. And there is irony, even tragedy, when that person who devotes his life to inquiry, to exploring the frontiers of knowledge, goes into a classroom and forgets that this is the nature of his calling or indulges in the mistaken belief that his students should in fact be doing something different in nature from what he does.

As we face up to the question of the student learning history in this way, certain other things become clear. One is that the silly academic arguments about what history should include—whether it should be wars and politics or whether it should be American studies, whether it is a social science or a humanity—these arguments become inconsequential. History becomes the exploration of human relationships in time past, lead where it may. Boundaries and labels become unnecessary. Unity turns out to come from method and from the philosophical and conceptual apparatus with which one approaches his task. At the same time the need becomes clear, and the temptations happily enormous, to do what good history teaching has always required: to present subjects for investigation in a way that makes clear the larger questions of human relationships with which the student is dealing, inviting him the more pointedly to bring to the exploration his own experience and to see its consequences as consequences for him. Thus a study of the impact of the New World's discovery on the European imagination can be seen as a study of the processes and implications of discovery itself; a study of the Missouri Compromise can be a study of the nature, processes, and limits of political compromise; a study of immigration can be a study in the making and change of social values.

Second, if we are interested in the student learning, we are interested also, necessarily, in the teacher teaching—in what it is that he does, and can do, to make learning possible. We are interested in how he sets up his course and how he goes about presenting it. We are convinced that the genuinely good teacher will build his own course: that a course and a curriculum grow out of local circumstances, that they must be built for the particular students who will take them. We are not interested in providing a packaged or a "teacher-proof" course, but in the preparation of materials out of which the teacher can build his own course. We are not talking about a new history course so much as about a new *kind* of history course, which should vary from place to place and teacher to teacher, ideally even from student to student.

We are not convinced that the course has to march from A to Z, "covering" what happened in between, after the fashion of the traditional course. Still less are we convinced that A has to be Plymouth Rock and Z Vietnam, or that they have to be points in time at all. It may be that the concept of the "posthole," which has become popular in recent years, is misleading. This is the notion that in a history course the student should stop off occasionally along the way to dig in depth into a particular subject, usually by looking at sources. He then comes out of his posthole and rides the fence—which is the traditional narrative—along to the next posthole. The concept implies an assumption that our work seriously questions. This is the assumption, all but universally held among teachers, historians, and publishers alike that sources are by their nature supplementary to the traditional course, which must take the form of the familiar narrative. We are frankly interested in the possibility that a history course might move more effectively not from A to Z but from the inside out, with a student starting somewhere, perhaps anywhere, and moving backward and forward in time in truly inductive fashion, as inquiry leads him.

To be sure history, viewed in one sense, is a chronological narrative; but more important than narrative, it is relationships, such as cause and effect, put down in time. To be sure, it is somehow critical that a student who has studied American history should know that the Revolution preceded the Civil War; but it by no means follows that the only way for him to do that—or even the best way—is to study the Revolution in October and the Civil War in January. The way to understand chronology is not necessarily to take up things in chronological fashion, but to take them up in a fashion that makes clear the significance of the fact that one thing happened before another, while another thing followed. It may be, in other words, if I may overstate my case, that a student will learn more about chronology and come to appreciate better the fact that the Revolution preceded the Civil War if he spends three weeks piecing together for himself the steps that led to war with Mexico in 1845, perceiving in so doing how critical order-in-time is for understanding. . . .

Inevitably we come finally to an interest in the training of the teacher who will teach history. There is no more fundamental problem. At the heart of it, it seems to me, is the fundamental fact that the teacher who would teach history well has got to be trained by the historian, and the historian is not doing the job well. So long as he sees the point of teaching history as simply the communication of conclusions about the past, he will not do the job better. He has got to get across to prospective teachers some sense of what history is, not just of what the conclusions of the historians are. The problem is not, as unthinking historians have put it from time immemorial—most recently a group at the University of Indiana—that teachers do not "know" enough history. It is that they do not know what history is and that they have never been encouraged to think about how it can be used in the growth and development of the human beings they teach.

The federal government has now committed itself, through amendment to the National Defense Education Act, to the expenditure of 140 million dollars, part of which will support a series of history institutes for teachers to be given at colleges and universities all over the land, beginning this coming summer. The notion is to bring teachers into contact with historians for six weeks or so of "recharging," and particularly to bring them up to date on the latest historical interpretations. To the extent that they stimulate and excite, these institutes will make livelier teachers, because livelier people. But I frankly doubt if, in the last analysis, most of them will accomplish much. So long as they teach conclusions, even new conclusions, they will not, it seems to me, be going to the heart of the problem. The real challenge is to get across to teachers not conclusions but the nature of a conclusion, and to give them some sense of how an awareness of that bears on what they might be doing in a classroom.

We have made few more interesting discoveries in the course of our project than the wholly accidental one that our summer writing sessions for teachers who are preparing units are enormously valuable for teacher training and re-training. We did not plan this and we make no conscious effort along that line. What we do is to provide our group with a library and six weeks of completely free time to put together a unit of historical sources designed for teaching purposes. The task requires them to do two things that a surprisingly large number have never done before. One is to be a historian—for they have to do research and work through a subject themselves to find their sources. The second is to think about how they can use history in a classroom and why they are there anyway, for they have to decide what should be in a unit and what should not. The results, in a number of cases, have been people who have gone back into their classrooms new people and wholly different teachers. The reason for this, I think, is that the experience they are getting is one not governed by the prevailing delusion that one can somehow, in the training of teachers, separate "content" from teaching skills—a delusion unfortunately embraced with as much ardor by the historian as by the professional educator. And it is an experience, too, that challenges fundamentally the prevailing nonsense that the "content" of a history course and the "facts" one teaches are necessarily the same thing.

I would like, finally, to make some general observations about some interesting things we are learning as, well-meaning innocents, we go about our activities. One is the profound truth of the observation that it is impossible to generalize about what is going on in American education today. Educators err in doing it; academics surely do. One is struck going from classroom to classroom, as I have been doing, by the real meaning of something we all know intellectually: this is that education is as good and as bad as what goes on in each individual classroom, and in a fundamental sense nothing else makes any difference whatsoever. Some of the best classes I have seen taught this year have been in the worst schools, and some of the worst have been in the best. It does not make sense, in my opinion, for anyone to say we have a good school, let alone a good school system. The most that one can say is that we have a school or a system in which there are a number of classes in which something is really happening—without deluding ourselves about what "something" means. What characterizes the best schools is that they have a large number of genuinely first-rate teachers and are most concerned with making it possible for them to teach, free from the incessant interruptions that bedevil the high school classroom and free from the appalling bureaucratic impedimenta that so often come between teacher and student.

We have had no more amusing or instructive experience this year than one that occurred last fall when we solicited the cooperation of a list of teachers to try out our material. Two on the list were in the same school, in one of the large cities. Back from one, in two days' time, came an enthusiastic letter saying she would be delighted to experiment with the materials, send them on. From the other we heard nothing until, six weeks later, long after we had exhausted our supply of units, there came a letter from the curriculum supervisor in the superintendent's office saying that the letter had been passed on to him by the principal, who got it from the department head, who got it from our second teacher; he had talked it over with the assistant superintendent and the two of them thought that such a request for cooperation ought rather to be addressed to the superintendent, whose name he willingly provided me. We dropped that. The first teacher has been using our materials all year, in some exceptionally lively classes. The moral is, I think, if I can say it without seeming to lecture, that no department head, in that capacity, can teach a class. No principal or curriculum supervisor or superintendent can. I suppose not even a member of a school board can. The most each can do is to hire the very best people he can find, and then get out of the way.

Secondly, I would be remiss, even ungrateful, not to tell you about one experience we have had with a school board—and to tell you something about costs. I am something of a hard-nosed skeptic, not an entrepreneur. I do not believe that money is a panacea for the ills of education or even that it will necessarily help at all, unless it is well spent. One cannot venture far into the world of education without being impressed at how much nonsense is bought by money. Yet I must tell you frankly that it will cost more to teach history with materials such as ours than it does to teach it with a textbook. The cost of material per student per course will double or triple. I am impressed also by the fact that it costs us more than five hundred dollars simply for the physical production and distribution of a single unit to our try-out schools, not beginning to count the cost of getting it written. Back in our indigent days, when it was often uncertain from month to month whether we would be able to continue, we had few more heartening expressions of support than the willing participation of the town of Amherst school board, which picked up the tab for two of our summer writers, together with the production of their materials. And we have had no more generous expression of confidence than their continued financial participation in the project to this day.

Finally, I must say this. One cannot move back and forth between a college campus and the schools, as we are doing in our project, without becoming painfully aware of how many of the problems one faces are rooted in the indifference of many historians, and the ignorance of most, as to what is going on in American education. If all too often, as historians are wont to complain, history is taught by the football coach, the fault lies in my estimation more with the historian than it does with the principal who makes the assignment. Until the historian himself makes clear to the world that the study of history could and should involve something more complicated and something more demanding than the rote "coverage" of facts, history will remain the easiest and the best course for the coach to teach. And if all too often the high school teacher of history is badly trained, the fault lies, in my estimation, not so much at the feet of those people who train him in methods courses, as it does at the feet of those who do not train him properly in the so-called "content" courses. The content of history is something more than the conclusions to which past historians have come. The role of history in education—if it is to have any role at all—is more than the inculcation of knowledge about the past. Until historians come to realize this and to accept the responsibility that only they can discharge, progress will be slow.

I cannot end on a negative note. We are one among a number of groups on a great crusade to bring about some badly needed changes in American education. We are trying to do our part to carry forward what is nothing less than a revolution going on in American education. We started with no axes to grind and with a considered belief that it was high time to stop pointing fingers and generalizing from ignorance and to do something practical. We are trying to let each step lead on to the next rather than following a blueprint, and we are trying to say some sensible things along the way. We are finding on all sides a heartening response—from the committee of educators and scholars who are so graciously and generously giving their time and ideas to the direction of the project; from the U.S. Office of Education, which gives us sustenance; from the College that sponsors us and the community of scholars that gives us a berth in Chicago; from the Amherst school board; from principals and supervisors, and most importantly of all, from teachers from one end of the country to the other who are in fact doing the work, giving us their time and energy, and making the whole project possible. With their support we hope that when we have finished our endeavors we shall have accomplished something genuinely worthwhile.

CHAPTER 28 World History: Examples

Maligned by scholars, badly taught by teachers, and often despised by students, the world history course in some form is probably with us for at least another decade. Few school systems seem ready to abandon it despite increasing criticism. Even the new curriculum projects make obeisance at its altar, although their directors propose some radical changes. Everyone who hopes to be a social studies teacher must face the fact that sooner or later he will probably teach something that passes as world history at some grade level to some group of students.

Courses in world history face the problem of coverage to an exaggerated degree. Any attempt to touch upon all the major civilizations of the past in one year can lead to nothing except superficiality. More than any other group of teachers, the teachers of world history must face squarely the problem of defining criteria for the inclusion of content.

Coverage presents even greater problems in the new world cultures courses. Throughout the nation, teachers have been asked to include additional material about the non-European world in their world history courses. In some schools, teachers have tried to add units about Southeast Asia or Subsaharan Africa to an already overcrowded year. Moreover, they have tried to organize materials around a chronological framework rather than approach the study of a culture area as an anthropologist would. New editions of conventional world history textbooks follow this trend.

Every world history teacher should declare his independence from the tyranny of the textbooks. At least four books of reading for world history courses are now on the market. Literally hundreds of paperback books about the nonwestern world written specifically for high school students have been published in the last five years. This vast quantity of supplementary material will permit every teacher to design his own course if he has the courage and the money for books to do so. In the meantime several groups of scholars are working on new approaches to world history.

452

The first such new approach is already on the market and is being used widely in hundreds of schools. It is the product of one of the first cooperative efforts between colleges and schools. Led by Professor Leften Stavrianos and several other faculty members from the Department of History at Northwestern University, and financed by a generous grant from the Carnegie Foundation, a number of university and high school teachers of history wrote and tested in the classroom a new global approach to world history. The material consists of a large textbook and an equally bulky book of readings. The two volumes place greater emphasis on the nonwestern world than is typical and use an approach derived partly from anthropology. Many teachers have received these volumes enthusiastically.

Chapter 28 represents a step beyond the approach of Professor Stavrianos. It consists of a unit on the Renaissance designed at the Carnegie Institute of Technology Curriculum Development Center. Three-fourths of the unit consists of source materials that challenge the student to make his own interpretation of the Renaissance, using the mode of inquiry of the historian. The final reading in the unit consists of a summary essay that places the Renaissance in the context of European history and summarizes conclusions that might be drawn from the three sets of source readings. As you read the chapter, think about the following questions:

1) To what degree is the material in this unit based on the teaching principles recommended by Brown and Bruner? For which of the two forms of classroom discussion described in Chapter 16 does this material seem to be designed? What might Ausubel (Chapter 8) think about Reading IV?

2) To what degree does the use of source material such as this demand a knowledge of the structure of social sciences generally? What does your conclusion indicate about grade placement of social studies courses?

3) Should an entire course in world history be built out of units like this one? What must be sacrificed if this procedure is followed? What goals would be implied?

THE RENAISSANCE IN ITALY

John M. Good · Edwin Fenton

STATING THE ISSUE

The cathedral dominated the medieval town. Each spire and buttress swept the eye to the heavens to emphasize to man his eventual destiny. The vast interior of the cathedral was called a nave, a word that derived from the Latin for boat. To medieval man this language symbolized that the church was a ship to help men cross life's tempestuous seas to their heavenly reward. In the Middle Ages men's lives focused mainly upon religion and the hereafter.

In 1492, an Italian mariner named Cristoforo Colombo launched three tiny ships on the face of the broad, unknown Atlantic. His goal was very much of this world: the riches of the Indies. His guide was not the word of God but man-made instruments and charts. His ships, instead of being symbols like the nave of the cathedral, were small wooden sailing vessels crowded with men and supplies. Columbus was of a new age; the Renaissance had begun.

What caused this dramatic period of European history to develop? The Renaissance covers several centuries. Its roots stretch well back into the Middle Ages when a number of forces working together began to transform traditional society. In this unit, we will be concerned with two major issues, the causes of the Renaissance and the major characteristics of Renaissance society. As you read, keep the following questions in mind: What caused the Renaissance? What were the personal characteristics of typical Renaissance men? What did these men value? How should a historian investigate these questions?

Reading I: The Emergence of the Renaissance

The Renaissance began in Italy sometime during the late Middle Ages. Like other periods of history, this one cannot be given a precise starting date. The characteristics of Renaissance society and the activities typical of Renaissance man developed slowly and at different rates of speed in different cities. The excerpts in Reading I present evidence which may reveal the reasons for the emergence of this dramatic period in Western history.

The interpretation which a student makes of this unit of work will result partly from two major causes working together. One will be the selection of source materials by the authors of this book. If they chose "representative" materials, then a student will have a chance to develop an "unbiased" account. If their selection of materials was unrepresentative, however, the interpretation will be unrepresentative in turn. The second will be the frame of reference of the student. As we have already learned, people often perceive events in keeping with their language, their culture, or their opinion of the nature of history. Study questions precede each excerpt from source materials in this reading. Keep them in mind as you read.

GENOA IN 1432*

One sided

The document which follows is a translation of a letter written in 1432 by Aeneas Silvius Piccolomini who later became Pope Pius II. The letter describes the city of Genoa and the life of her citizens.

1. How would you compare life in Genoa with life on a medieval manor?
2. How would you define the frame of reference of this future pope?

Would you were with me! You would see a city which has no equal anywhere on earth. It lies upon a hill over which rude mountains tower, while the lower city is washed by the waves of the sea. The harbor is bow-shaped so that the storms can not do the ships any harm . . . it constitutes thus a thoroughly reliable anchorage sought by ships big as hills, triremes and countless other craft. And what a coming and going there is! From the east they hail and from the west, so that you may see daily people of the most different sort with unimaginable rough manners and customs and traders with every conceivable ware. Right at the shore arise the most magnificent palaces, heaven-scaling, built of marble, decorated with columns and often too with sculptures. Under them runs an arcade for the length of a thousand steps where every conceivable object is for sale. . . .

Now as to the life and customs of the population. The men are substantial, well-grown, and impressive, carry themselves proudly and are in fact proud. They are gifted folk, not likely to be found inferior to any other people in the quality of their mind. Strenuous labors, night-watches, and self-denials they bear easily. Their deeds of bravery at sea are incredible; incredible too the perils they confront and the difficulties they master. Our helmsman, a certain Ottobono Imperiali, who has been living at sea now for twenty-three years, has never slept between walls, and never, as he told us, did he change his clothes, even when he was drenched with water. The advantages that come with profits and riches offer compensation for past hardships. In case of a war at sea one does well to take their experience and skill into account, for victory depends solely on them. Should they desire it, victory is certain; should they be contrary-minded, there is no prospect of success since they are the lords of the sea and every one trembles before them.

They dress nobly and elegantly. As for their women, they let them do as they please, for rather may it be said that the women wield the scepter than the other way about. They are not afflicted with thirst for education, though they learn languages as they need them. For other elements of the Liberal Arts they have little use, except as a possible relief from business. Every man

---

* Reprinted from Ferdinand Schevill, *The First Century of Italian Humanism* (New York: F. S. Crofts and Company, 1928), pp. 51–53. Used with the permission of Appleton-Century-Crofts.

selects a woman to whom he pays court. A strange thing is that they maintain irregular relations with other men's wives and at the same time are not in the least offended with the carryings-on of their own wives. Thus it happens that the women of this city enjoy great freedom; indeed it would not be an exaggeration to designate Genoa as the paradise of women. . . . Their dresses are luxurious, loaded with gold and silver trimmings and with jewels. On their fingers sparkle emeralds and diamonds supplied by India and Persia. For where it is a question of adornment they fear no expense. They bother neither about the household nor about needle and dishes, for every house enjoys abundant service. I remember a woman who was *not even a woman of rank* —when her son-in-law asked her what she had prepared for his breakfast, she made answer that she had not been in the kitchen for seven years. These women are all very easy-going, refuse to make an effort, and do not wait for the holidays to enjoy themselves with their admirers. They are always showing themselves in their best clothes. Indeed the more I reflect upon this city the more I am convinced that Venus in our time no longer dwells in Cyprus or on Cytheron but in this city of Genoa. Here seems to me to be her shrine. . . .

Even the nuns are not held to a rigorous standard. They go about at pleasure whither they will. It is incredible that this should not distract them from their purpose. Nor do they, as is said to be the case with us (i.e., the Sienese), curse their parents who confined them in the cloister. They are very numerous and much more merry than the married women, evidently because they do not bear the yoke of matrimony. . . .

THE CHRONICLE OF GIOVANNI VILLANI (1336–1338)*

Milan, Genoa, Venice, and Florence were the four most important commercial and industrial centers in Europe during the late Middle Ages. Venice never disappeared during the so-called Dark Ages; the other three declined seriously after the fall of Rome but began to revive in the eleventh and twelfth centuries. Florence had the most remarkable history of all. In a mere century and a half she rose to the heights of economic, political, and artistic excellence. The authenticity of the following account of the city by Giovanni Villani has been well established.

1. What was the origin of the economic strength of Florence?
2. How large a city was it? What were the people like? What was the relationship between the economic life and the remainder of the culture?

A close look at the figures of this period show that about 25,000 men in the 15-to-70 age bracket, all citizens and fit to bear arms, lived in Florence. The city's bread consumption indicated that some 90,000 mouths, including those

---

* Translated by Edwin Fenton from the *Chroniche Florentine* by Giovanni Villani.

of men, women, and children, must be filled. . . . And at this time there were already, it is calculated, about 1500 foreigners, transients, and soldiers, not counting the clerics and cloistered monks and nuns. . . . The total number of men in the territory and district of Florence in the period was estimated at 80,000. The rector's ceremony as he baptized infants—depositing a black bean for male infants and a white bean for female infants baptized in San Giovanni —showed a yearly total of from 5500 to 6000 baptisms per year, with the black beans outnumbering the white by some 300 to 500. The number of children learning to read ranged from 8000 to 10,000; those learning the abacus and algorism, from 1000 to 1200; and those learning grammar and logic in four large schools, from 550 to 600.

The workshops of the guild of wool merchants, the *Arte Della Lana,* numbered over 200 and produced some 70,000 to 80,000 pieces of cloth worth more than 1,200,000 gold florins. Over a third of this amount, after deduction of the profit of entrepreneurs, remained in the land as a reward for labor, and more than 30,000 people lived on this money. Thirty years before this, many more workshops—some 300—had produced more than 100,000 pieces of cloth; but the cloths at that time were coarser and much less valuable since the English wool was not then imported nor did laborers know the techniques of working it.

About twenty members of the guild of importers, refinishers, and sellers of Transalpine cloth, the *Fondachi* of the *Arte Di Calimala,* imported over 10,000 pieces of cloth worth 300,000 gold florins every year. Except for those that were reexported from Florence, these were all sold in the city.

Every year in Florence some eighty banks of money-changers struck about 350,000 to 400,000 gold florins and about 20,000 pounds of deniers of four petty each.

Merchants and mercers, including shoemakers, slipper makers, wooden shoemakers, stone and carpentry masters, and masters in many other crafts, were so numerous that some 300 left the city to do business. Florence housed as well 146 bakeries. Information furnished by the bakers, and a look at the amount of tax on grinding, show that 140 *moggia* of grain were needed every day, even though a majority of the rich, noble, and well-to-do citizens and their families spent four months of the year in the country.

Since at that period the people of Florence designed and constructed their buildings with the use of improved techniques and imported designs of every kind, the city itself contained many beautiful homes, parish churches of friars of every order, and magnificent monasteries. Every citizen, commoners as well as magnates, had built or was building as well a large and splendid estate in the country, with expensive mansion and fine buildings, spending money much more wildly on these estates than on their city houses and, it was said, committing sin on their country estates. Visiting foreigners who caught a glimpse of the luxury that bordered the city believed that such splendor was a part of the city itself, just as the environs of Rome formed a part of that city. Within a six-mile radius around the city of Florence, where costly palaces with towers, courts, and walled gardens existed, it was estimated that more than twice as many rich and novel mansions could be found as had been constructed within the walls of Florence itself.

COSIMO DE MEDICI: RENAISSANCE DESPOT*

> *The Medici of Florence became one of the most notable families of Europe in the fifteenth century. The family fortune was made in trade, manufacturing, and banking, beginning in the fourteenth century. In 1429, Cosimo de Medici fell heir to a vast store of wealth at the age of forty. Cosimo's grandson was Lorenzo the Magnificent; among his other descendants were two popes and two queens of France.*
>
> *Cosimo was a devoted businessman. He increased the family fortunes through loans to the popes and to kings. For thirty years he was the dominant figure in Florence, having complete control of the city, although he held no public office. A notable patron of the arts, Cosimo helped to set the tone that was soon to make Florence famous forever.*
>
> 1. What was the relationship between wealth and political power in fifteenth century Florence?
> 2. What did Cosimo use his wealth and political power for?

Cosimo di Giovanni de Medici was of most honourable descent, a very prominent citizen and one of great weight in the republic. He was well versed in Latin letters, both sacred and secular, of capable judgment in all matters and able to argue thereupon. . . .

Cosimo . . . had a knowledge of Latin which would scarcely have been looked for in one occupying the station of a leading citizen engrossed with affairs. He was grave in temperament, prone to associate with men of high station who disliked frivolity, and averse from all buffoons and actors and those who spent time unprofitably. He had a great liking for men of letters and sought their society. . . . His natural bent was to discuss matters of importance; and, although at this time the city was full of men of distinction, his worth was recognized on account of his praiseworthy qualities, and he began to find employment in affairs of every kind. By his twenty-fifth year he had gained great reputation in the city, and, as it was recognized that he was aiming at a high position, feeling ran strong against him, and the report of those who knew roused a fear that he would win success. . . .

(Cosimo) next considered how he might best gather together in these lodgings a company of worthy and learned men. First, he determined to collect a suitable lot of books, and one day, when I was with him, he said: "What plan can you suggest for the formation of this library?" I replied that if the books

---

* From Vespasiano Da Bisticci, *Renaissance Princes, Popes, and Prelates; The Vespasiano Memoirs: Lives of Illustrious Men of the XVth Century*, William George and Emily Waters, trans. (New York: Harper & Row, Publishers, Inc., 1963). Reprinted with the permission of Routledge & Kegan Paul, Ltd.

were to be bought, it would be impossible, for the reason that they could not be found. Then he went on, "Then tell me what you would do in the matter." I said it would be necessary to have the books transcribed, whereupon he wanted to know whether I would undertake the task. I said that I would. . . . He was anxious I should use all possible dispatch, and after the library was begun, as there was no lack of money, I engaged forty-five scribes and completed two hundred volumes in twenty-two months, taking as a model the library of Pope Nicholas and following directions written by his own hand, which Pope Nicholas had given to Cosimo. . . .

He knew the difficulty of ruling a state as he had ruled Florence, through the opposition of influential citizens who had rated themselves his equals in former times. He acted privately with the greatest discretion in order to safeguard himself, and whenever he sought to attain an object he contrived to let it appear that the matter had been set in motion by someone other than himself and thus he escaped envy and unpopularity. His manner was admirable; he never spoke ill of anyone and it angered him greatly to hear slander spoken by others. He was kind and patient to all who sought speech with him: he was more a man of deeds than of words: he always performed what he promised, and when this had been done he sent to let the petitioner know that his wishes had been granted. His replies were brief and sometimes obscure, so that they might be made to bear a double sense. . . .

He took kindly notice of all musicians, and delighted greatly in the art. He had dealings with painters and sculptors and had in his house works of divers masters. He was especially inclined towards sculpture and showed great favour to all worthy craftsmen. . . .

Reading II: An Artist of the Renaissance

Benvenuto Cellini——goldsmith, sculptor, lover, braggard, writer—has left us in his autobiography one of the best-known works of the Italian Renaissance. Through his words we can see much of Renaissance culture come to life. Cellini lived from 1500 to 1571 at the very height of the artistic outpouring for which the Renaissance is so well known. The following passages are all taken from the Autobiography.*

1. Who were Cellini's patrons? What were they interested in?
2. What were the sources of inspiration for Cellini's artistic works?
3. What sorts of things interested Cellini? Was he a well-rounded individual? Did he seem to care about what his contemporaries thought of him? about the judgment of history?
4. By what criteria did Cellini criticize Bandinello's statue? Would a medieval man use the same criteria?

* Reprinted from *The Autobiography of Benvenuto Cellini*, John Addington Symonds, trans. (New York: Modern Library), pp. 52–338 *passim*.

[Pope Clement VII summoned me to him, and said]

"I shall employ you on a very important work. This is the button for my cope. I want it to be about as big as a small trencher—a third of a cubit— and just as round. The design is to be a figure of God the Father, in half relief, and in the middle I want you to set that big, beautifully-cut diamond, as well as a large number of other priceless gems. . . . I want you to finish the work quickly so that I can get some enjoyment out of it. So go off and make me a good design."

While Florence was being besieged, the Federigo Ginori for whom I had made the medal of Atlas died of consumption and the medal came into the hands of Luigi Alamanni, who shortly afterwards brought it in person and made a present of it, together with some of his finest writings, to the French King, Francis. The King was tremendously pleased with the medal, and that brilliant man Luigi Alamanni told his Majesty something of the sort of man I was, as well as of my artistic talent. He praised me so highly, in fact, that the King showed that he would like very much to know me. . . .

I was working away, with all the diligence at my command, on the little model for the Pope's button. I made it exactly the same size as the morse itself was to be. Many members of the goldsmith's trade, who thought they could do it themselves, were extremely resentful about it. At the same time there was a certain Michele, who was very expert at engraving cornelians, who had come to Rome and been commissioned to repair the Pope's two tiaras since he was also a very able jeweller and had a fine reputation. When I began work on the little model, Michele, who was an old man, was very surprised that I had not approached him for advice, seeing that he was a clever craftsman and well in with the Pope. In the end, realizing that I was not coming to him he came to me. He asked what I was doing, and I told him: "What the Pope gave me to do."

Then he said that the Pope had commissioned him to supervise all the work done for his Holiness. My reply to this was that I would have to ask the Pope first, and then I would know what sort of answer to give him. He told me I would regret it, and he went off in a temper. . . .

Within a few days I had put the last touches to the model, and one morning I took it along to show the Pope. Traiano made me wait while he hurriedly sent for Michele and Pompeo, telling them to bring their designs with them. When they arrived we were shown inside, and they immediately began to hold out their designs for the Pope to see. As it turned out, the draughtsmen, not being jewellers, had no idea how to set the gems, and the jewellers had not given them any instructions (and a jeweller must when he is introducing figures among his gems know how to draw, otherwise his work will be worthless). And so in all their designs that marvellous diamond had been placed in the middle of God the Father's breast.

The Pope, whose judgment was very sound, saw what had happened and thought they were without merit. After he had inspected about ten of them he threw the rest on the floor, turned to me, who was standing on one side, and said:

"Let me have a glance at your model, Benvenuto, so that I can see if you've made the same mistake as they have."

I came forward and opened a little round box; the Pope's eyes seemed to light up, and he cried out:

"You wouldn't have done it in any other way, even if you were my very self. The others couldn't have thought up a better way of disgracing themselves."

Then a great number of important noblemen flocked round, and the Pope pointed out to them the difference between my model and the other designs. He praised it to the skies, with those two standing terrified and dumbfounded in front of him, and then he turned to me and said: "I can only see one snag, Benvenuto, but it's very important. It's easy to work in wax; the real test comes when one has to work in gold."

I answered him eagerly: "Holy Father, if it isn't ten times better than my model, we'll agree that I won't be paid for it."

At this there was an outcry from the noblemen present, and they protested that I was promising too much. But one of them, a very great philosopher, spoke in my favour.

"From this young man's physiognomy," he said, "and from his well-proportioned physique, I am certain of everything he promises, and more."

"And that's why I think so too," added the Pope. Then he called his chamberlain, Traiano, and told him to fetch five hundred gold ducats of the Camera. While waiting for the money the Pope examined more carefully the excellent way I had fitted the diamond in with the figure of God the Father.

What I had done was to place the diamond exactly in the centre of the whole work, with the figure of God the Father, gracefully turning to one side, seated above it, and so the design was beautifully balanced, and the figure did not detract from the jewel. With His right hand raised, God the Father was giving a blessing; and beneath the jewel I had placed three cherubs, supporting the diamond with raised arms; the middle one was in full, and the other two in half relief. Round about I had designed a crown of cherubs, beautifully arranged with the other gems. God the Father was draped in a flowing mantle, from which the other cherubs peeped out; and there were many other exquisite adornments, all enhancing this beautiful work. It was made in white stucco on black stone.

When the money was brought in the Pope handed it to me himself, and then, with great charm, begged me to do the work while he was still alive to enjoy it. He added that it would be well worth my while.

The Pope had just given me instructions to make this beautiful coin when Bandinello the sculptor came up. With his usual mixture of presumption and ignorance he said: "These goldsmiths must be provided with designs for such beautiful works."

I immediately turned to him and told him that I had no need of his designs for my work, but that I felt sure that before long my designs would deal some nasty blows to his. The Pope was delighted at what I said, and leaning towards me he added:

"Now go along, my dear Benvenuto, put all your energies into serving me, and pay no attention to what these idiots say."

So off I went, and in next to no time I made two steel dies. I stamped a coin, in gold, and one Sunday after dinner brought this coin and the dies along to the Pope. When he saw them he was astonished as well as delighted, not only because of my superb craftsmanship, which impressed him tremendously, but even more because I had been so incredibly quick about it. To add still further to the Pope's delight and amazement I had brought with me all the old coins that had been stamped years ago by those expert craftsmen who worked for Pope Julius and Pope Leo. Then, when I saw that he thought mine were superior, I took a petition from my breast pocket, in which I asked to be appointed superintendent of the dies. The job itself was worth six gold crowns a month, without counting the dies which were paid for by the Master of the Mint at the rate of a ducat for three.

The Pope took my petition and then turned to give it to his datary, telling him to have it seen to straight away. The secretary took it, and, as he was slipping it into his pocket, he commented:

"Holy Father, your Holiness should not be in such a great hurry; these matters call for a great deal of deliberation."

"I've heard what you say," replied the Pope. "Now give me that petition."

He took hold of it, impulsively signed it in his own hand, and then handed it back with the remark:

"I don't think you have any answer to that. Hurry the business up, now; that is how I want it. Benvenuto's shoes are worth more than the eyes of all those other numskulls."

I thanked his Holiness and went back to my work, overjoyed beyond words.

One feast day or other I went along to the palace, after dinner, and arriving at the Clock Hall I noticed that the door of the wardrobe was open. I approached nearer and then the Duke called out, greeting me pleasantly:

"You're welcome! Look at that little chest that the lord Stefano of Palestrina has sent me as a present: open it and let's see what it is."

I opened it at once and said to the Duke: "My lord, it's a statue in Greek marble, and it's a splendid piece of work: I don't remember ever having seen such a beautiful antique statue of a little boy, so beautifully fashioned. Let me make an offer to your Most Illustrious Excellency to restore it—the head and the arms and the feet. I'll add an eagle so that we can christen him Ganymede. And although it's not for me to patch up statues—the sort of work done by botchers, who still make a bad job of it—the craftsmanship of this great artist calls me to serve him." . . .

I did my best to make the Duke appreciate such beauty, and the fine intelligence and rare style that it contained. I held forth on these things for a long time, all the more willingly as I knew how much his Excellency enjoyed my doing so.

While I was entertaining the Duke in this agreeable way a page happened to leave the wardrobe, and, as he went out, Bandinello came in. When he saw him the Duke's face clouded over and he said with an unfriendly expression: "What are you after?"

Bandinello, instead of replying at once, stared at the little chest where the statue was revealed and with his usual malignant laugh, shaking his head, he started turning towards the Duke said: "My lord, here you have one of those things I have so often mentioned to you. You see, those ancients knew nothing about anatomy, and as a result their works are full of errors."

I remained silent, taking no notice of anything he was saying; in fact I had turned my back on him. As soon as the beast had finished his disagreeable babbling, the Duke said: "But Benvenuto, this completely contradicts what you have just been proving with so many beautiful arguments. Let's hear you defend the statue a little."

In reply to this noble little speech of the Duke's, so pleasantly made, I said: "My lord, your Most Illustrious Excellency must understand that Baccio Bandinello is thoroughly evil, and always has been. So no matter what he looks at, as soon as his disagreeable eyes catch sight of it, even though it's of superlative quality it is at once turned to absolute evil. But for myself, being only drawn to what is good, I see things in a more wholesome way. So what I told your Illustrious Excellency about this extremely beautiful statue is the unblemished truth; and what Bandinello said about it reflects only the badness of his own nature."

The Duke stood there, listening with great enjoyment, and while I was talking Bandinello kept twisting and turning and making the most unimaginably ugly faces—and his face was ugly enough already. Suddenly the Duke moved off, making his way through some ground-floor rooms, and Bandinello followed him. The chamberlains took me by the cloak and led me after them. So we followed the Duke till his Most Illustrious Excellency reached an apartment where he sat down with Bandinello and me on either side of him. I stood there without saying anything, and the men standing round—several of his Excellency's servants—all stared hard at Bandinello, sniggering a little among themselves over what I had said in the room above. Then Bandinello began to gabble.

"My lord," he said, "when I uncovered my Hercules and Cacus I am sure that more than a hundred wretched sonnets were written about me, containing the worst abuse one could possibly imagine this rabble capable of."

Replying to this, I said: "My lord, when Michelangelo Buonarroti revealed his Sacristy, where there are so many fine statues to be seen, our splendid, talented Florentine artists, the friends of truth and excellence, wrote more than a hundred sonnets, every man competing to give the highest praise. As Bandinello's work deserved all the abuse that he says was thrown at it, so Buonarroti's deserved all the good that was said of it."

Bandinello grew so angry that he nearly burst: he turned to me and said: "And what faults can you point out?"

"I shall tell you if you've the patience to listen."

"Go on then."

The Duke and all the others who were there waited attentively, and I began.

First I said: "I must say that it hurts me to point out the defects in your work: but I shall not do that, I shall tell you what the artists of Florence say about it."

One moment the wretched fellow was muttering something unpleasant, the next shifting his feet and gesticulating; he made me so furious that I began in a much more insulting way than I would have done had he behaved otherwise.

"The expert school of Florence says that if Hercules' hair were shaven off there wouldn't be enough of his pate to hold in his brain; and that one can't be sure whether his face is that of a man or a cross between a lion and an ox; that it's not looking the right way; and that it's badly joined to the neck, so clumsily and unskillfully that nothing worse has ever been seen; and that his ugly shoulders are like the two pommels of an ass' pack-saddle; that his breasts and the rest of his muscles aren't based on a man's but are copied from a great sack full of melons, set upright against a wall. The loins look as if they are copied from a sack of long marrows. As for the legs, it's impossible to understand how they're attached to the sorry-looking trunk; it's impossible to see on which leg he's standing, or on which he's balancing, and he certainly doesn't seem to be resting his weight on both, as is the case with some of the work done by those artists who know something. What can be seen is that he's leaning forward more than a third of a cubit; and this by itself is the worst and the most intolerable error that useless, vulgar craftsmen can make. As for the arms, it's said that they both stick out awkwardly, that they're so inelegant that it seems you've never set eyes on a living nude; that the right leg of Hercules is joined to that of Cacus in the middle in such a way that if one of the two were removed both of them—not merely the one—would be without a calf. And they say that one of the feet of the Hercules is buried, and the other looks as if someone had lit a fire under it."

The fellow couldn't stay quiet patiently and let me carry on describing the great defects of the Cacus. First, because I was revealing it clearly cause I was telling the truth, and second, the Duke and the others standing around. They were expressing their amazement and showed that they realized I was justified up to the hilt.

Suddenly the fellow cried out: "Oh, you wicked slanderer, what about my design?"

I replied that anyone who was good at designing would never make a bad statue, therefore I judged that his design was the same quality as his work. . . .

Reading III: Three Renaissance Writers

Most high school students associate the Renaissance with great painters, sculptors, and architects. Of course they are correct. But the Renaissance should also be remembered for its great contributions to western thought. Like many scholars during the Middle Ages, the men of the Renaissance redis-covered the great Greek and Roman classics, copied them, and translated them into the languages of the day. They also wrote great original works that have in turn become classics of their own.

The learned men of this period called themselves humanists, from the word *humanista,* a slang term coined by students for teachers of grammar, rhetoric, and other humane studies. The humanists were classical scholars. They learned Greek, Latin, and Arabic in order to study the classics in their original languages. They began to write in these languages and to publish learned treatises on the works of the ancients. They also wrote poems and other works in the vernacular.

The four excerpts in Reading III were written by three great Renaissance scholars. Study questions precede each excerpt. Think about them as you read.

TWO ASPECTS OF PETRARCH*

> The two readings below represent the work of the humanists at its best. They are from the pen of Francesco Petrarca (1304–1374), one of the greatest of the humanists. The first contains a letter to a friend about Cicero; the second is a sonnet addressed to Laura, whom Petrarch loved.
>
> 1. What does Petrarch think of the classics?
> 2. The poems addressed to Laura now seem far more significant to literary scholars than Petrarch's work with the classics. What atti-tudes are revealed here? How would you compare Petrarch's attitudes with those of medieval thinkers?

PETRARCH ON CICERO

I return to your Cicero. I could not do without it; the copyists are not competent to do it. What was left for me but to rely on my own resources, and press these weary fingers and this worn and ragged pen into the service? . . .

* Reprinted from J. H. Robinson and H. W. Rolfe, *Petrarch, the First Modern Scholar and Man of Letters* (New York, 1914). Copyright G. P. Putnam's Sons and Coward-McCann, Inc.

I must confess that I did finally reach a point in my copying where I was overcome by weariness; not mental, for how unlikely that would be where Cicero was concerned, but that sort of fatigue that comes from excessive manual labor. (writer's cramp) I began to have doubts about this plan that I was following and to regret having taken a task for which I was not trained; when suddenly I came across a place where Cicero tells how he himself compiled the orations of—someone or other; just who it was I do not know, but certainly not Tullius, for there is only one such man, one such voice, one such mind. These are his words: "You say that you have been in the habit of reading the orations of Cassius in your idle moments. But I," he jestingly adds, with his customary disregard of his adversary's feelings, "have made a practice of *copying* them, so that I might *have* no idle moments."

As I read this passage I grew hot with shame, like a modest young soldier who hears the voice of his beloved leader scolding him. I said to myself, "So Cicero copied orations that another wrote and you are not ready to copy his? What ardor! What scholarly devotion! What reverence for a man of godlike genius!" These thoughts were a spur to me, and I pushed on with all my doubts gone. If ever from darkness there shall come a single ray that can light the splendor of the reputation which his heavenly speech has won for him, it will come from the fact that I was so taken by his sweetness that I did a thing, itself most irksome, with such delight and eagerness that I scarcely knew I doing it at all.

One of Petrarch's Sonnets to Laura*

Loose to the breeze her golden tresses flow'd
Wildly in thousand mazy ringlets blown,
And from her eyes unconquer'd glances shone,
Those glances now so sparingly bestow'd.
And true or false, meseem'd some signs she show'd
As o'er her cheek soft pity's hue was thrown;
I, whose whole breast with love's soft food was sown,
What wonder if at once my bosom glow'd?
Graceful she moved, with more than mortal mien,
In form an angel: and her accents won
Upon the ear with more than human sound.
A spirit heavenly pure, a living sun,
Was what I saw; and if no more 'twere seen
T' unbend the bow will never heal the wound.

* Reprinted from Raymond Phineas Stearns, *Pageant of Europe: Sources and Selections from the Renaissance to the Present Day* (New York: Harcourt, Brace & World, Inc., 1961), p. 11

THE IDEAL OF THE WELL-ROUNDED MAN*

The well-rounded man represents the ideal of the Renaissance. Our best portrait of an ideal Renaissance type was written by Baldassare Castiglione in a book called The Courtier, *published in 1528. In this volume Castiglione revived the classical ideal of the well-rounded man and combined him with modern ideas of the humanities and a liberal education.*

1. What should an ideal man be able to do? How does this ideal compare with the ideal of the Middle Ages?
2. Is the ideal man mainly responsible for developing his personal qualities or should he concentrate on service to his fellow-man?

For this evening's game let us select someone from the company and give him the job of portraying a perfect Courtier, explaining all the conditions and special qualities that a Courtier must have; if he mentions something that is not correct, anyone may contradict him. . . .

Since one cannot spend all his time in every exercise and since repetition is tiresome, we must always vary our life with various occupations. For this reason I would have our Courtier sometimes take part in quieter and more peaceful exercises, and in order to escape envy and to seem agreeable to everyone, let him do what others do, yet never departing from praiseworthy deeds, and governing himself with that good judgment which will keep him from all foolishness; but let him laugh, joke, banter, frolic and dance, but in such a way that he shall always appear genial and discreet, and that everything he may do or say shall be stamped with grace. . . .

I would have him accomplished in letters, at least in those studies which are called the humanities, and able to speak and understand not only the Latin language but also the Greek. Let him know the poets, and the orators and the historians. Let him be proficient in writing, verse, and prose, especially in this vulgar tongue of ours; for besides the enjoyment he will find in it, he will never lack agreeable entertainment with the ladies, who are usually fond of such things. If other jobs or lack of study prevent his reaching such perfection, let him be careful to suppress his work so that others may not laugh at him, and let him show them only to a friend whom he can trust: because at least the exercise will enable him to judge the work of others.

My lords, you must know that I am not content with the Courtier unless he is also a musician, and besides being able to understand and read notes, he must be able to play different instruments. For music is the best relaxation or medicine for the troubled spirit and most becoming and praiseworthy in time of leisure and especially in the courts, where besides the relief from boredom that music gives us, many things are done to please the ladies, whose tender and gentle spirit is easily affected by harmony and filled with sweet-

---

* From Baldassare Castiglione, *The Book of the Courtier,* Edwin Fenton, trans.

ness. Thus, it is no surprise, that in ancient and modern times, musicians have always been favored and have found refreshing spiritual food in music. . . .

I wish to discuss another matter, which I think is very important and therefore think our Courtier should not overlook: and this is to know how to draw and to know the art of painting.

Do not be surprised that I want this art, which today seems to be that of an artisan and not for a gentleman; I remember having read that the ancients, especially in Greece, had the boys of noble birth study painting in school as an honorable and necessary thing and it was recognized as the first of the liberal arts, while at the same time by public edict forbidden to slaves. Among the Romans, too, it was held in highest honor. . . .

And truly one who does not honor this art seems unreasonable to me, for this universal fabric that we see—with the vast heaven so richly adorned with shining stars and in the middle the earth circled by seas, varied with mountains, valleys and rivers and decorated with so many different trees, beautiful flowers and grasses—may be said to be a great and noble picture, composed by the hand of nature and of God; and whoever is able to imitate it, seems to me to deserve great praise: nor can it be imitated without the knowledge of many things, as he who tries well knows. . . .

THE PRACTICAL POLITICIAN*

Niccolò Machiavelli (1469–1527) taught the world a lesson in practical politics. A Florentine lawyer, he had traveled widely in the employ of the government of his city. Everywhere he observed politics as they were actually practiced. Exiled from his native city in a change of administration, he wrote The Prince *as a guide book for a despot in order to try to gain favor and to set forth the techniques by which a prince might be able to unite all of Italy. Like other humanists, Machiavelli had read widely and he drew many of his examples from the classics as well as from his keen observations of contemporary life.*

1. How closely should a prince adhere to the moral teachings of the church?
2. What attitudes of life are revealed in this passage?
3. How would a medieval king react to Machiavelli's advice?

It is a good thing to be considered generous. But if liberality is not openly displayed for all to see, no one will ever hear about it, and under these circumstances a person would soon become known as a miser. For this reason many men who wish to earn a reputation for liberality depend upon lavish displays or costly shows which are easily seen. If a prince does this, he is

* From Niccolò Machiavelli, *The Prince*, G. C. Sansoni, ed. (Florence, 1899), Edwin Fenton, trans.

likely to spend most of his money on display, and if he wishes to keep his reputation for liberality he will have to impose heavy taxes and do everything possible to obtain more funds. This course of action will make his subjects begin to hate him; they will not even respect him because he will be poor. His liberality will have injured many and benefited only a few. . . . For these reasons a prince must not worry if he becomes known as a miser. . . .

Is it better to be loved more than feared or feared more than loved? Ideally, one ought to be both feared and loved, but it is difficult for the two sentiments to go together. If one of the two must be sacrificed, it is much safer to be feared than loved. In general men are ungrateful, dishonest, cowardly, and covetous. As long as you help them, they will do your bidding. They will offer you their blood, their goods, their lives, and their children when it appears that you will not need to take them up on the offer. But when you try to collect, they often go back on their word. If a prince has relied solely on the good faith of others, he will be ruined. Men are less afraid to offend a prince they love than one they fear.

. . . I conclude, therefore, with regard to being feared or loved that men have control of their love but the prince controls fear. The wise prince will rely on what he can control and not on what is in the control of others. He must be careful, however, not to make men hate him.

Everyone knows that it is a good thing for a prince to keep his word and live a faithful life. The history of our own times shows, however, that those princes who have done great things have had little regard for keeping faith. . . . A successful prince must imitate both the fox and the lion, for the lion cannot protect himself from traps, and the fox cannot defend himself from wolves. He must, therefore, be at the same time a fox to recognize traps, and a lion to frighten off wolves. . . . A prince ought not to keep his word when doing so would go against his best interest, and when the reasons which originally motivated him no longer exist. If men were all good, this rule would not be a sound one. But because they are bad and would not honor their word to the prince, he is not bound to keep faith with them. . . .

It is not at all necessary for a prince to have all the good qualities which I have named, but it is necessary to seem to have them. I will even go so far as to say that to actually have these qualities and to be guided by them always is dangerous, but to appear to possess them is useful. Thus it is well to seem merciful, faithful, sincere, religious, and also to be so. But a prince must always be ready to embrace the opposite qualities if the occasion demands it. New princes particularly are unable to live by these fine qualities. They are often obliged, in order to maintain their position, to act against faith, against charity, against humanity, and against religion. A prince must be ready to shift with the wind as the ups and downs of fortune dictate. He should not deviate from what is good if he can avoid it, but he should be ready and able to do evil when it is necessary. . . .

I conclude, then, that if fortune varies and men remain fixed in their ways, they will be successful so long as these ways fit the circumstances of the moment, but when the times call for other tactics they will fail. I certainly think that it is better to be impetuous than cautious, for fortune is a woman, and it is necessary, if you wish to master her, to conquer her by force. It can be seen that she lets herself be overcome by the bold rather than by those who proceed coldly. And therefore, like a woman, she is always a friend to the young, because they are less cautious, more fierce, and master her with greater audacity.

Reading IV: The Renaissance

At the end of the Middle Ages a combination of economic, political, and social changes brought about a great outburst of intellectual and artistic activity. Historians are unable to precisely identify this period of history that we call the Renaissance. Some aspects of Renaissance life were clear by 1250; others did not emerge until the sixteenth century. Moreover, the emphasis in Renaissance life differed from one place to another. The Renaissance began in Italy, where it was essentially secular, and spread to northern Europe, where religion played a more important role. Although the word "renaissance" means rebirth and refers to the revival of classical knowledge, there was much in the Renaissance that was entirely new. Everywhere, however, the age of the Renaissance marked the beginning of the transition from a rural agrarian economy to an urban commercial society typical of the modern world. The development of such a complicated historical period cannot be explained easily.

Major historical trends never result from only one cause. A number of events working together helped to bring about the triumph of Alexander the Great over the Greeks; another complex group of causes produced the fall of the Roman Empire. So it was with the Renaissance. A whole host of developments covering several centuries set the stage for the great outburst of intellectual and artistic activity that swept Italy. Major changes in the economy, a new political system, the weakening position of the Church, the rediscovery of the ancient world—all these factors and many others were at work. The chart lists some of the more important events that contributed to the emergence of Renaissance society. Study it carefully to discover the influences that helped to shape this new world. As you study the chart, try to determine how these influences were related to each other.

During the Middle Ages economic activity revived most rapidly in the Italian city states. This activity created the kind of dynamic urban life that set the stage for the Renaissance. In fact, vigorous economic activity had never ceased in Italy. She had been the center of the Roman world, and her cities, particularly Venice, remained the middlemen between Europe and the East throughout the Middle Ages. The Crusades increased the flow of people and trade through the Italian seaports; eventually Genoa, Pisa, and Florence

THE RENAISSANCE

	ECONOMICS	POLITICS	RELIGION	LITERATURE	PAINTING & SCULPTURE
1350	Venice, Genoa, Pisa & Florence all centers of trade and mfg. 30,000 employed in Florentine cloth trade. Bookkeeping & partnership arrangements develop in Italy. Eng- kings borrow from Flor- entine bankers	Rise of city state in Italy / Nobility being replaced by republics	1309–1378 Babylonian Captivity	1321 Dante died	1337 Giotto died
1400			1378–1407 Great Schism	1374 Petrarch died / 1375 Boccacio died / Greek taught in Flor- ence	
		Sforzas to power in Milan. Venice ruled by merchants' council	1447–1455 Nicholas V		1428 Masaccio died
1450	Economic prosperity spreads to N. Europe	1434 Cosimo de Medici to power in Florence	1458–1464 Pius II	1462 Cosimo de Medici founds Platonic Academy	
	1460 Prince Henry the Navigator dies				1466 Donatello died
	1488 Diaz rounds Cape of Good Hope	1492 Lorenzo / 1494 French invasion	1492–1503 Alexander VI		
1500	1492 Columbus sails		1503–1513 Julius II / 1513–1521 Leo X		1510 Botticelli died / 1519 Leonardo died / 1520 Raphael died
1550			1534–1549 Paul III, first in a line of reformer popes	1527 Machiavelli died	1564 Michelangelo died / 1576 Titian died

1407–1534 Renaissance Papacy

joined Venice as commercial centers. Sailors from those cities developed new ships, drew elaborate charts called *portolani* to guide them over the Mediterranean, and perfected new navigational instruments. Their sails soon filled the seas that bordered southern Europe.

Manufacturing and banking developed in the wake of the trading vessels. Money became the medium of exchange. Italian merchants seeking for goods to exchange for the spices and luxuries of the East encouraged the development of industry, including clothmaking and shipbuilding. To keep track of their new transactions, merchants invented double-entry bookkeeping, listing their assets and liabilities in parallel columns, an accounting technique essential to modern business practices. To handle this new wealth, some merchants eventually became bankers. From all these new economic activities— trade, manufacturing, and banking—a new class of wealthy men no longer dependent on land ownership for their prosperity emerged.

Large-scale manufacturing developed in the Italian city states. Raw materials such as wool and leather were imported from abroad and the finished products filled the holds of the merchants' ships. For this reason the merchants gained control of the manufacture of such goods as leather and cloth. They hired workers and paid them wages. This development helped to destroy the hold of the guilds, organizations of independent craftsmen who owned their own tools and raw materials and worked in small shops with little or no hired labor.

Other outlets for capital developed in banking and money lending. By the middle of the thirteenth century, they had become an indispensable part of Italian economic life. Merchants wished to pursue their profit-making activities without interference from political leaders. Cities such as Venice, Florence, Milan, and Siena had grown large, wealthy, and self-confident. In the thirteenth century they were a part of the Holy Roman Empire, which was ruled by German kings. The fact that the emperor lived in Germany and was involved in a struggle for power with the pope gave the city states an opportunity to play off emperor against church in order to win their own political freedom. By the end of the fifteenth century, all Italy except the kingdom of Naples in the south was controlled by independent territorial states. The map shows the major Italian city states in the year 1490.

Most of these new city states were ruled by despots. The Visconti and Sforzas of Milan and the Medici of Florence were examples. At first the cities were under the control of merchants and nobles. This rule was challenged in the thirteenth century by the merchants and bankers who, because of their wealth, were eager to direct the affairs of state. Guild masters, shop keepers, and professional men usually supported them rather than either the aristocracy or the proletariat. The struggle among these various groups resulted in an ineffectual republican government that gave way to one-man rule. Each despot owed his power to wealth and popular support. Most of them became patrons of the arts and sciences. The varied interests and in-

RENAISSANCE
ITALY

tense individualism of the "popular" despots was demonstrated in the works of art they commissioned and in their concept of a many-sided personality.

The rapid development of the city states destroyed the last traces of feudalism in Italy. The wealth and political power of merchants attracted feudal lords who allied themselves with the city states rather than with the popes and emperors. Soon the daughters of wealthy merchants began to marry the sons of impoverished nobles and the titled but less wealthy nobility acquired money. Because farming without capital was not profitable, land gradually passed into the hands of merchants and bankers who lived in the city. Because of this development the political authority of the town spread to the surrounding countryside. The cities were able to win control of rural areas partly because of their political and economic position and partly because the Church, whose power was declining, was no longer able to stand in the way.

The Church, which had been a very powerful organization in the Middle Ages, began to lose its hold at the same time that the strength of the Italian city states was growing. During these very years the papal power was also threatened by the rise of national states, particularly in France and England. The decline of the Church's power and influence gave the Renaissance a chance to emerge. Here was a case where the decay of an institution gave dynamic forces an opportunity to thrust ahead.

For centuries the papacy had functioned as the spiritual leader of Europe. During this period, in addition to their spiritual duties, the popes had concerned themselves with codifying canon law, developing the theory of papal supremacy, and launching the Crusades. When Boniface VIII tried to exert papal influence in 1300, however, he was opposed by the Italian city states and the rising national states to the north. Both Boniface's actions and his words demonstrated the growing weakness of the Church. He pushed the claims of the papacy to extremes, provoking the rulers of France, England, and the Holy Roman Empire to clash openly with him and his successors over questions of temporal and clerical power.

The Babylonian Captivity and the Great Schism that followed were proof that the Church was losing its hold. The Babylonian Captivity was a period of seventy years in which the popes lived in the south of France. This event came about when henchmen of the French king, Philip IV, severely manhandled Pope Boniface, who died three days later. Philip was able to get a French pope, Clement V, elected, and Clement established his court at Avignon. The papacy lost much respect during this period. At Avignon the court was corrupt, extravagant, and licentious. Moreover, a French pope who lived in France where he was dominated by a French king was not recognized elsewhere as the leader of a universal church.

Nor did the situation that followed increase the prestige of the Church. In 1377, an attempt was made to recall the French pope, Gregory XI, and the French cardinals who had elected him. This development resulted in a disputed election. Two popes were elected and two courts, one in Rome and the other in France, were set up. Each pope excommunicated the other and devoted much of his time and attention to denouncing his rival as "anti-Christ." This period, known as the Great Schism, lasted for thirty-nine years. The division in religious authority was finally ended by a series of councils that created a third pope before the schism was ultimately ended.

The first council, the Council of Pisa, began a series of meetings and a wave of controversy. The Church had to face the problem of whether the council or the papacy was supreme. While the controversy raged, the popes concentrated their attention upon financial and administrative tasks. They built up their arms and treasuries and set up highly centralized governments in the Italian papal states. Because they became secular rulers, they were soon treated as simply another force to be dealt with in a worldly way.

The Great Schism was ended at the Council of Constance in 1414, with the election of Martin V. The popes gradually recovered their position of power in the Church. They could never recover their universal moral control, however, nor the political supremacy they once enjoyed. In the meantime, a new secular culture had come into being.

The Conciliar movement also tried to reform the Church, but its attacks were directed against those who criticized Catholicism rather than at internal abuses. As a result, the members of the Roman Catholic Church in the West were divided in their allegiance. Furthermore, scholars called humanists, who had taken a renewed interest in the ancient world, began to criticize the institutions of the Church and to question its secular authority. Those who felt that the Church was no longer fulfilling its spiritual role questioned whether the worldly activities of the papacy and clergy served the people. Movements for genuine reform began, led by the Franciscan friars and by men such as Savonarola, John Wycliff, Peter Waldo, and John Hus.

In the meantime, the popes turned to Italian affairs and planned Crusades against heretics and Moslems. Many became patrons of the arts and sciences. One or two of the popes, such as Nicholas V who founded the Vatican library, were learned men. Other secularly oriented popes were Pius II, a humanist, Paul II, a lover of art, Alexander VI, who was the father of Caesar and Lucretia Borgia, and Leo X.

Patronage of the arts and sciences in Renaissance Italy came as the result of the new social and cultural life generated by the economic, political, and religious changes we have discussed. The transition from a rural to an urban life and the accompanying changes in class structure and distribution of wealth had a dynamic impact upon the intellectual and aesthetic life of Renaissance Italy. Wealthy bankers, merchants, and manufacturers commissioned painters, sculptors, and architects. Educated in Italy's new schools and having the wealth and leisure to indulge their tastes, the new men of wealth helped to promote a brilliant epoch of art. So did the new secular clergy and the despots who ruled the cities.

A new social structure and the intense interest in the arts influenced both the arts and their creators. The artist had a new role in society. If a painter, a poet, or a scholar without funds could interest a wealthy banker, merchant, duke, or clergyman, he could get money to support him while he worked. He not only received financial aid but often access to libraries, studios, and stimulating company, as well. When the search for works of art became competitive, good artists such as Michelangelo, Botticelli, Cellini, Raphael, and Titian became men of importance and wealth. The change in patronage from the Church to individuals and the change in the social status of the artist himself were reflected in the style, mood, subject matter, and techniques of art.

Each artist strove for unique methods and also tried out new materials. In their experiments they studied the human body carefully in order to render it more perfectly on canvas. Artists such as Leonardo Da Vinci and Benvenuto Cellini had a wide range of interests in sciences such as physics, astronomy, and mathematics. Much of their work was derived from Greek and Roman models. All these developments can be seen in their painting and sculpture.

The inheritance of the ancients and the inventiveness of the present created new forms and ideals in art unique to the Renaissance. Architecture, too, was influenced by the ancients. Renaissance architects measured the dimensions of Roman ruins in the Italian cities and began to use columns, arches, and domes, just as the Greeks and Romans had. Gothic art was ignored and many churches and public buildings were built in the "new" style by such men as Brunelleschi and Alberti. Monumental or free-standing sculpture in the manner of the ancients came into wide use. The pieces that the Renaissance artists created were left unadorned like those of the historic remains of Greece and Rome which they saw about them. Other artistic techniques developed by the Italian Renaissance artists were the use of perspective, new spatial relationships, and the wide use of color. The independence of expression so valued by the Renaissance artists contributed greatly to their work.

The Renaissance also saw an outburst of scholarship by writers who called themselves humanists. Inspired by the classics, Dante, Petrarch, Boccaccio, and a host of others began to imitate classic models and to write new works in the vernacular. The works they prized the most—their Latin letters written in imitation of men like Cicero—are little valued today, but some of their original compositions—Petrarch's sonnets to Laura, Boccaccio's *Decameron*, Dante's *Divine Comedy*, Machiavelli's *The Prince*—are universally recognized as classics in their own right. Through all of them run some common themes: individualism, secularism, skepticism, materialism, classicism, and the ideal of the well-rounded man. The painters and sculptors of the Renaissance had many of these same qualities. Together the writers and artists painted onto canvas, chiseled into stone, and lettered onto parchment the story of their lives and the enthusiasms of their age.

CHAPTER 29

American History:

Examples

The curriculum development projects have not yet published materials in American history. Within a few years, however, these projects will disseminate a host of new readings, largely based on inductive principles. The fact that not a single project is writing a conventional textbook for this field indicates the extent to which the leaders in curriculum development endorse inductive techniques. If teachers are to prepare themselves to teach the new social studies, they must learn to teach at least part of the time from readings and to handle their material inductively.

In the future whole textbooks containing source materials with expository material to link them together will be published for use in American history courses. In the meantime, however, teachers must rely on collections of readings to obtain source materials that can supplement textbook treatments. Some teachers are developing their own reading books by dittoing documents that are in the public domain and adding their own introductions and study questions. Others have been purchasing collections of documents designed for college students and assigning those whose reading level is within the grasp of secondary school pupils. A few general books of readings designed for high school are now beginning to appear.

In the meantime both D. C. Heath and Scott, Foresman and Company have published series of problems books specifically designed for inductive teaching in secondary school. One or more of these volumes can be purchased and used to supplement texts on a great variety of topics in American history. Chapter 29 contains a portion of one of these new volumes written by Edward H. Merrill of Brookline (Massachusetts) High School under the editorial direction of Van R. Halsey, one of the leaders in the curriculum development project in American history established at Amherst College in 1964 by a grant from the United States Office of Education. The Table of

Contents from the volume indicates the place of the passages cited in the entire unit of work. As you read, keep the following questions in mind.

1) What is the nature of the material used in these readings? How is the material arranged? How does both the kind of material and the pattern of arrangement resemble and differ from what you studied in Chapter 28?
2) Is this material suited to a discovery approach? What teaching strategies does the material itself imply?
3) What objectives are implied by the material? Is the balance between content and skills appropriate?

RESPONSES TO ECONOMIC COLLAPSE: THE GREAT DEPRESSION OF THE 1930's

Edward H. Merrill · Van R. Halsey

Contents

INTRODUCTION

PART I—THE NATURE OF THE DEPRESSION

A. Smashup—William E. Leuchtenburg
B. The World-Wide Nature of the Depression—
Robert R. Palmer with Joel Colton
C. Depression in Detroit from *When Detroit's Out of Gear* by Helen Hall
D. Song of Trouble—"Beans, Bacon and Gravy" from *American Folksongs of Protest,* edited by John Greenway
E. Statistics—Compiled by author from *Historical Statistics of the United States*

PART II—THREE TOTALITARIAN MODELS OF POLITICAL AND ECONOMIC ORGANIZATION

A. A Historian Views Economic Life Under Fascism—
Robert R. Palmer with Joel Colton

Reprinted from Edward H. Merrill and Van R. Halsey, *Responses to Economic Collapse: The Great Depression of the 1930's* (Boston: D. C. Heath and Company, 1964), pp. vii–ix and 1–3.

Introduction

This book of readings focuses your attention on the Great Depression which began late in 1929 in the United States and lasted until the fear of war and war itself required the complete use of the productive facilities and the manpower of our country. It does not describe all human phases of the depression in the United States nor analyze its causes. It is an attempt to give an understanding of the major features of the depression and to present the political and economic responses of Americans to an economic cataclysm. Although the main emphasis is upon the depression in the United States, the book also describes the manner in which the economic collapse shattered the lives of peoples all over the world.

Even before the depression began in the United States, two new ideologies, Communism and Fascism, had arisen to provide solutions for economic, political, and social problems. The depression helped to bring to power leaders of a third ideology—Nazism in Germany. To be sure, the Communists had been in power more than a decade before the depression began. Russia had passed through Lenin's war-communism and his New Economic Policy, and at about the time that the depression led other countries to spawn various solutions for it, the Soviets were carrying out the First Five-Year Plan. Also at this time, Mussolini, beset by economic problems stemming from the depression, marched further along the road he had chosen to travel. Hitler came to power in the midst of economic collapse.

The readings which follow are divided into four parts. The first introduces you to the nature of the depression in the United States and to its worldwide impact. The second describes how three European countries dealt with economic problems, and with what results. The third section contains some of the proposals for dealing with the depression in the United States, and the fourth comprises some analyses of Franklin D. Roosevelt and the New Deal.

The Nature of the Depression

Until 1929, years of hard times accompanied by failures of businesses and banks, unemployment, strikes of workers, and other evidences of economic misery were usually called panics. In your study of American history, you have been introduced to the panics of 1837, 1873, and 1893, to mention some of the worst of our economic upsets. The economic debacle which began in 1929 and continued into the 1930's is generally known as the Great Depression, because it was the worst upset which the American people had ever experienced. The purpose of this reading is not to give you an understanding of the causes of the depression. Its chief aim is to show you that the depression pervaded many areas of American life and affected the lives of millions of Americans. With the other readings in this section, it should help you answer questions about the nature of a great depression.

A. SMASHUP*

William E. Leuchtenburg

The prosperity of the 1920's produced the contagious feeling that everyone was meant to get rich. The decade witnessed a series of speculative orgies from "get-rich-quick" schemes to the Florida real estate boom, climaxed in 1928 and 1929 by the Great Bull Market. Before the war, stock market investment had been almost wholly a preserve of the wealthy; in the 1920's clerks and bootblacks talked knowingly of American Can or Cities Service and bought five shares "on margin." In later years it was frequently said that by the end of the twenties "everyone was in the market," but there were actually fewer, probably far fewer, than a million people involved. What is closer to the truth is that millions of Americans followed the market with avid interest; it became, remarks Professor Galbraith, "central to the culture."

No one can explain what caused the speculative wave of 1928. It is true that credit was easy, but credit had been easy before without producing a speculative mania. Moreover, much of the speculation was carried on at rates of interest which by any reasonable standard were tight. More important were the sense of optimism which permeated the decade and the conviction that, especially in the economic world, anything was possible. "We grew up founding our dreams on the infinite promises of American advertising," Scott Fitzgerald's wife Zelda once remarked. "I still believe that one can learn to play the piano by mail and that mud will give you a perfect complexion." The faith people had that they too could be rich was deliberately cultivated by responsible bankers and heads of investment trusts, who gave every indication of believing what they were saying. In an article called "Everybody Ought to Be Rich," John Raskob argued in the *Ladies' Home Journal* that anyone who saved fifteen dollars a month and bought sound common stocks would in twenty years be worth $80,000. Since commodity prices were remarkably stable throughout the boom, economists were reassured that, despite the speculative fever, the economy was basically sound.

The volume of sales on the New York Stock Exchange leaped from 236 million shares in 1923 to 1,125 million in 1928. That was a year when everything one touched seemed to turn to gold: industrial stocks went up the astonishing total of 86.5 points. Customers crowded into brokers' offices in midmorning and stood staring at the blackboard or inspecting the tape until closing time. They borrowed money, bought more stock, watched the stock go up, and borrowed still more money to buy still more stock. By 1928

* Reprinted from William E. Leuchtenburg, *The Perils of Prosperity, 1914–1932* (Chicago: the University of Chicago Press, 1958), pp. 241–263, *passim.* © 1958 by the University of Chicago.

the stock market was carrying the whole economy. If it had not been for the wave of speculation, the prosperity of the twenties might have ended much earlier than it did. Coolidge's deflationary policies had withdrawn government funds from the economy, consumers had cut spending for durable goods in 1927, and the market for housing had been glutted as early as 1926. But with the economy sparked by fresh funds poured into speculation, a depression was avoided and the boom continued.

The stock market frenzy began in March, 1928. On Saturday, March 3, Radio sold at 94½. By the next Friday it had surged to 108. On the next day it bounded to 120½. It seemed impossible, but when the market closed on Monday morning, Radio had gained another 18 points and was selling at 138½. The next morning Radio opened at 160, a gain of 21½ points overnight. And it did not stop. After a few days of relative quiet, Radio jumped 18 points on March 20. The Big Bull Market was under way. Not long before he left office, President Coolidge announced that stocks were "cheap at current prices." The summer of 1929 not only bore out his dictum but made the gains of 1928 look modest in comparison. In three months— from June to August—industrials climbed 110 points; in a single summer the value of industrial stocks increased by almost a quarter.

Even by the summer of 1928 the market had drawn people who never dreamed they would be caught in the speculative frenzy. How much longer could you hold out when your neighbor who bought General Motors at 99 in 1925 sold it at 212 in 1928? There were stories of a plunger who entered the market with a million dollars and ran it up to thirty millions in eight months, of a peddler who parlayed $4,000 into $250,000. The Bull Market was not simply a phenomenon of New York and Chicago; there were brokerage offices in towns like Steubenville, Ohio, and Storm Lake, Iowa. Even non-investors followed the market news; like batting averages, it touched the statistical heart of the country.

Men in Saginaw and Amarillo opened their newspapers and turned first to the stock market reports. They shared the same worries, often heard the same tips, that moved men to buy and sell in the canyons of Wall Street. In an era of prohibition, as Charles Merz points out, the broker's office took the place of the barroom; it had "the same swinging doors, the same half-darkened windows." In midmorning men would slump into the mahogany chairs of the smoke-filled room to search the blackboard or the hieroglyphics of the chattering ticker tape for news of the fate of Anaconda or Tel. and Tel.

In early September 1929, the stock market broke, rallied, then broke again. By early October, Radio had tumbled 32 points, General Electric over 50 points, Steel almost 60 points. Still there was no panic. "Stock prices," announced Professor Irving Fisher of Yale, in what was to become a classic statement, "have reached what looks like a permanently high plateau." In the last week in October the situation turned suddenly worse. On October 23, rails and industrials fell 18 points. On Thursday, October 24, prices broke violently, and a stampede set in. The gains of many months were wiped out in a few hours. Radio opened at 68¾, closed at 44½. For a few days a determined effort by bankers led by the House of Morgan held the market steady, but the next week the downward plunge resumed with reckless fury. On Monday U.S. Steel lost 17½, Westinghouse 34½, General Electric 47½. The next day, Tuesday, October 29, was a day of sickening disaster. The ticker closed two and a half hours behind; when the last sales had been listed, industrial stocks had zoomed down 43 points.

On November 13 the decline came to a temporary halt, as the market reached the lowest point it was to hit that year. On that day industrial stocks were 228 points lower than they had been in early September; their value had been cut in half. This was only the beginning of the end. In September industrials had stood at 452; in November, 1929, they were 224. On July 8, 1932, at the bottom of the depression, they would sink to 58. In three years General Motors plummeted from 73 to 8, U.S. Steel from 262 to 22, Montgomery Ward from 138 to 4.

The prosperity of the 1920's had been founded on construction and the automobile industry. Residential construction, which had stood at five billion dollars in 1925, was down to three billion by 1929. The automobile industry continued to grow, but after 1925 it grew at a much slower rate, cutting back purchases of steel and other material; the cycle of events, whereby an increase in car production produced rapid increases in steel, rubber, glass, and other industries, now operated in a reverse manner to speed the country toward a major depression. By 1929 the automobile industry—and satellites like the rubber-tire business—were badly overbuilt. Since there was no new industry to take the place of automobiles and no policy of federal spending to provide new investment (Mellon, in fact, was working in the opposite direction), it was inevitable that as investment fell off and the rate of production slackened in the key industries, a serious recession would result.

There was no single cause of the crash and ensuing depression, but much of the responsibility for both falls on the foolhardy assumption that the special interests of business and the national interest were identical. Management had siphoned off gains in productivity in high profits, while the farmer got far less, and the worker, though better off, received wage increases disproportionately small when compared to profits. As a result the purchasing power of the worker and the farmers was not great enough to sustain prosperity. For a time this was partly obscured by the fact that consumers bought goods on installment at a rate faster than their income was expanding, but it was inevitable that a time would come when they would have to reduce purchases, and the cutback in buying would sap the whole country.

With no counteraction from labor unions, which were weak, or from government, which had no independent policy, business increased profits at twice the rate of the growth in productivity. So great were profits that many corporations no longer needed to borrow, and as a result Federal Reserve banks had only minimum control over speculation. With no other outlet, profits were plunged into the stock market, producing a runaway speculation.

The policies of the ~~federal government in the~~ 1920's were disastrous. Its tax policies made the maldistribution of income and oversaving by the rich still more serious. Its monopoly policies added to the rigidity of the market and left business corporations too insensitive to changes of price. Its farm policies sanctioned a dangerous imbalance in the economy. Its tariff policies made a difficult foreign-trade situation still worse. Its monetary policies were irresponsible; at critical junctures, the fiscal policy of the Coolidge administration moved in precisely the wrong direction. The administration took the narrow interests of business groups to be the national interest, and the result was catastrophe.

The ~~market crash played a major role~~ in precipitating the Great Depression. *1929* It shattered business confidence, ruined many investors, and wiped out holding company and investment trust structures. It destroyed an important source of long-term capital and sharply cut back consumer demand. Yet business would have been able to weather even the shock of the crash, if business had been fundamentally sound. The crash exposed the weaknesses that underlay the prosperous economy of the twenties—the ~~overexpansion of~~ major industries, the maldistribution of income, the weak banking structure, and the overdependence of the economy on consumer durable goods.

During the 1920's almost seven thousand banks failed; no industrial nation in the world had as unstable and as irresponsible a banking system as the United States. "The banks," noted one writer, "provided everything for their customers but a roulette wheel." In the 1920's wrote Professor Schumpeter, "a new type of bank executive emerged who had little of the banker and looked more like a bond salesman"; the new type of banker-promoter financed speculation and loaded the banks with dubious assets. Nothing did more to turn the stock market crash of 1929 into a prolonged depression than the destruction of business and public morale by the failure of the banks.

A year after the crash, six million men walked the streets looking for work. By 1932, there were 660,000 jobless in Chicago, a million in New York City. In heavily industrialized cities the toll of depression read, as one observer noted, like British casualty lists at the Somme—so awesome as to become in the end meaningless, for the sheer statistics numbed the mind. In Cleveland 50 per cent were jobless, in Akron 60 per cent, in Toledo 80 per cent. In Donora, Pennsylvania, only 277 of 13,900 workers held regular jobs. In the three years after the crash, 100,000 workers were fired on the average every week.

By 1932, the physical output of manufacturing had fallen to 54 per cent of what it had been in 1929; it was a shade less than production in 1913. All the gains of the golden twenties were wiped out in a few months. By the last year of the Hoover administration, the automobile industry was operating at only one-fifth of its 1929 capacity. As the great auto plants in Detroit lay idle, fires were banked in the steel furnaces on the Allegheny and Mahoning. By the summer of 1932, steel plants operated at 12 per cent of capacity, and the output of pig iron was the lowest since 1896. Between 1929 and 1932, freight shipments were cut in half, and major railroad systems like the Missouri Pacific, the Chicago and North Western, and the Wabash passed into receivership.

The farmer, who had seen little of the prosperity of the 1920's was devastated by the depression. The crash—and the ensuing financial debacle—destroyed much of what remained of his foreign markets. American foreign trade declined from $10 billion in 1929 to $3 billion in 1932. Foreign capital issues fell from $1500 million in 1928 to the abysmally low figure of $88 million in 1932. As foreign nations erected new barriers to American products and unemployment cut heavily into the domestic market, crop prices skidded to new lows. Wheat fell from $1.05 a bushel in 1929 to 39 cents in 1932, corn from 81 cents to 33 cents a bushel, cotton from 17 cents to 6 cents a pound, tobacco from 19 to 10 cents a pound. The result was catastrophic. Gross farm income fell from nearly $12 billion to the pitiful sum of $5 billion.

Like a cold bay fog, fear of the bread line drifted up into the middle class. Detroit counted 30 former bank tellers on its relief-rolls. The universities graduated thousands of engineers, architects and lawyers who had not the slightest prospect of a job. With no hope of employment, young people postponed marriage or, if they were married, did not have children. In 1932, there were 250,-000 fewer marriages than in 1929, and the birth rate slipped from 18.8 to 17.4 per thousand. Hundreds of thousands of working women returned to their homes. Economy-minded school boards halted building projects and slashed teachers' salaries. Chicago teachers, unpaid for months, lost their savings, had to surrender their insurance policies, and were forced to borrow from loan sharks at 42 per cent annual interest. By the middle of 1932, over 750 had lost their homes.

The depression touched every area of American life. Bergdorf-Goodman slashed sables 40 per cent, Marcus and Company offered a $50,000 emerald ring for $37,500, and the Pullman Company cut rates on upper berths 20 per cent. The Yankees mailed Babe Ruth a contract for the 1932 season with a $10,000 salary cut, and the Giants offered their star first baseman, Bill Terry, 40 per cent less. The United Hospital Fund reported that donors not only reneged on pledges but even asked that the previous year's contributions be returned to them. Off Broadway, theater lights were darkened; on Fifth Avenue, strollers no longer heard the sound of riveters. The managers of the Empire State Building ended all pretext that its offices were rented; elevators stopped running from the 42d to the 67th floors.

Unable to pay rent or meet mortgage payments, many families were dispossessed from their homes. In empty lots on the edge of industrial cities, homeless men, sometimes with families, built crude shelters of packing crates and old pieces of metal. In the larger cities, whole colonies of these "Hoovervilles" were established. When municipal lodging houses became overcrowded, men huddled in empty freight cars or in shutdown factories. In New York's Central Park, a group of squatters nested in "Hoover Valley," the bed of a drained reservoir. In Arkansas, men were found living in caves. By the Salt River in Arizona, miners camped under bridges. In the great cities, girls slept in subways. Thousands of Americans wandered the country aimlessly, in quest of a job, or relief, or just sense of motion. In 1929, the Missouri Pacific counted 13,745 migrants; in 1931, 186,028. By 1932, there were from 1 to 2 million men, including a few hundred thousand young boys, roaming the country.

In the cities, long queues of hungry men, their shoulders hunched against December winds, edged along sidewalks to get a bowl of broth from charity "soup kitchens." While most families were able to make out on shorter rations, the plight of the utterly destitute—and by 1932, they numbered millions—was appalling. In the St. Louis dumps, small groups of men, women, and children dug for rotten food. In Chicago, they stood outside the back doors of restaurants for leavings or scoured the districts for spoiled fruit and vegetables. In the coal hills of Pennsylvania, families were fed on weeds and roots. While there were few deaths from starvation, 238 persons suffering from malnutrition or starvation were admitted to New York hospitals in 1931. Forty-five of them died.

In the three years after the crash, factory wages shrank from $12 billion to $7 billion. Although wages fell, the wage rate, which employers had promised Hoover they would maintain, held up remarkably well in the first two years of the depression. From the first, bankers declared a relentless war on the high-wage philosophy. The Commercial and Financial Chronicle conducted a persistent campaign for wage-slashing as "an intelligent step in the return of prosperity." "The man who relies upon the wage he receives for his daily toil," declared the Chronicle, "must realize that employers have suffered even as has the employee; and much beyond the same." On September 22, 1931, U.S. Steel announced a 10 per cent wage cut; General Motors, Bethlehem Steel, and other corporations immediately followed. The wage front was broken. Within a year, sweatshops had mushroomed all through the East. In one factory, 13-year-old packing girls were paid 50 cents a day; in another plant, apron girls received a daily wage of 20 cents.

In the spring of 1931, a slow upturn in production and employment led some economists to believe that the United States was pulling out of the depression. Then disaster struck from abroad. The withdrawal of American dollars from Europe after the 1929 crash had created serious financial stringency in Europe. In March, 1931, French bankers called in short-term German and Austrian notes, a move made partly for political reasons. Unable to meet the demands, the Kreditanstalt in Vienna buckled. The collapse of the greatest bank in Austria in turn set off a chain reaction. Heavy withdrawals of gold from Germany forced the Weimar Republic to default on its reparations payments. Fearing Germany would go Communist, President von Hindenburg appealed to Hoover for help.

In June, 1931, President Hoover proposed a one-year moratorium on reparations payments and intergovernmental debts. It was a superb move, but Hoover received so little cooperation from the French that much of its value was dissipated. In August, the British, who had gone to the aid of both Austria and Germany, were caught short themselves. In September, Great Britain abandoned the gold standard. The British decision marked the virtual end of the system of international exchange of nineteenth-century capitalism.

The American banking system was exceptionally vulnerable to these financial upheavals. In 1929, 659 banks failed; in 1930, 1,352; in 1931, 2,294. In November, 1930, a panic, starting in Nashville, swept through the Middle South and closed 129 banks. The following month, a little before Christmas, the Bank of the United States in New York City, an institution with 400,000 depositors, collapsed. The ruin of the Bank of the United States, which held the life savings of thousands of recent immigrants, affected a third of the people in New York City and was the worst bank failure in the history of the Republic. Millions of Americans who in 1929 had regarded banks as the epitome of security withdrew their money and hid it under flagstones. By the fall of 1931, a billion dollars had been taken from banks and put in safe deposit boxes or stuffed in old mattresses.   *Wide Implications*

The ~~European financial~~ debacle ~~created a fresh crisis in the United States~~. As Europeans demanded gold, American banks in turn had to call in their loans to American businesses, and a new wave of liquidations followed. When in October, 1931, Philadelphia's banks were threatened, President Hoover got the more substantial banks of the country to set up a National Credit Corporation so that strong banks could bolster the weak ones. The strong banks, animated by a sense of *sauve qui peut,* refused to cooperate.

In March, 1932, Ivar Kreuger, one of the most respected international financiers, committed suicide in his Paris apartment. When his affairs were disentangled, it was found that the Swedish Match King had fleeced American investors of a quarter of a billion dollars by duping Lee, Higginson and other presumably astute American investment firms. American financiers had permitted Kreuger to take $50 million in securities from the vaults of the International Match Company without anyone knowing it, and Lee, Higginson had sold Kreuger's issues to the American public without insisting on the elementary step of an independent audit. The same month, Samuel Insull's utility empire collapsed, with a total loss to investors of nearly $700 million. The stock of Insull Utility Investments fell from 107½ in 1929 to 1⅛ in March, 1932. Soon it was completely worthless. The scapegoat for other businessmen, Insull fled to Paris and crossed the Mediterranean in a dirty Greek steamer to avoid extradition to face a Cook County jury.

Nothing struck a harder blow at the prestige of American business than the phenomenon of want in the midst of plenty. While people went hungry, granaries bulged with wheat no one could sell. While people froze for lack of fuel in winter, snow drifted over the mouths of idle coal pits. With billions of dollars locked up in banks, Iowa towns issued scrip and stores in the state of Washington issued and accepted wooden money. Knoxville, Atlanta, and Richmond printed their own currency.

Abundance stalked the canefields and the grain belts. "From Ocala south and east to Orlando and the fertile Indian River region," reported one writer after a tour of Florida, "oranges and grapefruit hang heavy on the trees and cover the ground beneath." When a terrible drought struck the country in 1930, many farmers rejoiced, and stock prices soared on Wall Street. The Federal Farm Board urged southern planters to plow under every third row of cotton, and even the boll weevil was viewed with a friendlier eye. Brazil burned thousands of bags of coffee and shoved scowloads of coffee into the Atlantic. Rubber planters were jubilant when they discovered a new pest attacking their trees.

Technology was the god of the 1920's. When the depression struck, technology was denounced for bringing the curse of plenty. Men relentlessly sabotaged the production on which they had preened themselves in the Coolidge years. In 1932, Representative Hatton Sumners of Texas urged that the Patent Office cease giving patents on labor saving devices. In the winter of 1930, Newark abandoned machines for hand excavation, and Minneapolis used picks and shovels. Boston stored its snowloading machines to give men work with snow shovels that winter. When Henry Ford, who had done as much as any man to mechanize agriculture, hired men to harvest crops on his farms, he equipped them only with old-fashioned hoes. Kansas, the most highly mechanized agricultural state in the country, restored hitching racks in front of courthouses.

As the bread lines lengthened, the mood of the country became uglier. In July, 1931, 300 unemployed men stormed the food shops of Henryetta, Oklahoma. An army of 15,000 pickets marched on Taylorville, Illinois, and stopped operations at the Christian County Mines in 1932. In Washington, D.C., 3,000 Communist "hunger marchers" paraded. None of these demonstrations matched in importance the rebellion of American farmers. From Bucks County, Pennsylvania, to Antelope County, Nebraska, farmers banded together to prevent banks and insurance companies from foreclosing mortgages. When sheriffs attempted to carry out foreclosures, mobs of farmers brandishing pitchforks and dangling hangman's nooses, persuaded the sheriffs to retreat. In Iowa—the center of stable Republican farm life—once prosperous farmers, leaving their neat white houses and rich lands behind, barricaded highways to prevent milk from getting to market in a vain effort to force up prices. In a national radio broadcast, John A. Simpson, president of the National Farmers' Union, denounced the wealthy as "cannibals that eat each other and who live on the labor of the workers."

Nothing seemed more unreasonable to farmers than to deprive a man of a farm when, through no fault of his own, he could no longer meet his obligations, and, on this one question, the farmer was almost beside himself. A. N. Young, president of the Farmers' Union of Wisconsin, told a Senate committee: "They are just ready to do anything to get even with the situation. I almost hate to express it, but I honestly believe that if some of them could buy airplanes they would come down here to Washington to blow you fellows up. . . . The farmer is naturally a conservative individual, but you cannot find a conservative farmer today. . . . I am as conservative as any man could be, but any economic system that has it in its power to set me and my wife in the streets, at my age—what can I see but red?" For the first time in history, Lloyd's of London sold large sums of "riot and civil commotion insurance" to Americans.

Demanding immediate and full payment of bonuses for their service in World War I, an army of 15,000 to 20,000 unemployed veterans moved on Washington in the spring of 1932. The House passed the bonus bill, but when the Senate voted the bill down by an overwhelming margin, half the men left the city. The rest stayed on; they had no jobs, no homes, no place to go. Most of them lived in mean shanties on the muddy Anacostia flats, some camped in unused government buildings. General Glassford, the head of the District police, treated the men with decency and discretion, but, as the men stayed on day after day, Hoover and his officials panicked. On July 28, 1932, the Government decided precipitately to evict a group of bonus marchers from vacant government buildings on Pennsylvania Avenue. Two veterans were killed and several District police were injured in a scuffle that followed. President Hoover summoned the U.S. Army to take over.

With machine guns, tanks, and tear gas, brandishing sabers and drawn bayonets, the Army, in full battle regalia, advanced on the ragged group of bonus marchers. Led by the Army Chief of Staff, Douglas MacArthur (Dwight Eisenhower and George Patton were two of his junior officers), the Army dispersed the marchers and burned their billets. Hoover, whose attack on the veterans had aligned much of the country against him, made matters worse by releasing a report of the Attorney-General accusing the bonus army of being composed of Communists and criminals. General MacArthur, who called the veterans "a mob . . . animated by the essence of revolution" added to the sense that the government had lost its sense of proportion. If Hoover had "let it go on another week," MacArthur declared, "I believe that the institutions of our Government would have been very severely threatened."

B. THE WORLD-WIDE NATURE OF THE DEPRESSION*
Robert R. Palmer, with Joel Colton

The depression, in the strict sense, began as a stock-market and financial crisis. . . .

The crisis passed from finance to industry, and from the United States to the rest of the world. The export of American capital came to an end. Ameri-

* Reprinted from *A History of the Modern World*, by Robert R. Palmer with Joel Colton, pp. 779–781, *passim*, by permission of Alfred A. Knopf, Inc. Copyright © 1950, 1956 by Alfred A. Knopf, Inc.

cans not only ceased to invest in Europe, but sold the foreign securities they had. This pulled the foundations from under the post-war revival of Germany, and hence indirectly of much of Europe. Americans, their incomes falling, ceased to buy foreign goods; from Belgium to Borneo people saw their American markets slip away, and prices tumbled. In 1931 the failure of a leading Vienna bank, the Creditanstalt, sent a wave of shivers, bankruptcies, and business calamities over Europe. Everywhere business firms and private people could not collect what was owed them, or even draw on money that they thought they had in the bank. They could not buy, and so the factories could not sell. Factories slowed down or closed entirely. Between 1929 and 1932, the latter year representing the depth of the depression, world production is estimated to have declined by 38%, and the world's international trade fell by two-thirds. In the United States the national income fell from 85 to 37 billion dollars.

The world price of wheat fell incredibly. In 1930 a bushel of wheat in terms of gold, sold for the lowest price in four hundred years. Wheat-growers in all continents were faced with ruin. Growers of many other crops faced the same dismal prospect. Cotton and corn, coffee and cocoa all collapsed. Brazilian and African planters were caught by over-production and falling prices. In Java, where not only had the acreage in sugar been extended, but the unit yield of sugar from the cane had multiplied ten times under scientific cultivation over the past century, the bottom dropped out of prices in the world market. There were indeed other and more profitable forms of agricultural production—for example in oranges and eggs, of which world consumption was steadily growing. But the coffee planter could not shift to eggs, nor the Iowa farmer to oranges. Not to mention the requirements of climate, the ordinary farmer or peasant lacked the capital, the special knowledge, or the access to refrigerated transportation that these newer branches of agriculture demanded. For the one thing that the average farmer or peasant knew how to do—grow wheat and other cereals—the new wonderful world of science and machinery had too little place.

Unemployment, a chronic disease ever since the war, now assumed the proportion of pestilence. In 1932 there were 30,000,000 unemployed persons statistically reported in the world; and this figure did not include the further millions who could find work only for a few hours a week, or the masses in Asia or Africa for whom no statistics were to be had. The worker's wages were gone, the farmer's income now touched bottom; and the decline of mass purchasing power forced more idleness of machinery and more unemployment. Men in the prime of life spent years out of work. Young men could not find jobs or establish themselves in an occupation. Skills and talents of older people grew rusty; young people found no opportunity to learn. Millions were reduced to living, and supporting their families, on the pittances of charity, doles, or relief. Great modern cities saw an outburst of sidewalk-art, in which, at busy street corners, jobless able-bodied men drew pictures on the pavement with colored chalk, in the hope of attracting a few sixpences or dimes. People were crushed in spirit by a feeling of uselessness; months and years of fruitless job-hunting left them demoralized, discouraged, embittered, frustrated, and resentful. Never had there been such waste, not merely of machinery which now stood still, but of the trained and disciplined labor force on which all modern societies were built. And people chronically out of work naturally turned to new and disturbing political ideas.

C. DEPRESSION IN DETROIT*

Helen Hall

> *Obviously, the people of a city depending largely on the production of automobiles would be severely hurt by a depression. In the first year of the depression a social worker visited Detroit and graphically described the misery she saw.*

I have never confronted such misery as on the zero day of my arrival in Detroit. It was still dark at 7:30 when our train pulled in, and I had forgotten how cold cold could be until I stepped out on to the station platform that January morning. After breakfast at Franklin Street Settlement, we set out for the Department of Public Welfare. There we came upon muffled men and women at the entrance. They crowded the lower corridors and we had to push by. They were on the stairs and filled the upper halls, standing, waiting their turn. I wanted to look at them and see what type of men and women they really were, but I was ashamed to look. I felt suddenly conscious of the fur lining of my coat and the good breakfast I had eaten. Perhaps it was the bitter cold I had come in from and they had come in from that gave me the impression that they were congealed into one disconsolate lump.

When I came out two hours later the same lines were there, literally the same lines, for I recognized a red knitted cap on one of the men, such a sad little man, and his cap wasn't much nearer the window. And inside they were working fast and steadily and, it seemed to me, with great kindliness. In December alone the department had disbursed nearly a half million dollars in public relief. Two-thirds of the families had been driven to apply because of the unemployment of the breadwinner. In January the figure was to rise to $650,000. . . .

When I came to visit the homes of some of these men and women I could gauge something of the struggle that so often had gone on before they had

---

* Reprinted from Helen Hall, "When Detroit's Out of Gear," *Survey Graphic*, April 1930.

come to the welfare stations. Asking for help, even if the cause for it lies far outside our own control, means a serious breakdown in family pride and self-confidence, a self-confidence which seldom blossoms again with the same sturdiness. As one woman said to me, "My husband hated to go stand in those lines, but I drove him to it. We couldn't see the children starve. He don't seem to mind it so much now. . . ."

The Onottos were living on potatoes and pancakes when the father finally asked for help. He had been out since October from the Michigan Steel Corporation. Before Wesley Rollins finally appealed, he had carried his family for five and a half months, in spite of the serious illness of one of his children. . . .

The age factor may have entered somewhat into Henry Nelson's problem. He seemed anxious to sit down when we came in and steadied himself by the furniture, but I didn't know then that he was weak from lack of food. When the department had come in on the case he had had little or nothing to eat for three days. He was fifty-two, a bad age, practically hopeless for a job when young men couldn't get work, and he was aware of it; for he was an old Detroiter . . . and knew the ropes. But he had kept on trying because he had "the missus to look after." There were two sons and a married daughter. Both sons and the son-in-law had been out of work for three months. Four men workless and wageless in one family!

The lines at the city welfare stations are not the only ones. More of the automobile workers were to be found among the men and women shuffling dejectedly at the public and private employment offices, and again all of them at one time or another in those lines which run into the thousands before the gate of any of the large plants which are hiring help, and in lesser numbers, before the door of any plant, whether hiring or not.

For the men who are laid off still feel that they belong. They go back and back. Detroit is spread out. Even in normal times workmen sometimes travel two hours to work and two hours back. But when work is hard to get, they may spend the night in line waiting to be let in through the gates to the employment offices in the morning. In freezing weather they build fires to warm themselves, and what with the wet and the strain there are occasional fracases to get up front and a rush when opening time comes. Joe Smith told me that he was put through the line so fast at Hudson Motors that he had time to tell of only one thing he could do. So as he worked in four different departments, he changed hats and coats with friends and went through the line four times. . . .

It is inherent in most of us to long for a reasonable foothold in life. This quality was intensified in the Buchanans. They fought for it. They are both twenty-nine and both Scotch, coming to America by way of Canada. They have brought all their native thriftiness to bear on solving the problem of making a home for themselves and their five children, but this last period of idleness has discouraged them. Mrs. Buchanan said, with a roll to the r's:

"We have struggled for ten years and we are still in deep water. No movies, no fancy clothes, no radio, or no fuleishness (Sic). Just saving for our house. We lost the house we started to buy once, and it looks as though we were going to lose this one. We have paid $800 down on it and bought all our furniture, and are renting it furnished, and we wouldn't have any trouble if he were only working. We had $5000 paid on the last house and then we lost it. He was out of work for six months that time. This time he has been out seven weeks so far. Perhaps I shouldn't set such store by having a home of our own. . . . It's the insecurity that kills you, not the work or the saving."

D. SONG OF TROUBLE

John Greenway

> *President Hoover is said to have told Rudy Vallee, the crooner, that he would give him a medal if he could sing a song to make people forget their troubles and depression. Do popular songs give the historian any clues concerning the temper of the times? What popular songs of today would you recommend as indicative of the mood of your own generation? Why?*

Beans, Bacon and Gravy*

I was born long ago, in 1894,
And I've seen many a panic, I will own;
I've been hungry, I've been cold,
And now I'm growing old,
But the worst I've seen is 1932.

Refrain: Oh, those beans, bacon, and gravy
They almost drive me crazy,
I eat them till I see them in my dreams
In my dreams;
When I wake up in the morning,
And another day is dawning,
Yes, I know I'll have another mess of beans.

We congregate each morning
At the county barn at dawning,
And everyone is happy, so it seems;
But when our work is done

* Reprinted from John Greenway, *American Folksongs of Protest* (Philadelphia: University of Pennsylvania Press, 1953), pp. 64–65.

We file in one by one,
And thank the Lord for one more mess of beans.

We have Hooverized on butter,
For milk we've only water,
And I haven't seen a steak in many a day;
As for pies, cakes, and jellies,
We substitute sow-bellies,
For which we work the county road each day.

If there ever comes a time
When I have more than a dime
They will have to put me under lock and key;
For they've had me broke so long
I can only sing this song
Of the workers and their misery.

E. STATISTICS

The tables of statistics given below should be studied in relation to the description of the depression given in Reading A in this section and also in relation to the listing of New Deal legislation which is Reading K in Part III. The statistics cover six major areas. What do they add to your understanding of the nature of the depression? Do you think any of the statistics indicate the desirability or necessity of any of the legislation listed in Reading K in Part III? Can you establish any interrelationship between any two of the tables? What kind of a statement about the years 1929–39 could you make if you only had the statistics given here?

1. UNEMPLOYMENT, 1929–1941
(IN THOUSANDS OF PERSONS)

Year	Total Number Gainful Workers[1]	Unemployed
1929	49,180	1,550
1930	49,820	4,340
1931	50,420	8,020
1932	51,000	12,060
1933	51,590	12,830
1934	52,230	11,340
1935	52,870	10,610
1936	53,440	9,030
1937	54,000	7,700
1938	54,610	10,390
1939	55,230	9,480
1940	55,640	8,120
1941	55,910	5,560

SOURCE: Statistical Abstract of the United States, 200.
[1] Excluding persons in armed forces.

2. NATIONAL INCOME, 1929–1941
(IN BILLIONS OF DOLLARS)

Year	Total Income	Salaries and Wages Income
1929	87.4	50.8
1930	75.0	46.5
1931	58.9	39.5
1932	41.7	30.8
1933	39.6	29.3
1934	48.6	34.1
1935	56.8	37.1
1936	64.7	42.7
1937	73.6	47.7
1938	67.4	44.7
1939	72.5	47.8
1940	81.3	51.8
1941	103.8	64.3

SOURCE: *Historical Statistics of the United States,* 12.

3. NATIONAL INCOME—REALIZED PRIVATE PRODUCTION INCOME—MANUFACTURING AND CONSTRUCTION, 1929–1938
(IN MILLIONS OF DOLLARS)

Year	Manufacturing	Construction
1929	18,059	3,225
1930	15,958	2,910
1931	12,376	1,945
1932	8,528	932
1933	8,428	762
1934	10,471	928
1935	11,720	1,043
1936	14,138	1,447
1937	16,629	1,806
1938	12,208	1,359

SOURCE: *Historical Statistics of the United States,* 14.

4. FARM INCOME, 1929–1939
(IN MILLIONS OF DOLLARS)

Year	Net Incomes to Persons on Farms from Farming
1929	6,741
1930	5,114
1931	3,482
1932	2,285
1933	2,993
1934	3,531
1935	5,052
1936	5,361
1937	6,093
1938	5,041
1939	5,262

SOURCE: *Historical Statistics of the United States,* 99.

5. VALUE OF EXPORTS
(IN MILLIONS OF DOLLARS)

Year	Value
1929	5,241
1930	3,843
1931	2,424
1932	1,611
1933	1,675
1934	2,133
1935	2,283

SOURCE: *Historical Statistics of the United States*, 218.

6. BANK SUSPENSIONS
(IN THOUSANDS OF DOLLARS)

Year	Number of Suspensions	Losses Borne by Depositors
1929	659	77,000
1930	1,352	237,000
1931	2,294	391,000
1932	1,456	132,000
1933	4,004	540,000
1934	57	10,000
1935	34	4,000

SOURCE: *Historical Statistics of the United States*, 273–274.

CHAPTER 30 The New Curricula:
An Evaluation

The wave of curricular reform that began in mathematics and the natural sciences about a decade ago is beginning to revolutionize the schools. This volume has attempted to outline in inductive form the principles of the new curricula as they can be applied to the social studies. These principles, and the procedures for translating them into practice, are typical of the entire reform movement. Generalizations holding for PSSC physics also hold true for most of the materials produced at Project Social Studies centers. The new physics, the new math, the new language arts, the new social studies, and the new modern languages—soon to be followed by reforms in the fine arts and in vocational and technical subjects—will soon become the new curriculum, the standard fare for the mass of students in American schools.

For this reason, the concluding article in this volume concerns curriculum reform generally. The author, Evans Clinchy, who has been associated as an administrator and writer with Educational Services, Inc., a nonprofit corporation designed to develop curricula and new ways of training teachers for the schools, is well acquainted with the entire range of curriculum projects in all subjects. The common tendencies that he has underlined place the trends in the new social studies in a wider context.

Social studies teachers particularly ought to see this wider context clearly. More than any other teachers in the schools, social studies teachers have taken responsibility for seeing society in the whole and for making clear to the students the directions in which their world is moving. If they wish to assure the maximum opportunity for American education to accomplish its goals, they must be able to demonstrate to students—to future voters—the role of the schools in the society and the principles underlying excellence in education. This article delineates these principles and implies courses of action. As you read, keep the following questions in mind:

1) What common tendencies underlie the new curricula? Which typify the new social studies? Which principles of the new social studies are omitted from Mr. Clinchy's list?

2) What are the implications of these common tendencies for the following groups: curriculum builders, commercial publishing houses, the teachers of teachers, supervisors in charge of in-service programs, school administrators?

3) What is the future of reform in the social studies? Where will we go next? Why?

THE NEW CURRICULA

Evans Clinchy

About twelve years ago, some mathematicians and educators at the University of Illinois began to sense that the mathematics curriculum in the high schools of this country was not all that it could or should be. Calling themselves the University of Illinois Committee on School Mathematics, they set about the task of investigating "problems concerning the content and teaching of college preparatory mathematics in grades 9–12."

In 1956, a group of physicists under the leadership of Jerrold R. Zacharias and the late Francis L. Friedman, both of the Massachusetts Institute of Technology, formed another committee. This one was called the Physical Science Study Committee, or PSSC. These scientists, drawn from such diverse places as MIT, Bryn Mawr, Bell Labs, California Institute of Technology, and again the University of Illinois, set themselves a similar task. They, too, were appalled by the kind of teaching and learning that was passing for physics in most high schools. Zacharias and his colleagues devoutly desired, as did UICSM people in the field of math, to expose students to the kind of physics engaging the best scientific minds of the day. They began to construct a one-year course in physics that would do just that.

From this beginning in high school physics and math, the movement has spread in all directions—downward into the elementary schools, upwards into the colleges, out into biology, chemistry, the social sciences, even into some of the humanities, and, perhaps most significantly of all, into the fundamental field of why and how human beings are able to learn anything at all.

As of this moment, there is hardly any field that has not felt the impact of

Reprinted from Evans Clinchy, "The New Curricula," in Donald Gross and Judith Murphy, *The Revolution in the School* (New York: Harcourt, Brace & World, Inc., 1964), pp. 220–240.

this wave of reform. Almost every one of the traditional scholarly disciplines has a committee exploring the possibility of revising the teaching of its subject in the schools or of introducing the subject if it is not already being taught. There is, too, a great deal of healthy confusion and spirited competition amongst the various disciplines and the various projects, be they large or small. The situation is such that it will undoubtedly soon be worth an educational doctorate for the hapless schoolman who can do nothing more than simply keep all of the initials (BSCS, PSSC, SMSG, UICSM, etc.) straight and explain the difference between, say, CBA (Chemical Bond Approach) and CHEM Study (Chemical Education Material Study).

Some Common Tendencies *of new Curricula*

Out of this yeasty confusion, a few underlying similarities have begun to appear—general operational principles common to most significant and influential programs.

1. *The new curricular programs typically involve—and in most cases have actually been started by—men who are among the best minds a particular discipline has to offer.*

It is this involvement of first-rate scholars—and their commitment to their task—that is perhaps the single most striking feature of the new programs. For far too many years in the recent history of education, at least in this country, there has been a wide breach between the university scholars and the men and women who teach the subjects in school. This unnatural separation, often tinged with scorn on both sides, is in the process of repair, and it is interesting that in most cases it has been the scholars themselves who have first waved the flag of truce and urged a mutually profitable alliance.

One of the first achievements of this alliance has been to confer upon the entire field of curriculum design an aura of impressive intellectual respectability. It is no longer merely scholarly hack work or a get-rich-quick scheme to prepare material for the schools. Nor is it merely a matter of inevitable frustration after hours of fruitless committee work for a teacher nowadays to become involved in a serious, long-range concern over what he is teaching and how. And it is also possible for the general public to feel that at long last the efforts of able and intelligent men—scholars and teachers alike—are being turned to the all-important task of devising stimulating courses of study for its children.

A second achievement of the alliance is that in most cases the programs actually *are* intellectually respectable. Not all the programs are of equal worth, nor are they in all cases the best that could have been done under the circumstances. But the basic fact of importance is that fine scholars and intelligent teachers have sat down together to wrestle with the problem of what should be taught in our schools and that they have come up with some tentative answers. These answers are subject to infinite revision and refinement as experience is gathered in the classroom, but the initial framework of collaboration has in most cases produced programs that undeniably mark the beginning of a vast improvement in the quality of American schooling.

3 A third achievement of the new programs stems directly from the involvement and commitment of the scholars. It is that the scholars, once involved in constructing a program, become fascinated not only with the problem of what to teach, but with the problem of how the content should be taught. Once they have descended into the fiery furnace of the classroom and met the problems the classroom teacher must face daily, they are rarely the same again. They begin to wonder *why* it is so difficult to get across the principle of quadratic functions to fourth graders, or conversely, they are surprised to find that six-year-olds can handle complex geometric problems. They become curious to know how the children manage to do it. Many of the scholars tend, in short, to get themselves "hooked" on the process of education. If the new breed of cognitive psychologists is added to the list, then this is perhaps the first time in human history that so many richly endowed adults have lavished so much attention on what is or should be happening inside such small heads.

2. *The new programs tend to be national in scope and to be supported on a large scale.*

One of the most frustrating experiences an eager, energetic schoolman can have is to try to seduce historians or mathematicians or scientists, even those who may be living in his particular community and sending their children to the local schools, to work on the local curriculum. In most cases, the scholars simply do not have the time. Or they do not feel that the contribution they might make would have a broad enough impact. Or perhaps these are simply two ways of saying the same thing.

At any rate, it has been possible for the major revision programs to engage the attention and the energy of first-rate scholars (and first-rate teachers and school administrators) in part because the programs offer an opportunity to achieve a wide and perhaps lasting impact on the schools of this country. This does not mean that the men behind these programs feel that they are building *the* standardized, national curriculum in physics or chemistry or social studies, or that they have any desire to do so. Most of them are fully aware that the particular programs they design are only early prototypes, approximations, or best guesses. But they do want their time and effort to make a difference, and the national scope of the major programs gives them just this opportunity.

In addition to the lure of achieving an impressive impact on the schools, there is for these scholars and schoolmen the further enticement represented by money. Not, let us hasten to add, whatever money most of these men are paid in consultant fees or salaries, although these are not charity programs, and most of the men are paid for their services. It is, rather, the lure of those things which an adequate amount of money makes possible—a sufficient and able staff of colleagues, assistants, and administrators; the opportunity to experiment and test their ideas and to be wrong and start over; the opportunity gradually to expand, as the design grows and is transformed into teachable reality, into an increasing number of schools and, hopefully, into the minds of an increasing number of children.

These programs are expensive, of course, and well beyond the financial capacity of any individual school system and most states. The Physical Science Study Committee physics program, which so far has produced a one-year course for the high school plus an extension into advanced topics, has cost about $6,000,000 to date and will for a long time be in the process of revision. There have been, therefore, only two main sources of support for these programs—the Federal government and the private philanthropic foundations. The National Science Foundation has been the prime mover in science, engineering, and mathematics and recently in the social sciences as well. The U.S. Office of Education, through the National Defense Education Act and most recently through its Cooperative Research Program, has been and is becoming even more powerful a force. The private foundations, especially the Carnegie Corporation, the Sloan Foundation, and the Ford Foundation, have often provided crucial seed money for large-scale revision programs, although the full burden of a major program is beyond the resources even of Ford.

3. *The first step in the important reforms has been for the scholars to decide what is to be taught.*

This may seem at first glance to be a relatively simple task. After all, if you put the fifty top physicists or social scientists or mathematicians into a room for two weeks, surely they will be able to work out a neat plan for teaching everything that needs to be taught about physics or the social sciences or mathematics. They are all bright people, and they know their field better than anyone else. But that is not the way it works. The first thing that happens is a big fight, knock-down and drag-out style. At the end of the two-week or four-week or six-week period, the fighting may have to some extent subsided and the conferees will emerge with a rough, general plan. But it is very rough and very general, and not everyone at the conference will agree with it. In fact, some may have walked out in a huff after the first week.

What the fights are usually about is the matter of priority. If the field of knowledge is worth presenting to children, then it theoretically should have a set of prime principles or theoretical statements that to some extent summarize or at least make that importance clear. This set of theoretical principles is what Jerome S. Bruner, in his *Process of Education*, has termed the "structure" of the subject. It is these principles that should have priority. The time of the students is valuable, after all, and should not be wasted on trivia.

But, as groups of scholars have discovered, not every one of the best minds in a field has exactly the same view of what should have highest priority. These differences can be ironed out. Some honest and justifiable compromises can be arrived at. But it is a long and arduous process and one that is never complete. The disciplines that so far have had the easiest time of it are those that are by their very nature the most abstract, the most "mathematical" or "scientific." It is no accident that the first reforms were in the natural sciences and math. The very stuff of mathematics is its system of arbitrary symbolic abstractions. In physics, there is the atom of Bohr, Rutherford, and Schrodinger to be used as a central model.

But even in these cases, the agreement has not been complete. Only recently, a group of eminent mathematicians met in Cambridge, Massachusetts, to take a whole new look at the mathematics reforms that have been in progress now for thirteen years. This group, called the Cambridge Conference on Mathematics, included representatives of almost all of the significant reform movements. Recognizing that the work done so far has all been experimental, the Cambridge group proceeded to lay out a tentative over-all plan for what the mathematics curriculum from kindergarten through the twelfth grade should look like some thirty years from now when the plan might have a chance of becoming a reality. It is a bold and remarkable scheme, one that will undoubtedly receive wide attention. But again, it is mathematics.

If this process of reform is transferred to a field such as the social sciences, a quite different picture emerges. Here the scholars come from a wide variety of disciplines, each with its own peculiar view of man and society. There are social sciences, but there is as yet no such thing as social science. If history is admitted into this general field, as it should and must be, then the picture is even less clear. It is difficult enough to get a group of anthropologists and sociologists to agree on the "structure" of social science; it is well nigh impossible for social scientists and historians to arrive at a single set of guiding principles that both groups can uniformly salute. The best that can be hoped for in these fields is *a* set of basic principles or guidelines arrived at by one group composed of first-rate scholars who find that they can work profitably together. A different group would undoubtedly come forth with a different set of principles or assumptions, although there would most certainly be some similarities.

It thus becomes clear that "structure" is often a slippery term. In some cases what the best minds think should be taught is relatively clear and easily arrived at after a great deal of hard work. In other cases, the structure of a given curriculum will be the informed and intelligent but arbitrary opinion of a particular group and will be arrived at with great difficulty after a great deal of hard work. In all cases it will be subject to revision, for no field of inquiry stands still and quietly waits for the curriculum builders to catch up and keep abreast.

4. *Every significant reform has involved a deliberate effort to bring the curriculum up to date.*

When the university scholars first began to interest themselves in the content of what was being taught in the elementary and secondary schools, they were appalled at the obsolescence of the ideas and approaches they saw being presented to innocent American children. Indeed, it was this fervent desire to modernize the teaching of their various disciplines in the schools that first aroused the interest of many of these men.

"Modernize" in this sense can mean many things. It means first that the scholars wanted their subjects presented within the frame of reference used by the people working in the field at the present time. Newtonian mechanics, for example, had been one of the primary building blocks of the conventional physics course. Newtonian mechanics still works, so long as the body in question is not moving too fast or too slowly or is not too large or too small. In these special instances, the theories break down. The theoretical frame of reference of contemporary physics is Einsteinian, and it is difficult to teach high school students contemporary physics in an honest way without presenting it within this frame of reference. The PSSC physics course, therefore, pays a great deal less attention to Newtonian mechanics and works within a roughly Einsteinian frame. In this sense, the content of the physics course has truly been "modernized." *ZAHARIAS*

The desire on the part of scholars to have children learn within a contemporary intellectual framework means also that the new course of study often must deal with topics not typically included in the curriculum and must discard some of our most cherished practices. For example, many of the social scientists involved in recent attempts to revise the teaching of social studies have risen in revolt against the emphasis in the early grades upon "the friendly trashman" and the whole concentric process of moving from the child outwards through the family, to the community, the locality, the state, the country, and finally the world. The social scientists feel that this scheme provides little intellectual stimulation and as presently taught is almost always boring and often downright dishonest. *Oppose expanding environment*

This desire to have children deal with matters that are real and important (at least to the mind of the scientist and scholar) has led to some surprising results. Many people find it startling to hear scholars recommend that third graders should study the social organization of a baboon troop in order to make a comparison between human and non-human primate groups. Or to hear the mathematicians at the Cambridge Conference on Mathematics describe their program by saying that

> a student who has worked through the full thirteen years of mathematics in grades K–12 should have a level of training comparable to three years of top-level college training today: that is, we shall expect him to have the equivalent of two years of calculus and one semester each of modern algebra and probability theory.

Or to hear that Omar Moore at Yale has been able to teach three-year-old children to read, write, type, and take dictation.

The object of these men is not to startle but to expose children only—or at least primarily—to material that is relevant to the contemporary world and to the lives the children lead in it, material that is honest and honestly reflects the state-of-the-art in whatever field happens to be under study.

It is for these reasons that the more imaginative programs always seem to be radical revisions. In most cases they *do* depart radically from what is taught now, both in content and in spirit. But this appearance of radicalism comes not so much from any desire on the part of the scholars to be bold and brash. It is due more to the simple fact that our school programs have been allowed to fall so far behind that catching up requires drastic changes in what is taught.

5. *The current reforms almost always involve not only a radical approach to the content but also* explorations into new *and different ways of teaching and learning.*

Most of the scholars and schoolmen involved in the early curriculum reforms were interested right at the start in the improvement not only of what is taught, but how it is taught. They remembered, rarely with pleasure or respect, their own education; or they observed what was—or was not—happening to their own children in school; or, as schoolpeople, they saw what was actually going on in the classrooms.

One of the things many of these people most wanted to communicate to children was the pleasure, the sweat, and the rewards of intellectual inquiry. And not just for the students labeled "bright" or "academically talented," but for *all* students. The scholars felt that the particular substance that might be included in the new courses of study, while it was surely important and up to date, was in some sense less crucial than the way a scholar or scientist goes about finding the answer to a problem. The actual content of the new courses is doomed to obsolescence in all too short a time. Unless a student is able and eager to begin to smell out a problem; to be curious about its how and why; to work through the arduous but absorbing process of exploring data, worrying about it, making the intuitive hunches and leaps, and arriving at what is perhaps only an approximate or still ambiguous solution, then the new course has failed in some vital way.

This attitude has also been tied up with the desire to be honest about the state-of-the-art in the various scholarly disciplines and to be honest about the "conclusions" scholars reach and the methods by which they reach them. If the answers the scholars have are only approximate or are still ambiguous, as most of them tend to be, then the educational materials—the textbooks, the films, or whatever—should not give the impression that the answers are neat, firm, and forever, as most textbooks tend to make them. Rather, the content should be presented by both the materials and the teacher with all of the doubts and hesitancies and all of the messy incompletions that scholars themselves experience and must learn to handle.

In short, the scholars and scientists held the faith that students—all kinds of students at all ages—should and can be scholars and scientists themselves. Or at least that if the students are treated with respect and allowed to work through the same data that the scholars and scientists themselves work through, they can experience in some appreciable measure the excitement of the schol-arly chase and the satisfactions of intellectual mastery. In addition, they will, in theory, absorb and remember a great deal because they have actually worked through the material themselves and thus made it their own—again, the way a scholar or scientist might. (It should, however, be noted here that these theories about learning and teaching are not theories widely evident in the scholars' own colleges and universities.)

The kind of schooling these scholars were talking about, of course, was not new in the sense that it had never been talked about before. One predecessor had put the matter this way:

> *Discovery learning*
>
> Teach your scholar to observe the phenomena of nature; you will soon rouse his curiosity, but if you would have it grow, do not be in too great a hurry to satisfy this curiosity. Put the problems before him and let him solve them himself. Let him know nothing because you have told him, but because he has learnt it for himself. Let him not be taught science, let him discover it. If ever you substitute authority for reason he will cease to reason; he will be a mere plaything of other people's thoughts. . . . Undoubtedly the notions of things thus acquired for oneself are clearer and much more convincing than those acquired from the teaching of others; and not only is our reason not accustomed to a slavish submission to authority, but we develop greater ingenuity in discovering relations, connecting ideas and inventing apparatus, than when we merely accept what is given us and allow our minds to be enfeebled by indifference.[1]

This is not a quote from John Dewey or Jerrold Zacharias or Jerome S. Bruner, but from Jean Jacques Rousseau's *Emile*, published in 1762. But what the scholars and scientists discovered for themselves when they began to turn their theories into materials to be tried in the classroom was that they were talking about a quite drastic change in the prevailing mode of American schooling.

The prevalent style of American teaching has, for a wide variety of under-standable reasons, been too often limited to the rote acquisition of information ("rote" here meaning acquisition without real understanding) and repetitive drill. Too often the bench-bound student is asked simply to memorize facts, such as, in the words of Zacharias, "that damn list of Plantagenet kings." Or the student is asked to memorize the hard-won but always tentative conclu-sion of a scholar or scientist as if it were (and often in the form of) an im-mutable natural law—$R \times T = D$, or the rules of English grammar. After memorizing the rule, the student is then given a number of instances of the rule in the form of problems or exercises ("If Tom rows up the Mississippi at five miles an hour . . ." or "Parse this sentence . . .").

The scholars and scientists wanted to reverse this process by giving the instances first and asking the student, after he has begun to sense that a

---

[1] Jean Jacques Rousseau, *Emile,* trans. Barbara Foxley (London: J. M. Dent & Sons, Ltd., 1911), pp. 131, 139.

problem exists, to work through to the solution, law, or rule more or less on his own.

It was the early explorations of the curriculum reformers and the congruent growth of cognitive psychology that stirred up the enormous current interest in the whole process of how and why people, especially little people, learn. It is the combined and continuing efforts of the psychologists and the curriculum builders that will hopefully produce some remarkable improvements in what goes on in the classroom.

6. *The new programs almost always include the production of actual educational materials or specific directions for building instructional "models," and the exhaustive trial of these materials or models in the classroom before they are made widely available to the schools.*

It is all very well to develop fine theories and outlines and to set down on paper what should be learned and how. But it is quite another thing to translate these notions into hard materials, to establish priorities, and to devise instructional methods that actually work. Yet unless these steps are taken, very little is likely to happen.

A striking negative manifestation of this lesson has been the history of the reforms instigated in 1961 by the National Task Force on Economic Education, which was backed principally by the American Economic Association, with eventual collaboration from the Committee for Economic Development. The task force produced a program for extensive reforms, and the CED made available a list of study materials and a free sampling of publications to all the country's high schools. But two years later, in a dispassionate review of results thus far, the American Economic Association reluctantly concluded that "the task force report and related endeavors" had had virtually no impact on the schools. Nearly everyone, schoolpeople included, agreed that the scholarly recommendations were sound. But the classroom teachers, most of them with scant economics education themselves, needed more than broad outlines and lists of materials. They needed clear priorities on what to teach and when to teach it, and concrete demonstrations on *how* to teach it. In the words of Dr. Lewis E. Wagner, of the University of Illinois: "Teachers are going to need help, and in large doses." In particular Dr. Wagner emphasized the need for "model building"—specific and detailed examples demonstrating to the classroom teacher how a lesson or series of lessons could be built around an important fact or event or concept of economics, such as antitrust legislation or the Great Depression or the theory of wages. In the absence of such specific teaching aids—analogous to Zacharias' simple ripple-tank for demonstrating the property of waves—the average social-science teacher failed in his attempt to act on the task force recommendations.

In almost every case where a reform has made a difference, the people in charge of the intellectual structure have turned their hand to the business of designing at least sample materials if not complete courses. This process is important for a number of reasons. It enables the scholars to find out if the ideas they wish to communicate have been set forth with sufficient clarity to be understood by children, teachers, and ultimately by themselves. Sometimes, the scholars have learned as much about their subject from the process of curriculum building as the students have from taking the new courses. The process of designing materials also enables the scholars to find out if the ideas can be communicated in a way that distorts neither the ideas nor the scholarly process itself. It enables the scholars and schoolpeople to discover the proper level for particular ideas or particular forms of the ideas.

Once the materials have been designed in some tentative manner, the only way to see if they work is to try them out on children. Until the children, be they elementary school children or high school students, have actually worked their way through a unit or a course, the scholars have no way of knowing if the ideas have been communicated, if the scholarly process is unviolated, or if the first grade is really the best place to begin the teaching of geometry and high school the best place for calculus. This kind of information is what the scientific members of the curriculum building profession call "feedback," the indispensable knowledge that what you have designed works or does not work. *[margin note: knowledge derived from new ideas being tested.]*

Feedback is unobtainable, of course, without an extensive and intensive period of trial and experimentation. Many ideas that seem lucid when discussed among physicists or social scientists turn out to be slippery when presented to third graders. Even the experienced schoolmen and classroom teachers who help build the units and courses can be fooled, although their advice and counsel helps prevent gross errors. When errors of conception or execution appear, and they do with regularity, the offending material is scrapped or reworked until the children say that it is right at last. They say this by reacting to the material and working through it in such a way that the builders feel the ideas have been communicated and the children themselves are satisfied and even exhilarated by the experience.

Only after the ideas and the materials have passed through this period of test and trial can they be turned loose for wider use. It would be a careless teacher or school superintendent who would permit large numbers of children to be exposed to materials that had not proved themselves in this fashion.

7. *There is a tendency in the new programs to develop a greatly expanded range of integrated materials designed to foster the inductive, "work-through-the-problem-yourself" approach to instruction.*

The first breakthrough on the front of instructional materials came with the creation of the PSSC physics course. When the physicists sat down to design their materials, they knew that they wanted to do more than simply build a better textbook. They knew they wanted to use films made by real physicists speaking directly to the students about topics of common concern. They knew, too, that the schools lacked inexpensive but accurate laboratory equipment that the students could use to work through some of the basic physical problems. Following this train of thought and development, PSSC has created: a basic textbook, which carries only a part of the message; a series of almost sixty films; an array of inexpensive kits with which the students can construct such things as their own balances out of soda straws; laboratory and teacher guides; a battery of achievement tests (and a new College Board exam in physics); and a comprehensive series of paperback books for collateral reading.

All of these materials are created by the same group of people, and each part is designed to fit with every other part to produce a unified learning experience for the student. This has become something of a pattern, at least for the major revisions of science teaching such as the CHEM Study and the Biological Sciences Curriculum Study (which has so far produced not one, but three such courses).

This same basic philosophy, first articulated by Zacharias and Friedman, is spreading to fields other than high school science, such as science for junior high and the elementary schools and recently even to the social studies. Some of these reform movements have begun to carry these ideas even further.

As an instance of how some scholars and schoolmen feel constricted by existing types of material, take the conventional textbook. This is a curious instructional device with some distinct advantages. It is relatively inexpensive; it is easily and widely distributable; it makes available roughly the same quality and level of material in Birmingham, Alabama, and Scarsdale, New York.

But the textbook also has enormous disadvantages, even when produced by excellent scholars and teachers, which is not always the case. One major difficulty is the fact that most textbooks tend to be out of date by the time they are printed and distributed.

An even bigger disadvantage is the very nature of the typical textbook, the purpose for which it is written. In part, because the textbook is a book and is therefore a series of printed pages bound tightly together, the writer tends to take a given body of information and put it in some order, starting with introductory material on page one and ending with advanced material on the last page. In most cases the author becomes involved in a complex process of selecting the important ideas, concepts, or laws that he wishes to discuss, then summarizing the best available evidence that will support or illustrate them, and finally setting down the evidence and the conclusions derived from it in the most clean, neat, and efficient manner he can devise. The task of the student then, most typically, becomes one of reading the book, remembering what has been said, doing the exercises, at best understanding the material, and then repeating it during an examination which may or may not require him to use the material in some productive way. This is also the process embodied in the average educational film or film strip. Programed instruction carries this process to its ultimate, breaking the information and the ideas to be acquired into a series of small, utterly logical steps that carry the student inexorably from one fact or conclusion to the next, from little knowledge to whatever amount of knowledge is desired by the program builder.

The basic flaw in this process, in the eyes of many of the curriculum reformers, is that someone else does most of the job that they hope the students will perform for themselves. Instead of putting each student into the shoes of the scholar or scientist, the textbook approach *tells* the student what he should know. It robs him of the excitement of solving mysteries, of exploring and discovering things for himself, of building at least tentative—and perhaps deliciously grandiose—hypotheses. It robs him of pleasures of discourse and debate with his peers and the stimulation of the friendly acrimony that normally accompanies the educated exchange of views. The textbook approach also contributes to the misrepresentation of intellectual activity by making it appear clean, orderly, and final, rather than incomplete, tentative, and always subject to revision. In short, the textbook approach takes most of the pleasure out of using one's mind.

For these reasons, among others, the builders of some of the new programs are experimenting with ways of dispensing with textbooks altogether. In the study of history, for example, the students might be offered a loose collection of original documents (selected, of course, by the scholars but including some irrelevant pieces). Out of these comparatively raw materials, the student must fashion his own version of the origins of urban life in ancient Mesopotamia or the events leading up to and including the Battle of Waterloo. Whether his version be "right" or "wrong" is hardly the point here, so long as the rules of evidence are followed. What is important is that the student have the opportunity to build his own case and that he then be called upon to defend it against the onslaughts of differing views. Since, in theory, this kind of process would engage the interest of the students far more than reading a textbook, the students might well remember a great deal more history as well.

8. *The new programs and the material and methods they have produced tend to cast the teacher in a new and different role.*

Too often the typical task of the teacher in our classrooms today is to transfer the knowledge in his or her head into the heads of the students or to transmit a skill, such as reading, that the teacher possesses to the child who does not have it. Although the teacher is generally assisted in this task by a textbook and a small variety of other aids, the main responsibility for seeing that the children learn almost always rests with the teacher and no one else. If the teacher fails in his or her task, then the child fails, and ultimately the educational system fails. Since elementary school teachers rarely have fewer than 25 children to whom they must teach anywhere from three to five subjects a day, and since high school teachers average about 150 students a day in one subject, it is not humanly possible for even the finest teacher to discharge his responsibility adequately. All too often the teacher who bears this burden is not a fine teacher, full of knowledge and understanding, but a beleaguered soul one textbook page ahead of the students.

What many of the new programs are attempting to do is to make the teacher's burden more bearable and his task a great deal more sensible. The key to the problem is to transfer most of the responsibility for the content of schooling from the teacher to the materials and thus to the builders of the curriculum. This is where the responsibility belongs. If the material is thoroughly and imaginatively prepared, then the teacher need no longer be the world's greatest expert on a subject or fail at his job. The task of the teacher becomes not one of telling students what they should know or of assigning chapters in a textbook, but rather one of guiding the student through material that has been designed to engage his interest, to present him with intriguing problems, and to enable him to work through to at least tentative solutions largely on his own.

Far from eliminating the teacher from the educational scene, the new programs make him more important than ever. In some ways, the teacher's task becomes a good deal harder as well. While the written material, the films, the teacher guides, etc., may now contain the basic course material and an outline of the approach the teacher should take, it is more than ever up to him to make sure that the process works.

If the subject of the moment is an exploration of how the earliest cities developed out of the farming villages in ancient Iraq, then the problem becomes one of each child's working through the archaeological and anthropological evidence to build his own theory as to how this course of events came about and what changes thereby occurred in the life of the people. The evidence may be there in the form of films, or in bits and pieces of the excavated data reproduced on cards to be sorted by the children, or in translations of later texts, or in kits enabling the children to build models of the early villages and to chart the changes as the villages grow into cities. A methodology may be outlined in a teacher guide, but these methods are of value only if the children actually do work through them and actually do build their own hypotheses, argue about them, and arrive at tentative intellectual models of how it all must have happened.

Throughout this process it is *not the teacher's job to provide the* hypotheses or to explain what really did happen (especially in this case, since no one really knows), but rather to insure that both the verbally talented and the less verbally talented children are involved in the task of intellectual model building. Some of the children may be doing this primarily through extrapolating backward from the later Sumerian literary materials. Others may be doing it through the reconstruction of what the earliest cities must have looked like and how the change from the mud-hut villages to urban centers might have occurred, purely in architectural terms.

But it is hoped that both the analytical and imaginative powers of all the children will be engaged in the task. They will not be attempting to arrive at the "right" answer (the answer that, in their more conventional studies, they have learned the teacher wants them to get). Nor will they be asking the teacher to answer questions of substance. That is not what the teacher is there for. He is there to assist the children in the process of finding their own answers. In this sense, it is much harder to refuse to answer a question than it is simply to supply the answer when it is requested. The teacher finds himself involved in a quite different style of teaching, and thus in a new role.

9. Most of the major revisions have undertaken programs of training teachers to handle the new materials and new methods.

It is all very well to say that teachers should have a new role and a quite different kind of material to work with. It is quite something else actually to send forth into the classroom teachers who feel confident that they understand the materials and know how they themselves are supposed to operate.

It is difficult enough to do this in the case of the handful of teachers who may actually have worked on the development of the curriculum. It is quite another thing, if you are developing a unit to be used throughout the elementary schools of the United States, to be sure that 1,000,000 elementary school teachers are equipped to teach that unit.

Yet it is perfectly obvious, too, that unless this task is carried out, nothing of any real consequence is going to happen. In fact, it could be said that this is by far the most crucial part of any curriculum revision program. And it is also the problem that is farthest from being solved.

Some of the programs, such as PSSC, CHEM Study, BSCS, and others sponsored by the National Science Foundation, have used the twin devices of summer institutes and in-service institutes. Teachers spend four to six weeks in the summer, for instance, learning about a new curriculum from people who helped devise it. Or the teachers go to institutes conducted during the school year in their own geographic area. This is a feasible system if you are doing a one-year physics course. There are only 12,000 physics teachers in the country at the moment, and eventually most of these can be reached through the institute system. But those 1,000,000 elementary school teachers are a problem of another magnitude altogether.

In the longest of runs, the problem can only be solved by the production of teachers trained to handle the new curricula while they are being trained to be teachers in the first place—that is, in the existing teacher training institutions. But this will not happen for some time to come, and it does not solve the problem of retraining the teachers already in the schools.

Some newer methods of attack upon this problem are being explored. One is a much greater use of films in the training and re-training of teachers, films that among other things give the teachers a glimpse of the new materials actually being used in classroom situations. What the ultimate answers may be, however, no one can say at this time.

10. *Most of the people involved in curriculum revision are aware of the fact that the present programs are only the first step in a large, long-range effort.*

It has taken the Physical Science Study Committee almost seven years so far to bring its one-year high school physics course to a point where it is widely used, commands the respect of both the scientific and educational communities, and is almost ready to be radically revised. PSSC is ready for revision not because it is already out of date or because it has lost its value as a pedagogical innovation, but because the time is nearing for a second look at science teaching in general. PSSC is what is called in the trade a "first-generation" program, a first go-round. Much has been learned because of PSSC's experience and the experience of other high school science programs stimulated by PSSC. In addition, programs have been started in elementary and junior high science and in college physics. The question now becomes one of how all these programs relate to one another and to the over-all structure of the science which the curriculum builders wish to communicate. This requires even more thinking and will eventually necessitate new programs.

Most of the programs now in operation or in the planning stage are first-generation programs. Only mathematics has a "second-generation" project in the planning stage in the form of the Cambridge Conference on Mathematics. But even a second-generation program does not solve all of the problems or yield all of the answers. The curriculum builders in a sense are just beginning to discover what their field is all about and how little really is known about what the true capacities of children are and about how people learn. As feedback on the new programs and on children increases and as new programs are then built upon the new information, even the second-generation programs become obsolescent and will require further revision. The process is—fortunately or unfortunately—unending.

Some Problems, Dangers, and Limitations

The preceding (and quite sketchy) list of common tendencies among the new programs describes in some senses a success story. So far, many of the explorations into new ways of teaching have been highly productive. But this hardly means that all of them have been, or even that the successful ones will continue to be. In fact, it could be said that the new programs raise as many questions as they answer and uncover problems where none were thought to exist.

The whole area of evaluation is one such problem. Until recently evaluation of the results of a curriculum has been handled—and rather neatly, too—by simply giving the students a test. Since the aim of most curricula has essentially been to transfer into the head of a student a certain amount of factual knowledge or to train him to a certain degree of skill, it has been relatively easy to design a test which asks for the recall of the knowledge or requires the student to exercise his skill on particular problems. This has even been carried to the point of establishing national "norms," so that children can be rated as "fourth-grade level" in reading or "college level" in mathematics.

This kind of evaluative procedure obviously does not apply to the best of the new programs, whether or not it ever should have been applied to the older curricula. Recall of factual knowledge and the demonstration of rote skills are not what the programs are after. Yet it is no easy matter—in fact, it is as yet an unsolved problem—to design a method of finding out if a child's intuitive powers have developed to the point where he can be given a major, unsolved scholarly problem to sink his intellectual teeth into. On a purely practical level, school systems and parents have a right to know if their children are achieving what they are supposed to be achieving. In order to do any of these things, an entirely new system of looking at curricula and at what children do in school needs to be worked out.

Another unsolved problem lies in the quality of the teachers. Most of the new programs have quite consciously been designed to be taught by the teachers currently operating in our school systems—with the added benefit of all too brief periods of special training. But as Frances Keppel, the United States Commissioner of Education, has pointed out,

> serious limitations are imposed upon the student's ability to learn by the instructor's ability to teach. If the student is to be brought to the frontiers of knowledge, the teacher must know the whereabouts of those frontiers. If the student is to be encouraged to grope, the teacher must at least be able to suggest which of his roads are likely to be blind alleys.[2]

There is a real danger here that, unless the new curricula can obtain teachers of a much higher quality than the profession now seems able to attract, the second- and third-generation programs may never happen, because there will simply be no one able to teach them.

But both of these examples of major remaining problems are merely symptoms of a much more fundamental difficulty. Evaluation, teacher recruitment and training, the continuing development of new programs, further research into how people learn—all of these enormously important tasks depend upon the creation of a viable and permanent system of educational research and development that is an integral part of the larger American educational system. The current wave of reform is not the first that has hit American education. The deplorable history seems to be a burst of reform followed by twenty-five years of stagnation followed by another go at bringing things up to date. This is an exceedingly wasteful process.

One possible way to create a continuing and more efficient system of in-

2 Foreword to *Goals for School Mathematics: The Report of the Cambridge Conference on School Mathematics* (Boston: Houghton Mifflin Company, 1963), p. viii.

novation might be the establishment of a series of educational research and development centers or institutes, perhaps patterned after Educational Services, Incorporated, the private, non-profit organization that has grown out of the activities of the men who founded the Physical Science Study Committee. Even this step, of course, would not be sufficient, for institutions such as these would have to be intimately tied in with teacher training institutions, with operating school systems, and with the Federal government to insure that the innovations reached the schools and had an impact.

Whatever particular solutions are eventually arrived at, they will in the final analysis be largely a matter of American education facing up to what may be the distinguishing characteristic of our age, rapid and irrevocable change.

Index